W9-DGT-241

INTRODUCTORY SOCIOLOGY

CHARLES HORTON COOLEY
Late Professor of Sociology, in the University of Michigan

ROBERT COOLEY ANGELL
Associate Professor of Sociology in the University of Michigan

AND

LOWELL JUILLIARD CARR
Assistant Professor of Sociology in the University of Michigan

CHARLES SCRIBNER'S SONS
NEW YORK CHICAGO BOSTON ATLANTA
SAN FRANCISCO DALLAS

Printed in the United States of America

F

PREFACE

This volume is an attempt to present a systematic analysis of the phenomena of human association, especially as they appear under the conditions of modern life. The junior authors are convinced that our contemporary culture, dominated by science, the machine, and the city and strained by maladjustments issuing from the tremendous strides of material invention, can best be approached through the penetrating social theory of the late Professor Charles Horton Cooley. We have therefore undertaken to select from his *Human Nature and the Social Order* and his *Social Organization* the parts most appropriate to introductory classes and to combine them with new material.

In selecting from his works, we have included those portions which have been widely accepted by sociologists, and we have tried to exclude the abstract and speculative passages which are difficult for the beginning student to comprehend. What Professor Cooley wrote we have revised only slightly; newer developments in biology and social psychology have necessitated the few changes made. For the most part we have tried to introduce new material while letting stand what he wrote.

This new material is of two kinds: (1) new concepts and theories, and (2) data drawn from recent sociological research. Under the former head should be mentioned our treatment of culture (in the anthropologist's sense), of human ecology, of grouping, and of propaganda in relation to public opinion. The second form of supplementation is illustrated in almost every chapter. Because of this factual material the book is oriented more toward contemporary American life than were Professor Cooley's original works.

Those who are familiar with *Human Nature and the Social Order* and *Social Organization* will realize that we have introduced more systematization. Professor Cooley's books possess the fine organization characteristic of any slowly evolved organism, but this organization is subtle and best appreciated by the advanced student. We have, therefore, aimed to help the beginner by making the relations of the various parts more explicit and by arranging the chapters in a carefully planned sequence.

After an introductory chapter intended to arouse the student's interest in the problems of human association, our scheme has been to proceed from the basic concepts necessary to the analysis of even the simplest social life to those which are especially pertinent to our modern complex social organization. Human heredity, communication, human nature, primary groups, and culture are taken up in the first few chapters and should enable the student to understand the more developed aspects of personal behavior treated subsequently, such as the self, emulation, and conscience. With this foundation we are ready to grasp the effect of modern communication. In Chapter XII, then, we shift from a general treatment to one oriented toward modern life. We first see how modern communication has affected personality and enlarged social organization. This brings us to a general discussion of grouping under contemporary conditions in Chapter XV. The next thirteen chapters constitute from one point of view a detailed analysis of the functioning of different kinds of groups in modern life.

Thinking first in terms of residence groups, we take up the community, the region, the nation-state, and the world-market. Turning to the phenomena of economic stratification, we then deal with social classes. This is followed by chapters on groups functioning for purposes of adjustment—on public opinion, in short. Institutions such as the family, the school, and the church are treated next. The last chapter aims to show something of this history of social science, its relation to values, and the functions of both in solving social problems.

Throughout we have tried to keep description and evaluation distinct. But the beginner inevitably demands interpretation. Therefore we have from time to time woven into the conceptual analysis the problem approach, assuming certain values and pointing out the shortcomings of the actual conditions; but in fairness to the reader we have noted explicitly when we pass from description to evaluation.

An undertaking of this nature may seem to call for a statement as to the responsibility for the various parts of the work. Such a statement is peculiarly difficult in this case because the junior authors have radically revised each other's chapters and even changed responsibility in some instances. Professor Cooley actually wrote almost half the sentences in this book and contributed much more than half of the ideas. Only ten chapters are lacking in material from his pen; viz., I, VI, VII, XV, XVI, XVII, XVIII, XIX, XXI, and XXIX. The chief responsibility for all but the last of these rests with Doctor Carr, and in that he shares equally with Doctor Angell. Of the 19 other chapters, Doctor Angell is chiefly responsible for 13; viz., II, III, IV, V, VIII, IX, X, XI, XIII, XIV, XXV, XXVI, and XXVII. The chief responsibility for the remaining six—XII, XX, XXII, XXIII, XXIV, and XXVIII—lies with Doctor Carr.

It is because we revere the memory of Professor Cooley, because we feel an intense loyalty to him and to his sociological system that we have produced this book. We wished to see his sound theory, so cogently expressed, made accessible to the beginning student. We believe that he would have wished personal considerations to be sacrificed to the needs of sociology students. In this view Mrs. Cooley concurs, and we are glad to acknowledge her gracious acquiescence in this project.

To keep Professor Cooley's writing separate from our own by the use of quotation marks proved impracticable, because we were faced by the necessity of adding single sentences in the midst of his paragraphs and, *per contra,* of using in the body of our own writing short passages written by Professor Cooley. To have quoted incessantly would have rendered the text distracting.

The authors gratefully acknowledge the suggestions of their colleagues, Professors R. D. McKenzie, A. E. Wood, and R. H. Holmes. We are also indebted to Reverend H. P. Marley for his criticism of the chapter on the church, and to Mr. Karl Guenther for suggestions relative to the professional classes.

R. C. A.
L. J. C.

CONTENTS

ILLUSTRATIONS

TABLES

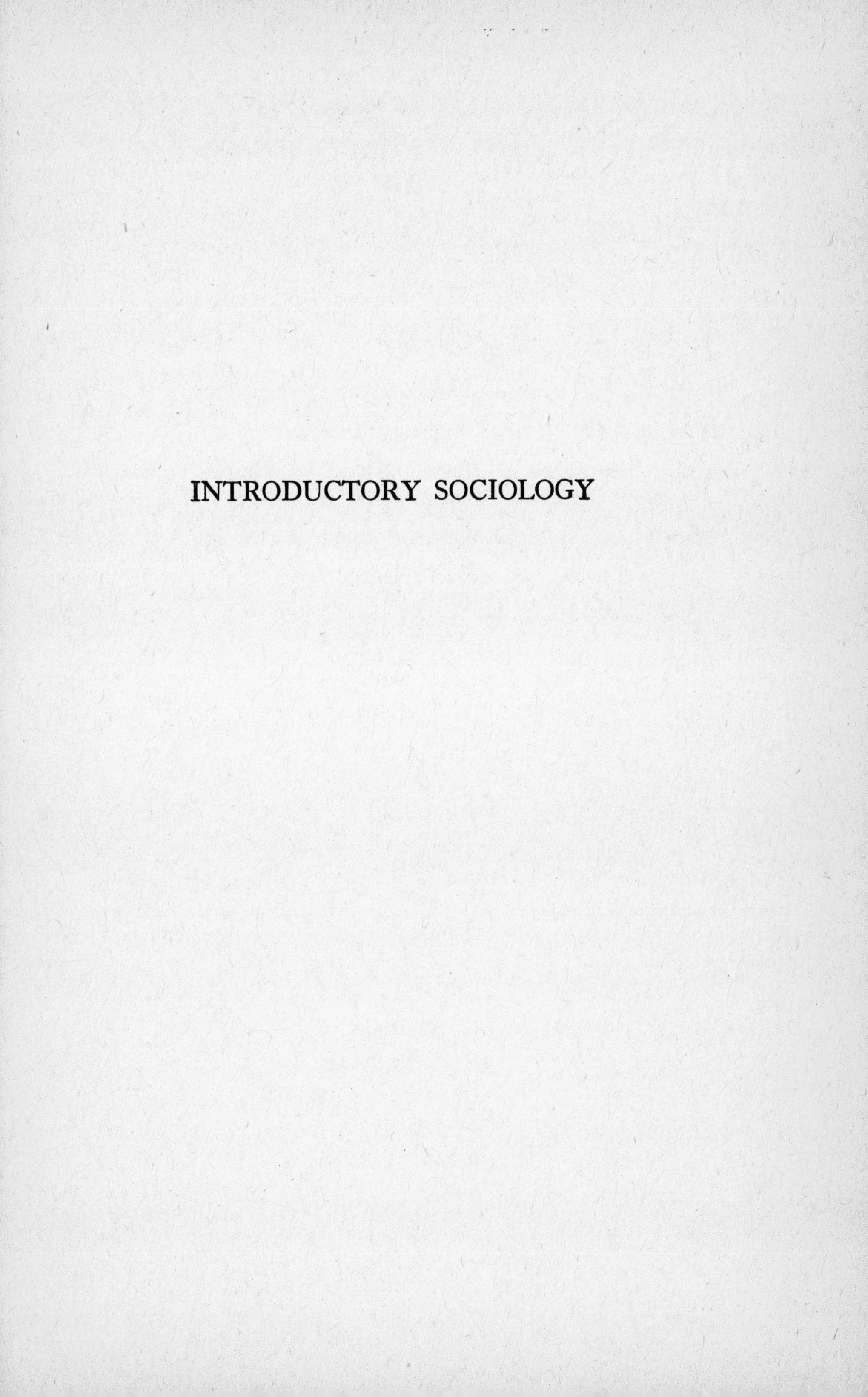

INTRODUCTORY SOCIOLOGY

CHAPTER I

THE PROBLEM OF LIVING WITH OTHERS

Of What Use Are Other People? Most of us take other people for granted. Since there have always been other people in the world around us and since we see no reason for expecting them suddenly to disappear, why bother to think about them except when we want them to wait on us, entertain us, or transact business with us? Living with others is so natural and so all-surrounding—like the atmosphere—that, while we may feel association where it touches us personally, we never stop to consider the phenomenon in its entirety.

Men have been associating for thousands, if not millions, of years and their animal predecessors were living in groups for ages before that, but the process of association itself has become an object of scientific curiosity only within the last century. Of course men have been thinking about certain phases of association for a much longer time. Plato and Aristotle, for example, concerned themselves with the problem of government twenty-three centuries ago and economic life has been studied systematically since Adam Smith's *Wealth of Nations* appeared in 1776. But scientific curiosity about the forms and processes of group-living in general may be said to date only from the work of Auguste Comte, a Frenchman, whose writings were published in the second quarter of the nineteenth century. It was Comte who invented the term sociology and applied it to the scientific study of the phenomena of group-living. Only within the last generation, however, and that mainly in America, have inductive studies rather than speculative treatises come gradually to constitute the main product of sociologists.

What a Scientific Interest in Living with Others Means. *The subject matter of this book, then, is human association, i.e.,* the phenomena of living with other people.

But before we even attempt to outline the problem we must

clarify our minds concerning the attitude with which we approach our task. To regard other people as phenomena is not at all the same as to regard them as friends, acquaintances, voters, or business prospects. As friends, acquaintances, voters, or prospects they are parts of our every-day world in which we have friendships to maintain, campaigns to win, businesses to carry on; they are parts, in short, of practical situations that we are seeking immediately to control. But as phenomena for scientific inquiry they cease to be objects of our will-to-do and become mere foci of observation, mere points, so to speak, in a world of truth. Our objective now is to understand rather than to do. Ultimately we may hope to use our understanding for practical purposes, but for the time being, and while we maintain the scientific point of view, our primary purpose is to understand.

Sociology, then, as a scientific discipline is not concerned with changing society, or with reforming it, or with maintaining the *status quo*. It is concerned wholly and solely with describing the phenomena of human association and trying to understand them. Whether the facts revealed and the uniformities discovered are pleasant or unpleasant has nothing to do with the case. The first task—and for many people the hardest—in approaching the study of social phenomena is to learn to set aside personal likes and dislikes, hopes and fears, and to view social behavior with the cold appraising eye of scientific curiosity.

Let us approach our analysis of association by first glancing at the human world in which we live and then tracing briefly the evolutionary path by which man and his social heritage have come to be what they are.

The Numbers and Distribution of Mankind Today. The human race, according to an estimate of the International Statistical Institute of the League of Nations in 1930, numbers approximately 2,000,000,000 people. It is believed to be increasing at a rate of from 12,000,000 to 30,000,000 a year. In this increase the share of the white race has been declining for more than a generation due to the falling birth rate in western Europe and the United States. Unless present tendencies reverse themselves, the United States, whose birth rate has now fallen below 19 per 1,000, will cease to grow by natural increase within another generation, *i.e.*, about 1960.

Including the Hindus, nearly 50 per cent of the world's population can be classed as white; about 40 per cent as yellow-brown, or Mongoloid; and about 10 per cent as black, or Negroid. Nearly half of mankind lives in Asia, about a quarter in Europe, and 11 per cent in the two Americas.

Three quarters of humanity are crowded into three centres of concentration—eastern Asia, India, and Europe. China, Japan, India, and Italy are the outstanding centres of high population pressure, while North and South America, Australia, and Africa are areas of low pressure. When we remember that the distribution of natural resources does not at all follow the pattern of population distribution, the pressure of the Japanese for expansion, the turmoil in India, and the restlessness of the Italians all become more understandable.[1]

The Way It All Began. Nobody knows how anything really began. Origins are all lost in obscurity. But this much we can say: Ages before there were any men in the world other animals had made the discovery that living together and protecting one another were biologically more economical than trying to go it alone. Fifty million years or so ago the ants whose fossilized remains are now found in the Baltic amber were living in colonies and carrying on ant affairs just as their descendants do today.[2] That our pre-human ancestors five or fifty million years ago in central Asia lived in groups larger than single families seems probable from the habits of certain of our distant cousins, the apes, and from the behavior of early men themselves. At least, pre-man was gregarious, and if recent theories concerning the origins of mankind are correct, association and mutual aid must have been of decisive importance in insuring survival in that desperate time when the disappearance of the forests north of the newly made Himalayas forced pre-man to the ground.

From Pre-Man to Man. Man and the anthropoid apes are both probably descendants of some tree-living form that existed many millions of years ago. It is needless for our purpose to speculate on which small mammal may have been our common ancestor. The lemur will do as well as any. The important thing

[1] For a discussion of population distribution in relation to resources, see Warren S. Thompson, *Danger Spots in World Population,* New York, 1929. See also *Recent Social Trends in the United States,* Report of the President's Research Committee on Social Trends, New York and London, 1933, Chapter I.

[2] See William Morton Wheeler, *Social Life among the Insects,* New York, 1923, p. 6.

here is that anywhere from five to fifty millions of years ago advanced anthropoid forms were swarming in the forests of central Asia. Recent discoveries in China are believed to indicate the presence there of tool-using, fire-making *men*—not mere anthropoids—more than a million years ago; and Professor Henry Fairfield Osborn, author of an authoritative book on the Old Stone Age, has multiplied by 100 his previous estimate of the length of time during which man has existed. Possibly there have been men for 50,000,000 years. The one thing certain is that all old estimates are being revised by new discoveries, and the tendency of these discoveries is to push the threshold of humanity farther and farther back into a past already incredibly distant.

Suppose the thing that has already been suggested actually happened, suppose the up-thrusting of the Himalayas ages ago trapped myriads of anthropoids north of the mountains in an arid land of disappearing forests. Only one possible path of survival would lie before them—to take to the ground and make the best of it. The forms that could change their ways of life to meet the new conditions—run on their hind legs, free their hands, live on smaller animals by hunting, band together for mutual protection—these forms would tend to survive and the less flexible, more old-fashioned forms would die out. In the end, the demands of communal living would weed out the smaller brains, the foolish ones who could not learn to talk.

How it actually happened we can only guess. But apparently sometime ages ago there were ape-men in lower Asia of the type of *Pithecanthropus erectus* whose skull-top, left thigh bone, and two molar teeth were found in 1891 by Dr. Eugene Dubois, a Dutch army surgeon, on the Bengawan River near Trinil in central Java. Most authorities agree that *Pithecanthropus erectus* was not one of our direct ancestors but an off-shoot of the direct line, an experiment, in other words, that failed.

The remains of other experiments have been found from time to time scattered in the river drift of those far-off ages. It is impossible here to do more than mention a few of the fragmentary remains from which scientists are slowly piecing together the story of man's long climb from the jungle. There is, for example, the lower jawbone of some form that must have been intermediate between pre-man and man. It was found 79 feet down in the Mauer sands near Heidelberg, Germany, in 1907. Then there are the fragments of a skull found in 1912 near Piltdown, Sussex, England. These are believed to be the remains of a somewhat more advanced race that had reached western Europe before 150,000 B.C.

With the fourth glaciation period from 100,000 to 50,000 years ago came a short, heavy-set, big-brained race, the Neanderthals, destined to be the last precursors of modern man in Europe. Since the first discovery of the remains of this race in a cave near Düsseldorf in 1856, skeletons or portions of skeletons have been found in more than twenty different places in Europe, and it is fairly certain that Neanderthal man was the master of Europe throughout the last ice age, a period of time at least as great as the 25,000 years that have elapsed since his disappearance. Physically, perhaps, the outstanding characteristics of the Neanderthals were the peculiarly prominent bony ridges above the eyes and the relatively small size of the frontal lobes of an otherwise large brain. Some authorities believe that the heavy brow ridges found among certain peoples in the British Isles and in western Europe may have come from Neanderthal blood. It has also been suggested that the ogre in our folk tales may be Neanderthal man as the folk memory has preserved him.

At any rate, Neanderthal was exterminated, or driven out, about 25,000 years ago by the first modern race to reach western Europe, Crô-Magnon man. The Crô-Magnon race was characterized by great stature, averaging more than six feet, and by disharmonic features, *i.e.,* a broad face and narrow head.[3] These characteristics were found in modern times among the Guanches of the Canary Islands.

On the mainland Crô-Magnon was apparently replaced gradually about 10,000 or 15,000 years ago by the three races which now dominate Europe—the Mediterraneans, or narrow-headed brunettes; the Alpines, or broad-headed blondes; and the Nordics,

[3] Anthropologists use the percentage ratio of the breadth to the length of the head as an index of biological relationship. A ratio of 80 per cent or more is called broad-headed; below 80, narrow-headed or long-headed. This ratio of breadth to length is called the cephalic index. The cephalic index, skin-color, and the shape of the hair in cross-section are the three indexes most used by anthropologists in classifying human types. It is important to remember, however, that no type appears in a pure form, *i.e.,* 100 per cent of a given population; and when two or more indexes are combined as a basis of classification the percentage of pure types rapidly decreases as the number of indexes is increased.

or narrow-headed blondes. Elsewhere the great Mongoloid and Negroid races were evolving.[4]

Evolving Man in an Evolving Environment. Thus, as is shown in the accompanying figure, we have behind us thousands of generations. More than 750 generations alone separate us from the first modern man in Europe, Crô-Magnon, as he replaces the Neanderthal. Nobody living today can begin to appreciate what life must have been like in the days of the Java ape-man; and the Java ape-man could certainly never have appreciated our life today. It is not merely that we are physically different, although our big brains are absolutely basic to any explanation of life as we live it. Over and above the biological differences that separate us from the ape-man there is an outward difference that the ape-man could never have grasped. On top of the natural physical environment such as the ape-man and his kind had to deal with, our bigger brains have built an *artificial environment* made up of ideas, tools, customs, institutions, skills, techniques of all kinds, man-made and absolutely essential to our well-being. This is the social heritage, or *culture*. Like our physical selves this also has evolved.

From Sticks and Stones to Steam and Stock Exchanges. It is so "natural" for us to sleep in beds, to wear clothing, to eat wheat bread, to warm ourselves at fires, to ride in wheeled vehicles, to talk as we please in our native tongue,—so easy and obvious to do these things,—that we never think of them as the accumulated inventions of uncounted myriads of men in the past. Yet like the soil in a rich bottom-land this social heritage is the accumulation of the deposits of many thousands of years. In the beginning it must have been altogether non-existent. True, animals have a kind of rudimentary social heritage in the form of forest paths, nests, beaver dams, and the like, and certain practices such as jumping with sticks and marching in line are passed about in a group of apes, but even the ape-man lived in a world so little altered by his own contriving that we can hardly credit

[4] How races originated is still a matter of dispute. Griffith Taylor, the Australian geographer, believes that the differentiation of human races occurred successively in central Asia, the original homeland, where the environmental stimuli were more intense. Other authorities, on the other hand, believe that differentiation occurred under the influence of widely differing environments, the Negroes in Africa, for example, and the Mongoloids, including the American Indians, in Asia. That races originated through cross-breeding is another theory to account for the same facts.

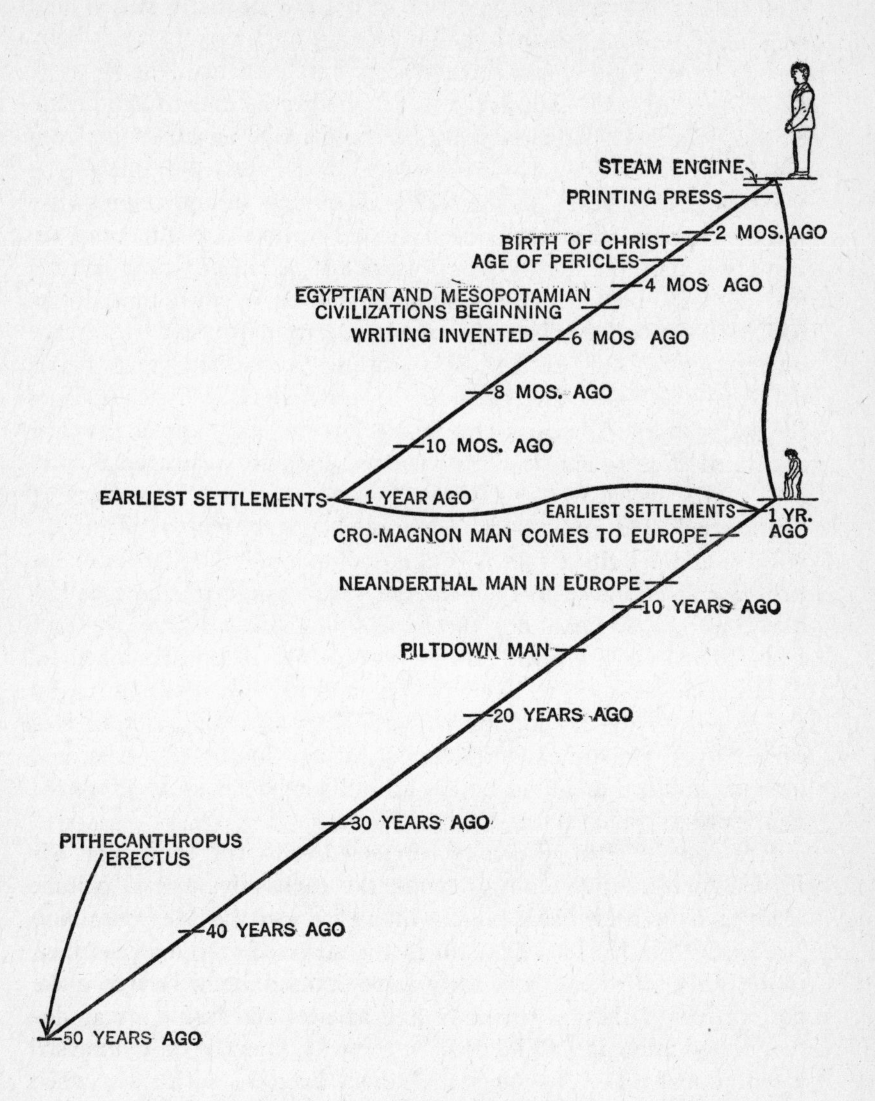

FIG. 1. How Man's Past Would Look if All Our Units of Time Were 10,000 Times Greater than They Are.

Adapted from James Harvey Robinson's *Mind in the Making*, pp. 82–4.

him with a social heritage at all. Possibly he used sticks and stones for striking, throwing, and poking, but if so he used them just as he found them, and there is no sure evidence that he used anything. Authorities disagree as to whether he could have had a language, although undoubtedly he could make an assortment of noises.

Gradually, however, as the slow millenniums dragged along, inventions grew from generation to generation. By the time of Piltdown man, possibly 150,000 years ago, a kind of rude culture had been in existence for a long time even in western Europe which seems to have been far removed from the centre of early inventiveness. This culture was passing from the stage of the eoliths, or dawn stones, such as the ape-man may have used, to the stage of the rough stones which were chipped or battered to a kind of edge to suit a dimly visioned purpose. With the arrival of Neanderthal in western Europe 50,000 years or so ago there is definite evidence of cultural advance, but it is still a culture so meagre and primitive that it is almost impossible for modern man to imagine existence in the Ice Age with such inadequate equipment. By 30,000 years ago the inhabitants of relatively backward Europe had long known how to make fire, to dispose of their dead, to chip stones, to live in caves, and to make their living by the chase. With the coming of Crô-Magnon about 25,000 B.C. came also finer stone work, wall paintings in the caves, lances, human skull-top drinking bowls, and other evidences of progress. But Europe was still far behind the East.

For some reason, probably connected with the protection afforded by the surrounding deserts, the early advances in culture seem to have been made chiefly in Egypt and the Mesopotamian Valley. While Europe was still in the stage of rough stone, men in the Valley of the Nile as early as 16,000 B.C. knew how to make pottery, could shoot with bows and arrows and had dogs as domesticated animals.[5] (The dog, by the way, was the only domesticated animal that the American Indians brought with them when they migrated from Asia by way of Bering Strait.) By 10,000 B.C. Egypt had reached the full Neolithic, or New Stone Age of domesticated animals, domesticated plants, and polished stone tools and weapons. Europe at that time was still lingering in the Rough

[5] This impressionistic sketch of the evolution of culture is adapted from A. L. Kroeber, *Anthropology*, New York, 1923, pp. 393 ff.

Stone Age. By 4500 B.C. the tribal period of Egyptian culture was giving way to little local kingdoms, the first evidence of man's ability to organize on a scale larger than face-to-face groups. Agriculture and animal breeding had now gone far enough to enable relatively large groups to live together. The stage was set for the invention of a calendar, metallurgy, writing, and the kingship.

By 4000 B.C. Egypt was beginning to use copper while western Europe was in its first phase of stone polishing.

Recorded history begins with the first dynasty in Egypt, possibly 4000 B.C., and with Sargon of Akkad, the first empire-builder in the Babylonian region, about 3750 B.C. Civilization, in other words, was in full flower in Egypt and Mesopotamia while Europe was still in the New Stone Age. As Kroeber says of Egypt:

> Hieroglyphic writing . . . had taken on substantially the forms and degree of efficiency which it maintained for the next 3000 years. An elaborate conventional system of this sort must have required centuries for its formative stages. A non-lunar 365-day calendar was in use. This was easily the most accurate and effective calendar developed in the ancient world and furnished the basis of our own. . . . Centuries must have elapsed while this calendar was being worked out.[6]

Egypt was using bronze by 2500 B.C. and iron by 1500. It is not believed that the Egyptians themselves discovered how to smelt iron, but that they acquired it from some other people around the eastern Mediterranean, or in western Asia. In the thirteenth century B.C. the Greek invaders who overthrew the Ægean culture of Crete, Mycenæ, and Troy were beginning to use iron. Italy learned the use of it from the Etruscans about 1100 B.C. Northern Europe did not reach the Iron Age till 500 B.C.

We have already suggested that the increasing efficiency of food-raising techniques and the lengthening arm of social control, by enabling more and more people to co-operate, were real factors in the evolution of culture. Cultural evolution has not only been an evolution of tools and material technologies but of social and economic organization as well. The economic historian Gras believes that in the beginning men lived by collecting what

[6] *Op. cit.*, p. 443.

nature offered. Later, when they started to cultivate animals and plants, there was a period of nomadism which preceded settled plant culture.[7] At least this may well have happened in many places.[8] Certainly with agriculture came permanent villages—at first probably free villages, unattached to any lord or protector; later, at least in Europe and apparently in Japan, dependent villages such as were common under the feudal system.

Gradually certain of these villages began to change their functions as there grew up within them a special class of people who made a business of trading. In other words, some of them became *towns*. We cannot go into the details of town organization, but it is interesting to note in passing that civilization as ordinarily understood is a product of town culture.

There have been no less than 18 civilizations. The first began apparently in Egypt, as we have seen, about 6000 years ago. Within a few hundred years and hardly a thousand miles away, a second centre arose in the Mesopotamian Valley.[9] From then down to our own day some civilization has always been carrying on somewhere in the world, although there have been curious recessions both in the old world and the new to lower levels of culture. One recession with which all of us are more or less familiar from our study of history was the period known as the Dark Ages, following the collapse of the Roman Empire in the West.

In terms of sheer duration the most lasting civilization seems to have been that of China which had reached a high level before the Greeks emerged from barbarism.

Along with these changes in food-techniques and changes in group organization there has also been going on a slow evolution in the control devices by which human activities are co-ordinated and unified. In the hunting stage of culture and even down into the late village stage, *kinship* constitutes the dominant regulating principle and *custom* the ruling power. Primitive man everywhere is custom-bound, hedged in by the mysterious sanctions of *taboo*. Rousseau's idyllic picture of the free and noble savage turns out

[7] Normal Scott Brien Gras, *An Introduction to Economic History,* New York, 1922.

[8] Anthropologists have long since shown that it is an error to believe that all groups inevitably pass through the same social or economic stages.

[9] The roll call of civilizations would include Sumerian, Akkadian, Babylonian, Assyrian, Chaldean, Persian, Egyptian, Cretan or Ægean, Chinese, Hindu, Greek, Roman, Arabian, Mayan, Toltec, Incan, Aztec, and Modern European.

everywhere to be merely a romantic fiction. Man is never so much a slave to custom and to his own dreadful imaginings as on the pre-literate level.

But with the coming of the town culture comes a decrease in the relative predominance of face-to-face groupings and an increase in those indirect kinds of association based on trade. To control these larger groups political *authority* develops, acting at first through military power and later, as in Roman times, through military power plus standardized codes of behavior known as the *law*.

Under rare conditions, if the total setting of culture and its environment is favorable, as it was in Athens during a few decades in the fifth century B.C., in Rome during the Republic, and in England and America during the nineteenth century, the escape from the tyranny of kinship and custom may result not in another and more far-reaching tyranny of authority, but in a society organized on the principle of *citizenship* and controlled by *public opinion*. Whether such a society so organized can maintain itself in the face of modern complexities is a question still unanswered.

Culturally, then, as well as biologically the world in which we find ourselves is a product of ages of evolution. What is the social situation that has emerged from all these ages of biological and cultural travail?

The Social World in Which We Live. Let us try to see our contemporary situation in its broad outlines. We find ourselves in a world organized for political action into some sixty-odd states and empires. Our own state, while it ranks as one of the great world powers, is only part of a much larger area covering western Europe and Canada in which, despite obvious differences in detail, the main elements of social life are very similar. Thus over most of western Europe and North America one finds private property, industrial capitalism, plow cultivation, schools, power-driven transportation, factories, the metropolitan organization of economic life, science, Christianity, monogamous families, and more or less representative government. In the United States particularly one finds an intensified form of the single family farm system, mass production, and an economic philosophy still dominated by pioneer individualism.

In this vast panorama of social life today what are the high points, the peaks, that dominate the picture as the Church dominated the Middle Ages? Three certainly stand out: *science*, the *machine*, and the *city*.

How Science Has Altered Life. Modern science is a development of the last three centuries. It has profoundly affected social life in three ways: (1) It has changed man's view of the universe and his conception of his own place in nature. (2) Its practical applications since the Industrial Revolution in the latter part of the eighteenth century in England have enormously decreased the burden on human muscles, enormously increased the social surplus and raised the standard of living, and vastly increased man's range of association and his power to affect his fellows for good or ill. (3) All of which has resulted in an increase in self-confidence among western peoples and a rebirth of the old Greek attitude that man's great adventure is here and now and not in some other world beyond the clouds.

The substitution of the scientific for the common sense and Biblical conceptions of the universe has not been accomplished, however, without great struggles, the echoes of which have not yet died away. The first clash came over the Copernican theory, which unceremoniously removed the earth from the centre of Creation. Before it became possible for good Christians openly to admit that the earth does move around the sun, Galileo had been forced to recant, Giordano Bruno had been burned at the stake and hundreds of lesser men had been killed, imprisoned or tortured. By the time the noise of that first battle had somewhat subsided the Darwinian theory appeared, and thinking men found themselves not only no longer resident at the centre of Creation but no longer even the favored children of that Creation. This was a very chilling discovery which two generations have been struggling with incomplete success to assimilate.

In the meantime it has gradually become apparent to all informed people that in place of a relatively simple world governed by the direct fiat of a personal God, science has gradually been substituting a highly complex universe governed, as the scientist sees it, by impersonal laws of cause and effect. Yet even these laws do not seem to be ultimate—modern physics, in the quantum theory which conceives of energy as passing from one level to another, so to speak, in jumps, or leaps, opens the door to further complexities.

No one can tell where science is taking us. Interstellar navigation, the conquest of death, nobody knows what, may lie ahead; for in the long perspective from the ape-man up, science is only an infant reaching for the moon. We assume that this is the kind of universe which it is good for man to understand; but that, of course, is a gesture of faith.

Meanwhile science must be counted as one of the great dynamic forces of modern life.

The Rôle of the Machine. Machinery has taken a load of toil off human shoulders, but it has not yet made man the free being that idealists consider possible. As machine production has become more highly developed, "more and more of the thought and will of the inventor, less and less of that of the immediate human agent, or machine tender, is expressed in the product."[10] Moreover, machine-production requires capital far beyond the powers of individual workmen to provide. In other words, the machine tends to dehumanize labor and to make it dependent on an external source of capital; *i.e.*, either on the private capitalist or on the state.

At the same time the machine has vastly increased the productivity of labor, increased per capita wealth, and raised the standard of living. For the first time in human history a great nation like the United States finds itself with productive power enough to give every normal individual reasonable economic security and a decent living. That millions do not have this security and do not have enough to maintain health and working efficiency is not the fault of the machine but of our methods of distributing the products of the machine. The mechanical engineer has done his job; the social engineer still has his to do.[11] Meantime the job of the social scientist is to formulate the principles which the social engineer will apply when people make up their minds whether or not it is a good thing for everybody to have as high a standard of living as the machine technology is ready to sustain.

Like its parent, science, the machine is a dynamic force in our social world. It creates overleaping economic ambitions on the one hand and bitter economic discontent on the other. It multiplies the

[10] John A. Hobson, *The Evolution of Modern Capitalism*, London, 1916, p. 71.

[11] Notice that this paragraph goes beyond mere description and assumes certain values. Whether poverty should or should not be abolished is a matter of opinion, but that the United States possesses productive power enough to feed and clothe all its normal citizens adequately is so generally admitted by all competent persons as to deserve rank as a fact.

opportunities for invention and draws people together in teeming centres where overcrowding, crime, and scores of other conditions become social problems of the first magnitude.

How the City Centralizes Co-operative Living. Cities are at least as old as civilization, which, as the word indicates, is a product of city-living. But the modern city and more particularly the organization of modern economic life around great metropolitan centres which dominate the activities of a region—these are products of science and the machine.

In its broadest outlines economic life in the United States is organized around 93 metropolitan centres of 100,000 or more and around more than 30,000 sub-centres of varying degrees of importance. The metropolitan centre, *i.e.,* the centre in which are concentrated the industrial and financial controls of a region, is the outgrowth of the last three centuries of town living. The beginnings date from the sixteenth century when London merchants began to organize their market to dispose of products outside of London. It was chiefly the pressure of this enlarging market that stimulated inventive activity among Englishmen in the eighteenth century and led to the invention of the steam engine, the various mechanical devices, and the new form of industrial organization, the factory, which characterized the Industrial Revolution.[12]

Like science and the machine which created them, modern cities are encouragers of social change. The changing needs of vast populations, the opportunities for individual profit by daring innovation, the focussing of all the forces of modern communication on an already highly stimulated group, the heightened competition of different races, different classes, and different business competitors, all these factors make for change.

From one point of view modern cities are focal points of social co-operation on a scale never seen before. Not only are they the organizing centres of their surrounding regions but they are the nodal points, so to speak, of a great network of exchange and competition that girdles the globe. The world market is no mere figure of speech. Under these conditions old attitudes and old ideas, appropriate enough for a slow-going, rural-village world such as our forefathers lived in, must be spliced and stretched and

[12] The factory itself, of course, was not new, since factories manned by slaves had existed in Roman times. It was the combination of steam power, mechanical power, and industrial discipline together that was unique.

sometimes changed altogether to meet new situations. *Science, the machine, and the modern city have given us a new social world and we can no longer rely on tradition to explain it to us or to control it for us.* Hence the growing emphasis on all the social sciences in the new education.

The Problem of Living in an Interdependent, Dynamic World. The problem is not merely one of the increasing size and complexity of social groups; it is in part a problem of changing the *values* of life to keep pace with our expanding powers. This was dramatically illustrated by the World War. There we had the spectacle of the very technological and scientific advances that had built the new world suddenly applied to the task of blowing it to pieces. The most ominous apparition that has issued from the smoking battlefields of Europe is scientific, mechanized warfare.

Scientific warfare means efficient warfare. It means increasingly efficient warfare—since no one can foresee an end of scientific discoveries. What this may mean a little comparison will make clear: Scientific warfare from 1914 to 1918 killed *twenty times as many soldiers per day* as pre-scientific warfare on the average could kill from the French Revolution to the German invasion of Belgium. In terms of soldiers killed per day, scientific warfare, in other words, even in its cradle, the World War, was 20 times as efficient as all the wars of the nineteenth century![13]

Now the important point is that, efficient as scientific killing had become by 1918, every expert agrees that it is many degrees more efficient today. We are probably prepared to kill from 30 to 40 times as many soldiers per day as the wars of the old-fashioned nineteenth century could dispose of. When we have perfected rocket planes and added germ-bombs and other devices to the list, instead of being able to account for only 6000 or 7000 per day as in the World War, we may be able to eliminate 100,000 or so a day. If the military prophets are correct, all this is just around the corner. It is the long look ahead, 100, 200, 500 years away, that really staggers the imagination. Either science will by that time have produced a situation in which any first-class power will be able to wipe out the entire human race in about one week, or the collapse of civilization will have wiped sci-

[13] See E. L. Bogart, *Direct and Indirect Costs of the Great World War*, New York, 1919.

ence itself out long before that time arrives. The only other possibility is that *Homo Sapiens* may have learned by that time how to get along without war.

Neither the Communists, on the one hand, nor the social pessimists, on the other, credit us, however, with that much sense. The Communists hopefully expect the next world war to bring about the inevitable collapse of capitalism, while the social pessimists see scientific warfare as the Frankenstein monster destined to end modern civilization and throw the western world once more back into the village economy of another dark age.

Yet war is only one of a host of problems each one of which has become more acute and more perilous as a result of science, the machine, and the city. With birth control widely practised, population growth in the United States slows down and we approach a stationary population—in a world in which the cradles of Russia and the Orient still teem with babies. In a world market dominated by a philosophy of each man for himself and the devil take the hindmost, economic security proves a will-o'-the-wisp and unemployment periodically throws millions on our streets. In cities, intent mainly on commercial prosperity, children grow up willy-nilly in the alleys and between the trucks; eventually these hoodlums present the bill for their lost childhood—at the point of a sub-machine gun. The school, the church, the family, all social life is feeling the impact of science, the machine, and city living.

The old world of our forefathers that held its breath at the terrific speed of 15 miles an hour and decided questions of practical improvement by references to the Bible[14]—the world that existed substantially from the time of Charlemagne to the days of Andrew Jackson—has been swept away. But we have yet to take down from the walls of our minds the pictures of that old world which no longer exists. With 11,000,000 men out of work in the winter of 1931–32 it was still possible to hear city people repeating the old village stereotype: "Anybody who really wants work can find it." In Andrew Jackson's day that would have been reasonably correct. In Herbert Hoover's day it was tragically false.

[14] In 1828 the school board at Lancaster, Ohio, refused to permit the schoolhouse to be used for a public meeting to discuss railroads, on the ground that if God had meant for man to travel at the incredible speed of 15 miles an hour He would have said something about it in the Bible!

Everywhere the conflict between old ideas and new conditions manifests itself. In their survey of Middletown, a representative mid-western manufacturing city, in 1922–24, the Lynds found that the city's life "exhibits at almost every point either some change or some stress arising from failure to change."[15] Throughout our social life this condition exists. *Thanks to the tremendous strides of physical science the material conditions of our lives have been changing faster than the ideas with which we control our collective behavior.* The result appears in madadjustment—maladjustment in industry, in family affairs, in government, in the church, in the school, in community life, in international relations. We are, so to speak, trying to drive a racing car with a buggy whip.

Thus we find ourselves living in a complex urban civilization, torn by national, racial, and class conflicts and bedevilled by a multitude of social changes which we only dimly understand. What are the basic processes underlying this complicated business of living with others? Why is life organized as it is, standardized as it is, regulated as it is? What forces are driving us on and what conditions determine our path?

As a first step toward answering these questions we must analyze the nature of man's heredity, the biological basis of association. To this analysis we turn in Chapter II.

STUDY QUESTIONS

1. Why was sociology so late in appearing as a subject of scientific study? What does it deal with?
2. As a sociologist, should it make any difference to you whether a given social condition is good or bad? Why?
3. How many people are there in the world and how are they distributed?
4. What bearing have the facts of population pressure in Japan on the Manchurian question?
5. What is the biological function of association?
6. Who was the Java ape-man and why is he significant?
7. Who was Neanderthal man? Cro-Magnon?
8. Distinguish the Mediterranean, Alpine, and Nordic races from one another. Define cephalic index.

[15] Robert S. and Helen M. Lynd, *Middletown,* New York, 1928. Middletown is Muncie, Indiana.

9. Roughly what is the time perspective of man's biological evolution? How long has culture been evolving?
10. Distinguish between the process by which biological evolution occurs and the process by which cultural evolution occurs.
11. How long have men known how to make fire?
12. Into what periods would you divide the evolution of tools?
13. Trace the evolution of social organization. Of social control.
14. What are the three outstanding features of modern culture?
15. In what three ways has science altered life?
16. In what way is science founded on faith?
17. What are outstanding effects of the machine?
18. If the machine can produce enough to feed and clothe all normal persons, why do we still have poverty?
19. Around how many centres is economic life organized in the United States? What do you understand by the term metropolitan pattern of culture?
20. What is the problem created for us by science, the machine, and the city?
21. What is the significance of the application of science to warfare?
22. How do you account for the fact that some people, in the midst of a depression, still say: "Anybody who really wants work can find it?"
23. What do you understand by the analogy, "trying to drive a racing car with a buggy whip"?

CHAPTER II

THE BIOLOGICAL BASIS OF HUMAN ASSOCIATION

Hereditary and Social Transmission. We have come in recent years to look upon all questions of human life from an evolutionary point of view. When regarded from this standpoint any personality appears to be at the confluence of two streams coming down from the past. Or perhaps we might better say that there is a stream with a road running along the bank—two lines of transmission. The stream is heredity or animal transmission; the road is communication or social transmission. One flows through the germ-plasm; the other comes by way of language, intercourse, and education. The road is more recent than the stream; it is an improvement that did not exist at all in the earliest flow of animal life, but appears later as a vague trail alongside the stream, becomes more and more distinct and travelled, and finally develops into an elaborate highway, supporting many kinds of vehicles and a traffic fully equal to that of the stream itself.

How does this idea apply to the life of a given individual? His body—and his mind, too, for that matter—begins in a minute, almost microscopic bit of substance, a cell, formed by the union of cells coming from the bodies of his parents, and containing, in some way not completely understood, tendencies which reach back through his grandparents and remoter ancestors over indefinite periods of time. This is the hereditary channel of his life, and the special kinds of cells in which heredity is conveyed—called the germ-plasm—are apparently the only source of those currents of being, those dispositions, capacities, potentialities, that each of us has at the beginning of his course.

The social origin of his life comes by the pathway of intercourse with other persons. It reaches him at first through his susceptibility to touches, tones of voice, gesture, and facial expression; later through his gradually acquired understanding of speech. What is reaching him of course is culture or the social heritage, of which language itself is one of the most important elements.

We may distinguish these two lines of history more clearly, perhaps, if we take a case where they are not parallel, where the road over which we get our social heritage, our culture, has not followed the stream from which we get our animal heritage, but has switched off, as it were, from another stream. Suppose, for example, that an American family in China adopts a Chinese baby and brings it home to grow up in America. The animal life history of that baby's past will lie in China. It will have the straight black hair, the yellowish skin and other physical traits of the Chinese people, and also any mental tendencies that may be a part of their heredity. But his social past will lie in America, because he will get from the people about him the culture traits that have been developed in this country. He will fall heir to the American political, religious, educational, and economic institutions; his whole mind will be an American mind, excepting only for the difference (if there is any) between his inherited aptitude to learn such things and that of the American children. The Chinese stream and the American road have come together in his life.

We have said that every person may be regarded as a point of meeting of these two lines of influence. He cannot, however, be thought of as the resultant of merely these two forces. He is directly affected to some extent by the natural or non-cultural aspects of his environment. During the whole pre-natal period, for instance, the individual is developing in reaction to certain surrounding biological conditions. It is only because these conditions are much the same for every member of the species that we think of them as unimportant. They may have a great deal to do with making us so similar. In a somewhat like manner we are directly affected by such pervasive natural factors as climate, though most of the effect of these has been embodied in culture—the siesta in tropical countries, for example.

The Mechanism of Hereditary Transmission. Each human individual starts as a fertilized egg in which are contained two complete sets of the hereditary carriers called genes. One of these sets has come from each parent and constitutes half of the genes which that parent possessed. Because of the way in which the germ cells of each parent divide before uniting to form the fertilized egg, the genes which the offspring receives are not identical with the sets passed to his parents by any two of his grandparents, but are rather a mixture from all four grandparents. The exact process need not detain us here but its significance in providing an infinite variety in the hereditary constitution of human beings is great. With the single exception of identical twins who are born of the same egg, each of us probably has a set of genes which have never before been together in the same combination.

It is important that during the life of the individual the germ cells which he is carrying and which may share in the production of new individuals are almost completely isolated. The result of this is that an individual's mode of life has no effect upon the heredity which he passes on to his children. An obvious example is that injuries or mutilations, such as the loss of a leg, are never inherited, not even if they are continued for generations, as was formerly the case with the feet-binding of certain classes of Chinese women. Thus the children of a great athlete gain no hereditary advantage from the fact that he has trained himself so well. Their genes would have been no different if he had never gone into athletics at all. They of course may receive an unusual hereditary equipment for athletics such as their father had, but this was in the father's germ-plasm at the beginning of his life and was not enhanced by his development. The only advantage which they will receive from his having become a great athlete is one of social transmission, since his example and advice will doubtless greatly aid them in developing their potentialities in this direction.

Though the mode of life of higher organisms in no way affects the hereditary stream, the sole changes in that stream are not merely those of recombination. Aberrations sometimes occur in the distribution of the genes so that an individual organism may receive either more or less than the two complete sets which are normal. Further, there sometimes occur changes, called mutations, in the nature of the genes themselves because of obscure chemical or physical processes. These changes have not been studied in man as yet, but we know that they must have occurred in the past in order to give the human race a type of heredity so different from that of the lower animals.[1]

Natural Selection. When we come to consider the hereditary equipment of a group of any sort, whether a tribe, a city, or a whole race, we meet the fact that it may be radically altered by selection. Since the germ-plasm carried by every individual is dif-

[1] For a full discussion of these matters, see H. S. Jennings, *The Biological Basis of Human Nature*, xiv.

ferent and since different individuals may vary greatly in the number of children they produce, the proportions of various sorts of heredity in the group may change greatly from generation to generation. An obvious case of this is where two contrasted races are living together. Imagine a purely hypothetical case of a county in the north in which there are equal numbers of Negroes and whites, but in which Negroes suffer disproportionately from tuberculosis so that the average number of children raised to maturity in the Negro families is only three while in the white families it is four. In the next generation the whites will outnumber the Negroes four to three, in the following generation sixteen to nine, and so on in geometrical ratio. The Negroes will be a rapidly dwindling fraction of the population.

If, instead of having two distinct races in the county, we had merely the white race, in which, however, there was a considerable difference in complexion among the family stocks represented, something analogous might take place. If the dark families were more prolific than the blonde, the population would darken *as a whole* and *vice versa.*

It is believed that the conditions of life are all the time tending to cause some types of heredity to increase at the expense of other types and so by an unconscious process changing the germ-plasm of the group as a whole. For example, the frontier conditions in the early history of America probably tended to produce a physically vigorous race; not because the undergoing of hardships had any direct effect upon the germ-plasm, but because the weaker sort of people would be likely to die out under hardships, and leave no children to inherit their weakness, while the stronger sort would leave large families and correspondingly increase the sort of germ-plasm that they carried. This process is what is known as "natural selection" or "the survival of the fittest," the discovery of which was the great contribution of Darwin. It should be clear that this process assumes hereditary variations and a certain set of conditions which act as a selective agent. In order to be selected the hereditary qualities have to be fitted to the particular conditions which the organisms are facing. Thus with the passing of the pioneer era in America the natural selection of the physically strong has undoubtedly been greatly diminished.

This process may in time produce very great changes. The difference in color between the black and white races (which are probably sprung from a common ancestry) is plausibly explained on the principle of natural selection by supposing that darker skins were associated with greater power of resistance to the actinic rays of the sun, or to the diseases of tropical climates, so that this kind of heredity would increase in such climates; just as many species of animals are known to develop colors that help their survival. Most animals, including birds, are so colored as to be hard to distinguish from their environment: it is a kind of camouflage, and helps them to escape the enemies who would otherwise devour them, or to approach the prey which would otherwise escape them.

Artificial Selection—Eugenics. Selection is, however, not necessarily an unconscious process produced by the working of "natural" forces. Animal breeders have for many centuries consciously selected those individuals which possessed the traits which they desired and bred them together in order to produce offspring of the greatest value. This artificial selection has been important in producing specialized types like the race horse and the cow of great milk-producing capacity. In man there has been some artificial selection through the incarceration of the feeble-minded and the prevention of their propagation. It might furthermore be argued that the members of each sex have consciously selected as their mates those members of the opposite sex who were most capable both physically and mentally, leaving the less capable to die without offspring. There is no proof that this has actually been the case. If it were true some might prefer to call it natural rather than artificial selection.

There has grown up of recent years a project for improving human heredity by artificial selection called eugenics. The objects are to stimulate the propagation of desirable types and to diminish or prevent that of undesirable types. There are two great obstacles which lie in the path of this movement. One is to get the public to accept the programme which the scientists advocate. Many believe it wrong to interfere in any way with propagation; and even those who would be willing to prevent propagation of defectives through segregation or sterilization would probably rebel if asked to make considerations of racial stock an important factor in their own marriage selections. The second and even greater difficulty is that defective genes are usually "recessive," not "dominant," so that only those who have both genes of the same pair defective exhibit the defect. Jennings estimates that there are about 30 normal persons carrying defective genes recessively for every one who, because he possesses two such genes, is himself defective. Thus preventing the defectives from propagating will only slightly decrease the number of defective genes in existence and will only slightly affect the number of defective in the next generation. The chief hope here is that scientists will discover a way of determining which individuals are carrying defective genes recessively. If this comes to pass and if people can be brought to accept the dictates of geneticists, eugenics will become a very powerful force for human welfare. Even at present the programme is a valuable one, though we must be careful not to be taken in by the extravagant statements of some of its proponents.[2]

Race Suicide. One phase of the problem of selection in human life which has caused considerable concern and to which eugenists have directed considerable attention is race suicide. By this term is meant the selective breeding of different classes in our society which is evidenced by the smaller families among the better educated and more prosperous and the larger families among the so-called "lower" classes. The assumption here is that the "better" classes have on the average better heredity and that therefore we are breeding future generations in a disproportionate degree from the poorer hereditary stocks. It is likened to the skimming of cream from the top of a pan of milk. The cream of our heredity is thought to rise to the higher positions in our society and then to be skimmed off by the small birth rate among those in such positions. If the underlying assumption is sound and if the process seems likely to continue indefinitely it is indeed a serious situation. There is a good deal of doubt on both these points, however. In the first place those who "rise" in our society may be better only in some respects, in aggressiveness for instance, and may be no better than those who do not "rise" in other traits like kindliness or stability. But beyond this Jennings maintains that biologically "the 'classes' do not perpetuate themselves as such. From the higher many lower are produced; from the lower, many higher. From the great mediocre group are produced more of the higher than the higher group itself produces; and

[2] For an excellent discussion of eugenics, see Jennings, *The Biological Basis of Human Nature,* x. Wiggam's popular books, *The New Decalogue of Science* and *The Fruit of the Family Tree,* have been responsible for a good deal of public misinformation on this subject.

more of the lower than the lower group itself produces."[3] Secondly, the fall in the birth rate in the "better" classes seems to be largely a result of the use of birth-control methods, a practice which is coming to be more common in all social classes. Thus it may happen that ultimately all social classes will have small families, each class just about reproducing its numbers, so that differential breeding will come to an end.

Heredity and Development. An individual's heredity is fixed at the moment of conception. After that all that takes place comes under the head of development. The relationship between these two has caused much controversy, but scientific opinion is now pretty well agreed that our heredity merely lays down general patterns which are filled in, revised, or even neglected by the developmental process. Jennings has stated the situation as follows: "The characters of the adult are no more present in the germ cells than is the automobile in the metallic ores out of which it is ultimately manufactured. To get the complete, normally acting organism, the proper materials are essential; but equally essential is it that they should interact properly with one another and with other things. And the way they interact and what they produce depends on the conditions. . . . Clearly, it is not necessary to have a characteristic merely because one inherits it. Or more properly, characteristics are not inherited at all; what one inherits is certain material that under certain conditions will produce a particular characteristic; if these conditions are not supplied some other characteristic is produced."[4] Thus we can think of heredity as bringing us certain tendencies to a definite sort of physical development and certain capacities or lines of teachability in the psychical realm as well. But all these potentialities are plastic in more or less degree, so that nourishment and stimulation will make a difference in the ultimate result. It has even been found that some defects in the genes can be compensated for by proper procedure. For instance, there is the case of the cretin, an individual undeveloped both physically and mentally, an imbecile dwarf, all because of innate defectiveness of the thyroid gland. If a child of this type is fed thyroid over a long period of time growth will gradually be resumed and the brain will develop normally.

[3] Jennings, *op. cit.*, p. 221.
[4] H. S. Jennings, "Heredity and Environment," *Scientific Monthly*, XIX (1924), pp. 230, 233.

Human heredity has not been nearly as thoroughly investigated as that of animals. In the latter case, scientists can control and vary the conditions of development almost at will so that the nature of the hereditary factor can be studied. With man this is impossible. Hence the greatest source of information on this subject is likely to be pairs of identical twins who have lived in very different situations from an early age. Investigations of cases of this kind have already been made and others are going forward. Even here, however, the two individuals will have had the same pre-natal environment in the mother's womb, a factor which is important and one which needs to be kept distinct from heredity. Most cases of venereal disease in children for instance are due to pre-natal contact, not to inheritance.

Culture in the Developmental Process. As far as our distinctively human traits are concerned, culture, working through social transmission, is the most important of the conditions of development. Most of the stimulation and teaching which cause the hereditary tendencies to develop in a particular way come from this source. It is thus that we learn to speak one language rather than another, feel patriotism for America rather than for Italy, to develop particular aims in life and kinds of ambition. Everything in the way of specific function must be learned in this way, no matter what capacity we have. When we say that a child is a born musician we mean, not that he can play or compose by nature alone, but that if he has the right kind of teaching he can rapidly develop power in this direction. In this sense and in no other can a man be said to be a born athlete, a born poet, or a born teacher.

Complementary Character of Heredity and Culture. At the moment of the individual's birth the two currents coming from the past, heredity and culture, begin a process of fusion which continues throughout the person's life. Nothing that he does—at least on the distinctively human level—thereafter can be ascribed to the influence of either stream alone, because everything is based on habits and experiences in which the two are inextricably intermingled. What heredity is, in its practical working at a given time, depends upon the total process itself, which develops some potentialities and represses others. And in like manner the effective environment depends upon the selective and assimilating activities of the growing organism. If you wish to understand the behavior of a person the main thing to do is to study his life-history back to its beginning in his conception and birth; beyond that you may, if you wish, pursue still farther the germ-plasm and the culture from which he sprang. These give us a background, like the accounts of a man's ancestry and early surroundings in the first chapters in his biography. But the life of William Sykes is a thing you must study directly, and no knowledge of heredity and culture can be more than a help to this.

Speech well illustrates the inextricable union of animal and social heritages. It springs in part from the native structure of the vocal organs and from a hereditary impulse to function through whatever organs we have. Perhaps a natural sensibility to other persons and need to communicate with them also enters into it. But all articulate utterance comes by social transmission; it is learned from others, varies with the environment and has its source in tradition. Speech is thus a socio-biologic function. And so it is with ambition and all our socially active impulses. We are born with the need to assert ourselves, but whether we do as hunters, warriors, fishermen, traders, politicians, or scholars depends upon the opportunities offered us in the social world.

Evidently it is wrong to regard heredity and social transmission as antagonistic. They are complementary, each having its own work to do and neither of any use without the other.

Which is stronger? Which is more important? These are silly questions, the asking of which is sufficient proof that the asker has no clear idea of the matter in hand. It is precisely as if one should ask, Which is the more important to the human race, man or woman? Both may be said to be infinitely important, since each is indispensable; and their functions being different in kind cannot be compared in amount.

Shall we say, then, that all discussions as to the relation between heredity and environing developmental conditions are futile? By no means. The fact is that, although it is plain that they are, in general, complementary and mutually dependent, we usually do not know precisely what each contributes in a given case, and so may be in doubt whether to seek improvement by working on the germ-plasm through selection or on the conditions influential in development. The truth is that for us heredity is the more important factor when it is the more variable factor and environing conditions are less likely to vary. Thus stature and skin color we think of as mainly hereditary because anything like normal nourishment and physiological influences will make the hereditary differences apparent; though this nourishment and these influences may alter the result if sufficiently abnormal. On the other hand, language, religion, and moral standards are thought of as due to cultural factors because it is these that vary so greatly; however, the normal hereditary capacity is not to be overlooked as a necessary condition to the development of these things. Between these extremes there are many differences of temperament and abilities concerning which it is doubtful what the contributions of the two streams are. Take, for instance, the Negro question. How far is the present inferior condition of that race remediable by education and social improvement, how far is it a matter of germ-plasm, alterable only by selection? The whole Negro-white problem hinges on this question, which we cannot answer with assurance.

There is an analogous problem with reference to criminals. How far, in just what sort of cases, may we safely trust to educational or deterrent measures as a preventative of crime? Should we also try to prevent propagation, and if so, when and how? And so with men of great intellectual ability. We need more of them. Will education do it, or shall we follow the teaching of Galton, the founder of eugenics, who held that we must above all things induce men of this sort to have more children? And again, with reference to the rich and powerful classes. Is their ascendancy that of natural ability, of a superior breed, and so, perhaps, just and beneficial? Or is it based on social privileges in the way of education and opportunity, and hence, as many think, unfair and detrimental? Unsolved questions of this kind arise whenever we try to make out just how we may better the course of human life. At present the best we can do is to try everything that seems likely to improve either the germ-plasm or the process of social transmission.

Man's Unique Hereditary Equipment. Although the transmission of heredity through the germ-plasm and its development under the influence of environing conditions is the same in man as in the other animals, the nervous structure on which behavior is based becomes largely fixed in the lower species at an early stage of the individual's development, whereas in man nervous pathways never become fixed, so that an indefinite growth and modification of behavior takes place. The mental outfit of the human child at birth is above all things teachable, consisting not of tendencies to do particular things, but of vague aptitudes or lines of teachability that are of no practical use until they are educated. The mental outfit of the animal, on the other hand, is incapable of the same variety of response but gives rise to activities which are useful with little or no teaching.

Roughly speaking, then, the early development of the other animals produces a mechanism like a hand-organ: it is made to play a few tunes; you can play these tunes almost at once with little or no training; and you can never play any others. The embryonic development of man, on the other hand, produces a mechanism—at least with reference to distinctively human traits—more like that of a piano: it is not made to play particular tunes; you can do nothing at all on it without training; but a trained player can draw from it an infinite variety of music.

A newly hatched chick is able to run about and to pick up small objects of a certain size and form which prove to be food and to sustain its life. It scarcely needs education, and breeders say that the products of the incubator, having no link with the past of their race except the germ-plasm, get along as well as those which have all a mother's care. A baby, on the other hand, takes a year to learn to walk and many, many more years to learn the activities by which he is eventually to get his living. He has, to be sure, a definite ability to draw nourishment from his mother, but this is only a makeshift, an animal method to help him out until his more human powers have time to develop. In general, his wonderful hereditary capacities are as ineffectual as a piano when the player begins to practice. Definite function is wholly dependent upon education.

Thus the plastic, indeterminate character of the human nervous system involves a long and helpless infancy; and this, in turn, is the basis of the human family, since the primary and essential function of the family is the care of children. Those species of animals in which the young are adequately prepared for life by earliest development have no family at all, while those which more or less resemble man as regards plasticity, resemble him also in having some rudiments, at least, of a family. Kittens, for instance, are cared for by the mother for several months and profit in some measure by her example and instruction.

More generally, this difference as regards plasticity means that the life activities of the animal are comparatively uniform and fixed, while those of man are varied and changing. Human functions are so numerous and intricate that no fixed mechanism could provide for them: they are also subject to radical change, not only in the life of the individual but from one generation to another. The only possible basis for them is an outfit of indeterminate capacities which can be developed and guided by experience as the needs of life require.

A flycatcher sits upon a branch where there are no leaves to interrupt his view. Presently he darts toward a passing insect, hovers about him a few seconds, catches him, or fails to do so, and returns to his perch. That is his way of getting a living: he has done it all his life and will go on doing it to the end. Millions of other flycatchers on millions of other dead branches are doing precisely the same. And this has been the life of the species for unknown thousands of years. They have, through the germ-plasm, a definite capacity for this—the keen eye, the swift, fluttering movement to follow the insect, the quick, sure action of the neck and bill to seize him—all effective with no instruction and very little practice.

Man has a natural hunger, like the flycatcher, and a natural mechanism of tasting, chewing, swallowing, and digestion; but his way of getting the food varies widely at different times of his life, is not the same with different individuals, and often changes completely from one generation to another. The great majority of us gain our food, after we have left the parental nest, through what we call a job, and a job is any activity whatever that a complex and shifting society esteems sufficiently to pay us for. It is very likely, nowadays, to last only part of our lives and to be something our ancestors never heard of. Thus whatever is most distinctively human, our adaptability, our power of growth, our arts and sciences, our social institutions, is bound up with the indeterminate system produced by the pre-natal development of our heredity.

Of course there is no sharp line, in this matter of teachability, between man and the other animals. The activities of the latter are not wholly predetermined, and in so far as they are not, there is a learning process based upon plasticity. The higher animals—horses, dogs, elephants, apes, for example—are notably teachable, and may even participate in the changes of human society, as when dogs learn to draw carts, trail fugitives, guide the lost, or perform in a circus. And, on the other side, those activities of man which do not require much adaptation, such as the breathing, sucking, and crying of infants, and even walking (which is learned without instruction when the legs become strong enough), are provided for before birth.

Instinct. This general discussion of animal and human development enables us to understand the place of instinct in human life. Animals, as we have seen, have definite and effective modes of acting which they do not have to learn, and it was these which first attracted the notice of scientists because of their contrast to human behavior. They were called instincts as opposed to the more rational or acquired activities of man. Darwin says in his *Origin of Species:*

"I will not attempt any definition of instinct . . . but every one understands what is meant when it is said that instinct impels the cuckoo to migrate and to lay her eggs in other birds' nests. An action, which we ourselves require experience to enable us to perform, when performed by an animal, more especially by a very young one, without experience, and when performed by many individuals in the same way, without their knowing for what purpose it is performed, is usually said to be instinctive.[5]

Men have few instinctive actions in this sense of the word. But when investigators began to study our behavior from the evolutionary point of view, they saw that if not instinctive in the strict sense, it had yet grown out of instinctive behavior, was historically continuous with it, and, in short, that there was no sharp line to be drawn, in this matter, between human and animal. The tendency seems to have been toward the breaking down of elaborate innate reaction patterns and the substitution for them of habits. This may very well have been fostered by natural selection working upon mutations in this direction, since individuals equipped with habits rather than instincts would have more adaptability and would be more likely to survive under changing conditions. Probably many of our reflexes like swallowing, blushing, and the knee jerk are remnants of once more inclusive patterns. The situation in man today is simply that his overt responses are largely habitual but that incorporated in these habits

[5] *Origin of Species* (New York: Appleton, 1873), p. 205.

are often reflexes which were, at a pre-human evolutionary stage, components of elaborate inherited patterns.

Though man does not show long trains of overt behavior based on inborn patterns he does seem to experience inner states, called emotions, which are unlearned. These emotions are a result of certain innate visceral reactions stimulated through the nervous system. What happens, then, is that these visceral reactions become "conditioned" to a great variety of external situations, and whenever one of these situations arises, the appropriate internal, innate pattern functions, giving us an emotion like fear, anger, or love. It is perhaps not inaccurate to speak of these patterns as instinctive emotions.

Although instinctive emotion probably enters in one way or another into most of the things we do, it enters in such a way that we can never explain developed human behavior by it alone. The previous conditioning process is always an indispensable cause as well.

If, for example, we say "War is due to an instinct of pugnacity," we say something that includes so little of the truth and ignores so much, that it is practically false. War is rooted in many instinctive tendencies, all of which have been transformed by education, tradition, and organization, so that to study its sources is to study the whole process of society. This calls, above all things, for detailed historical and sociological analysis: there could hardly be anything more inimical to real knowledge or rational conduct regarding it than to ascribe it to pugnacity and let the matter go at that.

Much the same may be said of the employment of a supposed gregarious instinct, or "instinct of the herd," to explain a multiplicity of phenomena, including mob-excitement, dread of isolation, conformity to fads and fashions, subservience to leaders, and control of propaganda, which require, like war, a detailed study of social antecedents. This is, as Professor Findlay remarks, "an easy, dogmatic way of explaining phenomena whose causes and effects are far more complicated than these authors would admit."[6] Indeed there is not any such evidence of the existence of a gregarious instinct as there is of an instinctive emotion of fear or anger; and many think that the phenomena which it is used to explain may be accounted for in other ways without calling in

[6] *An Introduction to Sociology,* p. 72.

a special instinctive tendency. It is perhaps the postulate of an individualistic psychology in search of some special motive to explain collective behavior. If you regard human nature as primarily social you need no such special motive.

Human History Only Possible with Plastic Heredity. Human history, in distinction from animal history, is a natural outcome of the biological basis of personality which we have outlined. It is a process possible only to a species having a teachable mental outfit, whose members can be organized into a plastic and growing social whole. This whole, responsive to the outer world in a thousand ways, and containing also diverse and potent energies within itself, is ever putting forth new forms of life, which we describe as progress or decadence according as we think them better or worse than the old. These changes do not necessitate, though they may accompany, alteration in hereditary capacities. The hereditary basis, the instinctive but teachable capacities, are relatively constant, and, so far as these are concerned, there is little or no reason to think that the Teutonic stocks from which a majority of Americans are sprung are appreciably different now from what they were when Cæsar met and fought and described them. If we could substitute a thousand babies from that time for those in our own cradles, it would probably make no perceptible difference. They would grow up in our culture, driving automobiles instead of war chariots, reading the newspapers and in general playing the human game as it is played today quite like the rest of us.

STUDY QUESTIONS

1. Do you think any animals have both heredity and social transmission?
2. What do you think of the view that many men of genius are lost to the world because of unfavorable environment?
3. Do you think the view that acquired traits are not inherited is hopeful or otherwise as regards the improvement of society? How does it affect the method of improvement?
4. Do you think that "selection," in the evolutionary sense, implies the action of will? Does it exclude will?
5. Just what is it that "survives" in an evolutionary sense? The individual? What else? In general what is the test of biological "survival"?

6. What illustrations of your own can you give of the operation of "natural selection" upon human life?
7. Many think that this operation is less favorable in civilized than in savage life. What can you say for or against this view?
8. Some hold that the anti-tuberculosis movement is harmful because it preserves weakly types that were better eliminated by the disease. What do you think?
9. What are some of the difficulties that beset the eugenics programme?
10. Just what would you understand by "race suicide," and in what respects does it seem to you a serious problem?
11. What reasons can be given for and against the proposition that the upper economic class is also the class of highest eugenic value? What are the practical bearings of the question?
12. Studies showing the existence of degeneracy in several generations of a family are usually interpreted as showing the preponderating influence of heredity. Is this an adequate interpretation?
13. "An interest in roast beef is hereditary; an interest in good literature is of social origin." What do you think of this statement?
14. How would you answer the question, Which is stronger, heredity or environment?
15. Show just how the question of heredity versus environment might arise in connection with a criminal; with a man of genius. Can you think of cases where it might arise other than those suggested in the text?
16. Illustrate from your observation the difference in teachability between human and animal heredity. How did this difference come about?
17. How is the helplessness of human infants related to the nature of our social life?
18. How would you distinguish the following: (*a*) animal instinct; (*b*) instinctive emotion in man; (*c*) habit in man?
19. What is meant by calling the explanation of human behavior by instinct alone "particularism"? Can you give other examples of this fallacy?
20. Show how the character of human heredity is the basis of social evolution.
21. How would you summarize the rôle of our biological inheritance in our social life?

CHAPTER III

THE PSYCHO-SOCIAL BASIS OF ASSOCIATION—COMMUNICATION AND SYMPATHETIC INSIGHT

Communication, the Basic Factor in Association. The psycho-social basis of all human association, of all distinctively human traits in personality, is communication. Communication may be defined as the process of sharing, or making common, any experience. Without taking part in such a process the mind does not develop a true human nature at all, but remains in an abnormal and nondescript state neither human nor properly brutal. This is vividly shown by those individuals who, having had the misfortune to become separated from their kind, have grown up among animals. Several of these so-called "feral" men have been discovered and all have lacked the qualities essential to human nature. Some have gone about on all fours, and all present more likeness to animals than to human beings.[1] Indeed they make relatively poor animals because they lack the instincts which would enable them to adapt themselves to the type of life animals lead. The truth is that our type of heredity implies a development under social conditions and if these conditions are lacking it is a liability rather than an asset.

We are, then, not born human but gradually become so as we develop through contacts with the minds of others. And it is likewise true that we will gradually lose our human characteristics if completely cut off from communication with others for a long period. If you go off alone in the wilderness you take with you a mind possessing memory and imagination which can continue the counterpart of social intercourse of a vivid sort for a long time, even in the absence of books or a radio to give you stimulation. This, and only this, keeps humanity alive in you, and just in so far as you lose the power of intercourse your mind decays. Prolonged

[1] For material on "feral" men see Park and Burgess, *Introduction to the Science of Sociology*, 1st ed., pp. 239–42; M. H. Small, "On Some Psychical Relations of Society and Solitude," *Pedagogical Seminary*, VII, pp. 32–36; and Paul C. Squires, "The Wolf Children of India," *American Journal of Psychology*, XXXVIII, pp. 313–15.

solitude, as in the case of sheepherders in remote places, or prisoners in solitary confinement, often has this effect. The mind cannot keep itself perpetually in motion without the rejuvenating experience of actual communication, and so must ultimately run down. A castaway who should be unable to retain his imaginative hold upon human society might conceivably live the life of an intelligent animal, exercising his mind upon the natural conditions about him, but his distinctively human faculties would certainly be lost, or in abeyance.

The Case of Helen Keller. A moving illustration of the need for communication is the case of Helen Keller, who was cut off at eighteen months from the cheerful ways of men by the loss of sight and hearing; and did not renew the connection until she was nearly seven years old. Although her mind was not wholly isolate during that period, since she retained the use of a considerable number of signs learned during infancy, yet her impulses were crude and uncontrolled, and her thought was so unconnected that she afterward remembered almost nothing that occurred before the awakening which took place toward the close of her seventh year.

The story of that awakening, as told by her teacher, gives as vivid a picture as we need have of the significance to the individual mind of the general fact and idea of communication. For weeks Miss Sullivan had been spelling words into her hand which Helen had repeated and associated with objects; but she had not yet grasped the idea of language in general, the fact that everything had a name, and that through names she could share her experiences with others, and learn theirs—the idea that there is *fellowship in thought.* This came quite suddenly.

"This morning," writes her teacher, "while she was washing, she wanted to know the name for water. . . . I spelled w-a-t-e-r and thought no more about it until after breakfast. Then it occurred to me that with the help of this new word I might succeed in straightening out the mug-milk difficulty (a confusion of ideas previously discussed). We went out into the pump-house and I made Helen hold her mug under the pump while I pumped. As the cold water gushed forth filling the mug I spelled w-a-t-e-r in Helen's free hand. The word coming so close upon the sensation of cold water rushing over her hand seemed to startle her. She dropped the mug and stood as one transfixed. A new light came into her face. She spelled water several times. Then she dropped on the ground and asked for its name, and pointed to the pump and the trellis, and suddenly turning round she asked for my name. I spelled 'teacher.' Just then the nurse brought Helen's little sister into the pump-house, and Helen spelled 'baby' and pointed to the nurse. All the way back to the house she was highly excited, and learned the name of every object she touched, so that in a few hours she had added thirty new words to her vocabulary."

The following day Miss Sullivan writes, "Helen got up this morning like a radiant fairy. She has flitted from object to object, asking the name of everything and kissing me for very gladness." And four days later, "Everything must have a name now. . . . She drops the signs and pantomime she used before, so soon as she has words to supply their place, and the acquirement of a new word affords her the liveliest pleasure. And we notice that her face grows more expressive each day."[2]

This experience is a type of what happens more gradually to all of us; it is through communication that we get our higher development. The faces and conversations of our associates; books, letters, travel, arts, and the like, by awakening thought and feeling and guiding them in certain channels, supply the stimulus and framework for all our growth.

"Communication" Among Bees. The fundamental forms of human communication are the pre-verbal and the verbal. The former involves the use of signs and the latter that of true symbols. Perhaps we can better understand their functioning if we observe a type of communication, so-called, in which learning seems to play no part in determining the effectiveness of the stimulus. For example, a scout bee on returning from a well-filled saucer of sugar-water will on entering the hive go through a kind of round-dance to attract the attention of other sugar-gatherers.[3] These others after following the dancer for a few moments will in turn rush off to seek out the source of supply. Experiments have demonstrated that they are guided in their search not by "ideas," or symbolical directions, but almost wholly by their sense of smell. If in their turn they find a well-filled supply they repeat the round-dance on their return to the hive; but if, on the other hand, they

[2] Helen Keller, *The Story of My Life*, pp. 316, 317.

[3] For a full description of "communication" among bees, see Karl V. Frisch, *Über die "Sprache" der Bienen*, Jena, 1928.

find only a meagre supply, they omit the dance. In this way the condition of the food-source is, so to speak, "communicated" to the hive-mates. But the process involves no communication of ideas and does not depend on real symbols at all. The odor of the food-source which is disseminated by the dance is practically a part of the food-supply itself which has been brought to the nest; it is not a different kind of stimulus such as a sound, for example, which the organism has learned to associate with the food-supply. On the human level the kind of influence exerted is analogous to that of the odor of a dinner attracting a hungry boy.

Pre-verbal Communication. Pre-verbal communication takes place through the expressions of the face—especially of the mobile portions about the eyes and mouth—the pitch, inflection, and emotional tone of the voice, and the gestures of the head and limbs. Such signs seem to be pre-human in their origin, since we find mammals the world over communicating by such means. What they communicate is, of course, much simpler than the substance of even the simplest conversation. Comparative psychologists are in substantial agreement that animal communication is limited to the emotional states of the organism, its wants and desires.[4] Factual description is quite beyond the scope of pre-verbal signs. A dog, for example, may excite another dog by barking, but he is quite incapable of telling the second dog that he had a cat up a certain tree day before yesterday.

The example just given suggests another characteristic of pre-verbal signs. Their use is quite involuntary until a high degree of sophistication on the human level has been reached. They are merely integral parts of total responses of the organism to which others come to attach meaning through experience. Gesture, such as reaching out the hand, bending forward, turning away the head, and the like, springs directly from the ideas and feelings it represents.

Eventually, however, the same thing happens to pre-verbal communication that happens to every other human tendency—cultural elaboration occurs. The stage, salesmanship, the motion picture,—various devices and techniques of this sort—are invented to capitalize the inherent possibilities. Thus it comes about that de-

[4] The language of parrots is only a seeming exception. Despite the claims of bird fanciers, scientists generally hold that parrots do not really understand the words that they repeat.

liberate control of pre-verbal signs becomes an important element of success in many situations. Successful acting, for example, seems to depend almost wholly on the proper control of pre-verbal signs. Anybody, as it were, can read lines; only an actor, deliberately yet unobtrusively controlling the play of pre-verbal communication, can make an audience feel the emotions behind the lines.

It is evident that pre-verbal signs are mainly relied upon to reveal feeling; for conveying ideational elements we chiefly use verbal symbols. But just because habitual states of feeling constitute the core of personality we are likely to judge other persons quite largely by their pre-verbal signs. If one is cheerful, confident, candid, sympathetic, he awakens similar feelings in others, and so makes a pleasant and favorable impression; while gloom, reserve, indifference to what others are feeling, and the like, have an opposite effect. We cannot assume or conceal these states of feeling with much success; the only way to appear to be a certain sort of person is actually to become that sort of person by cultivating the necessary habits. We impart what we are without effort or consciousness and rarely impart anything else.

If there is any truth in the belief that young children have an intuition of personal character quicker and more trustworthy than that of grown people, the reason is probably related to pre-verbal communication. In so far as children may be better judges of such simple qualities as sincerity and good will, a plausible explanation would lie in the fact that the faces they see and study are mostly full of the expression of love and truth. Nothing like it occurs in later life, even to the most fortunate. These images, we may believe, give rise in the child's mind to a more or less definite ideal of what a true and kindly face should be, and this ideal he uses with great effect in detecting what falls short of it. The adult loses this clear, simple ideal of love and truth, and the sharp judgment that flows from it. His perception becomes somewhat vulgarized by a flood of miscellaneous experience, and he sacrifices childish spontaneity to wider range and more complex insight, valuing and studying many traits of which the child knows nothing. It will not be seriously maintained, on the whole, that we know people better when we are children than when we are older.

In any assembled group of people such as an audience or a crowd there is a tendency for pre-verbal responses to build up an emotional tone more or less different from the tone that the mere words of the speaker would create. Each hearer is at least vaguely aware of the pre-verbal responses of his fellows about him and tends involuntarily to respond to their responses. Now under certain circumstances of dramatic excitement or tension this cumulative tendency of pre-verbal communication may easily transform an assembled group into a dynamic, emotion-charged mass known as a mob. One reason for this seems to be the fact that pre-verbal signs tend to transmit emotions much more rapidly than words can transmit ideas. Hence emotion, once the process is set going under proper conditions, tends to outrun ideas of control. When to the greater rapidity of emotional communication is added the factor of emotional cumulation, or reciprocal stimulation, already mentioned, the importance of pre-verbal communication in creating the mob situation becomes apparent. All this is, of course, impossible in the radio audience.

Pre-verbal signs, then, are chiefly useful for conveying emotion and giving an impression of the emotional, dynamic side of personality. All of us begin by using these signs and only gradually acquire the use of more complex ones. Pre-verbal signs do not, of course, cease to function as we grow up; they merely become overlaid, so to speak, with words.

Between purely pre-verbal and purely verbal communication there is a middle stage represented by gesture language. In the evolution of the race doubtless this was well organized before speech made much headway. Though it is now of little social importance it will serve to indicate the difference between the sign and the true symbol. A gesture whose meaning is only apparent in the context of a total act is a sign. Thus the clenching of the fists in the face of aggressive, threatening behavior on the part of another denotes determination to resist. The clenching of the fists as an isolated act means nothing. However, one could invent a conventional code in which the clenching of the fist always had a determinate meaning, such as "fight." This is what our pre-human ancestors no doubt did. In such a system each gesture is a symbol —that is, a stimulus referring to something beyond itself which does not have to be seen in a context of overt activity to be meaningful.[5] But pre-verbal symbols are clumsy and the range

[5] "A symbol may be defined as an act or object which is marked off by behavior as a substitute for a stimulus-act or -object and a response-act or -object,

of ideas that can be expressed is limited. Hence language everywhere supervened.

Importance of Speech. Speech, or a developed system of symbols, is an essential to human nature. Pre-verbal communication alone would scarcely be sufficient to give us that intercourse with others upon which the development of personality depends. Indeed speech may be regarded as the gate by which man emerged from his pre-human state. It means that, like Helen Keller, he has learned that everything has, or may have, a name, and so has entered upon a life of conscious fellowship in thought. It not only permitted of the rise of a more rational and human kind of thinking and feeling, but was also the basis of the earliest definite institutions. A wider and fuller unity of thought took place in every group where it appeared. Ideas regarding the chief interests of primitive life—hunting, warfare, marriage, feasting, and the like—were defined, communicated, and extended. Public opinion no doubt began to arise within the tribe, and crystallized into current sayings which served as rules of thought and conduct; the festal chants, if they existed before, became articulate and historical. And when any thought of special value was achieved in the group, it did not perish, but was handed on by tradition and made the basis of new gains. In this way primitive wisdom and rule were perpetuated, enlarged, and improved until they became such institutions, of government, marriage, religion, and property as are found in every savage tribe.

The languages now in existence are products of ages of evolution. Many humble inventors have contributed to their growth and are contributing today. Every man probably alters this verbal heritage in proportion as he puts his individuality into his speech. On the whole, however, the individual takes from language far more than he ever gives. It is language that extends the perceptible environment. Thanks to words each of us lives in a larger world than the one he merely sees, smells, and touches. It is language that puts our perceptible environment together for us and takes it apart. A name is a tool for cutting a little slice out of the flux of experience and fixing it in attention. Words give fixity

and which is also at the same time set off by behavior as different from them," *i.e.*, "as an act which is a stimulus-substitute for another act often not present, and at the same time is a stimulus for a response to . . . this other act, while the stimulus-substitute is also marked off by behavior as distinct from the other act and the response to it."—John F. Markey, *The Symbolic Process*, 1928, pp. 28 f.

and definition to experience. When one says "town" he not only marks certain phenomena off from all that is not town, but he lumps together certain characteristics such as houses, streets, people, stores, and the like.

A mind without words would make only such feeble and uncertain progress as a traveller set down in the midst of a wilderness where there were no paths or conveyances and without even a compass. A mind with them is like the same traveller in the midst of civilization, with beaten roads and rapid vehicles ready to take him in any direction where men have been before. As the traveller must pass over the ground in either case, so the mind must pass through experience, but if it has language it finds its experience foreseen, mapped out and interpreted by all of the wisdom of the past, so that it has not only its own experience but that of the race—just as the modern traveller sees not only the original country but the cities and plantations of men.

Spatially, as well as psychologically, language engulfs the individual. More than 160,000,000 people speak the English tongue and probably another 60,000,000 understand it. The sheer bulk of the 700,000 or more words in the English dictionary shows how infinitesimal must be the contribution of any one individual. In fact, the massiveness of language is one of the great obstacles to wider world organization today. According to the French Academy, there are more than 2796 different spoken languages, not to mention different dialects and systems of writing. Although only a few of these are of first importance, it remains true that even the most widespread language, English, is spoken by less than one tenth of the world's population.

Learning Language. Communication involves both giving and receiving, so that before the infant is truly human he must be able both to express and to understand verbal symbols. How are these goals achieved?

It is apparent that it is not our reflexes, but rather our plastic teachableness which makes possible these developments. Of the utmost importance is the baby's random, unorganized behavior. An infant is active a great deal of the time when he is awake, seemingly just working off his surplus energy. He moves his arms and legs, babbles and makes a variety of noises with his vocal apparatus, and watches things with his eyes. Gradually certain movements seem to succeed more than others in the sense that they give the baby greater pleasure in one way or another. Thus he learns to grasp his rattle and shake it. Habits are beginning to be formed out of this chaos of random movement.

At an early age other people come to be responded to by the infant in a degree disproportionate to the responses evoked by other objects in the environment. The human voice, for instance, soon comes to arouse greater interest and activity than other sounds of like intensity. This is undoubtedly because the voice has become associated with pleasant sensations such as feeding, rocking, stroking, etc. However, not all experiences with other people are pleasant, for there may be occasional slaps and rude treatment. When this occurs there is an accompaniment of frowns and harsh tones of the voice, so that the differentiation is soon made between those pre-verbal expressions which indicate approval and those which denote the opposite.

It is this developed interest in others working in conjunction with the random vocalizations of the infant which brings about the learning of language. The child perhaps first associates sounds with things or events when he sees a dog frequently in the act of barking, or when his mother repeats "daddy" to him whenever his father appears. Now if in his random vocalizations he has hit upon syllables similar to "bow-wow" and "da-da" and can reproduce them, he has taken the first step, for something he can say is now linked in his mind with some feature of the external world. From this point on it dawns upon the child that probably everything which others are saying in his presence has in a similar way some reference or meaning and it becomes one of the greatest interests of his life to discover what these meanings are.

A word is a vehicle, a boat floating down from the past, laden with the thought of men we never saw; and in coming to understand it we enter not only into the minds of our contemporaries, but into the general mind of humanity continuous through time. The popular notion of learning to speak is that the child first has the idea and then gets from others a sound to use in communicating it; but a closer study shows that this can be true only of ideas of concrete objects in the immediate environment, and is nearly the reverse of the truth as regards abstract thought.[6] Thus the word usually goes before, leading and kindling the idea—the

[6] In the evolution of the language all new ideas, whether concrete or abstract, precede the words which express them.

child would not have the latter if he did not have the word first. "This way," says the word, "is an interesting thought: come and find it." And so we are led on to rediscover old knowledge. Such words as *good, right, truth, love, home, justice, beauty, freedom* are powerful makers of what they stand for.

Interaction, the Life of the Mind. The human organism, like all organisms, is naturally active and needs outlets for energy. The ability to give and receive communications from the minds of others opens up fascinating new modes of functioning. We need no gregarious instinct to explain our natural sociability. The delight in companionship, so evident in children of all ages, may be largely ascribed to their need of stimulation. Thus they have a marked preference for active persons, for grown-up people who will play with them—provided they do so with tact—and especially for other children. It is the same throughout life; alone one is like fireworks without a match: he cannot set himself off, but is a victim of *ennui,* the prisoner of some tiresome train of thought that holds his mind simply by the absence of a competitor. A good companion brings release and fresh activity, the primal delight in a fuller existence. So with the child; what excitement when visiting children come! He shouts, laughs, jumps about, produces his playthings and all his accomplishments. He needs to express himself, and a companion enables him to do so.

The value for personal development of these social contacts through language is perhaps indicated by the fact that when left to themselves children continue the joys of sociability by means of an imaginary playmate. Although all must have noticed this who have observed children at all, only close and constant observation will enable one to realize the extent to which it is carried on. It is not an occasional practice, but, rather, a necessary form of thought, flowing from a life in which personal communication is the chief interest and social feeling the stream in which, like boats on a river, most other feelings float. After a child learns to talk and the social world in all its wonder and provocation opens on his mind, it floods his imagination so that all his thoughts are conversations. He is never alone. Sometimes the inaudible interlocutor is recognizable as the image of a tangible playmate, sometimes he appears to be purely imaginary.

The main point here is that these conversations are not occasional and temporary effusions of the imagination but are the naïve expression of the socialization of the mind that is to be permanent and to underlie all later thinking. The imaginary dialogue passes beyond the thinking aloud of little children into something more elaborate, reticent, and sophisticated: but it never ceases. Grown people, like children, are usually unconscious of these dialogues; as we get older we cease, for the most part, to carry them on out loud, and some of us practise a good deal of apparently solitary meditation and experiment. But, speaking broadly, it is true of adults as of children, that the mind lives in perpetual conversation. It is one of those things that we seldom notice just because they are so familiar and involuntary; but we can perceive it if we try to. If one suddenly stops and takes note of his thoughts at some time when his mind has been running free, as when he is busy with some simple mechanical work, he will be likely to find them taking the form of vague conversations. This is particularly true when one is somewhat excited with reference to a social situation. If he feels under accusation or suspicion in any way he will probably find himself making a defense, or perhaps a confession, to an imaginary hearer. A guilty man confesses "to get the load off his mind"; that is to say, the excitement of his thought cannot stop there but extends to the connected impulses of expression and creates an intense need to tell somebody. Impulsive people often talk out loud when excited, either "to themselves," as we say when we can see no one else present, or to any one whom they can get to listen. The fact is that language, developed by the race through personal intercourse and imparted to the individual in the same way, can never be dissociated from personal intercourse in the mind; and since higher thought involves language, it is always a kind of imaginary conversation. The word and the interlocutor are correlative ideas.

Thought and Communication Inseparable. The impulse to communicate is not so much a result of thought as an inseparable part of it. They are like root and branch, two phases of a common growth, so that the death of the one presently involves that of the other. Montaigne, who understood human nature as well, perhaps, as any one who ever lived, remarks: "There is no pleasure to me without communication: there is not so much as a sprightly thought comes into my mind that it does not grieve me to have produced alone, and that I have no one to tell it to."[7] and it was

[7] *Essay on Vanity.*

doubtless because he had many such thoughts which no one was at hand to appreciate, that he took to writing essays. The uncomprehended of all times have kept diaries for the same reason. So, in general, a true creative impulse in literature or art is, in one respect, an expression of this simple, childlike need to think aloud or *to* somebody; to define and vivify thought by imparting it to an imaginary companion; by developing that communicative element which belongs to its very nature, and without which it cannot live and grow.

Men apparently solitary, like Thoreau, are often the best illustrations of the inseparability of thought from communication. No sympathetic reader of his works can fail to see that he took to the woods and fields not because he lacked sociability, but precisely because his sensibilities were so keen that he needed to rest and protect them by a peculiar mode of life, and to express them by the indirect and considerate method of literature. No man ever labored more passionately to communicate, to give and receive adequate expression, than he did. This may be read between the lines of all his works, and is recorded in his diary, "I would fain communicate the wealth of my life to men, would really give them what is most precious in my gift. I would secrete pearls with the shell-fish and lay up honey with the bees for them. I will sift the sunbeams for the public good. I know no riches I would keep back. I have no private good unless it be my peculiar ability to serve the public. This is the only individual property. Each one may thus be innocently rich. I enclose and foster the pearl until it is grown. I wish to communicate those parts of my life which I would gladly live again."

Imaginary Persons Are Socially Real. It is worth noting here that there is no separation between real and imaginary persons. The test of social reality is influence upon our behavior, and it is well known that deceased persons, mythical heroes, characters in fiction, and others having no sensible presence may exert a greater influence than individuals physically close, like the crowd in a street car. Would it not be absurd to deny social reality to Abraham Lincoln, who is so much alive in many minds and so potently affects important phases of thought and conduct? He is certainly more real in a practical sense than most of us who have not yet lost our corporeity, and more alive, perhaps, than he was before he lost his own, because of his wider influence. And so

Colonel Newcome, or Romola, or Hamlet is real to the imaginative reader with the realest kind of reality, the kind that works directly upon his personal character. And the like is true of the conceptions of supernatural beings handed down by the aid of tradition among all peoples. What, indeed, would society be, or what would any one of us be, if we associated only with corporeal persons and insisted that no one should enter our company who could not show his power to tip the scales and cast the shadow?

Insight Essential to the Sociologist. If we are to understand social life, then, we must have insight into the minds of people, for it is there that we can perceive the influence of others upon them. A's idea of B is what is chiefly important as far as A's conduct is concerned, for it is that and not the real B which principally affects A; so that if we are to understand B's influence upon A we must have insight into A's mind. Weighing and measuring a person will give us little or no information upon him as a participant in social relationships. The physical factors most significant are the elusive traits of pre-verbal expression which do give some indication of the mind beneath, but in their observation and interpretation physical science is only indirectly helpful. What, for instance, could the most elaborate knowledge of his weights and measures, including the anatomy of his brain, tell us of the character of Napoleon? Not enough probably to distinguish him with certainty from a moron. Our real knowledge of him is derived from reports of his conversation and manner, from his legislation and military dispositions, from the impression made upon those about him and by them communicated to us, from his portraits and the like; all serving as aids to the imagination in forming a system that we call by his name.

The images which people have of each other, then, are solid social facts and the sociologist must make it his business to observe and interpret them. The intimate grasp of any social fact will be found to require that we divine what men think of one another. Charity, for instance, is not understood without imagining what ideas the giver and recipient have of each other; to grasp homicide we must, for one thing, conceive how the offender thinks of his victim and of the administrators of the law; the relation between the employing and wage-earning classes is first of all a matter of personal attitude which we must apprehend by sympathetic insight with both; and so on.

The Social Rôle of Sympathetic Insight. Sympathetic insight, however, is not just a tool of the sociologist. It is possessed in great measure by all human beings. It is really the great mark of distinction between man and the lower animals. Its roots lie, of course, in both our heredity and our culture. Without our natural teachability on the one hand and our developed language on the other we would be unable to share the mental states of our associates.

One's range of sympathetic insight is a measure of his personality, indicating how much or how little of a man he is. It is in no way a special faculty, but a function of the whole mind to which every special faculty contributes, so that what a person is and what he can enter into through the life of others are very much the same thing. A strong, deep understanding of other people implies mental energy and stability; it is a work of persistent, cumulative imagination which may be associated with a comparative slowness of direct sensibility. On the other hand, we often see the union of a quick sensitiveness to immediate impressions with an inability to comprehend what has to be reached by reason or constructive imagination.

Sympathetic insight is a requisite to social power. Only in so far as a man understands other people and thus enters into the life around him has he any effective existence; the less he has of this the more he is a mere animal, not truly in contact with human life. And if he is not in contact with it he can, of course, have only brutal power over it. This is a principle of familiar application, and yet one that is often overlooked, practical men having, perhaps, a better grasp of it than theorists. It is well understood by men of the world that effectiveness depends at least as much upon address, *savoir-faire,* tact and the like, involving insight into the minds of other people, as upon any more particular faculties. There is nothing more practical than social imagination; to lack it is to lack everything. All classes of persons need it—the mechanic, the farmer, and the tradesman, as well as the lawyer, the clergyman, the railway president, the politician, the philanthropist, and the poet. Every year thousands of young men are preferred to other thousands and given positions of more responsibility largely because they are seen to have a power of sympathetic insight which promises efficiency and growth. Without "caliber," which means chiefly a good imagination, there is no getting on much in the world. The strong men of our society, however much we may disapprove of the particular direction in which their understanding is sometimes developed or the ends their power is made to serve, are very human men, not at all the abnormal creatures they are sometimes asserted to be.

A person of definite character and purpose who comprehends our way of thought is sure to exert power over us. He cannot altogether be resisted; because, if he understands us, he can make us understand him, through the word, the look, or other symbol which both of us connect with the common sentiment or idea; and thus by communicating an impulse he can move the will. Sympathetic influence enters into our system of thought as a matter of course, and affects our conduct as surely as water affects the growth of a plant.

Selection in our Mental Life. A healthy mind, at least, does not spend much energy on things that do not, in some way, contribute to its development: ideas and persons that lie wholly aside from the direction of its growth, or from which it has absorbed all they have to give, necessarily lack interest for it and so fail to awaken the desire for further insight. An incontinent response to every stimulus offered indicates the breaking down of that power of inhibition or refusal that is the natural defense against the reception of material we cannot digest, and looks toward weakness, instability, and mental decay. So with persons from whom we have nothing to gain, in any sense, whom we do not admire, or love, or fear, or hate, and who do not even interest us as psychological problems or objects of charity, we can have no understanding except of the most superficial and fleeting sort. It should not be overlooked that a large class of people suffer a loss of human breadth and power by falling into a narrow and exclusive habit of mind; but at the same time personality is nothing unless it has character, individuality, a distinctive line of growth, and to have this is to have a principle of rejection as well as reception in understanding.

Perhaps those who most need the vigorous power of resistance to the numerous influences that in no way make for character development are those who live in the bustle of the modern city. Universal understanding is impracticable; what we need is better control and selection, avoiding both the narrowness of our class and the dissipation of promiscuous impressions. It is well for a man to open out and take in as much of life as he can organize into a consistent whole, but to go beyond that is undesirable. In a time of insistent stimulation, like the present, it is fully as important to many of us to know when and how to restrict the impulse to understand as it is to avoid narrowness. And this is in no way inconsistent with that modern democracy of sentiment which deprecates the limitation of mental sharing by wealth or position. Understanding must be selective, but the less it is controlled by conventional and external circumstances, such as wealth, and the more it penetrates to the essentials of character, the better. It is this liberation from convention, locality, and chance that the spirit of the time calls for.

The development of personality through sympathetic insight is guided and stimulated in its selective growth by feeling. The outgoing of the mind into the thought of another is always, it would seem, an excursion in search of the congenial; not necessarily the pleasant, in the ordinary sense, but of that which is fitting or congruous with our actual state of feeling. Thus we would not call Carlyle or the Book of Job pleasant exactly, yet we have moods in which these writers, however lacking in amenity, seem harmonious and attractive.

Differentiation of Insight in Modern Life. Since the life of this age is more diversified than life ever was before, the person who shares it through understanding evidences a greater variety of interests and affiliations. A man may be regarded as the point of intersection of an indefinite number of circles representing social groups, having as many arcs passing through him as there are groups. This diversity is connected with the growth of communication, and is another phase of the general enlargement and variegation of life. Because of the greater variety of imaginative contacts it is impossible for a normally open-minded person not to lead a broader life, in some respects at least, than he would have led in the past. Yet it is also true that there is demanded of us a more distinct specialization than has been formerly required. The complexity of society takes the form of organization, that is, of a growing unity and breadth sustained by the co-operation of differentiated parts, and the man of the age must reflect both the unity and the differentiation; he must be more distinctly a specialist and at the same time more a man of the world.

STUDY QUESTIONS

1. Would a baby reared alone from infancy among animals develop: (*a*) human characteristics; (*b*) distinctively animal characteristics; or (*c*) neither? Why?
2. Which in your opinion would make the better adjustment to prolonged solitude—(*a*) a primitive savage; or (*b*) a modern American? Why?
3. What is the significance of the case of Helen Keller for understanding human life?
4. Why do we not call the influence of one bee upon another communication?
5. Show how culture affects pre-verbal signs.
6. Compare what you might learn about a person (1) by seeing him frequently without exchanging words, and (2) by an intimate correspondence without seeing him.
7. Show how gesture language is intermediate between pre-verbal and verbal communication.
8. Show that speech, human nature, and cultural organization must have originated together.
9. What is meant by saying that language economizes experience?
10. "Language engulfs the individual." Point out at least two ways in which this is true.
11. Show how the random behavior of an infant lays the basis for his distinctively human development?
12. Why do babies come to respond to persons more intensely than to the inanimate objects in their environment?
13. Show just how a word enables us to form ideas that we could not otherwise have.
14. Children frequently have imaginary playmates. Does this prove the existence of a gregarious instinct? Why?
15. Is it true that an artist cannot create without an audience? Give your opinion, with reasons.
16. How do you reconcile a love of solitude with the social nature of the human mind?
17. How are we justified in saying that the test of social reality is mental rather than physical?
18. What is meant by saying that a sociologist must imagine imaginations?
19. "Sympathetic insight is a measure of personality." Give illustrations from your observation or reading.
20. What differences have you observed as to sympathetic insight between country people and city people? Between business

men, professional men and hand workers? Between men and women?

21. What ground is there for thinking that we may have too much sympathetic insight? Can you give illustrations?
22. "Our mental life is a work of art." In what sense? Do you agree?
23. By a comparison of activities show whether you share through sympathetic insight in more groups than your parents did at your age.

CHAPTER IV

HUMAN NATURE AND PRIMARY GROUPS

Why We Behave Like Human Beings. If one were to ask why we behave like human beings, the answer, unlike that given by a distinguished anthropologist,[1] would certainly include at least three factors: *Heredity, human nature,* and the social heritage, or *culture.* We have already considered the rôle of heredity in providing as the basis of human association the capacity for abstract thinking and the peculiar kind of plastic or unspecialized instinct characteristic of human beings. In later chapters we shall analyze those accumulated results of association which we call culture. Before attempting to do that, however, it is imperative that we see more clearly some of the psychological consequences of this process of living with other people. In other words, it is imperative that we consider the phenomena of *human nature,* and observe the basic forms of association, the *primary groups,* which are peculiarly important in affecting human nature.

Meaning of Human Nature. By human nature we mean those characteristics which are human in being superior to those of the lower animals, and also in the sense that they belong to mankind at large, and not to any particular race or time. These can perhaps be analyzed into (1) a highly complex yet flexible type of behavior, and (2) certain characteristic attitudes and sentiments which are always developed by close association with other people. Under the former head we would include the general results which flow from man's ability to use symbols for communication, such as conceptual thinking, imagination, idealization, foresight, and the ability to acquire or slough off behavior patterns without overt trial and error. We would include under the latter head such things as self-consciousness, enjoyment of approbation, pain at censure, a sense of right and wrong, rivalry, and hero-worship. These will vary in content from one culture to another but the general types will be found in all. For instance,

[1] The reference is to George A. Dorsey's, *Why We Behave Like Human Beings,* New York, 1925, in which almost the entire emphasis rests on heredity.

polygamy has been considered right in many tribes and peoples, though it is thought wrong by us; the heroes which the Viking children worshipped were very different from the big business men our children admire; the mediæval ascetics did not regard their physical bodies as parts of their selves, though the body is to us the very centre of our selves. But no matter how great the differences in content due to cultural differences, persons in all cultures have ideas of right and wrong, worship heroes, and feel self-conscious. Similarly men always seek honor and dread ridicule, defer to public opinion, cherish their goods and their children, and admire courage, generosity, and success.

The more insight one gets into the life of savages, even those that are reckoned the lowest, the more human, the more like ourselves, they appear. Take, for instance, the natives of Central Australia, as described by Spencer and Gillen,[2] tribes having no definite government or worship and scarcely able to count to five. They are generous to one another, emulous of virtue as they understand it, kind to their children and to the aged, and by no means harsh to women. Their faces as shown in the photographs are wholly human and many of them attractive.

And when we come to a comparison between different stages in the development of the same race, between ourselves, for instance, and the Teutonic tribes of the time of Cæsar, the difference is neither in human nature nor in capacity, but in organization, in the range and complexity of relations, in the diverse expression of powers and passions essentially much the same.

There is no better proof of the generic likeness of human nature than in the ease and joy with which the modern man makes himself at home in literature depicting the most remote and varied phases of life—in Homer, in the Hebrew scriptures, in the legends of the American Indians, in stories of frontier life, of soldiers and sailors, of criminals and tramps, and so on. The more penetratingly any phase of human life is studied the more an essential likeness to ourselves is revealed.

Primary Groups, the Nurseries of Human Nature. Now why should human beings exhibit this striking likeness? Some have said that it is because we have a common type of heredity.[3]

[2] *The Native Tribes of Central Australia,* London, 1899.

[3] Many writers have used the term human nature to mean merely man's biological nature, but we feel our definition is more nearly in accord with general usage, as when one says, "To resent an insult is human nature."

But obviously this is not enough—though it is an essential factor—since we have seen that our heredity without association leaves us unhuman. If human nature belongs, then, to men in association, what kind or degree of association is required to develop it? Evidently nothing elaborate, because elaborate phases of society have been transient and diverse, while human nature is comparatively stable and universal. But are there simple forms of association which could produce the observed result? It appears that there are, and we shall call them *primary groups*.

A primary group may be defined as a group of from two to possibly fifty or sixty people—*i.e.,* a small number—who are in relatively lasting face-to-face association for no single purpose, but merely as persons rather than as specialized functionaries, agents or employees of any organization. Type examples of the primary group are the family, or household group, the old-fashioned neighborhood, and the spontaneous play-group of children. In such groups all children everywhere participate, and the intimate association there realized works upon them everywhere in much the same way. It tends to develop sympathetic insight into the moods and states of mind of other people and this in turn underlies the development of both the flexible type of behavior and the common attitudes and sentiments which we have mentioned.

Human nature is, then, not something existing separately in the individual, but a *group nature or primary phase of society.* It is the nature which is developed and expressed in those simple face-to-face groups that are somewhat alike in all societies. Man does not have it at birth; he cannot acquire it except through fellowship; and it decays in isolation.

Characteristics of Primary Groups. The chief characteristics of a primary group are:

1. Face-to-face association.
2. The unspecialized character of that association.
3. Relative permanence.
4. The small number of persons involved.
5. The relative intimacy among the participants.

Such groups are primary in several senses, but chiefly in that they are fundamental in forming the social nature and ideals of the individual. The result of intimate association, psychologically, is a certain fusion of individualities in a common whole, so that one's very self, for many purposes at least, is the common life and purpose of the group. Perhaps the simplest way of describing this wholeness is by saying that it is a "we"; it involves the sort of sympathy and mutual identification for which "we" is the natural expression. One lives in the feeling of the whole and finds the chief aims of his will in that feeling.

It is not to be supposed that the unity of the primary group is one of mere harmony and love. It is always a differentiated and usually a competitive unity, admitting of self-assertion and various appropriative passions; but these passions are socialized by sympathy, and come, or tend to come, under the discipline of a common spirit. The individual will be ambitious, but the chief object of his ambition will be some desired place in the thought of the others, and he will feel allegiance to common standards of service and fair play. So the boy will dispute with his fellows a place on the team, but above such disputes will place the common glory of his class and school.

In primitive cultures, and even in advanced cultures before the growth of cities, the great bulk of human association occurs in primary groups. Probably the human race, all told, has lived more than 90 per cent of its total existence in such groups. That the home, the play-group and the neighborhood are relatively less prominent in modern American life than they were in Colonial days or among the original Americans themselves is not traceable to any decline in the absolute importance of the primary-group function itself but to the effects of modern communication, particularly the automobile, and to the resulting substitution of other less intimate forms of association.

It is well to remember, however, that no attempt to organize society on a non-primary basis has ever been permanently successful. Our own experiment in civilization is not escaping the difficulties that inevitably attend the effort to make large secondary groups such as corporations, cities, nations, satisfy the demands of human nature that issue from the primary group experience. As we shall see later, these difficulties are mainly difficulties of personality, of communication and of organization, but before attempting to analyze them more fully it is essential to understand more of the nature and functions of the groups themselves.

The Type Examples of the Primary Group. The most important spheres of this intimate association and co-operation, as we have said—though by no means the only ones—are the family, the spontaneous play-group of children, and the neighborhood, or "little community" of elders.[4] These are practically universal, belonging to all times and all stages of development; and are accordingly a chief basis of what is universal in human nature and human ideals. The best comparative studies of the family, such as those of Westermarck, Howard, or Briffault, show it to us as not only a universal institution, but as more alike the world over than the exaggeration of exceptional customs by an earlier school had led us to suppose.[5] Nor can any one doubt the general prevalence of play-groups among children or of informal assemblies of various kinds among their elders. Such association is clearly the nursery of human nature in the world about us, and there is no apparent reason to suppose that the case has anywhere or at any time been essentially different.

As regards play, we might, were it not a matter of common observation, multiply illustrations of the universality and spontaneity of the group discussion and co-operation to which it gives rise. The general fact is that children, especially boys after about their twelfth year, live in fellowships in which their sympathy, ambition, and honor are engaged even more, often, than they are in the family. Most of us can recall examples of the endurance by boys of injustice and even cruelty, rather than appeal from their fellows to parents or teachers—as for instance, in the hazing so prevalent at schools, and so difficult, for that reason, to repress. And how elaborate the discussion, how cogent the public opinion, how hot the ambitions in these fellowships!

Nor is this facility of juvenile association, as is sometimes supposed, a trait peculiar to English and American boys; since experience among our immigrant population seems to show that the offspring of the more restrictive civilizations of the continent of Europe form self-governing play-groups with almost equal readi-

[4] The neighborhood is to be distinguished from the community proper by the fact that within the neighborhood association is face to face while the community may be made up of a number of such neighborhoods. Under primitive or rural conditions the neighborhood may constitute the community, but in more advanced cultures the two are seldom identical.

[5] Edward Westermarck, *The History of Human Marriage,* London, 1891. G. E. Howard, *A History of Matrimonial Institutions,* Chicago, 1904. Robert Briffault, *The Mothers,* New York, 1927.

ness. Thus Miss Jane Addams, after pointing out that the "gang" is almost universal, speaks of the interminable discussion which every detail of the gang's activity receives, remarking that "in these social folk-moots, so to speak, the young citizen learns to act upon his own determination."[6]

Of the neighborhood group it may be said, in general, that from the time men formed permanent settlements upon the land, down, at least, to the rise of modern industrial cities, it has played a main part in the primary, heart-to-heart life of the people. Among our Teutonic forefathers the village community was apparently the chief sphere of sympathy and mutual aid for the commons all through the "dark" and middle ages, and for many purposes it remains so in rural districts at the present day. Terpenning's study of the neighborhood in America and in Europe, the open country neighborhood *vs.* the village neighborhood, is telling evidence of the importance of this form of association.[7] In America the intimacy of the neighborhood, which has never been that of the European village at best, has been further broken up by the growth of an intricate mesh of wider contacts which in cities at least often leaves us strangers to people who live in the same house.

Such Groups Primary in Social Organization Also. A secondary sense in which these groups are primary is that they do not change in the same degree as more elaborate relations, but form a comparatively permanent source out of which the latter are ever springing. Of course they are not independent of the larger society, but to some extent reflect its spirit; as the German family and the German school before the World War bore somewhat the print of German militarism. But this, after all, is like the tide setting back into creeks, and does not commonly go very far. Among the German, and still more among the pre-revolutionary Russian, peasantry were found habits of free co-operation and discussion almost uninfluenced by the character of the state; and it is a familiar and well-supported view that the village commune, self-governing as regards local affairs and habituated to discussion, is a very widespread institution in settled communities, and a continuator of a similar autonomy previously existing in the

[6] *Newer Ideals of Peace,* 177. Thrasher in *The Gang,* Chicago, 1926, presents much evidence of the same sort.

[7] Walter Terpenning, *Village and Open-Country Neighborhoods,* New York, 1931, p. 387.

clan. "It is man who makes monarchies and establishes republics, but the commune seems to come directly from the hand of God."[8]

These groups, then, are springs of life, not only for the individual, but for social institutions. They are only in part moulded by culture, and, to a considerable degree, express a universal nature. The religion or government of other civilizations may seem alien to us, but the children or the family group wear the common life, and with them we can always make ourselves at home.

From Animal to Man. In just what way is the primary group so powerful a humanizing agent? Biologically each of us is equipped with innate drives such as lust, greed, revenge, the thirst for power, and the like which are in their crudest forms not distinctively human drives at all but animal drives. The distinctively human level of behavior appears only when the raw instincts have been conditioned through sympathetic insight into *sentiments* such as love, ambition, and resentment. It is because we are always dealing with sentiments, *i.e., with instinctive emotions organized around ideas,* that attempts to explain human behavior by raw instinct are so hopelessly inadequate. *This humanizing of the animal drives is perhaps the greatest service performed by the primary group.* Other forms of association contribute in some degree to this same end, but the advantage of primary association is that it occurs spontaneously, over and over again, is not limited by conscious purpose, is accompanied by full and free play of pre-verbal as well as verbal communication with all that that implies for the emotional conditioning of personality, and finally, that it is a universal type of experience affecting the entire human race. For these reasons it produces as a matter of course a deeper psychological effect on more people per unit of time than society can manage to produce by elaborate social organization and deliberate effort.

Cyril Burt, for example, after a careful analysis of 200 juvenile delinquents, concluded that "Of environmental conditions, those obtaining outside the home are far less important than those obtaining within it; material conditions, such as poverty, are far less important than moral conditions, such as discipline, vice, and, most of all, the child's relation with his parents."[9]

[8] De Tocqueville, *Democracy in America,* Vol. I, Chap. V.
[9] *The Young Delinquent,* New York, 1925, p. 582.

Such evidence strongly suggests that *the primary group is a more efficient humanizer of animal drives per unit of time than any other form of association that man has been able to devise.*

Primary Ideals. Life in the primary groups gives rise to social ideals which, as they spring from similar experiences, have much in common throughout the human race. These naturally become the motive and test of social progress. Under all systems men strive, however blindly, to realize objects suggested by the familiar experience of primary association. Hence, again, the gravity of the increasing substitution of secondary for primary association in modern life.

Where do we get our notions of love, freedom, justice, and the like, which we are ever applying to social institutions? Not from abstract philosophy, surely, but from the actual life of simple and widespread forms of society, like the family or the play-group. In these relations mankind realizes itself, gratifying its primary needs, in a fairly satisfactory manner, and from the experience forms standards of what it is to expect from more elaborate association. Since groups of this sort are never obliterated from human experience, but flourish more or less under all kinds of institutions, they remain an enduring criterion by which the latter are ultimately judged.

Of course these simpler relations are not uniform for all societies but vary considerably with race, with the general state of civilization as we have already indicated, and with the particular sort of institutions that may prevail. The primary groups themselves are subject to improvement and decay, and need to be watched and cherished with a very especial care.

Neither is it claimed that, at the best, they realize ideal conditions; only that they approach them more nearly than anything else in general experience, and so form the practical basis on which higher imaginations are built. They are not always pleasant or righteous, but they almost always contain elements from which ideals of pleasantness and righteousness may be formed.

The Ideal of Group Unity. The ideal that grows up in familiar association may be said to be a part of human nature itself. In its most general form it is that of a moral whole, or community, wherein individual minds are merged and the higher capacities of the members find total and adequate expression. This ideal grows up because familiar association fills our minds with imaginations of the thought and feeling of other members of the group, and of the group as a whole, so that, for many purposes, we really make them a part of our selves and identify our self-feeling with them.

Of course children and savages do not formulate any such ideal, but they have it nevertheless; they see it: they see themselves and their fellows as an indivisible, though various, "we," and they desire this "we" to be harmonious, happy, and successful. How heartily one may merge himself in the family and in the fellowships of youth is perhaps within the experience of all of us; and we come to feel that the same spirit should extend to our country, our race, our world. As Thoreau said, "All the abuses which are the objects of reform . . . are unconsciously amended in the intercourse of friends."[10]

A congenial family life is the immemorial type of group unity, and the source of many of the terms—such as brotherhood, kindness, and the like—which describe it. The members become merged by intimate association into a whole wherein each age and sex participates in its own way. Each lives in imaginative contact with the minds of the others, and finds in them the dwelling-place of his social self, of his affections, ambitions, resentments, and standards of right and wrong. Without uniformity, there is yet unity, a free, pleasant, wholesome, fruitful, common life.

As to the playground, Mr. Joseph Lee, in an excellent paper on "Play as a School for the Citizen," gives the following account of the merging of the one in the whole that may be learned from sport. The boy, he says,

> is deeply participating in a common purpose. The team and the plays that it executes are present, in a very vivid manner to his consciousness. His conscious individuality is more thoroughly lost in the sense of membership than perhaps it ever becomes in any other way. So that the sheer experience of citizenship in its simplest and essential form—of the sharing in a public consciousness, of having the social organization present as a controlling ideal in your heart—is very intense. . . .
>
> Along with the sense of the team as a mechanical instrument, and unseparated from it in the boy's mind, is the consciousness of it as the embodiment of a common purpose. There is in team play a very intimate experience of the ways in which such a purpose is built up

[10] *A Week on the Concord and Merrimack Rivers,* p. 283.

and made effective. You feel, though without analysis, the subtle ways in which a single strong character breaks out the road ahead and gives confidence to the rest to follow; how the creative power of one ardent imagination, bravely sustained, makes possible the putting through of the play as he conceives it. You feel to the marrow of your bones how each loyal member contributes to the salvation of all the others by holding the conception of the whole play so firmly in his mind as to enable them to hold it, and to participate in his single-minded determination to see it carried out. You have intimate experience of the ways in which individual members contribute to the team and how the team, in turn, builds up their spiritual nature. . . .

And the team is not only an extension of the player's consciousness; it is a part of his personality. His participation has deepened from co-operation to membership. Not only is he now a part of the team, but the team is a part of him.[11]

Group unity, as this illustration implies, admits and rewards strenuous ambition; but this ambition must either be for the success of the group, or at least not inconsistent with that. The fullest self-realization will belong to the one who embraces in a passionate self-feeling the aims of the fellowship, and spends his life in fighting for their attainment. Moral unity, in short, may be viewed as the mother, so to speak, of all social ideals.

The Elements of the Ideal of Group Unity. The most salient principles of group unity may perhaps be distinguished as *loyalty, lawfulness,* and *freedom.*

Loyalty.—In so far as one identifies himself with a whole, loyalty to that whole is loyalty to himself; it is self-realization, something in which one cannot fail without losing self-respect. Moreover this is a larger self, leading out into a wider and richer life, and appealing, therefore, to enthusiasm and the need of quickening ideals. As Royce and others have shown, the individual for his own mental health needs to identify himself with something larger than his merely personal life; needs to find some idea, or cause or institution to whose service he can devote his life. One is never more human, as a rule never happier, than when he is sacrificing his narrow and merely private interest to the higher call of the congenial group. Without doubt the natural genesis of this sentiment is in the intimacy of face-to-face co-operation.

Among the ideals inseparable from loyalty are those of truth,

[11] *Charities and the Commons,* XVIII, pp. 486–91.

service, and kindness, always conceived as due to the intimate group rather than to the world at large.

Truth, or good faith toward other members of a fellowship, is probably a universal human ideal. It does not involve any abstract love of veracity, and is quite consistent with deception toward the outside world, being essentially "truth of intercourse" or fair-dealing among intimates. There are few, even among those reckoned lawless, who will not keep faith with one who has the gift of getting near to them in spirit and making them feel that he is one of themselves. Thus in the juvenile court of Denver, Judge Lindsey worked a revolution among the neglected boys of the city, by no other method than that of entering into the same moral whole, becoming part of a "we" with them. He awakened their sense of honor, trusted it, and was almost never disappointed. The same technique underlay Mott Osborn's success in winning the co-operation of the convicts at Sing Sing prison, a success so complete that on one occasion a party of "lifers" who had been sent in automobiles without guard to give a concert in a distant city fought their way back through a blizzard in order to keep faith with the warden and return to prison.

The ideal of service likewise goes with the sense of unity. If there is a vital whole the right aim of individual activity can be no other than to serve that whole. This is not so much a theory as a feeling that will exist wherever the whole is felt. It is a poor sort of an individual who does not feel the need to devote himself to the larger purposes of the group. In our society many feel this need in youth and express it on the playground, but never succeed in realizing it among the less intimate relations of business or professional life. Among the thousand evils of war at least one redeeming feature is the broad avenue of service that it opens up.

All over the world men acknowledge kindness as the law of right intercourse within a social group. This is as true among primitive savages as among the most advanced civilizations. Anthropological observers are united in their testimony that within their own groups the most ferocious cannibals, head-hunters, and blood-thirsty warriors become the kindest of parents and most considerate of friends. The head-hunters of Borneo are described as kind-hearted. Catlin says of the North American Indians, "to their friends there are no people on earth that are more kind."

Morgan extolls the kindness of the Iroquois to one another—an Iroquois "would surrender his dinner to feed the hungry, vacate his bed to refresh the weary, and give up his apparel to clothe the naked." Westermarck in his work on the *Origin and Development of the Moral Ideas* gives page after page of such testimony. Kropotkin adds similar evidence in his *Mutual Aid a Factor in Civilization.* The popular notion of savages as lacking in the gentler feelings is an error springing from the external, usually hostile, nature of our contact with them. Every culture has elements in it which strike outside observers as unkind or cruel. The white man recoils from the Indian practice of torturing prisoners of war, but in the United States in the last fifty years we have permitted more than 3200 Negroes to be lynched with varying degrees of brutality. Contrasts of opulence and poverty that fill a visiting Eskimo with disgust do not even attract the attention of the average New Yorker.

Ordinarily the ideal of kindness, in savage and civilized societies alike, applies only to those within the sympathetic group; the main difference between civilization and savagery, in this regard, is that under civilization the group tends to enlarge. One reason for the restriction is that kindness is aroused by sympathy, and can have little life except as our imaginations are opened to the lives of others and they are made part of ourselves. Even the Christian church, as history shows, has for the most part inculcated kindness only to those within its own pale, or within a particular sect; and the modern ideal of a kindness embracing all humanity (modern at least so far as western nations are concerned) is connected with a growing understanding of the unity of the race. Printing and the increased mobility of modern life have had much to do with this enlargement of sympathy. Today it is even possible to punish men for cruelty to animals whereas ten or twelve centuries ago in France a Frankish noble, returning cold from the chase, had the legal right to slit a serf up the middle with his sword and warm his feet in the man's entrails. The average American cannot understand how Frankish law could have been so needlessly cruel; no more can a visiting Eskimo understand the apparently needless cruelty of our own breadlines in the midst of plenty. Kindness is a universal ideal, but culture defines the group in which it operates.

Lawfulness.—Every intimate group, like every individual, experiences conflicting impulses within itself, and as the individual feels the need of definite principles to shape his conduct and give him peace, so the group needs law or rule for the same purpose. It is not merely that the over-strong or the insubordinate must be restrained, but that all alike may have some definite criterion of what the good member ought to do. It is a mere fact of psychology that where a social whole exists it may be as painful to do wrong as to suffer it—because one's own spirit is divided—and the common need is for harmony through a law, framed in the total interest, which every one can and must obey.

Nowhere is the need of common rules more apparent than on the playground. Miss Buck, the author of an instructive book on *Boys' Self-Governing Clubs,* suggests that the elementary form of equity is taking turns, as at swings and the like; and any one who has shared in a boy's camp will recall the constant demand, by the boys themselves, for rules of this nature. There must be a fair distribution of privileges as to boats, games, and so on, and an equal distribution of food.

No doubt every one remembers how the idea of justice is developed in children's games. There is always something to be done, in which various parts are to be taken, success depending upon their efficient distribution. All see this and draw from experience the idea that there is a higher principle that ought to control the undisciplined ambition of individuals. As Mr. Joseph Lee expounds the matter in the paper already mentioned:

> You may be very intent to beat the other man in the race, but after experience of many contests the fair promise of whose morning has been clouded over by the long and many-worded dispute terminating in a general row, with indecisive and unsatisfying result, you begin dimly to perceive that you and the other fellows and the rest of the crowd, for the very reason that you are contestants and prospective contestants, have interests in common—interests in the establishment and maintenance of those necessary rules and regulations without which satisfactory contests cannot be carried on. The child's need of conflict is from a desire not to exterminate his competitor, but to overcome him and to have his own superiority acknowledged. . . . The person whom you really and finally want to convince is yourself. Your deepest desire is to beat the other boy, not merely to seem to beat him. By playing unfairly and forcing decisions in your own favor, you may possibly cheat the others, but you cannot cheat yourself.
>
> But the decisions in most of the disputes have behind them the

further, more obviously social, motive of carrying on a successful game. The sense of common interest has been stretched so as to take the competitive impulse itself into camp, domesticate it and make it a part of the social system. The acutely realized fact that a society of chronic kickers can never play a game or anything else, comes to be seen against the background of a possible orderly arrangement of which one has had occasional experience, and with which one has come at last to sympathize; there comes to be to some extent an identification of one's own interests and purposes with the interests and purposes of the whole. Certainly the decisions of the group as to whether Jimmy was out at first, as to who came out last, and whether Mary Ann was really caught, are felt as community and not as individual decisions.

Of course the ideals derived from juvenile experience are carried over into the wider life, and men always find it easy to conceive righteousness in terms of fair play. "The Social Question," as John Graham Brooks remarked, "is forever an attack upon what, in some form, is thought to be unfair privilege."[12]

The law or rule that human nature demands has a democratic principle latent in it, because it must be one congenial to general sentiment. Explicit democracy, however—deciding by popular vote and the like—is not primary and general like the need of law, but is rather a mechanism for deciding what the rule is to be, and no more natural than the appeal to authority. Indeed, there seems to be, among children as among primitive peoples, a certain reluctance to ascribe laws to the mere human choice of themselves and their fellows. They wish to assign them to a higher source and to think of them as having an unquestionable sanction. Even American boys seem to prefer to receive rules from tradition or from their elders, when they can.

Freedom.—This is the phase of the social ideal which emphasizes individuality. The whole to which we belong is made up of diverse energies which enkindle one another by friction; and its vigor requires that these have play. Thus the fierce impulses of ambition and pride may be as social as anything else—provided they are sufficiently humanized as to their objects—and are to be interfered with only when they become destructive or oppressive. Moreover, we must not be required to prove to others the beneficence of our peculiarity, but should be allowed, if we

[12] *The Social Unrest,* p. 125.

wish, to "write *whim* on the lintels of the doorpost." Our desires and purposes, though social in their ultimate nature, are apt to be unacceptable on first appearance, and the more so in proportion to their value. Thus we feel a need to be let alone, and sympathize with a similar need in others.

This phase of idealism comes most vividly to consciousness when formal and antiquated systems of control need to be broken up, as in the eighteenth century. It then represents the appeal to human nature as against outworn mechanism. Indeed, did not the whole philosophy of the "natural rights" school of thinkers with its emphasis on the right to personal freedom, the right to labor, the right to property, the right to open competition largely spring from what the philosophers knew of the activities of men in small face-to-face groups? The reluctance to give up ideals like those of the Declaration of Independence, without something equally human and simple to take their place, need not look far for theoretical justification.

Yet here we encounter an apparent conflict between theory and practice. There seems to be no doubt that the primary-group experience is the source of our ideals of freedom; yet the closeness of association which exists in primary groups has been cited by some observers of primitive life as one reason for the cultural stagnation of such groups. Moreover, among ourselves there is no uniformity more deadly to the would-be innovator than the uniformity of the old-fashioned neighborhood. In such a setting the individual variant in religion or morals, for example, is discouraged with a promptness and efficiency unknown in the more impersonal areas of the city. As the history of civilization itself has shown, cultural innovations tend, on the whole, to come not from primary groups but from the secondary group centres, the cities. Paradoxically enough, the groups in which the individual is freest in his personal relations are thus the very groups in which he is least free to tamper with his group culture.

How is this paradox to be explained?

There is reason to believe that the freedom of association enjoyed in the primary group is a pre-cultural thing, a freedom inherent in the face-to-face relationship from the beginning, while the freedom to innovate is a relatively late cultural achievement, based not on the nature of the associative process but on certain ideas which are precipitates of that process, namely, ideas of right, of legal status, of privilege, and so on. The demand of the French revolutionists for equality was an echo of the primary-group experience; but the need of making such a demand was a product of a complex secondary situation in which many cultural barriers to free association had been set up. Accordingly we are not surprised to note that it was the secondary group centre, Paris, and not the primary-group centres of rural France that led the revolt.

If this theory is sound, the freedom enjoyed in primary groups is not based on cultural ideas of tolerance or formal freedom at all, but on the nature of the associative process, as we have said. Conversely, if the individual is comparatively unfree in the primary group to change the group culture the reason would seem to lie not in the essential nature of the face-to-face relationship but in the nature of the cultural ideals which the group holds. If those ideals include tolerance and personal freedom, there would seem to be no inherent reason why a family or a neighborhood, or any other face-to-face group could not react critically to its own culture.

STUDY QUESTIONS

1. What are the characteristics of human nature? Account for the transformation of biological nature into human nature.
2. Why is sympathetic insight needed to develop human nature?
3. Discuss the statement "Human nature is a group nature."
4. What are the principal characteristics of a primary group?
5. Explain the psychological nature of a primary group, illustrating from your observation.
6. What harm would it do one to grow up without experience of primary groups outside the family?
7. In just what senses are primary groups primary?
8. What is the difference between the neighborhood as a psychological unity and the neighborhood as a locality?
9. What evidence can you give that the primary group function of the family is changing?
10. What is meant by saying that the ideal of group unity is the mother of all social ideals?
11. Are primary ideals influential only in primary groups?
12. Explain the influence of the play group in developing a sense of fair play.
13. What ideals may be regarded as elements of group unity?

14. What does loyalty involve?
15. In what sense does a lawless boys' gang have a sense of lawfulness?
16. Explain the difference between freedom in the primary group and freedom in the secondary group.

CHAPTER V

THE INDIVIDUAL AND SOCIETY

Having seen in preceding chapters that human development is inevitably a social process, a give-and-take between the individual and his social environment, we may perhaps pause now in our more objective analysis of this process to ask what are the philosophical implications of this interactive relationship.

The Organic Theory. If we accept the evolutionary point of view we are led to see the relation between society and the individual as an organic relation.[1] That is, we see that the individual is not separable from the human whole, but a living member of it, deriving his life from the whole through social and hereditary transmission as truly as if men were literally one body. He cannot cut himself off; the strands of heredity and education are woven into all his being. And, on the other hand, the social whole is in some degree dependent upon each individual, because each contributes something to the common life that no one else can contribute. Thus we have a living organization composed of differentiated members, each of which has a special function.

This is true of society in that large sense which embraces all humanity, and also of any specific social group. A university, for example, is an organic whole made up of students, teachers, officials and others. Each member of the academic community functions in co-ordination with the rest to fulfil the aims of the whole. But note that it is precisely his individuality, his functional difference from the rest which gives each member his peculiar importance. The professor of archæology, for instance, has a part that no one else can play and his work is so planned as to bring under his influence those students who most need what he has to

[1] We do not mean that society is an organism in a biological sense, but rather that the parts are functionally related to each other and to the whole. This reciprocal influence and this integration seem to justify the use of the adjective "organic" though hardly the noun "organism."

give. Similarly even the lowliest freshman plays a unique rôle, since his needs and his choices help to determine the courses that are and shall be given, the manner of their presentation, and even, to some extent, the administrative organization. The whole is a network of interdependent parts, each one of which contributes to the functioning of the entire system.

The organic view stresses both the unity of the whole and the peculiar value of the individual, explaining each by the other. What is a football team without a quarterback? Almost as useless as a quarterback without a team. A well-developed person can exist only in and through a well-developed whole, and *vice versa.*

Falsity of the Antithesis, Society *vs.* the Individual. A separate person is an abstraction unknown to experience, and so likewise is society when regarded as something apart from persons. The real thing is human life, which may be considered either in an individual aspect or in a social, that is to say a general, aspect; but is always, as a matter of fact, both individual and general. In other words "society" and "persons" do not denote separable phenomena, but are simply collective and distributive aspects of the same thing, the relation between them being like that between other expressions one of which denotes a group as a whole and the other the members of the group, such as the army and the soldiers, the class and the students, and so on. This holds true of any social aggregate great or small; of a family, a city, a nation; of mankind as a whole: no matter how extensive, complex, or enduring a group may be, no good reason can be given for regarding it as essentially different in this respect from the smallest, simplest, or most transient.

So far, then, as there is any difference between the two, it is rather in our point of view than in the object we are looking at; when we speak of society or use any other collective term, we fix our minds upon some general view of the people concerned, while when we speak of persons we disregard the general aspect and think of them as separate. Thus "the Cabinet" may consist of President Lincoln, Secretary Seward, Secretary Stanton, and so on; but when we say "the Cabinet" we do not suggest the same idea as when we enumerate these gentlemen separately. Society, or any complex group, may, to ordinary observation, be a very different thing from all its members viewed one by one—as a man who beheld Grant's army from Missionary Ridge would have seen something other than he would by approaching every soldier in it. In the same way a picture is made up of so many square inches of painted canvas; but if you should look at these one at a time, covering the others, until you had seen them all you would still not have seen the picture. There may, in all such cases, be a system or organization in the whole that is not apparent in the parts. In this sense, and in no other, is there a difference between society and the persons of which it is composed; a difference not residing in the facts themselves but existing to the observer on account of the limits of his perception. A *complete* view of society would also be a complete view of all the persons, and *vice versa;* there would be no difference between them.

The antithesis, then, society *versus* the individual, is false and hollow whenever used as a general or philosophical statement of human relations. Whatever idea may be in the minds of those who set these words and their derivatives over against each other, the notion conveyed is that of two separate entities or forces; and certainly such a notion is untrue to fact.

Most people not only think of the individual and society as more or less separate and antithetical, but they look upon the former as antecedent to the latter. That persons make society would be generally admitted as a matter of course; but that society makes persons would strike many as a startling notion, though there is no good reason for looking upon the distributive aspect of life as more primary or causative than the collective aspect. The reason for the common impression appears to be that we think most naturally and easily of the individual phase of life, simply because it is a tangible one, the phase under which men appear to the senses, while the actuality of groups, of nations, of mankind at large, is realized only by the active and instructed imagination. We ordinarily regard society, so far as we conceive it at all, in a vaguely material aspect, as an aggregate of physical bodies, not as the vital whole which it is; and so, of course, we do not see that it may be as original or causative as anything else. Indeed, many look upon "society" and other general terms as somewhat mystical, and are inclined to doubt whether there is any reality back of them.

It follows that the individual can be separated from society only in an external sense. If you go off alone into the wilderness you take with you a mind formed in society and you continue social intercourse in your memory and imagination, or by the aid of books. This, and only this, keeps humanity alive in you, and just in so far as you lose the power of intercourse your mind decays. Long solitude, as in the case of sheep-herders on the western plains, or prisoners in solitary confinement, often produces mental degeneration.

At times in the history of Christianity, and of other religions also, hermits have gone to dwell in desert places, but they have usually kept up some communication with one another and with the world outside, certain of them, like St. Jerome, having been famous letter-writers. Each of them, in fact, belonged to a social system from which he drew ideals and moral support. We may suspect that St. Simeon Stylites, who dwelt for years on top of a pillar, was not unaware that his austerity was visible to others.

Organic Freedom. What freedom, then, has the individual under the organic view? The common notion of freedom is negative; that is, it is a notion of the absence of constraint. Starting with the popular individualistic view of things, the social order is thought of as something apart from, and more or less a hindrance to, a man's natural development. There is an assumption that an ordinary person is self-sufficient in most respects, and will do very well if he is left alone. But there is, of course, no such thing as the absence of restraint, in the sense of social limitations; man has no existence apart from a social order, and can develop his personality only through the social order, and in the same degree that it is developed. A freedom consisting in the removal of limiting conditions is inconceivable. If the word is to have any definite meaning in sociology, it must therefore be separated from the idea of a fundamental opposition between society and the individual, and made to signify something that is both individual and social. To do this it is not necessary to do any great violence to accepted ideas of a practical sort; since it is rather in theory than in application that the popular view is objectionable. A sociological interpretation of freedom should take away nothing worth keeping from our traditional conception of it, and may add something in the way of breadth, clearness and productiveness.

The definition of freedom which perhaps flows from the organic view is that it is *opportunity for right development.* A child comes into the world with an outfit of vague tendencies, for all definite unfolding of which he is dependent upon social conditions. If cast away alone on a desert island he would, supposing he succeeded in living at all, never attain a real humanity, would never know speech, or social sentiment, or any complex thought. On the other hand, if all his surroundings are from the first such as to favor the enlargement and enrichment of his life, he may attain the fullest development possible to him in the actual state of the world. In so far as the social conditions have this favoring action upon him he may be said to be free. And so every person, at every stage of his growth, is free or unfree in proportion as he does or does not find himself in the midst of conditions conducive to full and harmonious personal development. Thinking in this way we do not regard the individual as separable from the social order as a whole, but we do regard him as capable of occupying any one of an indefinite number of positions within that order, some of them more suitable to him than others.

This sort of freedom does not, then, mean that one can do things independently of society; rather one must work it out in co-operation with, and adaptation to, others. It implies teamwork. The individual has freedom to function in his own way like the quarterback of the football team, but, in one way or another, he has to play the game as life brings it to him.

The evolutionary point of view encourages us to believe that life is a creative process, that we are really building up something new and worth while, and that the human will is a part of the creative energy that does this. Every individual has his unique share in the work, which no one but himself can discern and perform. Although his life flows into him from the hereditary and cultural past, his being as a whole is new, a fresh organization of life. Never any one before had the same powers and opportunities that you have, and you are free to use them in your own way.

It is, after all, only common sense to say that we exercise our freedom through co-operation with others. If you join a social group—let us say a dramatic club—you expect that it will increase your freedom, give your individual powers new stimulus and opportunity for expression. And why should not the same principle apply to society at large? It is through a social development that mankind has emerged from animal bondage into that organic freedom, wonderful though far from complete, that we now enjoy.

So far as discipline is concerned, freedom means not its absence but the use of higher and more rational forms as contrasted with those that are lower and less rational. A free discipline controls the individual by appealing to his reason and conscience, and therefore to his self-respect; while an unfree control works upon some lower phase of the mind, and so tends to degrade him. It is freedom to be disciplined in as rational a manner as you are fit for.

Freedom and the Social Order. The social order is antithetical to freedom only in so far as it is a bad one. Freedom can exist only in and through a social order, and must be increased by all the healthy growth of the latter. It is only in a large and complex social system that any advanced degree of it is possible, because nothing else can supplant the multifarious opportunities by means of which all sorts of persons can work out a congenial development through the choice of influences.

In so far as we have freedom in the United States at the present time, in what does it consist? Evidently, it would seem in the access to a great number and variety of influences by whose progressive selection and assimilation a child may become, within vague limits set by the general state of our society, the best that he is naturally fitted to become. It consists, to begin with infancy, in a good family life, in intelligent nurture and training, adapted to the special traits of character which every child manifests from the first week of life. Then it involves good schooling, admitting the child through books and teachers to a rich selection from the accumulated influences of the best minds of the past. Free technical and professional education, so far as it exists, contributes to it; also the facility of travel, bringing him in contact with significant persons from all over the world; public libraries, magazines, good newspapers, and so on. Whatever enlarges his field of selection without permanently confusing him adds to his liberty. In fact, institutions—government, churches, industries, and the like—have properly no other function than to contribute to human freedom; and in so far as they fail, on the whole, to perform this function, they are wrong and need reconstruction.

Although a high degree of freedom can exist only through a complex social order, it by no means follows that every complex social order is free. On the contrary, it has more often been true in the past that very large and intricately organized states, like the Roman Empire, were constructed on a comparatively mechanical and unfree principle. There are serious objections to identifying progress, as Herbert Spencer sometimes appears to do, with the mere differentiation and co-ordination of social functions. But the example of the United States, which is perhaps as intricately differentiated and co-ordinated as any state that ever existed, shows that complexity is not inconsistent with freedom.

Strain Accompanying Enlargement of Freedom. The substitution of higher forms of control for lower, the offering of more alternatives and trusting the mind to make a right selection, involves, of course, an increased moral strain upon persons. This increase in moral strain is not in all cases exactly proportioned to the ability to bear it well; and when it is not well borne the effect upon character is more or less destructive, so that something in the way of degeneracy results.

Consequently every general increase of freedom is accompanied by some degeneracy, attributable to the same causes as the freedom. This is very plainly to be seen at the present time, which is one, on the whole, of rapid increase in freedom. Family life and the condition of women and children have been growing freer, but along with this we have the increase of divorce and of spoiled children. Democracy in the state has its own peculiar evils as we all know; and in the church the decay of dogmatism and unreasoning faith, a moral advance on the whole, has nevertheless caused a good many moral failures. In much the same way the enfranchisement of the Negroes is believed to have caused an increase of insanity among them, and the growth of suicide in all countries seems to be due in part to the strain of a more complex society. It is not true, exactly, that freedom itself causes degeneracy, because if one is subjected to more strain than is good for him his real freedom is rather contracted than enlarged. But it should rather be said that any movement which has increase of freedom for its general effect can never be so regulated as to have only this effect, but is sure to act upon some in an opposite manner.

Nor is it reasonable to sit back and say that this incidental demoralization is inevitable, a fixed price of progress. On the contrary, although it can never be altogether dispensed with, it can be indefinitely reduced, and every social institution or influence that tends to adapt the stress of civilization to the strength of the individual does reduce it in some measure.

STUDY QUESTIONS

1. What is meant by saying that there is an organic relation between society and the individual? Give your own illustrations.
2. What do you think of the proposition: "A man is social in so far as he is like others"?
3. Why can we say that the criminal is anti-social but not unsocial?
4. Explain the statement that a group is in one sense more than the sum of the individuals? Illustrate from your own experience.
5. Were primitive men more individual and less social than modern men?
6. Do religious hermits and the like prove that the individual can be separated from society? Explain your answer.
7. What would you give as the popular idea of freedom? What different idea arises from the organic view?
8. What is the relation between freedom and control? Give examples from your own observation of free and unfree control. Would you class control by propaganda in time of war as free or unfree?
9. Explain the relation of freedom to organization.
10. Many think that the American Indian was freer than the modern factory worker. What is your view?
11. What notably unfree conditions do you find in your home town?
12. Explain why new increments of freedom are likely to be accompanied by a certain amount of degeneracy. Illustrate from history or your own experience.

CHAPTER VI

CULTURE—THE ACCUMULATED RESULTS OF ASSOCIATION

Our Man-made Environment. Up to this point we have been discussing the biological and psycho-social bases of association, and the universal mind-set called human nature that results from it, very much as though all of these functioned somehow in a vacuum. It is time to come to terms with the environment in which association goes on.

This environment is of two kinds: (1) *The natural physical environment* of hills, rivers, forests, and the like; and (2) a *man-made environment* of roads, fields, houses, books, cities, families, and so on. This man-made environment which has been accumulating for hundreds of thousands, if not millions, of years, as we saw in Chapter I, has gradually been superimposed upon the natural environment until now it stands between us and the natural environment at nearly every point. For this reason we shall consider it first and then try to see how it has been adapted to the natural environment which underlies it. Our first task is to see this man-made environment itself, not only in its material forms—towns, fields, automobiles, etc.—but in its non-material forms as well—ideas, sentiments, customs, institutions.

Why We Don't All Dine at Different Hours. For a Haida Indian fish may talk, the dead may come alive, and live men may become invisible. Anything can happen, because primitive man, essentially like the child in our own culture, sees nature not as a unified process but as a succession of more or less unrelated episodes. The uniformity of nature, the principle underlying all modern science, has no existence for the primitive mind.

Just so, unreflective people usually fail to see the surrounding orderliness in human life. Things happen, but too often we cannot see the pattern according to which the particular episodes arrange themselves. Sometimes this is so because the pattern is very complex and can only be put together after long study and careful observation. But frequently it is so because we are so familiar with the pattern that we do not realize that it *is* a pattern at all. Take such a commonplace activity as eating, for example: On the basis of pure chance, *i.e.,* the unco-ordinated instincts of separate individuals, as many people should be eating at two o'clock or three o'clock or four o'clock in the afternoon as at any other hour. It is inconceivable that millions of people, starting their life careers at different times and growing at different rates, should all develop the same biological cravings at almost the same hour three times a day. The inconceivability grows when we discover that different nations eat at different hours, and that the old Romans, for example, used to eat four meals a day instead of three. Clearly mere instinct cannot explain the uniformity of a nation's behavior in even so simple a thing as the dinner hour.

Nor can habit explain it any better. The point is, Why do millions of habits happen so neatly to coincide?

The question meets us wherever we turn. In any ordinary crowd, for example, we find people wearing only a very few of the thousands of possible combinations of colors, cuts, and fabrics. Instead of thousands of possible noises that they might be making we find them making essentially the same sounds, *i.e.,* talking a common language. Instead of behaving in incalculably different ways we find them going through a kind of social ritual —getting up at a certain time, dressing in a prescribed way, eating certain standardized foods, going to predetermined places to do predetermined things, finding recreation in certain standardized ways; and at the end of a standardized time-unit called a "day" we find them returning again to certain predetermined places called "homes" to enter again into standardized relationships with certain predetermined individuals known as "members of the family." All this is obviously not a matter of chance. Something has operated to co-ordinate these millions of different habit-patterns; something has imposed a master-pattern in whose grooves the millions must run.

This master-pattern is the social heritage, or *culture.*

What Culture Does for Us. We are so accustomed to our own culture that most of us never stop to think what life would be like without it. We are so accustomed to hearing the wonderful qualities of man's biological heritage extolled that many of us assume that nothing else really matters. In the face of this comfortable assurance it is something of a shock to realize that if we were to be stripped of all the gifts of the past—fire, tools, shelter, language, iron, cereals, domesticated animals, the wheel, and all the rest—we should be poorer than the poorest savages, and millions of us would perish miserably within a month. Perhaps the best statement of what such a catastrophe would mean has been made by Graham Wallas:

> If the earth were struck by one of Mr. Wells' comets, and if, in consequence, every human being now alive were to lose all the knowledge and habits which he had acquired from preceding generations (though retaining unchanged all his own powers of invention, and memory, and habituation) nine-tenths of the inhabitants of London or New York would be dead in a month, and 99 per cent of the remaining tenth would be dead in six months. They would have no language to express their thoughts, and no thoughts but vague reverie. They could not read notices, nor drive motors nor horses. They would wander about, led by the inarticulate cries of a few naturally dominant individuals, drowning themselves, as thirst came on, in hundreds at the riverside landing places, looting those shops where the smell of decaying food attracted them, and perhaps at the end stumbling on the expedient of cannibalism. Even in the country districts, men could not invent, in time to preserve their lives, methods of growing food, or taming animals, or making fire, or so clothing themselves as to endure a northern winter. An attack of constipation or measles would be invariably fatal. After a few years mankind would almost certainly disappear from the northern and temperate zones. The white races would probably become extinct everywhere.[1]

If this picture of London or New York swept cultureless overnight is even approximately correct, is Wallas not justified in calling mankind parasitic on the social heritage? On the basis of an estimated Indian population of 800,000 in what is now the United States, Indian culture at the time of Columbus was supporting approximately one Indian to every 3.7 square miles of land area. Our own culture in the United States in 1930 was supporting 41.3 persons per square mile of land, or in round numbers 153 persons to every 3.7 square miles. Professor East of Harvard has estimated that by lowering our standard of living somewhat we might ultimately support about 111 per square mile, or 411 for every 3.7 square miles. With the imminence of a stationary population within the next generation due to birth control, it is un-

[1] *Our Social Heritage,* Yale University Press, 1921, p. 16.

likely that any such figure will ever be reached. The point is, a return even to the level of the Indian culture would necessitate the migration or death of more than 99 per cent of the people now alive in the United States; and the complete extinction of all culture would inevitably mean just what Wallas said it would—the extinction of the white races and the disappearance of man from the northern and temperate zones. This is the meaning of the statement that modern man is "biologically parasitic on culture."

What Is Culture? Culture is the entire accumulation of artificial objects and conditions, tools, techniques, ideas, symbols, and behavior-patterns peculiar to a group of people, possessing a certain consistency of its own, and capable of transmission from one generation to another.

Culture, in other words, is the sum-total of the *transmittible results* of living together.[2]

The Unit Parts of Culture—Culture Traits and Culture Complexes. For purposes of observation our cultural heritage may be broken up into units called *culture traits.* A culture trait is simply a unit of culture for purposes of observation. It is not a something whose identity can be fixed once for all; it must be redefined for each new inquiry. For example, from one point of view an automobile is a culture trait. One can observe the distribution of automobiles, and the relations of automobiles to other parts of culture such as railroads, living habits, and the like. Yet obviously the automobile is a cluster of many inventions, some of them, such as the wheel, dating back thousands of years, others, such as the internal combustion engine, much more recent in their origin. From this point of view the automobile is no longer the unit of our observation but must be considered as a cluster of units, or a *culture complex.* In the same way everything else around us from an airplane to a way of shaking hands may be regarded either as a culture trait, or, more synthetically, as a culture complex. A culture complex is a cluster of traits or separate inventions. Practically everything we use from the words of which this sentence is composed up to an automobile, a football game, or a national government is a complex of different unit inventions. Even so simple a thing as a pencil is a complex of

[2] Culture can be passed down from generation to generation. Human nature must be acquired anew by each generation.

four or five, and the use of such a substance as tobacco involves literally thousands of unit-inventions having to do with planting, harvesting, curing, marketing, and using it.

At any given time the culture of any people consists of thousands, if not of millions, of such trait-clusters, or culture complexes. In a single catalogue of one of our large mail-order houses, for example, there are listed more than 10,000 culture complexes, and some of them such as dictionaries are made up of thousands of other traits or complexes.[3] There are more than 1,700,000 patents on record at Washington, every one of them covering a multitude of traits. Nobody knows how many unpatented inventions are available. In the mass, including the material and non-material inventions together, we probably have at our disposal many millions of inventions carried along in the cultural heritage.

This total mass of culture traits and complexes as it exists at any given time is called the *culture base.*

Growth of the Culture Base. The most important thing to remember about the culture base is that bye and large, despite occasional recessions such as the destruction of the Minoan civilization and the fall of Rome, it tends to grow. When modern man entered Europe about 25,000 years ago he was a savage with a culture base smaller than that of any Andaman Islander or Veddah in the world today. Yet biologically he seems to have been practically as highly developed as any of his descendants. The differences between life in the Old Stone Age and life in modern Europe or America must be measured largely, not in terms of biological evolution, but in terms of cultural development, the accumulation of culture complexes.

What controls the growth of culture?

That question is much too complex to be answered in detail in an introductory course. Moreover many of the controls are still imperfectly understood. From what has been said, however, it seems to be clear that the growth of the culture base is not a function of any single set of variables such as biological or racial factors alone, but is rather a function of many different variables such as geographical conditions, contacts with other cultures, the size and organization of the group, hospitality to new ideas, and other factors.

In one sense culture tends to breed culture, *i.e.,* the larger the

[3] The English language contains more than 700,000 words, every one of which is a symbol-complex that refers in turn to other complexes.

culture base, other things equal, the more numerous are the challenges and opportunities for invention. Obviously until you have automobiles you can feel no need of having balloon tires, filling stations, and tourist camps. In the early ages cultural advance was very slow, chiefly for four reasons: (1) The culture base was small and the possibilities of improving existing inventions were therefore limited; (2) Primitive food-getting techniques enabled only a few people to live together—in the hunting cultures seldom more than 50 or 100. Under such circumstances the possibilities of biological variation were very limited. Even in modern America there is probably only about one patentee to every 500 people, and while the number of inventors would be considerably larger than the number of patentees, it is still apparent that many non-inventors are required to produce one inventor. Under primitive conditions the number required must have been much greater. By the law of averages, therefore, small primitive bands could have produced an inventive mind only once in generations. When one did appear his contribution to cultural change must have been much hampered, if not wholly prevented, by a third condition which endured for ages: (3) New ideas were regarded as dangerous and change was considered abnormal. This is still the attitude of most of mankind and even in the United States, Europe, and Japan only material innovation is welcomed. Until the discovery of the uniformity of nature and the consequent development of science this attitude of profound conservatism was probably justified—the world seemed full of uncertainty and danger and the obvious course of common sense was to cling to whatever security one's culture had already won. That most Americans today regard material invention as laudable while they still look with suspicion on new ideas in politics, law, economics, morals, and religion merely reflects the fact that physical science has succeeded in convincing us that physical nature is dependable and can be controlled within limits, while social science has not yet succeeded in introducing a feeling of similar stability and dependability into our conceptions of the social world. Tradition, not understanding, still rules society.

(4) A fourth factor, retarding the growth of the culture base until very recently, was the difficulty of communication. Before the invention of writing this difficulty severely limited the volume of culture that could be transmitted from one generation to an-

From Alfred Louis Kroeber's "Anthropology," published by Harcourt, Brace and Company.

FIG. 2. Culture Areas among the American Indians.

other, since without writing tradition rests solely on the memories of the old men. No civilization has ever been achieved without some means of permanent record. Furthermore, until the advent of printing and, more recently, electro-machine communication, the area within which even civilized men could co-operate on a basis of common understanding was very small. From Trinil Man to Andrew Jackson the world for the average man was the neighborhood. Conservatism and lack of contact worked together, each reinforcing the other, but the net result was stagnation.

Thus the size of the culture base, the small number in the group, primitive conservatism, and the lack of communicative devices, all conspired for many ages to retard cultural growth. Only gradually as these conditions changed did the rate of cultural accumulation change also. But it was with the radical transformation of the culture base of certain nations in western Europe which followed the growth of towns and the increase of trade contacts that the rate of cultural accumulation eventually began to rise toward its present level.

Important as the work of scientist and inventor is today, however, we must not forget that on the mere basis of probability it would be utterly impossible for any one city, or any one country, to produce one ten-thousandth of the cultural acquisitions actually at its disposal. Past generations and the rest of the world vastly outnumber any single group. The consequence is that most growth of the culture base comes not from within but from without. This brings us to the problem of the distribution of culture in space and to the phenomena of diffusion.

Variations in Culture from Place to Place—The Culture Area. Usually a trait or a complex such as the factory system starts in a centre of unusual activity and spreads. Now if human society were like a pond, traits would spread as ripples do, uniformly in all directions. Actually, however, society is not like a pond; mountains, seas, hostile peoples, social class lines, and other obstacles interfere with diffusion, while commercial contacts, trade routes, the borrowing of related traits, and other factors facilitate it. Consequently trait-complexes seldom spread evenly in all directions, and not infrequently, as in the case of newspaper circulations, automobiles, and Paris fashions, they also spread discontinuously, *i.e.,* they leave many places and many individuals untouched even within the limits of the area over which they do spread. Hence it is very difficult after the event to reconstruct a picture of the process that has produced a given situation. The problem is further complicated by modern developments such as advertising, propaganda, and increased mobility.

What we find is, of course, that most traits have definite limits of spread at any given time. Thus romantic love, for example, is fairly well localized in what we may call western civilization; the Orient and the rest of the world do not thus idealize the sexual relation. There is, in fact, as we suggested in Chapter I, a constellation of trait-complexes so definitely localized in western Europe and America as to justify the consideration of these regions as constituting one culture area. Within the western culture area in turn are lesser areas, as for example, the area covered by the single-family farm system, or the area covered by the Southern accent. It is perfectly possible to map such culture areas as definitely as temperature or rainfall can be mapped. Because of the discontinuous distribution of many traits, however, it is difficult to apply the culture-area idea to modern America.

Of What Is Culture Composed? Many attempts have been made to classify the culture complexes of which a given culture is composed.[4] One of the most useful classifications is that of the American anthropologist, Clark Wissler, who groups complexes into what he calls the "universal pattern," which is determined ultimately, Wissler believes, by our biological predispositions.[5] The universal pattern is made up of nine elements as follows: (1) Speech; (2) Material traits—objects and skills relating to them; (3) Art; (4) Mythology and scientific knowledge; (5) Religious practices; (6) The family and the social system; (7) Property; (8) Government; (9) War.

For our purposes, perhaps, it will be enough to distinguish three general classes of traits and complexes:

1. *Material objects.*
2. *Language.*
3. *Non-material patterns other than language.*

[4] For example, Gabriel Tarde, a French writer, distinguished "social realities" of six kinds: Language, religion, government, legislation, economic usages and wants, and morals and arts. Professor Small, following Ratzenhofer's analysis, classified on the basis of six "interests": Health, wealth, knowledge, beauty, sociability, and rightness. Professor Hayes divided social phenomena into three classes: Creeds and sciences; social sentiments; and the arts of life relating to two fields—material things and psychic possessions.

[5] *Man and Culture,* New York, 1923, p. 74.

1. Material Culture. The outstanding complex of our material culture is probably the power-machine-factory. In round numbers there are approximately 200,000 manufacturing establishments in the United States, and in 1929 they employed more than eight and a half million wage earners. In a world output of more than a billion and a half horsepower the United States uses probably half of it, and more than 75 per cent of that half, or about 600,000,000 horsepower, is developed in automotive engines alone.

A statistician has calculated by nations the relative output of work per person.[6] His figures give a rough index of the progress of the power-machine complex in the world:

TABLE 1

HOW NATIONS VARY IN UTILIZATION OF EXTERNAL ENERGY[7]

	Relative Work Output per Man
China	1
British India	1.25
Russia (before Five-Year Plan)	2.5
Italy	2.75
Japan	3.5
Poland	6
Holland	7
France	8.25
Australia	8.5
Czechoslovakia	9.5
Germany	12
Belgium	16
Great Britain	18
Canada	20
United States	30

While these figures are not to be taken too literally, they do suggest something of the enormous differential in efficiency that exists between the Occident and the Orient. When the terrific impact of western guns, western machines, and western ideas, is

[6] Mr. T. T. Read, quoted by Stuart Chase, *Men and Machines,* New York, p. 89.

[7] The figures given here represent a minimum estimate of differences among nations. The Columbia engineers and economists grouped together under the name Technocracy estimate, for example, that half of the installed horsepower in the world is in the United States and that the average utilization of energy per person per day in this country rose from 1,600 in 1800 to 150,000 kilogramme calories in 1932. See series in the *New Outlook* on Technocracy, by Wayne W. Parrish, beginning in November, 1932. Also, "Technocracy Speaks," Howard Scott, *The Living Age,* December, 1932, p. 297.

added to the existing population pressures in the East the turmoil there becomes somewhat understandable.[8]

As a recent writer puts it, machines surround us with walls of steel.[9] Machines supply us with communication, transportation, jobs, amusement, light, heat, power, food, water, books, newspapers, military protection, tell time for us, and carry us to the grave. If our direct contact with them does not on the average exceed about two hours a day and varies all the way from operating machines over which we exercise control to merely tending machines that control us, it is nevertheless a type of experience so dominant in our lives and so different from anything in past human history that no one studying American society can afford for one moment to ignore it.

But when we have admitted the power, the bulk, and the dominance of our material culture it is time to put it once more into perspective. We sometimes assume that material objects are what they are, so to speak, in their own right. This, of course, ignores the function of one whole side of culture, namely the whole machinery of symbolism which we have already discussed in Chapter III and need only refer to here.

2. **Language.** Language is the great repository of stored meanings by which man controls the behavior of others and passes along the experience of one generation to the next. The basis of all language is the *symbol.* The important point for us here is that through the use of symbols, *i.e.,* the language, man builds up an environment within an environment, an environment of meanings to which he responds and to which he adjusts behavior. Thus when Henry, the English trader, during his captivity with the Indians after the massacre at Michilimackinac during Pontiac's conspiracy, came across a wriggling object in the grass outside the Indian camp one day, he took it to be a rattlesnake and tried to kill it. The Indians were horrified. They said it was a messenger from the Great Spirit; and they insisted on burning much good tobacco to pacify it for the indignity which the stupid white man had so nearly heaped upon it.

Obviously the Indians were reacting to a different *meaning* than was Henry. That meaning was a cultural thing, a meaning transmitted by language symbols and created by the cultural con-

[8] See for example, Nathaniel Peffer, *China, the Collapse of a Civilization,* New York, 1930.

[9] Stuart Chase, *Men and Machines,* p. 108f.

text of Indian life. Thus while Henry and his captors all confronted the same physical object, they were responding to different cultural worlds, *i.e.,* to different environments.

Hence it follows that until you know what meaning a man attaches to a given event or circumstance you do not know what his real environment is. Until we know the meanings that men read into the objects around them, *i.e.,* until we have the key to the symbols to which they are responding, we do not know their effective environment at all. This is a fact of the utmost importance for the understanding of human behavior. The neglect of it leads to all sorts of false interpretations and misunderstandings. Nothing else so sharply marks man off from the animal as this, and nothing else is so often forgotten in attempts to explain human behavior as the mere expression of "instincts," "biological tendencies," and the like. Between man's innate biological capacities and tendencies and his actual behavior one must always take account of culture—both the symbols and the cultural pattern that the symbols stamp upon the individual. Thus we are brought to a consideration of still a third element in culture, the adjustment-pattern.

3. **Patterns of Adjustment—Folkways, Mores.** *Patterns of adjustment may be defined as those configurations of behavior and relationship that groups develop for furthering adjustment to situations that have been experienced over and over in the past.* At their simplest and most primitive level they appear as *folkways,* the spontaneous, unpremeditated, common ways of acting which men adopt in life situations in response to life-needs. Folkways were first identified and described by William Graham Sumner, late professor of sociology at Yale.[10]

It is necessary to see quite clearly what folkways are, how they originate, and how they change into something else.

Let us suppose that a pre-literate band, hard on the track of game, comes to a small stream that is too deep for wading. More or less random exploration of the bank ensues until some one finds a shallow place, which thereupon becomes the crossing place for the band. Note that no one says "Now we must cross here because if we don't we shall have bad luck," or "We must cross here because our ancestors have always crossed here." No one

[10] For a full discussion of the subject see Sumner's book *Folkways,* New York, 1907.

stops to think or to say anything—except perhaps to call to the stragglers that a crossing has been found. As Sumner aptly remarks, "Men begin with acts, not with thoughts."

So presently our primitives are on the other side. Now observe the course of events: If good luck attends the hunting, if all get safely back, if nothing goes wrong, the members of that band will have no cause to remember that ford with anything but approval. On subsequent visits to that locality those who were there before will direct the party thither, and if there is much crossing back and forth, paths will presently be beaten on the banks, making it easier still to head for that one particular crossing-place instead of any other. Thus the practice will grow up of crossing there. So far the fact that they are crossing there *and not somewhere else* has not been mentioned. Any other possibility has simply not occurred to anybody. And it is conceivable that it should not occur to anybody for a long time. Possibly for generations nobody will so far shake himself loose from the routine business of getting a living as to ask questions about so obvious a matter. In other words, while that condition lasts the practice of crossing at that particular place is a *folkway*. It is one of those taken-for-granted practices that abound in all societies.

But not forever can that condition continue. Soon or late something will happen to suggest an alternative mode of procedure. Some hunter, for example, intent on keeping sight of a strange bird, or seeking a shorter way back to camp, or trying to evade an enemy may flounder into the river away from the customary crossing-place. Perhaps he drowns; perhaps he merely gets a good wetting. In either event the old crossing acquires a new significance. It is a "safe" place now; other places have suddenly become charged with that mysterious menace of the preliterate world, "bad luck." If the group has advanced in its theology far enough to have peopled the world with spirits, the errant hunter is seen to have received a "warning" not to stray from ancient ways. And since the misdeeds of an individual are believed inevitably to involve the group, such tempting of the spirit-world must be repressed at all costs. Hence grows the tradition: Group welfare demands that every tribesman keep to the beaten track, cross at the accustomed crossing. The old men shake their heads, the warriors mutter; and the next straggler finds himself the target for a spear.

Thus our folkway has become a *mos,* or one of the *mores.* It is no longer common merely because it is obvious, spontaneous, convenient. Ideas of group welfare have become a part of it. Regardless of its convenience or lack of it, all *must* follow it. Even if the tribe has by this time moved several miles downstream, it is still necessary to go out of one's way to cross at the old place. Why? Because that is the "safe" place, that is the place which the spirits approve. When one tempts the spirits, game disappears, the water holes dry up, enemies sweep down on the village. Thus it is unhealthy to ask too many questions.

There is no tyranny more inexorable than that of the *mores.*

Yet we must not imagine that the *mores* are merely the peculiar ways of people who hunt with bows and arrows. They are the familiar ways of all of us as well, the "necessary" ways that all of us must follow in our daily lives. We no longer buttress them with spirit-sanctions, of course—we do not burn old women for witchcraft; but we denounce companionate marriage, we burn Negroes in the South, and we run Communists out of town. It is the *mores* that require women to dress differently from men and not to take the initiative in sex matters.

It is the *mores* in America that make it right to provide a surplus for dividends but wrong to agitate too boldly for a wage surplus. It is the *mores* that make Sundays different days from other days. It is the *mores* that determine most of our behavior most of the time.

It should be added, in contrast to Sumner's view, that the *mores* of a modern, dynamic society do not all originate in this slow process of evolution from preceding folkways such as we have just described above. In a dynamic society *mores* not only evolve from underlying folkways but they are also, so to speak, precipitated from overlying controversies. Protestantism, industrialism, the free wage labor system, each of these has been taken into the *mores,* but only after bitter struggles lasting in some cases for centuries. As a matter of fact, Christianity itself is more a product of conflict and controversy than of unconscious evolution from the folkways. Not only was there a sharp conflict between Christianity and paganism at the beginning, but within the Christian fold itself there were bitter controversies over the nature of the mass, the authority of bishops, the nature of God, and nearly every other detail that is now part of the orthodox faith of millions of people. In the same way there is now going on among the political thinkers and statesmen of the western nations a gigantic controversy over the problem of controlling war. Conceivably the outcome of that controversy may be just as authoritatively part of the *mores* of 3932 A.D. as the decisions of the Council of Nicæa in 325 A.D., for example, are part of the average Christian's faith today. In any event, conflict and controversy *which are completely decisive* must be recognized as important sources of the *mores* in dynamic societies.

The *mores,* then, are patterns of adjustment to which certain rationalizations or "reasons" have become attached. The reasons may not be the real reasons, but they are the ones which, given the cultural backgrounds of the group, seem satisfying and sufficient.

Intermediate Patterns—Conventionalized Practices. At one extreme, then, we have the unattended-to, unenforced patterns of the folkways; at the other, the highly rationalized, group-sanctioned patterns called *mores.* But obviously there are many patterns that can hardly be classified at either extreme. One of the essential characteristics of the folkways is that they are done without question and therefore without explicit awareness of them. Thus men wear notches in their coat collars and buttons on their coat sleeves, and sleep in beds without being explicitly aware of doing these things rather than something else. It simply never occurs to the average person to question the collar notches, sleeve buttons, or beds. In this sense, and in the further sense that nobody feels compelled to follow these practices by any ideas of group welfare or moral compulsion, notch- and button-wearing and bed-sleeping are folkways.

But as a result of modern conditions—travel, the newspaper, the motion picture, the radio—city-dwellers especially have been made *conscious* of many such practices, which still, however, remain on the enforcement level of the folkways. Thus, as a result of the struggle to change the moral prohibitions against women smoking, women of the upper and middle classes today find themselves practically free to smoke. Yet public opinion does not insist that they smoke. Probably among adults in cities, at least, no ideas of group welfare attach to the practice one way or the other. Thus the custom in cities is clearly neither a folkway nor one of the *mores.* We are conscious that women smoke, yet do not insist that they should smoke. In the same way smoking by men is not enforced by any ideas of group welfare, yet nearly everybody is perfectly conscious that men smoke. College men in American colleges have adopted the practice of going bareheaded —in their college towns. No ideas of group welfare attend this practice, yet because it varies from the practice of other people elsewhere, and of the college men themselves when not in the collegiate atmosphere, every one concerned is perfectly aware that such a practice exists. Examples of this sort could be multiplied almost indefinitely. Modern communication and the conflict of cultures under urban conditions have made us aware of all sorts of practices and beliefs which, so far as enforcement is concerned, remain practically on the level of the unattended-to and unenforced folkways.

Thus we are driven to recognize a type of adjustment-pattern intermediate between the folkway and the *mos.* These patterns which have passed beyond the unattended-to folkways and yet do not possess the group-welfare compulsiveness of the *mores* proper have no distinctive name. Neither tradition, custom, nor convention covers this particular characteristic. Tradition focusses attention on the time-perspective behind the particular adjustment-pattern. A custom may appear on any level of group consciousness and compulsiveness. And the term convention stresses the lack of inner necessity in the adjustment-pattern itself. Thus Sapir remarks, "It is a custom to write with pen and ink; but it is a convention to use a certain kind of paper in formal correspondence.[11]

Since no name exists, therefore for patterns of whose existence as patterns people are aware but which they do not enforce, we shall apply to them the term *conventionalized practices.* A conventionalized practice is simply any adjustment-pattern that people generally are aware of yet do not collectively enforce.

The Upper Limits of Compulsiveness. For the sake of completeness we should, perhaps, add that not only are there adjustment-patterns intermediate in conscious acceptance and compulsiveness between the folkways and the *mores,* but there are also patterns which lie either at the upper limit of the *mores* or beyond them. Such patterns are enforced not merely by public

[11] Edward Sapir, "Custom," *Encyclopædia of the Social Sciences,* Vol. IV, p. 658.

opinion, as the *mores* are, but by regularly constituted functionaries or authorities whose especial business it is to enforce them. The law is the supreme example of such a pattern, but the rules and regulations of any definitely organized body such as an army, a church, a lodge, or a university have something of this quality about them.

The Ascending Scale of Consciousness and Compulsiveness. We are thus brought to think of the adjustment-patterns that make up our non-material culture as forming a kind of ascending scale which gradually rises in conscious acceptance and compulsiveness from the unattended-to, unenforced folkways, through the attended-to but still unenforced conventionalized practices, to the attended-to, opinion-enforced *mores* and ultimately to the attended-to, authority-enforced institutional *mores*. Schematically all this might be expressed in a chart showing the various levels of consciousness and compulsiveness in adjustment-patterns:

TABLE 2

LEVELS OF ADJUSTMENT PATTERNS

Level	*Name of pattern*	*Characteristics*	*Examples*
5	Institutional *mores*	Attended-to Authority-enforced	Law, army orders, etc.
	(Threshold of authoritative enforcement)		
4	*Mores* proper	Attended-to Opinion-enforced	Moral code, value-beliefs about institutions, etc.
	(Threshold of group enforcement)		
3	Conventionalized practices	Attended-to Unenforced	Women smoking, custom of college men going hatless, etc.
	(Threshold of group awareness)		
2	Folkways	Unattended-to Unenforced	Notches in men's collars; buttons on sleeves; sleeping in beds; sitting in chairs, etc.
	(Threshold of common action)		
1	Non-unified, individual behavior, *i. e.*, behavior with no common pattern		

Customs and Institutions. With the fact clearly before us that adjustment-patterns vary in conscious acceptance and compulsiveness, we are now ready to ask in what other respects they vary. The most outstanding variations which we can consider here are probably those of *complexity* and *rationality.* It is in these respects particularly that a custom differs from an *institution,* although there are other differences. A custom is a relatively simple thing. Even if we recognize with the late Professor Hayes that a custom is composed of at least three distinct elements, *i.e.,* (1) the idea of a specific action propagated by mass suggestion; (2) general expectation that in a given situation the particular pattern will be followed; and (3) emotional familiarity with the pattern on the part of those concerned—even this leaves us with a comparatively simple phenomenon. Customs grow up apparently to control or unify specific actions; institutions to satisfy fundamental needs that may require *many kinds and combinations of specific actions.* In other words, there is a *rationality,* a *complexity,* and an *organization* in an institution that a custom does not have. Such an institution as the law, for example, or the church gives evidence of purpose, of a multiplicity of elements, of a definite patterning of these elements—of an adaptation of accepted means to rational ends, in other words—that no custom can show. We shall return to the discussion of these complex and highly important adjustment-patterns, institutions, in a later chapter.

For the moment it is enough to say that a custom can appear on any level of conscious acceptance and compulsiveness but that institutions stand definitely at the upper limit of the *mores.* In fact some sociologists tend to regard them as actually outside the *mores.* While there is much to be said for this view, we shall in this book use the term *mores* to refer to all those adjustment-patterns which are both attended-to and enforced, even though the enforcement as in the case of institutions may rest on definite authority and not merely on group opinion.

How Adjustment-Patterns Change. Adjustment-patterns vary not only in compulsiveness and complexity among themselves at a given time, but they also vary from time to time in their content. This is another aspect of the growth of the culture base which we referred to earlier in this chapter, but we are here concerned with the qualitative rather than the quantitative growth.

That the *mores* do change was admitted by Sumner, but his observations of such changes among primitive peoples gave him little hope that man would ever be able to control such changes. As he saw the matter, change could come only in response to three forces:

1. Changes in life-conditions—*i.e.*, food-supply, climate, etc.
2. Internal strain for self-consistency within the *mores*.
3. Failure of identical transmission from generation to generation.

Saturated as he was with the evidence of the inability of peoples on the Stone-Age level to readjust their *mores* to new conditions, he held out little hope that his own people could control the course of their own evolution through legislation or any other means of social control.

On the whole, in view of the Russian Five-Year Plan, modern propaganda, modern education, and the tremendous changes wrought in public attitudes by modern science since the sixteenth century, Sumner's view seems prematurely fatalistic. No people has ever yet made its own culture an object of attention. But there are many indications that if such an attitude of cultural curiosity became a part of the *mores* themselves the evolution of culture might be profoundly altered, if not actually controlled.

It is at least a working hypothesis that the uncontrollability of social evolution up till this time has issued less from the complexity or the fatality of the process itself than from man's own fatalism and lack of understanding. Until this hypothesis has been tested by an intelligent attempt to understand and control cultural change, it is surely premature to conclude that cultural change cannot be controlled.

Summary. We find ourselves in a man-made environment as well as one provided by physical nature. This man-made environment which we speak of as culture imposes the master-pattern which unifies and co-ordinates collective behavior. Without it we should be nearly helpless. For purposes of observation it consists of culture traits and culture complexes. The culture base is much larger today than it was a few centuries ago, although growth is not inevitable and recessions have occurred many times in the last few thousand years. Culture traits tend to spread, or diffuse, from centres of invention in a culture area.

Culture may be analyzed into material objects, language, and non-material adjustment-patterns. Non-material adjustment patterns consist of folkways, conventionalized practices, and *mores*. There is an ascending scale of conscious acceptance and compulsiveness from the folkways, through the conventionalized practices, to the *mores* proper and the institutional *mores*.

Adjustment-patterns differ in complexity and rationality, as we see by the contrast between customs and institutions. They also vary in content from time to time.

STUDY QUESTIONS

1. What is the general reason why advertising appears on the front page of English newspapers but not of American papers?
2. Several years ago a New York editor to win a bet entered the Canadian wilderness north of Quebec one day in the fall absolutely naked, and without matches, tools, food, or weapons of any kind. He had undertaken to support himself in the woods unassisted for several weeks. Assuming that he won his bet, did the experiment prove that man can exist without culture?
3. In what way was the fall of Rome in some measure analogous to the example of catastrophe imagined by Graham Wallas?
4. On the basis of the figures given in the text, how much more efficient is the plow and factory culture than the old Indian culture was?
5. Give examples of culture traits; culture complexes. What is the value of thus breaking up culture?
6. Show why the rate of invention is correlated with the size of the culture base.
7. What are four factors affecting the rapidity of cultural advance?
8. What proportion of the cultural traits observable in your home community originated there? (Take 10 traits at random.)
9. Why is the concept, culture area, more easily applied to primitive life than to modern civilization?
10. Name the three classes of culture traits herein adopted and give examples of each.
11. Distinguish between folkways and *mores*. Why do we have them? Could we abolish them?
12. How are customs and institutions related? How are customs and institutions related to culture traits?
13. In response to what three forces only did Sumner think the *mores* changed? Do you think recent tendencies bear out his view?
14. Do you think that innovations in law, religion, or morals will ever

be as indifferently regarded as innovations in airplane design or in automobile engineering? Are there any factors present in the one case that are not in the other?

15. In what way has the idea of culture enabled you better to understand the social life about you?
16. Contrast your man-made environment, or culture, with your natural environment.

CHAPTER VII

HOW EXTERNAL FACTORS CONDITION CULTURE

Early Recognition of Problem. The fact that external nature plays a great rôle in human affairs has been recognized at least since the days of Plato and Aristotle, both of whom mention distinctions between peoples based on differences in situation. Plutarch attempted to explain differences in the Athenian population by differences in atmosphere and altitude, and Montesquieu, many centuries later, in *The Spirit of the Laws,* even tried to trace political and civil liberty to the influence of climate on national character. Buckle, in the nineteenth century, and in more recent years, Miss Semple and Ellsworth Huntington, have refined and elaborated the theory of the controlling importance of geographical factors in human society. At the same time biologists, despite their usual preoccupation with heredity, have not failed to note the selective action of environment. Darwin, in fact, based his theory of natural selection on this; while some recent biologists tend to find in geological history the inciting causes of many of the great changes in organic evolution.[1] Obviously neither culture nor human association itself can be understood apart from the physical environment.

Constants and Variables in the Physical Environment. Broadly speaking the physical environment lays down the conditions and sets the limits under which and within which man must live; culture determines what those conditions and limits shall mean at any given time.

Certain conditions or forces such as gravitation operate as constants. Nobody can discuss the effect of gravitation on human behavior because nobody knows anything about human behavior apart from gravitation. What we are here concerned with, then, is not the constants in the physical world but the variables. Such variables include:

1. Natural resources:
    a. Soil and plants.

[1] See for example, Richard Swann Lull, *Organic Evolution,* New York, 1920, p. 672.

b. Animal life.
c. Minerals.

2. Climate.
3. Location relative to water, mountains, deserts, etc.
4. Position relative to other men and their activities.

1. **Natural Resources.** (*a*) *Soil and plants.*—The soil is our most valuable single natural resource, since from it comes 95 per cent of our food, 100 per cent of our clothing and a good share of our shelter.[2] It is not surprising, therefore, that variations in the fertility of the soil are associated with striking variations in the economic development and general progress of different regions. Thus central Illinois near Urbana, Champaign, and Bloomington is markedly superior to approximately the same extent of territory in southern Illinois near Centralia in all indexes of social and economic progress such as population, average size of farm, value of farm land per acre, percentage of population living in cities, per capita wealth, percentage of young people in school beyond the age of compulsion, and in the ratio of eminent men per 100,000 population.[3] The decisive difference between these two regions seems to be that in central Illinois the soil is more fertile than that around Centralia. The same condition accounts for variations in population density, per capita wealth, school facilities, and general social conditions as between good-soil areas in Michigan and poor-soil areas. The farm population per mile of road in the forest counties of the upper peninsula in 1930 for example was 7 as compared with 13 in the farm-urban counties in the southern peninsula. While climate as well as soil may be a factor in this difference, there is no question that the so-called forest counties in both peninsulas have poorer soils than the farm counties and that the poor soils seriously limit economic and social development.[4]

[2] The fact that beefsteaks and fur coats are not derived immediately from the soil like potatoes does not alter the ultimate source of both of them. All animals are dependent on plant life for food and plant life in turn depends on the chemical elements in the soil. It is estimated that all fisheries contribute only about 5 per cent of the food supply of the nation; the rest comes from the soil. Cotton, wool, flax, silk, rayon, fur and other materials used for clothing in this country come directly or indirectly from the same source.

[3] For details see Davis, Barnes, Huntington, and others, *Introduction to Sociology*, pp. 207f.

[4] P. A. Herbert, "Resources and Public Finances of Michigan in Relation to the Forest Tax Problem," *Progress Report of the Forest Taxation Inquiry, U. S. Department of Agriculture*, April 1, 1931, pp. 2f.

Of course man is absolutely dependent upon plant life either directly or indirectly for his existence. But, in addition, the character of the plant life in any area has much to do with the culture of the persons who live there. The cultivation of wheat, barley, oats, and rye has always been associated with Occidental civilization. The peoples of Europe have not only adapted their farming techniques, but their food habits and other aspects of their culture to these cereals. Similarly rice is the staple vegetable of the Orient, and maize held the same position in the culture of the American Indians.

(*b*) *Animal life.*—Civilization has been said to rest on the cultivation of cereals and the keeping of domesticated animals. The rôle of the horse since its introduction into Babylonia about 2000 B.C. and of cattle since Neolithic days need not be described here.[5] It is suggestive, however, that the word pecuniary which is so often used now to describe the profit-seeking, money economy, comes down from a Latin word, *pecus,* meaning cattle, which were once used as a medium of exchange.

One of the most striking examples of the importance of animals is supplied by Indian culture. The Indians came into America when they were apparently at the beginning of the New Stone Age. The only domesticated animal that they brought with them was the dog, and the only animal that they found in the two Americas fit for domestication was the llama in Peru. In other words, over the greater part of two continents they had no beast of burden or draft animal larger than the dog until the Spaniards reintroduced the horse which had become extinct in America ages before the Indians arrived. Lacking a real draft animal, the Indian never invented the wheel, and consequently never developed more than a rudimentary transportation complex. This deficiency in turn contributed to the retardation of Indian civilization even in the centres where it did develop.

Our present-day dependence on domesticated animals may be summed up statistically in the figures of the U. S. Census of Agriculture covering livestock on farms in 1930: For every person in the United States in 1930 there were 1.6 domesticated animals, exclusive of poultry, on our farms.[6]

[5] *Cf.* Kroeber, *Anthropology,* 433, 448, 455, etc.

[6] *Fifteenth Census of the United States, 1930: Agriculture—General Statistics, Summary for the United States, 1929 and 1930,* Bureau of the Census, Washington, 1932, pp. 58ff.

The rôle of wild animals and micro-organisms in affecting culture deserves far more space than we can give it here. Pre-literate man is, of course, largely dependent on game for his food supply. The culture of the Plains Indians was built on the buffalo as that of certain Eskimo tribes is in part, at least, on the caribou. The furs and skins of wild animals still constitute important articles of commerce in advanced cultures.

Micro-organisms have undoubtedly played an important selective rôle in history[7] and constitute today one of the chief barriers to the white man's exploitation of the tropics. Smallpox, measles, and scarlet fever have been important factors in the white man's victory over simpler cultures not only in North America but in the Pacific islands and elsewhere. Through long centuries of selection the white races have acquired a natural resistance to these diseases which the native races seem to lack. On the other hand, native races are more resistant to yellow fever, sleeping sickness and other tropical diseases than is the white man.

The account with animal life must not be closed until mention has been made of insects. While man has domesticated the bee—there were 3,107,000 hives reported in the United States in 1930—other insects cost him millions of dollars in crop losses every year. The experts on insects are telling us that the stupendous reproductive powers of the insect make it actually a potential menace to the entire human race. It is by no means certain, apparently, that man and not the insect is to be the dominant life-form on this planet. The answer may well be decided by man's success or failure in devising cultural protections against insect ravages in the future.

(*c*) *Minerals.*—Minerals are the raw materials of industrialism. As such their distribution, quality, and accessibility become determining factors in culture. Culture in its early stages needs only a few minerals, principally quartz and silicate of aluminum. Eventually copper and tin, and ultimately iron, coal, and petroleum become of prime importance. Economic development today rests fundamentally on iron, coal, and petroleum, although a number of other minerals such as manganese, chromium, tungsten, vana-

[7] Disease is believed, however, by some authorities not to have been an important factor for more than 10,000 or 20,000 years, *i.e.*, roughly since the beginning of the New Stone Age and the clustering of groups in more or less permanent settlements. For a discussion of this point, see Carr-Saunders, *The Population Problem.*

dium, nickel, copper, tin, aluminum, phosphate, and potash are of high importance for the making of alloys, for electrical work, for preserving food, for maintenance of soil fertility, and for other purposes.

It was the possession of cheap coal and iron that gave England her head-start over other nations in the industrial revolution, a lead which she maintained for practically 100 years. It is the almost total absence of coal and iron that today dooms Italy to subordinate rank as an industrial nation. Control of mineral resources, notably petroleum, outranks even the struggle for markets as a dominant factor in the foreign policy of every great nation.

With nearly 45 per cent of the world's coal, more than 42 per cent of the world's iron ore, and a large share of the world's petroleum, the United States finds itself in a very strong economic position. Yet so interdependent has the world become and so omnivorous is the appetite of the machine that even the United States must import more than thirty commodities essential to the conduct of war, the list including tin, nickel, and chromium.

Mining tends to run through a natural cycle. There is first a stage of prospecting, then a stage of development, then a stage of production culminating in the use of expensive machinery, and finally a stage of exhaustion and population decline.[8] Virginia City, Nevada, near the famous Comstock Lode silver deposits, is a typical example of a town that has passed through this cycle. In 1860 it had a population of 2,345; in 1900, 10,900; and in 1920, 1,200.

2. **Climate.** Books have been written on the influence of climate on human affairs. We can only suggest some of its more important effects.

Variations in climate seem to be associated with changes in ancient civilizations. Drought in Asia was probably one of the factors in the great folk-wanderings that drove the barbarians down on Rome. There is also evidence that the most advanced and progressive cultural areas today in Europe, North America and elsewhere tend to coincide with areas of the highest climatic energy, *i.e.,* areas of the most stimulatingly varied climate, such as one

[8] Lumbering passes through a somewhat similar cycle, but due to the replaceable character of timber the stage of exhaustion may be succeeded by a stage of reforestation and timber control.

finds in the north central and eastern parts of the United States.[9] Climate has probably been an important factor in racial differentiation. Certainly at present climate is the great barrier to the white man's occupation of the tropics.

Indirectly climate controls the distribution and centralization of population by controlling the water supply. Cities depend on surplus production. The production of surplus food depends in turn on a number of factors among which the amount and seasonal distribution of rainfall is of great importance. While it is, of course, possible to ship food into arid regions, the fact remains that for the mass of mankind it is easier to live near an abundant food supply. Hence cities tend to be more numerous in fertile, well-watered regions than in regions of infrequent rain.

As in the case of all other natural factors, however, the control exercised by climate is mediated by culture. At one extreme we find the rain-forest which modern culture has not yet subdued; at the other extreme, the desert which still defies us. Where the rainfall exceeds 60 inches, as in many parts of the tropics, ordinary agriculture is impossible. Where the average runs below 18 inches, as in the arid regions of the west and southwest from North Dakota to Arizona, present-day food-growing techniques cannot support dense populations. In between these limits of rain-forest and desert the climatic control obviously becomes less direct.

All over the world, however, climate continues to affect culture. Food, clothing, customs, and sometimes—as among primitive peoples—even religion, all reflect it. The Spanish siesta, the Eskimo igloo, the American irrigation ditch, each is an answer-back by a particular culture to a climatic problem.

3. **Location.** The location of a place is one of the most important environmental facts affecting it. This is true in a double sense: Location not only determines the relation of a place to natural features such as water supply, bodies of water, mountains, deserts, and the like, but it also determines spatial relations with reference to other places, and these in turn become important through the effect of culture traits such as highways, steamships, railroads, airplanes, and the like. We have to consider, therefore, two things: (1) *Location* pure and simple as it affects relationship to natural features of an area; and (2) *position,* or location in

[9] For the most detailed studies of the effects of climate on society, see the works of Ellsworth Huntington, particularly *The Pulse of Progress* and *Civilization and Climate.*

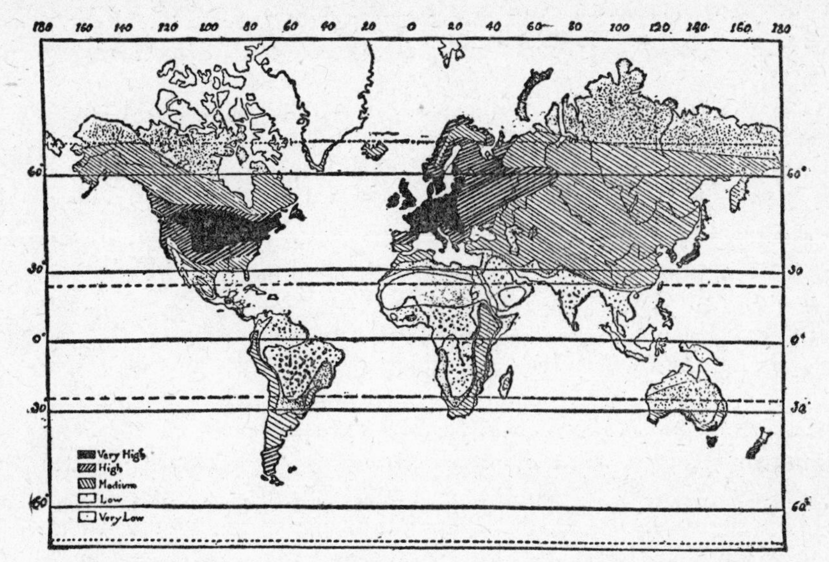

FIG. 3. The Distribution of Human Energy on the Basis of Climate.

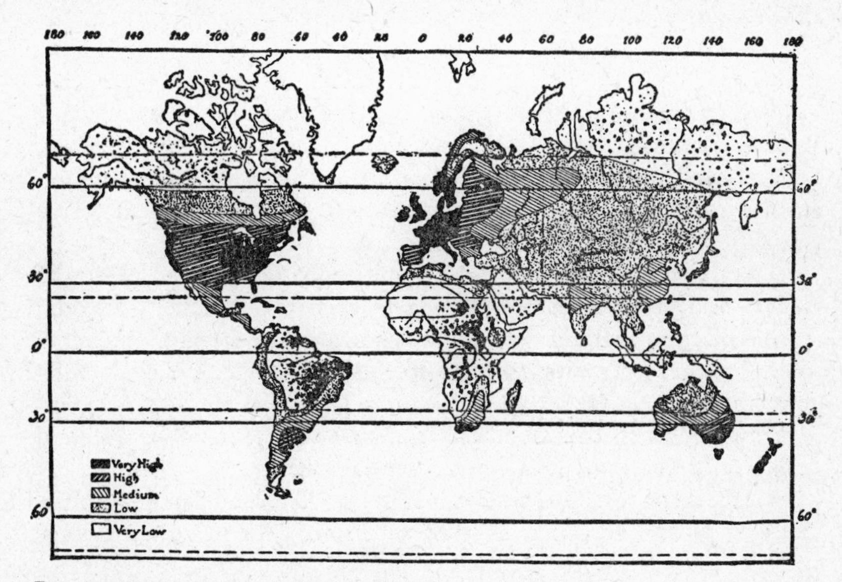

From Huntington's "Civilization and Climate."

FIG. 4. Distribution of Civilization.

terms of communication and transportation, with reference to other groups of people.

Location with reference to bodies of water is important because bodies of water—aside from their moderating influence on climate and their function as barriers in primitive days—may be utilized to provide drinking water, power, transportation, and recreation. It is location that forces New York and Pittsburgh to spend millions of dollars building bridges. The bridges, by improving communication and transportation, alter the cities' positions with reference to other cities, but the location of each city on two rivers has made the bridges necessary.

It is location with the accompanying difference in topography that accounts for the differences that exist between mountainous and flat country. Mountain regions have a reputation for being hard to govern, and the chronic turmoil in the Balkans is not all to be accounted for on the ground of exaggerated nationalism. Huntington has pointed out an interesting contrast between the rich Blue Grass region of Kentucky and the poor mountain regions, the feud country, only 60 or 70 miles away.[10] While population density is practically the same in each region, 47 to the square mile in the Blue Grass and 46 in the mountains, the average Blue-Grass family is 3.8 times as well off in income per head as are the mountain-dwellers. Isolation, ignorance, provincialism, spinning wheels, corn whiskey, family feuds, over-population, poverty, all attest the difficulties of transportation in the mountains—in other words, the importance of location as a factor in conditioning culture.

4. **Position.** Position is the culturally determined value of location. It is the relation that a place bears to other places in terms of the time and cost of transportation and communication. We shall have occasion to refer to this more at length in our discussion of regional organization in a later chapter, but it is important to grasp the idea here in connection with other external factors affecting the culture of a given place.

In the broadest perspective possible, all civilized communities may be said to be conditioned by position. Thus the town culture of ancient Egypt and Mesopotamia has been characterized as a river civilization; the Minoan and Græco-Roman civilizations have been called thalassic, or sea-conditioned; and modern civili-

[10] *Cf.* Davis, Barnes, and others, *Introduction to Sociology,* pp. 227ff.

zation is called oceanic. All of these terms obviously refer to the evolution of man's power to transport himself on water. An American naval officer, the late Admiral Mahan, was one of the first to recognize the decisive rôle of sea-power in history. The Roman victory over Carthage, England's victory over Napoleon, the Union victory over the South, and the Allied victory over the Central Powers can all be explained in terms of control of the sea. Whether the development of the airplane now means that the oceanic stage of civilization is passing into the aerial and that the decisive factor in future wars will be control of the air instead of the control of the sea, is a question for the future to answer.

The importance of position in determining a nation's fortunes has been demonstrated time and again. Why, for example, was it the Spanish and Portuguese and other peoples in the western part of Europe who were so eager to find a western route to the Orient, and why did Venice decline in importance after the discovery of America? Why have the English been especially interested in the New World, and why was Japan so backward in civilization a century ago? Such questions could be extended for pages, and the answers would always include a heavy emphasis on geo-cultural position.

Position conditions the destiny of cities. New York has become the greatest seaport in North America because of its situation at the greatest and most convenient ice-free natural gateway open the year round to European traffic.[11] Given iron in Upper Michigan and coal in Pennsylvania, the region from the Great Lakes to Pittsburgh was destined by position to be the scene of great industrial development when the cultural level demanded steel and supplied the means of transportation. The fact that settlement came from the East rather than the West foredestined the cities on the eastern side of the Michigan peninsula to greater importance than those on the western side. Position again favored Detroit as against its early competitors, Monroe and Port Huron. From nations to cities and even neighborhoods position is a decisive factor.

How the External World Limits and Patterns Culture. Let us summarize what we have been saying throughout this discussion. The four variables—resources, climate, location, position—affect human beings in a number of ways, the most impor-

[11] See Jones and Bryan, *North America,* New York, 1929, pp. 429–430.

tant of which for present purposes seem to be chiefly cultural. No doubt over a span of many centuries physical conditions also produce biological changes through natural selection. Thus the Indians of the high Andean plateaus are said to have an abnormal lung capacity as a result of the elimination of less sturdy types by the rigors of the high altitude. In the same way natives of the tropics and of the arctic regions have become heavily pigmented apparently as a protection against the actinic rays of the sun which are more intense in those regions. Other examples of the direct effect of geo-physical conditions on the physical type might be cited. It would also be possible to adduce evidence of the effects of climate, for example, on behavior. But since we are concerned primarily with association and its cultural results, these biological and psychological effects of environment may be left to the biologists and psychologists.

The physical environment has forced man to invent as a precondition of his own survival. Left without specific biological protection against darkness, rain, cold, food-shortage, and the other risks of a rude world, man has had to find a faster method of adaptation than the old method of biological mutation and selection. Culture is his answer. Culture-building is the distinctively human method of adaptation. Weapons, tools, clothing, houses, artificial lighting, coal mines, factories, these are man's devices for making himself secure in a niggardly environment. It follows necessarily that culture varies as environmental problems change. Homes in the South are not built for zero temperatures. Northern housing, games, customs, all reflect the cooler climate. The language and customs of the sea would be worse than useless on the Great Plains. All this needs only to be mentioned to be obvious.

But Nature not only challenges man to invent—she lays down the lines along which his inventions must run and sets limits within which his inventions must work. Other things equal, for example, islands cannot have populations as large as those of continents. Yet when cultural conditions change, an island obviously may contain many times as many people as at previous levels of development. In 1600, for example, Manhattan Island contained only a small Indian village. In 1930 it held more than 1,800,000 people. This means that the size of any group is determined partly by the geo-physical factors and partly by culture. The same intimate relationship appears in every field—until the invention of the airplane, for example, routes of migration and of commerce were rigidly determined by the location of rivers, passes, and the like. The explorers of America and the pioneers moved by water. Three centuries later the railroads were still following the valleys, but the motor roads were beginning to strike more boldly into the hills, and the airplane was flying over them. Thus even while location remains unchanged, position changes. The Erie canal, for instance, changed the relative position of New York and Philadelphia with reference to the West, and every improvement in transportation or change in freight rates has its repercussions in changes in traffic. Yet the great bulk of human transportation continues to follow the lines of easiest grade and lowest cost. Mountains, deserts, swamps, have always been obstacles and are such even today. Rivers, lakes, and oceans have only partially ceased to be barriers in becoming highways.

Gradually it has become apparent that culture tends on the whole to adapt itself to the main outlines laid down by the geo-physical characteristics of a region. Thus, basic contrasts in culture develop: the North differs from the South; the seaboard from the hinterland; the fertile-soil areas from the poor-soil areas. In a later chapter we shall have to examine the way in which culture tends to be organized in regions which express in some degree at least the basic geo-physical controls that underlie them. It is enough now to note that the geo-physical factors expressed in resources, climate, and location, and the positional factors resulting from cultural adaptation to location, provide the basic mold in which culture forms.

STUDY QUESTIONS

1. How long have theorists recognized the importance of the physical environment?
2. Why omit consideration of the constants in the physical environment?
3. List the variables considered.
4. Show from your own experience the effect of each on culture.
5. In what other ways than through culture do geo-physical factors affect human life?
6. Show how the Panama Canal changed the relative positions of New York and San Francisco but left their locations unchanged.

CHAPTER VIII

CULTURE AND PERSONALITY DEVELOPMENT

Since culture or the social heritage confronts the developing individual at every turn, it is apparent that he is largely shaped by its manifestations. However, there are marked differences in the complexity of the psychological processes through which culture affects the individual. In many instances the influence of culture is insidious, so that the traits creep into personality unaware. It is these situations with which we are concerned in this chapter. But where there is conflict, either between culture elements or between culture and non-cultural impulses, consciousness and, as we say, choice or will are brought to bear. The resulting behavior is then influenced by the self. We therefore leave the discussion of such situations until after we take up the self in the next chapter.

Suggestion. The process of insidious culture influence is usually called suggestion. It is that which accounts for the frequency with which we unintentionally take on the manners, habits of speech, religious, political and economic views, moral standards and other culture traits of those about us. This occurs when there is an absence of opposing stimuli which would force the mind to select, so that a comparatively mechanical process ensues which does not involve consciousness of what is happening. Thus it is a process of suggestion for most of us that leads to speaking the English language, because we have practically no choice in the matter. As children we are of course aware that we are learning to use words but we are not intentionally learning English instead of French. Similarly the sons of conservative fathers do not as children mean to hold conservative views; it is only the lack of competing stimulation which makes them do so.

Even when we have already developed habits of a certain kind we may be led to change them through suggestion. Professor Faris has put forward the interesting thesis that this happens as a result of subsequent mental rehearsal of events.[1] Thus a northerner who goes to live in the South may gradually pick up the southern

[1] "The Concept of Imitation," *Am. J. of Sociology,* XXXII, pp. 367–378.

accent without meaning to do so because in going over in his mind conversations that he has had with southerners he pronounces their words as they do, and thus his vocal apparatus becomes accustomed to this pronunciation. He is aware of the rehearsal but not of the fact that it is making him adopt a different culture trait. The same process may take place with respect to other sorts of habits.

It is evident that for the most part we acquire the folkways and *mores* of our own culture by suggestion. Indeed the great contribution of Sumner in his famous book[2] was his emphasis on the irrationality of these culture elements. Precisely because they surround us as we grow up and creep into our minds by the process of suggestion, we rarely bring to bear upon them our critical powers.

Cultural Definitions. It is easy to see that the habits developed through suggestion will influence our course of action in each new situation which confronts us. What is not so obvious is that these habits tend *to define the things perceived.*

The example given in Chapter VI of the snake, the English trader Henry, and the Indians not only exemplifies different lines of conduct in the face of the same object; it also shows that the thing itself was actually perceived differently. Take another instance. Before the rise of modern science very few colors were discriminated. A dozen color names, perhaps, were in common usage. But with the development of spectrum analysis, on the one hand, and of the chemical dye industry, on the other, new color names have been added to our vocabularies; and now we actually *see* differences in shade that our ancestors would not have discriminated—all because we have labels for them.

Generalizing this idea, social psychologists say culture tends to give us definitions of objects, activities, and situations. Their meaning for us and hence their effects upon us are determined in large part by the meanings which are handed down to us through social transmission. What impresses us as beautiful or ugly, worthless or valuable, good or bad is likely to be closely tied up with our particular cultural heritage. As Walter Lippmann has put it, "For the most part we do not first see, and then define, *we define first and then see.* In the great blooming, buzzing confusion of the outer world we pick out what our culture has already de-

[2] *Folkways.*

fined for us, and we tend to perceive that which we have picked out in the form stereotyped for us by our culture."[3] It has been proven by research that we have stereotypes in regard to various occupations, classes, and nationalities. We tend to see a school teacher, a radical, a big business man, a Turk in terms of conventionalized pictures. We perceive the traits and qualities emphasized by the stereotypes and pass over those that are incompatible. Similarly one who has been trained in the culture of cubist art will see a meaningful picture where another person not so trained will see nothing but a confused jumble of lines and masses.

Examples of this kind could be multiplied indefinitely. When a band strikes up "The Internationale" do a communist and a non-communist perceive the same thing? One will hear beautiful and stirring music played by worthy men on a splendid occasion. The other sees a bunch of no-good radicals playing a detestable piece of music in a slipshod way.

Mores define whole situations for us in a similar manner. A white child brought up in the South and used to the segregation of Negroes sees the portion of the street car reserved for them as a forbidden place. Whereas a northern child, not finding a seat among the whites, would naturally see a vacant seat among the Negroes as a place for him to sit. The *mores* of national pride and loyalty led the people in all countries at the outbreak of the World War to define the cause of their nation as a righteous crusade against the indefensible selfishness of the enemy. This is what is meant by saying that we "cut out" from our potential environment our actual environment. What actually stimulates us depends upon what we carry around with us in the way of habits and attitudes and this depends largely upon our culture. It should perhaps be emphasized that culture in modern life is highly differentiated so that persons living even in the same family may receive differing cultural influences. The worlds which twins "cut out" are not identical simply because two people cannot, even if they would, acquire exactly the same cultural patterns.

We have suggested in Chapter III that we use in a selective way our ability to understand others. We now see that this can be partly accounted for by stereotypes which make us well disposed toward certain types of persons and ill disposed toward other types. It is probable, however, that we do not rely wholly

[3]Lippmann, *Public Opinion,* p. 81.

on these cultural definitions but supplement them by insight gained from our own unique experience.

Thus we all build up both overt habits and mental attitudes through suggestion which tend to be perpetuated by the selective effect which these habits and attitudes have upon perception. It is a sort of vicious circle, and a circle which makes many of our social problems more acute.

Culture is a differentiated thing and each of us grows up under the influence of certain cultural streams—that of our social class, of our nation, of our historical epoch. We are swept along on the tide of our culture. This phenomenon may be compared to the situation of a yachting party whose craft has been stopped at some point on the Gulf Stream to permit them to go swimming in the ocean. Each swimmer realizes his movements relative to the other members of the party and to the yacht. But none is aware that swimmers and yacht alike are being borne along on the Gulf Stream. If all around us are subject to the same influence, we are no more conscious of it than of the revolution of the earth.

Influence of Class and National Cultures. There is nothing more important to understand, or less understood, than the class cultures in which nearly all of us live. We usually believe that the way we look upon social and economic questions is the natural way, the right way, not perceiving that it is a way imposed upon us by suggestion. The ideas which flow in upon us from the people with whom we associate determine the premises of our thought. There is something rather alarming to any one who wishes to see his country united, in the self-complacent ignorance which men in one class show regarding the ideas and feelings of their fellow citizens in another. It is rare to find among business or professional men any real comprehension of the struggles and aspirations of the hand-working class, while the contemptuous attitude of the native toward the immigrant, or of the white toward the Negro, is inevitably answered by resentment on the other side. The press, which ought to interpret social classes to each other, is itself divided on class lines, and the papers and magazines which the well-to-do man reads confirm him in his class bias, while the hand-worker feeds his upon labor and socialist publications. Nor do the common schools, for the most part, give the children instruction which prepares them for large and sympathetic views.

One result of all this is that it is easy, in times of excitement, for propagandists to arouse dangerous suspicions and hostilities of one class against another—as was shown in the trying period immediately following the World War. If we are to have friendly co-operation, among classes or among nations, we must begin by having more understanding.

The same thing is obviously true of one's national culture. The more thoroughly American a man is the less he can perceive Americanism. He will embody it; all he does, says, or writes, will be full of it; but he can never truly see it, simply because he has no external point of view from which to look at it. If he goes to Europe he begins to get by contrast some vague notion of it, though he will never be able to see just what it is that makes futile his attempts to seem an Englishman, a German, or an Italian. Our appearance to other peoples is like one's own voice, which one never hears quite as others hear it, and which sounds strange when it comes back from the phonograph.

Suggestion and the Historical Epoch. The control of those larger movements of thought and sentiment that make a historical epoch is still less conscious, more inevitable. Only the imaginative student, in his best hours, can really free himself from the limitations of his time and see things from a height. For the most part the people of other epochs seem strange, outlandish, or a little insane. We can scarcely rid ourselves of the impression that the way of life we are used to is the normal, and that other ways are eccentric. Dr. Sidis holds that the people of the Middle Ages were in a quasi-hypnotic state, and instances the crusades, dancing manias, and the like.[4] But the question is, would not our own time, viewed from an equal distance, appear to present the signs of abnormal suggestibility? Will not the intense preoccupation with material production, the hurry and strain of our cities, the draining of life into one channel, at the expense of breadth, richness, and beauty, appear as mad as the crusades, and perhaps of a lower type of madness? Could anything be more indicative of a slight but general insanity than the aspect of the crowd on the streets of Chicago?

An illustration of this unconsciousness of what is distinctive in our own time is the fact that those who participate in momentous changes have seldom any but the vaguest notion of their

[4] See the latter chapters of his *Psychology of Suggestion.*

significance. There is perhaps no time in the history of art that seems to us now so splendid, so dramatic, as that of the sudden rise of Gothic architecture in northern France, and the erection of the church of St. Denis at Paris was its culmination: yet Professor C. E. Norton, speaking of the Abbot Suger, who erected it, and of his memoirs, says, "Under his watchful and intelligent oversight the church became the most splendid and the most interesting building of the century; but of the features that gave it special interest, that make it one of the most important monuments of medieval architecture, neither Suger, in his account of it, nor his biographer, nor any contemporary writer, says a single word."[5] To Suger and his time the Gothic, it would seem, was simply a new and improved way of building a church, a technical matter with which he had little concern, except to see that it was duly carried out according to specifications. It was developed by draughtsmen and handicraftsmen, mostly nameless, who felt their own thrill of constructive delight as they worked, but had no thought of historical glory. It is no doubt the same in our own time, and Mr. Bryce has noted with astonishment the unconsciousness or indifference of those who founded cities in western America to the fact that they were doing something that would be memorable and influential for ages.[6]

Thus we see that our development takes place under the influence of many cultural streams of different kinds and sizes. Each of these separately, and all of them together, mold our personality without our realizing what is taking place. So great is their effect, however, that all of our later experience is colored by the habits and attitudes thus acquired.

STUDY QUESTIONS

1. Give examples from your own observation of unconscious control by suggestion.
2. Explain Professor Faris's notion that suggestion may operate to change habits by the process of mental rehearsal.
3. Why do other people rather than ourselves perceive our local accent? Give other illustrations of the principle involved.
4. What contrast, if any, do you notice between the trend of your mind at home and at the University? What do you ascribe it to?

[5]*Harpers*, Vol. 79, p. 770.
[6]*The American Commonwealth*, II, p. 705.

5. Explain how culture gives us definitions of objects and activities.
6. Give three examples of well-known stereotypes in American culture.
7. Give an example of a case in which a change in the definition of the situation necessitates changed behavior.
8. What examples can you give of the harmful or beneficial influences of class environment? How would you obviate the former?
9. Explain: "A 100 per cent American can have no standard by which to judge his country."
10. Is the "spirit of the age" a real thing? If so, what are its nature and importance?

CHAPTER IX

THE SELF

Personality. The personality of the individual comprises those qualities which are significant in his association with other people. This is, as we have seen, founded on human nature and conditioned by culture. But what of that more intimate thing we call the self, and how is it related to personality?

The Nature of the Self. By "self" is meant that which is designated in common speech by "I," "me," and "myself." It may be assumed that these pronouns have a substantial, important and not very recondite meaning, otherwise they would not be in constant and intelligible use by simple people and young children the world over. It is our purpose to discover this meaning and to show how the consciousness of self develops. Perhaps we may define the self as what the individual feels he is as a unique element in social relationships. It is thus different from personality in that it is subjective rather than objective, and only involves that which is felt to be in some degree distinctive. If we accept this definition, the self appears to be built up from two sources, one within personality and one without. The first we may call the my-feeling or sense of appropriation. There is no more hope of defining this feeling satisfactorily than there is of giving a formal definition of the taste of salt or the color red; we can expect to know it only by experiencing it. But as this feeling is quite as familiar to us as the taste of salt or the color of red, there should be no difficulty in understanding what is meant by it. One need only imagine some attack on his "me," say ridicule of his dress or an attempt to take away his property or his child, or his good name by slander, and self-feeling immediately appears. Another way to perceive this ingredient in the self is to listen to the talk of little children playing together, especially if they do not agree very well. They use the first person with none of the conventional self-repression of their elders, but with much emphasis and variety of inflection, so that its emotional animus is unmistakable.

Self-feeling of a reflective and agreeable sort is strongly suggested by the word "gloating." To gloat, in this sense, is as much as to think "mine, mine, mine" with a pleasant warmth of feeling. Thus a boy gloats over something he has made with his tools, over a bird he has brought down with his gun, or over his collection of stamps or eggs; a girl gloats over her new clothes, and over the approving words or looks of others; a farmer over his fields and his stock; a business man over his trade and his bank account; a mother over her child; the poet over a successful quatrain; the self-righteous man over the state of his soul; and in like manner every one gloats over the prosperity of any cherished idea.

But this self-feeling is not the whole story. It defines a field broader than the self, as is shown by the fact that we do not use "I" for all the things we speak of as "mine." The self is obviously an area of especially strong appropriative feeling in the centre of this larger area. This appears to be defined by the second factor—the use of "you" by others in addressing us. Just as we gradually learn what "beauty" must mean by hearing it in many contexts, so we evolve a notion of "me" by realizing what traits are common to the many instances when "you" is employed in referring to us. Since others regard each of us as a unique factor in social relations, and since the differentiated aspect of our lives is what needs to be sustained by purpose and endeavor, we tend to cherish as particularly dear those things which others seem to include in "you." Obviously, then, a fully developed self comes into existence only with the learning of language and the achievement of sympathetic insight.

The Self Not Merely the Physical Body. As many people have the impression that the verifiable self, the object which we name with "I," is usually the material body, it may be well to say that this impression is an illusion, easily dispelled by any one who will undertake a simple examination of the facts. It is true that when we philosophize a little about "I" and look around for a tangible object to which to attach it, we soon fix upon the material body as the most available *locus;* but when we use the word naïvely, as in ordinary speech, it is not very common to think of the body in connection with it; not nearly so common as to think of other things. One need only listen to ordinary speech until the word has occurred, say, a hundred times, noting its connections, or observe its use in a similar number of cases by the characters in a novel. Ordinarily it will be found that in not more than ten cases in a hundred does "I" have reference to the body of the person speaking. It refers chiefly to opinions, purposes, desires, claims, and the like, concerning matters that involve no thought of the body. *I* think or feel so and so; *I* wish or intend so and so; *I* want this or that; are typical uses, the self-feeling being associated with the view, purpose, or object mentioned.

The Social Reference of the Self. The self at any particular moment, then, is simply the system of objects and ideas which, because of the attitude of others toward us, we cherish as distinctively our own. It always possesses a social setting; that is, it is an assertion of the ways in which we are distinctive from our fellows. Its more aggressive forms tend to attach themselves to whatever one finds to be at once congenial to one's own tendencies and at variance with those of others with whom one is in mental contact. Agreeable to this view we find that the self manifests itself most conspicuously in an appropriation of objects of common desire, corresponding to the individual's need of power over such objects to secure his own peculiar development, and to the danger of opposition from others who also need them. And this extends from material objects to the attentions and affections of other people, to all sorts of plans and ambitions, including the noblest special purposes the mind can entertain, and indeed of any conceivable idea which may come to seem a part of one's life and in need of assertion against some one else. The attempt to limit the word self to the lower aims of personality is quite arbitrary; at variance with common sense as expressed by the emphatic use of "I" in connection with the sense of duty and other high motives, and unphilosophical as ignoring the function of the self as the organ of specialized endeavor of higher as well as lower kinds.

"I," since it asserts one's individual aspect of the social order, always implies the thought of others. Indeed, this is true of "my" and "mine" as well. Thus if we think of a secluded part of the woods as ours, it is because we think, also, that others do not go there. As regards the body it is doubtful whether we have a vivid my-feeling about any part of it which is not thought of, however vaguely, as having some actual or possible reference to some one else. Internal organs like the liver are not thought of as peculiarly ours unless we are trying to communicate something regarding them, as, for instance, when they are giving us trouble and we are trying to get sympathy. The reference to other persons involved in the sense of self may be distinct and particular, as when a boy is ashamed to have his mother catch him at something she has forbidden, or it may be vague and general, as when one is ashamed to do something which only his conscience, expressing his sense of social responsibility, detects and disapproves; but it is always there. There is no sense of "I," as in pride or shame, without its correlative sense of you, or he, or they. Even the miser gloating over his hidden gold can feel the "mine" only as he is aware of the world of men over whom he has secret power; and the case is very similar with all kinds of treasure. Many painters, sculptors, and writers have loved to withhold their work from the world, fondling it in seclusion until they were quite done with it; but the delight in this, as in all secrets, depends upon a sense of the value to others of what is concealed.

We have said that we think of the body as "I" when it comes to have a social function or significance, as when we say "I am looking well today," or "I am taller than you." We bring it into the social world, for the time being, and for that reason put our self-consciousness into it. Now it is curious, though natural, that in precisely the same way we may call any inanimate object "I" with which we are identifying our will and purpose. This is notably true in games, like golf or croquet, where the ball is the embodiment of the player's fortunes. You will hear a man say "I am in the long grass down by the third tee," or "I am in position for the middle arch." So a boy flying a kite will say "I am higher than you," or one shooting at a mark will declare that he is just below the bull's-eye.

The Reflected Self. Other people not only help to define the content of "I"; they are also the chief arbiters of the self's success. Any idea which a person cherishes will bring him great joy if his close associates approve of it, and sorrow if they do not. Thus we tend to cherish the reactions toward ourselves of our friends. This sort of self-feeling is usually called the reflected or looking-glass self. As we see our face, figure, and dress in the glass, and are interested in them because they are ours, and pleased or otherwise with them according as they do or do not answer to what we should like them to be; so in our imagination we perceive in another's mind some thought of our appearance, manners, aims, deeds, character, friends, and so on, and are variously affected by it.

A self-idea of this sort means to have three principal elements: the imagination of our appearance to the other person; the imagination of his judgment of that appearance, and some sort of self-feeling, such as pride or mortification. The comparison with a looking-glass hardly suggests the second element, the imagined judgment, which is quite essential. The thing that moves us to pride or shame is not the mere mechanical reflection of ourselves, but an imputed sentiment, the imagined effect of this reflection upon another's mind. This is evident from the fact that the character and weight of that other, in whose mind we see ourselves, makes all the difference with our feeling. We are ashamed to seem evasive in the presence of a straightforward man, cowardly in the presence of a brave one, gross in the eyes of a refined one, and so on. We always imagine, and in imagining share, the judgments of the other mind. A man will boast to one person of an action—say some sharp transaction in trade—which he would be ashamed to own to another.

The looking-glass self is related to character very much as credit is related to the gold and other securities upon which it rests. It easily and willingly expands, in most of us, and is liable to sudden, irrational, and grevious collapses. We live on, cheerful, self-confident, conscious of helping make the world go round, until in some rude hour we learn that we do not stand so well as we thought we did, that the image of us is tarnished. Perhaps we do something, quite naturally, that we find the social order set against, or perhaps it is the ordinary course of our life that is not so well regarded as we supposed. At any rate, we find with a chill of terror that the world is cold and strange, and that our self-esteem, self-confidence, and hope, being chiefly founded upon opinions attributed to others, go down in the crash. Our reason may tell us that we are no less worthy than we were before, but dread and doubt do not permit us to believe it. The sensitive mind will certainly suffer, because of the instability of opinion. As social beings we live with our eyes upon our reflection, but have no assurance of the waters in which we see it. In the days of witchcraft it used to be believed that if one person secretly made a waxen image of another and stuck pins into the image, its counterpart would suffer tortures, and that if the image were melted the person would die. This superstition is almost realized in the relation between the private self and its social reflection. They seem separate but are darkly united, and what is done to the one is done to the other.

Influence of Culture on Self-Feeling. It should be evident that the ideas that are associated with self-feeling and form the intellectual content of the self cannot be covered by any simple description, as by saying that the body has such a part in it, friends such a part, plans so much, etc., but will vary indefinitely with particular temperaments and especially with different cultures. The tendency of the self, like every aspect of personality, is expressive of far-reaching social factors, and is not to be understood or predicted except in connection with the surrounding life. The truth of this is perhaps most decisively shown in the fact that even those ideas that are most generally associated or colored with the "my" feeling, such as one's idea of his visible person, of his name, his family, his intimate friends, his property, and so on, are not universally so associated, but may be separated from the self by peculiar social conditions. Thus the ascetics, who have played so large a part in the history of Christianity and of other religions and philosophies, endeavored not without success to divorce their appropriative thought from all material surroundings, and especially from their physical persons, which they sought to look upon as accidental and degrading circumstances of the soul's earthly sojourn. In thus estranging themselves from their bodies, from property and comfort, from domestic affections—whether of wife or child, mother, brother, or sister—and from other common objects of ambition, they certainly gave a singular direction to self-feeling, but they did not destroy it: there can be no doubt that the feeling, which seems imperishable so long as mental vigor endures, found other ideas to which to attach itself; and the strange and uncouth forms which ambition took in those centuries when the solitary, filthy, idle, and sense-tormenting anchorite was a widely accepted ideal of human life, are a matter of instructive study and reflection.

Origin and Value of Self-Feeling. It is easier to experience self-feeling and to describe the objects to which it may attach itself than it is to explain its origin. It would seem as if there must be some instinctive basis for the feeling since it is so universal in man and manifests itself so early in life. If there is, it is not difficult to understand why self-feeling has survived in the selective process. This feeling stimulates and unifies the activities of human beings so that they accomplish more than they otherwise would. The first definite thoughts which a child associates with self-feeling are probably those of his earliest endeavors to control visible objects—his limbs, his playthings, his bottle, and the like. Then he attempts to control the actions of the persons about him, and so his circle of power and of self-feeling widens without interruption to the most complex objects of mature ambition. Although he does not say "I" or "my" during the first year or two, yet he expresses so clearly by his actions the feeling that adults associate with those words that we cannot deny him the rudiments of a self.

The correlation of self-feeling with purposeful activity is easily seen by observing the course of any productive enterprise. If a boy sets about making a boat, and has any success, his interest in the matter waxes, he gloats over it, the keel and stem are dear to his heart, and its ribs are more to him than those of his own frame. He is eager to call in his friends and acquaintances, saying to them, "See what I am doing! Is it not remarkable?" feeling elated when it is praised, and resentful or humiliated when fault is found with it. But so soon as he finishes it and turns to something else, his self-feeling begins to fade away from it, and in a few weeks at most he will have become comparatively indifferent. We all know that much the same course of feeling accompanies the achievements of adults. It is impossible to produce a picture, a poem, an essay, a difficult bit of masonry, or any other work of art or craft, without having self-feeling regarding it, amounting usually to considerable excitement and desire for some sort of appreciation; but this rapidly diminishes with the activity itself, and often lapses into indifference after it ceases.

Development of Self-Feeling. The manner in which this instinctive self-feeling is defined and developed by experience is well indicated by the child's learning the use of self words. It is obvious that these words must be particularly hard to master since, unlike other words, they have, apparently, no uniform meaning, but convey different and even opposite ideas when employed by different persons. The meaning of words is learned by associating them with other phenomena. But how is it possible to learn the meaning of one which, as used by others, is never associated with the same phenomenon as when properly used by oneself? The answer seems to be that the self-words are associated in the first instance with acts of appropriativeness such as grasping, tugging, screaming for toys, and the like. Others are heard to utter these words when performing such actions and the child naturally comes to use the same terms when himself acting similarly. The first-personal pronoun is a sign of a concrete thing after all, but that thing is not primarily the child's body, or his muscular sensations as such, but the phenomenon of aggressive appropriation, practiced by himself, witnessed in others, and incited and interpreted by an instinctive feeling. This seems to get over the difficulty of the apparent lack of common content between the meaning of "my" when used by another and when used by one's self.

The process by which self-feeling of the looking-glass sort develops in children may be followed without much difficulty. Studying the movements of others as closely as they do they soon see a connection between their own acts and changes in those movements; that is, they perceive their own influence or power over persons. The child appropriates the visible actions of his parent or his nurse, over which he finds he has some control, in quite the same way as he appropriates one of his own members or a plaything, and he will try to do things with this new possession, just as he will with his hand or a rattle. A girl six months old will attempt in the most evident and deliberate manner to attract attention to herself, to set going by her actions some of those movements of other persons that she has appropriated. She has tasted the joy of being a cause, of exerting social power, and wishes more of it. In such phenomena we have plainly enough the germ of personal ambition of every kind. Imagination co-operating with instinctive self-feeling has already created a social "I" and this has become a principal object of interest and endeavor. Progress from this point is chiefly in the way of greater definiteness, fulness, and inwardness in the imagination of the other's state of mind. A little child thinks of and tries to elicit certain visible and audible phenomena, and does not go back of them; but what a grown-up person desires to produce in others is an internal, invisible condition which his own richer experience enable him to imagine and of which expression is only the sign.

Selfishness. If the self and the self-feeling are healthy and respectable traits of human nature, then what are those things which we call egotism and selfishness? The answer to this appears to be that it is not self-assertion as such that we stigmatize by these names, but the assertion of a kind of phase of self that is obnoxious to us. There is nothing more respected—and even liked—than a persistent and successful pursuit of one's peculiar aims, so long as this is done within the accepted limits of fairness and consideration for others. Thus one who has acquired ten millions must have expressed his appropriative instinct with much energy and constancy, but reasonable people do not conclude that he is selfish unless it appears that he has ignored social sentiments by which he should have been guided. If he has been dishonest, mean, hard, or the like, they will condemn him. In short, any self-assertion is obnoxious to us and therefore selfish which seems to be characterized by a lack of appreciation of the social situation as we see it; the situation apparently has not awakened in the one we condemn the same personal sentiments that it does in us, and so his action wounds those sentiments. Since the judgment that a man is or is not selfish is a question of social evaluation it naturally follows that people disagree regarding it, their views depending much upon their temperaments and habits of thought. There are probably few energetic persons who do not make an impression of egotism upon some of their acquaintances; and, on the other hand, how many there are whose selfishness seems obvious to most people, but is not apparent to their wives, sisters, and mothers.

So far as there is any agreement in judgments regarding selfishness it arises from cultural standards of right, fairness, and courtesy. The selfish man is one in whose self, or in whose style of asserting it, is something that falls below these standards. This always signifies some sort of narrowness, littleness, or defect; an inadequacy of the imagination. The perfectly balanced and vigorous mind can hardly be selfish, because it cannot be oblivious to any important social situation, either in immediate intercourse or in more permanent relations; it must always tend to be sympathetic, fair, and just, because it possesses that breadth and unity of view of which these qualities are the natural expression. Provided it meets these tests even the most vigorous self-assertion will not be regarded as selfish. No one could be more ambitious than Martin Luther, or more determined to secure the social aggrandizement of his self; but in his case the self for which he was ambitious and resentful consisted largely of certain convictions regarding justification by faith, the sacrilege of the sale of indulgences, and, more generally, of an enfranchising spirit and mode of thought fit to awaken and lead the aspiration of his time.

Human Wishes. Since the theory that human beings are motivated by a definite set of specific instincts broke down there have been attempts to bring order out of the chaos of human behavior by the hypothesis of certain fundamental needs or wishes of the human personality. The most famous classification of this kind is that of W. I. Thomas,[1] who tentatively set up four fundamental wishes: the wish for security, that for new experience, that for recognition or prestige, and that for response or intimate fellowship and love. The desire for security would doubtless be largely based upon fear of anything which threatens the self. That for new experiences would be partly a result of the self's need for stimulation and growth; both intellectual curiosity and craving for excitement would be regarded as its manifestations. The desire for recognition would naturally develop because of the importance of the reflected self; functional activities which are stimulated by this wish we attribute to ambition, unimportant or foolish ones we lay to vanity. The desire for response would be connected with whatever instinctive tendencies toward love there are; Thomas regarded this wish as the main source of social idealism. Many writers have used these four wishes in analyzing the behavior of persons in social situations and, on the whole, the results have proved the value and essential accuracy of this formulation.

An alternative classification of the fundamental human needs would be threefold: the need for self-expression, for appreciation, and for a reasonable social security. No man can be content unless he has a chance to work out his personality, to form, strive for, and gratify reasonable ambitions. In connection with this, indeed really as a part of it, he needs fellowship and that appreciation by others which gives his self social corroboration and support. And, finally, he cannot take much satisfaction in life unless he feels that he is not at the mercy of chance or of other's wills, but has a fair prospect, if he strives steadily, of maintaining his position.

Discontent and the Unsatisfied Self. No man can study

[1] See *The Unadjusted Girl*, pp. 1–40.

sympathetically the actual state of men and women in our social order without being convinced that large numbers of them are denied some or all of these fundamentals of human living. We find, for example, workmen who have no security in their work, but are hired and fired arbitrarily, or perhaps lose their occupations altogether for reasons having no apparent relation to their merit. Very commonly the work itself does not admit of that exercise of the will and growth in skill and power which keeps the sense of self alive and interested. And if there is nothing in the work itself, or in appreciation by his employer, to gratify the self-feeling of the worker, it may well be that resentment and occasional rebellion are the only way to preserve self-respect. One of the great reasons for the popularity of strikes is that they give the suppressed self a sense of power. For once the human tool knows itself a man, able to stand up and speak a word or strike a blow. Many occupations, also, are of an irregular and nomadic character which makes it impossible for men and women to have that primary self-expression which we get from a family and settled home.

The Negro question includes a similar situation. There is no understanding it without realizing the self-feeling a race must have whose members, in a land where men are supposed to be equal, find themselves marked with indelible inferiority. And so with many other classes: with offenders against the law, for example, whom we often turn into hardened criminals by a treatment which destroys their self-respect—or rather convinces them that their only chance of self-respect is in defiance of authority. The immigrant has for the most part been treated purely as a source of labor, with little or no regard to the fact that he is a human being, with a self like the rest of us. The traditional treatment of children in school involves a similar question, and so does that of domestic workers, married women, and other sorts of people more or less subject to the arbitrary will of others.

In general it is clear that an unhealthy self is at the heart of nearly all social discontent. If individuals or classes find themselves leading a kind of life that does not fulfill the deep needs of human nature, they are certain to manifest their inner trouble by some sort of untoward behavior.

There seems to be some doubt whether it is possible to formulate a classification of fundamental needs or wishes that will hold good for all peoples. We have said that the wishes of Thomas have proved helpful in social research, but that may be because they have only been used in studying persons in Western civilization. Perhaps other classifications would be necessary for primitive peoples or for Oriental civilization. On this point Faris says: "The discussion has not reached an end and there is no warrant for asserting unanimity but the trend seems clearly in the direction of complete emancipation from the necessity of discovering or even the possibility of admitting any essential and definite elementary constituents in the developing individual. And this would have consequences of importance for sociology . . . for it would place the social group in a new perspective and enable us to find in the *mores* and institutions of a time and area those elements which were formerly asserted to exist in the psychophysical organism."[2]

Development Based on Instinctive Emotion. Though perhaps we cannot posit fundamental and universal needs of the human being we cannot escape the instinctive emotions discussed in Chapter II; and at this point it may be well to inquire how these instinctive emotions develop as the personality matures and the sense of self becomes well established. We will take anger as typifying this process.

Anger, like other emotions, seems to exist at birth as a simple, instinctive, animal-like reaction, and to undergo differentiation and development parallel with the growth of social insight. Perez, speaking of children at about the age of two months, says, "they begin to push away objects that they do not like, and have real fits of passion, frowning, growing red in the face, trembling all over, and sometimes shedding tears." They also show anger at not getting the breast or bottle, or when washed or undressed, or when their toys are taken away. At about one year old "they will beat people, animals, and inanimate objects if they are angry with them,"[3] throw things at offending persons, and the like.

This simple, animal sort of anger, excited immediately by something obnoxious to the senses, does not entirely disappear in adult life. Probably most persons who step on a barrel-hoop or run their heads against a low doorway can discern a moment of instinctive anger toward the harming object. But for a social, im-

[2] Ellsworth Faris, "Borderline Trends in Social Psychology," *Publications of the American Sociological Society*, XXV, no. 2, p. 39.

[3] Bernard Perez, *The First Three Years of Childhood*, p. 66.

aginative being, whose main interests are in the region of communicative thought and sentiment, the chief field of anger, as of other emotions, is transferred to this region. Hostility ceases to be a simple emotion due to a simple stimulus and, by a process of conditioning, comes to be aroused by all sorts of complex stimuli, which are accessible only through mental insight. Thus in this form anger may be regarded as a hostile comment on sympathetic insight. That is, we enter by personal imagination into the state of mind of others, or think we do, and if the thoughts we find there are injurious to or uncongenial with our conception of ourself, we feel a moment of anger.

This is forcibly expressed in a brief but admirable study of antipathy by Sophie Bryant. "A is drawn out toward B to feel what he feels. If the new feeling harmonizes, distinctly or obscurely, with the whole system of A's consciousness—or the part then identified with his will—there follows that joyful expansion of the self beyond self which is sympathy. But if not—if the new feeling is out of keeping with the system of A's will—tends to upset the system, and brings discord into it—there follows the reaction of the whole against the hostile part, which, transferred to its cause in B, pushes out B's state, as the antithesis of self, yet threatening self, and offensive." Antipathy, she says, "is full of horrid thrill." "The peculiar horror of the antipathy springs from the unwilling response to the state abhorred. We feel ourselves actually like the other person, selfishly vain, cruelly masterful, artfully affected, insincere, uncongenial, and so on."[4] And with similar meaning Thoreau remarks that "you cannot receive a shock unless you have an electric affinity for that which shocks you."[5]

Thus the cause of this sort of hostility is imaginative, an inimical idea attributed to another mind. We cannot feel this way toward that which is totally unlike us, because the totally unlike is unimaginable, has no interest for us. This, like all social feeling, requires a union of likeness and difference.

Resentment and Indignation. The commonest form of imaginative anger is grounded on social self-feeling, and comes under the head of resentment. We impute to the other person an injurious thought regarding something which we cherish as part

[4] *Mind,* new series, IV, 365.
[5] *A Week on the Concord and Merrimack Rivers,* pp. 303–328.

of our self, and this awakens anger, which we name pique, animosity, umbrage, estrangement, soreness, bitterness, heart-burning, jealousy, and so on; in accordance with variations which these words suggest. They all rest upon a feeling that the other person harbors ideas injurious to us, so that the thought of him is an attack upon our self. Suppose, for instance, there is a person who has reason to believe that he has caught you in a lie. It makes little difference, perhaps, whether he really has or not; so long as you have any self-respect left, and believe that he entertains the depreciatory idea of you, you must resent the idea whenever, through your thinking of him, it enters your mind. Or suppose there is a man who has met you running in a panic from the field of battle; would it not be hard not to hate him? These situations are perhaps unusual, but we all know persons to whom we attribute depreciation of our character, our friends, our children, our workmanship, our cherished creed or philanthropy; and we do not like them.

The resentment of charity or pity is a good instance of hostile insight. If a man has self-respect, he feels insulted by the depreciating view of his manhood implied in commiserating him or offering him alms. Self-respect means that one's reflected self is up to the social standard; and the social standard requires that a man should not need pity or alms except under very unusual conditions. So the assumption that he does need them is an injury —whether he does or not—precisely as it is an insult to a woman to commiserate her ugliness and bad taste, and suggest that she wear a veil or employ some one to select her gowns.

The word indignation suggests a higher sort of imaginative hostility. It implies that the feeling is directed toward some attack upon a standard of right, and is not merely an impulse like jealousy or pique. A higher degree of rationalization is involved; there is some notion of a reasonable adjustment of personal claims, which the act or thought in question violates. We frequently perceive that the simpler forms of resentment have no rational basis, could not be justified in open courts, but indignation always claims a general or social foundation. We feel indignant when we think that favoritism and not merit secures promotion, when the rich man gets a pass on the railroad, when a man breaks into a waiting line at the post office instead of going to the end, and so on. The attack in indignation is upon the self but upon the most impersonal aspect of the self—the standards which we cherish.

Three Levels of Instinctive Emotion. It is thus possible rudely to classify angers under three heads, according to the degree of mental organization they involve; namely, as

1. Primary, immediate, or animal.
2. Social, sympathetic, or imaginative of a direct sort. This is resentment and is caused by an idea imputed to some other person's mind attacking our naïve, narrowly personal self.
3. Ethical or highly rational. This is called indignation and is caused by behavior which outrages some standard which we cherish as part of our broader self.

Cultural standards play a rôle at the level of resentment in addition to their indicated relation to indignation. In this case the attack is not upon the standard, but the standard determines whether one should consider it an attack at all. Suppose for instance an American college boy should clap a foreign friend upon the back in the way that he does his American friends. The foreigner might very well judge that he was being insulted, simply because he is unfamiliar with our accepted mode of behavior. It is the same in war: soldiers do not necessarily feel any anger at other soldiers who are trying to shoot them to death. That is thought of as within the rules of the game. In the Spanish American War Admiral Cervera's chief of staff was reported to have said to Admiral Sampson, "You know there is nothing personal in this."

Thus we see that an instinctive emotion like anger is refined and differentiated as the conception of self arises out of social relations. It works into our complex life in innumerable ways and is in turn affected at every point by other influences.

Summary. The sense of self appears to spring from two sources, the my-feeling, based probably on instinctive emotion and developed in our contacts with others, and the definition of ourselves implied in the conduct of others toward us. The self appears always to have a social reference and one of its most striking phases is the reflected "I." Whether one is selfish or not is seen to depend upon the kind of self asserted. An analysis of the person's fundamental wishes or the needs of the self leads to the notion that an unhealthy self is at the bottom of most social discontent. Instinctive emotions like anger take on highly rational forms, influenced by cultural standards, with the development of the self.

STUDY QUESTIONS

1. From what two sources is the sense of self developed? Explain the contribution of each.
2. Why is not the naïve view that the body is the core of the self satisfactory?
3. Define the self, showing the importance of social factors.
4. How can you explain the application of "I" to inanimate objects, like a ball? Can you think of original examples?
5. Explain the "looking-glass self" and give your estimate of its practical importance.
6. Is it true that the self is molded by culture and varies with it? Prove your answer from observation.
7. Do you think it likely that the meaning of the word "I" is developed from a special sort of instinctive feeling? If so, explain the process.
8. Explain and illustrate the social function of the self-expressive impulse.
9. How do children learn the use of "I"? Can you contribute observations of your own?
10. How does the self grow and what happens when it stops growing?
11. Compare the conception of selfishness given in the text with your previous idea of the matter. What do you think of it?
12. Do you think there is any essential difference between the fourfold classification of human wishes as used by Thomas and the threefold classification suggested subsequently in the chapter?
13. Why is an unhealthy self a symptom of social maladjustment?
14. How does resentment imply sympathetic insight?
15. Differentiate indignation from resentment.
16. How is resentment related to accepted rules or principles?
17. Take the instinctive emotion of fear and show that it undergoes transformations similar to those of anger.

CHAPTER X

EMULATION

In this chapter we shall pursue further the relationship between the self and its social surroundings, both personal and cultural. Three sorts of emulation will be discussed—conformity, rivalry, and hero-worship.

Conformity and the Motives to It. Conformity means the molding of oneself to the dominant cultural pattern. It is a voluntary imitation of prevalent modes of action, distinguished from rivalry and other aggressive phases of emulation by being comparatively passive, aiming to keep up rather than to excel, and concerning itself for the most part with what is outward and formal. On the other hand, it is distinguished from imitation through suggestion by being intentional rather than involuntary. Thus it is not conformity, for most of us, to speak the English language, because we have practically no choice in the matter, but we might choose to conform to particular pronunciations or turns of speech used by those with whom we wish to associate.

The ordinary motive to conformity is the sense, more or less vivid, of the pains and inconveniences of not following the cultural pattern. Most people find it painful to go to an evening reception in any other than the customary dress; the source of the pain appearing to be a vague sense of the depreciatory curiosity which one imagines that he will excite. His social self-feeling is hurt by an unfavorable view of himself that he attributes to others. This example is typical of the way the group coerces each of its members in all matters concerning which he has no strong and definite private purpose. The world constrains us to its culture merely through the impulse, common to all, to despise peculiarity for which no reason is perceived. "Solitude is fearsome and heavy-hearted," and non-conformity condemns us to it by interrupting that relaxation and spontaneity of attitude that is required for the easy flow of sympathy and communication. Thus it is hard to be at ease with one who is conspicuously worse or better dressed than we are, or whose manners are notably different; no matter how little store our philosophy may set by such things. On the other hand, a likeness in small things that enables them to be forgotten gives people a *prima facie* at-homeness with each other highly favorable to understanding; and so we all wish to have it with people we care for. Thus we must conclude that conformity is not necessarily only a product of the self's fear of disapproval, but may also spring from the rational belief that such a course is functionally helpful.

In terms of our analysis in Chapter VI the cultural elements to which one conforms are those above folkways in the scale[1]—conventionalized practices, *mores,* and law. Obviously there is a stronger pressure exerted toward conformity the higher one goes in this scale.

The Social Demand for Conformity. It would seem that the repression of non-conformity is a natural impulse, and that tolerance always requires some moral exertion. We all cherish our particular culture and anything that clashes with it is annoying to us and likely to cause resentment. So our first tendency is to suppress the peculiar, and we learn to endure it only when we must, either because it is shown to be reasonable or because it proves refractory to our opposition. The innovator is nearly as apt as any one else to put down innovation in others. In periods of disorganization and change, such as ours is in many respects, people are educated to comparative tolerance by unavoidable familiarity with conflicting views—as religious tolerance, for instance, is the outcome of the continued spectacle of competing creeds.

Every profession, trade, or handicraft, every church, circle, fraternity or clique, has its more or less definite cultural standards, conformity to which it tends to impose on all its members. It is not at all essential that there should be any deliberate purpose to set up those standards, or any special machinery for enforcing them; they are enforced by the mere inertia of the minds constituting the group.

Thus every variant idea of conduct has to fight its way: as soon as any one attempts to do anything unexpected the world begins to cry, "Get in the rut! Get in the rut! Get in the rut!" and shoves, stares, coaxes, and sneers until he does so—or until he makes

[1] See page 94.

good his position, and so, by altering the standard in a measure, establishes a new culture trait to which to conform. There are no people who are altogether non-conformers, or who are completely tolerant of non-conformity in others. Mr. Lowell, who wrote some of the most stirring lines in literature in defense of non-conformity, was himself conventional and an upholder of conventions in letters and social intercourse. Either to be exceptional or to appreciate the exceptional requires a considerable expenditure of energy, and no one can afford this in many directions. There are many persons who take pains to keep their minds open; and there are groups, countries, and periods which are comparatively favorable to open-mindedness and variation; but conformity is always the rule and non-conformity the exception.

Value of Conformity. Conformity is a sort of co-operation: one of its main functions is to economize energy. The cultural standards which it presses upon the individual are often elaborate and valuable products of cumulative thought and experience, and, whatever imperfections they may have, they are, on the whole, an indispensable foundation for life: it is inconceivable that any one should dispense with them. If we imitate the dress, the manners, the household arrangements of other people, we save so much mental energy for other purposes. It is said with truth that conformity is a drag upon genius; but it is equally true and important that its general action upon human nature is elevating. We get by it the selected and systematized outcome of the past, and to be brought up to its standards is a brief recapitulation of social development: it sometimes levels down but more generally levels up. It may be well for purposes of incitement to goad our individuality by the abuse of conformity; but statements made with this in view lack accuracy. It is good for the young and aspiring to read Emerson's praise of self-reliance, in order that they may have courage to fight for their ideas; but we may also sympathize with Goethe when he says that "nothing more exposes us to madness than distinguishing us from others, and nothing more contributes to maintaining our common sense than living in the universal way with multitudes of men."[2]

Definition of Social Rôle. The cultural pattern to which one feels constrained to conform acts to define one's social rôle. This is simply a special case of the general proposition of cultural

[2] *Wilhelm Meister's Apprenticeship,* p. 16, Carlyle's translation.

definition discussed in Chapter VIII. Each of us tries to live up to the rôle in society which he finds himself playing. A young married man is likely to change markedly upon the birth of his first child because he is now a father and feels that he must play the part in the accepted manner. The differentiation of modern life has produced many recognized rôles and the behavior of each of us reflects this social patterning. Professor Burgess has made an interesting distinction between personality pattern and the social type.[3] By the former he means the integration of traits which characterize the typical reactions of a person toward others. It is developed under the simple conditions of association, as is human nature, and is the individualizing correlative of the latter. The social type, on the other hand, is a cultural product depending upon the rôle which a person finds himself playing. The same general personality pattern prevails throughout one's life, but the social type may change very markedly and very suddenly as a result of changed conception of rôle. Delinquent children become serious problems when they begin to identify themselves with the criminal social type.

Clashing Cultures and Mental Conflict. One of the frequent causes of severe mental conflict and personal disorganization is the incompatibility of two sets of cultural patterns to each of which the individual wishes to conform. A newly arrived immigrant, for instance, finds himself torn between the *mores* of his native land and those of America. He may try to solve the difficulty by assuming dual rôles, one to be played while he is among his countrymen and another while he mingles with Americans. There is another force which makes this almost impossible, however, where the *mores* are seriously divergent. This is the tendency toward consistency in behavior. If the person is to meet life successfully he must be an integrated whole. Though each of us adapts himself to different social situations and emphasizes different aspects of his personality, yet there must be at the bottom of all this variance a stable core of habits and attitudes or we are ineffective.

Factors in Non-Conformity. There are two factors in nonconformity: first, a rebellious impulse leading to avoidance of accepted cultural standards in a spirit of opposition without necessary reference to any other pattern; and second, the exis-

[3] In *The Jack Roller* (by Clifford R. Shaw), pp. 193–94.

tence of less popular, or more remote, but competing, cultural patterns. These two usually go together. One is led to a mode of life different from that of the people about him, partly by intrinsic contrariness, and partly by fixing his imagination on the ideas and practices of other perhaps very remote people whose mode of life he finds more congenial.

In respect to personal attitude, non-conformity requires the spirit of opposition. People of natural energy take pleasure in that enhanced feeling of self that comes from consciously *not* doing that which is suggested or enjoined upon them by circumstances and by other persons. There is joy in the sense of self-assertion: it is sweet to do one's own things; and if others are against him one feels sure that they *are* his own. To brave the disapproval of men is tonic; it is like climbing along a mountain path in the teeth of the wind; one feels himself as a cause, and knows the distinctive efficacy of his being. Thus self-feeling, which, if somewhat languid and on the defensive, causes us to conform, may, when in a more energetic condition, cause us to seek peculiarity; just as we rejoice at one time to brave the cold, and at another cower over the fire, according to the vigor of our circulation.

The second factor, the existence of less conspicuous cultural patterns to which the individual adheres, makes much non-conformity really remote conformity. The rebellion against cultural influence is only partial and immediate; and the one who seems to be out of step with the procession is really keeping time to another music. As Thoreau said, he hears a different drummer. If a boy refuses the occupation his parents and friends think best for him, and persists in working at something strange and fantastic, like art or science, it is sure to be the case that his most vivid life is not with those about him at all, but with the masters he has known through books, or perhaps seen and heard for a few moments. Environment, in the sense of social influence actually at work, is far from the definite and obvious thing it is often assumed to be. Our real environment consists of those images which are most present to our thoughts, and in the case of a vigorous, growing mind, these are likely to be something quite different from what is most present to the senses. The group to which we give allegiance, and to whose culture we try to conform, is determined by our own selective affinity, choosing among all the personal influences accessible to us; and so far as we select with any independence of our palpable companions, we have the appearance of non-conformity.

Naturally non-conformity is characteristic of the more energetic states of the human mind. Men of great vigor are sure to be non-conformers in some important respect; youth glories in non-conformity, while age usually comes back to the general point of view. "Men are conservatives when they are least vigorous, or when they are most luxurious. They are conservatives after dinner, or before taking their rest; when they are sick or aged. In the morning, or when their intellect or their conscience has been aroused, when they hear music, or when they read poetry, they are radicals."[4]

The value of non-conformity can hardly be overemphasized. If we had not been blessed through the ages with persons who desired to strike out new paths and who were willing to risk unpopularity in support of minority views we would have had neither the inventions nor the diffusion of culture which has developed us from our lowly beginnings.

Should One Conform or Not? Perhaps we may be permitted to digress from a strictly scientific analysis long enough to inquire what should be the individual's attitude toward conformity and non-conformity. A rational answer would seem to be: assert your individuality in matters which you deem important; conform in those you deem unimportant. To have a conspicuously individual way of doing everything is impossible to a sane person, and to attempt it would be to do one's self a gratuitous injury, by closing the channels of sympathy through which we partake of the life around us. We should save our strength for matters in regard to which persistent conviction impels us to insist upon our own way.

Society, like every living, advancing whole, requires a just union of stability and change, uniformity and differentiation. Conformity is the phase of uniformity, while non-conformity is the phase of differentiation and change. The latter cannot introduce anything wholly new, but it can and does effect such a reorganization of existing material as constantly to transform and renew human life.

Nature of Rivalry. We mean by rivalry a competitive striv-

[4] Emerson, *New England Reformers.*

ing urged on by the desire to win. It resembles conformity in that the impelling idea is usually a sense of what other people are doing and thinking, and especially of what they are thinking of us; it differs from it chiefly in being more aggressive. Conformity aims to keep up with the procession, rivalry to get ahead of it. The former is moved by a sense of the pains and inconveniences of differing from other people, the latter by an eagerness to compel their admiration. Winning, to the social self, usually means conspicuous success in making some desired impression upon other minds, as in becoming distinguished for power, wealth, skill, culture, beneficence, or the like.

On the other hand, rivalry may be distinguished from finer sorts of emulation by being more simple, crude, and direct. It implies no very subtle mental activity, no elaborate or refined ideal. If a spirited horse hears another overtaking him from behind, he pricks up his ears, quickens his pace, and does his best to keep ahead. And human rivalry appears to have much of this instinctive element in it. An eager person will not hear or read of vivid action without feeling some impulse to get into it; just as he cannot mingle in a hurrying, excited crowd without sharing in its excitement and hurry, whether he knows what it is all about or not.

The motive of rivalry, then, is a strong sense that there is a race going on, and an impulsive eagerness to be in it. It is rather imitative than inventive; the idea being not so much to achieve an object for its own sake, as to get what the rest are after. There is conformity in ideals combined with a thirst for personal distinction. It has little tendency toward innovation, notwithstanding the element of antagonism in it; but takes its color and character from the prevalent culture, accepting and pursuing the existing ideal of success. There is nothing so gross or painful that it may not become an object of pursuit through emulation. Charles Booth, who has studied so minutely the slums of London, says that "among the poor, men drink on and on from a perverted pride," and among another class a similar sentiment leads women to diet to a dangerous degree in order to achieve fashionable slimness.

Value of Rivalry. Professor William James suggests that rivalry does nine tenths of the world's work.[5] Certainly no motive

[5] *Psychology,* Vol. II, p. 409.

is so generally powerful among active, efficient men of the ordinary type, the type that keeps the ball moving all over the world. Intellectual initiative, high and persistent idealism, are rare. The great majority of able men are ambitious, without having intrinsic traits that definitely direct their ambition to any particular object. If their career is law, they strive to win cases and gain wealth and prestige, accepting the moral code and other standards that they find in actual use.

There is thus nothing morally distinctive about rivalry. It may be said, however, that it supplies a stimulus wholesome and needful to the great majority of men, and that it is on the whole a progressive force, utilizing the tremendous power of ambition and controlling it to the furtherance of ends that are socially approved. The great mass of what we judge to be evil is of a negative rather than a positive character, arising not from misdirected ambition but from apathy or sensuality, from a falling short of that active, social humanity which ambition implies.

Conditions for Sound Rivalry. If rivalry is to be morally sound two conditions must be satisfied. First, the goal of the race must be one receiving general social approval. The rivalry among the members of criminal gangs, for instance, could hardly be thought of as morally beneficent. Second, the rivalry must be disciplined and organized. This means, chiefly, that men must associate in specialized groups, each group pursuing ideals of technical efficiency and social service, success in this pursuit being the object of rivalry. Consider, for example, how achievement in athletics is attained in our colleges. In the first place, there is a general interest in sports and an admiration for success in them which makes it an object of general ambition. Many candidates are "tried out" and assigned, according to their promise, to special squads for training. In each of these little groups rivalry is made intense, definite, and systematic by traditions, by standards of accomplishment, by regular training, and by expert criticism and appreciation. Occasional public contests serve to arouse the imagination and to exhibit achievement. The whole social self is thus called in to animate a course of endeavor scientifically directed to a specific end. A similar method is used in armies and navies to develop excellence in marksmanship and the like. And is it not much the same in professional groups; among lawyers, for example, dentists, bacteriologists, astronomers, historians, painters, novelists, and even poets? In each of these fields we have the three essential elements to organized rivalry:

1. A selected group of candidates for distinction, watching one another's work, eager to excel, imagining the judgment of their fellows.
2. Well-defined standards both of technical efficiency and ethical conduct under which all are trained.
3. Expert criticism by leaders in the field.

The general fact is that the most effective way of utilizing human energy is through an organized rivalry, which by specialization and social control is, at the same time, organized co-operation. An ideal social system, from this point of view, would be one in which the work of individuals in each occupation, the work of occupations in relations to one another, and of nation in relation to nation, should be motivated by a desire to excel, this desire being controlled and subordinated by allegiance to common social ideals.

Hero-Worship. By hero-worship is here meant an emulation which strives to imitate some admired character in a spirit of loyal enthusiasm. The person who arouses the hero-worshipper's enthusiasm and endeavor does so because he bears a certain relation to the latter's aspirations, to his constructive thought. Hero-worship is thus selective and is significant of the special character and tendencies of the individual.

It has a great place in all active, aspiring lives, especially in the plastic period of youth. We feed our characters, while they are forming, upon the visions of admired models. As already pointed out, understanding appears to be an act of growth; and this is especially true of the sort of understanding we call hero-worship. All autobiographies which deal with youth show that the early development of character is through a series of admirations and enthusiasms, which pass away, to be sure, but leave character the richer for their existence. They begin in the nursery, flourish with great vigor in the school-yard, attain a passionate intensity during adolescence, and, though they abate rapidly in adult life, do not altogether cease until the power of growth is lost. All will find, if they recall their own experience, that times of mental progress were times when the mind found or created heroes to worship, often owing allegiance to several at the same time, each representing a particular need of development. We easily forget the varied and impassioned idealism of early life; but "the thoughts of youth are long, long thoughts," and it is precisely then and in this way that the most rapid development of character takes place. J. A. Symonds, speaking of Professor Jowett's early influence upon him, says, "Obscurely but vividly I felt my soul grow by his contact, as it had never grown before"; and Goethe remarks that "vicinity to the master, like an element, lifts one and bears him on."

As hero-worship becomes more imaginative, it merges insensibly into that devotion to ideal persons that is called religious. It has often been pointed out that the feeling men have toward a visible leader and master like Lincoln, Lee, Napoleon, or Garibaldi is psychologically much the same thing as the worship of the ideal persons of religion. That the personality toward which the feeling is directed is ideal evidently affords no fundamental distinction. So far as ideal persons are present to thought and emotion, and so work upon life, they are real, with that immediate social reality already discussed. The fact that they have attached to them no visible or tangible material body, similar to that of other persons, is indeed an important fact, but rather of physiological than of psychological or social interest.

STUDY QUESTIONS

1. Distinguish conformity from imitation due to suggestion.
2. Give an example of conformity from your own observation and analyze the motives. Do the same for non-conformity. How is each related to the self?
3. Which of the two, conformity or non-conformity, do you think needs more to be cultivated and why?
4. How does culture define one's social rôle?
5. Distinguish between the personality pattern and the social type.
6. Describe any cases of mental conflict resulting from clashing cultures which you have observed.
7. Do you think all non-conformity is remote conformity? Give evidence.
8. How is rivalry related to the self? Why is it so powerful a motive?
9. What conditions are requisite to a rivalry that is socially fruitful?
10. Explain and illustrate the action of hero-worship in the growth of the young. What ill effects, if any, have you observed?

CHAPTER XI

CONSCIENCE AND PERSONAL DEGENERACY

We have spoken of the *mores* or customary standards of right and wrong in Chapter VI. We must now consider the relationship between these elements of culture and the growing personality as it is manifest in conscience.

To have a conscience or a personal sense of right and wrong is a trait of human nature. It is a natural outgrowth of the human ability to see ourselves objectively through the minds of others. The particular standards of right which we cherish, however, vary tremendously. In the first place, they vary with culture; in the second place with the individual's life experiences.

Likenesses and Differences in the *Mores*. Comparative studies of moral ideas of different societies, such as William Graham Sumner's *Folkways,* nearly prove that "the *mores* can make anything right or anything wrong." Stealing, cannibalism, and many other things that we condemn, may be regarded as permissible, creditable, or even obligatory. Matters of decency, as in dress or manners, are almost wholly conventional, as appears, for instance, when Africans spit upon one as a sign of good-will. However, there seem to be about three things that are universally regarded as right:

1. Loyalty to one's own group. (Dante's judgment that traitors belong in the lowest pit of Hell expresses a universal sentiment of mankind.)
2. Kindness to members of the group.
3. Adherence to the customs of the group.

These are universal because they spring from universal conditions of social life. All men live in co-operating groups, and without loyalty and kindness they cannot co-operate successfully. And conservatism must be cherished, especially among savages, who have no recorded traditions, because it is the means of insuring stability and preserving the results of experience. Morals are profoundly functional, and beneath many strange divergences there is found a core of likeness corresponding to a similarity in the life process itself.

The differences in the *mores* are, however, much more striking than the likenesses, and they spring from the divergent situations in which various groups have evolved. Geographical and climatic factors, technical factors such as the degree of industrial development, even racial factors, all have their bearing upon the code of morality which a particular group works out. In the long run the tentative process[1] brings about a set of *mores* that is fairly well adapted to all the conditions which the group has to meet.

Conscience Also Dependent upon Special Heritages and Individual Experience. The consciences of the members of a particular cultural group will, then, have a certain similarity because of the common social heritage. In a highly developed and differentiated society like ours there are in addition special social heritages or special cultures which mold the consciences of those that come under their influence. The conscience of the doctor for instance is affected by the ethical standards of his profession; that of the old-family Virginian by the traditional morality of the gentry. Since each of us participates in many groups possessing such special *mores* the conscience of each one draws upon these sources as well as upon the general *mores* of our time.

There is a large realm of the individual's experience, however, which is important in conscience but which is not a matter of cultural standards. In some measure we create our standards of right and wrong on the basis of our own observation of social life. We may come to feel that there are certain conditions of privation which make stealing justified, though the surrounding culture condemns it under all circumstances. Or we may on the basis of our own experiences and contacts regard it as wrong to use positions of power to secure special privileges though it is not disapproved by the *mores*.

The Right as the Rational. What we judge to be right, then, is simply the rational, in a large sense of that word. The mind is the theatre of conflict of an infinite number of impulses, cultural and otherwise, among which it is ever striving to produce some sort of unification or harmony. This endeavor to har-

[1] A term used to describe the adaptive developmental interaction of social forms. See Cooley, *Social Process,* Chapter I.

monize or assimilate includes deliberate reasoning, but is something much more general and continuous than that. It is mostly an unconscious or subconscious manipulation of the materials presented, an unremitting comparison and rearrangement of them, which ever tends to organize them into some sort of a whole. The right, then, is that which stands this test; the sanction of conscience attaches to those thoughts which, in the long run, maintain their places as part of that orderly whole which the mind calls for, and which it is ever working with more or less success to build up. That is right which presents itself, after the mind has done its full work upon the matter, as the mentally necessary, which we cannot gainsay without breaking up our mental integrity.

According to this view of the matter, judgments of right and wrong are in no way isolated or radically different in kind from other judgments. Such peculiarity as they have seems to come chiefly from the unusual intensity of the mental conflict that precedes them. The slightest scrutiny of experience shows that the sharp and absolute distinction often assumed to exist between conscience and other mental activities does not hold good in life. There are gradual transitions from judgments which no one thinks of as peculiarly moral, through judgments which some would regard as moral and others would not, to those which are universally so regarded.

Of course, the view that the right is the rational would be untrue, if by rational were meant merely the result of formal reasoning. The judgment of right and the conclusion of formal thought are frequently opposed to each other, because the latter is a comparatively narrow, partial, and conventional product of the mind. The former is rational and mentally authoritative in a larger sense; its premises are immeasurably richer; it deals with the whole content of life, with instinctive emotions freighted with the inarticulate conclusions of a remote past, and with the unformulated inductions of individual experience. To set the product of a superficial ratiocination over the final output, in conscience, of our whole mental being, is a kind of pedantry. It is not here implied that there is usually an opposition between the two—they should work harmoniously together—but only asserted that when there is, conscience must be regarded as the profounder rationality.

On the other hand, the wrong, the immoral, is, in a similar sense, the irrational. It is that which, after the mind has done its full work upon the matter, presents itself as the mentally isolated, the inharmonious, that which we cannot follow without having, in our more collected moods, a sense of having been untrue to ourselves, of having done ourselves a harm. The mind in its fullest activity is denied and desecrated; we are split in two. To violate conscience is to act under the control of an incomplete and fragmentary state of mind; and so to become less a person, to begin to disintegrate and go to pieces. An unjust or incontinent deed produces remorse, apparently because the thought of it will not lie still in the mind, but is of such a nature that there is no comfortable place for it in the system of thought already established there.

The question of right and wrong, as it presents itself to any particular mind, is, then, a question of the completest practicable organization of the impulses with which that mind finds itself compelled to deal. The working out of the right conclusion may be compared to the process by which a deliberative body comes to a conclusion upon some momentous public measure. Time must be given for all the more important passions, prejudices, cultural standards, interests, and the like, to be urged upon the members with such cogency as their advocates can give them, and for attempts to harmonize these conflicting forces so that a measure can be framed which the body can be induced to pass. And when a decision is finally reached there is a sense of relief, the greater in proportion as the struggle has been severe, and a tendency, even on the part of the opposition, to regard the matter as settled. Those people who cannot achieve moral unity, but have always a sense of two personalities warring within them, may be compared to certain countries in whose assemblies political parties are so embittered that they never come to an understanding with one another.

Conscience the Only Guide to Conduct. It is useless to look for any other or higher criterion of right than conscience. What is felt to be right *is* right; that is what the word means. Any theory of right that should turn out to be irreconcilable with the sense of right must evidently be judged as false. And when it is urged that conscience is variable, we can only answer that, for this very reason, the right cannot be reduced to a universal and conclusive formula. Like life in all its phases, it is a progressive revelation out of depths we do not penetrate.

For the individual considering his own conduct, his conscience is the only possible moral guide, and though it differ from that of every one else, it is the only right there is for him; to violate it is to commit moral suicide. As a matter of fact, it will usually agree with the consciences of those in his own cultural situation so that he will have the feeling of group support. But sometimes it will disagree, and when it does it must be followed. Other tests become valid only in so far as conscience adopts them.

It must seem that any scientific study of the matter must consist essentially in investigating the conditions and relations of concrete right—the when, where, and why of what people *do* think is right. Social science can never be a final source or test of morality; though it can reveal facts and relations which may help conscience in making its authoritative judgment.

Factors Affecting Stability and Change in Conscience. Whether a person's life, in its moral or any other aspect, is obviously changeful, or, on the contrary, appears to be merely repetitive or habitual, depends upon whether the state of his mind, and of the conditions about it, are favorable to rapid changes in the system of his thought. Thus if he is young and vigorous, and if he has a natural open-mindedness and keenness of sensibility, he will be so much the more likely, other things equal, to incorporate fresh elements of thought and make a new synthesis, instead of running on habit. Variety of life in the past, preventing excessive deepening of the mental ruts, and contact with strong and novel influences in the present, have the same tendency.

The rigidly habitual or traditional morality of savages is apparently a reflection of the restriction and sameness of their social life; and a similar type of morals is found even in a complex society, as in old China, when the social system has become rigid by the equilibration of competing ideas. On the other hand, the stir and change of the more active parts of our society make control by mere habit impossible. There are no simple dominant habits; tendencies are mixed and conflicting, so that the person must either be intelligently moral or else degenerate. He must either make a fresh synthesis or have no synthesis at all.

What is called principle appears to be simply a habit of conscience, a rule formed originally by a synthesis of various impulses, but become somewhat mechanical and independent of its origin—as it is the nature of habit to do. As the mind hardens and matures there is a growing inaptitude to take in novel and powerful impressions, and a corresponding ascendency of habit and system; social sentiment, the flesh and blood of conduct, partly falls away, exposing a skeleton of moral principles. The sense of duty presents itself less and less as a vivid sympathetic impulse, and more and more as a sense of the economy and restfulness of a definite standard of conduct. When one has come to accept a certain course as duty he has a pleasant sense of relief and of lifted responsibility, even if the course involves pain and renunciation. It is like obedience to some external authority; any clear way, though it lead to death, is mentally preferable to the tangle of uncertainty.

Actions that appear memorable or heroic are seldom achieved at the moment of decisive choice, but are more likely to come after the habit of thought which produces the action has become somewhat mechanical and involuntary. It is probably a mistake to imagine that the soldier who braves death in battle, the fireman who enters the burning building, the brakeman who pursues his duty along the icy top of a moving train, or the fisherman who rows away from his vessel into the storm and mist, is usually in an acute state of heroism. It is all in the day's work; the act is part of a system of thought and conduct which has become habitual and would be painful to break. Death is not imagined in all its terrors and compared with social obligation; the case is far simpler. As a rule there is no time in a crisis for complicated mental operations, and whether the choice is heroic or cowardly it is sure to be simple.

The Right Not Social as Opposed to Individual. Those who accept this view of conscience will reject the opinion that the right is, in any general sense, the social as opposed to the individual. All our human thought and activity is either individual or social, according to how you look at it, the two being no more than phases of the same thing, which common thought, always inclined to confuse words with things, attempts to separate. The consideration of other persons usually enters largely into questions of right and wrong; but the ethical decision is distinctly an assertion of a private, individualized view of the matter. All will recognize that a strong sense of duty involves self-feeling, so that we say emphatically to ourselves *I* ought. It would be no sense of duty at all if we did not feel that there was something about it peculiar to us and antithetical to some of the influences acting upon us. It is important for many purposes to emphasize that the ethical self is always a public self; but it is equally true and important that it is always a private self.

In short, ethical thinking and feeling, like all our higher life, has its individual and social aspects, with no peculiar emphasis on either. If the social aspect is here at its highest, so also is the individual aspect.

The individual and the group are related in respect to moral thought quite as they are everywhere else; individual consciences and the social conscience are not separate things, but aspects of one thing, namely, the Moral Life, which may be regarded as individual by fixing our attention upon a particular conscience in artificial isolation, or as general, by attending to some collective phase, like public opinion upon a moral question. Suppose, for instance, one were a member of the Congress that voted the measure which brought the United States into the World War. The question how he should vote on this measure would be, in its individual aspect, a matter of private conscience; and so with all other members. But taking the vote as a whole, as a synthesis, showing the moral drift of the group, it appears as an expression of a social conscience. The separation is purely artificial, every judgment of an individual conscience being social in that it involves a synthesis of social influences, and every social conscience being a collective view of individual consciences. The concrete thing, the Moral Life, is a whole made up of differentiated members. If this is at all hard to grasp, it is only because the fact is a large one. We certainly cannot get far unless we learn to *see* organization, since all our facts present it.

Personal Authority and the Reflected "I" in Conscience. To a very large class of minds the notion of right presents itself chiefly as a matter of personal authority. That is, what we feel we ought to do is simply what we imagine our guide or master would do, or would wish us to do. This, for instance, is the idea very largely inculcated and practised by the Christian church. It is not anything opposed to or different from the right as a mental synthesis, but simply means that admiration, reverence, or some other strong sentiment, gives such overwhelming force to the influence of a certain example, that it more or less completely dominates the mind. The authority works through conscience and not outside of it. Moreover, the relation is not so one-sided as it would seem, since our guide is always, in one point of view, the creation of our imaginations, which are sure to interpret him in a manner congenial to our native tendency.

In one of Mr. Theodore Child's papers on French art he relates that Dagnan said after the death of Bastien-Lepage, "With every new picture I paint in future I shall try to think if he would have been satisfied with it." Almost the same has been said by an American author with reference to Robert Louis Stevenson. And these instances are typical of the general fact that our higher selves, our distinctively right views and choices, are dependent upon imaginative realization of the points of view of other persons. There is no possibility of being good without living, imaginatively, of course, in good company. The reflected "I" is too potent an influence for it to be otherwise.

The moral value of confession, and of all sorts of publicity, rests upon this basis. In opening ourselves to another we are impelled to imagine how our conduct appears to him; we take an outside view of ourselves. It makes a great difference to whom we confess; the higher the character of the person whose mind we imagine, the more enlightening and elevating is the view of ourselves we get. Even to write our thoughts in a diary, and so to confess, not to a particular person, but to that vague image of an interlocutor that connects itself with all articulate expression, makes things look different.

It is perhaps much the same with prayer. To pray is to confront our moral perplexities with the highest personal ideal we can form, and so to be unconsciously integrating the two, straightening out the one in accordance with the other. It would seem that social psychology strongly corroborates the idea that prayer is an essential aspect of the higher life by showing that thought is interlocutory in its very nature, and that aspiration almost necessarily takes the form of intercourse with an ideal being.

Whatever publishes our conduct introduces new and strong factors into conscience; but whether this publicity is wholesome or otherwise depends upon the character of the public; or, more definitely, upon whether the idea of ourselves that we impute to this public is edifying or degrading. In many cases, for instance, it is ruinous to a person's character to be publicly disgraced, because he presently accepts the degrading self that seems to exist in the minds of others. There are some people to whom we should be ashamed to confess our sins, and others, perhaps, to whom we should not like to own our virtues. Certainly it should not be assumed that it is good to have our acts displayed before the generality of persons: while this may be a good thing as regards matters, like the tax-roll, that relate to our obvious duty to the immediate community, it has in most things a somewhat vulgarizing effect, tending to promote conformity rather than a distinctive life. If the scholar's study were on the market-place, so that the industrious townspeople could see how many hours of the day he spends in apparent idleness, he might lack courage to pursue his vocation. In short, we need privacy as against influences that are not edifying, and communion with those that are.

Meaning of Personal Degeneracy. The question of personal degeneracy is a phase of the question of right or wrong and is ultimately determined by conscience. A degenerate might be defined as one whose personality falls distinctly short of a standard set by the dominant moral thought of a group. It is the nature of the mind to form standards of better or worse in all matters toward which its selective activity is directed; and this has its collective as well as its individual aspect, so that not only every man but every group has its preferences and aversions, its good and bad. Since there is nothing that interests us so much as persons, judgments of right and wrong regarding them have always been felt and expressed with peculiar zeal and emphasis. The righteous and the wicked, the virtuous and the vicious, the good and bad under a hundred names, have been sharply and earnestly discriminated in every age and country.

There is no sharp criterion of what is mentally and socially up to par and what is not, but there are large and important classes whose inferiority is evident, such as idiots, imbeciles, the insane, drunkards, and criminals; and no one will question the importance of studying the whole of which these are parts.

It is altogether a social matter at bottom; that is to say, degeneracy exists only in a certain relation between a person and the rest of a group. In so far as any mental or physical traits constitute it they do so because they involve unfitness for a normal social career, in which alone the essence of the matter is found. The only palpable test of it—and this an uncertain one—is found in the actual career of the person, and especially in the attitude toward him of the organized thought of the group. We agree fairly well upon the degeneracy of the criminal, largely because his abnormality is of so obvious and troublesome a kind that something in particular has to be done about it, and so he becomes definitely and formally stigmatized by the organs of social judgment. Yet even from this decisive verdict an appeal is successfully made in some cases to the wider and maturer thought of mankind, so that many have been executed as felons who, like John Brown, are now revered as heroes.

Causes of Degeneracy. Concerning the causation of degeneracy, we may say, as of every aspect of personality, that its roots are to be looked for somewhere in the mingling of hereditary and social factors from which the individual life springs. Both of these factors exhibit marked variation. In some cases the hereditary factor is so clearly deficient as to make it natural and justifiable to regard heredity as the cause; in a large number of cases there is good reason to think that social conditions are more particularly to blame, and that the original hereditary outfit was fairly good. In a third class, the largest perhaps of all, it is practically impossible to discriminate between them. Indeed, as we have seen, it is always a loose way of speaking to set heredity and environment over against each other as separable forces, or to say that either one is the cause of character or any personal trait. They have no separate existence after personal development is under way; each reacts upon the other, and every trait is due to their intimate union and co-operation. All we are justified in saying is that one or the other may be so aberrant as to demand our special attention.

Congenital idiocy is regarded as hereditary degeneracy, because it is obvious that no social environment can make the individual other than deficient, and we must work upon heredity if we wish to prevent it. On the other hand, when we find that certain conditions, like residence in crowded parts of a city,[2] are accompanied by the appearance of a large percentage of criminality among a population which there is no reason to suppose naturally deficient, we are justified in saying that the causes of this degeneracy are social rather than hereditary. Perhaps some of the criminality,

[2] See Clifford R. Shaw, *Delinquency Areas.*

in the latter case, is due to the conjunction of degrading surroundings with a degree of hereditary deficiency that a better training would have rendered harmless, or at least inconspicuous; but, practically, if we wish to diminish this sort of degeneracy, we must work upon social conditions.

A sound mental heredity consists essentially in teachability, a capacity to learn the things required by the social order; and the congenital idiot is degenerate by the hereditary factor alone, because he is incapable of learning these things.[3] But a sound heredity is no safeguard against personal degeneracy; if we have teachability, all turns upon what is taught, and this depends upon the social environment. Since the social surroundings of a person can be changed and his hereditary bias cannot, it is expedient, in that great majority of cases in which causation is obscure, to assume as a working hypothesis that the social factor is at fault, and to try by altering it to alter the person.

As a mental trait, marking a person off as, in some sense, worse than others in the same social group, degeneracy appears to consist in some lack in the higher organization of thought. It is not that one has the normal mental outfit plus something additional, called wrong, crime, sin, madness, or the like, but that he is in some way deficient in the mental activity by which sympathetic insight is created and by which all impulses are unified with reference to the general life. It would not be very difficult to take the seven deadly sins—Pride, Envy, Anger, Sloth, Covetousness, Gluttony, and Lust—and show that each may be regarded as the undisciplined manifestation of a normal or functional tendency.

Types of Personal Degeneracy. In the lowest phases mental organization can hardly be said to exist at all: an idiot has no character, no consistent or effective individuality. There is no unification, and no self-control and stable will; action simply reflects the particular animal impulse that is ascendant. Hunger, sexual lust, rage, dread, and, in somewhat higher grades, a crude, naïve kindliness, are each felt and expressed in the simplest manner possible. There can, of course, be little or no sympathetic insight, and the unconsciousness of what is going on in the minds of other persons prevents any sense of decency or attempt to conform to social standards.

[3] Though Jennings warns against assuming that just because a character is hereditary it is unalterable by the environment. *The Biological Basis of Human Nature*, p. 214.

In the higher grades we make the distinction between the unstable and the rigid varieties. There is one sort of person in whom the most conspicuous and troublesome trait is mere mental inconsistency and lack of character, and another whose members possess a fair degree of consistency and unity of purpose, but whose mental scope or reach of sympathetic insight is so small that they have no adequate relation to the life about them.

The unstable type possesses a conscience, but it is vacillating in its judgments, transient in duration, and ineffectual in control. We all probably can think of people conspicuously lacking in self-control, and it will perhaps be evident, when we reflect upon them, that their consciences are of this sort. The voice of conscience with them is certain to be chiefly an echo of temporary emotions, because a synthesis embracing long periods of time is beyond their range. They are likely to suffer sharp and frequent attacks of remorse, on account of failure to live up to their standards, but it would seem that the wounds do not go very deep as a rule, but share the superficiality of their lives. People of this sort, if not too far gone in weakness, are probably the ones who profit most by punishment, because they are helped by the sharp and definite pain which it associates with acts that they recognize as wrong, but cannot keep from doing without a vivid emotional deterrent. They also are the ones who, in their eagerness to escape from the pains of fluctuation and inconsistency, are most prone to submit blindly to some external and dogmatic authority. Unable to rule themselves, they crave a master.

With those of the rigid type, conscience exists and controls the life but it does not cherish the standards which are generally accepted. It may appear startling to assert that conscience may dictate the wrong, but such is clearly the fact if we mean what is wrong in the eyes of most people, though right in the eyes of the degenerate. The very worst men of the hard, narrow, fanatical, or brutal sorts often live at peace with their consciences. The usurer who grinds the faces of the poor, the unscrupulous speculator who causes the ruin of innocent investors to aggrandize himself, the fanatical anarchist who stabs the king or shoots a president, the Kentucky mountaineer who regards murderous revenge as a duty, are diverse examples of wrong-doers whose consciences not only do not punish, but often instigate their ill deeds.

The idea that crime or wrong of any sort is invariably pursued by remorse arises from the natural but mistaken assumption that all other people have consciences similar to our own. The

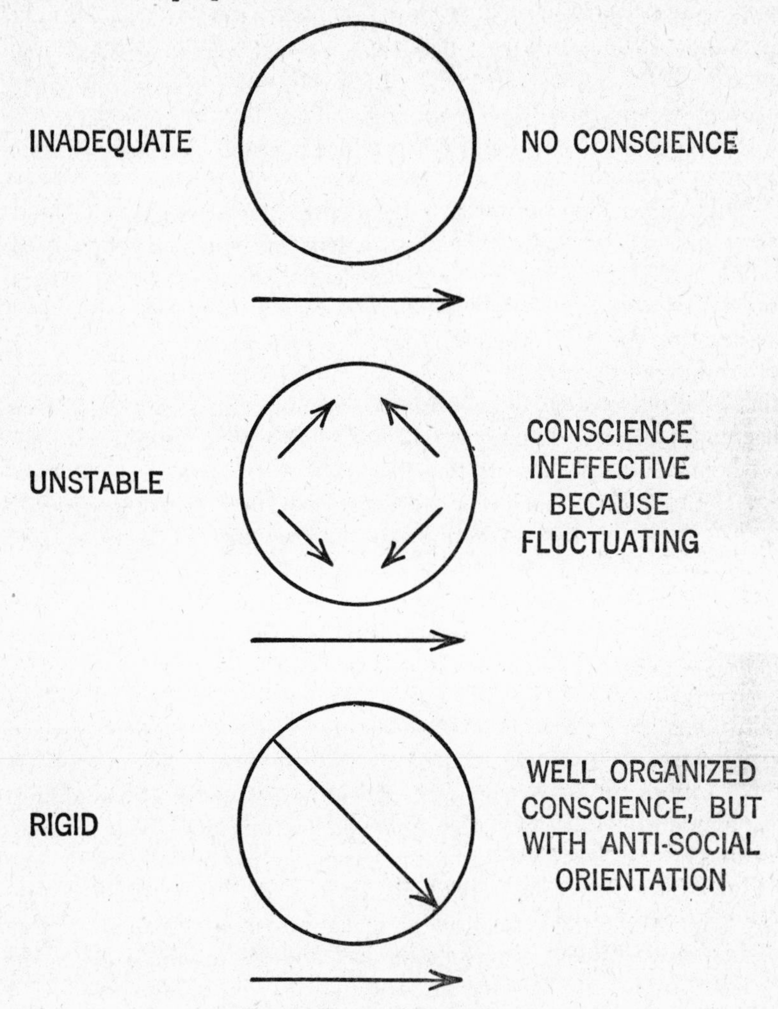

FIG. 5. Types of Degenerates.

The arrows within the circle indicate the orientation of the conscience of the degenerate; those outside, the orientation of the conscience of the normal person.

man of sensitive temperament and refined habit of thought feels that he would suffer remorse if he had done this deed, and supposes that the same must be true of the perpetrator. On the contrary, it seems likely that only a small proportion of those whom the general public regards as wrong-doers suffer much from pangs of conscience. All authorities agree that the mass of criminals, and the same is true of ill-doers within the law, have a habit of mind of which the ill deed is a logical outcome. That such people do have a definite code which they live up to is shown by the often-remarked "honor among thieves." It is impossible that mental organization should not produce a moral synthesis of some sort.

Such rigid degenerates are frequently the products of degenerate groups, groups which have degenerate *mores* of their own. Thus a boy who runs away from school, plunders freight cars, breaks windows, and the like, may do these things as a result of association in a delinquent "gang"—just as other boys under other influences turn their energies into athletics and the activities of Boy Scouts.[4] The group forms his conscience and what it countenances and admires will not seem wrong to him, no matter how the rest of society may regard it. If it becomes traditional for the members of a certain college fraternity to drink, gamble, and cheat their way through examinations, the freshmen will be likely to fall into these practices as a matter of course.

Responsibility for Degeneracy. What is the practical effect upon responsibility of the view that wrong does not originate merely in the individual will but has always a history in heredity and social transmission? It tends, not to diminish responsibility, but to change its character, to make it an organic whole, including every person whose will contributes to the wrong in question. It makes more people responsible, and mitigates, without removing, the blame that falls upon the immediate wrong-doer. When a boy is caught stealing brass fixtures from an unfinished house, the judge of the Juvenile Court will first of all blame the boy, but, far from stopping here, he will bring into court also the leader of his gang who set him the example, and his parents who failed to give him suitable care and discipline. The judge may well censure, also, the school authorities for not interesting him in healthy work and recreation, and the city government and influential classes for failing to provide a better environment for him to grow up in. The tendency of any study of indirect causes is to fix more and more responsibility upon those who have wealth,

[4] See Frederick Thrasher, *The Gang*.

knowledge, and influence, and therefore the power to bring a better state of things to pass. It is impossible not to see, as one looks into these questions, that there is little use in blaming or punishing those who have been brought up in demoralizing surroundings, and that the chief hope of improvement is in arousing the consciences of those who are able to do away with such surroundings and so check the evil at its source.

Punishment for Degenerate Conduct. Under the organic view punishment is not done away with: it has its uses as an influence upon the will, upon the wills of actual wrong-doers and of those who might become such. This view does tend, however, to depreciate the importance of punishment as compared with educational and constructive methods. If we can make the whole process healthy, vice, crime, and the like will be kept off as disease is from a healthy body.

In so far as we use punishment its efficiency depends mainly upon two things:

1. It must be evidently just; so that both the offender and the onlooker can see that it is what society must do for the protection of its members. If arbitrary, or gratuitously painful or humiliating, it arouses such resentment as one would feel at being mauled by a bully, thus brutalizing and alienating the offender. Much of our punishment is of this kind.

2. It must be reasonably certain. Otherwise those who contemplate a crime will take the chance. Under our present methods most offenders escape, and the criminal class regards punishment as merely one of the risks of a somewhat hazardous occupation.

Extent of Personal Degeneracy. The extent of personal degeneracy is incalculable because of the impossibility of setting a standard of normal conduct which all would accept. We can therefore merely cite a few figures relative to the more obvious and recorded type of degenerates.

In the United States about 47 persons out of every 100,000 are in institutions for the feebleminded or epileptic[5] and 245 are in hospitals for mental diseases.[6] Competent students believe that an equal number of the insane and ten times the number given for the feebleminded are outside of institutions. Of course many of

[5] Bureau of the Census, *Feebleminded and Epileptics in Institutions,* 1923, pp. 26, 70.

[6] Bureau of the Census, *Patients in Hospitals for Mental Disease,* 1923, p. 11.

the patients in hospitals for mental diseases will recover sufficiently to return to normal life activities, but their places will be filled by others.

In the field of delinquency and crime there are many studies. In Chicago it was found that the delinquency rates varied tremendously with the neighborhood. In the worst area more than one-fourth of the boys 10–16 were handled by the police probation officers in a single year while over a seven-year period 19.4 per cent came before the juvenile court. In the best area the seven-year percentage was .8. The corresponding figures for girls were 9.0 and .1. A rough calculation on this basis indicates that approximately one-third of 1 per cent of the total population of the city were juvenile delinquents in any one year.[7] In the field of adult criminality we find that there were 94.6 prisoners in federal, state, and county prisons for every 100,000 of the population in 1923.[8] In addition are those detained in police jails, which constituted a much larger, though more temporary, group. In the first six months of 1930, 2429 persons per 100,000 of the population were admitted to such jails.[9] This is about 52 times as many as were admitted to state and federal prisons. Taking into consideration all this evidence, a rough guess would place approximately 2½ per cent of the population in one of these categories of definite degeneracy. When we make allowance for uncaught criminals, drug addicts, alcoholics not counted in the above classes, prostitutes, and others of vicious morality the proportion might well rise to 4 per cent or more.

Summary. In this chapter we have tried to show that a person's conscience is dependent both upon the *mores* of his culture and upon his own peculiar life experiences. We have seen that the right is the rational for the person concerned and that what seems rational may vary with the individual's age, his admiration for particular leaders, and other factors as well as culture. Degeneracy appears as a falling away from a normal standard of conduct and its roots are seen to be both hereditary and environmental. Three types are perhaps distinguishable, the totally inadequate, the unstable, and the rigid. Under the organic view the responsibility for degenerate conduct cannot be laid solely upon the individual, nor is punishment dispensed with. Though

[7] Clifford R. Shaw, *Delinquency Areas,* pp. 88, 152, 213–14.

[8] Bureau of the Census, *Prisoners, 1923.*

[9] *National Commission on Law Observance and Enforcement,* No. 9, pp. 327–44. "Police Jails and Village Lockups."

there is no certain test for degeneracy, perhaps we may regard about one twenty-fifth of the population as degenerate.

STUDY QUESTIONS

1. Why do ideals of right vary with the group? Give examples from your observation.
2. Why are some ideals of right nearly universal? Illustrate.
3. What sources of moral principles other than the *mores* can you suggest?
4. Give a concrete example from your own experience illustrating the principle that the right is the rational.
5. May the decision of conscience be opposed to that of formal reasoning? Why?
6. If the wrong is the irrational, how do you explain the fact that we often do it?
7. When and why is the right the onward? When and why is it the habitual or static? Can you give illustrations from your observation? Would you expect to find that Chinese views of right are changing nowadays in this respect?
8. To what extent do you think we should act by a rule or principle in a moral crisis?
9. "Wrong is acting for ourselves: right is acting for others." What do you think of this principle? Can you frame one you think better?
10. What examples can you give of the influence of leadership on conscience?
11. Explain and illustrate the action of publicity on one's conscience. When may this action be degrading?
12. How may prayer be interpreted by social psychology?
13. Define degeneracy. Would you call a consumptive a degenerate?
14. May there be difficulty in distinguishing degeneracy from greatness? Why? Can you give examples of men of genius punished as criminals?
15. How far is it possible to distinguish between hereditary and social degeneracy? When would you stress the social causes and when the hereditary?
16. What three types of degeneracy may we distinguish?
17. What sorts of wrong-doers suffer pangs of conscience? What sorts do not?
18. Describe an example of group degeneracy from your observation, showing how the conscience of the individual is involved in it.
19. Just what is the practical effect of the organic view of conduct upon responsibility? Illustrate.

20. What do you think are the purposes of punishment? Under what conditions are these purposes realized?
21. Discuss the death penalty in the light of your answer to Question 20.
22. What is the estimated amount of degeneracy in the United States?

CHAPTER XII

THE CULTURAL ENLARGEMENT OF COMMUNICATION

Primary and Secondary Techniques of Communication. We have seen in Chapter III that words are important for the co-ordination of group life and for the building of tradition. During the long course of cultural evolution, therefore, men have been gradually improving the techniques on which group life rests. The net result of the accumulation of inventions in communication has been to raise the level of efficiency of communication far above that of primitive or tribal days.

As we have already seen, communication probably began on the pre-verbal level and eventually reached the level of speech. That is the level attained by primitive peoples all over the world. While some cultural inventions are involved in communication on this level, we can say in general that it still proceeds on the pre-literate or primary level, involving a minimum of cultural elaboration.

With the invention of writing, however, and especially with the invention of printing, the coming of railroad transportation, and the application of electricity to communicative purposes, a new level of efficiency is reached. That it is not all clear gain will be apparent, of course, to any one who will take the trouble carefully to compare the kind of information that is obtainable from a face-to-face interview with the information obtainable by letter. Yet obviously, despite the loss of directness and vividness, the newer cultural or secondary techniques more than make up in other respects what they lose in expressiveness.

The Four Elements of Communicative Efficiency. Communicative efficiency seems to be made up of four elements:

Expressiveness, or the range of ideas and feelings that a given set of symbols is competent to transmit.
Permanence, or the overcoming of time.
Swiftness, or the overcoming of space.
Diffusion, or the reaching of all classes of men.

We shall point out briefly how non-verbal arts have contributed to increase the expressiveness of communication as compared, for example, with mere verbal communication and then we shall go on to consider the further cultural elaboration of the pre-verbal and verbal forms by means of writing, printing, and the communicative uses of electricity and the machine.

Non-Verbal Aids to Expressiveness. There are from the start many side channels of communication. Thus among savage or barbarous peoples we everywhere find, beside gesture-language, the use of a multitude of other symbols, such as the red arrow for war, the pipe of peace, signal fires, notched sticks, knotted cords, totems, and, among nations more advanced in culture, coats of arms, flags, and an infinite diversity of symbolic ritual. The arts of painting, sculpture, music, dancing, and architecture, are perhaps the most important organized forms of non-verbal communication. Generally speaking, these arts seem to have two somewhat different functions: First, as mere picture- or image-writing, conveying ideas that could also be conveyed (although with a difference) in words; and, second, as the vehicle of peculiar phases of sentiment incommunicable in any other way. The importance of this second type of function of the non-verbal arts needs to be emphasized. One of the leading contemporary American poets once remarked that the wrong way to write a poem was to sit down with an idea. What he meant was that a poet, while using verbal symbols, was primarily concerned with sentiment and feeling. What he suggested was that poetry was a kind of hybrid art since the transmission of sentiment and feeling is peculiarly the function of the non-verbal arts. Thanks to these arts sentiment is cumulative in human history in the same manner as thought, though less definitely and surely. Thus Christian feeling, as it grew and flourished in the Middle Ages, for example, was fostered by painting as much, perhaps, as by the Scriptures themselves. In the same way Greek sculpture has been a channel by which Greek sentiment has flowed into modern life. The non-verbal arts have thus transmitted to us the sentiments and aspirations of many lands with a force and a directness utterly impossible through verbal symbols alone.

This function of the non-verbal arts is all too easily lost sight of in an age dazzled by the multiplication of techniques for increasing the efficiency of verbal symbols. If in later pages we stress the effects of these secondary verbal techniques, the student must remember that the non-verbal arts have a unique function which is of lasting social importance.

Writing as a Contribution to Permanence. Probably the most important cultural invention affecting the efficiency of communication was that of writing. Three stages have been distinguished in the evolution of writing:[1] First, the use of pictures of things and symbols of ideas—the pictographic stage; second, the representation of sounds by means of pictures or abbreviations of pictures—the transitional or rebus stage; and third, the phonetic stage in which the symbols no longer denote objects or ideas but sounds—words, syllables, or the elemental letter-sounds. Many nations have used pictographs. Only a few reached the transitional stage. And only one nation—some Semitic group around the eastern Mediterranean about 1000 B.C. or a little earlier—ever invented purely phonetic writing.[2] On the 22 non-pictorial characters standing merely for the sounds of consonants —it was the Greeks who added the vowels—on those insignificant little marks are based all the alphabets ever used in the world.

The importance of writing consists in this: By giving ideas a lasting record it makes possible a more certain, continuous, and diversified growth of the human mind. It does for the race very much what it does for the individual. When the student has a good thought he writes it down, so that it may be recalled at will and made the starting-point for a better thought in the same direction; and so mankind at large records and cherishes its thoughts.

Until writing is achieved the accumulation of ideas depends upon oral tradition, the capacity of which is measured by the memories of the people who transmit it. Without writing there can hardly be any science or any diversified literature. These require a means by which important ideas can be passed on unimpaired to men distant in time and space from their authors. Nor can stable and extended government be organized without it, for such government requires a constitution of some sort, a defi-

[1] Adapted from A. L. Kroeber, *Anthropology*, p. 263ff.

[2] "The earliest extant example of the primitive Semitic alphabet is on the famous Moabite Stone of King Mesha, who in the ninth century before Christ erected and inscribed this monument to commemorate the successful defense of Moab against the invading Hebrews. . . . It is . . . probable that the system was perfected, perhaps several centuries earlier, by a wealthier and more important people, one more in contact with foreign nations, such as the Phœnicians . . ." *op. cit.*, p. 271.

nite and permanent body of law and custom, embracing the wisdom of the past regarding the maintenance of social order. It is quite the same with religious systems. The historical religions are based upon Scriptures, the essential part of which is the recorded teaching of the founder and his immediate disciples. Without such a record Christianity, Buddhism, or Mohammedanism could never have been more than the faith of a small and transient sect. It is perhaps of some significance that none of the great ethical religions of mankind appeared in the world until after the invention of writing.

As for modern life, the whole structure and progress of it rests upon the preservation in writing of the achievements of the antique mind, upon the records, especially, of Judea, Greece, and Rome. To inquire what we should have been without these is like asking what we should have been if our parents had not existed. Writing made history possible, and the man of history with his complex institutions. It enabled a rapid and secure enlargement of that human nature which had previously been confined within small and unstable groups.

Printing and Diffusion. If writing, by giving thought permanence, brought in the earlier civilization, printing, by giving it diffusion, opened the doors of the modern world.

Invented first in China in the sixth century A.D. as a method of striking impressions from engraved blocks, and re-invented or decisively improved in western Europe in the fifteenth century as a method of securing impressions from movable letter-types, printing spread the records of the race before all who cared to read. The old monopoly of learning, so long held by the clergy in western Europe, was broken.

Printing brings a thrust toward democracy, because it puts knowledge within the reach of the common people. Everywhere in Europe the spread of printing was followed by a general awakening due to the unsettling suggestions which it scattered abroad. Political and religious agitation, by no means unknown before, was immensely stimulated, and has continued to the present time.

> When . . . on October 31, 1517, Luther's fateful theses were hung on the church door at Wittenberg, they were, as he tells us, known in a fortnight throughout Germany; and in a month they had reached Rome and were being read in every school and convent in Europe—a result manifestly impossible without the aid of the printing-press.[3]

[3] H. C. Lea, *The Cambridge Modern History,* Vol. I, pp. 684–85.

The printing-press and the cannon together are sometimes given credit for having sounded the knell of feudalism. In any event, the printing-press made possible that quickening and broad-

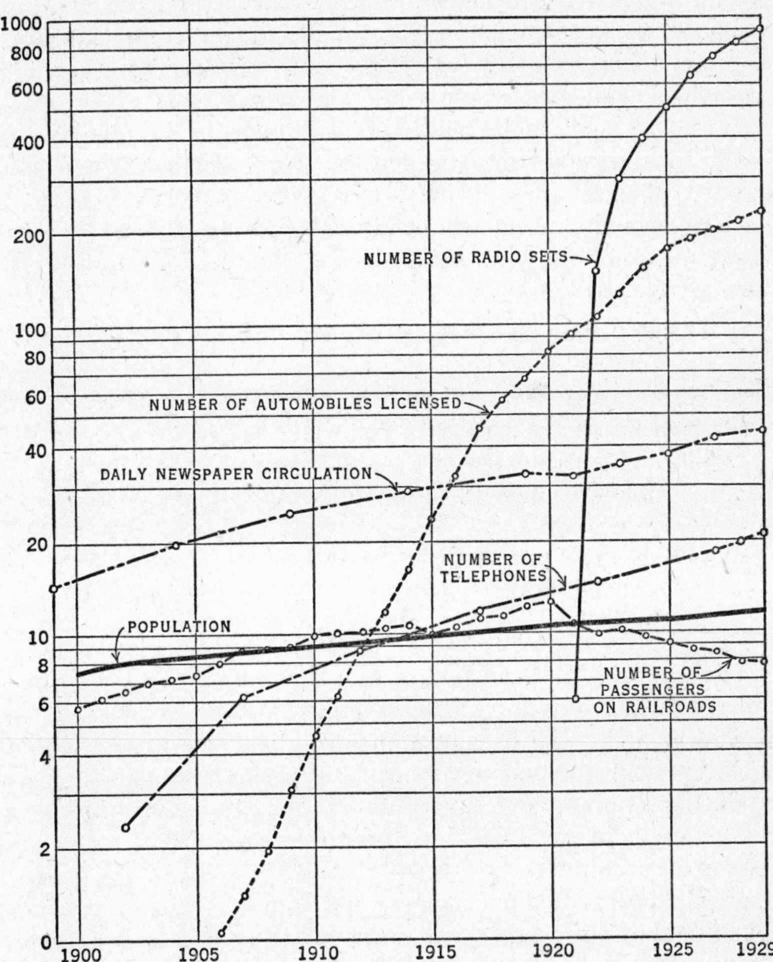

From "Communication" by Ernest W. Burgess in "American Journal of Sociology" XXXV, p. 1000.

FIG. 6. Rates of Increase of Different Agencies of Communication, or Their Use, in the United States, 1899–1929.

ening of mental life which so distinctively marks off the modern world from the Middle Ages.

Modern Inventions Add Swiftness to Diffusion. Modern communication obviously includes many more cultural devices than the non-verbal arts and writing and printing. Economic changes have made it possible to inundate a continent with cheap books, magazines, and newspapers. The rise of the postal system and the conquest of distance by the railroads, the telegraph, the telephone, the wireless, and the radio all contribute. And the arts of reproducing distant scenes and sounds—photography, photo-engraving, phonography, etc.—also play a part.

In the last analysis the modern contributions to communication rest distinctively on two great cultural achievements, the machine and the conquest of electricity. Let us try to see how electro-machine communication works. Together the machine and electricity do four things on a scale and at a rate which have never been approached before:

1. Through the press they function as the mass organizers of mind.
2. Through the telegraph and the telephone they lengthen the arms of point-to-point control.
3. Through the moving-picture and the radio they make possible the mass diffusion of sentiment and personality-impression.
4. Through the railroad, the steamship, the airplane, and the automobile they vastly increase individual mobility and fluidity.[4]

The Press—Mass Diffusion as a Factor in the Organization of Mind. Under the term press we here include all the machinery and social organization involved in the production of books, periodicals, and newspapers. The sheer volume of such production is impressive. Every month in 1927, for example, for every family in the United States there were produced on the average in round numbers 39 daily newspapers, 4 Sunday papers, 9 weekly papers and magazines, and 4 monthly magazines—a grand total of *more than 56 newspapers and magazines per family per month.*[5] In addition, and exclusive of textbooks, there was

[4] Mobility is change of residence; fluidity is change of place without change of residence.

[5] There were approximately 28,244,000 families in the United States on July 1, 1927, on the basis of the population estimates of the U. S. Census Bureau. The Census of Manufacturers that year found 2265 daily newspapers circulating 42,343,210 copies; 511 Sunday papers circulating 27,695,859 copies; 71 tri-weekly papers circulating 468,534 copies; 395 semi-weekly papers circulating 2,026,760; 7760 weekly publications circulating 55,985,413 copies; 238 semi-

printed an average of one book for every 2.3 families per month. While such figures gloss over very great inequalities in distribution between Park Avenue, for example, and the poorest hamlet in Mississippi, and ignore obvious differences in the quality of various publications—fiction and books for children, for example, constituting 40 per cent of all the non-textbooks published—nevertheless, they do suggest something of the volume of verbal diffusion issuing from the press.

Despite the supplementary services of radio, the lecture platform, newsreels, and other channels, it is mainly through trade journals, the newspapers, magazines, and books, *i.e.*, the press, that Americans keep in touch with current events and carry on the larger discussions essential to the process of collective readjustment by consent. As the Lynds found in Middletown and as any one can observe about him, the reading of serious books is, however, confined to a very small percentage of the population —university professors, teachers, lawyers, doctors, ministers, a few business men, and perhaps the wives of a few others. New ideas usually reach the mass of the people at second- or third-hand through fiction, and through popularized discussions in the magazines and in the Sunday papers. But the fact that they do tend to filter down in this way is of the utmost importance after all for social progress.

More impressive, perhaps, than its service in transmitting new ideas is the work of the press in drumming home old ones. Probably more than 90 per cent of the books published in 1927 and certainly much more than that proportion of the total content of magazines and newspapers tended on the whole to define the world in fairly stereotyped patterns. The net result of this, repeated 56 times per family every month, is inevitably to produce a certain uniformity of mental outlook. We must be careful, however, not to assume that this uniformity is necessarily the same

monthlies circulating 5,955,858 copies; and 2522 monthly publications circulating 120,693,490 copies. In addition and not included in the averages used in the text above, there were 477 quarterly magazines circulating 21,247,360 copies and 113 miscellaneous publications circulating 2,200,541 copies. Books published that year exclusive of textbooks totalled 143,645,880. Of these, 36,553,507 were fiction, 31,047,094 were juvenile, and 22,220,536 had to do with religion and philosophy; 6,281,165, poetry and drama; 3,075,121, biography; 2,493,510, law; science and technology, 2,392,044; travel, 1,190,569; medicine, 1,168,755; history, 1,462,193; fine arts, 943,952; sociology and economics, 875,191; agriculture, 282,861; and miscellaneous, 33,659,382.

for everybody, since all do not read the same publications, and we must not assume that it is the only effect produced by the press even on those concerned. As a matter of fact we have already suggested that the press functions as an agent of change as well as an agent of stability, and we shall have occasion to note later that it furthers individuality in some respects even while standardizing individuals in others. The social effects of modern communication are extremely complex and cannot be exhausted by a single generalization. The point that we are concerned with making here is simply that bye and large the press does function as a control device by which the current *mores* of the group impress themselves more or less unconsciously upon those who read. Thus, practically every newspaper read by whites in this country is edited as a matter of course wholly from the white man's point of view. This means that these papers are continually reinforcing that point of view in their readers. In a similar way other values embedded in the *mores* are pounded home in the press—the importance of private property, the value of education, the unseemliness of cruelty, and so on.

Furthermore, since newspapers and magazines are published in centres and carried out to readers, there is a tendency for the readers of each publication to be oriented more or less definitely toward the centre of publication. Thus there is built up, from the township weekly to the great national magazine, a series of overlapping circles of influence, each circle representing, so to speak, the orbit of orientation of a given publication.[6] How the newspaper functions in thus orienting its readers about its own community we shall see in a later chapter. For the moment we are interested merely in the general fact that the newspaper and periodical press does organize men's minds in this centre-oriented way. In other words, newspapers and periodicals do communicatively what banks, corporations, railroads, and similar agencies do economically—they tend to integrate modern society into con-

[6] Circle is, of course, only an approximate description. Ecological conditions control the shape of the area of influence. Thus obviously Lake Michigan destroys the circularity of the area of influence of *The Chicago Tribune* and the international boundary cuts through the middle of the potential area of the Detroit papers. Most of the popular magazines are published near the eastern seaboard and spread, therefore, farther west than east. Moreover, each newspaper tends to orient its readers toward a number of centres at once. Thus rural readers of a Detroit daily follow the *Chicago* grain reports, the *Detroit* automobile news, the State political news from *Lansing,* national political news from *Washington,* and financial news from *New York.*

stellations of sub-centres all oriented toward and dominated by the great metropolitan centres.

It thus becomes clear that the rôle of the press in the mass organization of mind is at least threefold: (1) it puts the group in touch with new events and new ideas; (2) it maintains the group pattern of established customs, practices, *mores;* and (3) it integrates the group about centres of social dominance.

The Lengthening Arms of Control—Telegraph and Telephone. If the unique importance of the press would seem to lie in its mass organization of the mind of the group through diffusion, the unique importance of the telegraph and the telephone would seem to consist in their capacity for an almost instantaneous exchange of symbols between designated distant points. While both have been used as adjuncts to the newspapers and periodical press and are by no means unimportant in that respect, it is well to remember that most of the quarter billion telegraph and twenty-seven billion telephone messages flashing about this country in 1930 had nothing to do with the press.[7] If communication be looked upon as a form of remote control of one individual by another, the social importance of the telegraph and telephone becomes obvious at once: Both have enormously multiplied the distance per unit of time over which designated individuals can be verbally controlled. Before the invention of the electric telegraph, for example, although experiments with semaphores and other devices were under way, the usual speed at which information travelled on land was approximately that of a horse, *i.e.,* less than ten miles an hour. Today it is possible to telegraph around the world in less than twenty minutes and to set up a direct speaking connection—given good weather—in less than ten minutes by radio-telephone from any telephone in America to any telephone in Europe, South America, Africa, or Australia. The net result of this increased reach of communicative control has been to speed up tremendously the tempo of modern life since so many more people can now affect us *in a given unit of time.* Another way of saying the same thing is to say that the area of association and control has been widened: a revolution in Buenos Aires this morning becomes spot news in our afternoon papers. When Lon-

[7] For purposes of comparison with the figures given on the press the telegraph messages averaged 1 to each family and a half per month and the telephone messages 80.2 per family per month. Every one of the 20,000,000 telephones in use in the United States averaged more than three calls a day in 1930.

don went off the gold standard in 1931, Canadian exchange felt the repercussion within the hour.

Far more than its per capita share of telegraph and telephone as well as postal business originates in the business district of a metropolitan centre. This is clear evidence of the control function of the telegraph and telephone since the business district is the control-centre of the economic and financial structure of the metropolitan area.

Thanks to the lengthening arm of control it has become possible to operate bigger units and more units from one central business office. The tendency in recent years has been for the central offices to move to the business centre while the operating plant gravitates toward the periphery where land is cheap.

Telephone and telegraph function as controls not only in directing and integrating production but also in facilitating the creation of great centralized agencies of distribution. In Middletown, for example, the extension of the general delivery system went hand in hand with the diffusion of the telephone and the automobile. While the chain store idea, dating from the old Hudson's Bay Company, is older than modern communication, the modern development of the chain store is closely related to the facility of control at a distance afforded by modern devices. In the same way the pre-eminence of certain market centres such as the Chicago live-stock market and the New York Stock Exchange is possible only because the prices established there can be flashed instantly to every part of the country.

In no small degree the increasing integration of business units and population aggregates within the modern metropolitan area can be traced to increased facility of control at a distance made possible by the telegraph and the telephone.

The Diffusion of Sentiment and Personality—Motion Pictures and Radio. About 15,000,000 people a day attend the 22,731 motion-picture theatres in this country.[8] This does not mean, of course, that the whole United States goes to a picture show once every eight days. Attendance habits vary widely in dif-

[8] Statement by N. D. Golden, assistant chief, Motion Picture Division, United States Department of Commerce, in *United States Daily,* May 3, 1930, as quoted by Malcolm M. Willey and Stuart A. Rice, "Communication," *American Journal of Sociology,* May, 1931, p. 976. Mr. Golden estimated that the talking picture which began to diffuse about 1927 originally increased attendance by about 15 per cent, but that attendance had again begun to decline in 1930.

ferent localities and among different classes. In a sample of 831 urban and rural homes in Washtenaw County, Michigan, for example, in 1924, it was found that from one third of the homes no one had attended a motion-picture show in more than a year and in a considerable percentage of these homes nobody had attended for five years or more. On the other hand, the 556 individuals who had attended within the year had averaged 16 attendances each in six months or approximately one every 1.6 weeks. More of the business class (*i.e.,* 85 per cent) than of the unskilled workers attended; but for each of the unskilled who did go (77 per cent), attendance during the preceding six months had averaged 20, the highest of all the groups. Only 31 per cent of the farmers had attended within the year, and these had averaged only seven attendances each in six months, or one every 3.7 weeks. What all this means is that the movies apparently reach certain strata of the population much more completely than they reach other strata.[9]

What do the movies do for the 15,000,000 who watch and hear them every day? We are here concerned not with the complete social effects of the movies but with their unique contribution as a medium of communication. From this point of view their contribution is similar in one respect to that of radio yet somewhat different. Both are highly efficient diffusors of sentiment and personality because of their capacity to transmit pre-verbal as well as verbal symbols. But the movies, and especially the talking pictures, are marked for their capacity to transmit entire visual situations.[10] We actually see the villain as well as hear his curses.

The result of this is, of course, that the movies have become powerful agents of diffusion. The spread of Paris styles, Grand

[9] Why they reach just whom they do is another question. For example, in the Washtenaw County study it was found that as the number of children in homes increased the number of movie attendances tended to increase, the correlation being .59 ± .016. Homes that reported no attendances in a year averaged 0.8 child per home; those reporting one attendance a week or less averaged 1.17 children; and those reporting more than one a week averaged 1.3 children. For purposes of comparison it may be noted that while only 66 per cent of the homes had been represented at the movies, 98 per cent took newspapers. The newspaper is thus the most pervasive medium of communication, exceeding even the radio, which reaches only about 60 per cent in this county.—L. J. Carr, *The Quantitative Aspect of Secondary Contacts in Relation to Group Adjustment to Change,* Unpublished doctoral dissertation, University of Michigan, 1925.

[10] Television, of course, shares this characteristic with the talking motion picture.

Rapids furniture, and similar traits has been greatly furthered by the screen. In fact so greatly has diffusion been furthered by American pictures that loud objections have been going up from three different groups of people—foreign business competitors, idealistic native sons abroad, and moral critics at home. The foreign business men complain that American movies make their customers want to buy American goods. The idealistic native sons point out that American movies are making America the joke of the world. As a popular magazine explains: "The world now knows all about us. Each American home contains a swimming-pool, a butler, and a pail of cocktails on the hearth. The American father signs checks, pushes buttons to summon servants, and entertains chorus girls. The American wife is usually arranging for the acquisition of her next husband. Every one is intent upon kissing or killing some one else. The greatest man in America is a little fellow with oddly arranged feet, a tiny black mustache, and a serious expression. America is a Never-Never Land, a phantasmagoria, a nightmare country. All the world laughs at an American. He is the everlasting lunatic. The movie masses see us that way—and seeing is believing. In nearly every land under the sun four out of five of the movies shown are made in America. The movie is our new ambassador—with plenary powers."[11]

If the American movie paints such a peculiar picture of America abroad it cannot be wondered at that critics abound at home. The overemphasis on sex has moved Professor Ross to declare that the motion picture is making Americans "the most erotic-minded people in the world." The pre-occupation with crime and violence has led to charges and counter-charges concerning the movie's share in America's high crime rate. Yet in a preliminary enumeration of ten causes of crime in 1927 the New York State Crime Commission did not even mention motion pictures. Studies of school children, however, in Chicago and elsewhere indicate that the moving-picture is so highly stimulating that it easily becomes a factor of difficulty in children already of a problem type.

We have been describing social reactions to the motion picture's effectiveness in transmitting situations. A less obvious effect is its diffusion of sentiment and personality by means of pre-

[11] Grant Overton, "The Movies Show Us to the World," *Colliers,* October 17, 1925, p. 14.

verbal symbols. The very processes of invention that have so largely robbed modern urban life of the personal touch have here, it seems, provided a kind of centralized substitute for the old type of personality experience. Instead of meeting his neighbors casually a dozen times a day the city dweller rushes frantically to work and rushes home again to submit himself in the evening to the tender ministrations of Hollywood or of the National Broadcasting Company. If the personality impressions that flicker from the screen or quiver on the air are perhaps somewhat stereotyped and frequently banal, the range of personalities accessible has at least been enormously increased. In place of meeting the same neighbors day after day one now watches a prime minister lay a cornerstone or tunes in on the President of the United States.

It is largely because of their efficiency in pre-verbal transmission that the motion pictures have tended to create an industry of capitalized personalities. Probably a larger percentage of the population of Hollywood than of any other city in the world is known by sight to millions everywhere. Paradoxical as it may sound, the public seem, really, to be more interested in the picture people than in their pictures—when a star dies his pictures usually die with him for no one will pay to see them. Probably this is only another way of saying that most of the Hollywood product has little permanent value as art.

In this diffusion of personality the radio also plays a part, although probably a less striking one because of its dependence on verbal symbols. The first official enumeration of radio sets by the Census Bureau, in 1930, revealed 12,563,000 sets in the United States, or radios in 40 per cent of the homes. Distribution varied greatly by states, 63 per cent of the homes in New Jersey having radios and only 5.4 per cent in Mississippi. Within states distribution was also far from uniform. To take Michigan as an example, there was a set for every 1.6 of the homes in Oakland county in the thickly settled Detroit area, but only one to every 5.3 homes in thinly settled Missaukee County in the north.

Not only is this variation in distribution a factor affecting the diffusion-effectiveness of the radio but variation in the number of sets actually operating at any given time is also a factor. "Investigations reveal that three out of every four sets owned are used at some time during each day, but that no more than half of the total sets are in use at any one time, even when the most popular programmes are on the air."[12] Studies sponsored by advertisers indicate that the effective listeners per set at any time should be taken as 3.1. The Census estimated total listeners in 1930 as 50,000,000.

Radio broadcasting as ordinarily understood began in 1920 when station KDKA of the Westinghouse Electric and Manufacturing Company, Pittsburgh, Pennsylvania, began the transmission of programmes on regularly published schedules. In November, 1930, there were 617 broadcasting stations in the United States and about 750 in the rest of the world. The 617 in the United States were divided into three classes, 242 being classed as local, 287 as regional, and 88 as clear channel, or higher-power stations. Many of these stations are linked together through the network of one of the two great broadcasting companies, the National or the Columbia, the former of which in 1930 included 75 stations and the latter 77.

In the main, radio has been used for advertising and for entertainment. Advertisers in 1929 paid $18,700,000 to three large broadcasting chains for time on the air. This was about 1.3 per cent of the estimated total of $1,400,000,000 which was spent for advertising in the United States that year.[13] Probably the percentage will increase somewhat as radio sets become more generally diffused. In 1929 the ten largest advertisers in the country spent 6.4 per cent of their total appropriations for broadcasting time and broadcasting talent. More than two thirds of all time on the air is devoted to entertainment. A considerable percentage of the remainder is used up on purely routine matters such as market reports and the weather. From one tenth to one fourth of the total is given to speeches, lectures, and news reports.[14]

[12] Data by John J. Karol, Director of Market Research, Columbia Broadcasting System, from unpublished manuscript. *Cf. Fortune,* II (December, 1930), 65ff.—As quoted by Malcolm M. Willey and Stuart A. Rice, "Communication," *American Journal of Sociology,* May, 1931, p. 974.

[13] *Editor and Publisher, The Fourth Estate,* October 11, 1930, p. 7. Of the total, newspapers received approximately 63 per cent; magazines 15 per cent; trade journals about 2.1 per cent; radio 1.3 per cent; and the remaining 18.6 per cent was divided among farm journals, billboard and sign advertising, car cards, and printed matter of various kinds.

[14] Officials of the N.B.C. in an interview estimated time given to news reporting at about 2.0 per cent. *Cf.* Malcolm M. Willey and Stuart A. Rice, "Communication," *American Journal of Sociology,* May 1931, p. 975, note 37. Newspaper publishers and editors were less worried about radio competition in the news field, however, than in advertising, although newspaper critics such as Silas Bent were pointing out that radio by developing a device like an automatic parlor ticker-press, radio-operated, might make the ordinary newspaper obsolete. *Cf. Ballyhoo,* 1927, pp. 308f.

The limited number of broadcasting wave channels available; the control of access to these channels by the Federal Radio Commission; the centralized control of the existing broadcasting stations through the great broadcasting chains; and the dependence of broadcasting on the national advertiser have all combined to make radio function as an agency of stabilization and conservatism rather than of intellectual stimulation and social readjustment. While both the Democrats and the Republicans have utilized the radio extensively in every campaign since the Democrats tried the risky experiment of broadcasting their national convention in 1924, controversial questions, especially of the non-political kind, have ordinarily been taboo in radio. This tremendously powerful device, in other words, has functioned—in so far as it has been permitted to function at all in this direction—more as a means of organizing action by extending control of existing officials than as a means of organizing mind through discussion and the canvassing of alternatives. Toward the intelligent discussion of social problems such as birth control, the distribution of wealth, and the control of war, the radio in its first decade at least had contributed very little.

Yet because it does offer a channel by which personal leadership can reach into millions of homes, the radio and its newest development, television, may be expected to play a vital part in every social crisis in which mass action and mass organization are essential.[15]

Transportation as a Factor in Communication. Up to this point in our discussion of secondary techniques by which symbols are transferred we have confined ourselves to devices whose essential function is to transmit symbols and nothing else. Obviously, however, we live in a world in which the movement of goods and people is just as important as the transmission of symbols. Moreover, this movement which we call transportation is an essential element in communication, not merely in the sense that paper, for example, must be transported to the printing-presses and that the newspapers, magazines, and books in turn must be transported to their destinations, but in the sense that transportation of people and mail by steamship, railroad, bus, private auto,

[15] The Spanish Revolution, for example, in 1931 was proclaimed over the radio.

and airplane is in itself a way by which communication is carried on.

The volume of such movement is staggering and its social consequences are incalculable.

In 1930, for example, more than 200,000 Americans were travelling abroad, and a total of 446,214 aliens were admitted to the country while 272,425 departed.[16] Within the country, airplanes, inter-city busses, railways, and private automobiles rolled up more than 475 billion passenger-miles in 1931, the equivalent of the migration of the entire city of Philadelphia from the earth to the moon. The relative contribution of each means of transportation to this staggering total can be expressed as follows:

Airplane	1
Motor bus	70
Railroad	228
Automobile	4,655

The part played by the private automobile is the striking thing in this picture of a people in motion. According to the facts shown in Figure 7, private automobiles totalled 447,000,000,000 passenger-miles in 1931. In 1922 the total,[17] as estimated by the National Automobile Chamber of Commerce, was 80,000,000,000, or less than a fifth of the total a decade later. While railroad passenger-mileage had been declining year by year, automobile travel had been increasing.

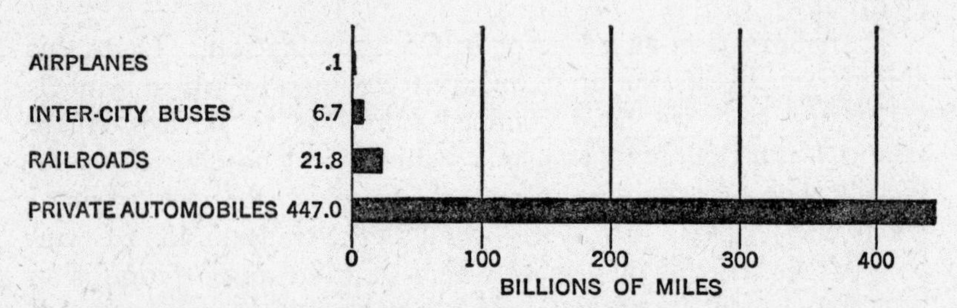

FIG. 7. Passenger Miles of Various Types of Carrier in the United States, 1931* (Billions of Miles).

* Except in the case of the airplane, for which the figures are those of 1930, given by Willey and Rice, *loc. cit.*, p. 971. The bus figure is taken from *Automobile Facts and Figures* (1932) and the railroad figure from *The Railroad Yearbook of Information* (1932). The private automobile figure is estimated by Professors Worley and Morrison of the Highway Engineering and Transport Department, University of Michigan.

16 Willey and Rice, *loc. cit.*, p. 971.

17 The number of passenger automobiles licensed in the United States in 1929 was 23,121,589; in 1922, 10,864,128; in 1915, 2,309,666; and in 1898, 800.

What this means is that Americans have been reshaping their travel habits, producing new institutions such as tourist camps, and modifying old institutions such as hotels, lodging houses, and hot dog stands. "Figures of the Department of Commerce for 1929 lead to an estimate of 110,000 wayside camps and refreshment stands in the country, of which 65,000 are permanent."[18] One result is a new problem of social control of the overnight stopping place. Another result that has come from the increased movement of women, thanks to the automobile and the touring complex, has been that the hotel proprietors have been driven to modify the furnishings of their establishments and in smaller communities greatly to improve their facilities. Increased fluidity is probably also the decisive factor in the peculiarly American habit of holding numerous conventions. In 1930 there were 15,653 conventions in the United States and Canada attended by 4,101,000 people.[19]

Much of this can be traced straight to the automobile. The relocation of population in and about our cities, the changing pattern of rural life, the exodus of the chaperone—in a thousand places the automobile is changing American culture and the forms of association.

The Enlargement of Association. Generally speaking the net result of all these devices for speeding up and enlarging communication has been to extend the range of human association in time and space. The stupendous consequences of this fact we shall have to examine more in detail in later chapters.

Summary. Cultural elaboration of communication, while it loses much of the expressiveness of pre-verbal symbols, vastly increases permanence, swiftness, and diffusion. From the start there are many non-verbal aids to expressiveness, valuable chiefly for transmitting sentiment and emotion. The invention of alphabetic writing about 1000 B.C. was the great decisive step toward permanence. Printing contributed mainly to diffusion. The more modern inventions have added to both speed and diffusion.

Mass organization of mind may be taken as the distinctive function of the press; extension of point-to-point control as the distinctive function of the telegraph and telephone; the mass diffusion of situations and of sentiment and personality-impressions

[18] Willey and Rice, *loc. cit.*, p. 969.
[19] *Loc. cit.*, p. 970.

as the distinctive functions of the motion picture and to some extent of the radio; while mobility and fluidity have been enormously increased by the railroad, the steamship, the airplane, and the automobile.

STUDY QUESTIONS

1. What do you understand by "secondary techniques of communication"? Would a set speech by a public speaker as part of a lecture programme be an example of primary or secondary techniques?
2. What are the four factors in communicative efficiency?
3. Explain how painting and sculpture increase the expressiveness of communication.
4. What are the stages in the evolution of writing?
5. Where and by whom was alphabetic writing invented?
6. What is the relation of writing to government? religion? literature? modern civilization?
7. Where and by whom was printing invented? Printing with movable types?
8. What great historical movement was significantly helped by printing?
9. What have been the effects of electricity and the machine on communication?
10. How many newspapers and magazines per month does the average family receive?
11. What are the three unique social functions of the newspaper?
12. What is the relation of point-to-point communication to the centralized organization of society?
13. How many people attend the motion-picture theatres every day?
14. In Washtenaw County, Michigan, in 1924 which social classes were attending most frequently? How much oftener does a business man go than a farmer?
15. What is the unique function of the motion picture and the radio?
16. What three groups of critics are especially critical of the average American movie?
17. What percentage of homes had radio sets in 1930? How did distribution vary as between New Jersey and Mississippi?
18. What factors decrease the effectiveness of the radio as a means of communication?
19. "The radio functions as an agency of stabilization and conservatism rather than of intellectual stimulation and social readjustment." Discuss critically. Why has this trend appeared?

20. What evidence can you think of to show the effect of the automobile on social habits and customs?
21. What has been the net effect of the cultural elaboration of communication?

CHAPTER XIII

PERSONALITY IN THE MODERN WORLD

How the Modern World Differs from the Old. The general character of the change which modern communication has wrought in human life is well expressed by the two words *enlargement* and *animation.* Social contacts are extended in space and quickened in time. The individual is broadened by coming into relation with a larger and more various life, and he is kept stirred up, sometimes to excess, by the multitude of changing stimuli which this life brings him.

It is a question of utmost interest whether these changes do or do not contribute to the independence and productivity of the individual mind. Do they foster a self-reliant personality, capable at need of pursuing high and rare aims, or have they rather a levelling tendency, repressive of what is original and characteristic?

Modern Communication and Individuality. Before the advent of modern communication most of the stimuli affecting a person came from local sources. This resulted in what we call provincialism. The individuality thus produced was of an involuntary sort, such as is evidenced by local dialects, local costumes, and local manners. Even today the mountain people of those sections of the South not yet reached by the new communication exhibit these types of individuality, perhaps better called peculiarities. And it is these things that make many European villages seem so picturesque. The opportunities are few, however, under this local régime for personal development along lines of special interest. The difficulties of getting in touch with others having similar tastes and thus building up a significant individuality are almost insurmountable. Thus the former situation fostered little individuality on the level of personal function, the only exception being where a particular art or craft was handed down locally, perhaps in a single family line.

Under modern communication stimuli are borne in upon us from great distances so that we are vital members of a much larger life. Whether or not this is productive of more individuality is a difficult question upon which eminent writers have different opinions.

It is clear that the local peculiarities of dress and dialect are disappearing. The talking pictures will have a great influence in standardizing speech, while women's fashions and many other things of ordinary consumption are already dictated from centres of dominance. Certainly a great deal is thus lost in the way of local color and atmosphere, of the racy flavor of isolated personalities and unconscious picturesqueness of social types. The diversities of dress, language, and culture, which were developed in Europe during the Middle Ages, when each little barony was the channel of peculiar traditions, can hardly reappear. Nor can we expect, in modern cities, the sort of architectural individuality we find in those of Italy, built when each village was a distinct social and political unit.

One might suppose, however, that on the level of personal function individuality would be increased. Modern communication makes it easier to get away from a given environment and to find support in one more congenial. The world has grown more various and at the same time more accessible, so that one having a natural bent should be the more able to find influences to nourish it. If he has a turn, say, for entomology, he can readily, through journals, correspondence, and meetings, get in touch with a group of men similarly inclined, and with a congenial tradition. And so with any sect of religion, politics, art, or what not; if there are in the civilized world a few like-minded people it is comparatively easy for them to get together in spirit and encourage one another in their special interest.

Something of this may be seen in the traditional contrast between cities and rural areas, the latter having more of the individuality springing from isolation, the former that springing from choice. The individuality of the city is less picturesque but perhaps more functional. There is more facility for the formation of specialized groups, and so for the fostering of special capacities. Notwithstanding the din of communication and trade, the cities are, for this reason, the chief seats of productive originality in art, science, and letters.

The difference is analogous to that between the development of natural species on islands or other isolated areas, and on a wide and traversable continent. The former produces many quaint species, like the kangaroos, which disappear when brought into contact with more capable types; but the continent by no means brings about uniformity. It engenders, rather, a complex relationship of related species and varieties, each of which is comparatively perfect in its special way; and has become so through the very fact of a wider struggle for existence.

Thus easy communication of ideas favors differentiation of a rational and functional sort, as distinguished from the random variations fostered by isolation. And it must be remembered that any sort is rational and functional that really commends itself to the human spirit. Even revolt from an ascendant type is easier now than formerly, because the rebel can fortify himself with the triumphant records of the non-conformers of the past.

Where men care to assert themselves, then, our new communication gives them greater opportunities for the development of individuality. In those aspects of their lives, however, which they do not feel particularly significant, they save their energies by conformity. It is this latter which has sired the ogre of standardization. Faced by the task of adapting to a more complex life and handicapped by the confusion of a new era, men have perhaps not had sufficient energy to choose with regard to all the significant matters, but have fallen back upon standardization. The criticism is especially pertinent with respect to ideas outside our own special interests. It is frequently said, and probably with some justice, that there is coming to be mass production of ideas as well as of material goods. The newspaper and the radio are particularly powerful agencies in this direction. Thus it may be that modern communication, though fostering functional individuality with respect to special interests, is creating so complicated a life as to frustrate it in other directions.

The action of the new communication is essentially stimulating, and so may, in some of its phases, be injurious. It costs the individual more in the way of mental function to take a normal part in the new order of things than it did in the old. Fortunately, from this point of view, our mental life is inclined to be rather sluggish, so that the spur of modern intercourse is for the most part wholesome, awakening the mind, abating sensuality, and giving men idea and purpose. Such ill effect as may be ascribed to it seems to fall chiefly under two heads, superficiality and strain, which are simply the evils which correspond to enlargement and animation.

Superficiality. There is a rather general agreement among observers that, outside of his specialty, the man of our somewhat hurried civilization is likely to have an impatient, touch-and-go habit of mind as regards both thought and feeling. We are trying to do many and various things, and are driven to versatility and short cuts at some expense of truth and depth. Ostrogorski, for instance, thinks that deliverance from the bonds of space and time has made the American a man of short views, wedded to the present, accustomed to getting quick returns, and with no deep root anywhere.[1]

In this matter, as in so many others, we should discriminate, so far as we can, between permanent conditions of modern life and what is due merely to the difficult transition from the older order. There is nothing in the nature of modern communication to prevent our social order from attaining an equilibrium of its own, though perhaps a moving one, with great advantage to our spiritual composure and productivity. In the meanwhile, it is beyond doubt that the constant and varied stimulus of a confused time makes sustained attention difficult. Certainly our newspapers and our popular literature are written for those who run as they read, and carry the principle of economy of attention beyond anything previously imagined. And in feeling it seems to be true that we tend toward a somewhat superficial kindliness and adaptability rather than a sustained passion of any kind. Generally speaking, mind is spread out very thin over our civilization; a good sort of mind, no doubt, but quite thin.

All this may be counteracted in various ways, especially by a thoroughness in education which would enable one to select for his careful attention the truly significant aspects of life, letting much that is trivial go by. Our trouble is perhaps to be regarded as a lack of maturity rather than an incurable defect.

Strain. Nervous strain, in spite of the alarming opinions sometimes expressed, is by no means a general condition in modern society, nor likely to become so; it is confined to a relatively small number, in whom individual weaknesses, or unusual stresses, or both, have rendered life too much for the spirit. Yet this number includes a great part of those who perform the more exacting in-

[1] *Democracy and the Organization of Political Parties*, ii, 579–88.

tellectual functions in business and the professions, as well as peculiarly weak, or sensitive, or unfortunate individuals in all walks of life. In general, there is an increase of self-consciousness and choice; there is more opportunity, more responsibility, more complexity, a greater burden on intelligence, will, and character. The individual not only can but must deal with a flood of urgent stimuli or be swamped by them.

Worse, probably, than anything in the way of work—though that is often destructive—is the anxious insecurity in which our changing life keeps a large part of the population, the well-to-do as well as the poor. Mr. H. D. Sedgwick in his study *The New American Type* which was based upon English and American portraits, some recent, some a century old, found that the more recent were conspicuously marked by the signs of unrest and strain. It is what we feel when we compare the people of Jane Austen with those, let us say, of Sinclair Lewis.

Another but probably more temporary source of strain is the conflict of culture which has been brought on through modern communication. The old, simple life has been superseded by one of much greater complexity, but the new organization is not yet mature. The result is that things are not well integrated, institutions are working at cross-purposes, and a person may find himself called upon to follow one set of standards in business, another at home, and a third in his recreational group. Not only has modern communication upset the former small community organization with its integrated institutions, but it also makes it easier for the person to ally himself with many groups. Thus the chance for conflict is even further enhanced. Inasmuch as there is a natural trend toward consistency in men's behavior, this situation of clashing standards and obligations introduces considerable strain. It will disappear only when our modern complex organization reaches a mature, even if moving, equilibrium.

The effects of strain may be seen in an increase of certain distinctly pathological phenomena. Most authorities believe that drug addiction, for instance, is becoming more prevalent in the United States. The number of persons per 100,000 being cared for in state hospitals for the insane rose from 204.2 in 1910 to 220.1 in 1920 and to 226.9 in 1927.[2] Though much of this increase is prob-

[2] H. M. Pollock, "State Institution Population Still Increasing," *Mental Hygiene*, XII, 103.

ably due to better diagnosis and stricter hospitalization, it is highly probable that some of it indicates an actually more frequent incidence of mental disease. The figures on suicide tell much the same story. On this point we cannot use the United States statistics because they have not been gathered long enough to give reliable trends, but all the European countries with the exception of Norway, Denmark, Germany, and Switzerland have shown marked increases since 1871.

Partly because of these signs of severe strain, many thoughtful people have welcomed the mental hygiene movement, which, since its inception in this country in 1909, has spread throughout the civilized world. Child guidance clinics, visiting teachers whose function is to aid problem children, mental health units in high schools, colleges, and industrial plants, and psychiatric social work are some of the many agencies which are fostering the aims of this movement.

Selection in the Mental Life. Under modern conditions, then, each one of us has, as a rule, a wider grasp of situations, and is thus in a position to give a wider application to his intelligence, sympathetic insight, and conscience. In proportion as he does this he ceases to be a blind agent and becomes a rational member of the whole. Because of this more conscious relation to the larger wholes,—nations, institutions, tendencies,—he takes a more vital and personal part in them.

At the same time, the limits of human faculty make it impossible that any one of us should actually occupy all the field of thought thus open to him. Although stimulated to greater activity than before, one must constantly select and renounce; and most of his life will still be on the plane of custom and mechanism. He is freer chiefly in that he can survey the larger whole and choose in what relations he will express himself.

Indeed, an ever-present danger of the new order is that one will not select and renounce enough, that he will swallow more than he can properly digest, and fail of the benefits of a thorough unconscious assimilation. These conditions demand that our educational system teach us to do some one thing well and at the same time lead us always to see the relation of that one thing to other aspects of the general life.

Modern Communication and Finer Achievement. Perhaps the supreme test of the efficacy of modern communication as it affects personality is whether or not it encourages the finer sorts of intellectual achievement. If, though giving the opportunity for a greater functional individuality, this is more than offset by superficiality and strain, we are condemned to an abundance of mediocrity but a dearth of true greatness. The answer to this question can hardly be sought in close induction from fact but must be formed on the basis of the broad principles at work in modern life.

There can be little doubt that America, where modern communication has had its greatest development, has been deficient in the production of great writers and artists. But in this, as in all discussion of contemporary tendency, we need to discriminate between modern communication and the transition which has followed from it. If America's weakness in finer intellectual achievement can plausibly be laid to temporary conditions flowing from transition, we may expect that these deficiencies will be made up when we become fully adjusted to modern communication.

It is true, as we shall see later, that modern communication provides some of the most essential conditions for democracy and that democracy, by demanding open opportunity and resisting hereditary stratification, will probably maintain a competition among persons more general, and as regards personal status more unsettling, than we have had in former times. But personal competition is the cause of only a small part of the stress and disorder of our time; much more being due to general changes in the social system, particularly in industry, which we may describe as transition. And moreover, competition itself is in a specially disordered or transitional state at present, and will be less disquieting when a more settled state of society permits it to be carried on under established rules of justice. In order to indicate the strength of the forces of transition we will discuss them under three separate heads: confusion, haste, and commercialism.

Confusion. With reference to æsthetic culture, not only the United States, but in some degree contemporary civilization in general, is a confused, a raw, society. Modern communication and the factory have disorganized the old institutions and the new ones are not yet perfected. It is our whole newspaper and factory epoch that is crude, and scarcely more so in America than in England or Germany. The main difference in favor of European countries is that the present cannot so easily be separated from the conditions of an earlier culture. The person seeking the finest sort of development is handicapped by this confusion in two ways.

First, the stream of culture in which he works and which he tries to express is immature. Works of enduring greatness depend, among other things, upon a certain ripeness of historical conditions. No matter how gifted an individual may be, he is in no way apart from his time, but has to take that and make the best of it as he can; the man of genius is in one point of view only a twig upon which a mature tendency bears its perfect fruit. In the new epoch the vast things in process are as yet so unfinished that individual gifts are scarce sufficient to bring anything to a classical completeness. The ideals themselves which a great art should express share in the general incompleteness of things and do not present themselves to the mind clearly defined and incarnate in vivid symbols. Perhaps a certain fragmentariness and pettiness in contemporary art and literature is due more to this cause than to any other—to the fact that the aspirations of the time are too much obscured to be clearly and steadily regarded. Americans may believe in democracy, for example, but it can hardly be said that they *see* democracy, as the Middle Ages, in their art, saw the Christian religion.

Secondly, confusion means that the aspiring individual does not receive the benefit of mature, specialized groups. What is involved may, perhaps, be made clearer by a comparison drawn from athletics. We find in our colleges that to produce a winning football team, or distinguished performance in track and field events, it is essential first of all to have a spirit of intense interest in these things, which shall arouse the ambition of those having natural gifts, support them in their training and reward their success. Without this group spirit no efficient organization, no high standard of achievement, can exist, and a small institution that has this will easily surpass a large one that lacks it. And experience shows that it takes much time to perfect such a spirit and the organization through which it is expressed.

In quite the same way any ripe development of productive power in literary or other art implies not merely capable persons but the perfection of a social group, whose traditions and spirit the individual absorbs, and which floats him up to a point where he can reach unique achievement. The unity of this group is mental, not necessarily local or temporal, and so may be difficult to trace, but its reality is as sure as the principle that man is a social being and cannot think sanely and steadfastly except in some sort of sympathy with his fellows. There must be others whom we can conceive as sharing, corroborating and enhancing our ideals, and to no one is such association more necessary than to the man of genius.

The group is likely to be more apparent in some arts than in others: it is generally quite evident in painting, sculpture, architecture, and music, where a regular development by the passage of inspiration from one artist to another can almost always be traced. In literature the connections are less obvious, chiefly because this art is in its methods more disengaged from time and place, so that it is easier to draw inspiration from distant sources.

It is readily seen that American conditions have not fostered groups of this character. Our most notable group of writers—flourishing at Concord and Boston about 1850—was connected with the maturing in partial isolation, of a local type of culture, which is now disintegrated and dispersed on the wider currents of the time.[3] Since the Civil War we have had a continuance of the westward movement, the movement from country to city, the development of large-scale industry with all the problems of displacement which it has involved, to say nothing of the headlong mixture of races, temperaments, and traditions that comes from the new immigration of peoples from the south and east of Europe. On top of all this we have had the turmoil of an economic system slowly and painfully outgrowing its governing philosophy, *laissez faire.*

From this point of view of groups and organization it is easy to understand why the "rugged individualism" of our epoch does not necessarily produce great individuality. Individual assertion may be aggressive and yet futile, because not based upon the training afforded by group organization—like the fruitless valor of an isolated, untrained soldier. It is this lack of differentiated "schools" of thought which underlies that comparative uniformity of American life which wearies the visitor from other shores. If we have a thousand towns, ten thousand churches, and a million homes built upon the same models and if our people and our institutions do not altogether escape a similar poverty of types, it is largely because we have not had sufficient opportunity for mu-

[3] *Cf.* Lewis Mumford, *The Golden Day.*

tual stimulation and support in artistic and intellectual groups. An old civilization has from its mere antiquity a richness and complexity of spiritual life that cannot be transplanted to a new world. The immigrants bring with them the traditions of which they feel in immediate need, such as those necessary to found the state, the church, and the family; but even these lose some of their original flavor, while much of what is subtler and less evidently useful is left behind. We must remember, too, that the arts in the Old World are chiefly the culture of a class, and that the immigrants have mostly come from a class that had no great part in it.

In short, our world lacks maturity of æsthetic and intellectual organization. What we sometimes call—truly enough as regards our economic life—our complex civilization is simple to the point of poverty in spiritual structure. We have cast off much rubbish and decay and are preparing, we may reasonably hope, to produce an art and literature worthy of our vigor and aspiration, but in the past, certainly, we have hardly done so.

Haste. Modern communication has brought in its train another condition, haste, which, with the superficiality and strain which attend upon it, is widely and insidiously destructive of good work in our day. This characteristic we may also come to condemn and avoid as our civilization becomes more mature. But in the meantime no other condition of mind or of society—not ignorance, poverty, oppression, or hate—kills art as haste does. Almost any phase of life may be ennobled if there is only calm enough in which the brooding mind may do its perfect work upon it; but out of hurry nothing noble ever did or can emerge. In art human nature should come to a total, adequate expression; a spiritual tendency should be perfected and recorded in calmness and joy. But ours is, on the whole, a time of stress, of the habit of incomplete work; its products are unlovely and unrestful and such as the future will have no joy in.

It is, to put the matter otherwise, a *loud* time. The newspapers, advertising, the radio, have an effect of din, so that one feels that he must raise his voice to be heard, and the whispers of the gods are hard to catch. Men whose voices are naturally low and fine easily lose this trait in our world and begin to shout like the rest. That is to say, they exaggerate and repeat and advertise and caricature, saying too much in the hope that a little may be heard. Of course in the long run this is a fatal delusion; nothing will really be listened to except that whose quiet truth makes it worth hearing; but it is one so rooted in the general state of things that few escape it. Even those who preserve the lower tone do so with an effort which is in itself disquieting.

Our strenuous state of mind comes mainly from having too many things to think of, from the urgency and distraction of an epoch and a country in which the traditional structures that support the mind and save its energy have largely gone to pieces. The endeavor to supply by will functions that in other conditions would be automatic creates a rush which imitation renders epidemic, and from which it is not easy to escape in order to mature one's powers in fruitful quiet.

The modern artist has too much choice. If he attempts to deal largely with life, his will is overworked at the expense of æsthetic synthesis. The result in most cases is, as has been said of architecture, "confusion of types . . ., an evident breathlessness of effort and striving for effect, with the inevitable loss of repose, dignity, and style."[4] A mediæval cathedral or a Greek temple was the culmination of a long social growth, a gradual, deliberate corporate achievement, to which the individual talent added only the finishing touch. The modern architect has, no doubt, as much personal ability, but the demands upon it are excessive; it would seem that only a transcendent synthetic genius of the calibre of Dante would deal adequately with our scattered conditions.

Commercialism. By commercialism, in this connection, we may understand a preoccupation of the ability of the people with material production and with the trade and finance based upon it. This is in part not a result of modern communication even indirectly, but of our character as a new country with stumps to get out and material civilization to erect from the ground up. In part, however, it flows from the increased emphasis upon business which the world markets opened up by transportation have brought about. In so far as it is due to this latter cause we may expect that we shall gradually get used to a world economic structure and that business services will come to receive no more than their share of attention.

The result at present is that ability finds a constant opportunity and incitement to take a commercial direction, and little, to follow

[4] Henry Van Brunt, *Greek Lines*, p. 225.

pure art or letters. A man likes to succeed in something, and if he is conscious of the capacity to make his way in business or professional life, he is indisposed to endure the poverty, uncertainty, and indifference which attend the pursuit of an artistic calling.

An even greater peril is the debasing of art by an uneducated market. There seem to be plenty of artists of every kind, but their standard of success is mostly low. The beginner too early gets commercial employment in which he is not held up to any high ideal. This brings us back to the lack of a well-knit artistic tradition to educate both the artist and the public. This lack involves the weakness of the criticism which is required to make the artist see himself as he ought to be.

The antipathy between art and the commercial spirit, however, is often much overstated. As a matter of history, art and literature have flourished most conspicuously in prosperous commercial societies, such as Athens, Florence, Venice, the communes of the thirteenth and fourteenth centuries, the trading cities of Germany, the Dutch Republic, and the England of Elizabeth. Nothing does more than commerce to awaken intelligence and enterprise. It is only the extreme one-sidedness of our civilization in this regard that is prejudicial.

It would seem, then, that conditions of transition furnish ample reason for our poor showing in art and literature. There is at least a strong probability that we shall become adjusted in a more mature way to modern communication and that when we do our capable personalities will find conditions congenial to the development of their talents.

STUDY QUESTIONS

1. What is the difference in emphasis which sets off this chapter from the one preceding? from the one succeeding?
2. Do you think *enlargement* and *animation* accurately describe the change in life wrought by modern communication? Draw on your experience with contemporary life for proof of your view.
3. What sort of individuality is produced by provincialism?
4. Discuss the effect of modern communication upon individuality. Do you think the view taken in the text is borne out by the differences between city people and those of isolated rural areas?

5. Do you think standardization is likely to go beyond its true function in modern life?
6. What are the causes for the superficiality so common today? What remedy can you suggest?
7. Does contemporary life overstimulate the individual? What causes of strain can you mention?
8. What is the mental hygiene movement?
9. Discuss modern communication and transition as possible causes of the inferior achievement of America in art and literature.
10. In what two ways are American writers and artists handicapped by confusion?
11. Explain: "Individualism may not be conducive to the production of great individuality."
12. In what ways are haste and commercialism hostile to æsthetic achievement?

CHAPTER XIV

THE ENLARGEMENT OF MEN'S MINDS

We Begin to Lift Our Eyes Above Foundations. We have now sketched some of the foundation-stones of our everyday social world—*human heredity, communication, human nature,* the *primary group, culture*—and we have seen also how the modern enlargement of communication has borne down on the individual through increased superficiality, strain, haste, and confusion. It is now time to turn our attention to the broader picture—the larger outlines of the social structure that stands on these foundations. We must see how on the basis of writing, printing, railroads, steamships, newspapers—in short, on writing, electricity, and the machine—human association has grown out of the old primary group that enclosed it in the beginning until now we find it organized in communities, regions, states, nations, and finally the world market. We must see how along with this stupendous growth has gone an increasing specialization and differentiation of classes, and how all this has reacted on those larger adjustment-patterns called institutions. And finally, we must see that in and through all this expansion of association and culture *what has really been expanding has been men's minds,* the range and depth and tempo of their social consciousness. This is so important for an understanding of the other changes which have occurred that we propose to devote a chapter to it here, since only in the light of this enlargement of human thought and feeling is it possible to see the real significance of modern public opinion, the community, the region, the nation, the world market, the modern class struggle, and the modern complexities of institutions.

Narrow Range of Early Group Consciousness. Many primitive tribes have almost no association beyond that of primary groups. For instance, the family, clan, and small village groups constituted all the social organization possessed by the Teutonic peoples before they took on Roman civilization. Within this narrow circle there was a vivid interchange of thought and feeling, a sphere of sympathy, loyalty, honor, and congenial intercourse. Here precious traditions were cherished, and here also was the field for an active public opinion, for discussion, leadership, conformity, and dissent.

When we say that public opinion is modern, we mean, of course, the wider and more elaborate forms of it. On a smaller scale group opinion has always existed where people have had a chance to discuss and act upon matters of common interest. Among our American Indians, for example, opinion was a most potent factor in all tribes, and this would be largely directed by those having popularity and power. Officers, in fact all persons, became extremely well known in the small community of an Amerind tribe. Every peculiarity of temperament was understood, and the individual was respected or despised according to his predominating characteristics.[1] The Germanic tribes were accustomed to assemble in those village moots to which the historian recurs with such reverence, where "the men from whom Englishmen were to spring learned the worth of public opinion, of public discussion, the worth of the agreement, the 'common sense' to which discussion leads, as of the laws which derive their force from being expression of that general conviction."[2]

Group opinion based on discussion, as every one knows, will appear among children wherever they mingle freely. Indeed, it springs directly from human nature, and is so difficult to suppress even by the most inquisitorial methods, that we may assume it to exist locally in all forms of society and at all periods of history. It grows by looks and gestures where speech is forbidden, so that even in a prison there is a group opinion among the inmates. But in tribal life these local groups contained all the vivid and conscious society there was, the lack of means of record and quick transmission making a wider unity impracticable.

In tribal life, then, group consciousness could be only local in scope. Beyond its narrow range the cords which held life together were of a subconscious character—heredity, of course, with its freight of mental and social tendency; oral tradition, often vague and devious, and a mass of custom which was revered without being understood. These wider relations, not being surveyed and discussed, could not be the objects of deliberate thought and will,

[1] F. S. Dellenbaugh, *The North Americans of Yesterday*, p. 416.
[2] J. R. Green, *History of the English People*, Vol. I, 13.

but were accepted as part of the necessary order of things, and usually ascribed to some divine source. In this way language, laws, religion, forms of government, social classes, traditional relations to other clans and tribes—all of which we know to have been built up by the cumulative workings of the human mind—were thought of as beyond the sphere of man's control.

The Problem of Enlarging Association. The problem of enlarging human association beyond the primary group has been mainly one of inventing more adequate mechanisms of (*a*) communication and (*b*) organization to extend the area of unity and co-operation without at the same time sacrificing the chief values of face-to-face association, namely, the realization of primary ideals.

Communication must be full and quick in order to give that promptness in the give-and-take of ideas and sentiments upon which unity depends. Gesture and speech insure this in the face-to-face group; but only the recent marvelous improvement of communicative machinery makes large groups organized on a free basis even conceivable. If there is no means of working thought and sentiment into a whole by reciprocation, the unity of the group cannot be other than inert and unhuman. This cause alone would account for the lack of extended freedom previous to the nineteenth century.

But in addition to quick and full communication there must also be forms and customs of rational organization, through which human nature may express itself in an orderly and effective manner. Even children learn the need of regular discussion and decision, while all bodies of adults meeting for deliberation find that they can think organically only by observance of the rules which have been worked out for such occasions. And if we are to have great and stable nations, it is easy to see that these rules of order must become a body of law and custom including most, if not all, of the familiar institutions of society. These are as much the product of progressive invention, trial, and survival as are the railroad and the factory, and they have in the long run the same purpose, that of the fuller expression of human nature in a social system.

Growth Through History of Social Consciousness. *The central fact of history, from a psychological point of view, may be said to be the gradual enlargement of social consciousness and* *rational co-operation.* Human nature, possessed of ideals moulded in the family and the commune, is ever striving, somewhat blindly for the most part, with those difficulties of communication and organization which obstruct their realization on a larger scale.

Throughout European history, at least, there has been an evident extension of the local areas within which communication and co-operation prevail, and, on the whole, an advance in the quality of co-operation as judged by an ideal unity. It has tended to become more and more free and human, more adequately expressive of communal feeling.

Perhaps all apparent departures from this tendency may plausibly be explained as cases of irregular growth. If we find that vast systems of discipline, like the Roman Empire, have broken down, we find also that these systems were of a low type, psychologically, that the best features of them were after all preserved, and the new systems that arose, though perhaps less in extent, were on the whole a higher and fuller expression of human nature.

In the later Empire, for example, it seems plain that social mechanism (in its proper kind and measure one of the conditions of freedom) had grown in such a way as to shackle the human mind. In order to achieve and maintain an imperial reach of control, the state had gradually been forced to take on a centralized bureaucratic structure, which left the individual and the local group no sphere of self-reliant development. Public spirit and political leadership were suppressed, and the habit of organized self-expression died out, leaving the people without group vitality and as helpless as children. They were not, in general, cowards or voluptuaries—it seems that the decline of courage and domestic morals has been exaggerated—but they had no trained and effective public capacity.

Opposition Between Freedom and Expansion. The growing states of the earlier world were confronted, then, whether they knew it or not, with an irreconcilable opposition between freedom and expansion. They might retain in small areas simple and popular institutions which nearly all the great people started with, and to which they owed their vigor; or they could organize on a larger scale a more mechanical unity. In the first case their careers were brief, because they lacked the military force to ensure permanence in a hostile world. In the latter they incurred, by the suppression of human nature, that degeneracy which sooner or later overtook every great state of antiquity.

The decay of the ancient and mediæval republics illustrates the failure which followed upon the embracing of the first alternative. They were too small to hold their own in a world that was necessarily, for the most part, autocratic or customary. Freedom, though itself a principle of strength, was on too little a scale to defend itself. The other horn of the dilemma resulted in deterioration by growth. If the small state grew in size, power, and diversity by the necessities of its struggles for existence—as did Rome, Athens, and a hundred other states—it sacrificed human nature to military expediency and developed a mechanical or despotic structure. This, in the long run, produced weakness, decay, and conquest, or perhaps revolt and revolution. The requirements of human nature—both direct, as expressed in social idealism, and indirect, as felt in the ultimate weakness and failure of systems which disregard them—are irrepressible. Montesquieu summed the whole matter up neatly when he said, "If a republic be small, it is destroyed by a foreign force; if it be large, it is ruined by internal imperfection."[3]

This was theoretically the prospect when the United States was formed. At the close of the eighteenth century public consciousness of any active kind was confined to small localities. Travel was slow, uncomfortable, and costly, and people undertaking a considerable journey often made their wills beforehand. The newspapers, appearing weekly in the larger towns, were entirely lacking in what we should call news; and the number of letters sent during a year in all the thirteen states was much less than that now handled by the New York office in a single day. People are far more alive today to what is going on in China, if it happens to interest them, than they were then to events a hundred miles away. The isolation of even the large towns from the rest of the world, and the consequent introversion of men's minds upon local concerns, was something we can hardly conceive. In the country "the environment of the farm was the neighborhood; the environment of the village was the encircling farms and the local tradition; few conventions assembled for discussion and common action; educational centres did not radiate the shock of a new intellectual life to every hamlet; federations and unions did not bind

[3] *The Spirit of the Laws,* Book IX, Chap. I

men, near and remote, into that fellowship that makes one composite type of man. It was an age of sects, intolerant from lack of acquaintance."[4]

In such a world it was no wonder that the United States Government, under the Constitution, was not in any sense a democracy and was not intended to be such by the men who framed it. It was expected to be a representative republic, the people choosing men of character and wisdom, who would proceed to the capital, inform themselves there upon current questions, and deliberate and decide regarding them. That the people might think and act more directly was not foreseen. The Constitution is not democratic in spirit, and, as Bryce has noted,[5] might under different conditions have become the basis of an aristocratic system.

That any system could have held even the original thirteen states in firm union without the advent of modern communication is very doubtful. Political philosophy, from Plato to Montesquieu, had taught that free states must be small, and Frederick the Great is said to have ridiculed the idea of one extending from Maine to Georgia.

Such democracy as the United States has achieved has arisen not, chiefly, because of changes in the formal Constitution, but as the outcome of conditions which make it natural for the people to have and to express a consciousness regarding questions of the day. It is said by those who know China that while that country was at war with Japan in 1894–95 the majority of the Chinese were unaware that a war was in progress. Obviously such ignorance makes the sway of public opinion impossible.

Communication and Democracy. If today, then, over much of the western world there is general awareness of public questions and an active attempt of great populations to deal with them more or less directly, the main cause must be sought in modern communication. It is modern communication that has rid us of the old dilemma between extension and freedom. If in turn it has created other dilemmas of its own, as we shall see in later chapters, that after all is the usual history of change. Over wide areas at least modern communication has made possible public opinion, which, when organized, produces national democracy. The whole growth of this is immediately dependent upon the telegraph, the

[4] W. L. Anderson, *The Country Town*, pp. 209–210.
[5] *The American Commonwealth*, Ch. 26.

newspaper, and the fast mail, for there can be no public opinion upon questions of the day except as the people are promptly informed of such questions and are enabled to exchange views regarding them.

The effect of all this goes far beyond politics. One is often impressed with the thought that there ought to be some wider name for the modern movement than democracy, which smacks so strongly of politics; some name which would more distinctly suggest the enlargement and quickening of the general mind, of which the formal rule of the people is only one among many manifestations. If we here use the term democracy for this more generic idea we must understand by it *a social system in which the self-expression of all the people plays an increasing part.* This clearly is not limited merely to a certain form of political organization.[6] As literature and daily life bear witness, it finds expression in many other fields.

From this point of view democracy is much more than the mere political accompaniment of the rise of the middle class, as some critics have contended. It is an expression of a certain level of communication and social organization and as such may persist in some form, whatever its political fortunes, so long as the underlying communicative techniques are available.[7]

The Growth of the Group-Self—Nationality. If modern communication has made democracy possible, it has also contributed strongly to that somewhat mystical extension of self-feeling known as nationality.

The group self, or "we," is simply an "I" which includes other persons. One identifies himself with a group and speaks of the common will, opinion, service, or the like in terms of "we" and "us." The sense of it is stimulated by co-operation within and opposition without. A family that has had to struggle with economic difficulties usually develops solidarity—"We paid off the mortgage," "We sent the boys to college," and the like. Indeed primary groups, simply because the members have many interests in common, are usually characterized by a "we" feeling. On a larger scale, a student identifies himself with his university when it is performing a social function of some kind, especially when it is contending in games with other institutions. "We beat Wiscon-

[6] Distinctions should be drawn between democracy as a form of government, as a method of conducting affairs through discussion, etc., and as a way of life.

[7] For further discussion see Chapter XXII, below.

sin," he says. Those who remained at home during the World War tell how "we" entered the war in 1917, how "we" fought decisively in the Argonne, and so on.

A nation, then, is a group of people numerous enough to be politically self-sustaining—although they may not actually be independent—who have a strong sense of "we" usually produced by a common social heritage of language, literature, traditions, customs, and are at the same time aware of the nation's unlikeness to other nations. It is a notable fact that the national self, indeed any group self, can be felt only in relation to a larger society, just as the individual self is felt only in relation to other individuals. We could have no patriotism unless we were aware of other nations and of our relationship to them.

Modern nations have been made possible by modern communication.[8] The members of such large groups could not be brought to feel as one without constant information concerning those outside the "we" group as well as those within it. The European peasant of 200 years ago thought in terms of local "we" groups, but had no conception of himself as an Englishman or a Frenchman. It was with the revolutionary awakening of the French people in 1789 to their unity as Frenchmen and not mere subjects of the French crown that nationalism started on its world march which has not yet ended. Most of the political history of the nineteenth century was dominated by nationalism: the liberation of Greece, the unification of Italy, the unification of Germany, the American Civil War, the turmoil in the Balkans, the emotional preparation for the World War—all these were the direct expressions of nationalism. For practical purposes, nationalism emerged from the World War as the dominant religion of western Europe and the United States, a religion that is even now disrupting the ancient Orient and threatening Europe with new wars.

It is obvious, of course, that the people who feel their identity as a nation and the political state which they may or may not control are two quite different things. The political state is a territory controlled by a single government. The "we" group, or nation, may correspond to this, but it need not and frequently does not. Thus, Poland maintained its nationality for more than a hundred

[8] Nationality as an ideal is, of course, much older. Thus Rose in his *Nationality in Modern History*, p. 9, speaks of Dante as the "father of Italian nationalism." English nationalism is sometimes traced back to the attack by the Armada in 1588.

years, from 1795 to 1918, without having any political existence at all. Similarly one government may include several nations, as the Austro-Hungarian Empire before the World War, and as Jugoslavia today. It was one of President Wilson's principles at the close of the World War that nationalities should have political self-determination, but this is a difficult principle to effectuate because national groups overlap and interpenetrate territorially.

Nationality and international organization are not in opposition, as so many thoughtlessly assume. We do not have less loyalty to our families simply because we are also loyal to our communities and our nation. A fraternity man is not on that account any less of an enthusiast for his university. In fact the smaller groups usually foster devotion to the larger. The effect of a definitely organized society of nations, in whose activities all took a generous interest, would be, not to diminish patriotism, but to raise its character, to make it more vivid, continuous, varied, and sympathetic. It would be like the self-consciousness of an intelligent individual in constant and friendly intercourse with others, as contrasted with the brutal self-assertion of one who knows his fellows only as the objects of suspicion and hostility. The patriotism of the past has been of the latter kind, and we have hardly considered its higher possibilities. The national "we" can and should be a self of real honor, service, and humane aspiration.

It is probably futile, however, to hope for one world state, since one of the prime requisites for "we" feeling is outside opposition, and this would be lacking. Temporary causes such as a world-wide insect pest or the return of the ice ages would undoubtedly bring all men to co-operate and feel loyalty to a common whole, but with the disappearance of the cause the group self would also probably disappear. We shall in all likelihood have to be content with nations motivated by high ideals working together as best they can in an international organization.

Enlargement of Feeling. We have already hinted that the enlargement effected through modern communication influences not only thought but feeling, favoring the growth of a sense of common humanity, of moral unity, between nations, races, classes. Among members of a communicating whole feeling may not always be friendly, but it must involve sympathetic insight. Even the animosities of modern nations are of a human and imaginative sort, not the blind animal hostility of a more primitive age.

The relations between persons or communities that are without mutual understanding are necessarily on a low plane. A really human fellow-feeling was anciently confined within the tribe, men outside not being felt as members of a common whole. The alien was commonly treated as a more or less useful or dangerous animal—destroyed, despoiled, enslaved. Even in these days we care little about people whose life is not brought home to us by some kind of sympathetic contact. We may read statistics of the miserable life of the Italians or Jews in New York or Chicago; of bad housing, sweatshops, and tuberculosis; but we care little more about them than we do about the sufferers from the Black Death, unless their life is realized to us in some human way, either by personal contact, or by pictures and imaginative description.

The work of communication in enlarging human nature is partly immediate, through facilitating contact, but even more it is indirect, through favoring the increase of intelligence, the decline of mechanical and arbitrary forms of organization, and the rise of a more humane type of society. History may be regarded as a record of the struggle of man to realize his aspirations through organization; and the new communication is an efficient tool for this purpose. Assuming that the human heart and conscience, restricted only by difficulties of organization, is the arbiter of what institutions are to become, we may hope the facility of intercourse to be the starting-point of an era of moral progress.

Trend Toward Humanism. We may call this wider reach and application of the sentiments that naturally prevail in the familiar intercourse of primary groups a trend toward humanism. Brief mention will be made of the increasing scope of the sentiments of justice, truth, kindness, and service.

As was pointed out in the discussion of primary ideals, the basis of all sentiment of this kind is the sense of community, or of sharing in a common social or spiritual whole, membership in which gives to all a kind of inner equality, no matter what their special rôles may be. The sense of justice is usually strong among the members of a sympathetic group, the basis of determining what is just being the perception of some purpose which every one is to serve, each in his own way, so that he who rightly holds a higher place is the one who can function best for a common good. It does not hurt my self-respect or my allegiance to remain a common seaman while another becomes captain of the ship, provided I recognize that he is the fitter man for the place; and if the distribution of stations in society were evidently of this sort there would be no serious protest against it. What makes trouble is the growth of an ideal of fair play which the actual system of things does not satisfy.

The widening of sympathic insight and the consciousness of larger unity have brought the hope and demand for a corresponding extension of justice; and all sorts of humanity—not to speak of lower animals—have profited by this wider sentiment. Classes have more understanding of each other; the personality of women and children is recognized and fostered; there is some attempt to sympathize with alien nations and races, civilized or savage, and to help them to their just place in the common life of mankind.

Our conception of international rights is coming to reflect the same view, and most Americans, for instance, desire that their country should treat other countries as one just man treats another, and are proud when they can believe that she has done so.

Truth is a kind of justice, and wherever there is identification of oneself with the life of the group it is fostered, and lying tends to be felt as mean and impolitic. Serious falsehood among friends is universally abhorred—by savages and children as well as by civilized adults. To lie to a friend is to hit him from behind, to trip him up in the dark, and so the moral sentiment of every group attempts to suppress falsehood among its members, however it may be encouraged as against outsiders.

Our democratic system aims to be a larger organization based on primary group principles, and, so far as it is so, it fosters this open and downright attitude of the individual toward his fellows. In idea, and largely in fact, we are a commonwealth, the members of which naturally feel loyalty one to another. Our disgust is therefore intense when one of our fellows tries to gain an advantage by false statements, as on an income tax return, or when class selfishness overrides community welfare as so often occurs *on both sides* in a strike.

The sentiment of mutual kindness or brotherhood flourishes most in primary groups. Under its influence the I-feeling becomes a we-feeling, which seeks no good that is not also the good of the group. And the humanism of our time strives with renewed energy to make the we-feeling prevail also in the larger phases of life.

Certainly there is, on the whole, a more lively and hopeful pursuit of the brotherhood of man under modern conditions than there ever was, on a large scale, before. One who is not deaf to the voices of literature, of social agitation, of ordinary intercourse, can hardly doubt this. The social settlement and similar movements express it, and so, more and more, does the whole feeling of our society regarding richer and poorer. Philanthropy is not only extending, but undergoing a revolution in principle from alms to justice and from condescension to fellowship. The wealthy and the educated classes feel, however vaguely, that they must justify their advantages to their fellow men and their own consciences by making some public use of them. Gifts—well meant if not always wise—to education, science, and philanthropy are increasing.

A larger spirit of service is the active side of this larger group feeling. A life of service of some sort—in behalf of the clan or tribe, of the chief, of the sovereign, of the Church, of God—has always been the ideal life; what is new is that the object of this service tends to become wider, with the modern expansion of the imagination, and to include all classes, all nations, and races, in this ideal scope. The narrower boundaries do not disappear, but as they become less distinct the greater whole tends to become more so.

In the modern world, the feeling that everybody ought to be doing something useful is becoming so established that in only a few countries is there now any influential class within which idleness is respectable. If it be true, as is asserted, that the children of the wealthy today are on the whole less given to sloth and vice than the same class in former times, the reason is to be found in a healthier, more organic state of opinion which penetrates all classes with the perception that the significance of the individual lies in his service to the whole. That this sentiment is gaining in our colleges is perhaps shown by the increasing popularity of courses that throw light on the nature and working of society, past or present, and upon the opportunities of service or distinction which it offers the individual. Classes in history, economics, government, sociology, ethics, and anthropology are larger year by year. And the young people, chiefly from the well-to-do classes, who seek these studies, seem to be adherents of the democratic idea that privilege must be earned by function.

Difficulties in Organizing Large-Scale Life Successfully. We may well believe that there is a trend toward humanism in sentiment and yet be doubtful of our ability to organize our larger life on the basis of the primary ideals. Indeed many thinkers are of the opinion that the obstacles to large-scale organization are so great that we shall never surmount them. Our society at the present time is full of confusion which often leaves the individual conscious only of his separateness, engaged in a struggle which, so far as he can see, has no more relation to justice and the common good than a dog fight. He infers that the world is a place where one must either eat or be eaten; the idea of the brotherhood of man appears to be an enervating sentimentalism, and the true philosophy that of the struggle for existence, which he understands in a brutal sense opposite to the real teaching of science.

There is a hiatus between our ideals and our achievements in many fields. We feel the new idealism, the sweep and exhilaration of a broader application of primary sentiment, but we practice, nevertheless, a thrifty exploitation of all the private advantages we can decently lay our hands on. Experience shows that until a higher sentiment, like brotherly kindness, attains some definite organization and programme, so that men are held up to it, it is remarkably ineffective in checking selfish activities. People drift on and on in lower courses, which at bottom they despise and dislike, simply because they lack energy and initiative to get out of them. How true it is that many of us would like to be *made* better than we are.

We have definitely left behind the old small-scale life of the village and surrounding countryside. We are committed to living in a wider world whose relationships are much more complex and where the mutual adjustments of people, groups, and institutions are much more difficult to make. It is not at all clear that human nature and human ingenuity are equal to the task of organizing and controlling this larger life successfully. We may be unable to foresee and forestall major maladjustments such as war, disastrous periods of unemployment, and the like. If the system proves so unwieldy that it has to be controlled by autocratic methods rather than by the democratic ones characteristic of the primary group, Western civilization is likely to fall of its own weight just as did the Roman Empire. Unless we can make our larger life one in which fundamental human needs are satisfied and one embodying in practical fashion the humanistic sentiment, men will become discontented and destroy it. The prevalence today of exploitation, ruthless competition, and waste only serve to show the immense task that confronts us.

Summary. On the foundation-stones of human heredity, communication, human nature, primary groups, culture, we find standing a social structure of communities, regions, nations, the world market, social classes, institutions. All this has been built up by the enlargement of human association from primary groups. But in this process of enlargement what has really been expanding has been the social consciousness of men.

Tribal consciousness was inevitably narrow. Only as communication and organization improved could association be enlarged. The central fact of history has been this gradual growth of social consciousness and rational co-operation. Until modern communication removed the barrier, all states faced an inevitable contradiction between extension and freedom. Even the United States in the beginning labored under this handicap and might well have failed had communication not improved. The effects of modern communication, however, go beyond political organization, as the spread of democracy in other fields indicates. Moreover, it has contributed to the spread of nationalism, or the enlargement of the group self, and to the enlargement of feeling which underlies the growing sense of moral unity between nations, races, and perhaps classes. Despite obvious shortcomings, recent generations have probably seen more evidence of justice, truth, kindness, and service on a larger scale than any preceding time.

The same forces that have brought about this enlargement of social consciousness have also created enormous problems which remain to be solved. There is no certainty that man can make the larger organization sufficiently flexible to serve the basic demands of human nature.

STUDY QUESTIONS

1. What five factors are suggested as particularly important foundation-stones of social organization?
2. What is the psychological significance of the larger social organization?
3. Contrast group consciousness in tribal life with similar phenomena among ourselves today.

4. What is necessary in order to have the primary ideals functional with respect to wider social relations?
5. What was the situation in the United States at the close of the eighteenth century with regard to public consciousness?
6. How do you account for the fall of the Roman Empire under the hypothesis that the central fact of history is the gradual enlargement of social consciousness?
7. With what dilemma were the states of the early world confronted?
8. What has been the political effect of modern communication?
9. How would you define democracy?
10. Define nationality. Why did the spirit of nationality grow in the nineteenth century?
11. Discuss "Patriotism will always be an insuperable bar to international organization."
12. What do you think are the possibilities of a world-wide "we"?
13. Do you agree that there is an enlargement of feeling resulting from modern communication? Give illustrations supporting your view.
14. Mention some tendencies of sentiment characteristic of modern life which might prove or disprove the existence of a trend toward humanism.
15. Will a trend toward humanism suffice to solve the problem of organizing the larger life ushered in by modern communication?

CHAPTER XV

GROUPING AND THE RISE OF NON-PRIMARY ASSOCIATION

Differential Association—the Fact of Grouping.[1] In Chapter IV we discussed the primary group and in Chapter XIV we implied at least the existence of publics and nations. We assumed, in other words, an obvious fact of the highest importance, namely, that living with others is not an all-alike process in which each individual mingles equally with every one else but is instead characterized by marked differences in degree. Each of us is constantly relating himself more closely to some people than to others even when the medium of communication is a letter, the telephone, the newspaper, or the radio. We could not possibly associate with every one in the world, even if we so desired. Differences in residence, in interests, in particular purposes, in social attitudes, in income, and in various other controlling factors limit and channel the flow of our associations. Instead of uniformity of association, therefore, *what we actually see about us is a process of differential association,* or association of varying degrees of nearness.

We refer to this fact by the term *group*. A group is any two or more persons who are temporarily or permanently set off from others by differential association, *i.e.,* by closer association with one another than with others during the time in question. Here, for example, is a student buying a newspaper from a newsboy on the street. The two for the moment constitute a group in contrast, say, to the rest of the townspeople. Yet the townspeople in turn are obviously in closer association with one another than

[1] Sociology has sometimes been defined as the science of group life. But this definition leaves it unclear whether the sociologist is primarily concerned with (*a*) human association, *i.e.,* the process of living with others; (*b*) phenomena involved in group living such as culture, population concentration, and so on; or (*c*) the phenomena of differential association, *i.e.,* grouping *per se*. In the present book we have chosen to consider that our subject-matter is human association and that the phenomena of group living are the results of previous association and conditioning factors for future association. Grouping is a phase of the associative process.

with the people of other communities in the United States, and the people of all these communities are in closer association with one another than with the residents of communities in Canada, or France, or Japan.

What Reality Has a Group? That people do associate in this way more closely with some persons than with others would seem to be obvious enough. But social theorists have been debating for many years whether groups are real things or not. This quarrel is an echo of the mediæval dispute between the Realists and the Nominalists in philosophy. The Realists held that only universals are real, *i.e.*, that any particular rose, for example, is only an imperfect copy of the universal, or ideal, rose. The Nominalists, on the other hand, said that the universal is a mere word and that only the particular, *i.e.*, the individual rose, is real. Social theorists who adopt the Realist point of view regard groups as having a reality over and above that of their individual members. Thus Hegel speaks of the state as the march of God in the world, German political theory before the war made the state an end in itself, and Mussolini gives the Italian state an existence over and above that of its functionaries and subjects. Durkheim, the French sociologist, in theorizing about the group mind as something over and above the individual mind, was taking the same point of view. As opposed to this position, the Nominalist denies the reality of any group larger than the number of people who can be observed by one person from one place at one time. Thus Professor Allport insists that publics, nations, and institutions have no reality as such and are mere figures of speech to link together the separate individuals who are the only realities.[2]

Neither of these theoretical positions seems likely to get us ahead in understanding the actual phenomena of differential association. The Nominalists seem to be right in their contention that the state is no mystical over-soul but merely human beings functioning in certain relationships to one another. On the other hand, the Realists have factual evidence on their side when they emphasize the reality of those functional relationships. It is true that differential association on a large scale cannot be observed in its totality by any one observer at one time and at one place. But neither can the solar system or the earth, for that matter.

[2] Floyd H. Allport, "Group and Institution as Concepts in a Natural Science of Social Phenomena," *Publications of the American Sociological Society*, Vol. XXII, 1928, p. 83.

Nobody denies that the earth is real merely because no scientist has ever yet seen it in its totality. It exists as an object of experience, *i.e.,* as a real thing, only through a symbolical representation of a complex of processes. In precisely the same way a university or the United States of America exists as an object of experience only through a symbolical representation of a complex of processes. Nobody has ever seen the United States of America any more than anybody has ever seen the earth. That is the truth in the Nominalist position. But the complex of differential association which we call the United States of America has precisely the same claim to be considered real that the earth has, namely, that such a symbolical construction unifies the phenomena before us better than any alternative construction. In its failure to see the reality of differential association and the necessity of dealing with all complex phenomena through symbolical representations the Nominalist position seems inadequate.

What Forms Does Grouping Take? Arranged in order of increasing size and decreasing intimacy, human groupings fall into four general classes:

I. *Intimate pair-groups* such as mother and child, husband and wife, lover and sweetheart. In a sense these are sub-primary groups.

II. *Primary groups* characterized by (1) face-to-face association, (2) small numbers, (3) unspecialized purpose, (4) comparative intimacy, (5) relative permanence. The home, the spontaneous play group, and the old-fashioned neighborhood are type examples, as we pointed out in Chapter IV.

III. *Quasi-primary groups.* These are organized face-to-face intimate groups, limited in some degree by special purpose and by the fact of organization. Boy Scout troops, college fraternities and sororities, luncheon clubs, etc., are examples. They have many of the characteristics of primary groups and may in fact perform many of the functions of primary groups, yet organization and the limitations of special purpose give them some of the characteristics of secondary groups.

IV. *Secondary groups.* These are groups wholly lacking in intimacy of association and usually in most of the other primary and quasi-primary characteristics. Crowds, communities, corporations, nations are among the examples. In general, secondary groups may be classified according as they are or are not basically organized around cultural elements. Six kinds of similarities seem to account for secondary groupings, as follows:

1. Culturally organized groups:

i. Status groups, *i.e.,* social classes.
ii. Nationality groups—nations.
iii. Residence groups—communities and regional groups.
iv. Attention-, interest-, and purpose-groups—publics, institutional groups, corporations, etc.

2. Groups not basically organized by culture:

v. Biological groups—age-groups, the sexes, races.
vi. Casual groups—crowds and assemblages, such as audiences, mobs, etc.

Primary groups we have already discussed in Chapter IV. Intimate pair-groups are usually sub-primary groups, or related in some way to primary groups, so they need not be discussed separately here. Since quasi-primary groups are hybrids and have some of the characteristics of both primary and secondary groups, it will be simpler to deal with the secondary groups directly and let the student make his own analysis of intermediate forms.

But before we turn to a discussion of secondary groups it is essential to realize how the rôle of such groups has been growing in modern society as the primary group has relinquished a larger and larger percentage of the average individual's life.

Decline of the Primary Group. To an extent unknown in any previous culture, modern civilization, in the United States at least, rests on non-primary forms of grouping. Other and more exciting forms of association are tending to crowd out the neighborhood, the home, and the spontaneous play-group. Thanks to electro-machine communication and to the automobile the great mass of Americans are no longer limited by vicinage in their associations: one's intimate friends need not and usually do not live near by. In our cities and in rural regions in which the old life has been disorganized by an influx of strangers, a neighborhood is no longer a distinguishable unit of social organization but a mere geographical expression. In Detroit, for example, the "neighborhood of the Dodge factory" is not a neighborhood at all, but a locality. Even under rural conditions neighborhoods are not all alike. Sanderson and Thompson in a study of the group relationships of 5143 farm families in Otsego County, New York, found at least seven types of neighborhood, *i.e.*, the hamlet, the institutional neighborhood, the business neighborhood, the ethnic neighborhood, the kinship neighborhood, the topographic neighborhood, and the village neighborhood. The average number of homes per neighborhood in that county was 14, and in 150 neighborhoods which averaged 12.5 homes each the area averaged 2.25 square miles.[3]

Similar studies in Wisconsin, Minnesota, and elsewhere show that rural neighborhoods differ greatly; but they are at least alike in this—the people in them do know each other personally and have regard for one another's opinions. It is this psychological unity that modern communication is destroying. In cities people not only know little or nothing about their next-door "neighbors," but have no desire to and feel no interest in their opinions whatever. Thus, McKenzie in his study of the neighborhood in Columbus, Ohio, found little real neighboring going on and although kinship was still a factor in organizing association, it was distinctly less of a factor than in rural communities. People of like attitudes toward the *mores* do tend to segregate into territorial publics, in the city, but the mobility of modern life tends to destroy real neighborhood solidarity.[4] The Lynds in their study of Middletown, *i.e.*, Muncie, Ind., found similar tendencies at work: "Vicinage plays a part in the forming of friendships," but more of a part among the working class than among the well-to-do.[5] On the whole since 1890 in Middletown the neighborhood has declined as "a place of most constant association of friends." Correlative with this decline in the importance of place as determining association has come an increase in the rôle of occupational associations such as the service clubs and of casual and purpose

[3] Dwight Sanderson and Warren S. Thompson, *The Social Areas of Otsego County*, Cornell University Agricultural Experiment Station, in co-operation with the U. S. Department of Agriculture, Ithaca, N. Y., 1923.

[4] R. D. McKenzie, "The Neighborhood; A Study of Local Life in the City of Columbus, Ohio," *American Journal of Sociology*, Vol. XXVII, September, November, 1921, January, 1922. "Mutual aid has almost ceased to be a factor in the fragmentary and casual relations between neighbors in the city environment."—p. 503.

[5] Robert S. and Helen M. Lynd, *Middletown*, New York, 1929, p. 273.

associations based on the automobile, the motion picture theatre, the bridge club, the golf club,[6] and the like.

The decay of the neighborhood in cities is part and parcel of the transformation that modern communication is working in all the primary groups. The family and the play-group likewise are showing the effects of the increased mobility of their own members and of the community about them. In Middletown far more of the activities of the members of the average household are now spent away from home than was true in 1890 and there is a tendency for different members to do different things. More women now work outside the home and the agencies drawing children away from home have greatly multiplied. In the three upper years of the Middletown high school the number of times the young people go out at night and the hours at which they get in are the two leading sources of friction between parents and children.[7] Approximately half of the boys and girls who answered the question were home less than four nights a week. Athletics, dramatics, committee meetings, Y. M. C. A., Y. W. C. A., the movies, auto-riding—"all extra-neighborhood concerns unknown to his parents in their youth—are centres of interest; club meetings, parties, or dances, often held in public buildings, compete for his every evening." No wonder that Middletown parents complained of the early sophistication of their children. Mobility has destroyed the old neighborhood, and mobility plus the rest of modern invention is truncating the socializing function of the family. Likewise the whole juggernaut of modern culture drives the play-group from the streets to take refuge in the alleys and vacant lots whence Young America issues presently as the gang, intent on business of its own for whose control we must organize playground movements and Boy Scout troops and all the rest of the institutional paraphernalia of a society that does not know how to build cities for children as well as for grown-ups.

What all this means is that from childhood up the rôle of the primary group is changing. Facing the decline of the old spontaneous face-to-face associations, we have been driven to set up all sorts of quasi-primary organizations such as neighborhood

[6] There were 458 active clubs in Middletown in the spring and summer of 1924, when Middletown's population was estimated at 38,000. Clubs were, however, largely business-class phenomena; the working-class home suffered from too much isolation rather than the reverse.

[7] *Op. cit.*, p. 134.

clubs, Scout troops, Rotary clubs, and the like, to re-establish consciously and purposively the semblance at least of the primary group experience. But no matter how informally such organizations may be conducted and no matter how much familiarity may spring up between members, they are still *ad hoc* organizations, set up for a purpose, with rules and formal organization, to do more or less mechanically and at some cost for a few people some of the things that formerly were done for all the people incidentally, spontaneously, and without costing a penny.

What the Increase in Secondary Association Means. The decline of the primary group and the corresponding increase in secondary association has one very immediate consequence: because of the nature of secondary association we are now associating more as mere functionaries and less as whole persons. What does this mean?

In primary groups people meet as persons, *i.e.,* unconstrained by artificiality, special purpose, limited contact, and the like. In secondary groups, on the other hand, they are functioning units in an organization, or mere acquaintances at best. *Secondary association is partial association.* It is association narrowed down by special purpose, by communication at a distance, by rules, by social barriers, or by the casual nature of contact. This means that under such conditions associating personalities present only special facets of themselves to one another. They cannot meet as whole persons.

Compare, for example, the degree of association that would exist between a student and a newsboy on the street and the same student and the newsboy if they were members of one family. As a seller of newspapers the newsboy is a mere functionary. The buyer knows nothing of his home background, his attitude toward his baby sister, his desire to be a football coach, his fear of the dark, and scores of other details of his personal life. As a mere newsboy, apart from the full context of his life, he is not a living personality at all; he is a specialized human atom, not a person.

Even those with whom we spend hours of our working lives each day seldom emerge as whole personalities. As students we listen to formal lectures from professors, and have no more conception of what the individual professors are like as persons than the professors have of what the individual students are like as persons. As business men we deal with customers and employees, but have neither time nor opportunity to go behind the specialized facet of his personality that each presents. As citizens and consumers we listen to political speeches and buy our household supplies from individuals who impinge upon us merely as functionaries, never as whole personalities.

Advantages and Dangers of Secondary Association. Suppose, now, we take the point of view of the social technologist who is interested in making primary ideals work in larger organizations.[8] What advantages and disadvantages do we find in secondary association? The advantages may be summed up as those resulting mainly from *specialization, impersonality, reach,* and *continuity.* The dangers lie chiefly in the *social illiteracy of the narrow specialist, in the functionary's tendency to disregard human values, in the inertia of great organizations,* and *in the resulting readjustment lag.*

It is only through division of labor that high civilization is possible. Correlative with this is the inevitable necessity of limiting association, of meeting for narrowly limited purposes and excluding everything else. Imagine trying to run a Twentieth Century Limited if the engineer and the passengers had to associate as persons with interminable questions on individual health, relatives, the number of the baby's teeth, and all that! If every manufacturer had to be personally interested in every one of his employees, industry would be limited to the level of the village blacksmith shop. In order to get things done interest in persons must be subordinated to interest in specialized function.

One danger involved in this concentration on function is what Stuart Chase has called "technological tenuosity"—*i.e.,* the danger that we may all become so highly specialized that the specialists will be unable to understand one another. Symptoms of such a condition have already appeared in our universities. Possession of a modern university degree does not guarantee that any two graduates will have any intellectual interests in common except perhaps a certain partiality for the football team. One may have specialized in Greek, the other in airplane design, and neither will have any conception of the other's specialty or of the personality interested in that specialty.

[8] Note that this section assumes certain values as worth while, namely, loyalty, truth, lawfulness, freedom, etc., the ideals developed in primary groups. See Chap. IV. Only by assuming values of some kind can we discuss the advantages and dangers of anything.

Impersonality in dealing with people and things is, like specialization, an enormous advantage. It simplifies decisions and cuts through complexities. Hence the functionary who insists on letting personalities affect his official decisions is a detriment to an organization. The Grand Duke Alexander of Russia, brother-in-law of the late Czar Nicholas II, insists that the great historical blunders of monarchs can usually be traced to their failure to remain functionaries, *i.e.*, to their acting as persons instead of official automatons. While this is probably only part of the story, as we shall see presently, it is a point worth emphasizing. The Kaiser, for example, was too much of a person to make a good emperor. As the Russian Grand Duke describes him,

> He was a great orator, a super-architect, a warrior extraordinary—and his speeches left Germany without a friend in the world. His artistic aspirations were responsible for the monstrosity of the Siegesallee, and his experiments in strategy, backed by those of his trusted friend von Kluck, immortalized Papa Joffre and saved Paris in the fall of 1914. . . . His quarrel with King Edward, his dismissal of Bismarck and his declaration of the submarine war—these are the three fatal mistakes of his reign and these are precisely the three things in his life that he enjoyed most. A ward politician would have known better. . . .[9]

History is filled wth similar examples of high-placed functionaries who let their personal likes and dislikes interfere with what should have been impersonal decisions, and all of us have had experiences with less highly placed functionaries who have done the same thing. Secondary organization demands impersonality in its functionaries.

But efficiency bought at this price comes high. It is a fatally short step from the impersonal to the inhuman. If we accept the development of personality as one of the ultimate tests of a civilization, any institution or function that does not contribute to that end becomes a social liability.[10] This means that any institution or function that does not contribute to the sanctity of life, to security, to mutual responsibility, to justice, and to other

[9] "Are Royalty People? They Dare Not Be, Says Grand Duke Alexander of Russia," *Detroit Times,* Oct. 30, 1932, pt. 4, p. 3.

[10] For a discussion of values see Chap. XXIX.

conditions necessary for the full development of personality is a source of illth, as Ruskin called it, and not of wealth or welfare. Under these circumstances the more narrowly efficient the functionary, the more of a social liability he becomes. It was a narrowly efficient military genius who betrayed the French Revolution for his own ends and set back the development of Europe for a generation. It was the narrowly efficient slave-owner who calculated coldly whether it was more profitable to work his slaves to death in five years or fifteen, and made slavery an abomination. It is the narrowly efficient employer today who calculates coldly how much of the burden of poverty and unemployment he can throw on his employees and on the community and who is making more and more people question the future of an acquisitive society. Impersonal efficiency uninspired by social ideals becomes a menace of the first order.

In addition to specialization and impersonality, secondary association also gives reach and continuity. It becomes possible with distance communication and partial association to build vast organizations such as the British Empire, the Roman Catholic Church, the Standard Oil Company, each of which covers a large share of the globe. At the same time it also becomes possible to escape the limitations of individual mortality—a secondary organization is an organization of functionaries not of persons. Persons die; functionaries are merely replaced—the function goes on. "The King is dead! Long live the King!"

But again this extension of association is purchased at a price. Large organizations have an inertia much greater than primary groups. An old-fashioned neighborhood might be poverty-stricken, but it would never generate a depression for the simple reason that it lacked the elaborate mechanism of exchange whose persistent derangement *is* the depression. Even a small business has an inertia, a routine, which is harder to change than that of a family. All of which means that, as compared with primary groups, there is more tendency for the adjustments reached by secondary groups to outlive the situations that give them birth. The readjustment process in a primary group, such as a household, a play-group, or an old-fashioned neighborhood, is a direct, face-to-face, give and take, dominated by outstanding personalities no doubt, but unhampered by difficulties of communication, censorship, propaganda, lack of interest, impersonality, legalism, and all the rest of the factors that hinder and delay secondary group action. Under these conditions the lag between need and readjustment tends to be longer in secondary groups than in primary.[11]

Clearly, then, the gain from specialization, impersonality, reach, and continuity that comes with secondary association carries with it corresponding losses. Social illiteracy, disregard of human values, social inertia, and the readjustment lag are tangible entries on the debit side of the ledger.

Kinds of Secondary Groups. Our first type of secondary group is that which is basically organized with reference to cultural elements. Social classes, for example, exist in and through the institutions determining the distribution of wealth. Labor unions, labor parties, the Grange, and similar organizations are institutional expressions of class interests. Every nationality group has its own institutions peculiar to its culture. Communities and regional groups are served by a complex of institutions. Attention-groups are served by some institutionalized communication service —a magazine, a newspaper, the radio. An attention-group whose members are not in presence is called a public. The term public also includes certain forms of interest-groups, or groups of people unified by a common practical interest. Such groups, while functioning as specialized members of a public, frequently seek to implement their interest with some organization in the way that the Prohibitionists, for example, formed the Anti-Saloon League. Such a specific implementing group may be called a purpose-group. A purpose-group is thus formed to do some specific thing. A football team, a corporation, or a committee furnish examples. In general, institutions are operated by interest-groups and purpose-groups. From this point of view the Republican Party, for example, the investors in the Standard Oil Company, and the school teachers of a State may be classified here.[12]

With the elaboration of all of these distinctions we are not here concerned. Each of the main types of culturally organized

[11] It is probably true that because of greater simplicity there are fewer maladjustments in primary groups than in secondary. But many of the existing maladjustments in primary groups are due to conditions created by maladjustments in secondary groups. For a discussion of the readjustment process in secondary groups see below Chaps. XXII, XXIII, and XXIV.

[12] It is obvious, of course, that one classification does not exhaust an individual's groupings. School teachers have a certain status as professional people, belong to various biological groups, residence groups, primary groups, and so on.

groups is discussed in detail in some later chapter.[13] We shall confine ourselves here, therefore, to the non-implemented groups —age-groups, the sexes, races, and casual groups. The first three of these differ from casual groups in this—that they are widely dispersed in space while casual groups are always presence-groups; *i.e.*, groups whose members are in presence in a given locality at a given time. Absence of institutional expression and lack of presence give biological groupings a more fluid and intangible character than either casual groups or the various types of culturally organized groups. Yet the biological factors, age, sex, and race, are real controls in channelling association.

Biological Groups. *Age-groups.*—Age probably plays a larger part in determining association in pre-literate cultures than in modern civilization. Even among pre-literates, however, it is seldom age alone that operates. Membership in an age-society of the Plains Indians, for example, seems to have been determined only in part by age and in greater part by the payment of fees.[14] In the same way in the United States today, it is possible to speak of infants, children, adolescents, the young unmarried set, younger and older married people, and so on; but the real significance of such classifications lies more in the cultural stages associated with different ages than in the age-differences themselves.

Age affects association in two ways: (1) through physiological and psychological differences in energy, stamina, physical alacrity, mental age, and so on; and (2) through differences in occupation, economic condition, marital status, and family responsibilities, *i.e.*, differences in cultural status, which are associated with age differences. The two together tend to keep members of each generation associating in the main with members of the same age-group, although age-groups as such have no group consciousness and no institutional organization.

Sex-groups.—From primitive days to the present the most fundamental cleavage in society has been that of sex. It was along this divide that the earliest division of labor ran—man's work and woman's work—and it still marks fundamental distinctions. Child-bearing is a biologically determined function, but around

[13] For attention-groups see Chaps. XXII, XXIII, XXIV. For residence-groups see the chapters on the Community and Regions, XVI, XVII, XVIII. For nationality-groups see Chap. XIX. For status-groups, Chaps. XX and XXI. For institutional interest-groups, Chaps. XXVI, XXVII, and XXVIII.

[14] Robert H. Lowie, *Primitive Society*, N. Y., 1920, p. 313 ff.

that function culture everywhere has added other functions. Home-making is a culturally determined function—and home-making was the occupation of 23 per cent of Middletown's population in 1924. Despite the employment of more than 10,000,000 women outside American homes, man still carries the heavier forms of labor and, apart from child-bearing, the riskier occupations, such as structural steel work and soldiering.

Along these lines, laid down by the biological and cultural division of labor based on sex, go marked differences in association. Outside of the family and except in the mating period, people spend most of their working and leisure hours in the company of members of their own sex. The result is that in every society two fairly distinct cultures exist side by side, a masculine culture and a feminine culture. Each has its own approved interests, its own approved attitudes, its own traditions, and its own organizations. The interests of each sex centre largely in the occupations which culture assigns to it—and since woman's main career is still marriage, it is inevitable that much of her distinctively feminine culture should be centred on mating, home-making, child-care, and the like. This means that feminine culture is predominantly a primary-group culture while a much greater emphasis is given in masculine culture to secondary-group relationships. In fact, secondary-group organization would seem to be largely a product of the masculine culture—a circumstance which may help to explain the common impression that in secondary-group association women find it harder to subordinate personalities, and, by the same token, harder to forget human values, than do men.

Traditionally the two cultures mark out separate paths for the little boy and the little girl in morals, in dress, in play, in life-interests, and in life-objectives. In Victorian days the difference was summed up in the phrase, "Woman's place is in the home."

All higher civilizations have been characterized by masculine privilege. On a more primitive level woman usually stands more nearly as man's equal; in fact, among many tribes the wife is the pivot on which family relationships turn and kinship is traced through the mother rather than the father. Some authorities believe that this was the original form of all social organization and that father-right, or organization around the father, is a later development than mother-right. In any event, among all the Indo-Germanic peoples and among the Semites and the Mongolians, *i.e.*, "among all the races who have developed the historic civilizations," father-right predominates.[15]

The subordination of woman takes many forms and varies in different cultures. It is vastly more pronounced, for example, in an ancestor-worshipping civilization such as the Chinese than in a juristic civilization such as the ancient Roman in which, after the Punic Wars, the women of the upper classes enjoyed more freedom than women were ever to see again until the twentieth century. In our own culture there are many traces of the lowly position which women occupied in western Europe during the dark ages and the centuries of feudalism. Woman's vicarious social position, *i.e.*, her usual dependence for social status on father or husband; her economic dependence; the double standard of morality; the passive rôle assigned to her in courtship; the fact that by custom the wife, not the husband, wears the wedding ring; the husband's right to determine the place of residence regardless of his wife's wishes—such a condition attests the existence of masculine privilege even after a century of feminist agitation.

With the cultural rediscovery of the individual that came with the romantic movement in the early part of the nineteenth century, a few women here and there began to demand consideration for women as persons and not mere members of a sex. When the agitation began not a college in the United States was open to women and not more than seven occupations were considered respectable.[16] In little more than a century American women won the right to an education, to support themselves in more than 300 occupations, to sue for divorce without social ostracism, and the right to vote. The birth-control movement may be interpreted as woman's fight for the right to control maternity. After these revolutionary changes in woman's status, leading feminists are eager to sweep away the remaining man-made restrictions. Thus Mrs. Bertrand Russell assails the conventional marriage as a

[15] *Cf.* L. T. Hobhouse, *Morals in Evolution,* New York, 1916, p. 162.

[16] The first institution for the higher education of women in this country was opened in Troy, New York, in 1821 by Emma Willard. Co-education began at the University of Indiana in 1868 and at the University of Michigan in 1870. *Cf.* E. P. Cubberley, *Public Education in the United States,* New York, 1919, p. 209. In 1840 Harriet Martineau found that self-repecting women could work only at teaching, needle work, keeping boarders, type-setting, book-binding, domestic service, or in the New England cotton mills. *Cf.* E. L. Bogart, *Economic History of the United States,* New York, 1907, p. 476.

"barrier to free public activity," that "burdens (the wife) forever . . . with her husband's duties and affairs," brings "looks of surprise and reproach if we enjoy other male society" and "constraint in the manner of men formerly our friends"; that makes "children, which, had we had them illegitimate, would have been our own, . . . now our husband's"; and, worst of all, humiliates the wife "with the looks and smiles of silly women broken into slavery, congratulating us on having done well and made ourselves secure for life."[17] The thrust of this attack is not at marriage, but at man's superiority in marriage. It is this superiority that feminism is frankly out to destroy.

Race-groups.—Race-groups are so closely related to status groups, or social classes, in this country that full discussion must be postponed until the forces that produce social classes are analyzed. This will be done in Chapter XX.

That race plays a part in limiting and controlling association is, of course, obvious wherever different races meet in this country. Two lines of explanation are available: (1) instinctive aversion on the part of the whites toward colored races; (2) that race prejudice is a culture trait which has grown up in situations of marked aggression and difference of racial status.

It is impossible to discuss these complicated theories here. Most sociologists agree that the instinct theory of race prejudice is inadequate to account for the facts and that some form of the culture-trait theory will ultimately prevail. This belief rests on five lines of evidence which can merely be referred to here without attempted proof: (1) *Historical evidence*—European whites have not always shown prejudice toward colored races. Portuguese court chronicles tell of the intermarriage of whites with former Negro slaves in Portugal a generation before Columbus; Spanish and French colonists intermarried with the Indians; white indentured servants in Virginia intermarried with Negro indentured servants in the sixteenth century before slavery had become an institution. (2) *Contemporary comparisons*—Race prejudice while marked in the Anglo-American cultures, is either absent or very weak in the Latin countries, particularly France, and in Slavic Russia. (3) *White inconsistencies*—Many white people, professing the most intense aversion to Negroes, have no aversion to comparatively intimate association with them

[17] Dora Russell, *Hypatia, or Woman and Knowledge,* New York, 1925, p. 38.

so long as the Negro maintains the social distance appropriate to a servant. Under these conditions Negroes ride in Pullman cars in the South and live in white homes. (4) *Genetic psychology*—White children do not show prejudice unless unfavorable reactions have been suggested by adults or by cultural stimuli such as games, nursery rhymes, etc. (5) *The effect of racial competition on prejudice*—Prejudice is most apparent where competition of races is keenest. Whites in a region previously free from prejudice show little or no feeling toward isolated individual invasions. Until competition for jobs, land, housing accommodations, or business is felt, prejudice is not apparent. This was the case on the Pacific coast with regard to Orientals prior to 1870, and in many northern communities with reference to Negroes today. In the South race feeling is keenest not in the Mississippi bottom lands where Negroes most outnumber whites, but in the poorer farming areas where the poor whites feel the competition most keenly.

Casual Groups. Casual groups are groups formed by the incidental convergence of individual purposes in a particular place at a particular time. A casual group is marked by three characteristics: (1) it has no history; (2) no lasting group purpose; and (3) it is always a presence-group.

Two main kinds of casual groups may be mentioned:

a. Crowds.—A crowd is a casual group in which attention is not focalized or concentrated on one object or person. People on the street, in a railroad station, in a hotel lobby, and so on, constitute crowds.

b. Assemblages.—A casual group with focalized attention is an assemblage. Three ways in which assemblages function should be distinguished:

(1) *Passive Functioning.*—An audience[18] is a passive assemblage. It is characterized by having no history, no common as distinguished from individual purpose, and by focalized attention and non-participation. Its dominant attitude is receptive.

(2) *Participant Functioning.*—Some audiences and most groups of spectators at baseball games, football games, prize fights, and the like, insist on taking part in the show, verbally if

[18] The term audience is here used to include groups of spectators as well as auditors. An audience as a casual group in presence should not be confused with certain hybrid forms of distance-groups such as the so-called radio audience which is in part an audience and in part a public.

not physically. The transition from a purely passive assemblage to a participant one is obviously easy, and the same group may function in both ways during an evening or an afternoon.

(3) *Aggressive Functioning.*—An assemblage whose members have become emotionalized, and eager for direct and possibly violent action is called a mob. Probably hundreds of mobs form in the United States every year. Labor troubles and race conflicts are particularly prolific in mob action.

Few objective studies of casual groups have ever been made. The late Professor Giddings gathered from his students statistics on the number of their casual groupings of certain kinds and found that 115 individuals reported 13,452 occasions on which they had unexpectedly hurried to a particular place where 10 or more other people assembled.[19] Of these occasions, 76 per cent were of minor importance; 18 per cent were of serious concern to individuals; and 6 per cent were of serious concern to communities, more than a third of such cases being due to floods, fires, or riots. Such figures do not, however, enable us to estimate how many casual groupings occur per day or per month in a community. The relative frequency of casual groupings in the life of the individual as compared with other kinds of groupings is still unknown.

Summary. A fact of great importance is that people do not associate equally with every one but tend to group. Groups have a reality of process symbolically represented. Four forms can be distinguished, intimate pair-groups, primary groups, quasi-primary groups, and secondary groups. Secondary groups, in turn, fall into those which are and those which are not organized around cultural elements.

In the modern world non-primary forms of association have become much more prevalent than in the past. This means that partial association as distinguished from full association is relatively more common. This kind of association carries with it the advantages of specialization, impersonality, reach, and continuity, and the dangers of technological tenuosity, disregard of human values, social inertia, and readjustment lag.

Of the groups not basically due to culture, biological groups are spatially distinguished from casual groups. Age affects asso-

[19] Franklin H. Giddings, *The Scientific Study of Human Society,* Chapel Hill, N. C., 1924, Chap. VII.

ciation directly by its effects on the individuals concerned and indirectly through cultural differences. Sex results in the development of two distinct cultures in each society which are now in America in more or less veiled conflict. Why race is a limiting factor in association is a matter of dispute, with sociologists tending to reject the instinct theory.

Casual groups may be classed as crowds and assemblages. Little scientific information exists on either.

STUDY QUESTIONS

1. What do you understand by the term differential association? Illustrate.
2. Define a group.
3. What does it mean to call Mussolini a Realist in his conception of the state?
4. In what sense is Professor Allport a Nominalist?
5. What reality has the United States of America as a group of people? How do you know?
6. What are the four fundamental forms of grouping?
7. Distinguish between primary groups, sub-primary groups, and quasi-primary groups.
8. Define a secondary group.
9. What two types of secondary groups were distinguished? Describe each type. What sub-groupings were differentiated?
10. Explain the decline of the primary group. Cite the evidence.
11. What is the outstanding significance of secondary association?
12. Indicate the advantages and dangers of secondary association.
13. Why is technological tenuosity a danger?
14. Why are graduates of different departments of a university likely to find it hard to carry on a conversation together?
15. What are the advantages and dangers involved in impersonality of function?
16. Define a functionary. In what way does a functionary differ from a person?
17. Explain why there is more social inertia in a bank than in a children's play group.
18. In what groups is adjustment lag likely to be most prominent?
19. In what way do biological groups differ from casual groups?
20. What are the three characteristics of casual groups?
21. How does age affect grouping? Give examples and explain.
22. Give examples of the different cultures produced by each sex.
23. Give examples of masculine privilege in our civilization.

24. What is the basic demand of the feminist?
25. What are the leading explanations offered for the part that race plays in channelling association?
26. What lines of evidence have led sociologists to reject the instinct theory of race groups?
27. What are the main types of casual groups? What functional varieties of the second can be distinguished?
28. Discuss the importance of casual groups.

CHAPTER XVI

THE COMMUNITY AND ITS STRUCTURE

What the Community Is and Does. We have discussed grouping and suggested some of the changes wrought by modern communication not only in a group itself and in its members but in the social life around it. Of the larger groups, the most important from many points of view is the *community. A community may be defined as a permanent, local aggregation of people, having diversified as well as common interests and served by a constellation of institutions.* A community may be no larger than a neighborhood within which all know each other and meet face to face; but ordinarily the term is applied to larger groups, or clusters of neighborhoods, whose members are united by their common interests in the school, the postoffice, the church, the stores, the factories, and the other institutions serving the people in a local area.

The community provides the immediate associational setting within which function the primary groups, including the old-fashioned neighborhood where it exists. It is through the institutions of the community such as the school, the newspaper, the library, and so on that the less personal aspects of culture are mediated to the individual. It is the community that provides the complex diversity of services made possible by division of labor and the cultural co-ordination of activity expressed in police protection, fire protection, health protection, education, the various types of economic activity, and so on. It is the community that bounds the average individual's goings and comings and sets the pattern of his life.

The Evolution of the Community. Without going back into the hypothetical beginnings of human and pre-human association, it is possible to watch the actual emergence of an American community from a pioneer settlement of colonial days. From a cluster of log cabins built in the summer of 1736, for example, the town of Keene, New Hampshire, became within a generation a "considerable village," which meant that it had a meeting-house and a fort, a sawmill, a school, and perhaps a blacksmith shop.[1] By 1787 there had been added a general store, a tannery, a grist-mill, and a tavern. As the years passed other services appeared: a printing-office, a weekly newspaper, a workhouse, a justice of the peace, a postoffice, a bakery, a nail manufactory, a grammar school, a "social library," a drugstore, and so on. In 1874 when the population had reached 6000 the town became a city. By that time it had added to previous services a municipal government, a municipal water supply, a railroad, a number of factories, sewerage, a bank, a Y. M. C. A., a building and loan association, a pottery, an armory and a militia company, various stores, a paid fire department, a police department, the usual complement of lawyers, doctors, and dentists, seven churches, a Masonic lodge, a lodge of Odd Fellows, a post of the G. A. R., and a number of women's organizations. In other words, from a pioneer neighborhood, with its simple face-to-face relationships and relatively undifferentiated economic and social life, Keene had evolved in less than a century and a half into a full-fledged community with complex division of labor and highly differentiated social interests, and it was on the way to further development represented by the telephone, paved streets, the high school, automobiles, recreation parks, and all the rest of the paraphernalia of a modern city that became common after 1874. Making allowance for local differences, the evolution of the town of Keene seems fairly representative of the development of many American communities.

Communities Simple and Complex. Our description of the evolution of the town of Keene has suggested an important characteristic of all communities, namely, the tendency for the absolute number of different functions carried on to increase as size increases. There is also a tendency for increase in size to bring with it an increase in the complexity of organization. Before the Revolution, for example, Keene, despite the geographical extent of a New England town, or township, was hardly more than a big "nucleated neighborhood." Gradually, however, the nucleus

[1] S. G. Griffin, *A History of the Town of Keene*, Keene, N. H., 1904, pp. 28 ff.

grew and became distinct from the surrounding farm area. By 1874, when this nucleus was incorporated as a city, it had long since outgrown the characteristics of a mere neighborhood—nobody could know personally 6000 people—and had become a cluster of neighborhoods.

Had Keene continued to grow as Detroit and Chicago and other cities did, it would presently have found itself consisting not only of a cluster of neighborhoods but of a cluster of minor communities, each of which in turn comprised a cluster of neighborhoods. Thus, Chicago, for example, is a collective term for a *metropolitan community* which consists of scores of minor communities within the corporate limits of the city itself, each minor community in turn consisting of multitudes of neighborhoods or quasi-neighborhoods.[2]

Communities, then, must be distinguished as simple and complex. Keene when it became a city was probably still a simple community. Chicago and Detroit have long since become complex communities, *i.e.,* communities including minor communities within them.

The Civic Community and the Service Community. It is also necessary to notice that with the improvement of transportation resulting from the invention of the automobile and the spread of good roads, there has been a tendency to return to one of the characteristics of the nucleated neighborhood, namely, the absence of definite demarcations between town and country. It is characteristic of the early village or hamlet stage of community development in eastern America that the fields run up to the back doors and farming operations are frequently carried on within a stone's throw of the main street. As the hamlet becomes a full-fledged village and later a small town or city, this interpenetration of town and country tends to disappear, a fact that is further emphasized by the hypothetical corporation line drawn around the village. With the coming of the automobile and the good road, however, there is again a blurring of the line between the

[2] Strictly speaking, the old neighborhood as it existed in pre-Revolutionary Keene has disappeared from our cities. A neighborhood in Chicago or Detroit is not a psychological unity, but a small area within which people are merely aware of fellow residents as functionaries rather than persons. Sometimes a neighborhood in this sense consists merely of part of an apartment building. It is in this sense that the term neighborhood or urban neighborhood is used with reference to cities.

nucleus and the surrounding territory, but the blurring this time is due not to the intrusion of agriculture into the town, but to the protrusion of the town into the country. This protrusion is seen in the scattering of homes along the main roads entering a city, in the extension into the country of city services such as gas, electricity, department store deliveries, daily newspapers, and the like, and in the movement of middle-class homes to the fringes and suburbs. All this means a breaking down of the sharp distinctions that characterize the middle period of community development. At the same time it means that the urban and especially the metropolitan community is no longer the same kind of thing that it was even a generation ago. There is growing up, in other words, a distinction between the *civic community* enclosed within the corporation limits and the broader *service community* which in the case of newspapers, for example, may extend for hundreds of miles from such a centre as Chicago or Detroit. We shall devote the remainder of this chapter to the civic community and consider the problems of the service community in a later chapter under the general title of the region.

Types of Communities. Apart from the complexity or simplicity of their organization, communities may be classified on the basis of the kind of economic activity that predominates in or about them. Thus there are agricultural communities, mining communities, manufacturing communities, resort communities, and so on. They may also be classified on the basis of their relation to other communities as for example *metropolitan communities* such as New York, Chicago, Detroit; *sub-metropolitan centres* such as Grand Rapids; *county centres* such as Ann Arbor, Michigan, although the county centre is not always the county-seat; *local centres* such as Dexter, Michigan, which are more than nucleated neighborhoods; and finally *neighborhood centres* such as Bridgewater, Washtenaw County, Michigan, which are merely the nuclei of rural neighborhoods. Between communities there exists a kind of ascending order of dominance which we shall have occasion to refer to again when dealing with regional organization.

The Ecology of Community Life. Community-living is from one point of view a way in which men distribute themselves in space. The scientific study of the distribution of human life and social forms in space and time and of the forces determining this distribution is called *human ecology.* McKenzie distinguishes five processes or forms in which this distribution occurs: *Concentration, centralization, segregation, invasion,* and *succession.*[3]

Concentration is the tendency toward increasing aggregation of population within a given area. The increase occurs through excess of births over deaths (natural increase) and through excess of immigration over emigration. The limit of purely rural concentration is probably found on the island of Java which under tropical conditions supports 1700 per square mile of tilled land. Japan with 2400 per square mile of tilled area (1924) is an example of high concentration based on partial industrialization. In the United States concentration has increased from 4.5 per square mile in 1790 to 41.3 in 1930, but is not expected to continue increasing after about 1960 unless the decline in the birth rate slows down or unless restrictions on immigration are again relaxed.[4]

Population Centres and Their Distribution. Within a given area, population seldom distributes itself in a uniform way. Men long ago discovered that life was easier when carried on by means of division of labor and co-operation with others than when carried on alone—and division of labor and co-operation, in turn, are easier when people live near one another than when they live far apart. Thus within an area of concentration appears the phenomenon of centralization, *i.e.,* grouping together into neighborhoods and communities.[5]

In 1930 there were over 18,000 incorporated and unincorporated centres in the United States. These ranged all the way from the country cross-road settlement up to New York City with its 6,930,000 inhabitants. In Michigan, for example, there were 475 incorporated places, ranging in size from Lake Angelus, Oakland county, with 27 inhabitants, to Detroit with 1,568,662. On the average there was one incorporated place in Michigan to every 121 square miles of land area, or one to every 2621 persons outside the incorporated places themselves. In general, population centres tend to be distributed according to population density, the more

[3] R. D. McKenzie, The Scope of Human Ecology, *Proceedings of the American Sociological Society,* Vol. XX, 1925.

[4] *Cf.* Louis I. Dublin, "Birth Control: What It Is Doing to America's Population," *Forum,* Vol. LXXXVI, Nov., 1931, pp. 270–275.

[5] In cities there is also a process of decentralization going on. Local business centres spring up, factories move to the outskirts, etc.

densely populated areas having more centres per 1000 square miles than the less densely populated areas. This suggests that in relation to its surrounding area each centre functions as a social and economic "service station," supplying commodities and services to the population in the area and drawing in turn from the area services and especially foods and raw materials for its own use and for distribution to other centres.

Segregation, Invasion, and Succession. Coincident with the processes of concentration and centralization are the processes of segregation, invasion, and succession going on within the centres themselves. Within each centre, or at least within those that have become communities as distinct from neighborhoods, there is constant going and coming and jostling of people and culture traits. Now in the long run this is a healthy process, but each individual and each business tries to minimize the jostling and competition by drawing together with kindred spirits. This process by which race and immigrant groups form "quarters," by which financial houses form the "financial district," by which retail stores form the "shopping district," and so on, is called *segregation.* Segregation in this sense is as natural as concentration, centralization, or any other ecological process. It is apparently an expression of the effort of each individual and each cultural unit to find the optimum conditions for normal functioning.

Unfortunately for those who desire peace without effort, the physical, human, and cultural environments will not "stay put." They are continually changing. In the average community, there is constant competition for places of heightened advantage, or of lessened pressure. Negroes, overcrowded in the Black Belt, move into white neighborhoods; chain stores, expanding, appear in the territory of neighborhood stores; business property drives out residential property. Every growing community is in a constant commotion of this kind. It is this process that is called *invasion.*

As a result of invasion the distribution of population elements and culture traits does not remain fixed. The city throws out "feelers of settlement" into the country; areas previously occupied by Germans come eventually to be Polish settlements; boarding houses invade the region contiguous to the business district and a residential district becomes a blighted area. Thus *succession* completes the process begun with concentration. In this perspective it is easy to see that communities are dynamic entities; restless, changing assemblages of people working out patterns of their own.

The Urban Pattern. As a result of centralization, segregation, invasion, and succession there exists at any given time in any fairly large community, *i.e.,* any community with intricate division of labor, a definite pattern of cultural distribution. In Chicago, where this pattern was first worked out, it has been found that there are five concentric zones or circles, each different from the others. The Loop, or business district, composes the central zone, or what would be the central zone if Lake Michigan did not cut the pattern in half. In that zone are concentrated the great financial institutions, the department stores, the most important office buildings, and so on,—the entire equipment, in other words, of domination and control. Around this central business district is a second zone, the Zone of Transition, from which the better families have fled before the impending advance of business. Behind the retreating better families have come the advance guards of the business centre—lodging-house keepers, cheap cleaning establishments, beauty parlors; a horde of little businesses and shady characters, all needing to be near the centre yet none prosperous enough to pay the high rentals demanded in the centre itself.

Beyond this Zone of Transition is a third zone, the Zone of Workingmen's Homes, and beyond that a fourth, the Better Residential Zone. On the periphery of the community is the Commuters' Zone. Thus Chicago presents the pattern of five concentric circles, or half circles, beginning with the central business district and extending back to the Commuters' Zone with its various residential suburbs scattered around the periphery, as shown in Figure 8 (p. 234).

While this concentric pattern is necessarily schematic and varies somewhat in details as peculiarities of topography, lakes, rivers, railroads, and other environmental controls interfere, it nevertheless expresses a tendency which can be recognized in other cities such as Montreal and Detroit. Until more specific studies have been made it is impossible to say whether the same pattern applies to all cities in our culture and to cities in other cultures. It seems probable, however, that when due allowance is made for local differences the pattern will be found applicable to most American cities. On this assumption it may be worth while to glance briefly at some of the characteristics of the more dynamic areas in the pattern, the Central Business District, the Zone of Transition, and the unorganized Fringe.

The Central Business District. Empirically the Central Business District in a metropolis such as Chicago or Detroit may

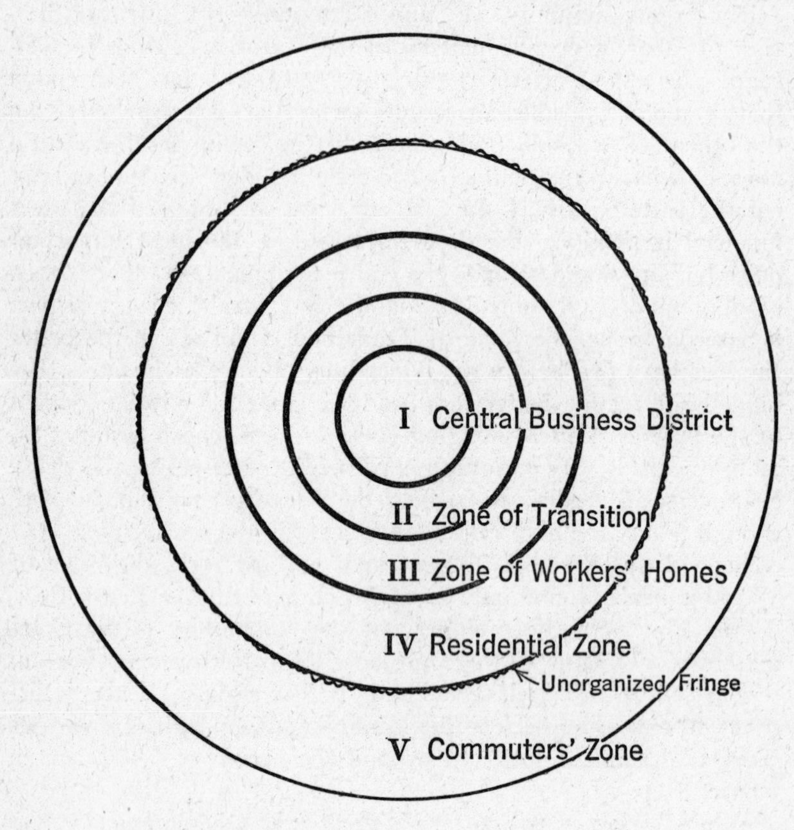

FIG. 8. Ideal Construction of the Urban Pattern.

be defined as the area within which real estate values exceed $1000 a front foot. In Chicago this area is known as the Loop. In Detroit it takes the form of an inverted T, with a stem extending about two miles north of the Detroit River. In this area are concentrated the financial, economic, and legal institutions and services that dominate and direct the activities not only of the rest of the metropolitan centre itself but of millions of people in the hinterland from which the metropolis draws its supplies and into which it extends its services and sends its products. Here are the great banks and trust companies, the great department stores whose deliveries reach out from 30 to 60 miles and whose mail-order business goes out hundreds of miles further; the great newspapers whose circulation areas cover whole States; the head offices of insurance companies, fraternal orders, manufacturing plants; the ticket offices of steamship and railroad companies. Here are the greatest traffic congestion and the greatest movement of pedestrians. In Detroit this central business district constitutes about one half of 1 per cent of the city area, yet it receives over 40 per cent of the mail,[6] carries on more than half of the telephone conversations, and controls probably 90 per cent of the community's serious economic activity. From the point of view of the number of people entering and leaving the district per unit of land area per day and from the point of view of the degree of control exercised over the rest of the community, both the civic community and the service community, the Central Business District is the most dynamic part of the city.

The Zone of Transition. On the other hand, the zone immediately around the Central Business District is highly dynamic in another sense. People change their residences here more often than anywhere else. Businesses come and go more rapidly than anywhere else. There is more crime and vice here than in any other zone. Personal disorganization is more prevalent and juvenile delinquency more frequent. The mile area just south of the Loop along the lake front in Chicago, for example, had a juvenile delinquency rate of 19.4 per cent in 1927, the highest in the city.[7] Studies in Chicago, Cleveland, Richmond, and other cities show that juvenile delinquency tends to peak up in the Zone of Transition, or blighted area, and to decrease steadily toward the better residential areas at the edge of the city.

From the point of view of community welfare, the blighted area presents some of the most difficult problems in the city. Like a beach deserted by one tide and not yet covered by another, it is

[6] The downtown area of Detroit, comprising about 3 per cent of the total area of the Detroit Postal District having city delivery, furnished 59.4 per cent of all letter collections in a sample two-day count in 1926.—Data furnished by Mr. Donald Marsh from unpublished studies of the Detroit central business district. The count covered an area somewhat larger than the central business district alone, which covers only half of one per cent of Detroit.

[7] Clifford R. Shaw, *Delinquency Areas,* Chicago, 1929. At the other extreme, a four-mile area on the north side had a delinquency rate of only 0.8 per cent.

a region of castaways and stranded failures: the rendezvous of prostitutes, dope fiends, professional criminals, homeless transients, and various other types of unadjusted humanity. Not only is the area always well supplied with the less desirable types of enterprise, but it is usually under-supplied with playgrounds, parks, libraries, Boy Scout troops, and other institutions making for healthful and worthwhile use of leisure time. Thus community resistance to the process of moral degeneration is weakest in the very area in which it should be the strongest. Since the better types of families tend to shun this area or to move out of it as soon as possible, it follows by a process of social selection that the area itself can provide little initiative toward its own regeneration. Hence the salvation of the blighted area, if any is to be found, must be sought in the community leadership supplied by other sections of the city.

The Unorganized Fringe. Cities grow by the more and more intensive occupation of land within the corporate limits and by the successive annexation of more and more territory. From less than 1 square mile in 1806, Detroit, for example, expanded to an area of more than 139 square miles in 120 years.

Frequently this process of expansion goes on with little regard for anything except the immediate needs of home-seekers and the immediate profits of the real-estate dealers who place the property on the market. The result inevitably is a sprawling, unorganized growth not unlike the original process that settled the frontier. Attracted by cheap land and low rentals, the more venturesome families go out beyond the usual community services and put up or occupy temporary homes. As compared with the residents of the older areas who have police protection, libraries, churches, organized centres of recreation, fire protection, hospital service, etc., the dwellers in these raw and inchoate sections of Chicago, Detroit, and other American cities can easily be regarded as living on a kind of urban frontier. The social consequences of this method of urban growth by extensions of population beyond the urban culture centre deserve more study than they have yet received.

STUDY QUESTIONS

1. "A community is a local aggregation of people who have interests in common." What elements are omitted in that definition?
2. Explain the order in which functions evolved in Keene, N. H.

3. What is the difference between a simple community structure and a complex one?
4. What is the civic community? the service community?
5. In what way does the interpenetration of town and country differ today in the average urban community from the condition in the old rural village?
6. Define ecology.
7. What are the oustanding ecological processes distinguished by McKenzie?
8. What general factor seems to be closely related to the distribution of population centres?
9. What do you understand by the ascending order of dominance as between communities?
10. Explain the process of segregation.
11. Why does invasion occur?
12. Draw the urban pattern from memory.
13. How many population centres are there in the U. S.?
14. Trace the process of succession in some area known to you—your city, your county, or your State.
15. In what sense is the Central Business District the most dynamic area in the city? In what sense is the Zone of Transition the most dynamic?
16. Apply the urban pattern to your own community, indicating clearly the Zone of Transition and the Unorganized Fringe if possible.
17. What specific observations can you make concerning the Unorganized Fringe of some city with which you are familiar?

CHAPTER XVII

THE COMMUNITY AS A CENTRE OF FUNCTION

The Functional Approach to the Community. From a functional point of view a community consists of an aggregation of people who are engaged more or less co-operatively in earning a living, making homes, rearing young, using leisure time, engaging in religious practices, joining in community activities, and in various ways providing informational, protective, and directive services.[1]

Each of these activities deserves a separate analysis, yet it is essential to see them here as aspects or phases of a more inclusive process, community life. In preceding chapters we have spoken of culture, primary groups, communication, public opinion, all of which appear of course in the community. In later chapters we shall analyze the phenomena of social classes, and of such specific institutions as the family, the school, the church. So long as we remember that it is the community that supplies the local stage, so to speak, on which primary groups, public opinion, social classes, the family, the school, and the church play their parts, it will be unnecessary to repeat here what is said elsewhere in more detail. For present purposes, therefore, we shall confine ourselves to certain other functions of community life—to economic functions, recreational functions, protective services, community information, and community control. Because there is great variation from community to community in the efficiency of these services we shall criticize as well as describe, assuming certain common-sense values such as the value of health, a decent childhood, protection against crime, efficient government, and so on.[2]

The Economic Organization of the Community. The community may be regarded as a focal point of production, distribution, and consumption. Slightly more than three fourths of

[1] The general organization of the discussion which follows is based largely on the functional analysis of Muncie, Ind., in *Middletown* by Robert M. and Helen S. Lynd, New York, 1928.

[2] We are here becoming social technologists in a sense rather than continuing as merely descriptive sociologists. The descriptive point of view is resumed after this chapter.

the males and one fifth of the females over 10 are gainful workers in the United States.[3] In a representative industrial community such as Middletown about 71 per cent of the gainful workers belong to the working class and about 29 per cent to the business and professional classes.[4] In terms of authority instead of occupation, about one seventh of any ordinary community give orders and about six sevenths take orders.

The basis of this division of income and authority in the United States is the system of private property rights in the means of production and distribution and in articles of consumption. This system, which is characterized by the use of wealth for the production of more wealth, by factory production, large-scale enterprise, minute division of labor, credit, centralized control, unequal distribution of wealth, cyclical fluctuations of prosperity and depression, and widespread belief in the efficacy of free competition for private gain, has created an interdependence of individual with individual and of community with community that makes contemporary social organization vastly more complex than any previous culture. Thus in Middletown, for example, there were about 400 different kinds of jobs by which individuals earned a living. But in addition to that maze of interrelationships, all the thousands of people working at these 400 jobs were working mainly for people in other communities who in turn were working for them. Nearly all the things that Middletown consumed—coal, building materials, clothing, food, automobiles, clocks, and the like,—were produced in mines or factories or on farms located elsewhere. To pay for what it consumed Middletown in turn produced glass bottles, insulators, automobile-engine parts, and various other articles nearly all of which were shipped out of town. Thus the process by which Middletown or any other community gets its living is an intricate process of production and exchange, with money and credit functioning as the mechanisms by which goods and services produced in one place are transformed ultimately into human satisfactions somewhere else. Over and above the evident element of competition is the even more fundamental fact of co-operation in a round-about process of want-satisfaction. In this process the relations of the various classes in the community and the relations of various communi-

[3] *Fifteenth Census of the United States: 1930. Occupation Statistics—United States Summary*, p. 8.
[4] See below, Chap. XX.

ties to one another will form the subject-matter of later chapters.[5]

The Community as a Place in Which to Play. We have just spoken of some of the outstanding features of the organization of work in an ordinary community. In the chapters on the family, the school, and the church we shall consider other basic aspects of community organization. For the present let us inquire into the community organization of leisure time. Thanks to the machine, the leisure time of adults has been increasing and with the present trends of labor-saving machinery it bids fair to increase still further in the future. From a time when the usual work day ran from sun-up to sun-down, the evolution of industry has resulted in the gradual reduction of hours until in 1924, for example, in 17 organized occupations three building trades had won the 40-hour week and none of the 17 worked longer than 54.[6] Constant displacement of men by machines and the depression which began in 1929 brought agitation for a 5-hour day and a 5-day week to spread existing jobs over more men. Whatever the outcome of this particular agitation, it seems clear that industry is tending in the direction of still shorter hours and more leisure, and both the schools and the community face increased responsibilities, the one for equipping pupils with interests and skills suitable for leisure, and the other for providing wholesome opportunities for satisfying those interests and exercising those skills.

Significantly enough, the growth of cities and the speeding up of urban transportation through the introduction of the trolley car and the automobile have worked together to make the leisure time of city children increasingly hazardous. In 1898, for example, horse-drawn vehicles and street cars together—there were no automobile fatalities—killed 201 persons of all ages in the streets of New York City, or about 5.8 per 100,000 population. In 1929, however, horses and street cars killed 74, and the automobile killed 1344, so that the total toll of street accidents per 100,000 had risen to 20.6, *i.e.,* to three and a half times the rate of 1898.[7] The failure of communities to foresee the needs of leisure time and to provide facilities for healthful recreation has driven millions of children to find their playgrounds in the streets and alleys.

[5] For a discussion of social classes see Chaps. XX and XXI. For a description of some phases of community interdependence see Chap. XVIII.

[6] *The American Labor Yearbook,* 1925, p. 26.

[7] Figures from *The World Almanac,* 1931, p. 563.

There they not only run the risk of accident but they also run an even more imminent risk of falling foul of the law. Experience in Chicago, Cleveland, Philadelphia, New York, and other cities has demonstrated that much of the juvenile delinquency that involves about 1 per cent of our juvenile population a year could be prevented simply by the provision of more supervised public playgrounds.[8]

Community provision for the play impulse began to take form between 1885 and 1895 when settlement houses and churches opened sand gardens for the smaller children in congested areas of the larger cities.[9] A few years later a few model playgrounds for older children appeared, and then in the more progressive cities a movement spread for equipping smaller parks as playgrounds. From 1905 to 1912 recreational centres were established in many cities, with Rochester, New York, leading the way in the wider use of the public schools. Civic art and welfare characterized the play movement on the eve of the World War. During the war the stress was on the development of local neighborhood centres, and following that there was an attempt to awaken backward communities to the need of organized recreation. The organization that finally emerged at the head of this movement was the Playground and Recreation Association of America which undertakes to furnish stimulus, guidance, and leadership for community recreational developments the country over.

The recreation movement has thus grown from an attempt to provide sand boxes for slum children to a recognized programme for providing recreation for all ages of all classes throughout the year. Private philanthropy has given way to public support and free play to organized, directed play. The objective is now not merely individual well-being but community integration. In 1926 790 cities reported play areas and a total public recreational expenditure of more than $19,202,000. Yet there were 320 cities of over 8000 population each without a single playground.

The slow growth of community interest in public recreation is

[8] Miriam Van Waters in *Youth in Conflict* estimated that 200,000 boys and girls passed through the juvenile courts in the United States in 1923. Since many of these were repeaters, the annual number of new cases would be somewhat less than the total number handled, but the number handled by the police is not included in the estimate.

[9] Summarized from Arthur E. Wood, *Community Problems,* New York, 1928, pp. 293 ff., and from Clarence E. Rainwater, *The Play Movement in the United States,* University of Chicago Press, 1922.

paralleled by community blindness to the need of controlling commercialized recreation. While most communities are now aware of the necessity of exercising some control over dance halls, pool rooms, moving-picture theatres, and the like, in the drafting of legal measures and in their enforcement when they have been passed there is usually a conflict between the demand for "chivalry toward youth," as Miss Van Waters calls it, and the demands of business men seeking profits by exploiting the play impulse. All too frequently fear of interfering with profits hampers public action intended to safeguard youth. Even service organizations such as the Boy Scouts, the Y. M. C. A., and the like can only partially offset such conditions, since they can seldom reach more than a minority of the young people involved and usually not the individuals who need their services most.

As a general conclusion concerning recreational conditions in most American communities, it is a safe generalization to say that every American community would benefit immeasurably by making a deliberate, conscious effort to provide more intelligently the conditions essential to healthy childhood. There is not a community in America in which the efficient rearing of children is regarded by more than a small fraction of the people as an objective equal in importance to profit-making, personal success, and a good time.

Protective Services in the Community. As a matter of fact if we are to criticize American communities for their inefficiency in child-rearing, there are other phases of community life that must not be overlooked. Protection of life and property is, of course, a major community objective. In 1930 there were in round numbers 73,000 firemen; 131,000 policemen not counting private guards and watchmen; and 41,000 marshals, sheriffs, and detectives.

Yet in spite of this small army of protectors it is common knowledge that in many communities the police department is paralyzed by political interference, which compels the enforcement officers to wink at the existence of "speak-easies," houses of prostitution, gambling houses, gang hang-outs, and the like, all of which in turn inevitably generate crime and contribute to further community disorganization.

The most notable exception to this very prevalent condition among large cities in 1930 was probably Milwaukee, Wis., which had the lowest burglary insurance rate in the country, did not let politicians tamper with the police department, and had had only three chiefs of police in 45 years.[10]

Inefficient as the average city police department is, however, the policing of rural communities is even worse. Under modern conditions the policing of rural areas over most of the United States is a joke. The chief protection now enjoyed by farmers from criminals is not from the sheriff miles away but from the fact that compared with banks, gas stations, and payrolls awaiting attack in the cities the average farm home has nothing to tempt the underworld.

In the same way, rural communities are inadequately protected against fire. While every city and practically every village now has fire-fighting equipment, it has only been with the coming of the automobile and the good road that the use of this equipment beyond the town has become feasible. Hence the growth of co-operative movements by which farmers, by subscribing a few dollars a year, can receive the services of the village fire-fighting equipment. Most of rural America in 1930 was still without such protection, however, and the rural fire loss was consequently more than $150,000,000 a year.

Along with the protection of life and property the protection of health has gradually been thrust forward by medical progress as another community objective of major importance. But it is still an objective whose attainment varies greatly in degree from community to community. The infant mortality rate, *i.e.*, the number of infants who die in their first year per 1000 live births, has long been recognized as a sensitive index of community health conditions. Taking 23 large American cities in 1930, infant mortality rates varied from 37.6 in Seattle to 92.7 in Denver.[11]

Health protection is the business of a large army of physicians,

[10] See "Wisconsin Gets Her Man," Ruth McDaniel, *North American Review*, June, 1929.

[11] The 23 cities and their respective infant mortality rates were: New York, 57.2; Chicago, 53.4; Philadelphia, 63.9; Detroit, 64.7; Los Angeles, 60.9; Cleveland, 54.5; St. Louis, 53.0; Baltimore, 65.6; Boston, 70.2; Pittsburgh, 69.2; San Francisco, 39.8; Milwaukee, 54.6; Buffalo, 67.3; Washington, D. C., 70.3; Minneapolis, 55.1; Cincinnati, 65.4; Newark, 52.1; Seattle, 37.6; Portland, 40.4; Denver, 92.7; Providence, 52.4; New Haven, 46.9; Bridgeport, 46.4. *Cf. World Almanac,* 1932, p. 382.

In 1927 the average for the 44 States in the U. S. registration area was 65, which placed the U. S. sixth among the 16 countries of the world whose rates were less than 100. New Zealand with a rate of 39 led the world. See *Encyclopædia of the Social Sciences,* Vol. III, p. 390.

nurses, druggists, and others who number in all more than 1,500,000.[12] This is nearly as many as the entire population of a city like Detroit in 1930, or about nine times as many as all the public peace officers in the United States. The Committee on the Cost of Medical Care in a comprehensive study covering several years found more than 143,000 physicians enumerated, or more proportionately than in any other country in the world. The geographical distribution of this army of healers is, however, very uneven.

In 1927 South Carolina and Montana had only 71 physicians per 100,000 people, while California, at the other extreme, had 200.

> Various state surveys show clearly that the larger cities are over-supplied with doctors relative to population, whereas smaller towns and rural districts are *relatively* under-supplied. Comparatively few recent graduates of medical schools are located in the small communities; the proportion settling in the larger cities is becoming progressively greater.[13]

In a similar way the 7000 hospitals in the United States with their 853,000 beds are likewise unevenly distributed. Over 40 per cent of the 3000 or more counties in the country have no hospitals for general community use. States show a range of from 1 bed per 154 persons as in Wisconsin to 1 bed per 749 persons as in South Carolina. Smaller cities have proportionately fewer hospital facilities than larger cities. Figure 9 shows the distribution of hospital facilities in October, 1928.

American communities are still highly individualistic in their approach to health problems. A survey of municipal health departments in 83 cities of more than 100,000 inhabitants, sponsored by the American Public Health Association, in co-operation with the United States Public-Health Service and with the assistance of the American Red Cross, revealed that in 1923 these 83 cities were spending for direct health service only 51.6 cents per capita.[14]

[12] Allen Peebles, *A Survey of Statistical Data on Medical Facilities in the United States,* The Committee on the Cost of Medical Care, Washington, D. C., 1929, p. 3.

[13] *Ibid.*, p. 3.

[14] Arthur Evans Wood, *Community Problems,* New York, 1928, p. 184, from Report of the Committee on Municipal Health Department Practice of the American Public Health Association in Co-operation with the United States Public Health Service, *Public Health Bulletin,* No. 136, July, 1923, United States Public Health Service. Fear on the part of the medical profession of "state medicine," *i.e.*, tax-supported medical service, has been one of the strongest factors in retarding changes in this field. Yet the inadequacies existing constitute potent sources of public dissatisfaction with the present organization of medical service.

One of the most striking conclusions in this study was that "the standard methods for the control of communicable disease formulated by the American Public Health Association and adopted by that body were not in general use at the time of this survey."[15]

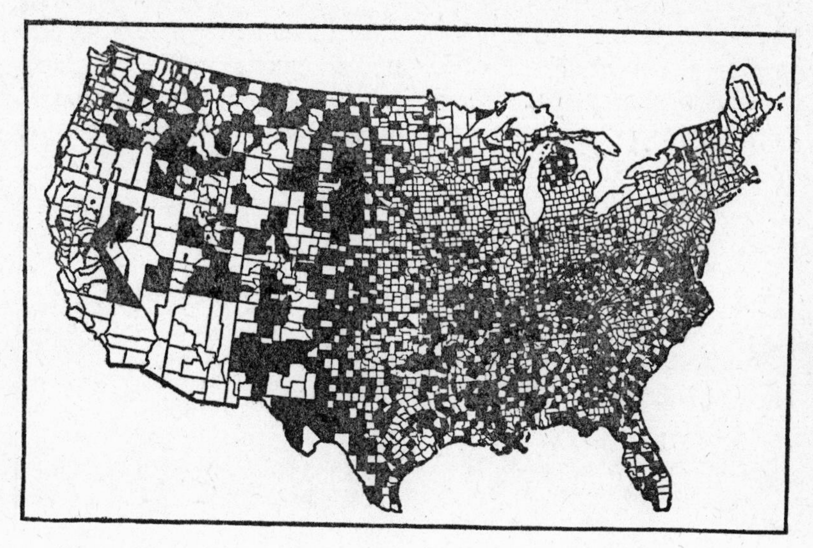

FIG. 9. Counties in the United States Without Hospitals for Community Use, October, 1928, Shown in Black.

Reproduced from *"A Survey of Statistical Data on Medical Facilities in the United States"* by Allen Peebles, The Committee on the Cost of Medical Care, Washington, D. C., October, 1929, p. 10.

The variation in distribution of nursing services needed for even moderate protection in a typical State is shown in Figure 10.

Caring for the Unable. There are four classes of dependents in American communities: the *normally dependent* children and old people; the *physically and mentally dependent, i.e.,* the sick, the injured, the blind, etc.; the *morally dependent,* or paupers,

[15] *Ibid.,* p. 184. It has become axiomatic among the socially informed that public health is *purchasable* and that it *pays.* In a city it costs at least $1.50 per capita per year to provide reasonably adequate health service. But New York City spends only 75 cents. How well public health pays can be illustrated in two ways. (1) During the depression of 1929–33 when cities were cutting teachers' salaries and closing playgrounds, nobody advocated the abolition of the public safeguards of water and milk supplies; (2) the Diphtheria Prevention Commission of New York estimates that an expenditure of $420,000 saved the lives of 1,400 children and nearly $3,500,000 *in three years.* J. A. Kingsbury, "Public Health Pays," *Survey,* February, 1932, p. 536.

FIG. 10. How Health Protection Varies by Counties.

who have given up the struggle to be self-supporting; and the *unemployed but employable.*

In Middletown, as we have already noted, more than a third of the community were classed as normally dependent, *i.e.,* too young or too old to work. Mills, compiling the statistics of illness and physical and mental defect in the United States for the Committee on the Cost of Medical Care in 1929, estimated that there were 900,000 mental defectives, 100,000 blind persons, 350,000 patients in hospitals for mental and nervous diseases, and 130,000,000 cases of disabling illness each year.[16] Estimates of the number of "social deserters," or paupers, run from 50,000 to 200,000. The unemployed are conservatively estimated to number more than 1,000,000 in so-called normal times and during the depression which began in 1929 the number increased to more than 10,000,000.

To care for these various types of dependents American communities have four institutionalized devices: *Individual gifts; group gifts* from churches, lodges, etc., usually at Thanksgiving and Christmas; *voluntarily supported social organizations;* and *tax-supported agencies.*

In colonial times it was assumed that the care of dependents whose relatives could not provide for them was an obligation of the local unit of government. Late in the nineteenth century part of this obligation began to be assumed by private charity, and many people gained the impression that the rich were now caring for the poor. Statistical studies in Manhattan in 1928, however, show that out of 357,825 persons who filed income tax returns, only 55,000, or about one out of seven, "subscribe to the city's three leading charities."[17] After summarizing similar figures from other cities, Epstein concludes that "the slackers in the United States are not the poor but the rich" and that, "When we talk of caring for unemployment and drought by private philanthropy we talk nonsense."

Private charity proved utterly unable to cope with relief demands during the depression of the early '30s. Reliable estimates indicated that during the first two years of the depression out of

[16] Alden B. Mills, *The Extent of Illness and of Physical and Mental Defects Prevailing in the United States,* The Committee on the Cost of Medical Care, Washington, D. C., 1929.

[17] "Do the Rich Give to Charity?" Abraham Epstein, *The American Mercury,* May, 1931.

every dollar spent for relief, 70 cents came from tax money and only 30 cents from private charity. Yet in 290 cities in 1931–32 the community chests applied to family relief alone no less than $35,000,000 out of their privately subscribed funds of $100,-000,000.[18]

Not only is private charity unable to cope with the relief problems created by mass unemployment, but old-fashioned methods of public charity are also going by the board. Since old age dependency and unemployment are persistent phenomena in the machine age, the demand has been growing in recent years for the removal of the stigma of charity from public provision for such dependency. The poorhouse, for example, as the community's solution of the problem of old-age dependency has been definitely losing caste in many States. The decline of the poorhouse can be measured by the number of States that have passed laws establishing old-age pension systems. In 1931 17 States had such laws providing for the payment of pensions to persons of 65 and upwards who have no income above $1 a day and no children able to support them, who have been in the State a certain number of years, and are citizens of the United States.[19]

The 1929 depression increased the agitation for measures designed to prevent unemployment dependency. After having denounced unemployment insurance for years, the American Federation of Labor in 1932 reversed itself completely and at its Cincinnati convention adopted a resolution demanding that kind of protection for all workers. Oddly enough, however, nearly six months before the largest body of organized workers in the country came to this conclusion the State of Wisconsin had put in force the first unemployment insurance law in the United States. The Groves Bill, which was signed by Governor LaFollette of Wisconsin in January, 1932, provides for an unemployment insurance fund by a contribution by employers and employees of 2 per cent of the payroll except for employees getting more than $1500 a year and for the employees of certain industries such as interstate railroads. Employers are given the option of setting up their own insurance plans provided they are at least as liberal as the State

[18] "Relief Crisis Near, Brownlow Declares," stenographic report of an address by Louis Brownlow, of the Public Administration Clearing House, Chicago, before the American Society of Newspaper Editors at Washington, April, 1932, as reported in *Editor and Publisher, The Fourth Estate,* April 30, 1932, p. 27.

[19] In New York State during the first ten months that the law was in operation applications totalled 77,158, of which 47,939 were granted.

plan. In a statement of public policy, the Groves law explains the theory underlying it: "The burden of irregular unemployment now falls directly and with crushing force on the unemployed worker and his family, and results also in an excessive drain on agencies for private charity and for public relief. The decreased and irregular purchasing power of wage-earners in turn vitally affects the livelihood of farmers, merchants, and manufacturers, results in decreased demand for their products, and thus tends partially to paralyze the economic life of the entire State. . . . Industrial and business units in Wisconsin should pay at least a part of this social cost, caused by their own irregular operations."

In general, in caring for dependents outside the home personal and semi-personal giving is being replaced by more organized charity and tends to function through trained social workers. The agitation for old-age pensions and unemployment insurance is indicative of deep-seated dissatisfaction with old methods of handling these problems.

Getting Information. Participation in community affairs and the making of intelligent decisions on common problems depend on the *information service* available to the community. Americans tend to rely largely on the newspaper for this service, supplemented to some degree by the radio and perhaps an occasional lecture or public meeting. Comparative surveys show that the newspaper is the most pervasive single medium of communication in the community (aside from the postal service), reaching a higher percentage of homes than the radio, the magazine, the telephone, or the motion picture. Under modern conditions it is practically a necessity in the conduct of group affairs.

Yet the fact remains that keeping the public informed of community affairs was only one of the functions of the 1923 commercial, or profit-seeking, daily newspapers published in 1931.[20] It is always easier to entertain people than to inform them or to make them think, hence the path to easy dividends lies in the direction of entertainment rather than community information. Thus in city after city we have the spectacle of pages of comics printed and waste-baskets full of community news ignored or rejected.

[20] *The International Yearbook of Editor and Publisher, The Fourth Estate,* January, 1932, listed 384 morning papers, 1539 evening papers and 513 Sunday papers.

Analysis of 12 issues of *The Toledo Blade, The Cleveland Press* and *The Saginaw Daily News,* July 11 to July 23, inclusive, 1932, covering a total of 124,178 column inches, revealed, for example, the fact that the percentage of total space devoted to local news averaged about 10 per cent for the three papers. Of this local news, approximately one third was devoted to recreation and amusement, about one fourth to police and governmental items, and about one sixth to business. All other local activities of churches, families, schools, the Federal government, State government, fraternal orders, public utilities, and the arts and professions together occupied on the average only about one third or one fourth of the total local space, or less than 3 per cent of the paper. While 12 issues of a daily paper constitute a very small sample and are not in any way conclusive evidence, the results at least suggest a certain indifference on the part of representative newspapers to large areas of community life.

Controlling the Community. Individual behavior in a community is largely determined by the beliefs, customs, and institutions which, taken collectively, constitute the *mores.* The institution charged most specifically with the control of behavior is *government.*

Most rural and urban communities have long ago outgrown their forms of local government. In the country the township, which is the local unit in most States, is generally moribund. Even the county fails to correspond to social and economic realities. Why, from a functional point of view, should there be a New York *County* in the midst of New York City, and why should the metropolitan area of Detroit be divided among no less than *five* counties? In the cities the condition is even worse, for most cities are still trying to operate under forms of government set up for semi-rural or village conditions. Because party organizations are needed to operate the State and national governments and because party organizations need local government jobs, or the prospect of government jobs, to hold the nucleus of the organization loyal, local government in America is still regarded as a political matter, when actually its main functions have to do less with policy-making than with business administration. This has been clearly recognized in England and especially in Germany where city management has long been a skilled profession.

Not only are we still thinking of local government in political terms, but we are still thinking of it in out-of-date political terms. In a small town a voter can vote intelligently on all the officials needed to operate his city government. He knows the candidates, and the functions of government are simple. But when the small town grows into a city of tens of thousands or a million inhabitants, government becomes so complicated that it is absurd to expect intelligent judgment from the voter on all the officials responsible for its various functions. Yet in only a small percentage of American cities has any attempt been made to readjust the structure of city government to its changing functions and increasing complexity. The situation in Detroit may be taken as typical. In 1835 the City of Detroit was performing 12 functions for the taxpayers; in 1921 it was performing 184.[21] Yet the only difference so far as the voter was concerned was that in 1921, instead of voting for a handful of candidates most of whom he probably knew personally, he was now called upon in a city of more than 1,000,000 people to vote for literally hundreds of candidates very few of whom he could possibly know even by reputation. Under such conditions which prevail in most American cities the wonder is not that we have scandals such as the Thompson régime in Chicago, but that municipal government works even as well as it does.

Two outstanding efforts have been made to adapt city government to the new conditions. The first, the commission form of government, originated in Galveston, Texas, after the hurricane of September, 1900, and spread slowly until in 1923 it had been adopted by 283 cities and retained by 214. The second radical departure from the old pattern is the city manager plan which seems to have been an outgrowth of the commission form and first appeared in 1908. By 1927 352 cities had adopted the city manager plan and 225 had retained it.[22] The main idea in both the commission form and the city manager plan is to centralize responsibility, eliminate "blind balloting" on the part of the average voter, subordinate politics, simplify administration, and bring better-trained men to the task of operating city governments.

Summary. From the point of view of functional unity a community is engaged in making a living in co-operation with other

[21] Dr. Upson, *The Growth of a City,* Detroit Bureau of Government Research, 1922.

[22] F. Stuart Chapin, *Cultural Change,* 1929, pp. 369 and 371.

communities; in making homes; rearing young; using leisure time; going to church; protecting health, property, and safety; keeping itself informed; and controlling itself through the institution of government. All of these functions as they are carried on in most American communities today show evidences of tardiness in readjusting to changed conditions. Business suffers from unemployment; recreational facilities are inadequate and not properly controlled; health protection is unevenly distributed; fire protection is largely limited to towns; police protection is a scandal in most of our large cities and feeble at best in the country districts; newspapers ignore whole sectors of community life to capitalize mass emotion; rural and urban government in most American communities is antiquated in structure and inefficient in operation. With so many maladjustments existing, American communities are interesting laboratories in which to study the process of social change.

STUDY QUESTIONS

1. What major functions are people in communities carrying on?
2. What do you understand by the expression "the community is the focal point of production, distribution, and consumption"?
3. What percentage of males over 10 are gainful workers? What percentage of females over 10?
4. In a representative industrial community what percentage of the population belong to the working class? What percentage to the business and professional classes? What percentage give orders?
5. What is the basis of this division of income and authority?
6. What are some of the outstanding characteristics of the existing economic system?
7. Illustrate in some concrete way from your own experience (*a*) the interdependence of people within a community; and (*b*) the interdependence of communities.
8. Why is the problem of leisure time becoming more important?
9. What evidence is there that working hours may eventually be even shorter than at present?
10. "The growth of cities and of machine civilization has made the business of being a child a risky occupation." Explain.
11. What percentage of the American people were living in cities of 8000 or more when the playground movement began? (Look up figures in U. S. Census.)

12. Trace the stages in the development of the recreation movement. How does the modern movement differ from its beginnings?
13. Give examples of the failure of the public to control commercialized recreation.
14. Why is the average police department inefficient?
15. Explain the comparative efficiency of the Milwaukee department.
16. What inequalities exist in the distribution of fire and police protection?
17. How many people are engaged in contributing to health protection?
18. What variations in infant mortality exist as between various large cities? Where does the U. S. rank in infant mortality as compared with other nations? Is your own community above or below the national average? (Look up health reports of your state board of health or write to your local health officer for information.)
19. What percentage of counties in the United States had no hospitals for general use in 1928?
20. What extremes of nursing protection exist among Michigan counties?
21. What does an adequate public health programme cost per capita?
22. What were 83 cities spending per capita in 1923?
23. What retrenchments were made in the public health budget of your community as a result of the depression which began in 1929? (Write to your local board of health.)
24. What are the various types of dependent persons? How many are there? How many unemployed?
25. How are dependents cared for? What evidence is there that private charity is not adequate?
26. What is the difference in point of view underlying the old-age-pension system as contrasted with the poorhouse system?
27. Explain the theory underlying the first unemployment-insurance bill passed in the United States.
28. What evidence is there to suggest that newspapers tend to neglect many community activities?
29. What are the outstanding defects in local government in the U. S.?
30. What two reforms have been attempted in city government? What percentage of cities have adopted them?
31. Why is there so much maladjustment in community life?

CHAPTER XVIII

REGIONS AND THE AMERICAN STATES

The Community as the Functional Centre of an Area. We have been considering the community as a centre of function. Inevitably we have had to imply that many of these functions are not confined to the limits of one town or city, and as a matter of fact we have seen that many of them involve a complicated give and take between various communities. It is necessary now to make the pattern of organization of this interdependence more explicit; to examine, in other words, some of the ramifications of the service community which surrounds and maintains the civic community. There are more than 18,000 population centres in the United States, incorporated and unincorporated, and our problem is to see how they are related to one another and to the scattered population in between.

Let us begin with the rural trade centre and its surrounding trade area. There are thousands of such trade centres scattered over the United States. They exist because agriculture is no longer self-sufficing but is conducted through a trading economy. According to Zimmerman, the cross-roads store is "the first sign of the appearance of non-agricultural activities and forms the first and most elementary variety of the trade centre."[1]

In a sense every trade centre, even the cross-roads store, is the centre of an ecological "region," *i.e.,* an area within which the inhabitants are oriented toward the centre for the services which it performs. But the term *region* is usually reserved for larger areas, each containing a constellation of centres. The smaller areas surrounding single centres are called *service-areas.*

The Service-Area. The first sociologists to realize the im-

[1] Carl C. Zimmerman, *Farm Trade Centres in Minnesota, 1905–29,* Bulletin 269, University of Minnesota Agricultural Experiment Station, September, 1930, p. 9. It is unnecessary to consider an even more elementary type of community, namely, the European peasant community. In such a community the village is not a trade centre *i.e.,* essentially a secondary group, but a neighborhood, *i.e.,* a primary group. For the implications of this see Walter Terpenning, *Village and Open Country Neighborhoods,* Century, 1931. This form of rural organization is not prevalent in the United States.

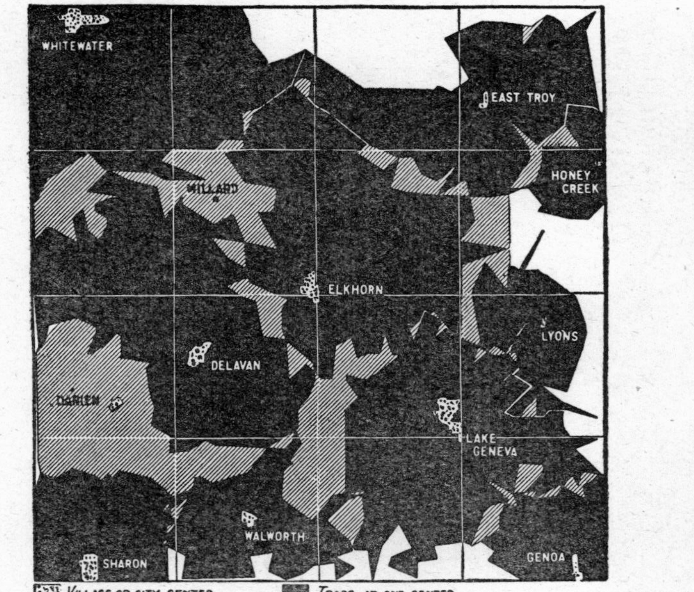

FIG. 11. Trade Communities.

Twelve villages and small cities situated in the county serve as trade centres for the farm homes precisely as for the village and city homes, and all the homes trading at the same centre form a trade community. Township lines six miles apart indicate the distance.

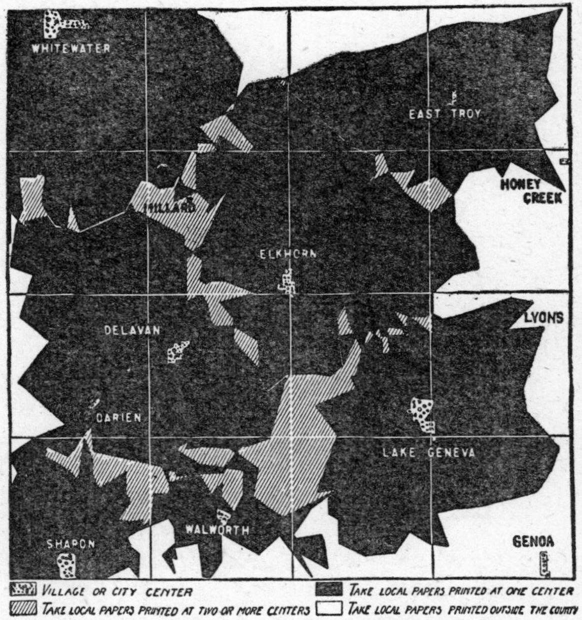

FIG. 12. Local-Paper Communities.

The homes taking the same local paper form a paper community. Such communities are pretty well defined and conform closely to the trade and banking communities.

From Galpin's "Rural Life." The Century Company.

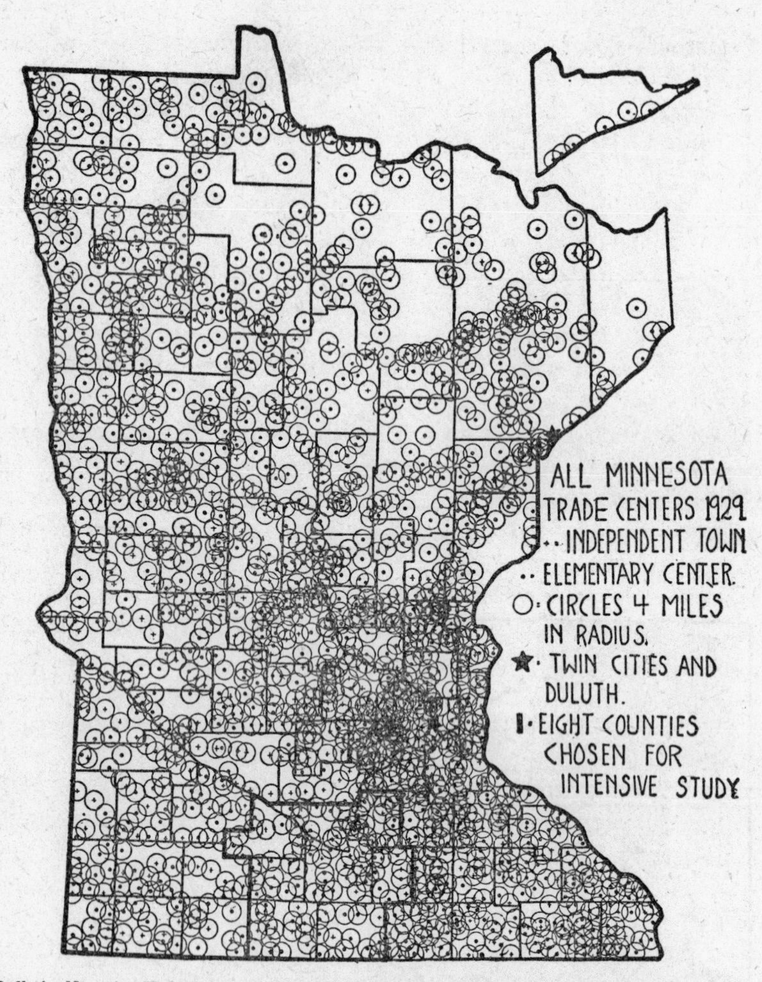

Bulletin No. 269, University of Minnesota Agricultural Experiment Station, p. 24.

FIG. 13. Location of All 1564 Trading Centres of Minnesota in 1929.

The independent centres are marked by a cross and the pure elementary centres by a dot. The circles are four miles in radius. The map attempts to show that the agricultural population of the state, even in 1929, is within approximately four miles or less of one or more trading centres. Further, the more highly developed areas, which are somewhat typical of the closely populated areas of the older settled sections of the United States, show that a two-mile radius circle would encompass most of the territory. The inclosed area in the southern part of the state is the eight-county section chosen for intensive study.

portance of the service-area seem to have been the students of rural life, headed by Professor Galpin. Before the World War Professor Galpin had begun to map what he called rural boroughs, *i.e.,* trade centres along with the trade areas that surrounded them. It was discovered that around each trade centre there is a definite configuration of population, a specific service-community, for each service provided, and that there is a distinct area, or general service-community, within which everybody looks to the given centre for all the services locally provided, *i.e.,* for retail buying, banking, high school, church, grain shipping, news, and so on, depending of course on the size of the centre. Figures 11 and 12 show the specific service-communities existing for two services, retail buying and local news, in Walworth County, Wisconsin, as delimited by Professor Galpin.[2] And Figure 13 shows the distribution of all the 1564 trade centres in Minnesota in 1929.[3] On the average there was one such centre to every 567 members of the rural farm population. The distribution of trade centres is probably controlled by population density, income, transportation facilities, cultural or racial background,[4] and by various geographical and historical factors.

The Region—Local, Sub-Metropolitan, and Metropolitan. In addition to the direct farm-to-trade-centre relationship, there is, as we have already said, an interrelationship of centres. There are communities in Minnesota and in northern Michigan, for example, whose main activities consist in providing the iron ore essential to the steel plants of Pittsburgh and Youngstown. Middletown makes engine parts for Detroit, Detroit makes automobiles for the world, and New York provides the necessary financial, wholesale, and terminal facilities needed by the commerce of a continent. From the cross-roads store to New York there is an ascending hierarchy of interdependence—the cross-roads store serves the people of a rural neighborhood; New York's banks, wholesale houses, magazines, factories, hotels, and docks serve communities scattered from Bar Harbor to San Diego.

[2] *Rural Life,* Century, 1918, pp. 74 and 77.

[3] Carl C. Zimmerman, *Farm Trade Centres in Minnesota, 1905–1929,* Bulletin 269, University of Minnesota Agricultural Experiment Station, September, 1930, p. 24.

[4] The first four were the factors found to be controlling the distribution of retail centres in Baltimore by the Department of Commerce investigators in 1930. *Cf.* Inez K. Rolph, "The Population Pattern in Relation to Retail Buying," *American Journal of Sociology,* Nov., 1932, p. 368.

Let us be careful here, however, to emphasize again the distinction between a trade area and a region. The cross-roads store provides goods and services for individual consumers directly and it does nothing else. The neighboring village, while it is still mainly concerned with rendering services to the rural population within a radius of five or ten miles, has taken on two more functions: A part of its energy is devoted to providing goods and services for its own population; and a part goes, let us say, to the service of the cross-roads stores in its territory, *i.e.,* to the minor trade centres. The area of service of the village is somewhat larger than that of the cross-roads store, and the services involved are beginning to become more specialized and complex. Its area might thus be called a village region.

One step farther on and we have reached the small town, or county centre, which in news, banking, government, and other functions usually serves a number of villages. The area dominated by such a centre may be called a *local region.* A number of local regions will usually have certain interests centering in a city which can be spoken of as a sub-metropolitan centre dominating a *sub-metropolitan region.* Grand Rapids is an example of such a city, and most of western Michigan constitutes the Grand Rapids sub-metropolitan region.

Villages, local centres, and sub-metropolitan centres in turn all are oriented toward some one of the various metropolitan centres which dominate metropolitan regions in the United States.

In contra-distinction to a service-area in which services flow direct to the consumer, a region, then, may be defined as that area of dominance of any centre within which its services tend to flow to other centres and indirectly to the consumer. Let us illustrate this constellational pattern of community interdependence with such a familiar matter as the gathering and distribution of news.

The Constellational Pattern of News Distribution. The narrowest circle within which news circulates is the neighborhood, *i.e.,* the area within which people know each other by their first names and meet face to face. This is the area of gossip. Under rural conditions it is easy to distinguish neighborhoods. As we have already pointed out, the disappearance of such personal neighborhoods is one of the disorganizing factors in urban life. Many neighborhoods have no centre, *i.e.,* no nucleus where people congregate to gossip and exchange news. In such unorganized neighborhoods news circulates by word of mouth, of course, but less efficiently than in neighborhoods that have a general store, garage, post office, or some other focal point of meeting. Such focalized, or nucleated neighborhoods, constitute the first step up from the unorganized neighborhood toward the village, the city, and the metropolis. The cross-roads store constitutes such a neighborhood focus.

But the affairs of one neighborhood are not usually known directly to another neighborhood. Rumor passes from neighborhood to neighborhood sometimes, but the more usual link for news is the local correspondence that appears in the village weekly. It is the village weekly that ties up with the village the various neighborhoods in the service-area of the village and thus creates the mental correlate of the service-community.

In turn, the affairs of one village, or village service-area, are seldom known directly to the inhabitants of another village. Their most continuous and reliable source of information about neighboring villages is the local daily, usually published in the county seat or in the nearest small city of 5000 or more. Just as the village weekly links together the neighborhoods in the village region or service-area, so the small town daily links together the villages in the local region. Carrying this a step farther, we find that the affairs of one small town and its local region are known to people in another local region mainly through the city newspapers and through the news services supplied from the nearest metropolitan or sub-metropolitan centre. It is in these metropolitan or sub-metropolitan centres that the dispatches from local correspondents to the city papers are assembled and edited by the various press services and then distributed to all the local papers in the city's region.

Thus in the gathering and distribution of news there exists a definite constellational pattern, with the neighborhoods clustering around the village, the villages around the county-seat or local town, and the towns around the metropolitan or sub-metropolitan centre. A similar constellational pattern can be traced in the distribution of telephone service, in the distribution of automobiles, and in many other services. It is true, of course, that the parcel post, magazine advertising, retail delivery by automobile, and similar developments have tended to extend the service-areas of the great cities, but such extension does not seriously affect the general pattern of regional organization. Most services, most of the time, are still organized on the constellational pattern, centre-to-centre, with control tending to gravitate toward the metropolis itself.

For every centre superior to the cross-roads store, then, we must distinguish a service-area of direct service to consumers and a region of indirect, or centre-to-centre, service to consumers. For some services the two may be the same, as in the case of radio broadcasting. For others, as in the case of newspapers and banking, the direct service-area is probably smaller than the indirect, or centre-to-centre, service-area or region.

Local and Sub-metropolitan Regions. The village service-area is usually no larger than five or possibly ten miles in radius. But as the centre increases in population the services provided become more complex and the area served tends to enlarge. It becomes harder, therefore, to delineate regions and even city service-areas. Since it is impossible for an investigator to visit every home in a state or even in one county, some method of delineation by indexes must be used.

One of the most useful that has been suggested is the area dominated by the newspapers published in a given centre, *i.e.,* the area within which 50 per cent or more of the newspapers circulated are from the centre in question as compared with other centres of the same class.[5] In Figure 14 the local, sub-metropolitan, and metropolitan regions in lower Michigan as delineated by this method are shown. It should be clearly understood that newspaper circulation is only one index of a city's regional dominance. Just as the weekly newspaper area does not wholly coincide with the trade area around a rural village (see Figures 11 and 12), so the daily newspaper circulation area around any city probably does not correspond to the parcel-post area, the banking area, the radio-listener area, and so on. Yet a certain amount of correspondence probably exists, and this correspondence is prob-

[5] The comparison is always between centres of the same class. Thus in most local regions more of the local dailies than of the distant metropolitan dailies circulate, yet as compared with a competing metropolitan centre a county such as Jackson or Calhoun, for example, in Michigan, would be classed in the Detroit region rather than the Chicago or Toledo regions. (See Fig. 14.) This method of delineating regions was first used by Prof. R. E. Park, of Chicago.

ably closer in the village and local areas than in the sub-metropolitan and metropolitan regions.

Two things are particularly to be observed with reference to the regions depicted in Figure 14: one is that they do not in any way conform to the political boundaries of cities, counties, or states; and the other is that their actual configuration is probably to be explained largely in terms of history, transportation, competition and culture.

The smallest local region in lower Michigan in terms of square miles is that dominated by *The Ann Arbor Daily News*—Area 3. This barely crosses the boundaries of the adjoining counties to the north, east, and southeast, but is crowded out of a portion of its own county by competition from the rival regions, Nos. 12 and 1 (Jackson and Adrian), to the west and south.

The largest local region, exclusive of Grand Rapids, in terms of mere area is that dominated by *The Bay City Times*—Area 5. This covers all of eight counties and parts of seven more, most of which, however, are very sparsely populated. In all, the region had an estimated population of only 130,000 in 1930.

On the western side of the state Grand Rapids dominates a region (Area 11) which can probably be classed as sub-metropolitan. With a population of 168,000, it is the centre of news dominance for 17 entire counties and for parts of 8 others, an estimated population of 664,000, or 13 per cent of the state.

Grand Rapids dominates this region because of its predominance during the lumbering days of a generation ago, because of its superior transportation facilities, and because no other centre has been able to put its papers into the region on equal terms with the Grand Rapids papers.

That mere size of a centre is not always a good index of its regional dominance appears from a comparison of two of these centres in Michigan, Grand Rapids, and Flint. In 1930 Flint was only 7 per cent smaller than Grand Rapids, but its newspaper region, one of the smallest in the state, included only one county and parts of five others. Exclusive of Flint itself, this region had an estimated population of 88,000 as against nearly 500,000 in the Grand Rapids region outside of Grand Rapids. In terms of numbers served, Grand Rapids was thus 5.6 times as much of a regional centre as was Flint.

Metropolitan Regions. Authorities differ as to how many

By courtesy of Kenneth McGill, Earhart Fellow, University of Michigan, 1931.

FIG. 14. Metropolitan and Sub-Metropolitan Newspaper Circulation in Michigan.

metropolitan centres there are in the United States. Gras, basing his definition on financial dominance, contents himself with a dozen. The 1930 Census, however, on the basis of areas of 100,000 dominated by cities of 50,000 or more, distinguishes 93. These 93 covered only 1.2 per cent of the land area of the country, but they contained approximately 45 per cent of the population.

For Census purposes Grand Rapids ranks as a metropolitan centre. For present purposes it is of no importance whether it is called a metropolitan centre or a sub-metropolitan centre. In any event there are larger centres whose dominance tends to overlie that of the smaller centres. This is the case in Michigan with Detroit and in the north Middle West with Chicago.

As compared with newspaper competition from Chicago and Toledo, Detroit newspapers completely dominate 49 of the 68 counties in lower Michigan and dominate 12 others partially. In the upper peninsula, while neither Detroit nor Chicago circulation is much of a factor, such metropolitan circulation as there is belongs to Detroit east of a line from Manistique to Marquette and to Chicago west of that line.

The line or rather zone of competitive equality, as we may call it, is shown in Figure 14. To the south, west, and northwest, then, Detroit's newspaper dominance is limited ultimately by competition from rival centres. To the north and east the limitation is mainly physical and cultural in addition to competitive. North and east from Marquette to Sault Ste. Marie and on down to Detroit, there is a physical barrier of lakes and rivers—Lake Superior, the St. Mary's River, Lake Huron, the St. Clair River, Lake St. Clair, and the Detroit River. This barrier is effectively broken through at only three places—Sault Ste. Marie, Port Huron, and Detroit itself.[6] But at each of these three places the international boundary interposes an intangible cultural barrier, which is apparently more resistant to newspaper penetration than are hundreds of miles of native territory. Southward, Detroit papers push their way 40 miles, or two thirds of the distance to the rival centre, Toledo. Westward, they span nearly half of the 272 miles to Chicago. Northward, they dominate the entire 400 miles of territory to Lake Superior. But eastward, they fade away

[6] Boats cross at various other points on the St. Mary's River, the St. Clair River, and the Detroit River, but the main lines of transportation cross at the points indicated.

less than a mile from the Detroit River. One railroad tunnel, a vehicular tunnel, a suspension bridge, and half a dozen railroad and passenger ferry lines link the two shores of that river. The transportation problem facing the Detroit circulation managers, therefore, is certainly no greater than similar problems facing New York papers at the Hudson and East Rivers. Yet the New York papers blanket their territory for hundreds of miles beyond the rivers, because, aside from the physical barrier which has been overcome there just as it has been overcome at Detroit, no cultural barrier exists. It is this cultural barrier, the international boundary, plus the Canadian competition which flourishes behind it, that dams the flow of Detroit circulation along the international transportation routes.

The net result of all these forces—American competition, physical barriers, the international boundary, and Canadian competition—has been to produce a curiously lopsided and irregular region, some 400 miles long by 100 wide, with the centre of dominance far down on the extreme eastern border barely 40 miles from the southeastern corner. Assailed by rivals on the south and west and hemmed in by the Great Lakes and Canada, Detroit has been able to dominate only 80 per cent of the counties of its state and many of those only partially.

In contrast to the partial state dominance exerted by such a centre as Detroit stands the picture of multi-state dominance wielded by such centres as New York and Chicago. The dominance of New York's financial institutions in the fiscal and industrial affairs of the country is too well known to need elaboration. Some conception of the range of Chicago's dominance may be gathered from Figure 15, showing the area tied up to Great Lakes shipping ports by the structure of freight rates for fifth-class freight in 1924. As the heavy line indicates, all or a considerable portion of the people of 24 states from western New York to eastern Idaho are more or less directly tributary to the Great Lakes shipping routes. This area in 1930 had an estimated population of more than 44,000,000, or about 36 per cent of the United States. In terms of freight rates, Chicago itself was the centre of dominance for the area extending from eastern Indiana to eastern Idaho and as far south as Little Rock, Arkansas. From Louisville, Kentucky, for example, the fifth-class rate per 100 pounds in November, 1924, was 30 cents to Chicago, 31.5 to

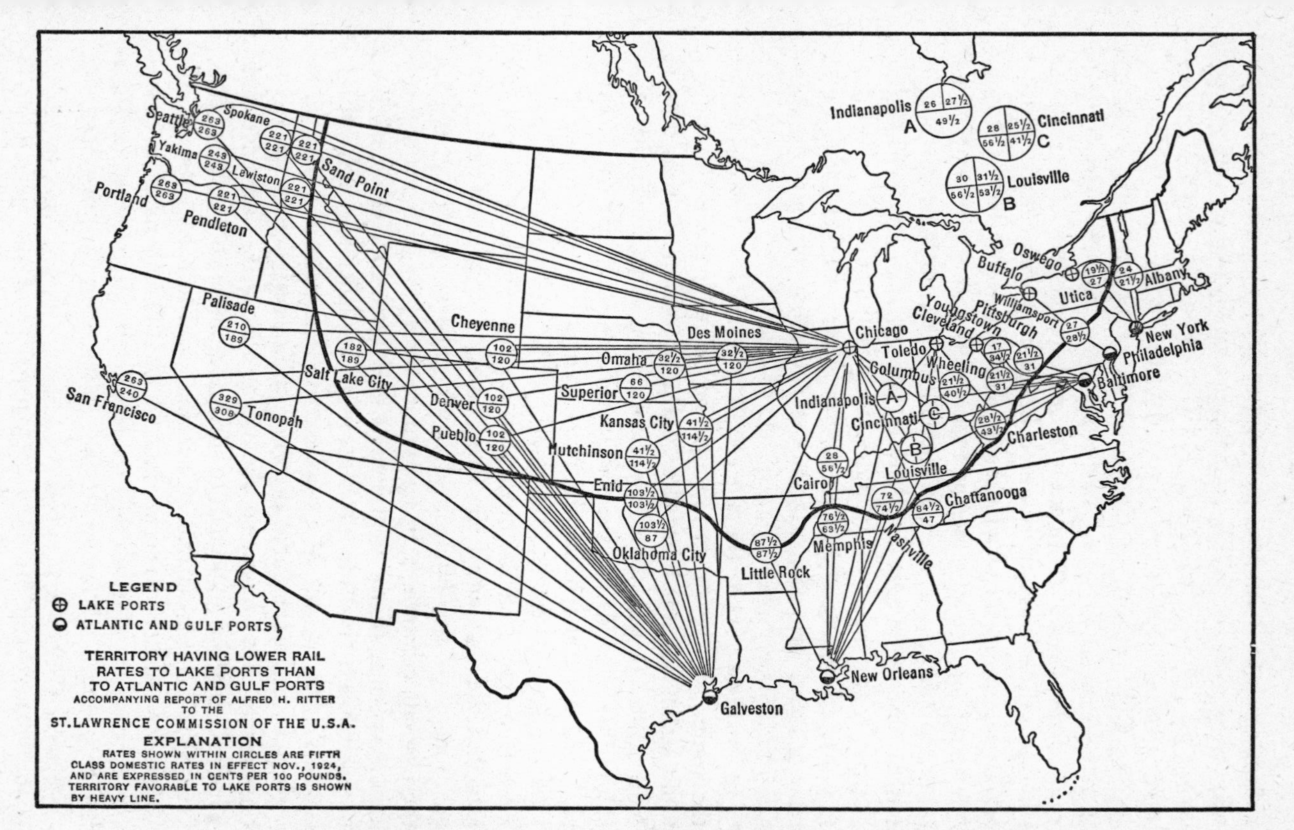

Fig. 15. Territory Having Lower Rail Rates to Lake Ports than to Atlantic and Gulf Ports.

Toledo, 53.5 to Baltimore, and 56.5 to New Orleans. In the same way from Salt Lake City, Utah, practically equidistant as the crow flies from both Chicago and Galveston, the rate to Chicago was 7 cents per 100 pounds *lower* than to the Gulf.

The Competition of Centres. It is apparent that a change in freight rates of even a few cents a hundred would divert a portion of the stream of business from Chicago, say, to Toledo or to some other centre. Any other factor that changed the cost of transportation in terms of time and money would have the same effect. At any given time, in other words, the various regional centres of the country are in a condition of unstable equilibrium with reference to one another. A new road, a new railroad, a change in freight or postal rates, the opening of a new form of transportation, any one of a score or more of other factors may change the distribution of services and stimulate the growth of one centre or region at the expense of another.

In the early part of the nineteenth century, for example, before the coming of the steamship and the railroad, the settlers in the Ohio Valley felt far more closely drawn to New Orleans than to New York. It was to New Orleans, not New York, that they shipped their goods. As the continent developed, four cities on the seaboard entered into a strenuous competition for metropolitan predominance—Boston, New York, Philadelphia, and Baltimore. At the beginning of the nineteenth century Philadelphia held the lead, but the opening of the Erie Canal, in 1825, capitalizing the advantages of the Hudson-Mohawk gateway, gave New York the ultimate advantage. In 1930 more than half of the entire foreign commerce of the continent passed through New York harbor. Its closest rival was not Boston, or Philadelphia or Baltimore or New Orleans, but Montreal.

Just as the Erie Canal diverted millions of dollars' worth of business to New York, so the Great Lakes-St. Lawrence Ship Channel may be expected to divert millions of dollars from New York to Montreal, Cleveland, and other ports on the Great Lakes-St. Lawrence route. What this can mean in a specific case can be illustrated by the estimated effects of such a channel on the cost of raw materials delivered at Akron, Ohio, the rubber capital of the country,

In 1919, Akron produced 48.5 per cent of the rubber manufactures of the country, and 95 per cent of the 344,860 tons imported into the United States in 1922 came through the port of New York. Laid down at Akron, the rate per ton of rubber from Europe was $15.40. By the St. Lawrence Ship Channel, permitting ocean steamers to reach lake ports direct, the estimated cost would have been $10.40, a saving of $5.00 a ton, or 32 per cent.[7] Had the St. Lawrence Ship Channel been in operation in 1922, in other words, most of Akron's rubber would have passed through Montreal instead of through New York. Hence, we see one of the reasons for the bitter opposition of New York shipping and financial interests to the deepening of the St. Lawrence waterway, and hence, also, the reason for the activities of the Great Lakes-St. Lawrence Tidewater Association, composed of the representatives of 23 states whose freight rates would be lowered by the deepening of the St. Lawrence.[8]

This competition of centres goes all the way down to the struggle for survival between cross-roads hamlets. In Minnesota, for example, between 1905 and 1929, 320 trade centres disappeared while 356 new centres came into existence.[9] The same thing is going on in all states. Since the coming of the automobile and the good road many sections of the country have found themselves with more small centres than they need—farmers can now drive 10 or 15 miles as easily as they could formerly drive 2. Moreover, many of the old centres are now off the main roads and no longer serve the needs of the people at all. With the widening of the service-area and the shifting of transportation routes a new distribution of trade centres becomes inevitable. Thus we find the Eastern and Middle-Western states dotted with little hamlets drowsing in the service-shadows of more successful rivals.

Regions and Political Divisions. As we have already seen in our consideration of the local newspaper regions in Michigan, the Detroit newspaper region, and the Chicago freight-rate area, economic and cultural regions do not coincide with political areas. Yet we cannot conclude that the political boundaries are therefore

[7] Alfred H. Ritter, *Transportation Economics of the Great Lakes-St. Lawrence Ship Channel,* Great Lakes-St. Lawrence Tidewater Association, Washington, D. C., Nov., 1925, pp. 96–97.

[8] The Great Lakes-St. Lawrence Tidewater Association was composed of representatives of Ohio, Indiana, Illinois, Michigan, Wisconsin, Minnesota, Iowa, Montana, Missouri, North Dakota, South Dakota, Nebraska, Kansas, Colorado, Wyoming, California, Idaho, Utah, Oregon, South Carolina, West Virginia, Kentucky, and Washington.

[9] Carl C. Zimmerman, *op. cit.,* pp. 30–31.

meaningless for regional activities. Such a conclusion would be very far from the facts. Actually we have seen how the international boundary bisects the Detroit newspaper region, and Rice in his study of the diffusion of political attitudes toward the LaFollette movement in 1924 in the Northwest found likewise that political boundaries were by no means unimportant. He concluded that

> State boundaries interpose a real barrier to similarity in the vote . . . within contiguous areas. . . . The influence of state boundaries is reduced within areas in which retail shopping relationships prevail with reference to a common trading centre.[10]

The township and the county are political units that were developed before the coming of the railroad and the automobile, to say nothing of the airplane and radio. Hence, since they are essentially political units of the "horse-and-buggy culture," they are unadapted to the cultural and economic situation of today. Even the geographical state as we find it in this country is inadequate to deal with regional problems growing out of railroad regulation, control of airplane traffic, industrial disputes, and the like. From a nation of scattered and more or less isolated farms and villages, the United States in little more than a single century has grown into a closely knit, continental market organized into metropolitan, sub-metropolitan, and local regions whose problems need to be considered in the light of fundamental cultural and economic unities. Delay in readjusting political forms to changed economic and social conditions has been one of the prolific sources of difficulty in American life for many years.

The nearest approach in American political life to the metropolitan region in the scope of its organization is the state.

The American States. Historically the early states of the American commonwealth expressed a certain unity of origin. They were the lineal descendants of the Colonies, and throughout the early period the inhabitants of each colony felt themselves much more closely bound to residents of the same colony than to other colonials. Even during the Revolution, for example, it was difficult to interest Virginians in the troubles of Massachusetts, and had the English Government not surpassed itself in stupidity the colonies could never have been brought to form even so loose

[10] Stuart A. Rice, *Quantitative Methods in Politics,* New York, 1928, p. 155.

a union as the Confederation. The adoption of the Constitution did not essentially change the psychology of the average man. If it was no longer the colony which he regarded as peculiarly his we-group, it was the state, which for many years amounted to practically the same thing. Not until after the Civil War can we really think of the United States as a *nation* instead of a federation of nations. In 1835, for example, it was still possible for a Michigan governor to mobilize an army for the invasion of Ohio in order to settle the disputed location of the state boundary. Only prompt action by President Jackson in removing the Michigan Commander-in-Chief prevented actual hostilities. An attempt of this sort by any governor today would be laughed out of court; loyalty to the nation has long since swallowed up pioneer provincialism.

The point is, with the coming of the railroad, the telegraph, and the daily newspaper, economic activities have flowed naturally over broader and broader areas until the state has become a mere political and administrative convenience. It is still the unit of basic legislative control in semi-local matters, but its territorial boundaries seldom coincide with the economic and cultural regions that express the most vital interests of the people.

Under these circumstances there is a certain artificiality in any statistical index based on states. Yet the Census tabulates its material in this way and it is impossible to make more realistic comparisons until the delimitation and analysis of regions has progressed much farther than it has today.

Variations in Social Conditions by States. The accumulation of statistical information in recent years has made possible certain broad comparisons between states with reference to health, wealth, education, production of distinguished men, fertility in patentable inventions, public order, and the like. One of the most comprehensive comparisons of this sort was *The American Mercury's* answer to the question, Which is the worst American state?[11] On the basis of more than 60 different indexes, "the worst state" turned out to be Mississippi which on the average ranked 48.6 out of a possible 49. Massachusetts stood first with an average rank of 2.6, and Connecticut second with an average rank of 3.0. The ranking of the states is shown in Table 3.

[11] Charles Angoff and H. L. Mencken, "The Worst American State," *The American Mercury,* Vol. XXIV, September, October, and November, 1931, pp. 1ff.

TABLE 3

AVERAGE RANK OF AMERICAN STATES IN WEALTH, EDUCATION, HEALTH, AND PUBLIC ORDER

1. Massachusetts
2. Connecticut
3. New York
4. New Jersey
5. California
6. District of Columbia
7. Minnesota
8. Iowa
9. Illinois
10. Oregon
11. Rhode Island
12. Michigan
13. Maine
14. Washington
15. Wisconsin
16. New Hampshire
17. Ohio
18. Nebraska
19. Utah
20. Kansas
21. Pennsylvania
22. Vermont
23. Colorado
24. Indiana
25. Nevada
26. Delaware
27. Missouri
28. Maryland
29. North Dakota
30. Wyoming
31. Montana
32. Idaho
33. South Dakota
34. West Virginia
35. Arizona
36. Oklahoma
37. Florida
38. Virginia
39. Texas
40. New Mexico
41. Kentucky
42. Louisiana
43. North Carolina
44. Tennessee
45. Arkansas
46. Georgia
47. South Carolina
48. Alabama
49. Mississippi

In average intelligence as measured by the Army mental tests, Oregon stands first, with an Alpha test median score of 79.9. Mississippi stands last with a score of 41.2. In fertility in patents, Connecticut with an average of 74.4 patents per 100,000 population from 1916 to 1925, stands first with Mississippi again at the bottom with only 4.4. In percentage of distinguished men in *Who's Who,* 1930–31, New England leads the country with Vermont and New Hampshire topping the list at 85 and 69 per 100,000, respectively, while Oklahoma comes last with 0.6. The healthiest state for babies in 1929 was Oregon with an infant mortality rate of 47.9. The unhealthiest was New Mexico with a rate of 145.5 per 1000 live births.

Such specific comparisons could be extended for pages. The general trend of them, however, is clearly that the Northern states tend to outrank the Southern in health, wealth, education, public order, average mental test scores, patenting activity, distinguished men, and other indexes of cultural conditions.

With this glance at inter-community organization from the rural trade centre to the metropolitan region and the administrative state, we are now ready to go on to a consideration of social organization on a world scale—the nation-state, the world market, and the two forms of super-national organization which are now so prominent, namely, imperialism and federation.

STUDY QUESTIONS

1. How many population centres are there in the United States? Why do they exist?
2. What is the service-area?
3. How many service-areas are there around any given centre?
4. What factors probably determine the distribution of trade centres?
5. What is a rural borough?
6. What is the problem that exists in the relations of the trade centre to the service-area in rural territory?
7. Define a region as distinguished from a service-area.
8. What do you understand by the constellational pattern of news distribution?
9. What are the outstanding facts concerning the local regions distinguished in Michigan?
10. What is the relation of size to regional dominance? Note that the evidence given is negative rather than positive. What positive relationship can you discover?
11. How many metropolitan centres did the 1930 Census enumerate?
12. What is a metropolitan centre as the Census defines it?
13. What part of Michigan is included in the Detroit area of newspaper dominance? What part is excluded?
14. Explain the peculiar shape of the Detroit region. What factors are involved?
15. How much more of a barrier is the international boundary than is competition with other centres in the U. S.? How much more than mere distance?
16. What percentage of the population of the United States is included in the area of Chicago's transportation dominance as measured by fifth-class freight rates in 1924? What percentage in the area of lake port dominance in general?
17. How did the Erie Canal affect the dominance of New York?

How is the Great Lakes-St. Lawrence Ship Channel likely to affect it?

18. What evidence can you cite of the competition of rural trade centres?
19. What is the relation of regions to political boundaries?
20. What are the outstanding differences between states? What states lead in intelligence? In health? In productivity in distinguished men? In patents? In general biological and cultural standing?

CHAPTER XIX

NATIONS, THE WORLD MARKET, AND THE PROBLEM OF WAR

The Nation-State. Over and above the divisions we have just considered stands the nation-state, or major state proper. There were 65 such major groupings in the world in 1932, although more than 300 distinctive governmental areas could be distinguished, not counting provinces, parts of the United States, and the like.

A major state, as political scientists usually define it, has five essential attributes: (1) population; (2) territory; (3) government; (4) sovereignty; and (5) law.[1] For our purposes it will be necessary to discuss only population and sovereignty.

Population.—In the days of the ancient city-state Plato held that the ideal size of a state was 5040 inhabitants. From this point of view the most ideal modern state would be the Republic of Andorra on the southern slope of the Pyrenees with a population of 5232. Unfortunately for the ancient ideal, however, times have changed, and Andorra, under the joint protectorate of its neighbors, France and Spain, finds itself one of the most insignificant states in the world even though it is not actually the smallest.[2] At the other extreme stand such great political aggregations as the United States, which in 1930 had 123,000,000 inhabitants, or 6.1 per cent of the world's population, and was outranked among the effective states of the world only by the Union of Soviet Socialist Republics with its 161,000,000 people, or 8 per cent of mankind.[3] If, instead of considering separate states, we talk in terms of governmental organization, however,

[1] *Cf.* R. G. Gettell, *Problems of Political Evolution,* N. Y., 1914, p. 53.

[2] The smallest state in the world is the State of Vatican City, established by treaty between the Papacy and the Italian government in 1929. It covers 108 acres and in 1930 contained 632 inhabitants.

[3] As effective states both China and India, although represented in the League of Nations, and enumerated among the 65 major groupings mentioned above, may here be disregarded. Although both are more populous than either Russia or the United States, they are so little unified and so lacking in sovereign independence that they can hardly be classed as effective states, however important the fate of their five or six hundred millions of people may be.

both Russia and the United States are outranked by the greatest grouping of human beings ever achieved, the British Commonwealth of Nations, which brings nearly one fourth of the human race under the British flag.

So much by way of a world view. Let us turn now to the population of continental United States itself. Of the 123,000,000 human beings who in 1930 made up the United States, about 78 per cent were native whites, 11 per cent foreign-born, 10 per cent Negroes, and a fraction more than 1 per cent belonged to other races.[4]

Three significant trends in population must be noted. (1) Both foreign-born and Negroes are decreasing relative to the rest of the population; (2) age distribution is shifting markedly toward the less active periods of life; (3) and the fall in the birth rate portends the end of population growth and a possible decrease in population within the next century.

The percentage of foreign-born reached its high point since the Civil War in 1910 when 14.6 per cent of our population claimed foreign birthplaces. In 1920 the percentage had declined to 13.1. With the establishment of the policy of immigration restriction after the World War, with the growth of Russia as a competitor for working-class immigrants,[5] and with the exodus of foreign-born exceeding their influx here during such a depression year as 1931, the prospect is for a continued decline in the percentage of foreign-born.

Negroes have been increasing in absolute, but decreasing in relative, numbers almost steadily since the first census in 1790. At that time they numbered 757,000, or more than 19 per cent of the population. In 1930, while they numbered nearly 12,000,000, they constituted less than 10 per cent of the total. Predictions of future Negro population growth place the upper limit within the next century at from 15,000,000 to 18,000,000.

The fall in the birth rate, due largely to birth control but in part to the aging of our immigrant population, is decreasing the percentage of people in the active years of life and increasing the percentage past middle age. Between 1918–21 and 1928–29 the standardized birth rate of native-born white women, 15 to 44

[4] Percentages given in round numbers. Actual figures: Native whites, 77.8 per cent; foreign-born, 10.9; Negroes, 9.7; Other races, 1.6.

[5] *Cf.* Walter Duranty, "U. S. A. and the U. S. S. R.," *The Survey Graphic*, Nov. 1, 1932, p. 533.

years of age, fell from 89 per 1000 to 77, *a decline of 13 per cent.* The rate for foreign-born white women of the same ages fell from 141 to 95, *a decline of over 32 per cent.* And the rate for Negro women fell from 99 to 88, *a decline of 11 per cent.*[6] Altogether this collapse of the birth rate is one of the most revolutionary things that has ever happened in America. No one can yet foresee how far it will go, and its ultimate consequences are beyond prediction. Notice in Figure 16 that there are more children now living in the 5–9 and 10–14 age groups than in the 0–4 group. According to the calculations of Dublin and Lotka, true natural increase ceased in 1932 or 1933, and all apparent increase will cease by 1960.[7] This means, of course, a gradual decrease in the percentage of young people and a gradual increase in the percentage of older people in American communities. When a stationary population is reached, instead of having approximately half of the population in the active years 20 to 49, as in 1920, only 42 per cent will be in that period; while the percentage 50 and over will have risen from 15 to 26. Such a fundamental shift in the age distribution of the population will mean a lessening of demand for new dwellings and new subdivisions as well as for elementary teachers; an increase in the pressure on the standard of living which will then have to be maintained by a smaller percentage of the population; an increase of the conservatism that goes with age; and fundamental readjustments in our social and economic arrangements for caring for older people who are now being thrust out of industry in increasing numbers after the age of 40. The youthful phase of American history is over.

Even more serious is the prospect of the ultimate effects of the

[6] P. K. Whelpton, "Population: Trends in Age Composition and in Specific Birth Rates, 1920–1930," *American Journal of Sociology,* May, 1932, pp. 855–861.

[7] Louis I. Dublin and A. J. Lotka, "The Present Outlook for Population Increase. *Publications American Sociological Society,* May, 1930, Vol. XXIV, p. 106. True natural increase is the excess of births over deaths as corrected for the effects of the falling birth rate and population growth itself. The falling birth rate means in general that 1000 babies born in 1930 will not have the same reproductive value thirty years later that 1000 babies born in 1900 had in 1930. Hence, relatively, the 1930 birth rate *seems higher* than it effectively is. In the same way the fact that population is growing at all means that there is a higher proportion of young people in the population than would be true in a stationary population. Hence the death rate *seems low,* since young people have a lower death rate than older people. The apparent difference between the birth rate and the death rate, which in the U. S. in 1929 was 7.0 per 1000 population, must thus be greatly reduced. Dublin and Lotka calculate that the true or corrected difference between the two rates would approximate zero in 1932.

falling birth rate on the international position of the United States. Dublin estimates that if present tendencies are not checked population may actually begin to decline after 1960 until by 2100 A.D. the United States may contain only 75,000,000, or about the

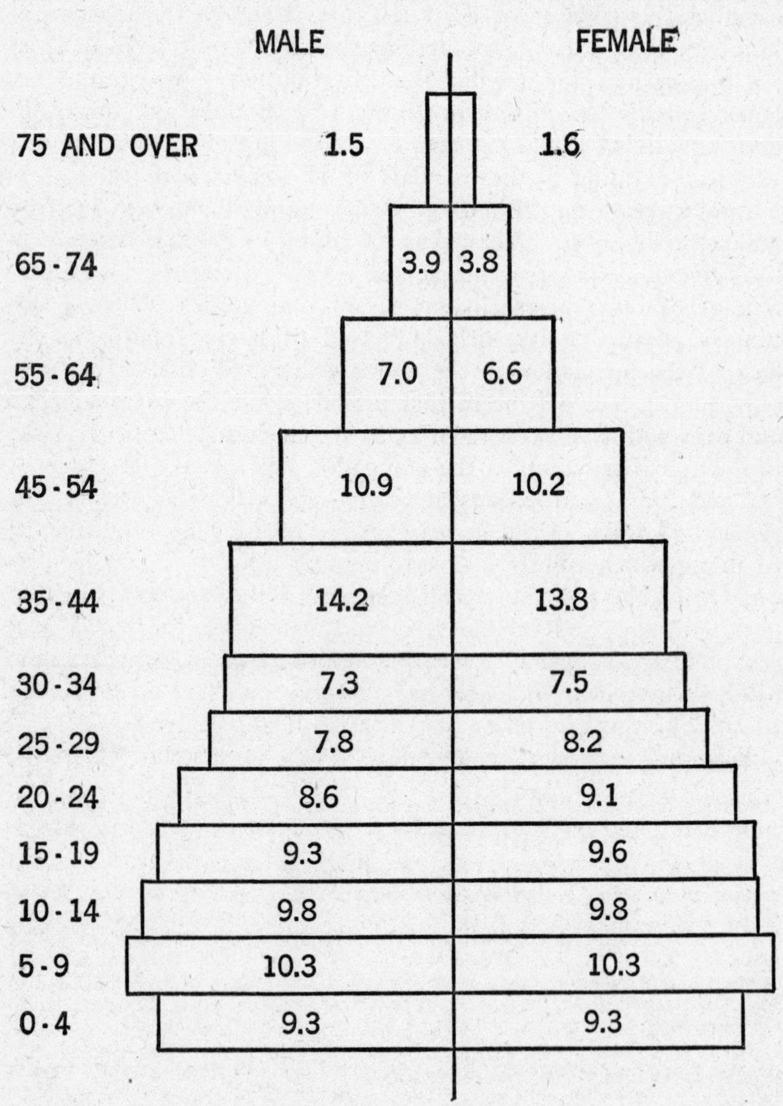

FIG. 16. Population Pyramid, U. S., 1930, Showing Percentages of Each Sex in Each Age Group.

same number as in 1900.[8] But whereas in 1900 Japan, for example, had less than 50,000,000 population, in 2100 Japan will probably have more than 90,000,000 herself and will undoubtedly be heading an empire of more than 130,000,000.[9] Russia at the same time will have from 200,000,000 to 250,000,000, if not more. Thus, if present tendencies continue, the United States may look forward to finding itself far outclassed in population by both Russia and Japan within the next two centuries. All of which may in due time involve far-reaching questions of international relations and external sovereignty.

Sovereignty.—This is the name given to the internal supremacy of the state over all persons and associations within it and to its external independence of other states. Both in regard to its internal and its external aspects the old theory of the absolute sovereignty of the state has had to be modified to fit such complex facts as trusts, labor unions, international alliances, the League of Nations, and so on. It is from such facts that Laski argues that authority can no longer be thought of as unitary and absolute within the state, but must be conceived as pluralistic and relative. The fetish of unity and absoluteness, he insists, is a heritage from mediævalism.[10] In the same way the change in world conditions, the growth of what Graham Wallas so aptly calls the Great Society, has made the old ideas of the sovereign independence of each state nothing more than anachronisms. Whatever the theory may be, a nation like Great Britain, for example, in which more than 15,000,000 of the population depend for their existence on food grown outside the British Isles, is not and cannot be independent. For the last three centuries at least there has been growing up a series of economic relationships between nations which have finally become so far-reaching and yet so closely integrated as to tie all nations together in the network of the world market. In the presence of this overmastering fact the stereotyped idea of the sovereign independence of the nation-state must be revised.

[8] *Cf.* Louis I. Dublin, "Birth Control: What it is Doing to America's Population," *Forum,* Vol. LXXXVI, Nov., 1931, pp. 270–275.

[9] Prof. Raymond Pearl has placed the upper limit of population of Japan proper at 86,641,000 which will not be attained until 2100 A.D. or thereabouts. In 1930 Japan proper had 64,450,000 and the Japanese Empire had 91,337,000. See Pearl, *Studies in Human Biology,* Baltimore, 1924, p. 627; 1930 statistics from *World Almanac,* 1932, p. 674.

[10] Harold J. Laski, *Authority in the Modern State,* Yale University Press, 1919, p. 23.

The World Market. Strictly speaking, the world market is the creation of the steamship and the railroad. Thanks to modern means of transportation, the United States now draws rubber and coffee from Brazil, silk from Japan, tungsten from China, chromium from India and South Africa, nickel from Canada, nitrates from Chile, and so on. In return, American wheat helps to feed Europe, cotton from the Southern States competes in England with cotton from India and Egypt, American-made farm machinery gathers the harvests of the Argentine, and typewriters and automobiles made in the U. S. A. are sold in South Africa and in Sweden. In 1930 the value of imports into the United States was in round numbers $3,061,000,000 and the value of exports $3,843,000,000. The interdependence of nations—as well as of communities and regions—is easily proven. Nearly one third of the population of Great Britain and one fourth that of Germany are dependent upon foreign markets for their livelihood. Again, the United States, which is probably the most self-sustaining nation in the world, is dependent on other nations for over 30 minerals essential to the conduct of an important war. Year by year the peoples of the world have been growing more and more dependent on international co-operation for the flow of goods and services on which normal life depends. This means that on a world scale, just as we have already found true on the community and regional scale, economic life has outrun political organization.

Super-National Organization. Efforts to organize social structure on a scale commensurate with the expansion of economic activity find two main channels of expression: (1) *Economic imperialism;* and (2) *The League of Nations.*

Economic Imperialism.—As Moon says, "the realms conquered by military emperors of past ages were baubles, trifles compared with the far-flung dominions which have been won, more often with the pen than by the sword, in our own supposedly prosaic generation. . . . Imperialism is the most impressive achievement and the most momentous world-problem of our age."[11] In the mid-Victorian period empire-building was in disrepute in Europe. Business men were inclined to look upon empires as expensive luxuries. Then came the decline in the supremacy of the English cotton mills and iron works, the revolution in transportation and

[11] Parker Thomas Moon, *Imperialism and World Politics,* New York, 1927, p. 1.

communication, the demand for tropical products, and the need of investing "surplus capital." Governments awoke to the desirability of promoting business, and nationalism, which is the doctrine of the independent sovereignty of kindred peoples, discovered that one of the best ways of promoting business was to dominate the "independent" peoples living in the undeveloped regions of the world. Hence, the scramble for colonies, spheres of influence, foreign markets, and all the rest, that led inexorably to the World War.

In this scramble the United States has not been backward. In the short space of one generation from 1897 to 1926, inclusive, the United States, in its operations south of the Rio Grande alone, set up two republics, made five protectorates, intervened by force no less than 30 times in the affairs of nine so-called independent states, annexed Porto Rico, built the Panama Canal, set up a naval station, and increased American investments from $300,-000,000 to $3,000,000,000. In commercial value, the colonial empire of the United States in 1923–24 ranked second only to that of Great Britain.[12] Between them "ten imperialist nations possess colonies and protectorates which, taken together, are seven times the size of Europe and half the earth's total land surface. Six hundred million human beings, a third of the human race, are directly subject to the imperialist domination"[13]—and another third are indirectly subject to it. Facing on the one hand, the demands of the subject peoples for "self-determination," *i.e.*, the right of independent existence as nations, and on the other, the competition of rival imperialisms with one another, and aware of the fact that the progress of science was making it altogether possible that another major conflict might jeopardize civilization itself, European and American statesmen emerged from the World War with a willingness to experiment with some form of world organization that might control national antagonisms and at least restrain the more aggressive forms of imperialism. The organization which was set up for this purpose is the League of Nations.

The League of Nations.—The League of Nations may be de-

[12] The total commerce of the chief colonial empires was estimated by Moon as follows: British (1923–24) $11,079,000,000; American (1923–24) $1,542,-000,000; French (1922) $906,000,000; Dutch (1924) $898,000,000; Japanese (1923) $607,000,000; Portuguese (1924) $59,000,000; Belgium (1924) $44,000,-000; Italian (1922–23) $21,000,000.—P. 519.

[13] Moon, *op. cit.*, p. 513.

scribed as an attempt to enlarge the political organization of the world to cope with its enlarged economic structure, *i.e.*, imperialism and the world market. It came into existence January 20, 1920, when the Treaty of Versailles became effective.

In briefest outline, the League in 1932 was composed of 55 member states—the entire world, in fact, except Afghanistan, Brazil, Costa Rica, Ecuador, Egypt, the Hedjas and Nedj, Soviet Russia, and the United States of America. The basis of organization is the so-called Covenant, or constitution, which binds each member-state to submit all controversies with other member-states to a third party—to the League Council or to the Permanent World Court—before resorting to war; to refrain from warlike preparations for at least 90 days after an award has been made; to submit to further attempts at settlement if the first one fails; and to bring pressure, economic or military, on any member-state that refuses to abide by these conditions, or on any non-member that starts a war. The organs of League organization are the *Council* or executive body, of 14 members, five of whom permanently represent France, Germany, Great Britain, Italy, and Japan;[14] the *Assembly,* which acts as a forum of discussion and elects the nine non-permanent members of the Council; the *Permanent Court of International Justice* which is open to every nation of the world but to which nine nations including the United States do not belong; and the *administrative bodies* which include the Permanent Secretariat and various special commissions.

The refusal of the United States to follow the lead of the founder of the League, Woodrow Wilson, and the exclusion of Soviet Russia have seriously crippled the effectiveness of the League during its early years of existence. Lack of confidence of member-states in the League's disinterestedness on the one hand and in its power to enforce its decisions against powerful nations, on the other, as evidenced by its inability to control Japanese aggression in Manchuria in 1931–32, have also weakened its influence. Nevertheless, the League forms an interesting experiment in international co-operation in the years following the World War.

Whether the League is to be the final answer to the problem of world organization on a supernational scale cannot be de-

[14] A seat on the Council is reserved for the United States, if and when this country decides to join.

termined for at least another generation. Some students of international affairs believe that instead of a single world league there will evolve possibly three leagues—the present League sheared of its non-European members; an Asiatic league headed perhaps by Japan; and a league of the American nations including the United States. Even such an arrangement would leave Russia out of the picture and at best would bear a very suspicious resemblance to the old balance-of-power idea that broke down with the World War.

Despite the existence of the League and the widespread demand in many nations for the abolition of war, the world a decade after Versailles was rent by more hatred and was staggering under a heavier burden of armament than in 1914.[15]

War as a Factor in World Organization. War has been the court of last resort for the settlement of inter-group disputes for at least 15,000 years and possibly much longer. Some anthropologists believe that primitive man on the level of savagery did not engage in organized group-fighting, although spontaneous fighting for an immediate objective such as the possession of game or a waterhole no doubt did occur. From this point of view war as organized, institutionalized group-fighting for a common purpose by means of mass destruction of life and property probably did not appear until men had acquired enough permanent possessions to tempt envious neighbors. But from some such beginnings in plunder raids the pressure for survival has led everywhere in the higher cultures to (1) the evolution of a special fighting class, (2) the development of traditions glorifying successful war, and (3) the invention of highly specialized weapons primarily for use in war. In the end, every great nation as the surviving product of this process today finds itself part of a system which has given us wars in 91 per cent of the last 3400 years and bids fair to give us many more unless a radical change of attitude and world organization can be achieved in the meantime.[16]

[15] It is estimated that the world is spending about $5,000,000,000 a year on armaments.

[16] In 1864 Odysse-Barot, *Lettres sur le Philosophie de l'Histoire,* p. 20, counted 8,397 solemn agreements of peace and friendship that had been violated between the formation of the Amphictyonic League in 1496 B.C. and the signing of the treaty between England and France on January 23, 1861. Altogether there had been 3130 years of war as against only 227 years of peace. Quoted in Wallace, *The Trend of History,* p. 233, note. In the 71 years between 1861 and 1932 there were at least 15 years of war, not counting colonial squabbles and the like, making 3145 years of war out of the last 3428, or 91.7 per cent.

The fruits of past wars—the present distribution of world power, the survival of the great political ideas of the modern world such as liberty, nationalism, kingship, etc.,—all these are apparent enough. What the fruits might have been of centuries of peace we can only guess. Unquestionably war is a time-honored method of settling international disputes, but it seems a highly irrational and wasteful method. If it has eliminated many of the unfit in days past, it has also eliminated many of the fit and has probably retarded cultural development as much as it has advanced it. Thus the Napoleonic wars are said to have reduced the average stature of the French nation by over two inches, and the incessant wars on the continent are blamed for the failure of European peasants to develop any of the great breeds of domestic cattle. It is from areas of long-continued peace such as England that the great improvements in domestic animal breeding have come. Thus, while invading armies were sweeping away the scrawny herds on the continent time after time, English farmers, secure for 800 years behind the English Channel, were breeding century after century the Clyde and Suffolk horses, the Durham, Hereford, Devon, and Angus beef cattle, the Jersey and Guernsey milkers, the Berkshire, Yorkshire, and Tamworth hogs, the Brahma, Plymouth Rock, and Orpington hens, and the Cheviot, Oxford, Southdown, and Shropshire sheep.[17]

British and American statistics also show that while war stimulates the invention of military devices, it decreases the number of non-military inventions that are patented, so that the total number of patents applied for or patents issued during such a struggle as the American Civil War or the World War markedly decreases.[18] In addition to such evidence there is the inevitable dislocation of

[17] Sidney Hillyard, "Animal Husbandry and War," *The Scientific Monthly*, March, 1928.

[18] The first year of the Civil War coincided with a drop in the number of applications for patents at Washington to the level of 1854, the Spanish-American War coincided with a drop to the level of 1881, and American participation in the World War saw the application curve fall nearly to the level of 1895. In each case recovery was fairly rapid. See reports of the Commissioner of Patents for the years mentioned. In England, according to statistics gathered by E. Wyndham Hulme, former librarian of the British patent office, the World War cut a notch in the volume of British patents that brought the number in 1916 below the number issued in 1885. See Hulme, *Statistical Bibliography in Relation to the Growth of Modern Civilization*, London, 1923, Appendix. On the average, the three American wars coincided with a recession equivalent to more than 15 years. The recession in Britain during the World War was equivalent to 31 years.

educational and social services in a nation at war; the disorganization of the world market following a world war; the sucking up of a disproportionate amount of national revenue for war purposes—in his message to Congress, December 6, 1929, President Hoover announced that 72 per cent of the federal budget was devoted to wars past or wars to come; and more important still, the lowering of the standard of living, the increase of social unrest, the trail of revolution and near-revolution left by such upheavals as the Napoleonic wars and the World War. All this means that war is after all apparently a method of achieving roast pig by burning down the house. When to all this is added the fact that the conscription of science in the World War now gives us the certainty that every succeeding war will be more deadly than the last—in soldiers killed per day the World War, for example, was more than 20 times as "efficient" as the average war of the nineteenth century—it becomes clear that a great deal more than mere sentimentalism is involved in the modern world-wide agitation for peace. Many people agree with the late Lord Bryce's remark: "We must destroy war, or war will destroy us."

From the standpoint of social technology what can we say of this problem?[19]

The will to control war is probably more widespread and articulate in the world than ever before, but it is still an appalling distance from its goal. The difficulties of controlling war may be summed up under three heads: (1) The prevalence of attitudes that assume or imply war, *i.e.*, belief in its inevitability, the prevalence of narrow nationalism, etc.; (2) the presence of fundamental conflicts of national interest; and (3) the lack of adequate machinery for discovering and settling such conflicts peaceably.

(1) As to the inevitability of war, the overwhelming opinion of American psychologists is that there is nothing biologically inevitable about it.[20] Such inevitability as it seems to possess from

[19] As we shall point out in the final chapter, technology inevitably involves moral values. These enter in the selection of the problem and in the interpretation of the facts, *i.e.*, in evaluating their meaning. The remainder of this chapter is evaluative, the assumption being that civilization is worth preserving and that war is a menace to it.

[20] Answering a questionnaire submitted by Dr. John M. Fletcher of Tulane University, asking whether "there are present in human nature ineradicable instinctive factors that make war between nations inevitable," 345 out of 378 members of the American Psychological Association, or 91 per cent, said "No"; 11 said "Yes"; and 22 were non-committal. News release, *Science Service*, dated New Orleans, January 13, 1932.

our record of the last 34 centuries, for example, issues not from man's biological nature, but from the defects of his social systems.

(2) Such defects seem to produce fundamental conflicts that are only doubtfully open to complete settlement by discussion and negotiation. Such conflicts, for example, as those arising from the unequal distribution of raw materials necessary for industrial development, from the opposing claims of communism and capitalism, and from differential population pressures are so basic and so charged with emotional values for millions of people that the *status quo* seems essentially fragile and impermanent.

(3) Yet because of (*a*) the lack of international organs of opinion, (*b*) the lack of world patriotism as compared with national patriotism, (*c*) the limitations inherent in international law,[21] and (*d*) the skepticism of great nations toward the principle of world federation, the world finds itself with inadequate machinery for readjusting the strains that today threaten the *status quo*. Every one of the conflicts mentioned above issues from what some great nation or group of nations regards as a vital interest. Any attempt, for example, to bring about a more equitable division of the coal resources of the world would instantly be resisted by the United States which has nearly half of the world's supply. Professor Thompson's proposal that the white race peaceably renounce to Japan and China millions of its broad acres, which the white birth rate gives no promise of ever being able to fill, is merely ignored as the idle theorizing of a professor. Traditionally and psychologically even those who talk most loudly of controlling war are ill-prepared to face the sacrifices that would be demanded of the great nations if they were seriously to set about organizing the world on a basis of impartial justice for all irrespective of race, wealth, or nationality. Yet a world organized on any other basis is probably doomed to be continually in a condition of unstable equilibrium with millions of people dreaming of righting their "wrongs" by the only method open to them, namely, force.

Under these conditions the problem of destroying war before it destroys civilization seems obviously one of the major issues now confronting mankind.

Summary. The nation-state is the most widespread inde-

[21] International law as contrasted with domestic law has two defects: It is not enacted law since there is no international legislation; and it is not explicitly enforceable law since there is no international police force. Its efficacy depends on the consent of the parties involved.

pendent grouping in world affairs. Certain distinct trends are visible in the population of the United States and in the evolution of national sovereignty. In a world market super-national organization seems inevitable and this has appeared in the form of imperialism on the one hand and federation on the other. The court of last resort for the settlement of national disputes remains, however, war. Because the enlistment of science makes warfare so much more "efficient," war is regarded by many thoughtful people as a menace to civilization. Yet the will to peace is still far from its goal.

STUDY QUESTIONS

1. What are the attributes of a nation-state?
2. What is the population of the three or four most effective governmental groupings in the world?
3. What are the percentages of native whites, foreign-born, and Negroes in the United States?
4. What three major trends are discernible in the population of the United States?
5. What factors may be expected to cause a decline in the percentage of foreign-born?
6. What has been the trend of Negro population?
7. What are the predicted limits of Negro population within the next century?
8. How much has the crude birth rate fallen in the United States in recent years? (Look up figures in the World Almanac, the Statistical Abstract of the United States, the American Yearbook, or some other source.)
9. Why is the decline in the birth rate called one of the most revolutionary things that has happened in American history?
10. When, according to the statisticians, will visible natural increase disappear?
11. In 1960 what will be the proportion of the population 20 to 49 years old? What will be the proportion 50 and over? How will these percentages compare with the condition in 1920?
12. What are some of the problems that this shift in age distribution will bring to the front?
13. How is the falling birth rate likely to affect the international position of the United States?
14. What is sovereignty?
15. How have old ideas of internal and external sovereignty been revised and why?

16. What do you understand by the world market?
17. Point out some of the foreign commodities used in your community.
18. What is modern imperialism? How does it differ from the older type?
19. How does the United States rank as an imperialistic nation?
20. What is the structure of the League of Nations?
21. What three cultural elements have the higher cultures evolved in connection with war?
22. What percentage of the years in the last 34 centuries has been free from war?
23. What are some of the advantages of past wars?
24. What is the effect of war on animal breeding? On qualities of population? On invention? On social services? On national budgets? On the future of civilization?
25. What types of difficulty confront those who would control war?
26. Explain what is meant by describing the world *status quo* as one of unstable equilibrium?

CHAPTER XX

SOCIAL CLASSES

The Fact of Stratification. In every society complex enough to have division of labor, association tends to stratify on levels determined by economic power and function. The groups thus formed are called social classes. *A social class may be defined as a major group within an economic system whose members are recognizably and significantly alike in their relations to a basic division of economic power or function.* In other words, a social class is an economic group whose members are alike in their relations to the process of getting a living.

How Are Classes Formed? What determines any one's social position? Aside from luck, there are but two principles available: caste or competition. Caste is the principle of distributing social functions and social privileges on the basis of inheritance—like father, like son.[1] Competition is the principle of distributing functions and privileges on the basis of comparative efficiency. The presence of caste is revealed by two crucial attitudes: (1) a sentiment against intermarriage; (2) the practice of judging individuals on the basis of their group memberships rather than their individual merits. The taboo on intermarriage is, of course, aimed at protecting the caste at the source, while the refusal to judge individuals on their own merits prevents competition from affecting the distribution of functions and privileges. In this way inheritance alone is made the only principle that operates. Which principle shall predominate in a given culture at a given time is not, however, a matter of chance.

The Conditions that Determine Caste. There are two general classes of conditions that control the strength or prevalence of caste in any culture: (1) human nature conditions, particularly parental affection and the suggestibility of children; and (2) social conditions, such as population differences, the rate of social change, and the state of communication and enlightenment.

1. **Human Nature Conditions.** (1) *Parental Affection.*—

[1] The term caste is also used to refer to the group determined by this principle.

The desire to secure for one's children whatever desirable thing one has gained for oneself is a perennial source of caste, and this endeavor seems to flow from the attitudes developed in ordinary family life at least in western European, in American, and in Oriental culture. The desire is not confined to any one class—a few years ago in Chicago only the son of a plumber was permitted to learn the plumber's trade.

(2) *Suggestibility of Children.*—Apart from parental intention, there is a strong drift toward inheritance because of mere familiarity. It is commonly the line of least resistance. The father knows much about his own trade and those closely related to it, little about others; the son grows into his point of view. Of course he may lack the ability to perform the paternal function; but this, though common enough, does not affect the majority of cases. The functions that require a peculiar type of natural ability, while of the first importance, since they include all marked originality, are not numerous. Sound character and good training with fair intelligence are ordinarily sufficient. Even in the learned professions the great majority of practitioners probably hold their own by common sense and assiduity rather than by special aptitude. The mass of men are guided chiefly by early surroundings and training, which determine for them, in a general way, what sort of life they will take up, and contribute much to their success or failure in it. Society, even in a comparatively free country, is thus vaguely divided into hereditary strata, or sections, from which the majority do not depart. Great as the movement from class to class may be here as compared, say, with India, it is nevertheless true that the great majority remain in the classes in which they are born. This is a fundamental fact which the American tradition of encouraging ambition too often tends to obscure. Traditionally the American reaction to an individual's unfortunate economic condition has been to advise him to work hard and get ahead in the world. Practically for more than half of the population that advice is simply futile.

Parental affection and the suggestibility of children, then, are human nature conditions operative everywhere, at least so far as we know. Not everywhere, however, do they result in caste. In other words, while they are the necessary conditions of caste they are not the sufficient conditions. These must be sought in social factors.

2. Social Conditions Affecting Caste. (1) *Likeness or Unlikeness of Population Elements.*—The most important sorts of such differences are perhaps three: (*a*) differences in race; (*b*) non-racial differences due to immigration or conquest; and (*c*) differences due to differentiation of social function.

(*a*) *Racial Differences.*—Two races of different temperament and capacity, distinct to the eye and living side by side in the same community, tend strongly to become castes, no matter how equal the social system may otherwise be. The difference, as being hereditary, answers in its nature to the idea of caste, and the external sign, color, serves to make it conscious and definite.

The most striking example of this is found in the race situation in the South. The fact that many Negroes are equal, and some superior, in ability to the majority of the whites does not, in the opinion of the latter, make it just or expedient to treat them apart from the mass of their race. To dine with a Negro, to work or play by his side, or to associate in any relation where superiority cannot be asserted, is held to be degrading and of evil example, no matter what kind of Negro the individual may be. It is the practice and policy of the dominant race to impress upon the Negro that he belongs by birth to a distinct order out of which he can in no way depart. If he wishes to mingle with whites it must be as an acknowledged inferior. As a servant he may ride in the same railway car, but as a citizen he may not do so.[2]

Thoughtful whites, while condemning obvious excesses such as lynching, justify their attitude on the ground that a race is an organic whole—bound together by heredity, social connection and traditions—and that it is practically necessary to recognize this in dealing with race questions. Individuals cannot in practice be separated from their families and other antecedents, and the whites feel that even if they could be, the example of mixture on an equal footing would be demoralizing to both.

The more intelligent Negroes, while usually insisting on the need of maintaining biological distinctness, favor the abolition of

[2] Whites both North and South usually have less objection to the physical proximity of Negroes who "keep their place," *i.e.*, preserve social distance, than they have to the loss of social distance even when the Negroes are out of sight. Thus over 70 per cent of certain classes at the University of Michigan in 1929 said they would have no objection to living in the same house with a Negro servant, but more than 80 per cent of them said they would seriously object to having a Negro family live on the same street even though several blocks away.

the caste system and urge the judging of each individual on his own merits. They condemn compulsory segregation and race prejudice. Survival of the Negro as a separate race, however, would seem to depend on the building of race pride in the Negroes themselves,[3] *i.e.*, on the growth of a Negro demand for biological segregation.

In the white man's own culture the race question creates a fundamental conflict. Science, religion, the democratic spirit, the constant change and bustle of the machine age itself, all these are hostile to the old caste spirit. Yet of the 11,891,000 Negroes in the United States in 1930, 9,361,000, or more than 78 per cent, lived in the South, and in 280 counties they outnumbered the whites. More than 57 per cent of these southern Negroes lived on farms or in rural villages, and one out of every five could not read or write.[4] Perhaps the most basic fact in the whole situation is that under present conditions the Negro is a source of docile, cheap labor in the South. That the present caste attitude tends on the whole to keep him docile and cheap is not a factor tending to weaken that attitude.

In the North the conflict in the white culture comes to the surface: Theory and practice do not always coincide. The Negro has the ballot and certain civil rights according to law, but it is a matter of common knowledge that equality of treatment is the exception rather than the rule. Since the ebbing of the idealism or fanaticism of the Civil War the average Northerner in personal relations has tended to accept the Southern caste attitude toward the Negro race without, however, taking over the Southerner's kindliness toward the individual Negro. The result is a confused

[3] That segregation and prejudice are not maintaining biological distinctness of races is shown by the increase in the percentage of mixed bloods among the Negroes since 1850. At that time 11 per cent were mixed bloods. In 1930 the percentage was 16. In this increase of mixed bloods intermarriage is only a small factor—it is a crime in the South and relatively infrequent in the North. Far more crossing occurs through casual association and concubinage, *i.e.*, at the initiative of the white man, than occurs through intermarriage. The white man's concern over intermarriage, *i.e.*, the gesture of social equality, and his relative unconcern over the actual biological facts of illicit crossing is indicative of the relative weight of social as compared with biological factors in the whole situation. Although race prejudice undoubtedly discourages intermarriage, it contributes to race crossing by belittling the Negro in his own estimation and by making Negro women more accessible to white men outside of marriage.

[4] In the North and West less than 12 per cent of the 2,500,000 Negroes there lived outside the cities and more than nineteen out of every twenty could read and write. Illiteracy for the whites in 1930 averaged 2.7 per cent for the United States.

uncertainty of both whites and Negroes which was increased by the Negro migrations from the South in 1915–17 and 1924–25.[5]

While the white attitude toward the Negro continues to constitute our greatest race problem, the same caste tendency has appeared on the Pacific coast toward the Chinese, Japanese, and Filipinos and in the Southwest toward the Mexicans. In 1930 there were 74,000 Chinese, 138,000 Japanese, 45,000 Filipinos, and 1,422,000 Mexicans in the United States. The number of Mexicans had doubled in ten years, thanks to the application of the quota laws to European immigration and to the continued demand of American employers for cheap labor.[6]

Unfortunately the caste attitude of whites toward other races has tended to retard real understanding of race as a factor in society. Since Gobineau's *Essay on the Inequality of Human Races* in 1854, writers have tried to "prove" some race "superior" or "inferior" to all other races. The fact that anthropologists are still quarrelling among themselves as to what constitutes a race; that the extremes of any given race always differ far more from each other than the average of that race differs from the average of any other race; that the weight of authority is that no method has yet been devised for unscrambling race and culture;[7] and that culture is a product of many variables including climate, location, cultural borrowings and the like, with race merely one among all these variables—facts like these do not discourage popular writers with enough imagination.[8] Thus we have the Industrial Revolu-

[5] About a million and a third more Negroes came North from 1915 to 1930 than moved South. Most of these migrants to the North settled in the industrial centres, particularly New York, Cleveland, Youngstown, Chicago, Toledo, Detroit. In 1920 Detroit's Negro population numbered 40,838; in 1930 it was 120,066. The inevitable result of this concentration was overcrowding, infiltration into white neighborhoods, increased competition with white workmen, and increased race tension.

[6] Cheap labor means labor with a low standard of living. The chief sociological justification for limitation of immigration lies in the value of protecting the so-called American Standard of Living.

[7] Concerning the value of the Army mental tests for this purpose, see A. L. Kroeber, *Anthropology,* New York, 1923, p. 75 f.

[8] For a statement of the racialist point of view see Madison Grant, *The Passing of the Great Race;* Lothrop Stoddard, *The Rising Tide of Color.* For a somewhat emotional refutation of that point of view see Geo. A. Dorsey, Race and Civilization, in *Whither Mankind,* edited by Charles A. Beard, p. 229. A more scientific discussion will be found in Kroeber. The one fact that every student of race questions should bear in mind is that while *socially* we tend to treat races as units, all members of which are alike, *biologically* every race with reference to any given characteristic or combination of characteristics is distributed along a scale instead of being concentrated at one point on the scale.

tion, the poverty of the Negro, and innumerable other cultural characteristics attributed straight to race and to race alone. However satisfying that may be emotionally, it has no value for the scientific understanding of what race is and how it is related to culture.

(*b*) *Immigration and Conquest.*—When peoples of the same race mingle by migration, the effect, as regards classes, depends chiefly on their states of civilization and on the character of the migration, whether friendly or hostile. The peaceful advent of kindred settlers like the English immigrants to the United States creates no class divisions. If they differ in language and customs, like the Germans, or are extremely poor and ignorant like many of the Irish, they are held apart for a time and looked down upon, but as they establish themselves and gradually prove their substantial equality with the natives, they may become indistinguishable from the latter. In the years immediately before the World War, however, the arrival by millions of peoples somewhat more divergent—especially Italians, Slavs, and Jews—had introduced distinctions in which racial as well as cultural differences play a part.

Conquest has been one of the main sources of caste the world over. The hostile tradition it leaves may continue indefinitely; servile functions are commonly forced upon the conquered, and the consciousness of superiority leads the conquerors to regard intermarriage as shameful. Such differences were found among the Teutonic tribes, in England after the Conquest, in India, and elsewhere.

(*c*) *Differences due to Differentiation of Social Function.*—The unlikeness out of which caste grows may not be original, as in the case of race differences or conquest, but may arise gradually by the differentiation of a homogeneous people. Any distinct social group, having its special group sympathies and traditions, has a tendency to pass on its functions and ideas to the children of its members, promoting association and intermarriage among them, and thus taking on a caste character. Accordingly, any increase in the complexity of social functions—political, religious, military, or industrial—such as necessarily accompanies the enlargement of the social system, may have a caste tendency, if conditions are otherwise favorable.

Something of this sort seems to have followed upon the conquest by the Germanic tribes of Roman territory, and the consequent necessity of administering a more complex system than their own. As the new order took shape it showed a tendency toward a more definite inheritance of rank and function than existed in the tribal society.

The feudal system also was based on inheritance of function, and had two well-defined castes, the knightly, consisting originally of those whose ability to maintain a horse and equipment placed them in the rank of effective warriors, and the servile. Between these marriage was impossible. Intercourse of any kind was scanty. Socially and psychologically the mediæval nobility lived in their caste, not in the world at large. The plain people were regarded with a contempt at least as great as that felt in our day for the Negro in the South.

In India also the elaborate caste systems, although due in part to conquest, seem also to have come about by the hardening of occupation-classes. The priests, powerful because of their supposed intercourse with superhuman powers, taught their mystic traditions to their children and so built up a hereditary corporation, known, finally, as the Brahman caste. The military caste was apparently formed in a similar manner, while in industry, "veneration for parental example and the need of an exact transmission of methods"[9] rendered all employments hereditary.

(2) *The Rate of Social Change.*—Since caste is a way of organizing society on the basis of inheritance of function, it is obvious that a settled stage of society is favorable, and change hostile, to the growth of caste. Whatever breaks up existing customs and traditions tends to abolish hereditary privilege and throw men into a rough struggle, out of which strong, coarse natures emerge as victors, to found, perhaps, a new aristocracy. Thus the conquest of southern Europe by northern tribes led to a period of somewhat confused readjustment in which men of natural power bettered their status. In the same way the relative openness of classes in our own day may be due as much to confusion as to a permanent decline in the caste principle.

(3) *The State of Education and Enlightenment.*—Since caste is an organization of the social mind on a biological principle it is simpler to apply than is the principle of competition which requires selection on the basis of individual capacity and preference. Competition requires, therefore, a somewhat more advanced state

[9] Samuel Johnson, *Oriental Religions, India,* p. 241.

of communication and enlightenment than does caste. Evidently caste means the subordination of reason to convenience, of freedom to order. From the point of view of the value of personality, the ideal principle is not biological but moral, based, that is, on the spiritual gifts of individuals without regard to descent. Caste, then, is something which, we may assume, will give way to this higher principle whenever the conditions are such as to permit the latter to work successfully; and this will be the case when the population is so mobilized by free training and institutions that just and orderly selection on the basis of individual merits is practicable.

The diffusion of intelligence, rapid communication, the mobilization of wealth by means of money, and the like, mark the ascendancy of the human mind over material and biological conditions. As such, they make for competition rather than caste.

In this way, then, human-nature conditions and social conditions work together to produce the kind of class system that exists in any given country at any given time: Always and everywhere, so far as we can see, parental affection and the suggestibility of children tend toward caste; but only when marked population differences are present or when the rate of social change is slow, when the state of education and enlightenment is relatively low, or when all three of these social conditions exist together, only under those circumstances, do the human nature conditions actually work out in caste.

Social Classes in the United States. The facts of American life have so long belied the old stereotype of political clap-trap—"the United States is a nation without classes"—that every intelligent person is prepared, of course, to recognize that instead of being without classes the United States has a very complicated system of functional, property, and racial classes, membership in which is only very partially determined by competition.

About 40 per cent of the population are gainful workers. Of the 48,829,000 gainful workers in 1930, 21 per cent were in agriculture and 79 per cent were in non-agricultural pursuits.[10] The

[10] *Fifteenth Census of the United States; 1930.* Population Bulletin, Second Series, United States Summary, p. 57. Of the 38,357,000 engaged in non-agricultural pursuits in 1930, approximately 39 per cent were in manufacturing and mechanical industries; 19 per cent were in trade; about 12 per cent were in domestic and personal service; about 11 per cent in transportation; and not quite 9 per cent in the professions.

percentage of non-agricultural workers has tended to increase steadily since the coming of the Industrial Revolution and the growth of cities. In 1790 less than 10 per cent of the population was non-agricultural. Yet disproportionate as the increase of the non-agricultural elements has been, the increase in the percentage of the national income going to those classes has been even greater. Figures on relative distribution of income in the early years are hard to obtain, but during the last quarter-century it is estimated by Professor Taylor of Northwestern, that the share of the agricultural classes decreased from one fifth to less than one tenth of the total income, while the farming classes themselves were shrinking only from one third to about one quarter of the total number. These facts of population drift and the shifting of economic power go far to explain current conflicts between farm and city.

1. **Agricultural Classes.** Leaving aside racial class differences, there are three principal classes among the 10,471,000 gainful workers on America's 6,288,000 farms: (1) *Farm owners.* These have been decreasing since 1910 and in 1930 numbered only 3,500,000, *i.e.*, 9 per cent less than in 1920 and approximately one third of all the gainful workers engaged in agriculture.[11] (2) *Tenant farmers.* In 1930 these numbered 2,600,000, or 8.5 per cent more than in 1920, and constituted about one fourth of the gainful workers in agriculture. About 38 per cent of all farms are tenant-operated. Tenancy is most prevalent in the high-land-value States such as Illinois, Iowa, Nebraska, and Kansas, and in the South where about three quarters of a million Negroes are tenant farmers. In Michigan the percentage of tenancy has remained practically stationary for 30 years—15.8 per cent in 1900 and 15.14 per cent in 1930.[12] In general, tenant farmers tend to be less efficient than farm owners, have a lower standard of living, and participate less generally in community affairs. Their access to the land, *i.e.*, to the means of production, depends on their making *rental bargains* with landlords. Rent is usually paid in farm products, although many tenants pay in cash. (3) *Farm laborers.* Nearly 42 per cent of all gainful workers in agriculture are la-

[11] Only 1,569,000 of these, or not quite one fourth of all farm operators, owned their farms free from mortgage debt. *Fifteenth Census of the U. S., 1930*—Agriculture, General Statistics, Summary for the U. S., 1929 and 1930, pp. 10–12.

[12] *Fifteenth Census of the U. S., 1930*—Agriculture-Michigan. Second Series, p. 5.

borers. Paid wage workers, however, constitute only about two thirds of the total number of farm laborers, since more than 15 per cent of all gainful agricultural workers are unpaid members of farm families. These unpaid family workers are an important factor in retarding or preventing the spread of the corporation farm, and in keeping down the wages of agricultural labor generally.

The farm wage worker obtains access to the means of production through the *wage bargain* between himself and the farm operator, *i.e.,* farm owner, tenant, or farm manager.[13] For a variety of reasons farm wage workers receive lower wages than wage workers in urban industries, and their wages fluctuate less violently than urban wages. Thus in 1914, for example, when in 18 typical manufacturing cities including Chicago and Detroit 1,002,481 wage earners received an average for the year of $629.62 each, the Department of Agriculture estimated average yearly farm wages without board at $356.64. No doubt free rent, free garden produce, and the like frequently add materially to the real value of the farm laborer's wages, but during normal times there remains a cash differential favoring urban labor. On the other hand, the greater security and slower pace of agricultural labor go far to offset the cash differences. Agricultural labor is subjected to far less violent vicissitudes of tenure and pay than is labor in urban industry.

Farm wage laborers like wage laborers in urban industry have been seriously affected by the increasing mechanization of their industry. The increasing use of tractors, combines, and similar labor-saving devices forced many farm laborers into the cities during the decade of 1920–30. Despite a reverse current of migration to the farms, set in motion in 1929 by the depression, there was a net loss of farm wage workers, between 1920 and 1930. It is probable that as agriculture becomes more efficient the 1930 ratio of 1 agricultural worker to 3.7 non-agricultural workers will be increased.

2. **Non-agricultural Classes.** In functional terms, the 38,357,000 non-agricultural workers in the United States fall into three groups: (1) the business class; (2) the professional class; and (3) the wage-working class.

(1) **The Business Class.** This is the profit-seeking class,

[13] There were 55,000 farm managers in agriculture in 1930, an 18 per cent decrease from the number in 1920.

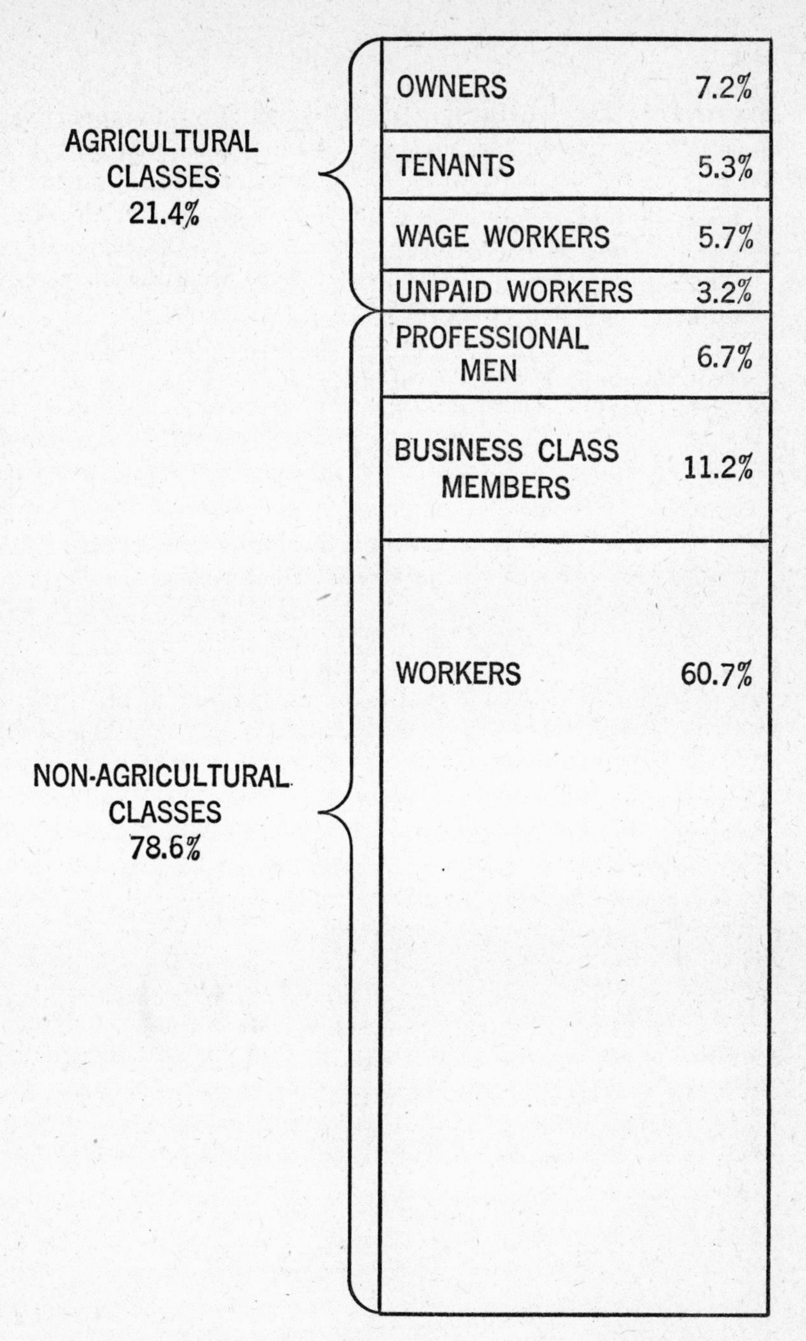

FIG. 17. Occupation Classes Based on 1930 U. S. Census and *Middletown.*

commercial and industrial, and its executive and salaried agents. Probably in actual numbers it does not exceed 15 per cent of the total number of non-agricultural gainful workers, or about 11 per cent of all the gainful workers in the United States.[14] In power and wealth, however, it far outweighs all the other classes put together.

The business class dominates American society through (*a*) economic power; (*b*) political power; (*c*) control of the press; (*d*) influence over the professional class; and (*e*) prestige.

(*a*) *Economic Power.*—Immediate power over goods and services, based on the legal institution of private property, is the foundation of the business man's control of the economic system. More accurately, perhaps, the power of the business class rests on its ownership and control of a disproportionate percentage of the total property. Whether this is a good thing or a bad thing is beside the point. It is essential to face facts before attempting evaluative judgments, and we are here concerned merely with describing what is, not with defending it or with attacking it.

Approximately 13 per cent of the population owns 87 per cent of the wealth of the nation. In terms of income, about half of the total income goes to one fifth of the income receivers, and probably over 80 per cent of all income receivers get less than $2,000 a year.[15] In 1927 it was estimated that less than 2 per cent of the gainfully employed had incomes of $5,000 or more.[16]

Obviously economic power is in the hands of a comparatively small number of people. Actual control is even more highly concentrated than is ownership and income. The agency through which this has been brought about is the corporation. The corporation was an important legal invention of antiquity which modern business has used to bring together the capital of many shareholders to finance large enterprises that would have been impossible without some such device. But if the corporate form of organization

[14] Owners, managers, and officials in logging, mining, manufacture, transportation, trade, public service, and domestic and personal service numbered approximately 3,784,111 in 1930. Including foremen and minor officials, 1,664,905, makes a total of the owning and directing class of 5,449,016, or 14.2 per cent of the 38,357,000 non-agricultural gainful workers and 11.2 per cent of the 48,829,000 gainful workers of all occupations. *Fifteenth Census of the U. S., 1930*—Occupation Statistics, U. S. Summary, Table 13.

[15] Cf. *Income in the United States, Its Amount and Distribution, 1909–1919,* National Bureau of Economic Research. At that time 86 per cent were getting less than $2,000 a year.

[16] On the basis of the 4,122,000 income tax returns filed that year. Of these, 3,234,000 were estimated to have incomes less than $5,000.

facilitated the mobilization of capital, it also lent itself to manipulation. By means of interlocking directorates, holding companies, and the like, control of a large percentage of American corporations has been concentrated in a few hands.

"The relative growth of the large companies has been such in the last 20 years that if the same rate were maintained all corporate wealth would be in the hands of 200 companies within 50 years—a concentration of economic power unknown in the world's history, unless it be compared to the present control of Soviet Russia."[17]

Ownership has actually been divorced from control in many cases.[18] When the banking house of Dillon, Read & Co., for example, reorganized the Dodge Brothers Motor Company they sold to eager investors millions of dollars' worth of non-voting stock in excess of the amount that the bankers had paid to the Dodge estate, thus not only getting their money back with a handsome profit but also retaining full control of the corporation at the same time. American legal practice permits management to apportion earnings and assets arbitrarily among the various participants in a corporation, thus enhancing one class of securities at the expense of another. By various other devices stockholders have been shorn of power until they frequently find themselves merely in the position of interested spectators. And if even the stockholders, *i.e.,* the owners, cannot hold management to an accounting, what of the public? While we have been evolving complicated political machinery by which even the poorest immigrant after a short residence here can vote on the behavior of his political representatives, no recognized way exists, so long as no law is violated, by which life-long American citizens can hold accountable the managers of great corporations. Yet corporate decisions concerning hours, wages, working conditions, and the like frequently affect a community far more profoundly than do the usual decisions of political lawmakers and executives.[19]

[17] A. A. Berle, Jr., and Gardiner C. Means, *Encyclopædia of the Social Sciences,* Vol. IV, p. 422.

[18] *Cf.* William Z. Ripley, *Main Street and Wall Street.* Another interesting development is the growing significance of the technical staff in the management of business. The technicians are more concerned with efficient production than with profit-making and hence are in a strategic position to represent community interests as against the narrower interests of capital on the one side or labor on the other.

[19] For example, the community leadership of a city of more than 100,000 in the Middle West was badly disorganized in the spring of 1932 when a great corporation, in the course of a reorganization of its various plants, discharged all the higher executives in two of its local companies. For years the men let go

(*b*) *Political Power.*—This derives only in part from direct corruption, vast as that is, but even more from roundabout and perfectly legal pressures in the shape of inducements—trade to the business man, practice to the lawyer, employment to the hand-worker, campaign contributions to the politician. Influence of this kind makes almost every rich man a political power, even without his especially wishing to be. But when wealth is united to a shrewd and unscrupulous political ambition or when it sets out to control legislation and the enforcement of the laws, as it seems to have done during the famous "graft cases" in California and later in the Mooney case, the American theory of government breaks down.[20] Probably it is not too much to say that except when public opinion is unusually aroused, wealth can generally have its way in our politics if it makes an effort to do so. How difficult it may be, however, to arouse public opinion was shown in the Teapot Dome scandal in which for months most of the press actually tried to discredit the Senate investigation.

(*c*) *Control of the Press.*—While many people persist in thinking of newspapers as "tribunes of the people," the average commercial paper in the United States is a business enterprise, owned by business men and deriving more than 75 per cent of its revenues from advertising contracts distributed by other business men. Although under a certain compulsion to interest everybody, the average paper tends on the whole to express the attitudes and points of view of the business class more sympathetically than it does those of any other class. As the Lynds observed in *Middletown:*

"It is usually safe to predict that in any controversy the two leading

had been the stand-bys in educational, religious, civic, and charitable work in the city. In the same way, the decisions of corporation executives, as in most of our industrial cities during the depression of 1929, may throw thousands of families on the public relief agencies through unemployment, yet the public has no voice in the decisions.

[20] The graft cases grew out of the bribing of public officials in San Francisco by business interests about the time of the earthquake. No business men were ever convicted although the officials were caught accepting bribe money. The Mooney case came to national attention during the war when President Wilson asked the governor of California to intervene to prevent the execution of a radical labor agitator, Tom Mooney, who had been convicted of murder in connection with a bomb explosion during a "preparedness day" parade in 1916. Judge, jury, and others connected with the case, with the exception of the former district attorney who prosecuted Mooney, have since charged that the conviction was a "frame-up," one crucial witness was discredited by his own letters, another admitted that his testimony was false. Mooney's sentence was commuted to life imprisonment. He was still in prison in January, 1933.

papers may be expected to support the United States in any cause, the business class rather than the working class, the Republican party against any other but especially against any 'radical' party."[21]

So closely integrated is the average newspaper with the whole complex of bank loans, advertising, luncheon clubs, and the like, that to explain the prevalent business class tone of the commercial press it is quite unnecessary to look for deliberate dictation by advertisers.[22] Actually the larger the newspaper the more improbable, if not impossible, such dictation becomes; yet at the same time the larger the newspaper the closer becomes the integration of the whole enterprise with the business community.[23] In extreme cases when an industry dominates a community completely, as not infrequently happens in one-industry regions during a strike, the newspapers become utterly subservient. The most notorious example of this was the behavior of seven Pittsburgh newspapers during the great steel strike of 1919, when ordinary demands for abolition of the 12-hour day and recognition of the union were misrepresented as red Bolshevism and no effort was made to present the men's side of the controversy at all.[24] Resenting the unfairness of the Associated Press reports of that strike, labor newspapers organized their own news association, the Federated Press. Class journalism of any kind does not, however, solve the problem of how to place impartial news on class questions before the public.

(*d*) *Influence on the Professional Class.*—The influence of the business class on professional men is real but largely indirect. The abler men of this sort are generally educated and self-respecting, have a good deal of professional spirit and are not wholly dependent upon any one employer. At the same time they get their living largely through the rich, from whom the most lucrative employment comes, and who have many indirect ways of making and marring careers. The ablest men in the legal profession are in close relations with the rich and commonly become capitalists

21 *Middletown*, p. 476–7.

22 Upton Sinclair's *Brass Check* probably overstates the facts here.

23 Silas Bent in *Ballyhoo* points out that crusading is more characteristic of medium-sized papers than of large ones. Big papers represent investments of millions of dollars.

24 Cf. *Public Opinion and the Steel Strike*, Commission of Inquiry, Interchurch World Movement, New York, 1921, p. 111.

themselves; physicians are more independent, because their art is not directly concerned with property, yet they look to wealthy patients for their most profitable practice; clergymen are under pressure to satisfy wealthy parishioners; and teachers must win the good will of opulent citizens who control educational boards. Even the man of letters is not immune, despite William Dean Howells's dictum that the rich can do nothing to make or mar a book. Unsympathetic critics contend that young writers who start with magazine writing are likely to be stereotyped and stunted by the commercial pressure for "pleasant endings," by the widespread taboo on "sociological" stories, and by the preoccupation of editors with romances of "escape from reality" and with the trivialities of leisure class life.

(*e*) *Prestige.*—For most Americans, to succeed is to become a successful business man. The ideal of pecuniary success has so permeated all classes that it is difficult for many people to appreciate real achievement unless it carries a market value. Years ago Thorstein Veblen pointed out that the old barbaric awe of physical prowess has gradually been transformed into awe of economic power and that the most evident manifestation of economic power today is "conspicuous consumption," *i.e.*, the unnecessary consumption of goods and services for the purpose of impressing others with the possessor's economic importance.[25] Thus all of us are impressed by surplus servants, excess automobiles, jewels, private yachts, and the like. So to its other sources of power the business class adds power over the imagination. Thus indirectly as well as directly the business class tends to dominate American society.

(2) **The Professional Class.** There were approximately 3,253,000 persons, or about 7 per cent of the gainful workers, classified as rendering professional and semi-professional service in 1930. Professional people are the main sources of new ideas and discoveries. They are also the principal source of distinguished people in each succeeding generation.

Professor J. McKeen Cattell found the ratios in which various occupations had produced scientific men per unit of population to be as follows: Professional class, 13.9; manufacturing and trade, 1.04; agriculture, 0.48;[26] Visher in his study of the occupa-

[25] *The Theory of the Leisure Class.*
[26] *American Men of Science,* 1921, pp. 783–4.

tions of 18,400 Americans listed in *Who's Who* found the number produced in each class to be as follows per 10,000 persons: Clergy, 315; other professions, 142; business men, 80; farmers, 9; skilled and semi-skilled laborers, 4; unskilled laborers, 0.013.[27] Other studies reveal similar tendencies.[28]

In outlook and sympathies most professional people probably lean toward the business point of view. That schools, for example, might be controlled by teachers instead of business men is regarded as "radicalism" even by most teachers themselves. Yet the class consciousness of professional people is probably increasing and has already won some notable points of vantage.

The first professional organization in America was the Ministerial Association of Boston which was formed in 1690.[29] The first organization of national importance was the American Medical Association which was organized in 1847. Its greatest growth has come since 1900. The membership in 1931 was 98,341.

The next great professional organization to appear was the National Teachers Association, the forerunner of the present National Educational Association. The N. T. A. was organized in Philadelphia in August, 1857, when there were already existing 23 state educational associations. The name was changed in 1870 to the National Educational Association. In 1930 the N. E. A. had 216,188 members. Since 1901 a considerable number of classroom teacher organizations have also appeared. A. R. Lang in 1922 found that of 59 such associations 50 per cent had been organized in the preceding six years.[30] One of the pioneers in the classroom teacher movement has been the Chicago Teachers Federation under the leadership of Catherine Goggin and Margaret Haley. Since 1912 the classroom teachers' organizations have

[27] Stephen S. Visher, "A Study of the Type of the Place of Birth and of the Occupation of Fathers of Subjects of Sketches in Who's Who," *American Journal of Sociology,* Vol. 30, March, 1925, p. 553.

[28] See, for example, Edwin L. Clarke, "American Men of Letters," *Columbia University Studies,* Vol. LXXII, 1916, pp. 74–76, and Pitirim Sorokin, *Social Mobility,* New York, 1927, p. 289. Of men of letters Clarke found the following percentages from each class of homes: Professional 32.8; business, 15.1; agricutural, 13.9; mechanical, clerical, unskilled, 4.8; unknown, 33.4.

[29] William W. Sweet, *The Story of Religions in America,* N. Y., 1930, p. 93.

[30] A. R. Lang, "Classroom Teachers' Organizations," *1923–24 Yearbook of the National League of Teachers Associations,* p. 28. See also M. David Hoffman, "Status of Voluntary Teachers Associations in Cities of 100,000 Population or More," *Bulletin 1930, No. 36, U. S. Dept. of the Interior, 1931,* p. 6, Hoffman's study covers 137 teacher organizations from 1840 to 1927.

been organized nationally in the National League of Teachers Associations which is committed to securing for the classroom teacher a greater share in the control of the school system.

On the college level, professional organization as it relates to class status as distinguished from scientific or technical achievement finds expression in the American Association of University Professors which was founded in 1915 and had as its first president John Dewey. In 1932 the A. A. U. P. had about 12,000 members, or about one fifth of the number eligible for membership.

After the teachers, the next group of professional workers to band together on a national scale for mutual protection and advancement were the lawyers who in 1878 formed the American Bar Association. In 1931 this organization had 27,000 members, or about 20 per cent of the lawyers of the country.

All professional groups are showing increasing self-consciousness of common interests as professional workers, and in some instances this increased self-consciousness is achieving social recognition. In California, for instance, the members of the state bar association control admission to the bar. In Mississippi a few years ago when the governor forced a hand-picked board of regents of the state university to dismiss certain strong-minded members of the medical faculty the American Medical Association compelled their reinstatement, with ample guarantees of future security, by threatening to have all Mississippi medical graduates barred from practice in every other state in the Union. In Chicago and Milwaukee, classroom teachers have strong professional organizations. In fact, it was largely through the Chicago teachers' organization that the tax scandals of the Thompson régime were uncovered. Even newspaper reporters have attempted quasi-professional organization.[31]

As the realization grows that for the majority of any nonbusiness class, hope of improvement in the future lies in raising the status of the class rather than in changing the status of the

[31] The difficulty in professionalizing journalism lies in the fact that unlike the lawyer or doctor, the editor and reporter must work with large amounts of invested capital which the owners control. In Scranton, Pa., in 1930 there was a flourishing "union" of editorial workers which had for several years maintained a salary scale from 21 to 28 per cent above the average of typical dailies in towns of similar size. Cf. *Editor and Publisher and Fourth Estate,* October 25, 1930, p. 50.

individual, the class consciousness of professional people may be expected to increase.[32]

(3) **The Wage-working Class.** In round numbers there were probably 29,600,000 wage-workers and minor salaried workers in non-agricultural industry in 1930. In other words, approximately 60 per cent of all gainful workers are non-agricultural wage-workers. Since in the business and professional classes together in 1930 there were only 8,702,000, and since only a minority of the business and professional groups are ever replaced by former wage-workers in any generation, it is obvious that the vast majority of non-agricultural wage-workers are fated to remain wage-workers all their lives despite openness of classes and American optimism.[33]

It is this optimism, perhaps, which has blinded most Americans to the fact that freedom as applied to class conditions has two distinct aspects. There is, on the one hand, (*a*) *freedom to rise from one class to another, i.e.,* freedom of individual opportunity, or *carrière ouverte aux talents.* This kind of freedom is chiefly for the man of exceptional capacity and ambition. It is important, but not more so than the other kind, namely, (*b*) *freedom of classes,* or freedom within the class.[34] This second kind of freedom means justice, opportunity, humane living for the less privileged groups as groups; not opportunity to get out of them, but opportunity to be something in them; a chance for the teamster to have comfort, culture, and good surroundings for himself and his family without ceasing to be a teamster.

Freedom to rise has been much better understood in the United

[32] For those who object to the term class consciousness, the important thing would seem to be not class consciousness in itself, but class consciousness subordinated to a larger loyalty to community and nation. The business class has the most highly developed class consciousness in the country, as the existence of employers' associations, luncheon clubs and the like indicates. It is not class consciousness itself that is dangerous, but exclusive class consciousness without broader loyalties and tinged with bitterness and hatred.

[33] The effect of traditional attitudes appeared in striking contrast to the facts in Middletown: While in six Middletown plants employing an average of 4240 workers there was one promotion to foreman in every 424 eligible men during 23 months, January 1, 1923, to October 1, 1924, more than half of the senior class of the Middletown high school marked as true or probably true the statement that "Failure to succeed in life is absolutely the individual's own fault." *Op. cit.,* p. 66. For a full examination of the evidence of class mobility see Pitirim Sorokin, *Social Mobility.*

[34] This discussion of freedom implies values; first, the value of freedom itself, and second, the value of personality. For a brief consideration of values, see Chapter XXIX.

States than has freedom within the class. That it is wrong to keep a man down who might rise is quite familiar, but that those who cannot rise, or do not care to, have also just claims is almost a novel idea, though they are evidently that majority for whom our institutions are supposed to exist. Owing to preoccupation with the ideals of enterprise and success, a certain neglect, and even reproach, have rested upon those who do quietly the plain work of life.

It may even be argued that success in the United States during the nineteenth and early twentieth centuries was too much on the tontine plan, where one puts all he has into a pool in the hope of being one of a few survivors to get what the rest lose. From the point of view of wholesome social conditions, it is no doubt a great thing that every child in the United States can aspire to be president or to be head of the Standard Oil Company, but it is equally important that he should have a chance for full and wholesome life in the much more probable condition of clerk or mill hand. While we must admire the heroes who have risen from the ranks, we must also remember that they do and should constitute only a small minority of the human race.

The main guarantee for freedom of this latter sort, freedom within the class, is some kind of class organization which shall resist the encroachment and neglect of which the weaker parties in society are in constant danger. Those who have wealth, position, knowledge, leisure, may perhaps dispense with formal organization (though in fact it is those who are already strong who most readily exert their strength in this way), but the multitudes who have nothing but their human nature to go on must evidently stand together or go to the wall.

The efforts that working people have made to meet this need of organization to achieve more freedom within their class will be analyzed in the next chapter. For the moment we must ask what are the conditions under which the majority of plain people actually live out their lives? How much less free are they as handworkers than they would be as members of the business or professional classes? What does America's blindness to the problem of freedom within the class mean to the great majority of our urban workers?

The Economic Watershed—and What It Means. Dividing Middletown into the business-professional class on the one hand

and the working class on the other, the Lynds found a kind of economic watershed down which income coursed, plentifully on one side and not so plentifully on the other. If the Middletown ratios hold for industrial cities generally, 29 out of every 100 industrial urban workers would live on the business-professional side of this watershed, and 71 would live on the working-class side. What does it mean to live on one side rather than the other? Since we have described the power of the business class, let us here confine ourselves to the working-class side of the watershed. Life on the working-class side entails for the average man nine handicaps affecting principally health, economic status, and civic security. These may be summarized as follows:

(*a*) *Handicaps affecting health.*

i. Higher infant mortality.

Evidence: U. S. Children's Bureau study in Baltimore, 1915, showing almost uniform increase in infant mortality in white homes as income of the father fell below $1850 per year. At $1850 per year and up only 38.3 babies died; below $450, 164.8 per 1000 died. Studies in Johnstown, Pa., and eslewhere confirm this. The correspondence is so striking and the effect of improved sanitation, free medical service, etc., so apparent that the importance of the environmental factors must be admitted, even when full account is taken of the fact that some of the higher rate among the poor may be due to the presence of parents of biologically inferior stamina on that social level.[35]

ii. Higher percentage of stunted and diseased children.

Evidence: Studies of the stature of school boys in Liverpool, Eng., show that at the age of 7 the sons of wealthy citizens average 4.4 inches taller than the sons of unemployed or casual laborers, while at 14 the difference is 6.5 inches. Granting again the biological factor which is undoubtedly present, the close correspondence of height and social class through four gradations—casual laborers, laborers, well-to-do, and wealthy—exceeds the exactness normally experienced in the sorting out of biological qualities by any social system. Hence the inference that some at least of the stunting is due to environmental factors.[36] As to disease, the mor-

[35] *U. S. Children's Bureau, Publications No. 119,* pp. 94–97.

[36] H. M. Vernon, *Industrial Fatigue and Efficiency,* p. 165, quoted by Queen and Mann, *Social Pathology,* New York, 1925, p. 260.

bidity rate of working-class districts is higher than the better residential sections.[37]

iii. Higher risks of accident, unemployment, and of old age dependence.

Evidence: Accident insurance rates are higher for hand-workers than for white-collar workers. 8,000,000 to 11,000,000 estimated unemployed and under-employed in the winter of 1931–32. 3,100,000 unemployed or on involuntary lay-off without pay in the U. S. in April, 1930.[38] From 1,000,000 to 2,000,000 unemployed in U. S. at all times. Maintenance of poorhouses and adoption of old age pension laws notoriously are for the benefit of the working class, not the business class which does not need them. 17 states had old age pension laws in 1932.

iv. Shorter average life.

Evidence: Higher insurance rates for workers whose average duration of life is "about eight years shorter than the other classes in this country."[39]

(*b*) *Economic handicaps.*

v. Inadequate housing.

Evidence: In Detroit, 1928, the average number of persons per room in the city as a whole was 0.7681; in working-class districts the average ran from 10 to 26 per cent above this; in middle-class areas it ran below. Authorities estimate that on the basis of the present distribution of wealth over 66 per cent of the people cannot afford to pay more than $4800 for a house. Under recent conditions in the building industry the needed homes cannot be built for such a price. Hence the impasse: Overcrowding on the one hand and idle construction workers on the other.[40]

vi. Less average schooling *per unit of ability.*

Evidence: Most of the A and B brains in this country are

[37] *City Health Bulletin, Detroit Department of Health,* July and August, 1929. Vol. XIII, Nos. 7 and 8, p. 10 f.

[38] *15th Census of the United States,* 1930: United States Summary—Unemployment, p. 2.

[39] L. J. Dublin, *Health of the Workers,* pp. 8 ff., cited by Pitirim Sorokin, *Social Mobility,* p. 263.

[40] In 1920, 62.5 per cent of all dwellings in the U. S. were rented. Of the others, 38.3 per cent were mortgaged. In other words, less than one third of all dwellings were owned free of debt. This included both rural and urban dwellings. *Less than one third* of the non-agricultural classes own their own homes, free or mortgaged.

in the non-white-collar occupations, yet most of the college and normal students come from the white-collar homes. Lehman and Stoke have shown that farmers, artisans, semi-skilled and unskilled on the basis of the Army test percentages produced 2,010,000 A and B men in 1920, while the professional and clerical groups together produced only 1,372,000.[41] In 1929–30 Woody and Keeler found that out of 5715 Michigan students attending the University of Michigan, Michigan State College, and all the other institutions of higher education in the state, including normal colleges, farmers, artisans, and semi-skilled classes contributed just 33.3 per cent, while the clerical, business, and professional classes contributed over 53 per cent.[42] In Middletown the Lynds found economic factors playing a powerful rôle in determining who should go to college.[43]

vii. Lower incomes and lower standards of living.

Evidence: Average income of 100 working-class families in Middletown in 1924, $1495. Minimum health and decency budget for family of five, 1924, $1,920.87. Over 80 per cent of all income receivers get less than $2000. Only 4,122,000 income tax returns filed in 1927, 31,527 of them by millionaires, out of over 45,000,000 income receivers.

viii. Little property protection for dependents.

Evidence: Statistics of estates left by decedents in the United States. In 1928 these averaged $28.61.[44]

(c) *Civic insecurity.*

ix. Inequality before the law.

Evidence: Report of the United States Industrial Relations Commission, 1915, that "denial of justice in the creation, adjudication and enforcement of the law" is one of four basic causes of industrial unrest.[45] In 1916–17, the Boston

[41] Harvey C. Lehman and Stuart M. Stoke, "Occupational Intelligence in the Army," *American Journal of Sociology,* July, 1930, Vol. XXXIV, p. 15.

[42] Unpublished results of study by C. Woody and L. W. Keeler, University of Michigan. In 13 per cent of the cases the parental occupation was unknown.

[43] *Op. cit.,* pp. 185–186. Girls in high school, for example, felt "out of it" unless they could afford silk stockings. Both in Middletown and in the state generally economics rather than intelligence was selecting the college students.

[44] The range by states was from $1.96 in Idaho to $229.22 in Delaware. *Cf.* Chas. Angoff and H. L. Mencken, "The Worst American State," *The American Mercury,* Vol. XXIV, September, 1931, Table 8.

[45] The other causes were "unjust distribution of wealth and income"; "unemployment and the denial of an opportunity to earn a living"; and "the denial of the right to form effective organizations."

Legal Aid Society found that out of 551 cases that needed court action, 129, or 23 per cent, could not be brought because the clients could not pay the ordinary court costs. R. H. Smith in *Justice and the Poor* concluded that "the rich and the poor do not stand on an equality before the law." Evidence of the political and legal inequalities affecting the working class could be extended many pages.

Summary. In every society above the hunting stage association tends to stratify on levels determined by occupation and economic power. The individual's place in the system is determined by one of two principles—caste or competition. Which of these principles predominates at a given time is the result of human-nature tendencies intensified or modified by social conditions such as population differences, the rate of social change, and the state of education and enlightment.

In the United States there is a complicated class system based on occupation, wealth, and race. The racial situation in the South is an example of a caste society which has grown up in the midst of otherwise free institutions. Aside from the racial castes, classes may be divided into agricultural and non-agricultural. Agricultural classes consist of farm owners, farm tenants, and farm wage laborers, all of whom have been profoundly affected by the increasing mechanization of agriculture especially since the World War. The non-agricultural classes consist of the business class which dominates the country, the professional class, and the wage-working class, which latter includes more than half of all gainful workers. In Middletown 71 out of every 100 gainful workers were classified as members of the working class. This class finds itself on the relatively disadvantageous side of the economic watershed, handicapped by higher health hazards, lower income, and greater civic insecurity than other classes.

STUDY QUESTIONS

1. What is a social class?
2. What kinds of social classes are there?
3. Define caste.
4. How can one determine when a caste situation exists?
5. What human nature conditions determine the strength or prevalence of caste?
6. What social conditions affect caste?

7. What is the conflict created in white culture by the race question?
8. What race questions are there in the U. S.?
9. How many Negroes are there in the United States? What percentage of them live in the South? In how many counties do they out-number the whites?
10. What is the relation of the Negro's economic condition to the problem of race relations in the South?
11. In what way has the white man's caste attitude toward colored races interfered with a scientific understanding of race as a factor in society?
12. In what way do non-racial differences affect caste?
13. How do the rate of social change and the state of education and enlightenment affect it?
14. What basic social differences are there in the United States?
15. What are the two groups of occupational classes?
16. How many farm owners are there? Tenant farmers? Farm laborers?
17. On what does the farm laborer's livelihood depend?
18. Compare farm wages with urban wages.
19. What are the non-agricultural classes?
20. At a maximum estimate, what percentage of the gainful workers of the nation belong to the business class?
21. What are the sources of business-class power?
22. What percentage of the population gets less than $2000 a year?
23. What are the facts of economic concentration?
24. A recent writer says that the corporation has done for capital what the factory did to labor, namely, separated control from operation. What did he mean?
25. "No recognized way exists by which life-long American citizens can hold accountable the managers of great corporations, so long as no law is violated, although corporate decisions . . . frequently affect a community far more profoundly than do the usual decisions of political law-makers and executive." Discuss the principle implied in that statement.
26. Give evidence of the political power of the business class.
27. Discuss the control of the press by the business class. In what sense is the usual indictment overdrawn? In what sense is it true?
28. How are young writers influenced by the business class?
29. Explain conspicuous consumption as an element in business class prestige.
30. What percentage of the gainful workers belong to the professional class?
31. In what way is the professional class important?

32. What evidence is there of increasing class consciousness among professional people? What reason is there to believe that this will increase in the future?
33. Is class consciousness necessarily a bad thing? Which class has the most highly developed class consciousness in the United States today?
34. What percentage of the gainful workers belong to the wage-working class?
35. Explain class freedom. What type has been neglected in the United States?
36. What is the economic watershed?
37. List the disabilities existing on the wage-working side of that watershed.

CHAPTER XXI

CLASS TENSIONS IN THE MODERN WORLD

The Fact of Class Tension. The present social system based on private capitalism has evolved as every one knows from a preceding system which was based on feudal land rights. Under our system during normal times it is probable that more people enjoy a higher standard of living, more leisure, greater freedom, and more human dignity than was ever true under any preceding system. Yet the present system because of the very conditions and ideals generated by it is afflicted by serious maladjustments which threaten to destroy it unless they can be removed. But before any maladjustment in society or anywhere else can be removed it must be understood, and to understand these conflicts in our present culture we must face them as unemotionally as we can, trace their origins, and observe how men are actually trying to deal with them.

The Rise of Capitalism. Modern capitalism is a complex type of society which, while it did not reach full development until the nineteenth century, can be traced back in its origins to the thirteenth. The first treatise on bookkeeping was published by an Italian, Leonardo Pisano, in 1202, and dates the small beginnings of modern business. Many other things had to happen, however, before the world was ripe for the appearance of a United States Steel Corporation or a Ford Motor Company. J. A. Hobson, the English economist, has enumerated five conditions which were essential to the appearance of capitalism: (1) surplus production, part of which was saved; (2) a proletariat, or laboring class deprived of the means of earning an independent livelihood; (3) industrial technique sufficiently advanced to make profitable the use of indirect methods of production by group-labor using tools or machinery; (4) large, accessible markets; and (5) the capitalist spirit, or the desire and the capacity to apply accumulated wealth to profit-making by the organization of industrial enterprise. The surplus necessary for European capitalism came from three sources: ground rents, gold and silver mining, and the exploitation of colonies. This surplus passed into the hands of "business men" who probably came originally from a number of different sources; from members of the landed aristocracy who had entered city life; from feudal officers who had access to public resources; from enterprising burghers; and from the Jews who being under no religious restrictions on "usury" took the lead in money-lending.

At the same time, while the nascent business class was slowly learning how to make profit and how to control a business enterprise, the dependent working class necessary for later developments was being produced by successive revolutions in agriculture. In England enclosures and improvements in tillage were the great instruments by which small farmers and laborers were shaken loose from the land. The process extended over several centuries but by the mid-eighteenth century it had gone far enough to provide the mobile working force needed by the oncoming Industrial Revolution.

As the handicraft system under the guilds in the early towns had passed away it had been replaced or overlaid—for traces of it still remained—with a system of domestic industry in which manufacture was carried on in individual households. In the country agriculture and manufacture were not only carried on in the same locality but by the same people. Specialization was still incomplete.

> The simplest structure of "domestic" manufacture is that in which the farmer-manufacturer is found purchasing his own material, the raw wool or flax if he is a spinner, the warp and weft if he is a weaver, and, working with his family, produces yarn or cloth which he sells himself, either in the local market or to the regular master-clothiers or merchants. . . . The weak point in this economy lay in the trouble and uncertainty of marketing the product. It was here that the merchant, who represents the earliest form of industrial capitalism, presses in upon the self-employing artisan-capitalist. . . . From the habit of selling his product to a specialist middleman, it is a small step to receiving "orders" from the latter.[1]

It was also a small step to complete dependence on the middleman for raw materials as well as orders. This was the normal condition of the cotton trade in England by 1750. In the stocking-

[1] J. A. Hobson, *The Evolution of Modern Capitalism,* New York, 1916, p. 56.

trade capitalism had encroached one step further on domestic industry: Not only were the artisans dependent on the merchants for orders and for raw materials but the frames used for weaving were also owned by the merchants and rented out to the workers. Thus for *orders, materials,* and *tools,* workers in the stocking-trade were already dependent on the merchant-capitalist even before the Industrial Revolution.

The Coming of Machinery. By the middle of the eighteenth century the capitalist spirit, reinforced by the religious frugality of Puritan days, had permeated large sections of the English public. English victories in the wars with Spain, Holland, and France had opened India and the Americas to commercial exploitation. Markets were expanding. Protected by the Channel and with their own house in order, thanks to the revolutions of the seventeenth century, Englishmen were free to grapple with the problem of increasing the output of industry to take advantage of the opportunities opening before them. The net result of all these forces was the remarkable series of inventions that revolutionized industry and produced the modern factory system.

The Industrial Revolution was at least four revolutions in one: (1) The *mechanical revolution, i.e.,* the substitution of machinery for human skill; (2) the *revolution in power, i.e.,* the substitution of steam for human and animal muscular power; (3) the *revolution in industrial organization, i.e.,* the substitution of the factory for the domestic workshop; and (4) the *revolution in transportation, i.e.,* the substitution of the steamship and the railroad train for the sail boat and the stage coach. The actual story of that tremendous series of events, probably the most momentous in human history since the birth of Christianity, is too well known to need recounting here. How the great inventions of Kay, Hargreaves, Arkwright, and Crompton swept the spinners far ahead of the weavers even before Watt's steam engine, patented in 1769, began to be applied to spinning in 1790; how Cartwright, Horrocks, and others were thus stimulated to perfect the power-loom which reduced hand-weavers to beggary but multiplied output many-fold; and how from textiles the great idea spread to the iron trade, to shipbuilding, and to all the rest—these facts we need not dwell upon. The point is, *for the first time in human history man had gotten his hands on a source of gigantic power, dependable, controllable, flexible, and he had discovered how to use that power to produce goods and services in quantities undreamed of before. For the first time in human history it became possible to look forward to a time when meagre living need no longer be the inevitable lot of the majority of mankind.*

Yet the first impact of the new inventions on the old order was anything but reassuring.

What Machinery Did to the Workers. The Industrial Revolution enormously accelerated the capitalist evolution which was already in progress before the great inventions. It did this in a number of ways.[2]

1. The new machinery was too expensive for the small, independent worker. Hence the worker lost the ownership of the mechanical means of production, his "tools."

2. The new machinery was too heavy to be installed in workmen's homes and the new power could not be economically applied to isolated machines. Hence, the new machinery and the new power were concentrated in factories, and the workman lost control of his workshop.

3. The new machinery made possible the division of the productive process into small units which could be performed with little skill and training. Hence the worker lost his trade education, his skill, and his control of the trade and trade conditions.

4. For economy all machines in a plant had to be run together. Hence the individual worker lost control of his hours of work.

5. The capitalist now determined the location of the factory. Hence the worker lost control of his place of residence and became in most cases the tenant at will of the employer or the landlord.

6. The cutting up of the manufacturing process by machinery into small and simple tasks made possible the employment of weak and unskilled workers, *i.e.*, the employment of women and children, and thus increased the supply of available labor and lowered wages. Hence the worker lost control of apprenticeship, a process which has continued until since the advent of the automatic machine one great manufacturer is quoted as saying that he "wouldn't have a man in the plant who couldn't learn his job in four days."

7. The net result of all these changes was to produce congested manufacturing centres in which old modes and regulations of life

[2] Adapted from Robert Franklin Hoxie, *Trade Unionism in the United States*, New York, 1920, pp. 241 f.

no longer operated and in which housing and sanitary conditions were horrible beyond description.

Morality degenerated to the lowest possible depths. Poverty, drunkenness and vice held undisputed sway. Thus, within a generation, was the industrial worker of England, from an independent, skilled, tool-owning producer of goods for sale, or a worker in process of becoming such, a country or small town dweller, comfortably housed, fed and clothed, living a life governed by definite customs, based on definite religious, ethical and social concepts, protected by an intricate legal code, reduced to an unskilled wage-worker dependent upon a master to whom he was merely a part in the process of production, ill-paid, ill-housed, ill-clothed, ill-fed, deprived of the ordinary conditions and standards of life—the basis of a new and distinct class in society.[3]

How Changing Conditions Changed Men's Minds. Long before the Industrial Revolution, with the break-up of the old mediæval system in Europe, the young nation-states that had gradually emerged had begun the development of a system of centralized control of economic life. In England, for example, from the time of Henry VII on,

there was a constant extension of the sphere of government until it came to pass laws upon and provide for and regulate almost all the economic interests of the nation. . . . Thus, instead of industrial life being controlled and regulated by town governments, merchant and craft guilds, lords of fairs, village communities, lords of manors and their stewards, or other local bodies as in medieval days it was now regulated in its main features by the all-powerful national government.[4]

This system of centralized regulation for the purpose of strengthening the state was known as *Mercantilism*. For a century or more as the old mediæval system of local and personal loyalties passed away Mercantilism was the prevailing economic philosophy in western Europe. Gradually, however, as commerce expanded, enterprising individuals began to chafe at the restraints imposed by government.

Now it happened at about this time, in the seventeenth and eigh-

[3] *Op. cit.*, p. 243–244.

[4] Edward P. Cheyney, *An Introduction to the Industrial and Social History of England,* New York, 1919, p. 173 *passim.*

teenth centuries, that, because of political conditions in England and later in France, social theorists in those two countries were trying busily to explain the origins of government. The evolutionary theory of social development was still unknown, and for several generations the explanation that carried the most intellectual authority was the so-called *Social Contract Theory.* According to this theory, which dates from an English philosopher, Thomas Hobbes (1588–1679), and was elaborated by John Locke (1632–1704), the philosopher of the "Glorious Revolution" of 1688, and later by Jean Jacques Rousseau (1712–78), man had originally existed in a state of nature under natural law, as the Roman Stoics had once taught, but to avoid the pains and uncertainties of such an existence in which every man was at war with every one else, men had by means of the social contract given up some of their originally unlimited freedom for the sake of orderly government and security. Now in the state of nature, as Hobbes had conceived it, each man had had a right to anything he could take—in other words, private property did not exist. But for John Locke this was an unsatisfactory explanation. It is a natural law, he said, that each man is entitled to the fruits of his own labor. Therefore, in a state of nature private property is a natural right since it is the fruit of the labor of each individual for himself. It is thus a more basic right than any right of government, for governments exist by virtue of the social contract, but private property exists by virtue of a law which antedates the social contract, namely, the law of nature.

Thus for political reasons, at the very time when the rising business class was beginning to chafe at the restrictions imposed by governments, there had been evolved a theory of society by which government was made subordinate to property and the right to private property was regarded as a natural right beyond the power of governments to change.

There was presently to appear a logical statement of the business man's claim to be let alone not only on the ground of natural law but on that of expediency as well. This statement came in one of the great books of the world, Adam Smith's *Wealth of Nations,* published in 1776 and ordinarily regarded as dating the beginning of the science of economics. In this book, Smith, arguing that the individual is inevitably a better judge of his own interests than any governmental official can possibly be and that an Unseen Hand co-ordinates the activities of all individuals under the benign rule of the natural laws of supply and demand,[5] demolished Mercantilism as an economic theory and turned men's faces toward the new doctrine of *laissez-faire.*

Laissez-faire is that general economic attitude or philosophy which assumes property as a natural right superior to government and demands that government keep "hands off" except to provide police protection and enforce contracts.[6] Carried to its logical extreme as in Herbert Spencer's philosophy, *laissez-faire* even denies the right of the state to educate children at public expense on the ground that the state has no right to interfere with the natural relationship between parent and child. In some form *laissez-faire* with its background of natural law has formed the working philosophy of the business class in England and the United States for more than four generations.

Natural Law and *Laissez-Faire* Individualism in America. In America conditions were peculiarly favorable to the new point of view. It was a new country of rich natural resources which had been settled for the most part by enterprising members of the middle and lower classes who were not averse to bettering their economic condition. Pioneer conditions put a high premium on individual initiative. Traditions were few and weak. Unlike the situation in England, rural conditions here, even after the coming of the factory, continued for generations to encourage individualism. The government and the legal system were deeply colored by the natural rights philosophy which formed the social outlook of the leaders of the Revolution. The Constitution is based definitely on the notions of natural order and natural rights, and these have

[5] The Unseen Hand theory ignores half the facts—conflict of interest is just as real as harmony of interest. For example, in a depression it is to the interest of the individual employer to reduce expenses by reducing wages and laying off men, but such action lowers the total buying power of the community and increases the number of unemployed, *i.e.*, tends to injure every other business man in the community. Another example of the actual conflict between the individual interest and the community or collective interest is found in the waste of natural resources such as coal, timber, or oil when individuals are left free to make as much profit as they can regardless of long-time needs. Uncontrolled competition, *i.e.*, *laissez-faire* individualism, is blamed by business men themselves for the existing demoralization in the oil fields and the wasting of two barrels of oil for every one that has been extracted.

[6] In cold logic, *laissez-faire* would not even require the enforcement of contracts. As a recent economist points out, "Would not a customer who refused to pay his bills soon experience difficulty in getting dealers to sell to him?" See S. H. Slichter, *Modern Industrial Society,* p. 49.

been powerful influences in shaping the development of American law which fundamentally still assumes a natural order of social relationships given once for all. This is a thoroughly eighteenth-century and pre-evolutionary point of view.[7]

To such individualists and believers in natural rights the capitalist attitude in the midst of America's natural resources was thoroughly congenial. Profit-seeking was early recognized and encouraged by the national government itself. So eager, in fact, were all classes for economic well-being that even the most vehement partisans of *laissez-faire* individualism could not afford to be wholly consistent—it was business men themselves who were the most earnest advocates of protective tariffs and the policy of spending public money for public improvements. This did not, however, weaken their allegiance to the *laissez-faire* principle when it was a question of society's control of business. Legal regulation of working hours, the control of railroad rates, abolition of child labor, proposals of this kind aroused the most influential classes in the country for generations to insist that government should keep its hands off the natural laws of supply and demand.

Twilight of *Laissez-Faire* Individualism. Looking back from a vantage point of more than a century and a half it is obvious now that the philosophy of *laissez-faire* had no sooner been formulated by Adam Smith than the conditions out of which it had grown, namely, pre-machine capitalism, began to pass away. In England the Industrial Revolution swept away the independent workers whom Smith had seen and replaced them with the proletariat of the cities, utterly dependent on great corporations with which individually they were no match at all in the wage-bargain. That pre-machine capitalism passed away more slowly in America is perhaps one of the reasons why the individualistic philosophy lingered so persistently when the more advanced industries had long been on a machine-collectivist basis.

New conditions, however, both abroad and in America drove practical men and theorizers alike to new positions. Critics like

[7] For a discussion of the conflict in American law between the absolutistic or static concept of social relationships and social rights implied in the natural rights philosophy and the evolutionary concept which developed in the nineteenth century see Hoxie, *Trade Unionism in the United States,* pp. 212 ff. The evolutionary concept assumes that there is no natural order of social relationships given once for all, but that social relationships change and that justice does not consist in protecting or restoring natural rights but in changing or adapting rights and law to meet the particular needs and circumstances of developing social conditions.

Carlyle and Ruskin, revolutionists like Karl Marx, business men like John D. Rockefeller, social theorists like Lester F. Ward, men of many different temperaments and points of view, joined hands in this, that by word or deed they repudiated *laissez-faire*. Reform, Communism, the trust movement, social telesis, each in a different way denies the basic philosophy of "let alone."

Then came the World War when every western nation as a matter of military necessity scrapped whatever of *laissez-faire* remained and went as far as it could in the direction of national planning and controlled production.[8] Out of the war crisis came the Russian revolution and the Communist attempt at national planning in peace time, followed by the Italian Fascist experiment in the same direction for the defense of capitalism. Before the world had yet taken stock of either venture the depression of 1929 arrived, and confronting the spectacle of more than 10,000,000 Americans hunting for jobs economists debated the merits of industrial planning and a Senate committee took the testimony of industrial leaders on its feasibility.

It is impossible to review the evidence of social trends over the span of a century without coming to the conclusion that for better or worse *laissez-faire* individualism is a receding point of view.

Social Reactions to the Factory System. Up to this point we have been tracing the rise of the business man, the unprecedented impetus given to him by the Industrial Revolution for which he was largely responsible, the consequences of that revolution on the workers of the time, and the changing social philosophies that the business man brought with him. It is now time to ask what has been the reaction of society to its new master and his new machines, particularly in America.

That reaction has been so complex that generations of novelists, reformers, labor leaders, economists, business men, social workers, and sociologists have not yet completed the description of it. In the nature of the case, all we can attempt here is to suggest some of the outstanding results of the new order. These may be summarized under three heads: (1) the appearance of a new social class, the proletariat; (2) industrial unrest; and (3) readjustments to unrest.

1. **The Proletariat Emerges.** We have already seen how

[8] The setting up of the War Industries Board in the United States is an example.

the independent artisan-producer of England was transformed by the Industrial Revolution into a propertyless machine-hand dependent on his employer for access to the means of production. For millions of English workers this transformation occurred between 1760 and 1820. In America the process was somewhat different and did not really get under way until the period of the restrictions on importations that ushered in the War of 1812. It was another generation before factory production had superseded older methods in any industry. Even in textiles the factory did not become dominant until about 1830,[9] and the country continued to be primarily an agricultural nation until long after the Civil War. It was 1880 before the value of manufactured goods exceeded the value of agricultural products, and even then, despite the substitution of machinery for men on the farms which had been going on for almost half a century, 44.3 per cent of the gainful workers were still in agriculture and only 21.8 per cent were in manufacture. Only 28.6 per cent of the population was urban. But the tide had turned and while agriculture continued to grow for another thirty years, manufacture grew much faster. By 1929–30 the value of manufactured products was many times that of agriculture, the percentage of agricultural workers had fallen to 21.5 while manufacture claimed 29.2 per cent, and 56.2 per cent of the population was now classified as urban. Between 1880 and 1930, in other words, the factory system, which had been preparing its victory in the protective tariff policy established as a revenue measure during the Civil War, definitely strode to the front and captured America.[10] From the Civil War on, the factory system, with the way cleared by the elimination of the rival slave labor system in the South, became the most dynamic factor in American life.

Into this system, by the million, were swept the surplus young men and young women, released by machinery from the farms, and the swarming masses of European peasants who were com-

[9] E. L. Bogart, *Economic History of the United States,* New York, 1915, p. 166. A spinning jenny was operated in Philadelphia in 1775. The first cotton factory in the U. S. was erected at Beverly, Mass., in 1787. Samuel Slater opened his first mill at Pawtucket in 1789, the real beginning of the factory system in the U. S.

[10] The war-time tariff was really established by the victory of the New England Radicals in the elections of 1866 which were fought not on the issue of the tariff but on that of "keeping the traitors out of office" at the South. See Beale, *The Critical Year.*

ing here in shiploads to find liberty and economic opportunity and remaining to build our railroads and stoke our blast furnaces. These and their descendants, with more than 2,000,000 Negroes from the South, today form the proletariat of the northern industrial cities, the new job-dependent class created by the evolution of capitalism.

In America the beginnings of that class go back, beyond the beginnings of the factory system itself, back into Colonial days, and it is back to those times that we must go to find the beginnings of industrial discontent which the factory system has intensified and generalized.

2. **Industrial Unrest.** Discontent of the wage-worker with his lot first appears definitely in America when the increasing specialization of capitalism at the end of the eighteenth century separated the wage-earning function from the employing and price-fixing functions. To understand this we must see clearly that because of frontier conditions, free land, sparse population, difficulties of transport, and the like, capitalism followed a slightly different course in Colonial America than it did in England. In the earliest colonial period the artisan was an "itinerant, travelling laboriously to the farm or plantation of his employer who was also the consumer of his product."[11] Then came the custom-order and the retail-shop stage when the consumer travelled to town and the merchant or pedler, not the artisan, travelled to the consumer. In these stages wage-earning, price-fixing, and profit-making were combined, and combined often in the same individual. It was only with the extension of the market that followed the levelling of political barriers with the adoption of the Constitution that a new stage began to appear which the factory and later improvements in transportation were to bring to full maturity. In this stage with its wholesale markets, its credit system, and its separation of the merchant-capitalist, or capitalist-wholesaler, from the manufacturer on the one hand and the retailer on the other,

> the manufacturer was at first merely an incipient employer without capital—the "boss," the contractor—the successor of the master workman—whose function was merely that of driving the wage-bargain. The distinction between the employer and the wage-earner at

[11] John R. Commons and Associates, *History of Labour in the United States*, New York, 1921, Vol. 1, p. 6.

the time was not so much the amount of his income or his possession of capital, as the contingent and speculative character of his income. His profit was the margin between the prices he paid for labor and the prices he received from the wholesale-merchant, or merchant-capitalist, for his product.[12]

It was this pressure of the evolving employer that gave rise to discontent among wage-workers.

The coming of the factory and the widening of the area of competition as transportation improved merely intensified and diffused an attitude that had already begun to appear even before the Industrial Revolution reached America. The factory brought discipline, "the discipline of a power driven by a competition that seemed as inhuman as the machines that thundered in factory and shed."[13] The railroad and the steamship brought job-seekers from the ends of the earth and intensified the other insecurities of a system that could not foresee the needs of a world market. Added to these economic forces were psychological factors inherent in modern culture: Literature, science, social theory, education, religion, all these were enhancing the value of the individual, while the factory was making him merely a cog in a machine. The cult of progress issuing from physical science and modern invention was making men impatient with the pains and discomforts of life. The decline of otherworldliness in religion was making men doubt whether the injustices of this world would ever be set right in another, and the break-down, as the century wore on, of the old American formula of "hard work—thrift—independence" was adding to the growing sense of frustration and bewilderment. Then in the early years of the new century and following the World War there came the spectacle of aggressive working-class movements in England and Russia striking out for mass improvement.

All these factors acting in conjunction with the original resentment of low wages and long hours, insecurity of livelihood, and inequality before the law have produced a deep-seated discontent with modern industry that is one of the most outstanding features of modern society.

3. **Efforts to Escape, Remove, or Control Discontent.** Readjustments to industrial dissatisfaction appear in four forms:

[12] *Ibid.*, p. 7.

[13] J. L. and Barbara Hammond, *The Town Laborer*, London, 1919, p. 19.

(1) Among exceptional individuals readjustment takes the form of personal escape from the wage status; (2) among working people it takes the form of the labor movement; (3) among employers it takes the form of repression, concession, and psychological control; and finally, (4) in the state it takes the form of coercion and repression on the one hand and social legislation and administrative regulation on the other.

(1) **Individual Escape.** It is impossible to estimate the percentage of each generation of wage-workers who succeed in climbing into the business, professional, and farm-owning classes.[14] Unquestionably a considerable number do and the proportion is probably greater than in any other industrial nation. At the same time there is, of course, a reverse current of business, professional, and farm-owning individuals who slip back into the wage-earning class. Times of depression speed this downward movement just as boom times speed the upward movement. The most that can be said with assurance is that of the total number of individuals born on the wage-earning level in any generation only a minority ever succeed in entering the business, professional, or farm-owning groups. The majority spend their lives as wage-earners. *Individual escape, then, is no solution for the bulk of industrial unrest.*

(2) **The Labor Movement.** The wage laborer's reaction to the Industrial Revolution began with the protests and riots that marked the introduction of the new machinery in English villages; but generations had to pass before laborers could develop solidarity enough and economic and political competence enough to affect the institutions with which they had to deal. To mitigate or remove the disabilities of the wage status working people have moved along three lines: (*a*) *co-operation;* (*b*) *trade unionism;* and (*c*) *political action.*

(*a*) **Co-operation.**

The idea of eliminating profit by co-operatively managed factories and bulk purchases of food and clothing is as old as the Industrial Revolution itself. In 1767 in Great Britain "through

[14] The most comprehensive study of changes in class levels that has been made to date is that of Professor Sorokin, *Social Mobility*. Unfortunately he was not interested in this specific question and while his tables show what percentage of certain college and business groups have come from lower economic strata they do not show what percentage of the lower economic strata have gotten to be college and business men.

philanthropic efforts advances of money were made to the poor to build mills for grinding wheat or to finance bulk purchases of consumption needs."[15] The present movement in Great Britain, which enrolls 6,000,000 members and employs a quarter of a million, dates back to the founding of the Rochdale Equitable Pioneers Society in 1844. In the United States, apart from insurance, telephone, and building and loan societies, consumer's co-operation has had little development.[16] In 1930 there were probably 2000 consumers' co-operative societies in the country, about half of them operating general merchandise stores in small towns. A relatively recent development has been the growth of credit unions for providing credit facilities for members.[17] In October, 1930, there were about 1500 such societies, over half of them in New York and Massachusetts, with 300,000 members and assets of $47,000,000. Forty-five per cent of the members were industrial workers, 30 per cent were government or public utility employees, and 20 per cent were from rural areas.

On the whole, the co-operative movement has not seriously affected the capitalistic form of organization in the great industries and services, such as fuel, light and power, transportation, manufacturing, and banking. Nor has it affected the basic causes of unrest.

(*b*) **Trade Unionism.**

We have already seen how industrial discontent antedated the machine factory. Unionism, which is the outgrowth of that discontent, antedates it also. The first trade union was organized and the first strike in America occurred in 1786 in Philadelphia when the printers walked out in a demand for a minimum wage of $6 a week.[18] Cordwainers, bakers, shipwrights, and carpenters in Philadelphia and other seaboard cities organized local trade unions during the closing years of the eighteenth century. These unions had nothing to do with the factory, which had barely arrived; they were attempts on the part of wage-earners to block the efforts of the early manufacturers to force down wages, disregard apprenticeship rules, and so on. But despite

[15] Fred Hall, "Consumers' Cooperation in Great Britain and Ireland," *Encyclopædia of the Social Sciences,* Vol. IV, p. 363.

[16] Albert Sonnichsen, "Consumers' Cooperation, United States and Canada," *Encyclopædia of the Social Sciences,* Vol. IV, pp. 393 ff.

[17] Roy F. Bergengren, "Credit Cooperation," *idem,* p. 394.

[18] John R. Commons and Associates, *History of Labour in the United States,* New York, 1921, Vol. 1, p. 25.

sporadic strikes there was little evidence of an awareness of common interests as between the different trades. Such an awareness does not appear until 1827 when, again in Philadelphia, "American wage-earners for the first time joined together as a class, regardless of trade lines, in a contest with employers."[19] According to Commons, *that strike in 1827 in Philadelphia marks the beginning of the American labor movement as distinguished from mere unionism.*

The Troubled History of Unionism.[20]—It is unnecessary to detail here the somewhat confused history of unionism in America—the demands for free public education in the thirties, the humanitarianism of the forties, the expansion after the Civil War, the upheaval and reorganization of the eighties that produced the American Federation of Labor, the craft union conservatism[21] dominant after the eighties, and the confusion and decline that followed the World War. From a peak membership of 4,078,000 in 1920 the American Federation of Labor fell off to 2,961,000 in 1930, a loss of 27 per cent in ten years. Fundamental changes in social conditions were under way that the unions were slow to meet. The demand for increased efficiency in industry, the increasing competition of the unskilled through the automatic machine, the advent of the Negro in the North, the increasing difficulty of separating economic from political action, the precarious legal position of unionism before the courts, technological unemployment —these and other problems which old policies had not solved were pressing for attention as the decade closed.[22]

Two Basic Types of Union.—Fundamentally there are two types of union, *business, or bargaining,* unions like the A. F. of L. unions and the Railway Brotherhoods, and *revolutionary unions* like the Amalgamated Garment Workers and the Industrial Workers of the World.

Business unions, which in 1930 included more than 90 per cent

[19] *Ibid.*, p. 25.

[20] For the history of unionism in the United States see the work by Commons and Associates referred to above.

[21] A craft union is a union based on craft or trade skill. The basis of American unionism after the organization of the American Federation of Labor in 1886 has been predominantly craft skill. Hence the problem created by the increasing use of automatic machinery which dispenses with skilled operatives.

[22] Technological unemployment is unemployment due to displacement of men by machinery. Always present since the Industrial Revolution, this type of unemployment became a serious problem in the decade following the World War because of the increasing rapidity of industrial change.

of all the union men in the United States, accept the wage system, but seek by means of collective bargaining—backed up by strikes if necessary, and crystallized in trade agreements—to secure higher wages, shorter hours, and so on. Except for the Plumb Plan sponsored by the Railway Brotherhoods after the war, the policies of business unionism in America have raised no questions concerning the ownership and control of industry.

Revolutionary unions raise precisely these questions, but their tactics differ. Although revolutionary in theory, the Amalgamated Garment Workers with a membership of approximately 150,000 under the leadership of Sidney Hillman, by employing efficiency experts, extending credit to employers and so on, in the decade after the World War actually co-operated more effectively with employers than did any of the so-called business unions. At the other extreme, the most striking example of revolutionary unionism in the United States during the war period and the early years following was the I. W. W., the Industrial Workers of the World, a small, numerically unimportant, Syndicalist organization that gained notoriety by violent strikes in the lumber camps of the Northwest and in the hop fields of California. Unlike the business unions, the I. W. W. regards open conflict as the normal relation between employer and employee and idealizes sabotage or any other means by which the employer may be damaged and ultimately driven out of industry. At the sixteenth annual convention of the I. W. W. in 1924 its dues-paying membership was officially reported as 37,600.[23]

The Functions of Trade Unions.—Theoretically the function of revolutionary unions is to hasten the elimination of the employer, that is to say, the taking over of industry by the workers. The business unions have as their chief function the improvement of the wages, hours, and working conditions of their members by means of collective bargaining with the employers. They are limited in this function by many factors—the ignorance and disloyalty of their own members; the resistance of the employer; pressure from the state; economic conditions; and so on. In order to function effectively, therefore, they are driven into various supplementary activities, such as workers' education, insurance, po-

[23] The *American Labor Yearbook*, 1925, p. 104. For a sympathetic interpretation of the I. W. W. as an expression of the migratory worker's reaction to unsatisfactory working conditions see Carleton Parker, *The Migratory Worker and Other Essays.*

litical log-rolling, and the like. With profits at stake on the one side and bread and butter on the other, neither employers nor union men have been over-nice in their choice of weapons when conflicting demands have led to open conflict. The history of the labor movement in this country is marred by violence, frequently culminating in riots and "massacres." To a degree unknown in Europe, the federal and state governments have permitted employers to hire armies of private guards or even to pay the salaries of public peace officers, *i.e.*, actually to take over the police function of the state for private purposes. *Had the unions even attempted to do the same there would have been an instant public outcry.* The inevitable result has been violence. Out of this school have grown the predatory union, preying on employers, workers, and public alike, and the labor racketeer, using his labor connections to intimidate the politicians and violence to intimidate employers and non-union men. Neither the predatory union nor the labor racketeer, however, is the essence of unionism. Both represent perversions of the movement brought about in part by the employers themselves and in part by the callous indifference of the public.

The Strength and Distribution of Unionism.—In 1920, the year in which the American Federation of Labor reached its peak membership, 1 out of every 5 workers in the non-agricultural working class was a member of a labor union. Out of a working class of 23,518,000, unions claimed 4,924,000, or 20.9 per cent.

In 1930 the ratio was 1 in 8. Out of a working class of approximately 29,600,000, not over 3,700,000, or 12.5 per cent, were union members. Absolutely and relatively the unions had lost ground during the decade.

The same tendency may have held in the world at large. In 1920 world trade union membership, including 13,000,000 in Germany, 8,493,000 in Great Britain and 5,222,000 in Russia, totalled 46,114,000. In 1922 as a result of depression, onslaughts by employers, and governmental repression, nearly every country except Russia showed a decline and the total was only 39,951,000, a loss of 13.3 per cent in two years.[24]

The figures from Germany, Great Britain, and Russia suggest, however, the much greater strength of unionism abroad than in the United States. As a matter of fact, in the United States union-

[24] The *American Labor Yearbook,* 1925, pp. 294–295.

ism claims as many as one fourth of the wage workers in only three classes of industry—mining, transportation, and construction—and in none of these does the percentage exceed 41 per cent. Table 4 shows the percentage of wage workers organized in the major divisions of industry in 1920.

TABLE 4

PERCENTAGE OF WAGE WORKERS ORGANIZED IN 1920[25]

Industry	Per cent
Mining	41.0
Transportation	37.3
Building trades	25.5
Manufacture	23.2
Stationary firemen	19.9
Stationary engineers	12.4
Clerical occupations	8.3
Public service	7.3
Professional service	5.4
Domestic and personal service	3.8
Trade	1.1

Unionism Fails to Remove Discontent.—These figures indicate quite clearly that unionism during its first century in the United States had affected only a minority of the wage workers, had affected that minority chiefly in the manual-labor occupations, and had left the so-called white-collar occupations almost untouched. As a matter of fact, trade unionism had made little headway in organizing four classes of wage workers—the white-collar class, the unskilled, women workers, and the Negro. Predominantly it had been a movement of skilled, white, male workers in mining, transportation, and the building trades.[26] As a remedy for discontent, unionism, even if it had been fully successful as far as it went, still left untouched at the end of its first century the great majority of the wage workers whose bargaining-power was the weakest. In other words, unionism had signally failed for the great mass of workers to remove the causes of discontent.

(*c*) **The Labor Movement in Politics.** The first workers' political parties in history appeared along the eastern seaboard of the United States in the thirties of the last century. These parties

[25] *Ibid.*, p. 49.

[26] The percentage of women organized in non-agricultural industry in 1920 was 6.6. Outside of manufacture, *i.e.*, the clothing trades particulary—and transportation, organization of women was negligible. The percentage organized in manufacture was 18.3; transportation, 6.5; clerical occupations, 2.7; professional service, 1.5; domestic service, 0.6; and trade, 0.5.

were unlike the workers' parties which were later to spring up in other countries in that they were not primarily conscious of the disabilities of the wage status as such so much as they were conscious of certain specific disabilities of citizenship which interfered with the individual's chance of escaping from the wage status. With the granting of some of their demands and the collapse of the unions in the panic of 1837, workmen lost interest in separate parties and from then until well into the present century played little part as a separate political force in American political struggles.[27]

Leaving aside various Utopian attempts such as Brook Farm and others, the first realistic challenge to the capitalist system in the name of the working class[28] appeared in 1847 when Karl Marx and Friedrich Engels issued their famous *Communist Manifesto,* ending with the words, "The proletarians have nothing to lose but their chains. They have a world to win. Working men of all countries, unite!" In the sixties, appeared *Das Kapital* by Marx, the book which did for the labor movement what Adam Smith's *Wealth of Nations* had done for capitalism, *i.e.,* provided it with a point of view and a philosophy of its own. As Laski says, "Marx found communism a chaos and left it a movement."

In *Das Kapital* Marx developed four main ideas: (1) the *materialistic interpretation of history, i.e.,* that economic factors have been the determining factors in history; (2) the *surplus-value theory, i.e.,* that the surplus value produced by labor over and above what is returned to it in the form of wages is appropriated by the capitalist who produces nothing; (3) the *theory of the class struggle, i.e.,* that between the capitalist and the proletariat there is a basic conflict that can only be solved by a violent revolution in which the class-conscious members of the working class seize power and eliminate the capitalists; and (4) the *theory of increasing misery, i.e.,* that by the law of their own existence the rich must continue to get richer and the poor poorer until inevitably the working class is driven into revolt to fulfil its historic destiny, the capture of the state.

The Fortunes of Marxism.—In 1864 Marx and others organ-

[27] Under Gompers the policy of the American Federation was to eschew separate political action but to "swing the labor vote" to the party which offered labor the most satisfactory platform.

[28] Leadership of the early labor movement frequently came from outside the working class. Both Marx and Engels were born in middle-class homes.

ized the First International which was wrecked by the secession of the Anarchists under Bakunin in 1873.[29] In 1889 the various Socialist and labor parties which the Marxians had formed in Europe organized the Second International which in turn fell to pieces at the outbreak of the World War in 1914 when the workers in the various warring countries heeded the call of the fatherland rather than the call of the international working class.[30]

Following the breaking away of the Anarchists, another cleavage gradually appeared in the radical labor movement. In some countries such as Great Britain, where labor had by this time acquired the suffrage, various leaders became convinced that the Marxian method of violent revolution was unnecessary. Thus in England a group of leaders, including the dramatist, George Bernard Shaw, began to "educate" the public along socialistic lines. Because they adopted the delaying tactics of the famous Roman general, Quintus Fabius Maximus Verrucosis, the movement was known as Fabian Socialism. In general, this philosophy of evolutionary Socialism formed the working basis of the British Labor Party whose leaders, under Ramsay MacDonald, thanks to the support of the Liberal Party in Parliament, finally set up the first Labor Government in the history of Great Britain on January 22, 1924.

In the meantime, the First Russian Revolution had swept away the old Czarist régime in 1917, and, attempting to temporize with the demands of the soldiers and peasants for peace and land, had been followed by the Second Revolution in which the Bolshevik wing of the Russian Communists under Nicolai Lenin seized power in November, 1917. Here for the first time in human history a class-conscious group of the proletariat found itself in control of a great state. Contrary to Marxian theories, this had happened, however, not in the most advanced capitalist country but in the most backward. The struggle of Communism to maintain itself under these conditions against counter-revolution, famine, and foreign invasion and to transform Russia from an agri-

[29] As Communism represents one extreme pole around which society may be organized, *i.e.*, complete group control of the individual, so Anarchism represents the other pole, namely, complete abolition of all group control of any kind. In between these extremes in the order of their approach toward Anarchism would come Socialism, Syndicalism, and *laissez-faire* individualism.

[30] The Second International was later revived as the organization of the Socialists as distinguished from the Communists who in 1919 organized the Third International.

cultural into an industrial nation cannot be described here. The point is, the capture of Russia by Communism revived the prestige of violence as a method of social change even in America, and the Russian Five-Year Plan as an effort to organize industry toward the more efficient satisfaction of human needs later caught the imagination of many Americans who themselves had no sympathy with either Communism or Socialism.

Reverberations of the Russian revolution have been world-wide, just as a century before the echoes of the French Revolution eventually reached South America and the Balkans. In Italy the threat of a Communist rising in 1921–22 was one of the main factors in uniting millions of Black Shirts under Mussolini's dramatic revival of state absolutism. In the large perspective of world events the significance of the Fascist dictatorship would seem to be that in its resort to violence it furnishes the possessing classes of the world with a foil to Communistic violence.

Labor Politics in America.—In America radical labor movements down to 1932 at least had played less part in politics than had the efforts of American farmers to remedy agricultural ills by political means. While the Socialist vote increased nearly 10 times in 20 years, two generations after *Das Kapital* it was still less than a million, or not 4 per cent of the total presidential vote, and after the withdrawal of the old leader, Eugene V. Debs, it fell back again in 1924 to the level of 20 years before. Comparatively the high point was reached in 1912 when the Socialist candidate, Debs, polled 5.9 per cent of the total vote. In 1932 the Socialist candidate, Thomas, polled about 2.5 per cent.

As for the Communists, there was truth in a Socialist leader's sneer that "more people march with them than vote for them." In 1924, for example, in a total vote of over 29,000,000 the Communist party polled only 36,000 votes and in 1928 in a total vote of nearly 37,000,000 it polled only 48,000. Table 5 (p. 334) shows the political fortunes of labor parties in the United States from 1892 to 1932.

As a result of the decline of unionism during the 1920's and the sufferings of the unemployed during the depression of 1929, agitation for the formation of an independent labor party similar to the British Labor Party increased.[31] Politically as well as eco-

[31] See, "We Need a Labor Party—Now!" Paul Hutchinson, *Forum*, May, 1932.

TABLE 5[32]

LABOR VOTE IN 11 PRESIDENTIAL CAMPAIGNS

Year	*Socialist Party*	*Socialist Labor*	*Communist Party*	*Farmer Labor*	*LaFollette Combination*	*Total Vote*
1892	....	21,512	....	....	....	12,064,767
1896	....	35,454	....	....	....	13,827,212
1900	94,768	32,751	....	....	....	13,979,134
1904	402,400	33,724	....	....	....	13,524,349
1908	420,820	13,825	....	....	....	14,887,594
1912	897,011	29,079	....	....	....	15,031,169
1916	585,113	14,398	....	....	....	18,486,489
1920	919,799	44,271	....	265,411	....	26,674,171
1924	....	36,428	36,386	....	4,822,858	29,090,208
1928	267,835	21,181	48,228	....	....	36,798,669
1932	881,951	35,034	102,785	7,431	....	39,734,351

nomically the decade of the thirties opened with labor uncertain and drifting toward new alignments.

Programmes of Labor Radicals.[33] Communism—In *Das Kapital* Marx provided the theoretical basis of Modern Communism which was later supplemented by the writings of Lenin, the Bolshevik leader of the Russian Revolution. In general, Communism aims at the complete socialization of production and consumption, *i.e.,* collective ownership of farms, factories, railroads, banks, and all other productive enterprises, and collective control of income, housing, and other details of consumption. This objective of complete socialization of production and consumption is to be attained by a violent revolution led by the class-conscious minority of the proletariat, *i.e.,* the Communists, when the capitalist system breaks down either because of increasing injustice and suffering due to economic depression or because of disorganization following an unsuccessful war. Out of the revolution is to emerge a dictator-

[32] Figures from *The American Labor Yearbook,* 1931, p. 139, except those for 1932, which are from the Associated Press news releases of December 24, 1932, from Washington.

[33] The programmes here sketched include only Communism and Socialism which both here and in Europe are the outstanding radical movements. Minor movements not here discussed include Syndicalism and Anarchism. Theoretically Anarchism stands for utter freedom of the individual, *i.e.,* the abolition of all institutional and coercive controls from the family to the state. Syndicalism would abolish the state and turn industry over to syndicates or guilds of workers.

ship of the proletariat similar to the Soviet dictatorship in Russia which is to carry on through the period during which the last remnants of capitalism and the capitalist class are being exterminated and the new system set up in its place. Ultimately, the theory holds, this dictatorship will liberalize itself and a measure of freedom will be restored.

Socialism.—Hostile like Communism to the capitalist system, but less extreme both in aims and methods, Socialism seeks to socialize the most important forms of production like the great industries, the railroads and the banks, but would let individual consumption alone. The ideal is production for use not profit. As the New York City Socialists defined it in a resolution adopted December 27–28, 1930, "Socialism is the movement through which the working class, as fast as it becomes self-conscious and self-reliant, seeks to win liberty as well as material well-being for all the people through the democratic socialization of the means of wealth production. State ownership and control of industry, under whatever form, is not a realization in whole or in part of the Socialist ideal, unless the state is a responsible instrument for the freely determined will of the people. In accordance with its essentially democratic aim the Socialist movement relies upon democratic methods. . . . It specifically rejects the theory that the desired reorganization of society is to be effected through the action of a resolute minority, exercising a dictatorship over the rest of the working class and over society as a whole."[34]

The Great Issue Confronting Capitalism.—For centuries in political science one of the great issues has been the reconciliation of government with liberty. Today in Europe and America the great social issue is the reconciliation of liberty with economic security. Capitalism has failed to provide economic security for the wage worker, but it does provide, at least for business and professional people, economic, political, and civil liberty. To obtain economic security for the workers Communism abolishes all three forms of liberty. Seeking the same end, but by less radical means, Socialism would retain political and civil liberty. The problem which these radical movements pose for capitalism thus appears: *Can Capitalism meet the worker's demand for economic security and still retain economic, political, and civil liberty?* Or will the Communist threat of violent revolution drive Capitalism

[34] *The American Labor Yearbook,* 1931, p. 148.

into the arms of revolutionary Fascism which seeks the economic security of capitalism by abolishing all liberty whatsoever?

(3) **The Employer's Reaction to Unrest and the Labor Movement.** Speaking generally and allowing for exceptions, the employer's first reaction to unrest almost from the beginning seems to have been repressive. That is, by discharging the first workers who become openly critical, by blacklisting "agitators" and union organizers, and by employing labor spies to keep an eye out for union sympathizers, employers have endeavored to repress labor's reaction to unsatisfactory conditions. These early methods are still in use, but have been supplemented with concessions and with the attempt to apply modern psychological principles to the management of labor. Concessions take the form of welfare work, profit-sharing, company insurance and pensions, stock-subscription plans, and the like. The purpose of these is to improve or remove some of the conditions which cause unrest. The attempt to allay unrest by more skillful management of labor has found expression in works councils or employee representation plans, which union men call company unions; in personnel management; in propaganda; and in various other ways.[35]

Another reaction of employers has been to form employers' organizations matching the unions. Because employers are fewer in number, have more money, are better informed, and can retain the services of higher-priced advisers, employers' organizations in most industries have been much stronger than the unions which they faced.

On the whole, the reactions of employers have removed some of the conditions contributing to unrest, but they have left untouched such factors as the *distribution of wealth, inequality before the law, economic insecurity,* and the prevailing *autocratic control of industry.*

(4) **Public Action to Control Unrest.** Since politics reflects economics, as James Harrington pointed out nearly 300 years ago, and since economic power in this country has been in the hands of the business and farming classes, federal and state action with reference to industrial unrest has presented a confused picture of re-

[35] *Cf.* James Myers, *Representative Government in Industry,* New York, 1924. Out of 1000 plants having some form of employee representation in 1924, however, only a handful were regarded by disinterested observers as being really a means of giving labor a voice in management instead of being merely another method by which management could control labor.

pression, official violence, partial reforms, and long-delayed readjustments to new conditions. Saturated with the prevailing ideology of *laissez-faire* individualism and with a background of rural and village conditions, the American public for generations remained unable to understand what was happening in our industrial cities. Thinking in terms of village or small-town stereotypes from a rural past which regarded poverty as a symptom of personal inefficiency, the average American of the professional and business classes has had little conception of the enormous inequalities of wealth-distribution in the United States and the formidable amount of poverty prevalent even during so-called normal times. The estimates of social workers and economists that from 10 to 25 per cent of the population are always actually unable to maintain health and working efficiency because of low income usually arouse one of two characteristic defense-reactions among members of the more comfortable classes: either the figures are questioned and the amount of poverty is asserted to be much less than the experts estimate it; or the figures are accepted and an attempt is made to justify them by citing some personal experience with "lazy workmen," or by quoting some quasi-scientific facts to show the "natural inferiority" of the poorer classes. Both the denial of the facts and the attempt to justify them betray a defective sense of community responsibility, a defective we-feeling. All parts of society being interdependent, the evils of poverty are not confined to one class, but spread throughout the community. The influence of a low standard of living is felt in political corruption, in the prevalence of vice, in the inefficiency of labor, and in the existence of disease- and crime-breeding slums whose ramifications reach into the servants' quarters and affect the burglary insurance rates of every well-to-do home.

A generation ago comfortable people might defend themselves against any feeling of responsibility for poverty by calling the poor the biologically unfit on the way to elimination. But with millions of people driven below the poverty line by mass unemployment in every depression, and with child labor, industrial accidents, preventable disease, and other purely social maladjustments working to the same effect year in and year out, in the midst of overstocked warehouses and overflowing flour bins, it is simply social illiteracy to go on thinking of poverty as nothing more than a biological phenomenon. Many poor people are biologically subnormal—and probably more are subnormal than one would find among the well-to-do—but millions are perfectly normal biologically and are merely the victims of gross social maladjustments. As a matter of fact, the failure to distinguish the biologically normal victims of social maladjustments from the biologically subnormals is not only stupid—it is downright poor sportsmanship. The self-respecting poor who maintain themselves against great odds and refuse to become permanently dependent on charity are not only struggling to preserve themselves but to preserve the ideal of self-support. That ideal is the moral basis of modern industry; the moral basis, in other words, of the prosperity of the prosperous. The poor who keep up the struggle are, thus, literally fighting in the front line trenches to preserve the system whose officers and camp-followers so commonly condemn them.

Neither the facts of wealth-distribution nor the industrial conditions underlying them have yet been grasped by public opinion in this country. For years the very existence of a proletariat was denied; or if its existence was admitted, to point the fact out was regarded as un-American and subtly disloyal. Under these conditions, complicated further by the division of powers between federal and state governments, public action has been confused and halting. Certain States like Wisconsin have stood out for years as leaders in social legislation for protecting the weak-bargaining groups in industry. Others like South Carolina and Mississippi had not even gotten around to enacting workmen's compensation laws by 1930.[36] Even the public protection of children in indus-

[36] Workmen's compensation laws, which were regarded as radical prior to 1900, were passed by most States between 1900 and 1912. By 1930 only four States remained without such laws—Arkansas, Florida, Mississippi, and South Carolina. The theory of workmen's compensation legislation is simply that the cost of industrial accidents should be spread by insurance in the same way that the cost of fire and death is spread. Under the rules of the old common law, which had grown up for governing pre-machine industry and had been carried on down, an injured workman in order to recover from his employer had to prove that no fellow servant as distinguished from the employer had been responsible for the accident, that he had not assumed the risk when he took the job, and that he had not contributed to the accident through negligence himself. These rules, fair enough under domestic industry, had long been inapplicable to factory conditions, but it required generations of agitation to outlaw them. Under the compensation acts an injured workman receives a stipulated amount for each type of injury merely by filing a claim and without having to bring suit. In New York State, for example, permanent total disability is compensated at the rate of two thirds of the average weekly wage for the period of the disability, but is not to exceed $25 a week. To protect employers New York has a State insurance fund in which more than 23,000 employers were insured as of January 1, 1930.

try required a long struggle and was still far from its goal in 1932. Agitation for child-labor legislation began in New England early in the nineteenth century, but it was near the end of the century before laws were enacted. Laws reducing the hours of child labor to 12 a day were bitterly resisted, and an attempt by Congress to prohibit interstate traffic in the products of child labor was declared unconstitutional by the Supreme Court. A constitutional amendment to give Congress the power to pass such legislation and thus overcome the court's decision was submitted to the States in 1924, but was ratified by only five—Arizona, Arkansas, California, Montana, and Wisconsin. Forty-one legislatures, including those in Illinois, Michigan, Ohio, and Pennsylvania, refused to ratify. In 1926, in the midst of growing technological unemployment and only four years before the relief agencies were to be swamped with more than 8,000,000 unemployed, the legislatures of New York, Virginia, and Massachusetts actually discussed bills to increase the child-labor force of the nation by lengthening the hours of working children, by lowering the legal age limit, and by permitting the employment of 12-year-old boys outside of school hours![37] In 1930, when the Census enumerators were finding more than 3,100,000 workers unemployed or on involuntary lay-off without pay, they also found more than 554,000 boys and girls under 17 in the various occupations exclusive of agriculture, and nearly 200,000 of these were under 16.

Refusal of the courts to give up eighteenth-century conceptions of natural rights in the face of twentieth-century facts has been another evidence of public inability to appreciate changed conditions. Immigrant laborers seeking jobs with a great coal company have been regarded as possessing "freedom of contract" although not one of them had money enough to leave town, while attempts of their fellows to organize in order to bargain on somewhat even terms with the great corporations have been held to be illegal interferences with this hypothetical right of "free contract."

In the enforcement of the law, once it has been passed and upheld by the courts, there has been a tendency to regard property rights as more fundamental than other rights. This, of course, accords with John Locke's eighteenth-century theory that prop-

[37] Within seven years of these discussions child labor was abolished by President Roosevelt as an emergency measure under the terms of the National Industrial Recovery Act of 1933.

erty is a natural right antedating government which exists only through the social contract; but it is not in accord with twentieth-century social theories, with the demands of wage-workers, or with the "square deal" ideals of liberals like Theodore Roosevelt. During strikes or other times of acute labor unrest the property point of view actuating the police and the military has frequently led to gross violations of civil liberties despite the fact that these are guaranteed by the very same constitutions that empower public officials to protect property.[38]

All in all, public readjustment to unrest and the labor movement has been confused and partial. Down to 1932 at least the American public has had a very inadequate conception of the economic forces at work in our industrial centres and has not faced the contradictions existing there between actual conditions and the ideals and purposes for which the great majority of people believe American institutions exist. The implicit belief in a static social order achieved through the American Revolution and preserved through the Civil War has made it very difficult for many people to see that the social order like everything else is in process of evolution and that the price of survival in a dynamic world is constant readjustment.

Summary. Capitalism is the product of a long evolution marked by a number of cultural revolutions in agriculture and in industry. The coming of the factory stripped control of industry from the worker. Complete dependence on the job followed, accompanied by low wages, long hours, undesirable living conditions, economic insecurity, and rigid discipline. The business class, on the other hand, developed or adopted a philosophy which told them that these things were inevitable and that the state could do nothing about it. This philosophy was clearly a product of pre-machine capitalism, but it has lingered on into the factory age, rationalizing the resistance of the business class to efforts toward social control of industry.

Out of poverty, unemployment, inequality, and other disabilities the modern emphasis on the value of the individual, the pos-

[38] Instances of this are too numerous to cite in detail. One of the most flagrant examples of the disregard of civil liberties for the protection of property interests was the behavior of the authorities in the areas in Pennsylvania affected by the great steel strike of 1919. In Ohio towns also affected by the strike civil rights were upheld. Cf. *Public Opinion and the Steel Strike,* Commission of Inquiry, Interchurch World Movement, New York, 1921.

sibility of progress, changing religious ideas, the closing door of opportunity, and foreign labor movements have all combined to crystallize industrial discontent. The majority of wage-workers cannot escape the wage status. To improve their own condition they have tried co-operation, trade unionism, and political organization. Co-operation has made little progress. Trade unionism from 1920 to 1930 was receding and had made little impression on the white-collar workers, the unskilled, women, and Negro workers. Politically, in contrast to the aggressive labor parties abroad, American labor had almost nothing to show for its first century as a "movement." Meanwhile employers had developed powerful methods of repressing, resisting, or diverting labor organization, and the public, inadequately aware of what was happening, had developed no clear policy concerning the social control of industry. Faced with the problem of reconciling economic security with liberty, most Americans were still limited in their social outlook by the natural rights philosophy of the eighteenth century and the belief in a static social order which that philosophy implies. Meanwhile the evolution of industry was increasing the tension for social readjustments to economic realities.

STUDY QUESTIONS

1. What were the sources of modern capitalism?
2. What do you understand by the capitalistic spirit?
3. From what three sources was the surplus wealth necessary for early European capitalism derived?
4. Trace the transition from the domestic system of manufacture to the factory system. For what elements of their occupation were workers in the stocking-trade in England dependent on the merchant capitalist even before the coming of machinery?
5. What four revolutions are included under the term Industrial Revolution?
6. What was the basic significance of the Industrial Revolution?
7. What changes in the life of the average worker did machinery make?
8. Trace the evolution of economic ideas from feudal days to Adam Smith.
9. What is the difficulty with the theory of pre-established harmony of interests as assumed by *laissez-faire?*
10. What do you understand by *laissez-faire?*

11. Is a protective tariff consistent with *laissez-faire?* Is a child-labor law? Is an economic dictatorship, as advocated by Owen D. Young in June, 1932?
12. Did the United States adhere to a policy of *laissez-faire* during the World War? Why not? Did any nation?
13. In what sense may the *laissez-faire* philosophy be called an adjustment to a past situation?
14. What are the types of social reaction to the Industrial Revolution mentioned in the text?
15. What is the proletariat?
16. When did the United States become a manufacturing nation?
17. When did industrial discontent first appear in America? Why?
18. What was the effect of the factory on industrial discontent?
19. What psychological factors in modern culture contribute to industrial discontent?
20. What are the four types of readjustment to discontent that have appeared?
21. Is individual advancement a solution to the problem?
22. What are the three forms taken by the labor movement?
23. Why has the co-operative movement been more successful abroad than in America?
24. When did the labor movement begin in America?
25. What are the reasons for calling the decade of the 1930's a period of readjustment in the labor movement?
26. What are the two basic types of union?
27. What is the function of a radical union? What are the functions of a conservative union?
28. Why has the history of the labor movement in this country been marked by so much violence?
29. Discuss the strength and distribution of unionism.
30. What four groups of workers has the union movement left almost untouched?
31. On the basis of the evidence, what hope do you see in the American union movement for the removal of industrial unrest?
32. What were the four ideas set forth by Karl Marx in *Das Kapital?*
33. In what sense was Karl Marx the Adam Smith of the labor movement?
34. What is the difference between the Second International and the Third International?
35. What is the broader significance of Fascism?
36. To what extent has labor radicalism expressed itself in American politics? What is the evidence?
37. Distinguish between Communism and Socialism.

38. What is the fundamental problem posed by these radical movements for the capitalist system?
39. In what way has the employer usually reacted to labor unrest?
40. Have the employer's reactions removed the basic causes of unrest?
41. Why has public action concerning industrial unrest and its manifestations been confused and ineffective?
42. In what sense is it stupid and unsportsmanlike to regard the poor as all biologically unfit?
43. In what sense is the struggle over child labor an example of the conflict between individual and collective interest?
44. Would you call the judicial view of freedom of contract as frequently applied to poor immigrant laborers an example of cultural lag?
45. What is the basic philosophical difficulty underlying the public's failure to appreciate the facts of industrial unrest?

CHAPTER XXII

PUBLIC OPINION

The Problem. In a previous chapter we discussed the folkways and the *mores, i.e.,* those culturally given patterns of adjustment and co-ordination that have been evolved for dealing with situations that have come up over and over in collective experience. Customs, institutions, and values are important types of such patterns. But customs, institutions, and values, in the nature of the case, are the generalized results of multitudes of specific instances. In other words, no custom, institution, or value covers all the details of any actual situation. Every situation has elements of uniqueness or difference that distinguish it from every other situation, and some situations have so many such elements of uniqueness that we call them new situations.

Thus it becomes important to ask, how do people collectively adjust and co-ordinate behavior in the actual situations which they encounter from day to day. Within the limits of the folkways and the *mores* how is group-living carried on?

The Basic Adjusting and Co-ordinating Process—Talking-over. In small, unorganized groups under normal conditions in our culture the ordinary adjustments and co-ordinations of day-to-day existence are made by a more or less informal process of comment and response. No authority exists and domination by force is not only unnecessary but frequently impossible. Under such circumstances talking-over is the usual means of adjustment and co-ordination.

Whether this has always been true it is impossible to say. We know that in many preliterate groups such as most of the North American Indian tribes, even while a certain authority might be lodged with head men or chiefs, talking-over rather than ordering and obeying was the process by which difficulties were usually ironed out and behavior co-ordinated. Thus Radin tells us concerning the Winnebagoes that, "No important undertaking was ever attempted without the holding of a council."[1] One of the

[1] Paul Radin, "The Winnebago Tribe," 37th Annual Report, Bureau of American Ethnology, 1915–16, *House Document 102.*

early French explorers observed that the Tocobaga Indians of Florida "decide upon nothing until they have held a number of councils over it."[2] Major Long tells how, in the face of a shortage of provisions among the Omaha one June, "the customary council was called by the chiefs to deliberate on further arrangements."[3] In fact, among most of the tribes the council was a prominent feature of Indian life. Moreover talking-over was not confined to the council. Henry, the English trader, who was captured at the massacre of Michilimackinac during Pontiac's conspiracy, recounts several incidents in which talking-over was the process by which Chief Wawatam's family met the situation.[4] John Hunter, who lived as an Indian with the tribes west of the Mississippi for many years, found talking-over was the means by which opinion was organized for war among the young men of the Kansas, the Kickapoos, and the Osages.[5] Catlin observed its use among the Sioux and other tribes in the Northwest.[6] The Jesuits on the St. Lawrence, Lewis and Clark, Major Pike, Colonel James Smith, Christian Friedrich Post, and other observers who came in contact with the Indians all testify to the same effect. In other culture areas the same phenomenon has been noted. In certain African villages common affairs are talked over daily by the men in a group before the headman's hut. In Hawaii the early missionaries found the natives eager to talk over the new religion—"many of the people in the house continued talking . . . till almost daylight."[7] Malinowski observed that in the Trobriand Islands the *kula* expeditions formed the subject-matter of conver-

[2] Jacques LeMoyne, "Narrative of LeMoyne, an Artist who accompanied the French Expedition under Laudonniere, 1564." Trans. from the Latin of De Bry, Boston, 1875, pp. 11–12. Quoted *Bulletin 73, American Bureau of Ethnology*, p. 375.

[3] *Evidence of John Daugherty, deputy Indian agent for the Missouri, as reported from Notes of Mr. Say, compiled by Edwin James—Account of an Expedition from Pittsburgh to the Rocky Mountains in 1819, 1820,"* London, 1823, p. 183.

[4] For example, the time when human bones were discovered in Henry's cave of refuge on Mackinac Island.

[5] John Dunn Hunter, *Manners and Customs of Several Indian Tribes Located West of the Mississippi*, Philadelphia, 1823, p. 330.

[6] G. Catlin, *North American Indians.* See, for example his account of the return from Washington of the Young Assinneboin, The Pigeon's Egg Head, Vol. II, pp. 198 ff.

[7] William Ellis: *The Journal of William Ellis, A Narrative of a Tour through Hawaii, or Owhyhee; with Remarks on the History, Traditions, Manners, Customs, and Language of the Inhabitants of the Sandwich Islands,* Hawaii Gazette Co., Ltd., Honolulu, 1917, reprinted from the London edition, 1827.

sations for months and that all the details were thoroughly discussed beforehand.[8]

It seems clear, therefore, that *underlying and surrounding the adjustments achieved by ordering and obeying there is from a very early level of social life a more generalized and fluid process of comparison of experience and exchange of ideas which may be called the talking-over process.*

In preliterate cultures this is wholly a face-to-face process. Moreover, in such cultures the range of subjects that can be talked over is very limited. The process is wholly conservative; designed to impose the pattern on the individual rather than to change the pattern itself. Even in Greek and Roman days, while a certain amount of questioning of customary ideas might on occasion be tolerated, the process was still limited spatially to the range of a man's voice. Hence there was no such thing as a public in the modern sense and larger group readjustments depended in the main on authority and force.

This was essentially the situation down to the appearance of modern means of communication, little more than 100 years ago. Talking-over was a process confined to small groups, and since only the groups at the top of the social order had any means of keeping in touch with events beyond the neighborhood, only such groups were in a position to direct the collective life with even a semblance of intelligence. Hence the impossibility until the nineteenth century of anything resembling democracy on a scale larger than that of the ancient city-state.

The Talking-over Process in the Electro-Machine Culture. Modern communication and the social changes associated with it have carried the talking-over process from the primary-group level of the neighborhood to the secondary-group level of the public. For personal and intimate adjustments talking-over still remains one of the fundamental processes; but it has now taken on important functions of adjustment and co-ordination on a scale unknown before the advent of the newspaper and the telegraph. Thanks to the transformation wrought by modern communication the individual finds himself facing a larger environment, to deal with which he must co-operate with more people, in a world in which fewer things can be taken for granted than ever before.

The inevitable result of this, in a culture in which the elimina-

[8] Bronislaw Malinowski, *Argonauts of the Western Pacific.*

tion of conflicting interests by force is not a recognized method of adjustment, is to increase the amount of talking-over that occurs.

How much such talking-over is actually going on in the United States at any given time cannot even be estimated. The mere volume of communication[9] gives little indication of the amount devoted to discussion, and the thousands of printed pages required every year to record the sessions of Congress and of our various State legislatures represent only a minute fraction of the discussions actually carried on in committee rooms, cloak rooms, hotel rooms, and the like, to say nothing of the discussions on non-political as well as political issues in the newspapers, in the magazines, around the firesides, and so on.

But the matter does not end there. Explicit discussion is itself only part of the picture. In addition to the discussions in which issues are *explicitly* stated there is a type of discussion, or talking-over, in which the issues are *implicit* in situations and characters. This is the type of talking-over represented by our more serious novels and plays. Instead of using the *contention* these use the *character* as the unit of argument and dramatize the social and psychological rather than the merely logical implications of a question.

Literary drama may be regarded as intelligence striving to interpret the social process in art. Forms like the play and the novel should be the most effective agents of social discussion; and, in fact, the more searching, in a moral sense, are the questions to be discussed, the more these forms are in demand. In an ordinary political campaign, where there is little at issue beyond a personal choice of candidates or some clash of pecuniary interests, the usual appeals through newspaper editorials, interviews, and speeches may suffice. But when people begin to be exercised about really fundamental matters, such as the ethics of marriage, the ascendancy of one social class over another, the contact of races, or the significance of vice and crime, they show a need to see these matters through novels and plays. In no other way is it possible to present such questions with so much of living truth, and yet so simplified as to make a real impression.[10]

[9] See above, Chap. XII.

[10] Examples of implicit discussion include the more significant works of Dickens, Ibsen, Galsworthy, Shaw, Bennett, Wells, Upton Sinclair, Sinclair Lewis, O'Neill, Willa Cather, Frank Norris, Sherwood Anderson, and many other writers.

The Occasions for Talking-over. Thus we have to visualize as going on about us a continuous process of experience-exchange by which each of us keeps in touch with what our friends and neighbors, our political leaders, our editors, our authors, our cultural innovators, are thinking about those aspects of the world which, because of some defect, gap, inconsistency, or inadequacy in the folkways and the *mores* have happened to obtrude upon attention. We do not talk over the accepted things, the things that do not obtrude. No sane person discusses with his family the desirability of abolishing beds. Even the most rabid egalitarian has not yet discovered the gross indignity involved in having to walk on the *sidewalk* while vehicular traffic occupies the middle of the street. Conceivably beds and sidewalks should both be abolished, but the problems seem not to have obtruded. Hence there is no occasion to talk them over. So long as all of us agree, there is nothing to discuss. The talking-over process, then, is essentially a process of adjustment and co-ordination in situations which for some reason have not been handled satisfactorily on the unquestioning level of the folkways and the *mores*. It may be that the traditional patterns are too general, or they conflict, or the situation is new and unprovided-for, or some individual or group is repudiating the old patterns altogether. In some way the old adjustments break down. On such occasions, if there is time to talk, if the participants have a common language, and if they are disposed to listen as well as talk, the talking-over process begins to operate. It becomes, in other words, a means of collective adaptation to a life situation.

Talking-over as an Adaptive Process. As Mumford long ago pointed out, the process of adaptation takes two main directions —"that of maintaining and that of changing existing customs and institutions."[11] From this point of view talking-over is both a conservative and a readjustive process. In a rural neighborhood when Farmer Brown's boy runs away to town it is gossip that indelibly impresses on the minds of the remaining youth the desirability of helping the old folks. In university circles, when a so-called liberal meeting turns out to have been called apparently to spread radical propaganda, it is the protests of indignant conservatives that make the liberals more wary next time. When justice

[11] Eben Mumford, "The Origins of Leadership," *American Journal of Sociology,* XII, 234.

miscarries in some notorious case it is the outcry and the public agitation that make judicial officers everywhere more conscious of their stewardship. On the positive side, it is the adulation and vociferous approval that greets such a feat as that of Lindbergh which makes a million boys yearn to fly the Atlantic. Thus, from neighborhood gossip to the widest reaches of public opinion, the talking-over process functions in part to preserve current adjustment patterns either by whipping the unapproved variant back into line or by welcoming the approved variant, such as Lindbergh, with ticker-tape and confetti.[12]

But in addition to this conservative function, which was apparently the predominant function in all early societies, the talking-over process also operates, under certain conditions, to change existing customs and institutions. In a dynamic society suffering from maladjustments and cultural lag in nearly every field because of the different rates of social change, it becomes of the utmost importance to understand the nature and limitations of the talking-over process as an agency of readjustment. The remainder of this chapter will be devoted to an analysis of the talking-over process from this point of view.

The Natural History of the Readjustive Process. We have said that readjustment through talking-over begins in a situation of doubt or difficulty. The doubt or difficulty obtrudes on attention, and the simple and obvious thing to do, given time, a certain mutual interest, and a common universe of discourse, is to begin comparing notes with others in the same predicament. The immediate objective is to define the difficulty and suggest ways out. Conceivably the process may stop there. A scientific society, for example, will spend hours or months wrangling over the definition of a word or the phrasing of a formula, but no collective action will even be thought of. Increased mental clarification or organization of the individual mind is the result sought. The practical man frequently regards such performances as a waste of time.

For dealing with the practical world, merely to organize ideas is seldom enough; separate individuals must be interested in a common objective and co-ordinated in actively seeking its attainment. This calls for the enlistment of co-operation, division of labor, maintenance of morale, and the release of action—in short,

[12] Part of New York's way of showing its approval of a celebrity is to throw rolls of ticker-tape and bunches of confetti from the windows of the skyscrapers along the line of march.

for leadership and social organization. When the interest shifts from the mere organization of ideas to the organization of social action the first symptom is usually the formation of a nucleus of leadership—one or more individuals who devote themselves to the business of "putting over a programme"; *i.e.,* winning enough adherents to their policy to change the existing pattern. They are now functioning in a definite interest-group which, as it grows, attracts attention and inevitably opposition from rival interest-groups.

The struggle then becomes one of rival interest-groups for the support of those members of the public-at-large who can be induced to pay attention to the question at issue. At any given time there are always many such struggles in progress. Some of them such as the cash payment of the soldiers' bonus, for example, have a definite political objective; others like birth control and evolution, while they may have political echoes, are mainly directed toward changing the moral code, the popular conception of religion, and the like. Occasionally some such struggle may issue in a clear-cut decision: The voters repudiate the League of Nations or vote down Free Silver. Frequently, however, as in most moral questions, the position of women, etc., no such decision by the counting of noses is ever reached. A certain fixity of opinion gradually emerges from the discussion, other issues crowd to the front, and the question that had everybody by the ears in 1890 becomes by 1930 a foregone conclusion that nobody bothers to talk about. Thus, among educated people in the United States, for example, evolution which was still a matter of dispute in 1890 was by 1930 an accepted *fact.* Everybody agreed that something of the kind had happened, and the only question now concerned the processes by which it had come about. On the other hand, new issues had arisen such as birth control, the League of Nations, unemployment insurance, and the like. This is reasonably typical of the readjustments brought about by the talking-over process.

In the nature of the case, however, the process is not uniform and it is subject to many hindrances and limitations.

Diversity of the Talking-over Process. At any given time there are as many different talking-over processes going on as there are different groups seeking adaptation. Thus the family, the club, the schoolroom, the party, the union, and so on, are all carrying forward their own separate adjustment processes while their members are also participating in the general processes of community, state, and national adjustment.

In addition to this there are different levels of maturity in each process. At the earliest, most superficial level one finds that little attention has been given to a difficulty and it has been very imperfectly discussed. Individuals at this stage may have an impression of the situation but can hardly be said to have a mature opinion. Collectively, there exists merely what has been called *popular impression,* a facile, shallow, transient reaction to events, analogous to the unconsidered views and utterances of an individual. It may happen that ninety-nine men in a hundred hold "opinions" today contrary to those they will hold a month hence—partly because they have not yet searched their own minds, partly because the few who have really significant and well-grounded ideas have not had time to impress them upon the rest. Much that passes as public opinion is really nothing more than popular impression. Such, for example, was the "opinion" that a Pittsburgh newspaper secured from its readers in the summer of 1908 when Doctor Cook and Admiral Peary came out of the north within a few weeks of each other, each claiming to have discovered the North Pole. The Pittsburgh newspaper readers voted overwhelmingly for "Doc" Cook, and the editor remarked complacently that since public opinion had spoken, the opinions of a few scientists to the contrary really mattered very little. Unfortunately for the editor, however, public opinion, even in Pittsburgh, eventually accepted the verdict of the scientists and the popular impression evoked by the referendum was speedily forgotten.

The controversy over the discovery of the North Pole illustrates the gradual maturing of attitude through continued attention and discussion. As people have time to compare ideas, to follow up the obscurer implications of their own opinions, and to take account of the facts and arguments advanced by the better-informed and the clearer-headed, there comes about a certain organization of ideas and attitudes in individual minds and a drawing together into more or less permanent alignments of those persons who favor similar kinds of action. This is the level of *public opinion,* properly so-called. In the nature of the case it is not reached over night, and because of the psychological and social momentum behind it, its judgments are not to be taken lightly. It is not always right. But at least it never makes the absurd mistake of passing snap judgment on a highly technical matter about which it knows nothing.

The precipitates of old controversies sink to the level of the *mores.* Those *mores* which have to do with the ethics of conduct may be called the social conscience. It is the social conscience that includes, as Mecklin says, the "mature and unchallenged moral sentiment of the community. The social conscience represents the tested conclusions of the social order."[13] We do not discuss on the level of the social conscience; we take for granted. In all discussions of crime and punishment, *we take it for granted* that murder is wrong. In all discussions of child welfare, prison reform, and the like, *we take it for granted* that cruelty is wrong. In all discussions of free speech, hours of labor, and the like *we take it for granted* that slavery, serfdom, and peonage are wrong. In every discussion there are certain ethical values that remain unquestioned.[14] It is these values that have reached the unquestioned level of the *mores* that constitute the social conscience.

The talking-over process uses these values. From discussion to discussion the unquestioned values may vary. But in every discussion, to enable it to proceed at all, there are certain ethical values which, within the limits of that particular discussion at least, are never questioned.

To the complexity of different groups seeking adjustment, some on the level of popular impression, some on the level of public opinion, we must add, then, the underlying substratum of ideas and sentiments that nobody questions.

How the Individual Participates. Up to this point we have been viewing the talking-over process in terms of its adaptive utility for group-living. It is time to come nearer to the process and ask how the individual participates.

The most brilliant analysis of how the individual takes part is probably that given by Mr. Walter Lippmann in his book, *Public Opinion.*[15] In the first place, says Mr. Lippmann, each one of us has to deal, not merely with the visible, verifiable environment in which we move about each day, but also with an unseen, invisible, relatively unverifiable environment that we merely read about and hear about at second hand. All sorts of things happen in that in-

[13] John M. Mecklin, *Introduction to Social Ethics,* p. 150–151.

[14] For an attempt to study the social conscience objectively, see G. C. Cox, *The Public Conscience,* New York, 1922.

[15] Harcourt Brace and Co., New York, 1922.

visible environment that affect our lives: Wars break out, stock markets crash, racketeers run wild. Willy-nilly we are compelled to readjust to those changes. What are the variables that control our relations with that world out there? Chiefly three: (1) Our points of *contact* with it; (2) the *stereotyped expectations* of what we shall find in it; and (3) the *interest* that is aroused.

Let us examine briefly what Mr. Lippmann means by these variables which control the individual's impressions of the unseen environment.

1. **The Barriers Between the Individual and the Unseen World.** The flow of information from the unseen environment is highly selective, partial, and fleeting. The individual's contact with the unseen environment is limited by four factors: (*a*) Censorship and ideas of privacy; (*b*) political, economic, and social restrictions on the diffusion of ideas once they have been put in circulation; (*c*) limitations of time and attention given by the average person to collective affairs; and (*d*) the highly selective nature of the symbols in which the unseen environment is reported.

(*a*) Wartime furnishes the best examples of censorship, but it exists in a measure wherever there is organization on a large scale. Even in the most democratically conducted community nobody on the outside knows everything that goes on in the mayor's office, the board of education, the office of the chief of police. But in addition to what is concealed because publication is not believed to be in the public interest there are many things which are regarded as none of the public's business. Standards vary. As Mr. Lippmann says, "The sale of a piece of land is not private, but the price may be. Salaries are generally treated as more private than wages, incomes as more private than inheritances. A person's credit rating is given only a limited circulation. . . . There was a time when the affairs of all corporations were held to be as private as a man's theology is today. There was a time before that when his theology was held to be as public a matter as the color of his eyes. But infectious diseases, on the other hand, were once as private as the processes of a man's digestion."[16]

Thus access is limited at the source by censorship and privacy.

(*b*) After a version of the facts has been set in circulation, however, many forces limit and channel the diffusion that ensues.

[16] *Op. cit.*, pp. 44–45.

The self-imposed canons of the social set, for example, shut out a world of information. People devoted to bridge and motoring have no attention to waste on the League of Nations and unemployment insurance. The needs of business require that one read certain papers and associate with certain people. Specialization, from the turret-lathe up, tends to narrow the range of contacts that the individual has with the world outside.

(*c*) The pressure of modern life tends to narrow his contacts still further. Within the limits of the newspapers and the magazines that he does read, the average person samples very sketchily. Studies of the reading habits of some 4000 urban newspaper readers show that between 70 and 75 per cent spend about 15 minutes a day reading newspapers.[17] Even if that time were doubled to allow for error of estimate, it would still be a woefully short period in which to keep in contact with the current affairs of 123,000,000 people.

(*d*) In the 15 minutes of contact with the unseen environment that the average reader has, despite limitations at the source, limitations on diffusion, and limitations on attention, what sort of information comes through? Only a fraction of the reality. The difficulty is that "men command fewer words than they have ideas to express" and the words themselves may mean one thing to the one person and another to another. When the Associated Press reports, for example, that the marines have landed somewhere to "repel an attack by bandits," is it bandits that the marines are chasing or "patriots" or "recreant debtors," or what? The reporter must call them something, since the marines are going in; but whatever he calls them, he must single out one or two characteristics out of a complex and ignore the rest. Nine times out of ten he tends to pick out the characteristic that strikes *him* as important. Yet whether the important thing about those bandits is their banditry or the fact that they are not infrequently in their own eyes brave men fighting for a principle, this obviously depends upon the point of view. Few of us stop to analyze the symbols to which we respond, and no verbal report of any social situation can convey more than a minute fraction of the complex reality.

Thus as barriers between the individual and the unseen environment stand censorship, ideas of privacy, restrictions on diffusion,

[17] George Brutton Hotchkiss and Richard B. Franken, *Newspaper Reading Habits of College Students,* New York, 1920; W. D. Scott, *The Psychology of Advertising,* 1916.

limitations of time and attention, and the incapacity of word symbols to transmit all of reality. These, however, constitute only the first of our three sets of variables controlling our impressions of the world. The second set consists of those stereotyped expectations with which the individual himself faces the world.

2. **Stereotypes.** The rôle of the stereotype, *i.e.,* the expectation which dominates perception, in personality organization has been discussed above in Chapter VIII. We are here interested only in the way in which stereotypes condition the talking-over process.

Since stereotypes are the spectacles through which our minds see the world, they are the definers of our "facts." The most famous example in all history, perhaps, is Aristotle's definition of a slave: "He then is by nature formed a slave, who is fitted to become the chattel of another person, and on that account is so." In other words, whoever is a slave, is a slave by nature, and you discover who are slaves by nature by observing who are fitted to perform servile work, namely, slaves! That the greatest intellect of antiquity should have used such an argument seems incredible except for the fact that this is precisely the way the stereotype works: It is a form of perception. It stamps its own mark on the data while they are on the way to consciousness. Aristotle did not see *men* who had become *slaves,* but he saw slaves who were obviously not men like himself.

In the same way the average white Southerner does not see a man like himself who happens to be black; he sees a Negro, who is in the very act of perception recognized as inferior. The timid conservative does not see his milkman or his coal man or the friendly electrician when he hears the term "labor"; he sees a "menace," a "threat," a "mob." A well-to-do, otherwise normal, woman once confessed that she was afraid to drive through the main street of a certain Detroit suburb even in daylight—"You never know what those foreigners will do!" "Those foreigners" meanwhile, were ordinary Polish immigrants, most of them immensely proud of their Americanization papers and no more formidable than the lady's butler. She was suffering from a stereotype developed by newspaper over-emphasis on a few spectacular crimes committed in that area.

Since stereotypes are all-pervasive, it is as impossible to escape them as to escape one's culture. They *are* one's culture from one important point of view. For most of us progress is a stereotype science is a stereotype, democracy is a stereotype, competition is a stereotype. Acquiring an education is largely acquiring the accepted sets of stereotypes in different fields—biology, economics, history, mathematics, and so on. Real education should, of course, be more than this. It should be a training in the discounting of stereotypes as well as in their acquisition. But even the scientist fails here. Within his own field the scientist realizes that his conceptions, his stereotypes, are all more or less tentative and subject to revision. He is modest and undogmatic. But take him out of his field, let the biologist begin talking economics, or the chemist begin discussing juvenile delinquency, and the scientist becomes a layman like the rest.

The importance of all this for the talking-over process is very great. As Lippmann says,

> the pattern of stereotypes at the centre of our codes largely determines what group of facts we shall see, and in what light we shall see them. This is why, with the best will in the world, the news policy of a journal tends to support its editorial policy; why a capitalist sees one set of facts, and certain aspects of human nature, literally sees them; his socialist opponent another set and other aspects, and why each regards the other as unreasonable or perverse, when the real difference between them is a difference of perception.[18]

Here is the crux of the difficulty of organizing men's minds. Opponents do not see the same facts and judge them differently; they *actually see different facts.* This means that every discussion should begin with a fundamental examination of the expectations of the participants. Until they have at least been made aware of their own stereotypes, talking-over can only make them more acutely conscious of their differences.

Stereotypes, then, constitute the second set of variables that control the individual's impression of the unseen environment. The interests enlisted constitute the third set.

3. **The Sentiment as the Key to the Organization of Action.** Stereotypes and barriers to contact explain the difficulties of organizing men's minds. But it is the sentiment that explains the organization of action when opinions differ. A sentiment, as we have mentioned in a previous chapter, is an organization of emotion around the idea of an object.

[18] *Op. cit.*, p. 125.

How does this organization come about? By a process very similar to, if not identical with, the formation of the conditioned reflex in the dog. A child, let us say, experiences the usual care and protection furnished by the mother. Long before a time that he can consciously remember, his mother has been feeding him, soothing him, giving him his first sense of happiness and security. Throughout childhood it is Mother who bandages up the bunged toe, irons out childish difficulties, and praises him for each little achievement. Thus, there is developed a firm association between his idea of his mother and a multitude of emotional experiences running back to the cradle and beyond.

How strong this association may be was illustrated by an incident that occurred in one of the great mid-western hospitals in the winter of 1930. A young man had been terribly injured in an automobile accident and lay dying on a bed in a private room. His head was swathed in bandages—his forehead had been crushed under the instrument board of his machine—and after three hours on the operating table he had been brought back unconscious and barely breathing. The surgeon, giving him only a few hours to live, had told the nurse to let the mother visit him. Knowing his condition and that it was probably her last chance to say goodbye, the woman bent over the bed.

She called him by name—there was no sound or sign. His hand lay inert in hers. Dropping to her knees, she called again.

"Don't you know me, dear? It's Mother."

At that word "Mother" something like a miracle happened. The figure stirred, tried feebly to turn its blind and bandaged face toward the voice, groped weakly with its free hand. A moment—then the death-stupor came down again. But for that moment that word, that voice, had reached down through the numbness and the darkness and the drugs, down through the ether and the codein, to touch some spark of life that still remembered. There in the dark on the edge of the grave the last thing in that boy's mind that still lived was his memory of his mother.

Just as that dying boy could be moved by touching the deepest sentiment in his personality, so normal people are moved by the same psychological mechanism. Motherhood, home, love, patriotism—these are sentiments whose roots run deep in every one of us. As these roots and others like them grow they leave behind a surface-growth of symbols—words and rituals associated with, and ordinarily regarded as expressive of, the sentiments that lie beneath. Now the process of motivating collective action consists mainly of seizing hold of these symbols and pulling on the sentiments with which they are connected. But since the same emotions are organized around many different ideas even in the same personality, it thus becomes possible by this means to produce common collective action out of individuals who hold quite different opinions. In fact that is precisely what is done in every political campaign.

Probably the most lucid analysis ever made of this process is that of Mr. Lippmann in his discussion of Mr. Hughes's first speech after accepting the Republican nomination for the presidency in 1916 and of President Wilson's famous Fourteen Points. It is impossible here to do more than suggest the method which Mr. Lippmann analyzes in detail.

Briefly it consists of using sentiment-symbols rather than idea-symbols and stating objectives in general terms rather than specific programmes. One paragraph from Mr. Hughes's speech will illustrate the sentiment-symbol technique.

"This *representative* gathering is a happy augury. It means the strength of *reunion*. It means that the party of *Lincoln* is restored."

As Mr. Lippmann says, the underscored words are binders.

Lincoln in such a speech has, of course, no relation to Abraham Lincoln. It is merely a stereotype by which the piety which surrounds that name can be transferred to the candidate who now stands in his shoes. Lincoln reminds the Republicans, Bull Moose and Old Guard, that before the schism they had a common history.[19]

President Wilson's Fourteen Points are beautiful examples of the same technique. Point No. 8 said: "And the wrong done to France by Prussia in 1871 in the matter of Alsace-Lorraine, which has unsettled the peace of the world for nearly fifty years, should be righted . . ." Mr. Lippmann's analysis of this masterpiece of wartime diplomacy deserves to be quoted at length:

Every word here was chosen with meticulous care. The wrong done should be righted; why not say that Alsace-Lorraine should be re-

[19] *Op. cit.*, p. 199.

stored? It was not said, because it was not certain that all of the French *at that time* would fight on indefinitely for re-annexation if they were offered a plebiscite; and because it was even less certain whether the English and Italians would fight on. The formula had, therefore, to cover both contingencies. The word "righted" guaranteed satisfaction to France, but did not read as a commitment to simple annexation. But why speak of the wrong done by *Prussia* in *1871?* The word Prussia was, of course, intended to remind the South Germans that Alsace-Lorraine belonged not to them, but to Prussia. Why speak of peace unsettled for "fifty years," and why the use of "1871"? In the first place, what the French and the rest of the world remembered was 1871. But the formulators of the Fourteen Points knew that French officialdom planned far more than the Alsace-Lorraine of 1871. The secret memoranda that had passed between the Czar's ministers and French officials in 1916 covered the annexation of the Saar Valley and some sort of dismemberment of the Rhineland. It was planned to include the Saar Valley under the term "Alsace-Lorraine" because it had been part of Alsace-Lorraine in 1814, though it had been detached in 1815. . . . By insistence on "1871" the President was really defining the ultimate boundary between Germany and France, was adverting to the secret treaty, and was casting it aside.[20]

Both Mr. Hughes and President Wilson faced the task of getting united action out of people whose opinions differed. Both worked in essentially the same way: by appealing to established sentiments and by concealing the points at which policies conflicted. After the talking-over process has done its best to unify policy there not infrequently remains an unresolved conflict of interest and ideas, even at the moment when collective action becomes imperative. It is in this situation that leadership resorts to the sentiment-symbol and the generalized objective.

Thus the individual's relation to the talking-over process is conditioned not only by limitations on contact and by his own stereotypes, but also by the way in which leadership manipulates his interests. We are thus brought to a further phase of the talking-over process, the phenomenon of leadership.

Summary. We have seen that as a process of control and co-ordination, if not of readjustment, the talking-over process appears on a very early cultural level. With the advent of modern communication it broadens from the old face-to-face primary

[20] *Op. cit.*, pp. 213–214.

group to the impersonal public. It becomes implicit as well as explicit, using fictitious characters and situations as well as contentions stated in argument in order to clarify situations. Always and everywhere it is essentially a process of adaptation, both in its tendency to maintain old adjustments and in its tendency to work out new ones.

Readjustment by discussion tends to follow a pattern which begins with attention, leads to attempts to define the difficulty and suggest ways out and possibly to the emergence of a nucleus of leadership and the conflict of rival interest-groups. Frequently there is no formal decision, but merely an organization or crystallization of the minds of individuals with reference to the point at issue. At any given time this process is going on in many different groups and going on at different levels of maturity, or mental organization. The most superficial level is that of popular impression. A more mature and organized level is that of public opinion proper. Underlying both is the level of the *mores,* which so far as they refer to matters of ethical conduct, constitute the social conscience. In this whole process individual participation is limited by three sets of variables: contacts with the unseen environment; stereotypes; and the interests aroused by leadership.

The next step, therefore, in our analysis is a consideration of the nature of leadership and the methods used in the modern electro-machine culture.

STUDY QUESTIONS

1. Why is talking-over called the basic readjustment process?
2. How does talking-over in the electro-machine culture differ from the same process in previous cultures?
3. What conditions cause people to talk things over?
4. Trace the natural history of the talking-over process.
5. What is meant by speaking of the diversity of the process?
6. What are the levels of maturity in the process?
7. What factors does Lippmann distinguish as controlling individual participation in the talking-over process?
8. What four barriers limit contact?
9. Define a stereotype.
10. What is a sentiment?
11. Why are sentiments important in the talking-over process?
12. Why is it risky for a leader to be too specific in stating his objectives when trying to corral votes?
13. What is public opinion?

SUGGESTED ASSIGNMENT

Apply the ideas of this chapter to an analysis of the talking-over process as it appears (*a*) in the reports of speeches, meetings, etc., published on the front page of a newspaper, and (*b*) in the editorials.

CHAPTER XXIII

PUBLIC OPINION AND LEADERSHIP

We have seen that the talking-over process involves a give and take of experience. This give and take may be face-to-face or at a distance, and it may take the form of mere comparison of notes, of actual disagreement, of fiction, and so on. At whatever distance and under whatever form, it is always characterized by the transfer of *initiative, i.e.,* control of attention passes from person to person.

This control of attention, which the speaker or the writer in the talking-over process normally possesses if only for a moment, is the first step in leadership.

It is obvious, of course, that leadership is a much bigger thing than the mere control of attention. One could control a certain amount of attention by standing on his head on his front porch; but no one would confuse the act with leadership. *Leadership is directive initiative exercised for purposes of group adjustment under circumstances that enhance the element of personal ascendancy rather than force or authority.*

The problem immediately before us is to understand the psychological nature of leadership, the social functions of leaders, and the interplay of leaders and led in the increasing application of human intelligence to group adaptation.

The Need of Leadership. We are born with a vaguely differentiated mass of mental tendency, vast, and potent, but unformed and needing direction. There is explosive material stored up in every individual, but it cannot go off unless the right spark reaches it, and this spark is usually some sort of personal stimulus, some living trait that sets life free and turns restlessness into power. The prime condition of personal ascendancy is the presence of undirected energy in the person over whom it is to be exercised; it is not so much forced upon us from without as demanded from within. All views of life are fallacious which do not recognize the fact that the primary need is the need to do.

When a child begins to acquire some control over his activities he welcomes eagerly whatever he can participate in and so stimulate and guide those activities. The playthings he cares for are those that go, or that he can do something with—carts, fire-engines, blocks, and the like. Persons, especially those that share his interests, maintain and increase their ascendancy which was begun in the first place because they offered a greater amount and variety of sensible stimulus than other objects. Other children, preferably a little older, and of more varied resources than himself, are particularly welcome. Among grown-ups he admires most those who can do something that he can understand, whom he can appreciate as actors and producers—such as the carpenter, the gardener, the maid in the kitchen. One youngster, for example, invented the happy word "thinger" to describe this sort of people, and while performing similar feats would proudly proclaim himself a thinger. Himself constantly trying to do things, the individual learns to admire those who can do things better than himself, or who can suggest new things to do. His father sitting at his desk probably seems an inert and unattractive phenomenon to the child, but the man who can make shavings or dig a deep hole is a hero; and the seemingly perverse admiration which children at a later age show for circus men and for the pirates and desperadoes they read about, is to be explained in a similar manner. What they want is *evident* power.

The Value of the Obvious and the Dramatic. But the boy who as a youngster cherishes the hope of becoming a pirate or a policeman or an airplane pilot grows up to be a lawyer or a machinist or a farmer. The individual's conception of personal power changes as he matures. Every occupation has its heroes, men who stand for the idea of power, or efficient action as understood by persons of a particular training and habit. It should be observed, however, that the simpler and more dramatic or visually imaginable kinds of power have a permanent advantage as regards general ascendancy. Only a few can appreciate the power of Darwin, and those few only when the higher faculties of their minds are fully awake; there is nothing dramatic, nothing appealing to the visual imagination, in his secluded career. But we can all *see* Grant or Nelson or Napoleon at the headquarters of their armies or on the decks of their ships, and hear the roar of their cannons. They hold one by the eye and by the swelling of an emotion felt to be common to a vast multitude of people. There is always something of the intoxication of the crowd in the submission to this sort of ascendancy.

Not an inconsiderable part of the art of leadership under modern conditions is the art of imparting this air of the obvious and the dramatic to things that may be very abstruse and dull. The ability to "dramatize himself" is an invaluable accomplishment for any candidate. Some men such as Theodore Roosevelt possess this ability to a high degree. Others like Taft seem almost wholly to lack it. For years Roosevelt was always doing or saying something that caught at least, if it did not startle, the popular imagination. The fact that he timed most of his White House announcements for Monday morning when the newspapers are less pressed for space than on other days of the week, proves that it was not all a matter of spontaneous accident. In the decade following the World War the most consummate master of personal dramaturgics was undoubtedly Mussolini. Knowing well the value of conflict as an interest-arouser, he was forever leading a crusade of some kind, first against Communism, then against democracy, then against marriage-slackers, and so on. Whatever one may think of these methods, they are undoubtedly effective in creating a powerful stereotype of the leader as a man of action and power.

What Followers Demand of Leaders. If we ask what are the mental traits that distinguish a leader, the only answer that takes account of differing situations seems to be that he must be, in one way or another, a great deal of a man, or at least appear to be so. He must stand for something to which men incline, and so take his place by right as a focus of their thoughts. This means that he must possess, on the one hand, a significant individuality, and on the other, a certain breadth of sympathetic insight.

Significant individuality is hard to define. It means above everything, perhaps, freshness of appeal and the impression of power and mastery. It is because a man cannot stand for anything except as he has a significant individuality, that self-reliance is so essential a trait in leadership: except as a person trusts and cherishes his own special tendency, different from that of other people and usually opposed by them in its inception, he can never develop anything of peculiar value. Emerson's essay on self-reliance only formulates what has always been the creed of significant persons.

Yet to unfold a special tendency and give vogue to it, depends upon being in touch, through sympathetic insight, with the current of human life. All leadership takes place through the communication of ideas to the minds of others, and unless the ideas are so presented as to be congenial to those other minds, they will evidently be rejected. It is because the novelty is not alien to us, but is seen to be ourself in a fresh guise, that we welcome it.

The impression of power and mastery frequently runs ahead of the deed and controls the minds of men without apparent reason. Most men of executive force possess something of this direct ascendancy, and some, like Napoleon, Cromwell, Bismarck, and Andrew Jackson, have had it in pre-eminent measure. Such men are only striking examples of what we are all familiar with in daily life, most persons of decided character having something imposing about them at times. Notwithstanding the mystery that is often made of this, it appears to be simply a matter of impulsive personal judgment, an impression of power, and a sense of yielding due to interpretation of the visible or audible symbols of personality which we discussed in a previous chapter.

Bismarck may be taken as an example of almost irresistible personal ascendancy in face-to-face relations. He had the advantage of an imposing bulk and stature which, however, many men of equal power have done without. But much more than this were the mental and moral traits which made him appear the natural master in an assembly of the chief diplomats of Europe. "No idea can be formed," says M. de Blowitz, "of the ascendancy exercised by the German Chancellor over the eminent diplomatists attending the Congress. Prince Gortchakoff alone, eclipsed by his rival's greatness, tried to struggle against him."[1] His "great and scornful pride," the absolute contemptuous assurance of superiority which was evident in every pose, tone, and gesture, accompanied, as is possible only to one perfectly sure of himself, by a frankness, good-humor, and cordial insight into others which seemed to make them one with himself, participators in his domination; together with a penetrating intelligence, a unique and striking way of expressing himself, and a perfect clearness of purpose at all times, were among the elements of the effect he produced. He conciliated those whom he thought it worth while to conciliate, and browbeat, ignored, or ridiculed the rest. There was nothing a rival could say or do but Bismarck, if he chose, would say or do something which made it appear a failure.

[1] *Harper's Magazine,* Vol. 78, p. 870.

Other examples of personal ascendancy would include General Grant, the elder J. P. Morgan, Napoleon, Cromwell, and many other commanders, financiers, public speakers, and statesmen. Even authors exercise an ascendancy at a distance. Darwin, for example, conveys an impression of utter candor and honesty that few people can resist.

How Closely Do Fame and the Actual Person Correspond? The fame and power of a man often transcend the man himself. The reason is that the function of the great and famous man is to be a symbol, and the real question in other minds is not so much, What are you? as, What can I believe that you are? What can you help me to feel and be?

Perhaps the most notorious example of this fact in all history was the idea of the Pope, as it was entertained by the religious world before the Reformation, and the Pope himself, as he appeared to his intimates. The visible Pope was often and for long periods at a time a depraved and insignificant man; but during those very periods the ideal Pope, the Pope of Europe's thought, might and often did flourish and grow in temporal and spiritual power. The former was only a symbol for the better definition of what the world needed to believe, a lay figure for garments woven by the co-operative imagination of religious men. The world needed to believe in a spiritual authority as a young girl needs to be in love, and it took up with the Papacy as the most available framework for that belief, just as the young girl is likely to give her love to the least repugnant of those who solicit it. The same is true in a large measure of the other great mediæval authority, the Emperor, as Mr. Bryce so clearly shows in his history of the Holy Roman Empire. It holds true in some degree of all those clothed with royalty or other great offices today.

In fact, the gap between the public which needs to believe in its leaders and the men who do the leading at a distance under modern conditions has led to the development of a deliberate technique for creating stereotyped conceptions of the leaders which frequently have only a remote connection with the realities behind them. In the Middle Ages the process was unintentional and more or less inevitable. Today it is not infrequently deliberate and highly technical.

In the parlance of the publicity agents this process is known as "shirt-stuffing." Sometimes the same result is achieved by the tendency of newspaper correspondents to cater to the public demand for a simple and obvious stereotype. During the Coolidge administration, for example, the President was pictured as "Silent Cal." By constant reiteration this characteristic came to be generally associated with Coolidge in the public mind. Yet actual comparisons showed that Coolidge issued more statements and made more speeches in a given length of time than President Harding, who had not been regarded as reticent at all.

Apparently there is no necessary connection between fame and reality, although in the long run only those who create an impression of sincerity will exercise enduring influence over others. We all pose more or less, under the impulse to produce a desired impression upon others. As social and imaginative beings we must set store by our appearance; and it is hardly possible to do so without in some degree adapting that appearance to the impression we wish to make.

The same impulse to show the world a better or idealized aspect of ourselves finds an organized expression in the various professions and classes, each of which has to some extent developed a cant or pose, which its members assume unconsciously, for the most part, but which has the effect of a conspiracy to work upon the credulity of the rest of the world. There is a cant not only of theology and of philanthropy, but also of law, medicine, teaching, and even of science. In general imposture is probably of considerable importance, but it is probably never of the first importance. In the long run mankind seems to have a correct intuition in the choice of leaders although all of us are subject to be duped in matters in which we have no working knowledge but some emotional excitement.

Do Leaders Lead or Are They Symbols of Inevitable Tendencies? Turning now from the psychological phases of leadership to its social manifestations, the first question that confronts us is, paradoxically enough, whether there are such things as leaders at all. Do leaders really lead or are they merely the spearheads, so to speak, of tendencies that thrust them forward? This question was first raised by the conflict between the hero-worship of Carlyle and Spencer's explanation of history in terms of tendency. Carlyle saw all history as the record of the deeds of great men; Spencer saw it as the unrolling of elemental forces which the great men here and there expressed.

If one keeps in mind the fact that the relation between the individual and society is an organic relation, that each conditions the other, it appears to be clear that the individual *is* a cause at the same time that he expresses the tendencies that have conditioned him. It is false to set over against individuals something called "impersonal tendency" as though it were a separate thing. There is no such disembodied tendency. Tendencies express themselves through human beings. And a man of genius may make a decisive contribution that changes the flow of causation so that the tendency issues after him in results quite different from those that would have appeared without him. Would the life we receive from the last century have been the same had Darwin, Lincoln, and Bismarck not lived? Take the case of Darwin. No doubt his greatness depended upon his representing and fulfilling an existing tendency, the tendency toward scientific explanation of the world, and this tendency entered into him from his environment, *i.e.*, from other individuals. But it came out of him no longer the vague drift toward evolutionary theory and experiment that it was before, but concrete, common sense, matter-of-fact knowledge, thoroughly Darwinized, and so accredited by his character and labors that the world accepts it as it could not have done if he had not lived.

Perhaps the most dramatic demonstration in modern times of the power of personality to affect events was the return of Lenin from exile in April, 1917, when all the other Bolshevik leaders then in Russia were agreeing with the middle class *duma* leaders that because of Russia's lack of industrial development a bourgeois republic on the model of the French must precede any attempt of the workers to govern themselves. Under the dominance of this idea the workers' Soviets had been doing their best for weeks to turn what power they had over to the *duma*. Lenin had hardly reached Bolshevik headquarters in Petrograd, however, before he was lashing out in a thunderlike two-hour speech, sweeping aside democracy, legislative agrarian reform, and all the other policies of the Soviets and the *duma*, and demanding the taking of the land by the peasants, abolition of the *duma* and seizure of power by the Soviets of workers, soldiers, and peasants' deputies. So completely did Lenin break with the prevailing leadership of his party that most of the Bolsheviks who heard him were simply dumfounded. Outsiders who heard of his proposals refused to take them seriously, and Kerensky, whom the Bolsheviks were to overthrow a few months later, even spoke patronizingly of "setting Lenin right."

Yet within a month Lenin had won his party. The party then proceeded before the end of the summer to win control of the Soviets; and in another handful of weeks the Soviets had taken charge of all Russia. There has seldom been a more spectacular demonstration of the power of a single personality to transform events.

Clearly the leader does make a difference even in the very inner circles of the economic determinists, themselves, who have been talking most loudly of "inevitable tendencies." Trotsky, who organized the final seizure of power by the Soviets and who was for years Lenin's right-hand man in the government of Russia, puts it as succinctly as could be desired:

> Without Lenin the crisis, which the opportunist leadership was inevitably bound to produce, would have assumed an extraordinarily sharp and protracted character. The conditions of war and revolution, however, would not allow the party a long period for fulfilling its mission. Thus it is by no means excluded that a disoriented and split party might have let slip the revolutionary opportunty for many years. The rôle of personality arises before us here on a truly gigantic scale. It is necessary only to understand that rôle correctly, taking personality as a link in the historic chain. . . . Lenin was not an accidental element in the historic development, but a product of the whole past of Russian history. . . . Lenin did not oppose the party from outside, but was himself its most complete expression.[2]

In other words, personality expresses the tendency and in turn crystallizes and directs the tendency which it expresses. To oppose either the leader to the tendency or the tendency to the leader is thus a false antithesis—one implies the other.

The Average Man's Share in Group Adjustment. But when we talk of tendencies, what is it we are talking of? The function of leaders such as Lenin in defining and organizing the confused tendencies in the public mind is evident enough. What is difficult is to see the tendencies that they define and organize. If society today is more humane, more free, and on the whole, more

[2] Leon Trotsky, *The History of the Russian Revolution,* New York, 1932, Vol. I, pp. 330–331. Trans. by Max Eastman.

honest than civilizations in the past, it is not merely because of the easing of the economic struggle and the contributions of distinguished men. Movements aiming to raise the dignity of human life have generally been pushed on, if not initiated, by the common people, rather than by privileged orders, or by conspicuous leadership of any sort. This seems to be true of Christianity in all ages, and of the many phases of modern democracy and enfranchisement. In American history particularly, both the Revolution which gave us independence, and the Civil War which abolished slavery, were more generally and steadfastly supported by the masses than by the people of education or wealth. Mr. Higginson, writing on "The Cowardice of Culture,"[3] asserts that at the opening of the Revolution the men of wealth and standing who took the side of liberty were so few that they could be counted, and that "there was never a period in our history, since the American Nation was independent, when it would not have been a calamity to have it controlled by its highly educated men alone." In England also it was the masses who upheld abolition in the colonies and sympathized with the North in the American struggle.

It was the common people and not the ministry or the bar or the well-to-do that forced the establishment of our system of free public education. It is the demand of the common people today for economic security that is forcing a re-examination of the foundations of our economic order. The ideas and the specific programmes are supplied by leaders; but the demand comes from below and not from above.

Why the Masses and "the Classes" Do Not See the World Alike. The reason for this is more or less obvious. Wealth, culture, reputation bring special gratifications. These foster special tastes, and these in turn give rise to special ways of living and thinking which imperceptibly separate one from common sympathy and put him in a special class. If one has a good income, for instance, how natural it is to spend it, and how naturally, also, that expenditure withdraws one from familiar intercourse with people who have not a good income. A man with $10,000 a year and a man with $1000 have the weather and the baseball scores, perhaps, in common, but little else.

Conspicuous and successful persons are more likely than the

[3] *Atlantic Monthly*, October, 1905.

commonalty to be institutionalized, *i.e.*, to have sacrificed kindly interest in people to a technical interest in their specialty. To succeed one must ordinarily serve institutions. In its very essence an upper class is institutional since it is control of institutions that makes it an upper class, and men can hardly keep this control except as they put their hearts into it. Successful business men, lawyers, politicians, clergymen, editors, and the like, are such through identifying their minds, for better or worse, with the present activities and ideals of commercial and other institutions.

> Seldom does the new conscience, when it seeks a teacher to declare to men what is wrong find him in the dignitaries of the church, the state, the culture, that is. The higher the rank the closer the tie that binds those to what is but ought not to be.[4]

Whether we like it or not the fact seems clear that the humbler classes are somewhat less entangled in the established order. Surely the mechanic who sells to the times only his eight or ten hours of muscular work is less committed to the defense of the industrial system than is his employer. He is also less called upon than the lawyer, the merchant, or the statesman to "make believe" for the sake of controlling others. And he looks upon his pay as so much for so much time. But in the professions, and still more, in commerce and finance, there is, as a rule, no definite measure of service, and men insensibly come to base their charges on their view of what the other man will pay, thus perilously accustoming themselves to exploit the wealth or weakness of others. All of which means that the wage workers are less institutionalized than the business and professional classes and are, therefore, more free to express broadly human sentiments, to be interested in people rather than merely in output or "results."

How the Masses Deal with Complex Situations. If the contribution of the average man, then, to group adjustment is likely to be sentiment or feeling rather than ideas, how do groups of people handle situations in which ideas are important? Various mental tests of large samples of the population have shown that probably not over 20 per cent of any ordinary group can be rated as superior in problem-solving ability while 60 per cent rate normal or average, and the remaining 20 per cent run from dull to

[4] Henry D. Lloyd, *Man the Social Creator,* p. 101.

feeble-minded. At best not more than one in five has the wits to handle ideas, and actually only a fraction of our upper fifth has the necessary information, the necessary training, the necessary interest, and the necessary *disinterestedness* to reason well on any given question. Does this mean that only groups of college professors can carry on affairs by discussion and that the masses must always look to authority for their answers? Various critics of democracy have come to almost this conclusion.

Now whatever one may believe concerning the desirability or undesirability of democracy, this particular criticism of co-operative group adjustment seems to be quite superficial. For one thing, within the limits of the *mores* and the existing social organization, groups always tend to act through their most competent members. For another thing, the average man makes little attempt to deal directly with ideas that lie outside of his own field of competence: he aligns himself with leaders who, he believes, *can* deal with the specific problems at issue.

Let us try to see more specifically in the next two sections what we mean by groups "tending to act through their most competent members," and by individuals adjusting by judging persons instead of ideas.

Leadership as Selected Competence. The idea that group thought or action must, in some way, express the working of an average or commonplace mind seems clearly fallacious. It would be more correct to say that it is representative, *i.e.*, that the preponderant *feeling* of the group seeks definite and effectual expression through individuals especially competent to give it such expression. Take, for instance, the activities of one of our colleges in intercollegiate athletics or in debates. What belongs to the group at large is a vague desire to participate and excel in such competitions; but in realizing itself this desire seeks as its agents the best athletes or debaters that are to be found. A little common sense and observation will show that the expression of a group is nearly always superior, *for the purpose in hand,* to the average capacity of its members. It is not necessarily superior morally or æsthetically or economically; but it is simply more effective in the direction determined by the prevalent feeling. If a lynching is in prospect, the brutality for the time-being ascendant may act through the most brutal men in the crowd; and in like manner a money-making enterprise is likely to function through the shrewdest agents it can find without regard to any moral qualities except fidelity to itself.

This is not to say that groups inevitably function through morally undesirable agents. That depends on the moral character of the purpose in hand. If the life of the group is deliberate and sympathetic, its expression may be morally high, on a level not merely of the average member, but of the most competent, *i.e.,* of the best. Group-will may be above or below the average, but it will almost always be different. One mind in the right, whether on statesmanship, science, morals, or what not, may raise all other minds to its own point of view just as one mind in the wrong may debase all the rest. This is the way in which sound social judgments are reached in matters so beyond commonplace capacity as science, philosophy, and much of literature and art. The world makes no mistake as to Plato, though, as Emerson said, there are never enough understanding readers alive to pay for an edition of his works.

It is natural for an organism to use its appropriate organ, and it would be as reasonable to say that the capacity of the body for seeing is found by taking an average of the visual power of the hand, nose, liver, etc., along with that of the eye, as that the capacity of a group for a special purpose is that of its average member. If a group does not actually function through its most competent instruments, it is simply because of imperfect organization.

How the Average Man Adjusts to Ideas. Some one has said that for each of us, outside the field of our practical experience, reasoning is mainly a process of rearranging our prejudices. Less cynically we might describe it as a process of rearranging our stereotypes.

Fortunately, however, problems of group adjustment do not reach us merely as abstractions. We are not asked to pass judgment, for example, on the technicalities involved in American membership in the League of Nations, but on acceptance-of-the-League-as-advocated-by-Wilson and rejection-as-advocated-by-Senator-Lodge-and-the-Republicans; we are not asked to approve or to disapprove of secession in the abstract but to follow Abraham Lincoln or Jefferson Davis, and so on. We are never solving group problems in a copy book; we are always accepting or refusing to accept some policy or programme proposed by, and in our minds identified with, some *person* whom we trust or distrust. From one point of view this confusion of issues with personalities is merely one more complicating factor in a process already almost hopelessly complex. From another point of view, however, it is singularly simplifying. For the plainest men have a certain shrewdness in judging human nature which makes them good critics of persons even when they are thoroughly impenetrable to ideas. This shrewdness is fostered by a free society, in which every one has to make and hold his own place among his fellows; and it is used with much effect in politics and elsewhere as a guide to sound ideas.

In the 1896 campaign, for example, on the issue of coining silver freely at a rate much above its bullion value, two facts impressed observers: first, the inability of most men, even of education, to reason clearly on a somewhat abstract question lying outside of their daily experience; and, second, the tendency of all sorts of people to decide the issue on the basis of their confidence in leaders. It was common to hear men say that they should vote for or against the proposition because they did or did not trust its conspicuous advocates; and obviously many were controlled in this way who did not acknowledge it, even to themselves.

Probably it is true that the masses cannot think on abstract questions. But it is also true that abstract thinking is not the process by which the average man reaches the conclusions on which he acts. When he does not rely directly on authority as in scientific questions, he tends to pass judgment on the persons involved in an issue rather than on the issue as such. Probably it would be correct to say that the more technically competent an individual is to judge a given question the more likely he is to base his judgment on the merits of the issue rather than on the personalities involved. But the average person listening, for example, to a strange speaker or picking up a book by an unfamiliar author is inclined to ask "Who is he?" rather than "What is the merit of this idea?" Outside of the fields of our daily experience or special competence we react to ideas as refracted by personality rather than to ideas as such.

Since most people have far more experience in dealing with people than with ideas and are more competent to do it, this tendency makes possible co-operative group adjustments in situations in which domination or authority would be the only possible source of control if each individual had to disregard every personal influence and lay his course of action solely on the basis of the cold reason implicit in the facts so far as he could understand them. The ability to handle ideas thus symbolically through persons is of high importance, then, for the development of a free and flexible society. But it carries its own penalty in its train, namely, the closing of our minds to ideas that are not expressed by persons who fit our stereotype of acceptable people. To find our way about among strange new ideas that we feel ourselves personally incompetent to analyze, each of us develops a set of stereotypes of the kind of persons whose opinions we deem important and more especially stereotypes of the kind of persons whose opinions we shun and repudiate. Thus a Republican knows in advance that a Democrat must be wrong on the tariff no matter what he says, and a prohibitionist knows that a wet can't possibly reason correctly on the liquor question. On economic and social issues you have only to label an opponent a "red" or a "Bolshevik" to close the minds of all timid conservatives to anything he says about the weather or the state of the crops. "Label thinking" of this kind is the inevitable accompaniment of mediocre intelligence, a deluge of new ideas, and an acute sense of the dangers of making a mistake.

The Rôle of Intelligence in Group Life. In this chapter we have discussed the general nature of leadership, the social function of leaders, and the interplay of leaders and led. Our consideration of this last point has raised the question of the rôle of intelligence in society. What is intelligence and how does it express itself in group living? The answer to that question will form the subject-matter of the next chapter.

STUDY QUESTIONS

1. What is the first step in leadership?
2. How is leadership defined? Would an inventor be a leader under this definition? Would an author? A political speaker? A composer? A salesman?
3. In what sense is leadership implicit in the follower?
4. What is meant by "dramatizing oneself"?
5. What, in general, does the follower demand of the leader?
6. What does the term "shirt-stuffing" mean?

7. Can you think of any examples of theological, legal, medical, or scientific cant?
8. What is meant by the question, Do leaders really lead?
9. What are the three theories of leadership bearing on this question?
10. What is the average man's share in group adjustment?
11. Explain what is meant by calling successful persons institutionalized.
12. In what two ways do groups of ordinary people deal with complex situations?
13. In what sense would you say leadership is selected competence?
14. What is the method by which the average man adjusts to an idea that lies outside his own field of competence?
15. What is the importance of this method?
16. What penalty must we pay for using it?

CHAPTER XXIV

PUBLIC OPINION AS GROUP INTELLIGENCE

The Blindness of Social Evolution. In the past social evolution has been very little affected by human foresight and intelligence. Any page of history will show that men have been unable to foresee, much less to control, the larger movements of life. Even great statesmen have lived in the present, feeling their way and having commonly no purpose beyond the aggrandizement of their country or their order. Such partial exceptions as the framing of the American Constitution by the light of history and philosophy, or the adoption of the Five-Year Plan in Russia are confined to recent times and excite a special wonder. Foresight has been alive only in details, in the smaller courses of life, in what each man was doing for himself and his neighbors, while the larger structure and movement have been subconscious, and for that reason erratic and wasteful. For it is just as true of large groups as of individuals that if they blunder on without knowing what they are doing, much of their energy is lost. A society which planned intelligently and on a large scale would have the same sort of superiority to present society as man has to his sub-human progenitors. But the very idea of Progress, of orderly improvement on a great scale, is only a few centuries old and its general acceptance in the *mores* even in America is a matter of little more than a century. For ages in all cultures the prevalent view was that the actual state of things was, in its general character, unalterable. If we are still groping and ineffective in our efforts to master many of our modern problems, it is well to remember that the conscious effort to master them began only yesterday, and that millions of people still cannot see the very communities in which they live, so intent are they on individual purposes.

The Planlessness of American Life.[1] For the most part social phenomena of a large sort are not willed at all, but are the unforeseen results of diverse and partial endeavors. It is seldom that any large plan of social action such as was devised during

[1] For a glimpse of what planning would mean, see the When-We-Choose-to-Plan issue of the *Graphic Survey*, March, 1932.

the World War is intelligently drawn up and followed out. Even a crisis such as the depression beginning in 1929 which Justice Brandeis characterized as "more serious than the war itself," may fail to crystallize intelligent collective planning. Each interest works along in a somewhat blind and selfish manner, grasping, fighting, and groping. As regards general ends most of the energy is wasted. Between 1855 and 1929, for example, there had been no less than 19 well-marked periods of general unemployment, yet when the 1929 depression began America had no plan for dealing with its unemployed, and no individual community had anything more intelligent to offer than soup kitchens and welfare baskets. Worse yet, two and a half years after the depression started the country still had no plan and none of the big cities had a plan.

> Without plans, without strong national leadership, with meagre and uncertain funds, these cities have someway, somehow, muddled through the winter, keeping their people alive but at what cost of broken spirit and human suffering only God knows.[2]

Here again, nobody *intends* this result. They merely do not, with sufficient determination, intend anything else. The wrongs that afflict society are seldom willed by any one or any group, but are the by-products of acts of will having other objects; they are done, as some one has said, rather with the elbows than the fists. There is surprisingly little ill-intent, and the more one looks into life the less he finds of that vivid *chiaroscuro* of conscious goodness and badness which his childish teaching had led him to expect. Racketeering and corruption are real enough and in a few cities they have become problems of the first magnitude, but even there the great majority of the people mean well and do not consciously will to let their community be looted by gangsters and politicians. Even the gangsters and the politicians are usually only doing what they think they are forced to do in order to hold their own. Moreover, to a man who has seen a machine gun used in France it may not seem particularly wicked to use one in a beer war in Chicago. And this will be especially true if one has spent his childhood in some crime-breeding slum which nobody intended to create but which nevertheless exists because everybody has been too short-sighted and too busy to plan effectively for its

[2] "How the Cities Stand," *Midmonthly Survey,* April, 1932, p. 71.

removal. Unemployment, crime, and poverty, like our other problems, while very real and very terrible, are less the results of individual ill-will than of collective stupidity.

If this conclusion does not make them any less real or any less terrible, it at least shifts the point of attack from human depravity to human intelligence.

The Nature of Intelligence. Intelligence has been variously defined, but the substance of most definitions seems to reduce it to the power or capacity to act successfully in new situations. Essentially intelligence is a kind of foresight, a mental reaction that anticipates the operation of the forces at work and is prepared in advance to adjust itself to them. As distinguished from the animal mind, human intelligence is able to bring more factors into relationship, to distinguish more clearly the relationships themselves, and to construct patterns or plans of behavior for the control of future situations.[3] It is this last characteristic that underlies that type of behavior known as intelligent foresight.

Intelligence works by a tentative method, feeling its way. Our mental staging of what is about to happen is almost never completely true, but in proportion as we are "intelligent" it approaches the truth, so that our action comes somewhere near success and we can the more easily make the necessary corrections. Even in dealing with human relations intelligence works in the same way. But it is a grave error to think of it as working by itself in a kind of social vacuum. While the thinking is always done by individuals, it is done under conditions provided by the group, with the intellectual tools provided by the group culture, on subject-matter more or less directly concerned with group-living and for purposes not infrequently concerned with problems of group adjustment.

Suppose, for example, that a man is to select a college for his son to attend. Here is a problem for his intelligence, but it is also a social problem, a situation in a drama wherein the man and his son and others are characters, and the man's aim is to understand and guide the development of that drama so that it may issue as he wishes. He brings before his mind all that he has been able to learn about the teachers at the college, the traditions and surrounding influences, as well as the disposition and previous history of the boy, striving all the time to see how things will develop if he

[3] From years of experiments with rats and human beings, Prof. J. F. Shepard, University of Michigan, is convinced that plan is the distinctive characteristic of human mentality. *Unpublished lectures.*

does send him. The better he can do this the more likely he is to act successfully in the premises, *i.e.*, the more intelligent he is.

Adjustment as a Product of Many Minds. Now the process that goes on in this case is not the work of one individual mind in a vacuum but of that mind reacting to memories of social experiences in the past, to such current information as it can pick up, and to such forecasts of future social situations as it can develop. The father's information comes to him through other people who share in forming his ideas. Quite probably he discusses the matter with his friends; certainly with his wife; and possibly it may be a matter for a family council. A complete view of the mental processes involved in sending that boy to college would undoubtedly show a number of minds co-operating in various ways to bring out of one or two of them a decision which may not be at all the decision that the father alone would have given had his mind been working in a social vacuum. The actual adjustment to the new situation in such a case, then, is a co-operative product, the result of pooling the suggestions of a number of minds. Here obviously intelligence works through a social process, a process of give-and-take, suggestion, comparison, criticism, selection, and synthesis. If we say that it is always the individual who thinks, we should also add that the protection which enables him to think, the intellectual tools with which he thinks, the stimulus and the subject-matter of his thought and the objectives for which he thinks are usually provided by his culture and his group.

The Group Implications of Intelligence. It is easy to pass from what seems to be an act of merely private intelligence through a series of steps to a view of the matter in which it becomes distinctly public or societal, *i.e.*, a co-operative process aiming at collective adaptation to new situations. The groups in which men have lived—the family, the tribe, the clan, the secret society, the village community, and so on to the multiform associations of our own time—have had a group intelligence of this kind, working itself out through discussion and tradition, and illuminating more or less the situations and endeavors of the group.

The results of past experiment and foresight are preserved in the *mores; i.e.*, in the customs, institutions, and values implicit in the social heritage. Attention is thus left free to deal with new difficulties. By means of discussion, criticism, controversy, the tentative process repeats itself, the intelligence of each grasping such factors as his contacts, stereotypes, and interests have prepared him to appreciate, and each contributing something from mere vague desires to definite and specific plans. In the end, if conditions are suitable, a new level of adjustment will be reached on which, in turn, new difficulties will be encountered.

Factors Conditioning the Play of Intelligence in Groups. Group adaptability, which is what we seem to mean by intelligent group-living, may be said to depend on five conditions: (1) communication; (2) the quantity and quality of new ideas available; (3) the group attitude; (4) the total situation, *i.e.,* the time available, the number of problems pressing for solution, etc., and (5) organization.

Ease of communication, the quantity and quality of new ideas available, and the group attitude are closely related. Every group needs to have what we call in the individual "a fertile mind," so that a goodly number of intelligent ideas may be available to meet new situations through the usual methods of discussion and trial. Thus, if a group of boys have to camp in a rocky place where no tent-stakes can be driven, their success in putting up the tent will depend upon having among their number those whose ingenuity or experience will suggest good plans for using stones or logs instead of stakes.

To insure a high quality of ideas in the highly complicated situations of modern life it is essential to draw on experts. But experts are not merely individuals with a certain skill or technique. They attain their expertness and exercise it only through participating in highly specialized or functional groups which, by selection and training, have come to represent as nearly as may be the highest attainable faculty in a given direction. Inevitably, such groups are not large since high specialization implies high selection. Thus, for example, in 1930 there were, in the United States, only 6097 aviators, 12,449 authors, 22,000 architects, and so on.[4] For fertility of ideas specialized groups must be encouraged and protected.

But the encouragement of recognized lines of special thought is by no means sufficient. It is equally important that we have the utmost freedom of proposal and discussion for projects originat-

[4] *Fifteenth Census of the United States:* 1930, Occupation Statistics, Abstract Summary for the United States.

ing in unforeseen and unaccredited quarters. The specialist, whether lawyer, economist, biologist, business man, minister, socialist, anarchist, or what-not, is, after all, likely to be an expression of what has already been worked out, an organ of an institution. He does not confront the new situation in the naïve and unbiased manner that may give value to the views of people of inferior training. Urgent contact with a situation may also lead to fruitful originality that more specialized training overlooks. Workmen in the shop have suggested innumerable improvements which the designer in his office would never have thought of; and practicable ideas of economic and social betterment originate largely with those who have most reason to feel the inadequacy of the actual condition of things. At any rate, their point of view is essential to the formulation of a good plan. Here we reach the question of group attitude itself.

Why Tolerance Matters. There are, in general, four reasons why expression of extreme views is essential to the efficiency of intelligent readjustment: (*a*) *They may be right.* As Mill says, "All silencing of discussion is an assumption of infallibility." From all that science can tell us today the notion that the world is flat was a preposterous error. Yet millions of people once believed it to be self-evidently true. Probably half a million people in western Europe were burned to death as witches between the fifteenth and the eighteenth centuries. A few centuries before Christ, human sacrifice was deemed indispensable by the ancestors of the same western Europeans. Pages could be filled with similar instances of monstrous errors which were once regarded as beyond question. "Complete liberty of contradicting and disproving our opinion is the very condition which justifies us in assuming its truth for purposes of action; and on no other terms can a being with human facilities have any rational assurance of being right."[5]

(*b*) *They contribute to the complete picture of the actual situation.* Whether we like it or not, evolution, birth control, Socialism, Communism, atheism, pacifism, and various other emotion-arousing doctrines are part of our actual environment. They exist because of man's persistent effort to reach an optimum adjustment to life-conditions. They represent somebody's attempt to reach a more satisfactory adjustment to the world as he sees it.

[5] John Stuart Mill, *An Essay on Liberty,* 1859.

Unless we are to assume that the human mind is to give up its struggle for adaptation or that life-conditions are suddenly to become completely satisfying to everybody, it is merely stupid to imagine that extreme points of view will not continue to appear. And it is even more stupid to imagine that intolerance and coercion can eliminate them once for all.

It would, of course, be untrue to say that persecution never achieves its purpose, for the history of heresy shows that on more than one occasion the Church, for example, was able to stamp out weak and insignificant bands of fanatics. Yet it would be equally untrue to hold that persecution always succeeds, as the Reformation, the rise of science, and the Russian Revolution all bear witness. The broad fact seems to be that while intolerance carried to the extreme may silence a particular doctrine for a time, it has never yet been able permanently to repress doubt itself. If the Roman persecutions under the sanction of pagan *mores* and an autocratic emperor were unable to eradicate the strange new doctrine called Christianity, even in Rome itself, how much more efficient must persecution be in our day to eradicate evolution, birth control, Communism, and similar heresies which are no longer confined to one jurisdiction but scattered widely over the world? Even within the United States itself what chance is there for efficient persecution? Diligent hanging, deporting, and shooting might, indeed, drive heresy underground for a time, but it would hardly extirpate it; it would still remain a *fact* as the experience of the late Russian czars well illustrates.

The plain fact seems to be that, lacking a return to pagan callousness and imperial despotism, persecution in the modern manner can only be a matter of local mob action and temporary success. Really efficient persecution has been outlawed by modern *mores*.

What this means is that whether we like it or not most of us are going to have to get along in a world containing many wild ideas. We may refuse to notice them; we may denounce them as a menace; or we may throw their adherents into jail and shoot a few of them at sunrise; but whatever we do the ideas will still remain. The logical conclusion seems to be that it is the part of intelligence to take account of factors that cannot be eliminated. If we cannot destroy the ideas by force, then, the intelligent thing to do would seem to be to try to understand why men hold such ideas. It is intelligent not to stop with an emotional reaction to the strange, the different, the unpleasant, but to try to understand why the strangeness, the difference, and the unpleasantness exist.

For this reason, because they are part of reality and cannot apparently be eliminated by force, extreme ideas have a rational claim for an opportunity to reach our minds.

(*c*) *Extremists often become less extreme when forced to examine their own ideas.* Extreme views often represent an individual's intense reaction to a part of life. When, by criticism and discussion, he is compelled to take account of other aspects of experience he not infrequently finds himself driven to modify his theories. This is as true of the extreme conservative as of the extreme radical. In so far, however, as an individual is using extreme views as a platform, so to speak, on which to assemble supporters rather than as a means of organizing his own ideas, criticism may be less potent. When it is a question of a conflict of groups rather than one of principles it is seldom the leaders that desert first. One of the important values of toleration, however, is that it tends to keep the struggle on the level of ideas, thus permitting imaginative experiments and new combinations, instead of forcing it to the level of group action.

(*d*) *Radical groups force the discussion of principles and thus serve to educate all concerned.* To quote Mill again:

> He, who knows only his own side of the case, knows little of that. His reasons may be good, and no one may have been able to refute them. But if he is equally unable to refute the reasons on the opposite side, if he does not so much as know what they are, he has no ground for preferring either opinion. . . . If either of two opinions has a better claim than the other, not merely to be tolerated, but to be encouraged and countenanced, it is the one which happens at the particular time and place to be in a minority. That is, the opinion which, for the time being, represents the neglected interests.

The Illusion of Tolerance. The question of free speech is surrounded by a kind of illusion. We think of it as a matter that was important in the past, or still is, perhaps, in other circles of society but not in ours. We are confident, if we think of the matter at all, that we are not interfering with free speech, nor are any of those other liberal-minded people, our friends and associates. But this is what people have always believed. We know how humane and broad-minded the Emperor Marcus Aurelius was, and also how he regretted the turbulence of the Christians and the severity he felt compelled to use toward them—the same occurrences which have come down to us in the Christian tradition as martyrdoms. Torquemada, of the Spanish Inquisition, was a humane and liberal-minded man in his own view and that of his associates, and so were the burners of witches, the German officials in Belgium, and indeed nearly all of those we look upon as persecutors.

The plain truth is that we are all engaged with more or less energy in endeavoring to force upon others those modes of thought and behavior which we, as a result of our habit and environment, have come to look upon as decent and necessary. That is all that Torquemada did, and we are doing no less, although we are somewhat more humane in our methods and more aware in a vague way of something called free speech. But always tolerance is a matter calling for eternal vigilance and courage, not only in resisting the unconscious encroachments of others but in keeping our own minds open and flexible. The easy thing is stagnation; the hard thing is growth.

Intolerance in the Modern World. In January, 1932, Mr. Bruce Bliven, managing editor of *The New Republic,* in an address at Yale University, said that "even if we consider freedom in its lowest terms, meaning the right of the individual to express his political views, we see the world today more completely muzzled than it has been in peace times for many generations." The evidence consisted of 160,000,000 Russians, 40,000,000 Italians, 350,000,000 Indians, and 65,000,000 Japanese, all denied the right of free political discussion. In the United States he distinguished four kinds of censorship beyond the inhibitions imposed by the individual upon himself: the censorship of the audience, *i.e.,* the pressure on speaker and editor from hearer and reader to say what they want to hear; the censorship of material interests; governmental censorship in peace time; and governmental censorship in time of war or revolution. He predicted that free speech is on the way out because the world "is entering an era of unexampled economic stress and strain."

> Freedom of speech had its rise with *laissez-faire* economics; and if I am right in believing that *laissez-faire* is finished forever, then I think I am justified in predicting that in the future we shall see populations

marshalled for predetermined purposes—told certain things and kept in ignorance of other things, to further these purposes.[6]

Whatever one may think of Mr. Bliven's predictions, it is impossible to ignore the magnitude of the obstacle presented to collective intelligence by two expressions of group attitudes of which the World War first made us acutely conscious—censorship and propaganda.

Censorship as a Factor in American Life. In May, 1930, the American Civil Liberties Union published a list of more than 38 federal, state, and municipal laws, court decisions, and administrative rules restricting free speech, free press, freedom of assembly, and other phases of civil liberty. We are not here concerned with the question of whether or not such restrictions should or should not be imposed. That is a question to be answered on the basis of one's social and political philosophy—the process of co-operative readjustments by public opinion is only one method by which groups meet new situations. In times of crisis, in times when unsolved problems accumulate too rapidly, in times when prejudice and emotion raise the threshold of tolerance, in such times talking-over is not the process used. Then recourse is had to authority or to authority concentrated in dictatorship. This has happened at least twice in the history of the United States—once during the Civil War when Lincoln wielded what amounted to dictatorial powers in suspending the writ of habeas corpus, etc., and again during the World War when President Wilson functioned at the head of an enormous bureaucracy built up to win the war. What we are concerned with now is merely the fact that such restrictions on the free play of collective intelligence exist.

These restrictions include the following: Decisions of the United States Supreme Court upholding the right of Congress to penalize expressions of political and economic views; rulings by the Post Office Department prohibiting the dissemination of birth-control information; various rulings by the Radio Control Commission governing the establishment and conduct of radio stations; state laws against sedition, criminal syndicalism, and criminal anarchy in 32 states; prohibition on the teaching of evolution in 3 states; laws barring atheists from testifying in court or holding public office in 6 states; exclusion of Negroes from the

[6] *Editor and Publisher The Fourth Estate,* January, 23, 1932.

ballot in 10 states; censorship of movies in 6 states; laws against dissemination of birth-control information in 13 states; and various municipal ordinances penalizing the distribution of literature in public places, requiring permits for meetings even in private halls, etc., etc. The sheer bulk of the official restrictions on free speech, free assembly, and free press, is certainly impressive.

But far more important than these official restrictions, important as they are, must be ranked the unofficial restrictions imposed by the *mores* and the practices of American communities. Ideas of privacy and of secrecy, as they restrict the individual's access to facts, we have already spoken of in Chapter XXII. But added to such ideas are the widespread fear of antagonizing business interests and the active hostility of nearly every one to criticism that affects himself or his own interests. Business organizations which permit criticism by their own employees could probably be counted on the fingers of one hand. In so far as a business organization, like an army, exists to get things done, not to organize ideas, repression of criticism within the organization might be defended, if the business psychology were not carried over into the community. But in community after community a critic can say anything he pleases about politicians in general or about conditions in the abstract, but he may actually have to take his life in his hands as Don Mellett did in Canton, Ohio, if he becomes too specific about conditions in the home town. In other words, because of the prevailing intolerance, many American communities are not really talking over their major problems at all, but are simply muddling through on the basis of stereotyped ideas and antiquated social organization, and wondering vaguely why community affairs are managed so inefficiently in comparison with the local utility company or the trunk-line railroad! *So long as it is hamstrung by intolerance, whether expressed in a Post Office ruling or in the social frigidity of the local sewing circle, collective intelligence cannot deal effectively with group problems.*

The Reason for Censorship. All restrictions on the free play of ideas may be traced to fear. In war time it is fear of the enemy; in peace time, fear of change, fear of the different, fear of the half-suspected weaknesses in one's own nation or community or social position.

Under modern conditions free speech in war time will probably never exist. Every modern state has within it so much social dynamite, so much discontent and unrest, that it would be suicidal to permit the enemy propagandist free rein. Yet the silencing of criticism may be almost as dangerous as the attack of the enemy. This was illustrated by Great Britain's experience in the early days of the war when Lord Kitchener refused to send high explosive shells to France until the resulting sacrifice of British lives was exposed by Lord Northcliffe's newspapers. The inability of the American people to agree on a constructive peace programme at the end of the World War is another example. Suppression of discussion during the war had prevented the organization of ideas essential to public agreement on what to do with the victory once it was gained.

In peace time intolerance rests on the fear that ultimately other people are not as reasonable as we are. Adjustment by discussion always assumes two things: the objectivity of truth; and the reasonableness of those concerned. Intolerance always denies one or both of these assumptions. Either the belief that is not to be discussed is so esoteric that ordinary minds could not appreciate it, or ordinary minds are held to be incapable of reasoning under the circumstances. We have already seen how stereotypes and sentiments complicate the circumstances. And we have also seen how the average man's tendency to handle ideas through personality-symbols somewhat simplifies the process.

Yet the matter does not end there, for modern communication has not only carried discussion from the face-to-face group to the public but it has also enormously enlarged the scope of the nonrational techniques hitherto employed in face-to-face groups only. Winged with propaganda, *persuasion* has become a major technique of mass control. Thus all those who were already inclined to distrust the processes of change are now given an additional reason for fearing the process of co-operative readjustment. There is reason for asking whether it is not becoming less rational rather than more intelligent. Like censorship, propaganda seems to be one more obstacle to the free play of collective intelligence.

Let us examine briefly the nature of propaganda and some of its major manifestations, before continuing our discussion of the factors controlling the play of group intelligence.

Propaganda as Mass Persuasion. Propaganda, in the simplest possible terms, is "the art of disseminating conclusions."[7] It

[7] Definition by Professor F. E. Lumley.

is a method of short-circuiting the talking-over process so that while the victim thinks he is making up his own mind he is really having it made up for him. Typically the method of operation is to create an association in the mind of the victim between a certain line of conduct and powerful sentiments of approval or disapproval which the propagandist knows to exist. Thus during the war at a time when Great Britain was worrying about the attitude of the Chinese toward the Allies, there came across the desk of one of the British officials one morning two photographs: one, a picture of some German dead awaiting ordinary Christian burial; the other, a picture of a pile of horses back of the German lines on their way to the rendering works. It flashed across the mind of the British officer that the Chinese have a deep reverence for their dead. A moment's work with scissors and pastepot sufficed, therefore, to transform the German funeral picture into a picture of "German Dead on Their Way to the Rendering Works." Duly disseminated in China, this picture played its part in intensifying the anti-Germanism of the ancestor-worshipping Orientals.

History of Propaganda. While America did not become propaganda-conscious until the World War, propaganda is at least as old as Christianity and possibly much older. Plato proposed using it in *The Republic* to impose his hierarchy of social classes on the people, but it was Christianity that provided the first large-scale demonstration of propaganda in the ancient world.

The term itself was not invented till 1622 when Pope Gregory XV created the Congregation of the Propaganda, composed of cardinals and charged with the management of Catholic missions all over the world. Propaganda has been a factor in every modern war, although not so great a factor as in the World War. But even at the Battle of Bunker Hill handbills were circulated among the British troops offering every man who would come over to the colonists $7 a month, fresh provisions, and a good farm.

American social development from Revolutionary days down has been replete with the liberal use of this technique. The anti-slavery agitation, the growth of the labor movement, the spread of prohibition sentiment, the perennial battles over the tariff were all carried on in part at least by propaganda.

The World War elicited the most terrific propaganda barrage ever known. Literally every government realized that while the military front depended on the economic front, both depended on the psychological front. When America entered the war in 1917 a gigantic propaganda bureau was organized under George Creel, which, in the course of a year and a half, sent out more than 6,000 news releases; enlisted 75,000 Four-Minute Men who delivered 755,190 speeches to more than 300,000,000 people; dispatched moving pictures to foreign countries in a great "battle for the mind of mankind"; and organized chambers of commerce, churches, schools, artists, newspapers, and innumerable other agencies for the most stupendous "educational campaign" ever conceived. To date, this war effort of Mr. Creel's bureau probably sets the high-water mark of propaganda.[8]

Prevalence of Propaganda in Peace Time. Peace-time propagandists, however, have not permitted the lessons learned during the war to be forgotten. In 1922 in California, propagandists for and against 13 initiative and referendum measures spent more than a million dollars to "educate" the voters. Of the total, California power companies spent $501,605 to defeat the Water and Power Act for whose adoption other citizens spent only $159,990.[9] The demand for the return of the bodies of American soldiers from abroad is said to have been "stimulated" by the undertakers and casketmakers.[10] Following the war, business interests conducted a subtle campaign for lower taxes, one of the main targets being the school tax. The depression of 1929 brought this campaign into the open with a deliberate drive to slash school budgets.

From its inception the school has been a storm centre of propaganda. The use that the German Government made of its school system to teach militaristic nationalism is well known. Efforts to use the American school system in the same way to disseminate conclusions rather than methods of thinking have not been wanting. From 1903 to 1923, for example, the number of prescriptive laws attempting to determine what the schools should and should not teach increased from 564 to 926.[11] Between 1921 and 1929, 30 state legislatures faced bills to outlaw the teaching of evolution, and in 2 states—Tennessee and Mississippi—such bills ac-

[8] See G. Creel, *How We Advertised America*, N. Y., 1920.

[9] Albion Guilford Taylor, "Labor Policies of the National Association of Manufacturers," *University of Illinois Studies in the Social Sciences*, Vol. 15, March 1927, p. 72.

[10] E. K. Strong, Jr., "The Control of Propaganda," *Scientific Monthly*, Vol. XIV, March, 1922, pp. 234 f.

[11] D. J. K. Flanders, *Legislative Control of the Elementary Curriculum.*

tually became laws. In Arkansas the first anti-evolution initiative measure in history carried almost 2 to 1 and became law.[12] As a counter move to the various campaigns to restrict the school, the school men developed a technique of publicity aimed to "sell the school to the community."

One of the most far-reaching campaigns of propaganda ever planned in peace time was that of the public utility interests as revealed by the investigations of the Federal Trade Commission in 1928 and 1929. Propaganda operations of the utility companies included the subsidizing of college professors, the dissemination of the private utility point of view on public ownership through textbooks in 491 New York high schools, and the investment of nearly $11,000,000 in thirteen newspapers in various parts of the country.[13]

The revelation that the utility interests were trying to use the schools for propaganda purposes led to counter-propaganda under the slogan "Save Our Schools" with Bishop Francis J. McConnell of the New York Methodist Episcopal Church acting as national chairman and John Dewey as vice-chairman of the counter-propaganda organization.

The whole incident vividly illustrates the difficulties of talking over any public question under modern conditions. Propaganda enormously increases the power of aggressive leadership to control attention and dominate action. When you can assure a million homes a week that your profit on meat is only "one tenth of a cent a pound," as certain packers did in a dispute with the government a few years ago, you have a certain advantage over any ordinary person who might wish to question your figures. When the questioner is no longer ordinary but one possessed of propaganda resources of his own, such a difference of opinion becomes a spectacle for the gods. Witness the "debate" between the tobacco interests and the candy industry. The slogan "Reach for a Lucky Instead of a Sweet" precipitated a propaganda war that threatened before it was patched up to reverberate in anti-cigarette laws and crusades against women smoking.

[12] Maynard Shipley, *The War Against Evolution,* Science League of America, San Francisco, 1929.

[13] *New Republic,* June 27, 1928, p. 135, and verbatim report of the testimony before the Federal Trade Commission of President Graustein of the International Paper and Power Co., as published in *Editor and Publisher The Fourth Estate,* Vol. 61, No. 50, May 4, 1929, pp. 7–30.

How Propaganda Distorts the Adjustive Process. Propaganda does three things to the talking-over process: (1) It tends to derationalize it; (2) it shifts the emphasis from the examination of ideas and relationships to the mass recruitment of adherents; and (3) by removing still farther from the average individual the possibility of participating actively in the larger organization it enhances the power of organization and wealth to impose behavior patterns on the group.

Control by propaganda is control on a distinctly lower psychological level than control by education or by rational discussion. Modern propaganda extends persuasion from the face-to-face group and the crowd, in which it has always functioned, to the distance group, which has until almost the last generation been free from it. Now reason involves the making of distinctions of likeness and difference; but persuasion works in an almost diametrically opposite way by obscuring differences and creating psychological linkages without logical foundation. To control behavior by propaganda is to secure action without integrating the proposed behavior with the totality of the individual's past. Under such conditions interest shifts to action tendencies. We no longer care about the merits of prohibition, for example, we hope merely to enlist opponents and adherents.

It is the scope on which this persuasive technique operates that creates the modern problem. Not only is it possible to box entire states in a propaganda barrage in a few hours but no poor-but-honest citizen any longer has a chance to be heard. The leaders of the new profession of public relations counsel associate with millionaires and charge like corporation lawyers.

On the great contemporary issues, then, such as railroad valuation, control of electrical power, prohibition, disarmament, and so on, only those commanding great newspaper or broadcasting properties, hundreds of thousands of dollars for publicity purposes, or prestige enough to make their opinions news of national importance, can participate in "discussion by competitive propaganda." *The net effect of the development of modern propaganda has probably been to make it more difficult for the weak, the unorthodox, and the unorganized to participate in the co-operative control of collective behavior.*

Crowd-Mindedness. Certainly it has lent much force to the arguments of critics who have contended that the public tends to behave like a crowd. The psychology of crowds has been treated at length by Sighele, LeBon, and other authors, who having made a specialty of man in the throng, are perhaps inclined to exaggerate the degree in which he departs from ordinary personality.[14] The crowd mind is not, as is sometimes said, a quite different thing from that of the individual, but is merely a collective mind of a low order which stimulates and unifies the cruder impulses of its members.

The peculiarity of the crowd-mind is mainly in the readiness with which any communicable feeling is spread and augmented. Just as a heap of firebrands will blaze when one or two alone will chill and go out, so the units of a crowd "inflame each other by mutual sympathy and mutual consciousness of it."[15]

It must be admitted that modern conditions and particularly the development of the art of "ballyhoo" by the newspapers and of propaganda by the advertising men and public relation counsels enable such contagion to work on a larger scale than ever before, so that a wave of feeling now passes through the people very much as if they were physically a crowd—like the wave of resentment, for instance, that swept over the American people when the battleship *Maine* was destroyed in Havana harbor in February, 1898, or the Lindbergh baby was kidnapped in March, 1932. Popular excitement over athletic contests is another example. And when a war breaks out, the people read the papers in quite the same spirit that the Roman populace went to the arena, not so much from any depraved taste for blood, as to be in the thrill. Even the so-called individualism of our time and the unresting pursuit of business are in great part due to the contagion of the crowd. People become excited by the game and want to be in it whether they have any definite object or not.

All of this is definitely analogous to crowd-mindedness, and propaganda plays its part in helping to create it on a large scale.

Yet it is difficult to evaluate the ultimate influence of all these factors. Granting the formidable character of the obstacles to group intelligence which censorship and propaganda have reared, it remains true that in matters regarding which they have a trained habit of thought men are little likely to be stampeded. A veteran army, for example, is not a crowd no matter how numerous or

[14] Scipio Sighele, *La folla delinquente,* French translation, *La foule criminelle;* Gustave LeBon, *Psychologie des foules,* English translation, *The Crowd.*
[15] Whately in his note to Bacon's essay on "Discourse."

concentrated, and a public that is used to talking things over may work its way through situations that would stampede a less experienced group. Having been disillusioned by the World War experience, the present generation, for example, is somewhat more skeptical of propaganda than in the pre-war days. But mere skepticism is not enough unless people know that they are being subjected to propaganda. The most effective propaganda is that which is not recognized as such.

All in all, propaganda must be added to censorship as one more difficulty in the way of organizing group life intelligently.

Let us now return to our analysis of the conditions controlling group intelligence.

The Total Situation as a Factor in Group Intelligence. In addition to the factors of communication, fertility in ideas, and group attitude, the play of intelligence in group adjustment is conditioned by the total situation, *i.e.,* by the imminence of crisis and the number of problems pressing for solution.

Talking-over takes time. When the house is burning down, when the nation is facing an ultimatum, when a catastrophe has happened, there is no time for general group discussion. The group must act and act at once.

Under such circumstances the tendency in organized groups is to act on the decisions of the recognized officials and leaders. In unorganized groups the first dominant personality who seems to have a practicable plan will almost certainly control action. *Thus, the effect of crisis on intelligent control is to narrow the circle of those whose intelligence affects group behavior.*

The rate of social change is another environmental factor working in the same direction. A group can concern itself with only a few problems at a time. This means that public opinion can deal with only the more general aspects of any question that does come up, since administrative details are too numerous, too complex, and too changeable for general appreciation; and also that in a rapidly changing culture such as our own there is a very real danger of confusion and ineffectiveness due to the multiplicity of problems demanding attention. In the end the failure to make the necessary readjustments must result in an accumulation of maladjustments such, for example, as we are apparently suffering from in our economic and political systems. Under such circumstances a crisis or a succession of crises may be regarded as more or less inevitable. But as we have already seen, in a crisis there is no time for collective intelligence to function through discussion. The circle of intelligence narrows, therefore, and the more intense the crisis, *i.e.*, the more urgent the demand for action, the narrower the circle is likely to become. Hence, the call for dictatorship.[16]

From this point of view censorship and propaganda become even more ominously significant since both constitute hindrances to the free play of collective intelligence. The rate of social change being what it is in the United States, there would apparently be a real problem of readjustment through discussion quite apart from the added difficulties of artificial limitations and non-rational barriers.

The Organization of Group Intelligence. Communication, fertility in ideas, the group attitude, and the total situation constitute four of the five conditions controlling group adaptability. The fifth is the organization of the group itself.

Organization may be considered with reference to the organization of ideas; and with reference to the organization of action, *i.e.*, the articulation of group opinion with group action. We shall confine ourselves mainly to the first.

What we have already said about specialized groups, censorship, and propaganda, all bears, of course, on the problem of organizing the group for the organization of ideas. In general, the group needs a generalized information service such as that supplied by the sciences, a current information service such as that supplied by the press and the radio, and, furthermore, it needs facilities for discussion. It is with reference to this last need that modern tendencies again are creating a problem. In the old rural culture face-to-face discussion groups were matters of course. At the meeting house, at the post office, at the general store, people met in informal groups and mulled over their common problems. For the individual the value of actually participating, thus, in the growth of a collective opinion was certainly very great, and within the limits of provincial stereotypes and narrow interests the community was probably, as a result, more intensely a community than any modern group of the same size.

The modern urban resident lacks this recurring face-to-face

[16] For example, the statement of Mr. Owen D. Young, president of the General Electric Co., and a prominent spokesman for the big business group, that what was needed in the U. S. to deal with the depression was a dictatorship. See news dispatches, June, 1932. The crisis of 1933 illustrates the point.

challenge to justify his own opinions. He undoubtedly has a wider range of information at his disposal than was true a generation ago and his prejudices in many ways are less intense. But the hurly-burly of urban life, the disappearance of the neighborhood, the preoccupation with earning a living, the impersonality of association, the whole pattern and tempo of city living have combined to discourage face-to-face discussion. In consequence discussion in the average urban community tends to be carried on *for the public* by a few leaders rather than *by the public* for itself. One evidence of this tendency is the American passion for being talked at—the insistence that no club meeting, banquet, or public assembly is complete unless somebody makes a speech. Discussion *for,* not *by,* is a predominant pattern of urban life.

The articulation of group opinion with group action is achieved in various ways, principally by *representation,* by *election,* and by *direct pressure* through personal influence, newspaper publicity, lobbies, mass-meetings, and the like. The consideration of group organization from this point of view belongs properly to political science. Of more immediate concern here is the question of how collective intelligence attains the kind of organization implied by policy and plan.

The Problem of Organizing Foresight. As we have said, social development in the past has been largely blind and unplanned. It is evident that many of our difficulties in cities, in our economic life, and in other fields have arisen because of this very blindness and lack of plan. The problems of readjustment in the immediate future, therefore, seem to call particularly for some kind of conscious and intelligent self-direction by the groups concerned. Intelligence used in this way for the deliberate self-direction of any social group may be called *group will.*

Deliberate self-direction expresses itself in many ways. Government, as the most definite and authoritative expression of public choice, is perhaps the most obvious agent of group will. But only a small part of the collective foresight practised in America finds expression through government. In a larger sense group will embraces the thought and purpose of all institutions and associations that have any breadth of aim. The most evident advantages of government as a social instrument are its power and reach and its definite responsibility to the people. Its defects are its tendency to become too mechanical, too rigid, too costly and inhuman.

By and large the special demand for the extension of governmental powers seems to spring chiefly from three conditions: the need of controlling the exorbitant power of private economic associations, the need of meeting novel problems arising from life in great cities, and the need of reducing the waste and suffering inevitable in a régime of *laissez-faire*.

Yet the main source of a more effective public will is to be sought not, peculiarly, in the greater activity of government, but in the growing efficiency of the intellectual and moral processes as a whole. This general striving of the public mind toward clearer consciousness is too evident to escape any observer. In every province of life a multiform social knowledge is arising, and mingling with the higher impulses of human nature, is forming a system of rational ideals, which through leadership and emulation gradually work their way into practice. Compare, for instance, the place now taken in our universities by history, economics, political science, sociology, and the like, with the attention given them, say, in 1875, when some of them had no place at all. Or consider the multiplication since the same date of government bureaus—federal, state, and local—whose main function is to collect, arrange, and disseminate social knowledge. If governments are becoming more and more vast laboratories of social science, there is likewise an increase in the number of private benefactions, institutionalized in the form of foundations, for the study and improvement of social conditions. New conditions are confronting us with staggering problems calling for readjustment and reorientation, but American society is steadily, if somewhat slowly, improving its organization for gathering and interpreting the facts.

Trends in Self-Direction. Four tendencies in the growth of group will may be noted: (1) *Idealism is becoming more organic.* Much energy has been wasted, or nearly wasted, in the exclusive and intolerant advocacy of special schemes—single tax, prohibition, state socialism, and the like—each of which has been imagined by its adherents to be the key to the millennium. Gradually, however, the interconnectedness of social ills has become more apparent. No one reform can accomplish very much. Advance must be all along the line.

(2) *Moral standards are slowly being revised to comprehend the life they aim to regulate.* Many of the prevalent moral ideas still reflect the simpler stage of society in which they were

evolved. The acts to which they apply may still need to be condemned, but other evils have since sprung up that need condemnation more. Murder, rape, and the like, while by no means under adequate control, are still relatively obvious and simple. Everybody condemns them and no great organization or social philosophy upholds them. Graft, stock-market manipulation, and the like, are, on the other hand, not adequately penalized in the moral code. *The most dangerous immorality is that which makes use of the latest engines of politics or commerce to injure the community.* High-pressure salesmanship, for example, is responsible for a considerable share of the corruption that exists in private as well as in public business. One expert gives it as his considered opinion that the public school built without graft forced in by contractors, salesmen, and other business men, is the rare exception, not the rule. Wrong-doers of this kind are usually decent and kindly in daily walk and conversation, as well as supporters of the church and other respectable institutions. For the most part they are not even hypocrites, but men of dead and conventional virtue, not awake to the real meaning of what they are doing. But as fast as science enables us to trace the outcome of a given sort of action we need to create a corresponding sense of responsibility for that outcome. Thus we face the necessity for revising our moral codes to make them grip the realities of modern life.

(3) *Group will is tending to express itself through indirect service.* The problem here is to energize the service. The groups we serve—the nation, the educational institution, the oppressed class—have become so vast, and often so remote from the eye, that even the ingenuity of the newspaper and magazine press can hardly make them alive for us and draw our hearts and our money in their direction. Propaganda serves as a partial answer, but except in war time seldom speaks in the name of the nation or the community. Increasingly, we take part through agents acting on our behalf, such as the American Red Cross, the National Tuberculosis Society, and the like.

(4) *A final tendency observable in the trend of public will is that toward a greater simplicity and flexibility of structure in every province of life: principles are taking the place of formulas.* In the early history of science the body of knowledge consists of a mass of ill-understood and ill-related observations, speculations, and fancies, which the disciple takes on the authority of the mas-

ter: but as principles are discovered this incoherent structure falls to pieces and is replaced by a course of study based on experiment and inference. So in the early growth of every institution the truth that it embodies is not perceived or expressed in simplicity, but obscurely incarnated in custom and formula. The perception of principles does not do away with the mechanism, but tends to make it simple, flexible, human. The modern world, then, in spite of its complexity, may become fundamentally simpler, more consistent, and reasonable. The tendency is to demand that all things, institutions as well as social classes, justify themselves by function: How well are they doing the thing they are supposed to do?

On the whole, many of the problems which afflict us today, crime, poverty, unemployment, war, are problems *precisely because intelligence in group affairs has reached the point at which we are beginning to realize the needlessness of the blind blundering of the past.* Organized foresight cannot yet do much toward controlling the future. But it can at least do something toward reducing the costs of social change. Obviously, social change is all around us. It is the rôle of intelligence to seek to understand it and to plan accordingly.

Summary of the Discussion of Public Opinion. We have now in barest outline sketched something of the process by which groups adjust and co-ordinate behavior within the limits of the folkways and the *mores.* Fundamentally, in our culture, except in time of crisis or in cases set apart for the decisions of authority, the process is mainly one of comment and response, discussion, controversy. We have seen how modern communication has extended this process from the old face-to-face group to the modern public. We have observed the adaptive nature of the process, the various stages through which it passes, and the different levels of mental organization involved in it. We have watched the individual participate, subject to the limitations of contacts, stereotypes, and interest. We have called attention to the rôle of the sentiment in the formation of groups, and attempted to analyze the nature and functions of leadership. We have seen that the leader and the group's idea of the leader may not correspond, but that the leader is a veritable cause even while he expresses and embodies the tendency of his group. It is as a contributor to the tendency that the common man plays his part, a part that should not be overlooked despite the fact that it is different from the part played by the leaders. In dealing with complex situations the masses tend to act through selected competence and through the personality-symbol.

Until almost yesterday complex situations were little understood and individual intelligence, so far as it existed, was limited to purely personal concerns. The prevalent planlessness of American life illustrates this fact. Only slowly is intelligence being applied to collective problems, subject always to five controlling conditions: communication, the supply of good ideas, group attitudes, the total situation, and group organization. Many factors interfere with the free play of ideas: intolerance, censorship, propaganda, crisis, lack of face-to-face discussion groups, and so forth. Ultimately the problem of applying intelligence to collective living becomes one of organizing foresight. Four tendencies in this direction may be observed: Idealism is becoming more organic; moral standards are becoming socialized; indirect service plays a more prominent rôle; and organization is becoming more functional.

STUDY QUESTIONS

1. To what degree has the present condition of your community been planned?
2. In what way does the recognition of the lack of plan in American life change one's conception of social problems such as unemployment, crime, poverty, and the like?
3. What is the tentative method? How is it related to intelligence? What do you understand by the term intelligence?
4. If it is true that it is the individual who does the thinking, to what extent is it also true that intelligence is a group matter?
5. What five factors condition the play of intelligence in groups?
6. Why is the encouragement of specialized groups important?
7. What are the four reasons why tolerance matters?
8. What is meant by the illusion of tolerance?
9. What right have you to try to persuade or convince another person to accept your view of anything?
10. What ground is there for pessimism concerning the future of tolerance?
11. Name five kinds of restriction that interfere with the free play of ideas in your community.
12. What is the ultimate reason for censorship?
13. In what way does propaganda interfere with group intelligence?

14. Define propaganda. How is it to be distinguished from personal advocacy? From education? From advertising?
15. When did propaganda originate? When did the term originate? When did Americans generally become aware of propaganda?
16. Name some of the incidents in which the school has figured as the storm centre of battles over censorship or propaganda or both.
17. In what three ways does propaganda distort the talking-over process?
18. Is the net effect of modern developments of censorship and propaganda to increase or decrease equality of opportunity in America?
19. What is the effect of crisis on the talking-over process?
20. How does the rate of social change affect it?
21. From what two points of view may group organization be considered?
22. What two types of organization does any group need for dealing with ideas?
23. What do you understand by the statement that discussion for, not by, is a predominant pattern of urban life? What difference does it make?
24. In what three ways is group action articulated with group opinion?
25. What is group will?
26. What three conditions in particular have led to the demand for the extension of governmental powers?
27. What four tendencies, or trends, in group self-direction can be distinguished?

SUGGESTED ASSIGNMENT

Outline the conception of public opinion presented in this and the two preceding chapters. Show the relation of this conception to the ideas developed in other chapters.

CHAPTER XXV

INSTITUTIONS

In this chapter and the three following we take up once more our analysis of social life from the standpoint of culture. Now, however, we are ready to deal with the more complex elements in culture and to see them as they function in relation to the wider setting of life due to modern communication.

What Is an Institution? *An institution is a complex, integrated organization of collective behavior, established in the social heritage and meeting some persistent need or want.* Since the locus of an institution is in the public mind, it is related to, and a product of, public opinion, though often seeming, on account of its permanence and the visible customs and symbols in which it is clothed, to have a somewhat distinct and independent existence. Thus the political state and the church, with their venerable associations, their vast and ancient power, their literature, buildings, and offices, hardly appear even to a democratic people as the mere products of human invention which, of course, they are.

The great institutions are the outcome of that organization which human thought naturally takes on when it is directed for age after age upon a particular subject, and so gradually crystallizes in definite forms—enduring sentiments, beliefs, customs, and symbols. And this is the case when there is some deep and abiding interest to hold the attention of men. Language, government, the church, law, and customs of property and the family, systems of industry and education, are institutions because they are the working out of permanent needs of human nature.

Every institution holding its own in the world has a special character and function which explains its power to live. It is only thus that it is able to enlist a share of human vitality in its service. Commercial institutions, for example, have in general obvious functions, but the needs which are being served by some of our less basic institutions like, for instance, Rotary Clubs are not so apparent. Consider college football. There is something more in it that the obvious athletic functions; you could not explain its growth without going into crowd psychology, its exploitation by an organized athletic interest attached to the educational system, and the use of the game by college officials as a means of mobilizing alumni.

The intimate and distinctive character of an institution might be compared to the theme of a symphony, continually recurring, and of which the whole organism of the music is a various unfolding. Like that it is a pattern running through the web which this particular loom turns out.

Distinction Between an Institution and a Group. We should be clear as to the distinction between an institution and a group. The latter is primarily an aggregation of persons, like a children's play-group, a board of directors, a military regiment, or a family. It is a configuration or pattern of particular personalities. These group members may or may not be participating in an institution, that is, in a socially established pattern of collective behavior. Thus, a newly formed play-group has no institutional character, a boy-scout troop is a group which is participating in an institution. Sometimes the group is co-extensive with the institution, as for instance the membership of the Daughters of the American Revolution; often the group is less extensive, sharing the institutional behavior with other small units as do the local chapters of the same organization. The officers and soldiers of a regiment form a group which may have a few distinctive institutional traits of its own but which, on the whole, participates in the institutional pattern of the larger military system. Thus we would call *a* family a group, but *the* family is an institution, a mode of thought and action in which thousands of particular families participate. When family groups are so participating, much of the personalities of the members may have little to do with the institution; only certain typical habits and interests indicate the institutional character of their behavior. And on the other hand, the institution is more than a group; its vitality consists in an organic whole of transmitted ideas which has the power to enlist the activities of a group, but does not, for the most part, originate with the group, and cannot be explained as a mere product of their personalities. Language is, perhaps, the most striking example of this, since there is the merest shadow of a group which corresponds to the institution.[1]

[1] Perhaps two kinds of institutions should be distinguished: Those which pattern the relationship of symbols, *e.g.*, language; and those which pattern the relationship of people, *e.g.*, the family, the state, etc

The various institutions of any social order are not separable entities, but rather phases of a common and at least partly homogeneous body of thought, just as are the various tendencies and convictions of an individual: they are the organized attitudes of the public mind, and it is only by abstraction that we can regard them as things by themselves. We are to remember that the social system is above all a whole, no matter how the convenience of study may lead us to divide it.

The Individual and the Institution. In the individual the institution exists as a habit of mind and of action, largely unconscious, because largely common to all the group: it is only the differential aspect of ourselves of which we are commonly aware. But it is in men and nowhere else that the institution is to be found. The real existence of the Constitution of the United States, for example, is in the traditional ideas of the people and the activities of judges, legislators, and administrators; the written instrument being only a means of communication, an Ark of the Covenant, ensuring the integrity of the tradition. If all existing copies should be burned, the Constitution would not have ceased to exist.

The individual is always cause as well as effect of the institution: he receives the impress of the state whose traditions have enveloped him from childhood, but at the same time impresses his own character, formed by other forces as well as this, upon the state, which thus in him and others like him undergoes change.

An institution is a mature, specialized, and comparatively rigid part of the social structure. It is made up of persons, but not of whole persons; each one enters into it with a trained and specialized part of himself. Consider, for instance, the legal part of a lawyer, the ecclesiastical part of a church member, or the business part of a merchant. In antithesis to the institution, therefore, the person represents the wholeness and humanness of life. A man is no man at all if he is merely a piece of an institution; he must stand also for human nature, for the instinctive, the plastic, and the ideal.

The saying that corporations have no soul expresses well enough this defect of all definite social structures, which gives rise to an irrepressible conflict between them and the freer and larger impulses of human nature. Just in proportion as they achieve an effective special mechanism for a narrow purpose, they lose humanness, breadth, and adaptability. As we have to be specially on our guard against commercial corporations, because of their union of power and impersonality, so should we be against all institutions.

The institution represents might, and also, perhaps, right, but right as organized, mature, perhaps gone to seed, never fresh and unrecognized. New right, or moral progress, always begins in a revolt against institutions.

There is a painting which may be said to set forth to the eye this relation between the living soul and the institution.[2] It represents St. James before the Roman Emperor. The former is poorly clad, beautiful, with rapt, uplifted face; the latter, majestic, dominant, assured, seated high on his ivory chair and surrounded by soldiers.

Of course the institutional element is equally essential with the personal. The mechanical working of tradition and convention pours into the mind the tried wisdom of the race, a system of thought every part of which has survived because it was, in some sense, the fittest, because it approved itself to the human spirit. In this way the individual gets language, sentiments, moral standards, and all kinds of knowledge: gets them with an exertion of the will trifling compared with what these things originally cost. They have become a social atmosphere which pervades the mind mostly without its active participation. Once the focus of attention, and effort, they have now receded into the dimness of the matter-of-course, leaving energy free for new conquests. On this involuntary foundation we build, and it needs no argument to show that we could accomplish nothing without it.

Thus, all innovation is based on conformity, all heterodoxy on orthodoxy, all individuality on solidarity. Without the orthodox tradition in biology, for instance, under the guidance of which a store of ordered knowledge had been collected, the heterodoxy of Darwin, based upon a reinterpretation of this knowledge, would have been impossible. And so in art, the institution supplies a basis to the very individual who rebels against it. In America it is not hostile criticism but no criticism at all—sheer ignorance and indifference—that discourages the artist and man of letters and makes it difficult to form a high ideal. Where there is an organized tradition there may be intolerance but there will also be intelligence.

[2] By Mantegna

Thus choice, which represents the relatively free action of human nature in building up life, is like the coral insect, always working on a mountain made up of the crystallized remains of dead predecessors.

Morality of Institutions. It is a mistake to suppose that the person is, in general, *better* than the institution. Morally, as in other respects, there are advantages on each side. The person has love and aspiration and all sorts of warm, fresh, plastic impulses, to which the institution is seldom hospitable, but the latter has a sober and tried goodness of the ages, the deposit, little by little, of what has been found practicable in the wayward and transient outreachings of human idealism. The law, the state, the traditional code of right and wrong, these are related to personality as a gray-haired father to a child. However world-worn and hardened by conflict, they are yet strong and wise and kind, and we do well in most matters to obey them.

Thus, it is from the interaction of personality and institutions that progress comes. The person represents more directly that human nature which it is the end of all institutions to serve, but the institution represents the net result of a development far transcending any single personal consciousness. The person will criticize, and be mostly in the wrong, but not altogether. He will attack, and mostly fail, but from many attacks change will ensue.

Phases of Institutional Growth. The structure of an institution does not bear a constant relationship to the needs of the persons participating in it. We may roughly distinguish four periods of institutional organization: (1) incipient organization, (2) efficiency, (3) formalism, and (4) disorganization. The last three of these may be looked upon as stages in a recurrent cycle, once the process has been inaugurated by the first period. (See Figure 18.) We must be careful to make no assumptions regarding rhythm, regularity, or equal intervals in each stage. All that is meant is that each preceding stage will at some time give way to the one following, that there is a natural sequence of cause and effect which swings the institution through the cycle.

Institutions arise in a variety of ways so that little can be said about the period of incipient organization except that it is characterized by a tentative seeking for adjustment. Some institutions begin in social movements, like Christianity or communism, with great enthusiasm; after a time patterns of collective action are laid down and passed on. Other institutions begin in a cool and calculating manner like the League of Nations.[3] Still others are unconscious growths out of the folkways and *mores* like the family.

In discussing the relationship between the individual and the

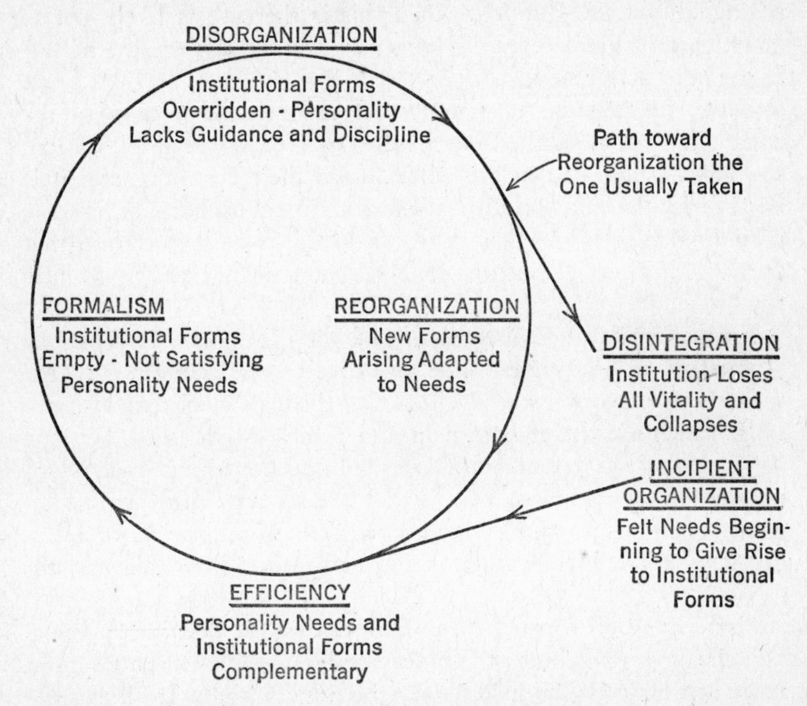

FIG. 18. The Cycle of Institutional Development.

institution we have suggested the potential value each possesses for the other. When these potential values are being realized practically we have the stage of efficiency. Then is personality working hand in hand with the institution, supplying it with fresh life and new points of view, while receiving from it the wisdom and guidance of the past generations of participants.

But since in the very nature of the case institutions can live only through symbols, there is a constant tendency for the symbol to obscure the human purpose implicit in it. When this happens the institution has passed into the phase of formalism.

[3] For a discussion of these two types of institutions, see Everett C. Hughes, *The Growth of an Institution: the Chicago Real Estate Board,* pp. 8, 9.

Formalism. By formalism we mean too much mechanism in an institution. It is by no means easy, however, to determine whether this condition exists or not. Mechanism becomes an evil no doubt when it interferes with growth and adaptation, when it suppresses individuality and stupefies or misdirects the energies of human nature. But just when this is the case is likely not to be clear until the occasion is long past and we can see the matter in the perspective of history.

Thus, in religion, it is well that men should adhere to the creeds and ritual worked out in the past for spiritual edification, so long as these do, on the whole, fulfil their function; and it is hard to fix the time—not the same for different churches, classes, or individuals—when they cease to do this. But it is certain that they die, in time, like all tissue, and if not cleared away presently rot.

Formalism is an overemphasis of mere symbols, is what we stigmatize as "red tape." The aim of all organizations is to express human nature, and it does this through a system of symbols, which are the embodiment and vehicle of the idea. So long as spirit and symbol are vitally united and the idea is really conveyed, all is well, but so fast as they are separated the symbol becomes an empty shell, to which, however, custom, pride, or interest may still cling. It then supplants rather than conveys the reality.

Underlying all formalism, indeed, is the fact that it is psychically cheap; it substitutes the outer for the inner as more tangible, more capable of being held before the mind without fresh expense of thought and feeling, more easily extended, therefore, and impressed upon the multitude. Thus in our own architecture or literature we have innumerable cheap, unfelt repetitions of forms that were significant and beautiful in their time and place.

Effect of Formalism on Personality. The effect of formalism upon personality is to starve its higher life and leave it the prey of apathy, self-complacency, sensuality, and the lower nature in general. A formalized religion and a formalized freedom are, notoriously, the congenial dwelling-places of depravity and oppression.

When a system of this sort is thoroughly established, as in the case of the later Roman Empire, it confines the individual mind as in a narrow cage by supplying it with only one sort of influence.

The variation of ideas and the supplanting of old types by new can begin only by individuals receiving stimulation of a sort that conflicts with the ruling system; and in the absence of this, an old type may go on reproducing itself indefinitely, individuals seeming no more to it than the leaves of a tree, which drop in the autumn and in the spring are replaced by others indistinguishable from them.

Among the Hindus, for instance, most children are brought up from infancy in subjection to ceremonies and rites which stamp upon them the impression of a fixed and immemorial system. These control the most minute details of their lives, and leave little room for choice either on their part or that of their parents. There is no attempt to justify tradition by reason: custom as such is obligatory.

Intolerance goes very naturally with formalism, since to a mind in the unresisted grasp of a fixed system of thought anything that departs from that system must appear irrational and absurd. The lowest Chinaman unaffectedly despises the foreigner, of whatever rank, as a vulgar barbarian, just as Christians used to despise the Jews, and the Jews, in their time, the Samaritans. Tolerance comes in along with peaceful discussion, when there is a competition of various ways of thinking, no one of which is strong enough to suppress the others.

In America and western Europe at the present day there is a good deal of formalism, but it is, on the whole, of a partial and secondary character, existing rather from the inadequacy of vital force than as a ruling principle. The general state of thought favors adaptation, because we are used to it and have found it, on the whole, beneficial. But dead mechanism is too natural a product of human conditions not to exist at all times, and we may easily find it today in the church, in politics, in education, in industry—wherever there is a lack of vital thought and sentiment to keep the machinery pliant to its work.

Thus our schools, high and low, exhibit a great deal of it, in spite of recent movements to "humanize" education. Routine methods, here as everywhere, are a device for turning out cheap work in large quantities, and the temptation to use them, in the case of a teacher who has too much to do, or is required to do that which he does not understand or believe in, is almost irresistible. Indeed, they are too frequently inculcated by principals and training schools, in contempt of the fact that the one essential thing in real teaching is a personal relation between teacher and pupil. Drill is easy for one who has got the knack of it, just because it requires nothing personal or vital, but is a convenient appliance for getting the business done with an appearance of success and little trouble to any one.

Even universities have much of this sort of cant. In literature, for instance, whether ancient or modern, English or foreign, little that is vital is commonly imparted. Compelled by his position to teach *something* to large and diverse classes, the teacher is led to fix upon certain matters—such as grammar, metres, or the biographies of the authors—whose definiteness suits them for the didactic purpose, and drill them into the student; while the real thing, the sentiments that are the soul of literature, are not communicated. If the teacher himself feels them, which is often the case, the fact that they cannot be reduced to formulas and tested by examinations discourages him from dwelling upon them.

In like manner our whole system of commerce and industry is formal in the sense that it is a vast machine grinding on and on in a blind way which is often destructive of the human nature for whose service it exists. Mammon—as in the painting by Watts—is not a fiend, wilfully crushing the woman's form that lies under his hand, but only a somewhat hardened man of the world, looking in another direction and preoccupied with the conduct of business on business principles.

Disorganization. The apparent opposite of formalism, but in reality closely akin to it, is disorganization or disintegration. One is mechanism supreme, the other mechanism going to pieces; and both are in contrast to that harmony between human nature and its instruments which is desirable.

Disorganization is a term which may be used with reference to either specific institutions or the general conditions of a particular society. In the latter case it merely means that general order and discipline are lacking. Though there may be praiseworthy persons and activities, society as a whole wants unity and rationality, like a picture which is good in details but does not make a pleasing composition. Individuals and special groups appear to be working too much at cross purposes; there is a "reciprocal struggle of discordant powers" but the "harmony of the universe" does not emerge. As good actors do not always make a good troupe nor brave soldiers a good army, so a nation or a historical epoch—say Italy in the Renaissance—may be prolific in distinguished persons and scattered achievements but somewhat futile and chaotic as a system.

As applied to a specific institution, disorganization implies that there is a relative lack of integration. Perhaps there is factional strife within the institution or perhaps it has become a case of every man for himself with no devotion to common aims and purposes. At all events, the mechanism or structure which is so essential to the successful patterning of collective behavior is inadequate.

The Effect of Disorganization upon Personality. Disorganization appears in the individual as a mind without cogent and abiding allegiance to a whole, and without the larger principles of conduct that flow from such allegiance. The better aspect of this is that the lack of support may stimulate a man to greater activity and independence, the worse that the absence of social standards is likely to lower his plane of achievement and throw him back upon sensuality and other primitive impulses; also that, if he is of a sensitive fibre, he is apt to be overstrained by the contest with untoward conditions. As we saw in Chapter XIII there is considerable evidence of such strain in contemporary American life. How soothing and elevating it is to breathe the atmosphere of some large and quiet discipline and how rarely in our day is a man dominated by restful and unquestioned faith in anything!

The fact that great personalities often appear in disordered times may seem to be a contradiction of the principle that the healthy development of individuals is one with that of institutions. Thus the Italian Renaissance, which was a time of political disorder and religious decay, produced the greatest painters and sculptors of modern times, and many great personalities in literature and statesmanship. There are two explanations of this. One is that occasionally there is a spur in the troubles of a confused time which may excite a few individuals to heroic efforts, just as a fire or a railroad disaster may be the occasion of heroism. If they are of great natural capacity they may be able to draw upon the well-organized institutions of the past in spite of the disorganization of the present and thus rise to great achievement. The other explanation is that some institutions may not share in the general disorganization of the time, but may be highly developed, as were the arts during the Renaissance. Thus, though the society as a whole may be disorganized and personalities not well integrated, one particular institution and the habits of individuals which correspond to it may be in a healthy state.

The Transition from Formalism to Disorganization. It looks at first sight as if formalism and disorganization were as far apart as possible, but in fact they are closely connected, the latter being only the next step after the former in a logical cycle—the decay of a body already dead. Formalism in an institution is likely to produce sensuality, avarice, selfish ambition, and other traits representing personal disorganization, because the merely formal institution does not enlist and discipline the soul of the individual, but takes hold of him by the outside, his personality being left to torpor or to irreverent and riotous activity. So in the later centuries of the Roman Empire, when its system was most rigid, the people became unpatriotic, disorderly, and sensual. This situation is certain to be ended sooner or later either by the natural disintegration of the institution through lack of interest or by revolt from the meaningless routine on the part of interested persons critical of the system.

We see the first stage of this process in a school whose discipline is merely formal, not engaging the interest and good-will of the student. Such a school is pretty certain to turn out unruly boys and girls, because whatever is most personal and vital in them becomes accustomed to assert itself in opposition to the system. And so in a church where external observance has been developed at the expense of personal judgment, the individual conforms to the rite and then feels free for all kinds of self-indulgence. In general, the lower "individualism" of our time, the ruthless self-assertion which is so conspicuous, for example, in business, is not something apart from our institutions but expresses the fact that they are largely formal and inhuman, not containing and enlarging the soul of the individual.

The second stage of the process is exemplified in the casting aside of the traditional school routine or the external formulas and rites of the church. The anomaly of the formalism situation, where the real purposes of the institutions are not being achieved, becomes apparent to those interested and the outworn shell is broken. First come the destructive critics and, if the institution is reorganized, the constructive critics follow. But there is always a period, long or short, in which disorganization is prevalent and personality loses the guidance which a sound institution can give.

The real opposite of both formalism and disorganization is, of course, efficiency—that wholesome relation between individuality and the institution in which each supports the other, the latter contributing a stable basis for the vitality and variation of the former.

Disorganization in Contemporary Life. In so far as it is true that the larger interests of society are not impressed upon the individual, so that his private impulses co-operate with the public good, ours is a time of moral disintegration. A well-ordered community is like a ship in which each officer and seaman has confidence in his fellows and in the captain, and is well accustomed to do his duty with no more than ordinary grumbling. All hangs together, and is subject to reason in the form of long-tried rules of navigation and discipline. Virtue is a system and men do heroic acts as part of the day's work and without self-consciousness. But suppose the ship goes to pieces—let us say upon an iceberg—then the orderly whole is broken up and officers, seamen, and passengers find themselves struggling miscellaneously in the water. Rational control and the virtue that is habit is gone, each one is thrown back upon undisciplined impulses. Survival depends not upon wisdom or goodness, but upon ruthless force, and the best may probably perish.

Here is "individualism" in the lowest sense, and it is the analogue of this which is said, not without some reason, to pervade our own society. Old institutional forms are passing away and better ones, we hope, are preparing to take their places, but in the meantime there is a lack of that higher discipline which prints the good of the whole upon the heart of the member. In a traditional order one is accustomed from childhood to regard usage, the authority of elders, and the dominant institutions as the rule of life. "So it must be" is one's unconscious conviction, and, like the seamen, he does wise and heroic things without knowing it. But in our own time there is for many persons, if not most, no authoritative canon of life, and for better or worse we are ruled by native impulse and by that private reason which may be so weak when detached from a rational whole. The higher morality, if it is to be attained at all, must be thought out; and of the few who can do this a large part exhaust their energy in thinking and do not practice with any heartiness the truths they perceive.

We find, then, that people have to make up their own minds upon their duties as wives, husbands, mothers, and daughters; upon commercial obligation and citizenship; upon the universe and the nature and authority of God. Inevitably many of us make a poor business of it. It is too much. It is as if each one should sit down to invent a language for himself; these things should be thought out gradually, co-operatively, each adding little and accepting much. That great traditions should go rapidly to pieces may be a necessary phase of evolution and a disguised blessing, but the present effect is largely distraction and demoralization.

The Reorganization Process. The fact that the breaking up of traditions throws men back upon immediate human nature has, however, its good as well as its bad side. It may obscure those larger truths that are the growth of time and may loose pride, sensuality, and skepticism; but it also awakens the child in man and a childlike pliability to the better as well as the worse in natural impulse. We may look, among people who have lost the sense of tradition, for the sort of virtues, as well as of vices, that we find on the frontier: for plain dealing, love of character and force, kindness, hope, hospitality, and courage. Alongside of an extravagant growth of sensuality, pride, and caprice, we have about us a general cult of childhood and womanhood, a vast philanthropy, and, at least in many quarters, an interest in the welfare of the masses of the people. The large private gifts to philanthropic and educational purposes, and the fact that a great deal of personal pride is mingled with these gifts, are equally characteristic of the time.

A period of disorganization, then, creates a great need, and furnishes a fruitful soil, for constructive leadership. In order to reorganize institutions successfully and bring them back to the stage we have termed efficiency, there must arise persons of vision and forcefulness to formulate and build the new order. Our own civilization is in great need of such leadership at present. If institutions generally can be brought to that healthy development which is one with the healthy development of personalities, then once more will we have to face the age-long problem of keeping them in that condition and warding off the insidious advent of formalism. It takes intelligent guidance not only to create efficient institutions but to keep them efficient, for the path of least resistance will always be the lapsing into the mechanical.

STUDY QUESTIONS

1. Explain the nature and origin of institutions. How do you explain the sudden rise of revolutionary institutions like communism in Russia?
2. What is the difference between the concepts, institution, and group?
3. What is the general value of institutions to personality? Of personality to institutions? Illustrate from your own experience.
4. Why does moral progress always begin in a revolt against institutions?
5. Discuss the question whether the moral standards of institutions are necessarily lower than those of persons.
6. What four periods of institutional organization can you name? Give examples of each. Which are involved in a recurring cycle?
7. Explain formalism and discuss its effect upon personality.
8. Explain disorganization and show how it follows naturally from formalism.
9. How would you explain the fact that the great art of the Italian Renaissance was produced in a time of much disorganization?
10. What grounds are there for calling our age a period of disorganization in institutions?
11. What are the obstacles to personal achievement in a period of disorganization?
12. What does a period of reorganization require?

CHAPTER XXVI

THE FAMILY

In Chapter IV we spoke of the family as perhaps the most important of the primary groups. Here we are to consider it as an institution. We should be clear as to the difference between the two. As a primary group the family affords an opportunity for early and intimate association which is all-important in the development of human nature on the one hand, and the more elaborate social structures on the other. It performs this simple service in all cultures. One might argue that this function is institutional, that the family is the way, established in the social heritage, of meeting this need. Be that as it may, a family group would perform this primary group function even if it were not the method established by tradition. When we speak of the family as an institution we are thinking of the whole complex of established ideas and practices which characterize the family in any particular culture. These ideas and practices vary, naturally, with the needs of the situation. Thus, though the family as a primary group everywhere operates in the same way, as an institution it operates very differently under different circumstances.

The Family in Primitive Life. Primitive life offers a fascinating variety of customs with reference to the forms of marriage, the composition of the family group, and the functions of the group. Marriage may be by capture, by purchase, by mutual consent and cohabitation, or by arrangement between parents while the parties are still infants. The family group in primitive life is usually larger than in modern life, being composed in many cases of all the descendants of a living ancestor. Where the system is patrilineal the family would consist typically of an old man and his wife, their sons and their wives, their unmarried daughters, and their grandchildren (except married granddaughters). If descent is matrilineal it would be an old woman and her husband, their daughters and husbands, their unmarried sons, and their grandchildren (except married grandsons). Thus in a matrilineal system the fathers may be much less important to their children than maternal uncles, who may have a very close relation to their nephews. In such a system the husbands may not even reside in the household. These relationships may be further complicated by the practice of either polygyny or polyandry. Also, in many tribes there is some variety of fosterage—children reared by others than their own parents, though still in family groups.

Family functions vary widely. To quote Margaret Mead, "There are societies where the men take meals entirely outside the home; others in which religion is entirely socialized; others in which the economic unit is far larger than the biological family. The degree to which the family serves as a transfer point of civilization differs depending on whether religious instruction is given by the father to the son, as among the Omaha Indians, or is made a group function with formal initiation ceremonies; whether children learn crafts from their parents or receive formal instruction from experts, as in Samoa and among the Maori. Some societies rely heavily upon the family group to dispense economic and social instruction to the children; others rely upon age groups, special ceremonies or formalized instruction. The family may comprise almost the entire social world of the child, as among some particularly nomadic groups. The biological family may be obliterated by a much larger group, so that the child is required to adjust to a group of some 15 or 20 persons. Male club houses may result in boys leaving home at an early age and in the realignment of old and young along sex lines."[1]

The Family in Mediæval Times. Of fundamental importance to the understanding of the contemporary family in America is its progenitor, the mediæval family. This, like other mediæval institutions, was dominated by comparatively settled traditions which reflected the needs of the general system of society. Marriage was thought of chiefly as an alliance of interests, and was arranged by the ruling members of the families concerned on grounds of *convenance,* the personal congeniality of the parties being little considered.

We know that this view of marriage has still considerable force among the more conservative classes of European society, and that royalty or nobility, on the one hand, and the peasantry, on the other, adhere to the idea that it is a family rather than a personal

[1] "Family," *Encyclopedia of the Social Sciences,* VI, p. 65.

function, which should be arranged on grounds of rank and wealth. In France it is hardly respectable to make a romantic marriage, and Mr. Hamerton tells of a young woman who was indignant at a rumor that she had been wedded for love, insisting that it had been strictly a matter of *convenance*. He also mentions a young man who was compelled to ask his mother which of two sisters he had just met was to be his wife.[2]

Along with this subordination of choice in contracting marriage generally went an autocratic family discipline. Legally the wife and children had no separate rights, their personality being merged in that of the husband and father, while socially the latter was rather their master than their companion. His rule, however—though it was no doubt harsh and often brutal, judged by our notions—was not so arbitrary and whimsical as would be the exercise of similar authority in our day; since he was himself subordinate not only to social superiors, but still more to traditional ideas, defining his own duties and those of his household, which he felt bound to carry out. The whole system was authoritative, admitting little play of personal choice.

In mediæval times the family bulked larger in the whole social scheme than it does today because it performed many functions which have since been entrusted to other institutions. On the economic side the family produced most of the goods which it consumed, so that it was nearly a self-contained unit. Later, with the beginnings of manufacture, the household was still the place where the industrial processes were carried on, though it no longer remained essentially independent. Education and recreation were also largely functions of the family. In a simple economy there was neither the need for the special institutions we have for those purposes nor the means for supporting them. Moreover, the family was to a far greater extent than now the protector of its members. There were no police and fire departments and no insurance to provide for old age. Being adapted to these conditions, the law allowed much more in the way of private redress for wrongs to family members than it does today. In the United States we need only go back 100 years to find a situation very similar in all the region west of the Alleghenies. And remnants of the old order may still be found among the mountaineers of Kentucky and Tennessee.

The Family's Loss of Functions. The first great force

[2] *French and English,* p. 357.

which has broken up the old family pattern is, then, the specialization in other institutions of functions that used to be performed in the family. Only in rural areas is the household much of a productive unit and even there it is less so than formerly. Our pioneer ancestors made their own clothes, prepared almost all their food, made their candles and soap, built their own houses, and cut the wood for their fuel. Now we have great industries devoted to these tasks and the family members leave their homes to perform the necessary work in mines, shops, and factories.

The final stage in this process is seen in the decline of such traditionally domestic occupations as baking, canning, laundering, and sewing.

Between 1899 and 1929, for instance, the value of the product of commercial bakeries in dollars of equal purchasing power increased about twice as fast as the number of families in the United States. Unpublished data of the U. S. Bureau of Home Economics indicate that 90 per cent of urban households now use baker's bread exclusively. In the period above mentioned the value of the product of commercial canneries has increased more than twice as fast as the number of families and the increase in quantity has been much greater than that of the value in dollars. Between 1919 and 1929 the work done in power laundries increased 110 per cent while the number of urban families increased only one third. A decline in the value of sewing machines manufactured between 1919 and 1929 coupled with an increase by 20 per cent in the number of families would seem to show that this traditional activity is also leaving the home.

Furthermore, it seems apparent that there is less cooking of meals in the home.[3] The number of delicatessen dealers who sell foods ready to be served has increased about three times as fast as urban families since 1900, while the number of waiters and the number of restaurant keepers also increased enormously.

[3] Nowhere in this chapter have we considered the very important matters of housing and home equipment. This is because our whole analysis is in terms of personal relations rather than material culture. One of the best recent studies of these objective matters was that made by R. O. Eastman, Inc., for the *Literary Digest* entitled *Zanesville and 36 Other American Communities: A Study of Markets and of the Telephone as a Market Index.* (1927). Approximately 70 per cent of the 4596 Zanesville homes were owned by the families living in them, but their average value was only $5048. 38 per cent of these homes had no bathrooms, but 73 per cent had electricity, 96 per cent gas, and 90 per cent running water. Furnaces were found in only 38 per cent of the homes. The most widely used electrical device was the electric iron, found in 59 per

In addition to the loss in economic function, the family plays a much smaller rôle than formerly in education. The whole public school movement, the growth of public libraries and many other developments point in this direction. It must not be forgotten, however, that even today the family is of vital importance in the development of character and that much incidental learning takes place through the association in the home circle.

There is no need to dwell upon the institutionalization of recreation outside the home which has taken place of recent years. The moving-pictures, dance halls, amusement parks, and summer camps at once come to mind. And in our larger cities, homes are so small and spacious yards so rare that the community has had to set up playgrounds in order to provide opportunity for healthful recreation.

The protective function has been likewise largely shifted from the family to other agencies. Besides our public fire and police services we have all sorts of institutions to care for the unable. The law no longer allows a family to redress wrongs inflicted upon a member but entrusts that responsibility to the public prosecution. It even protects minor members of a family against exploitation by parents through child-labor laws.

The family, then, plays a smaller rôle because it has fewer functions. However, such a far-reaching change in the ordering of life could not take place without much dislocation and maladjustment. There was bound to be a cultural lag—a passing on of ideas and sentiments appropriate to the mediæval situation, but quite unsuited to the conditions faced by the contemporary family. The traditional domination of the husband and father over his wife and children, the emphasis upon the family line and family property, especially the homestead, and the inculcation among women of the purely domestic virtues, all continued after the conditions to which they were adapted had disappeared. Thus the family came into a state of formalism. The dissolution of the old pattern which has brought the family to its present disorganized state was the work of a second great force which we must now discuss.

cent of the homes; the vacuum cleaner was next with 52 per cent. 92 per cent had no servants and hired no outside help. 70 per cent of the families had incomes of $2000 or less and only 2 per cent had more than $5000. These figures suggest that modern conveniences are by no means completely diffused as yet even in an up-to-date town. A slum area of a big city would show far less satisfactory conditions. For a careful discussion of the problems of housing see Arthur Evans Wood's *Community Problems,* New York, 1928.

Growth in the Spirit of Individualism. The spirit of individualism, the notion of the supreme worth of the individual, began to appear in late mediæval times. The feudal system was decaying and people were being thrown more on their own initiative. In the religious sphere the Reformation gave impetus to the idea. The commercial cities which began to spring up offered great opportunities for self-assertion. A little later the beginnings of science put the more intelligent in a questioning frame of mind. They became skeptical not only of traditional explanations concerning the physical world, but of the accepted social organization. The discovery of the New World gave those with a taste for adventure and a desire to free themselves from the irksome requirements of the old order a chance to escape and attempt the development of one allowing more self-expression, and pioneer conditions in America continued to foster individualism until late in the nineteenth century. In the political sphere this spirit gave rise to the democratic movement which burst into the open on both sides of the Atlantic with the American and French Revolutions. Part of the same stream of thought was the freeing of the slaves, while more recently we have had another expression of it in that movement known as the emancipation of women.

This spirit of individualism was on the increase all during the period that the functions of the family were on the decrease. While formalism was creeping in on the one hand, a force which would destroy the outworn shell was developing on the other. Thus there was bound to come about a crisis in the institution's history. The old authoritative family was tried and found wanting. But of course a new institutional pattern to fit the new conditions has not been immediately forthcoming. The result is that natural confusion following the break-down of formalism which we call disorganization.

Marriage in Modern Life. In considering the family in modern life the first thing to note is that there is no evidence of any disinclination toward the married state. Even after making allowance for the changes in age grouping in the population and various other factors, Ogburn finds that there was a larger percentage of the people of the United States married in 1920 than in 1890.[4] The family may be somewhat disorganized but it shows little tendency to disappear.

[4] *American Marriage and Family Relationships,* Chap. XI.

Eugenists are, however, concerned over the declining marriage rate among those whom they conceive to represent the better stocks, the college graduates. For example, Banker found that in 1917 the percentages of men and women graduates of Syracuse University who were married were as follows:[5]

TABLE 6

PERCENTAGES OF SYRACUSE UNIVERSITY GRADUATES OF CERTAIN CLASSES WHO WERE MARRIED UP TO 1917

Classes	*Women*	*Men*
1862–71	87	87
1872–81	81	90
1882–91	55	84
1892–1901	48	73

Whether we agree or not that this is serious from the point of view of hereditary stock, there can be no doubt that there is a waste here from the point of view of social transmission, since college-trained persons can provide an environment for their children more stimulating than the average.

Family Disorganization. The disorganization of the family in our time is evidenced both in its structure and its spirit. City life, which is becoming more and more typical, gives us no definite pattern of family relationships. There are all sorts of variants such as the companionate marriage, the family in which the mother of small children works away from home, the family of the man who works at night so that his children scarcely know him, and the single-child family where the home life all revolves about the child. Moreover, there is a subtle change in spirit. The decay of settled traditions, embracing not only those relating directly to the family but also the religious and economic ideas by which these were supported, has thrown us back upon the unschooled impulses of human nature. In entering upon marriage the personal tastes of the couple demand gratification, and, right or wrong, there is no authority strong enough to hold them in check. Nor, if upon experience it turns out that personal tastes are not gratified, is there commonly any insuperable obstacle to a dissolution of the tie. Being married, they have children so long as they find it, on the whole,

[5] *Journal of Heredity,* VIII, p. 213.

agreeable to their inclinations to do so, but when this point is reached they proceed to exercise choice by refusing to bear and rear any more. And as the spirit of choice is in the air, the children are not slow to inhale it and to exercise their own wills in accordance with the same law of impulse their elders seem to follow. "Do as you please so long as you do not evidently harm others" is the only rule of ethics that has much life; there is little regard for any higher discipline, for the slowly built traditions of a deeper right and wrong which cannot be justified to the feelings of the moment.

Decline in the Birth Rate. One of the very marked changes in family life during recent decades is the sharp decline in the birth rate. In the United States in 1880 there were nearly 40 children born yearly per thousand of the population whereas in 1927 it was about 21.[6] The causes of this decline are, of course, very complex and difficult to get at. Some of them may be regarded as quite rational adaptations to changed conditions, not necessarily showing any falling off in family morale, while others seem to indicate a definite spirit of individualism.

First it may be noted that modern medicine has greatly reduced the rate of infant mortality so that families may raise the same number of children to maturity with fewer births. Again, under former conditions, both on the farms and in the towns, many parents regarded a large family as an economic asset and expected to make their children pay for themselves after they were 14 years old. There has recently arisen a great movement for child welfare which has resulted in child labor and compulsory school laws. To the degree that the shrinking birth rate reflects the present inability of parents to exploit their children, it cannot be regarded as a symptom of disorganization.

On the positive side it is widely claimed that the smaller family, especially among the well-to-do, represents, not selfishness on the part of parents, but concern for the best development of those children that they do raise. It is obvious that there are not the easy opportunities for making an independent start in life that there were in pioneer days, and that to fit a young man or woman to take his or her place successfully requires more of an investment on the part of the parents. They therefore often feel that it is better to give many advantages to two children than few to four.

After all is said, however, there undoubtedly is some shirking

[6] Louis I. Dublin, "The Great American Family," *Survey*, LIX, 267.

of parenthood for merely selfish reasons. Freedom of opportunity diffuses a restless desire to rise in the world, beneficent from many points of view but by no means favorable to natural increase. Men demand more of life in the way of personal self-realization than in the past, the consequence being that marriage is often postponed and the birth rate in marriage deliberately restricted. And the trend of things is bringing an ever larger proportion of the people within the ambitious classes and subject to this sort of checks.

The spread of luxury, or even comfort, works in the same direction by creating tastes and habits unfavorable to the bearing and rearing of many children. Among those whose life, in general, is hard these things are not harder than the rest, and a certain callousness of mind that is apt to result from monotonous physical labor renders people less subject to anxiety, as a rule, than those who might appear to have less occasion for it. The joy of children, the "luxury of the poor," may also appear brighter from the dullness and hardship against which it is relieved. But as people acquire the habit, or at least the hope, of comfort they become aware that additional children mean a sacrifice which they often refuse to make.

These influences go hand-in-hand with that general tendency to rebel against trouble which is involved in the spirit of choice. In former days women accepted the bearing of children and the accompanying cares and privations as a matter of course; it did not occur to them that anything else was possible. Now, being accustomed to choose their life, they demand a reason why they should undergo hardships; and since the advantages which are to follow are doubtful and remote, and the suffering near and obvious, they are not unlikely to refuse.

The distraction of choice grievously increases the actual burden and stress upon women, for it is comparatively easy to put up with the inevitable. What with moral strain of this sort and the anxious selection among conflicting methods of nurture and education it possibly costs the mother of today more psychical energy to raise four children than it did her grandmother to raise eight.

One small study of the reasons for few children in modern families was conducted by Ruediger.[7] Fifty-three graduate and upper-class students gave the principal reason for the failure to have more children in the cases of 300 couples with whom they were

[7] "Causes of Small Families," *Journal of Educational Sociology,* IV, 517–22.

personally acquainted who had either no children or only one child. The distribution of principal reasons was as follows:

TABLE 7

REASONS ASSIGNED FOR SMALL SIZE OF 300 FAMILIES

Reason	Per cent
Health of the mother	26.3%
Sterility	19.7
Economic	20.7
Personal	23.3
Late marriage	5.0
Miscellaneous	5.0
	100.0%

We may perhaps assume that the reasons listed as "personal" were rather selfish and hence an indication of individualism in the family. "Economic" undoubtedly also includes some of the same type, though the welfare of the children themselves was probably here the chief concern. It must be remembered that, since the couples studied were the intimate friends of college students, the sample was far from representative of the American population in general.

Gainful Employment of Married Women. Another marked contrast with the old family pattern is the gainful employment of married women outside their homes. In the United States about one tenth of all wives are in this category and slightly more than half of them (53 per cent) have children. 40 per cent have infants under 5. Studies by the U. S. Women's Bureau indicate that the great majority of working wives are employed because the family greatly needs their economic contribution, not because they are desirous of so doing.[8] In fact the working of the wife usually means a double load, for she commonly does the housework in addition to her gainful employment. But even though she has no selfish aims and is working wholly for the welfare of the family, the absence from the home of a mother with young children indicates a state of disorganization in the institution.

There is, of course, a small class of married women who work because of a desire for comfort and luxury or because they wish to express themselves in some other way than through their homes. Where the children are grown up and the routine housework can be satisfactorily taken care of in other ways this raises no prob-

[8] "The Share of Wage-Earning Women in Family Support," *Bulletin of the Women's Bureau*, No. 30, 1923.

lem. Where, on the other hand, such employment comes in conflict with a healthy family life the case is different. Many feel that the mother's first duty is to her family rather than herself under such circumstances. It is not impossible, however, that some compromise will be worked out either through the more general adoption of part-time work for married women or through a redivision of function which would give the husband a larger share in the activities of home-making.

Certainly nothing in modern civilization is more widely and subtly beneficent than the enlarged sphere of women's social function. It means that half of human nature is newly enfranchised, instructed, and enabled to become a more conscious and effective factor in life. The ideals of home and the care of children, in spite of the pessimists, are changing for the better, and the work of women in independent careers is often in the direction of much-needed social service—education and philanthropy in the largest sense of the words. Any one familiar with these movements knows that much of the intellectual and most of the emotional force back of them is that of women. One may say that the maternal instinct has been set free and organized on a vast scale, for the activities in which men excel are those inspired by sympathy with children and with the weak or suffering classes.

Children in the Modern Family. There is a very general belief that modern children are unduly independent, that they are suffering from individualism in the family. The family has always had the responsibility of socializing children, of developing them emotionally so that they would be able to adapt themselves readily to the demands of the larger society. There are several difficulties in the way of its fulfilling that function today.

In the first place the family is not the centre of general association and recreation that it once was. What, with apartment-house life, the development of clubs of all sorts, the decline in household economic activity, and the importunities of the agencies of commercialized recreation, the family members do not find themselves associating so much in the home circle as they used to. Communal work and play make for a discipline for all and the children are likely to see that there are rules and conditions of life above immediate pleasure. But, especially with the well-to-do classes, whose labors are rarely such as children may share, there is little chance for this development.

The smaller number of children in the average family is also a factor in the situation. Where there are only one or two children there is great danger that they will be spoiled. Not merely is discipline lacking, in many instances, but the affection which might be supposed to go with indulgence is turned to indifference, if not contempt. As a rule we love those we can look up to, those who stand for a higher ideal. In old days parents shared somewhat in that divinity with which tradition hedged the great of the earth, and might receive a reverence not dependent upon their personality; and even today they are apt to be better loved if they exact respect—just as an officer is better loved who enforces discipline and is not too familiar with his soldiers. Human nature needs something to look up to, and it is a pity when parents do not in part supply this need for their children.

The general sentiment of the times must be counted as a third factor in producing the "wildness" of modern youth. It would be strange if children were not hospitable to the modern sentiment that one will is as good as another, except as the other may be demonstrably wiser in regard to the matter in hand. Willing submission to authority as such, or sense of the value of discipline as a condition of the larger and less obvious well-being of society, is hardly to be expected from childish reasoning, and must come, if at all, as the unconscious result of a training which reflects general sentiment and custom. It is institutional in its nature, not visibly reasonable.

But the child, in our day, finds no such institution, no general state of sentiment such as exists in Japan and existed in our own past, which fills the mind from infancy with suggestions that parents are to be reverenced and obeyed; nor do parents ordinarily do much to instil this by training. Probably, so great is the power of general opinion even in childhood, they would hardly succeed if they tried, but as a rule they do not seriously try. Being themselves accustomed to the view that authority must appeal to the reason of the subject, they see nothing strange in the fact that their children treat them as equals and demand to know "Why?"

In short, the child, like the woman, helps to bear the often grievous burden of disorganization; bears it, among the well-to-do classes, in an ill-regulated life, in lack of reverence and love, in nervousness and petulance; as well as in premature and stunting labor among the poor.

Perhaps no better proof of the failure of the family properly to socialize the child can be adduced than the number and variety of movements calculated to improve the home relations of the child. Of recent years there have developed many types of parental education, of which the Child Study Association of America may be taken as a type. Again, there are psychiatric child-guidance clinics, visiting teachers who try to co-ordinate the activities of the home and the school, and juvenile courts which aim, among other things, to make the home relations more wholesome.

Divorce. Perhaps the most striking indication of family disorganization is the great increase in the number of marriages that break up through desertion, separation, and divorce. Because it is impossible to secure accurate figures on the amount of desertion and separation the divorce rate is usually used as the index of marriage dissolution. While it is probably sufficiently accurate for comparative purposes it must be remembered that in an absolute sense it always understates the case.

The following table which is abridged from a more comprehensive one in Lichtenberger's definitive work, *Divorce,*[9] shows the trend of divorce in the United States as compared with other countries.

TABLE 8

DIVORCES PER 100,000 POPULATION

Country	1920	1910	1900	1890
United States	139	92	73	53
Japan	94	113	143	269
France	71	37	25	17
Germany	63	24	15	13
Holland	29	16	10	8
Sweden	21	11	8	6
Australia	19	12	10	6
England and Wales	17	3	2	1

Another way of showing the increase in the United States is to compare in various years the number of mariages with the number of divorces. The following is also abridged from Lichtenberger:[10]

[9] New York, 1931, p. 110.
[10] Page 152.

TABLE 9

MARRIAGES TO ONE DIVORCE

Year	Marriages
1925	6.7
1920	7.7
1910	11.0
1900	12.3
1890	16.3
1880	23.8
1870	33.7

Thus we find that there was approximately five times as much divorce in 1925 as in 1870 and almost three times as much as in 1890. By 1929, indeed, the proportion was still greater, for the divorces per 100,000 of the population reached 166 in that year. When one considers that about one out of every six marriages now contracted will come to grief in the divorce court some day the situation seems appalling, but when one realizes that only one out of about 125 existing mariages is dissolved in any one year[11] the family does not seem so completely unstable.

Furthermore, divorce is, in the majority of instances, resorted to by couples rather recently married and without children. Of the 1924 divorces two fifths were granted before the marriage had endured 5 years, and two thirds before 10 years. The separation which actually breaks up the marriage probably occurs on the average a year before the divorce is granted. Of the 1929 divorces 37.2 per cent involved children, 57.1 per cent involved no children and in the remaining 5.7 per cent the record did not specify as to children.

The increase in divorce indicates a loosening of marriage ties. These ties are of two sorts—personal and institutional. By the former is meant those bonds which spring more directly from natural impulse and which may be roughly summed up as affection and common interest in children. The institutional are those that come more from the larger organization of society, such as economic interdependence of husband and wife, or the state of public sentiment, tradition, and law.

The Personal Ties in Marriage. As regards affection, present conditions should apparently be favorable to the strength of the bond. Since personal choice is so little interfered with, and the whole matter conducted with a view to congeniality, it would seem that a high degree of congeniality must, on the whole, be secured.

[11] Lichtenberger, *op. cit.*, p. 423.

And, indeed, this is without much doubt the case: nowhere, probably, is there so large a proportion of couples living together in love and confidence as in those countries where marriage is most free. Even if serious friction arises, the fact that each has chosen the other without constraint favors a sense of responsibility for the relation, and a determination to make it succeed that might be lacking in an arranged marriage. We know that if we do not marry happily it is our own fault, and the more character and self-respect we have the more we try to make the best of our venture. There can hardly be a general feeling that marriage is one thing and love another, such as may prevail under the rule of *convenance*.

Yet it is not inconsistent to say that this aim at love increases divorce. Since it is expected that the contracting parties are to be made happy, it follows that, if they are not, the relation is a failure and should cease; the brighter the ideal the darker the fact by contrast. Where interest and custom rule marriage those who enter into it may not expect congeniality, or, if they do, they feel that it is secondary and do not dream of divorce because it is not achieved. The woman marries because her parents tell her to, because marriage is her career, and because she desires a wedding and to be mistress of a household; the man because he wants a household and children and is not indifferent to the dowry. These tangible aims, of which one can be fairly secure beforehand, give stability where love proves wanting.

And while freedom in well-ordered minds tends toward responsibility and the endeavor to make the best of a chosen course, in the ill-ordered it is likely to become an impulsiveness which is displayed equally in contracting and in breaking off marriage without good cause. The conditions of our time give an easy rein to undisciplined wills, and one index of their activity is the divorce rate. Bad training in childhood is a large factor in this, neglected or spoiled children making bad husbands or wives, and probably furnishing the greater number of the divorced.

The Institutional Ties. As regards institutional bonds there is, of course, a great relaxation.

Thus economic interdependence declines with the advance of specialization. The home industries are mostly gone, and every year more things are bought that used to be made in the house. Little is left but cooking and that, either as the task of the wife or in the shape of the domestic-servant question, is so troublesome that many are eager to see it follow the rest. At one time marriage was, for women, about the only way to a respectable maintenance, while to men a good housewife was equally an economic necessity. Now this is true only of the farming population, and less true of them than it used to be; in the towns the economic considerations are mostly opposed to married life.

Besides making husband and wife less necessary to each other, these changes tend to make married women restless. Nothing works more for sanity and contentment than a reasonable amount of necessary and absorbing labor; disciplining the mind and giving one a sense of being of use in the world. A regular and necessary task rests the will by giving it assurance, while the absence of such a task wearies it by uncertainty and futile choice. Just as a person who follows a trail through the woods will go farther with less exertion than one who is finding his way, so we all need a foundation of routine, and the lack of this among women of the richer classes is a chief cause of the restless, exacting spirit, harassing to its owner and every one else, which tends toward discontent, indiscretion, and divorce.

If economic interdependence does form a bond, we should expect rural divorce rates to be below urban. Such is the case, as the following table shows, though the difference is not great:

TABLE 10

1929 DIVORCES PER 100 MARRIAGES IN STATES AND CITY COUNTIES[12]

State		*City County*	
California	29.1	San Francisco	37.9
Colorado	18.3	Denver	30.3
Louisiana	10.4	New Orleans	11.4
Maryland	8.4	Baltimore (city)	21.5
Missouri	25.6	St. Louis (city)	36.4
New York	4.2	New York	2.1
Pennsylvania	11.1	Philadelphia	12.1
Illinois	18.8	Cook (Chicago)	23.0
Ohio	23.3	Cuyohoga (Cleveland)	27.9
Massachusetts	11.3	Suffolk (Boston)	13.1

The single exception to the general rule, New York City, may perhaps be explained on the basis of the sentiment against divorce among the immigrants and among the Catholics who form so large a proportion of the population of that city.

The importance of the economic bond is perhaps also demonstrated by the figures on divorce by occupation. The farmers have

[12] Adapted from Lichtenberger, *op. cit.*, p. 120.

the lowest rate of all, while the highest rates are found among the actors, musicians, and commercial travellers. The farmer is tied to the land and needs a woman to help operate the farm; the other occupations listed are notoriously footloose.

Public sentiment is, perhaps, the strongest of all institutional factors in relation to the dissolving of marriage ties by divorce. Migrations and other sorts of displacement, by liberating persons from the pressure of community disapproval, tend to raise the rate. Thus, in new countries, in pioneer areas and among those classes most affected by economic change divorce is most frequent. To have an effective public opinion holding people to their duty it is important that men should live long in one place and in one group, inheriting traditional ideas and enforcing them upon one another. All breaking up of old associations involves an individualism which is nowhere more active than in family relations.

No further proof of this principle is needed than the statistics of divorce by geographical regions of the United States. These show that there is a solid band of states along the eastern and southern coasts from Maine to Louisiana, with the single exception of Florida, which have rates lower than that for the country as a whole. On the other hand, all the states in the Southwest, in the mountain region, and on the Pacific coast have rates higher than the average for the country as a whole. In the Middle West those states which are mainly agricultural like Wisconsin, Minnesota, and the Dakotas have low rates, while those which are highly industrialized like Ohio, Michigan, Illinois, and Indiana have high rates. The differences are very great. Disregarding Nevada whose rate is eight times that of any other state, the figures run from 348 divorces per 100,000 population in Oklahoma to 41 in New York and none in South Carolina. The total picture is one of traditionalism in the East and Southeast contrasted with the pioneer spirit in the West.

Some will perhaps argue that it is not a matter of public sentiment but merely a matter of the different laws in the different states. Thus South Carolina allows no divorce for any cause. But surely the laws must reflect to some extent the will of the people. And if it is hard to secure a divorce in New York but easy in Oklahoma it must be largely because the residents of those states have differing views with regard to the justifiability of divorce.

A third institutional bond is the church. Christian teaching is the chief source of the ideal of marriage as a sacred and almost indissoluble bond, and church organization has been the main agent in enforcing this ideal. The Roman Catholic Church has never admitted the possibility of absolute divorce, and to her authority, chiefly, is due its rarity in Italy and Spain; while in England, the Established Church, not much behind Rome in strictness, has been perhaps the chief cause of conservatism in English law and sentiment. And the other Protestant churches, though more liberal, are conservative in comparison with the drift of popular feeling. What has weakened this institutional bond is not so much that the churches have relaxed their standards as that the people are less controlled by the disciplinary authority of the church than formerly.

The Broader Implications of Divorce. The evil involved in divorce is largely an old evil in a new form; it is not so much that new troubles have arisen between husband and wife as that a new remedy is sought for old ones. They quarrelled and marriage vows were broken quite as much in former times as now, as much in England today as in America; the main difference is in the outcome.

Moreover, the matter has its brighter side; for divorce, though full of evils, is associated with a beneficent rise in the standing of women, of which it is to a certain degree the cause. The fact that law and opinion now permit women to revolt against the abuse of marital power operates widely and subtly to increase their self-respect and the respect of others for them, and, like the right of workmen to strike, does most of its good without over-exercise.

All competent observers agree that little can be done to reduce family disintegration by tinkering with the divorce laws. People are not likely to remain together if they feel like separating just because the law makes divorce difficult. A much more promising method of approach is through making marriages inherently stable from the beginning. The chief factors here are better training for marriage, laws which will make hasty and ill-considered marriages impossible, and a public sentiment which lays less emphasis than at present upon romantic love as the sole element in choosing a mate.

Whether the family will ever become as well integrated with its fewer functions as it formerly was with its more numerous ones is a moot point. At any rate, it will probably not remain as disorganized as at present. Most people believe that the changes which have caused the decay of old family traditions and disciplines are on the whole progressive and that, once we have passed through this period of falling back on human impulse and reason, there will again develop a sound institutional structure.

STUDY QUESTIONS

1. Differentiate between the family as a primary group and as an institution.
2. In view of the wide diversities in family organization and function in different cultures do you feel we are justified in bringing them all under one conceptual head:—the family? If so, what common factors make this seem legitimate?
3. How was the mediæval family strikingly different from that of our time?
4. How is the present state of the family related to changes in industry and communication? Name several functions that have been lost.
5. What forces have given rise to the so-called "spirit of individualism" in family life?
6. What forces are responsible in your opinion for the declining marriage rate among college graduates, when the general rate shows no diminution?
7. Discuss what you conceive to be the reasons for the sharp decline in the birth rate.
8. Do you believe that the increasing percentage of married women gainfully employed argues more selfishness in modern wives? Give reasons for your view.
9. Discuss the changed relationship of the child to the home in modern life.
10. What is the relative per cent of divorce in the United States as compared with other countries? in the United States today as compared with 50 years ago?
11. What is the geographic distribution of high and low divorce rates among the American states?
12. Explain the personal and institutional causes tending to increase divorce.
13. How would you answer the question, "Is the family degenerating?"

CHAPTER XXVII

EDUCATIONAL INSTITUTIONS

We shall discuss in this chapter institutions of education other than the family. The latter obviously deserves to be included in the general category because of its perpetual importance in the social development of the young, but its trends have already been discussed.

Education in Primitive Life. Since the culture base among primitive peoples is small, there is not the need for complex educational procedure. Most of that which it is necessary to acquire can be "picked up" by the members of the rising generation in the informal life of the family, the play group, and the community. And what little there is in the way of institutional organization varies widely from one group to another. Indeed, it is almost impossible to make valid generalizations about primitive education. In some instances the tribe seems to entrust the passing on of traditional lore to a story-teller or historian; in other cases public assemblies at which tribal ceremonies are performed and tribal deeds glorified play an important rôle; again one may find an elaborate institution of fosterage in which the child is given over to others than his own parents for rearing. Perhaps the primitive institution which has attracted the most attention is the initiation ceremony at puberty. This is a very widespread practice, the aim being to signalize the achievement of maturity by an elaborate ritual which will impress the initiates with the seriousness of their new rôle. Quite frequently there is an extended course of instruction in the moral standards and religious practices of the tribe. Usually the initiation of the boys leads to membership in a secret society of the adult men which acts as an educational agency to some extent. Not infrequently there is a "men's house" set apart for the members of the secret society to which the women and children of the tribe are not admitted. Association of the young men with their elders under these circumstances may take on some of the features of a modern school.[1]

[1] For primitive educational institutions see: Dudley Kidd, *Savage Childhood;* W. D. Hambly, *Origins of Education among Primitive Peoples;* Nathan Miller, *The Child in Primitive Society;* Arthur J. Todd, *The Primitive Family as an Educational Agency.*

It is interesting that educational institutions do not, to quote Margaret Mead, "correlate with the amount of esoteric lore to be learned or the difficulty and intricacy of any technique which is to be handed down from specialists in one generation to novitiates in the next. . . . The formal training given in the Whare Wananga, the sacred college of the Maori, observed all the customary formalities of instruction such as common residence, a teaching class, examinations, and graduation. . . . Among the Zuni, on the other hand, where there is apparently far more ritual to be memorized, no such institution developed. A similar contrast is found between instruction in the art of housebuilding in Samoa and among the Indians of the northwest coast of America. Housebuilding in Samoa although not remarkably complicated was in the hands of a definitely recognized group of craftsmen, and apprenticeship to this group and recognition by it were necessary before an individual could become an accepted housebuilder. No such institution is found on the northwest coast, although more elaborate houses are constructed."[2]

Evolution of Educational Institutions Since the Middle Ages. In order to understand the system of educational institutions which has developed in the last half century it is necessary to obtain a glimpse of the evolution that lies behind. Before the Renaissance the most important agencies of formal education were the monastic schools. These, of course, were designed to train the youths who were entering the church as their profession. The great mass of the people learned what they needed to know at home or through apprenticeship. With the revival of intellectual interest and the founding of universities in the twelfth century, Latin schools of various sorts sprang up which served as a preparation for the universities. But these grammar schools were still for the chosen few who were destined to enter the professions or become civil officials. Slightly later came the forerunners of our modern elementary schools—the vernacular schools for the training of young men to become craftsmen and merchants. These were necessitated by the rise of free cities and the increasing importance of trade and manufacture.

The Renaissance produced a quickening of the mental life which was reflected in part in the establishment of new kinds of schools, notably the *gymnasium* in Germany and the public

[2] Margaret Mead, "Primitive Education," in *Encyclopedia of the Social Sciences.* V, 402.

schools such as Winchester and Eton in England. The Reformation led to a broader development, in as much as the Protestants believed that the surest guide to salvation was the reading of the Bible. Hence the need for universal education in the vernacular. The invention of printing at about the same time did much to make this increased mastery of reading by the masses a possible objective. It was not, however, until the eighteenth century that anything like a system of universal elementary education was anywhere achieved.

The great changes in educational institutions which have taken place in the past 150 years stem from the great social changes wrought by the application of scientific knowledge to the processes of production and communication. The Industrial Revolution coupled with modern methods of transportation has completely altered the economic organization, while ease of communication has given birth to a spirit of nationalism and has made possible large-scale democracy. The working out of these forces has produced a wholly new type of life, a life more complex than any which has gone before. As we saw in Chapter XIII the individual finds it necessary to be at the same time more specialized and more co-operative. The whole situation has become more than ever organic in that each member of society plays a more distinctive rôle and is more inseparably linked with the whole. The rapid changes have also produced much confusion which is in itself an important aspect of the general situation.

The adaptation of educational institutions to this increasingly diversified, confused modern life have illustrated strikingly the tentative character of social process. There have been many trials and not a few errors, but still the half-intelligent, half-blind process of adjustment goes forward. We have by no means reached the end of the road and there is still much cultural lag in education, but today there is a remarkably ramified system which has grown up in response to the demands created by the modern situation.

Change in Control. One of the most important changes is the passing of the great majority of schools from the hands of the church to the state. With the growth of nationalism came the feeling that the state must take the responsibility for so important a task as the education of its citizens. The church, which had been for centuries the only institution with any breadth of vision, had at last to bow before the superior power of this spirit of nationality. At first the state system extended only through the elementary school, the more advanced education being left to academies and colleges under private control. In 1821, however, was established in Boston the first public high school, and at about the same time the first state universities were set up. Thus, in America, the state system is complete from kindergarten through graduate school. But it must be remembered that over half of the students in colleges and universities in the United States are still enrolled in sectarian or other private institutions.

Increasing Amount of Formal Education. Perhaps the most striking change is the great increase in the amount of formal education given. One crude index of this trend is the rapid decline of illiteracy. Although there had been much educational expansion previous to the beginning of the nineteenth century, more than half the people in Western Europe and America at that time were illiterate. Today in the same countries practically all children have a few years of schooling. In the United States in 1930 only about 2 per cent of those between the ages of 10 and 14 were illiterate. It is reliably estimated that the average number of days of schooling in 1800 per adult person was only 80; by 1840 it had risen to 208; by 1870 to 582; by 1890 to 776; by 1920 to 1200; and it has risen more since.[3] The following table shows the percentages of certain age groups attending school in 1930.

TABLE 11

PERCENTAGES ATTENDING SCHOOL ACCORDING TO 1930 CENSUS

Ages	*All*	*Urban*	*Rural*
5–20	69.9	72.3	67.6
Males	70.2	73.7	66.7
Females	69.7	70.9	68.5
5	20.0	29.6	10.8
6	66.3	76.6	56.4
7–13	95.7	97.3	93.3
14 and 15	88.8	92.7	85.0
16 and 17	57.3	60.5	53.9
18–20	21.4	22.5	20.0

The mounting cost of education is another way of showing the growth of educational institutions. Between 1870 and 1930 the

[3] U. S. Bureau of Education, *Biennial Survey of Education*, 1924–26, p. 559.

value of public-school property was multiplied by 44, amounting in the latter year to more than six billion dollars. During the same period annual expenditures multiplied more than 34 times. Even allowing for the decreased value of the dollar, the great increase in national wealth, and the growth in population between these dates, the increase in outlay for education has been tremendous.

The forces which have led to this increased institutional education are so familiar as to need little emphasis. Democracy demands at the very least the literacy of its citizens. Beyond that the intelligent participant in modern life needs to know a great many things with which the ordinary contacts and associations in the family and the community will not supply him. And then there are the greater demands in the way of vocational training which our increasingly specialized industrial order makes. Taken together, these needs seemed so great that compulsory education laws were adopted. Massachusetts was the first of the United States to pass such a law, in 1852. It merely required attendance for eight weeks a year from eight to fourteen. Other states rapidly followed suit, with Mississippi bringing up the rear in 1920. There are wide variations at the present time among the different states both as to the ages within which schooling is compulsory and the minimum number of months in the school year.

Change in Objectives and Curricula. A third important shift has to do with the objectives of formal education and the curriculum to encompass those objectives. To quote Professor Smith: "Quite inevitably the extension of educational privileges from upper to lower social levels led to a differentiation of school purposes. When education was confined to the priesthood its aims were primarily religious and theological. After the admission of the lay nobility the avocational aim became prominent. For the aristocrat, leisure time preponderated; hence he desired an education which would enable him to spend his free hours more pleasantly and profitably. In so far as education was an upper-class privilege, and a badge of distinction within these classes, it must be kept remote from the plebeian mind and free from economic utilitarianism. Its objectives, therefore, clustered about the classics, philosophy, and polite accomplishments. As professional training in law, medicine, and teaching developed, and as the upper commercial classes began to patronize the schools, the idea of education for vocational purposes again became prominent.

Still more of the utilitarian motive came in as the small business proprietors and skilled tradesmen entered the educational clientele, and when the doors of the school were finally opened to the great masses, efficiency became the watchword."[4] Efficiency is coming to be thought of in broad terms, however, and covers the individual's social and political relations as well as his purely economic ones.

Institutions and curricula suited to the needs of modern life have been slowly evolving, though not without much travail. We shall take them up, so far as possible, in the order of the child's progress through them.

The Earliest Years. First, then, is the nursery school. This is a very recent development and only a comparatively small number of them are actually in operation. Two forces are perhaps mainly responsible for this growth—an increasing body of knowledge about infant health and child psychology which has made some believe that home care needs to be supplemented with the more informed care of such an institution, and the decline in the birth rate which has more frequently meant that a child has no playmates in the home.

Though nursery schools are not numerous enough to prove much, the trend toward formal education for the younger age-groups is fully demonstrated by the figures on kindergarten attendance. Between 1890 and 1924 the number of children in kindergartens in the United States multiplied approximately 19 times. This startling increase may in part be laid to the very general feeling that children who have the benefit of kindergarten experience find it easier to adjust to the work of the regular grades. Also, the decline of opportunity for healthful play in and about the home, especially in our cities, has been an important factor.

The Elementary Level. The figures in the above table indicate quite clearly that school attendance at the elementary level is practically universal in this country, as indeed it must be under our laws. Since, however, the elementary school was naturally the first unit developed, the gains in attendance here in the last fifty years are not nearly so great as at other levels. There has been somewhat of a revision of the curriculum in recent years especially in our city school systems, though here also the change is

[4] Walter R. Smith, *Principles of Educational Sociology*, p. 108.

not as great as in secondary and higher education. The religious emphasis which was formerly so strong has largely disappeared while other matters such as citizenship-training are receiving greater attention. Now, as always, however, chief emphasis is on the tool subjects which will enable the child to enter into the intellectual inheritance of the race. With regard to the recent changes the Lynds, comparing the Middletown school curriculum of 1890 with that of 1924, found the following:

"In the culture of thirty-five years ago it was deemed sufficient to teach during the first seven years . . . the following skills and facts, in rough order of importance:

a. The various uses of language (overwhelmingly first in importance).

b. The accurate manipulation of numerical symbols.

c. Familiarity with the physical surroundings of peoples.

d. A miscellaneous group of facts about familiar physical objects about the child—trees, sun, ice, food, and so on.

e. The leisure time skills of singing and drawing.

Today the things for which children are sent to school fall into the following rough order:

a. The same uses of languages.

b. The same uses of numerical figures.

c. Training in patriotic citizenship.

d. The same familiarity with the physical surroundings of peoples.

e. Facts about how to keep well and some physical exercise.

f. The same leisure time skills of singing and drawing.

g. Knowledge and skills useful in sewing, cooking, and using tools about the home for the girls, and, for the boys, an introductory acquaintance with some of the manual skills by which the working class members get their living."[5]

Secondary Education. At the secondary level three developments are particularly important: (1) the great increase in attendance; (2) the changes in curriculum; and (3) the junior high school movement. Under the first head we merely need note that in 1890 only about 6 per cent of the children of the appropriate ages were attending secondary schools, while in 1930 it was more than half.

The high school curriculum has changed more radically than

[5] *Middletown,* pp. 189–90.

that of the elementary school. Here is where the pressure for vocational education has been most strongly felt. No longer is the high school merely a preparatory institution for those going to college. In 1890 Middletown High School students had no option, except that of pursuing Latin or English. In 1924 there were 12 different courses of which 7 were frankly vocational; *viz.*, shorthand, bookkeeping, applied electricity, mechanical drafting, printing, machine shop, manual arts, and home economics. In some cities the movement has resulted in the establishment of separate technical high schools. But supplementing this emphasis upon practical courses has developed a greater concern with effective social and civic participation. Consequently there is a general tendency at least in the urban high schools to make the programme centre more and more around the social sciences and history.

The junior high school, which has had such a rapid spread, attempts to make the transition easier between the prescribed work of the elementary school and the more independent and elective work of the senior high school. By separating the seventh, eighth, and ninth grades in a special institution there is an opportunity to develop an explorative programme which will aid the pupil in finding what his capacities are and which of the differentiated senior high school courses would be most suitable for him.

Other Developments. A special type of institution which has had a great growth in America since the World War is the continuation school. It is designed to meet the needs of the child who has had to go to work in his middle 'teens before he has completed an adequate school training. In 1928 there were 320,000 schools of this type in the United States. In more than half the states attendance is compulsory for certain age groups where the population is sufficiently dense to support such schools. Thus agricultural groups are usually unable to profit by this continuation work. Most frequently four hours of attendance per week is required, though some states, like Wisconsin, enforce a more rigorous requirement. The ages within which attendance is compulsory vary among the states, the upper limit being either 16, 17, or 18.

All through the public school system there has been a tendency to relieve pupils of expense and throw the whole cost of education upon the taxpayer. In most states textbooks are now furnished free and in many instances transportation is by school bus. During the depression beginning in 1929 many schools took the further step of giving lunches to the needy among their pupils.

Rural education has presented a particularly difficult problem. Many of the country school districts have been too poor to have a suitable school plant or to pay for a good teacher. Doctor L. A. King found that in 18 typical Pennsylvania counties in 1920, 25 per cent of the teachers in one-teacher schools had received no secondary education, that only 22 per cent had finished a four-year high school course, and that 76 per cent had received no normal school training. In these same schools 30 per cent of the teachers each year were beginners and another 37 per cent were new to the particular job, leaving only 33 per cent who were in the same school as the previous year.[6] To this handicap of poorly prepared teachers are added serious limitations in the way of curricula and equipment. Most rural schools cannot afford even the simple courses in scientific agriculture which would bring the pupils into a more vital relation with their surroundings. Hence has developed the movement toward consolidated schools in rural areas. Some states, like Indiana, have almost no one-teacher schools left. By consolidating several school districts, building a modern well-equipped schoolhouse, and using buses to transport the children, most of the handicaps of rural education are removed.

Colleges, universities, and professional schools enrolled in 1928 868,793 students in the United States and normal schools add another quarter million. All these institutions together enrolled only 150,000 in 1890. Thus higher education is no longer for the select few. To meet the needs of its enlarged clientele as well as to adjust to the newer fields of knowledge opened up by the advancement of science and the development of large-scale industrial enterprise has required great curricular changes. The demands for more specific professional training brought the differentiation of schools of law, medicine, and engineering. More recently have been added many more special courses, such as agriculture, forestry, business or commerce, dentistry, and education. Even in the liberal-arts colleges there has been a great expansion in the subjects offered, so that the required curriculum

[6] U. S. Bureau of Education, *Bulletin 34*, 1922.

has had to be abandoned and the elective principle put in its place. The growth in collegiate work in modern languages, the natural sciences, history, and the social sciences has been tremendous.

There is a trend in all our educational institutions to make the classroom procedure less formal. This is probably a result of two forces: the general philosophy of individualism and self-expression which flowered with the French Revolution and has been strongly affecting human affairs ever since; and modern psychology which has proved the great importance of interest in the learning process. Various "new schools" have sprung up which carry this principle to the extreme of having no formal class work at all, while even the more conservative institutions are experimenting with the "socialized recitation" and the "project method."

Certain new sets of activities in addition to those added to the curriculum seem to have come into educational institutions at all levels in response to the changed conditions of life. We will discuss (1) extra-curricular activities, (2) educational guidance, (3) school health work, and (4) mental hygiene.

Extra-Curricular Activities. Starting at the college level, extra-curricular activities have come to flourish vigorously in our secondary schools and are now found to some extent even in the elementary grades. They tend to be supervised by the educational personnel, especially at the lower levels. Their development is probably due in part to the decline of the home as an economic unit, since children, having fewer chores to do around the house, naturally are eager to express themselves in some way during their leisure hours. Athletics, student publications, student self-government, musical clubs, and the like furnish interesting outlets for their energies. These activities are probably also in part a reaction to an educational régime which traditionally has given the young people little opportunity for self-expression in the academic work.

Participation in extra-curricular activities is very widespread, especially at the high school level. A recent study of California high schools indicated that 68 per cent of the pupils took part in some form of these activities.[7] Much has been written about them, both favorable and unfavorable, but the indications are that they

[7] Study by Miss A. L. Dement cited in Smith, *Principles of Educational Sociology*, p. 685. Is should perhaps be pointed out that achievement in extra-curricular activities is more easily appreciated by the general public than achieve-

will continue to play an important rôle in our educational institutions for some time to come. There is at present a tendency to incorporate them more and more into the regular curriculum by giving credit points for satisfactory participation.

Educational Guidance and Hygiene Programmes. With the differentiation of curricula in the senior high school and the opportunity for more or less exploration in the junior high school there has developed a strong movement for educational guidance. This work is entrusted either to specialists or to teachers or administrative officers particularly well qualified for the task. Not only are the pupils advised as to which courses they are probably best fitted to pursue but they may also receive counsel regarding participation in extra-curricular activities. In many large city school systems the guidance effort culminates in a placement bureau which tries to find suitable jobs for those who are leaving the school to work, or to secure entrance to the proper higher educational institution for those who are able and qualified to pursue their training further.

The school nurse, the school doctor, and the school dentist are now part of the regular personnel of our more advanced elementary and secondary school systems and at the college level there is usually complete health service. The reason for the taking over of this function by educational institutions is probably that medical knowledge has gone ahead so fast as to outstrip the family's or the individual's appreciation of it. Hence, if the young person is to have the benefits which can accrue from this knowledge, the school, as the most far-reaching of our institutions, must assume the burden.

As a sort of connecting link between this interest in health on the one hand, and the educational and vocational guidance movement already mentioned on the other, there have grown up measures for dealing with the "problem child." Here the chief concern is mental health. At the elementary level the visiting-teacher movement seems the most promising method of handling these cases. The visiting teacher is a trained social worker who attempts to obtain a complete picture of the case in hand by consulting with the parents in the home, observing the child in school,

ment in scholarship because the returns are obvious in the short run. Football victories and class plays are more tangible than intellectual development. There is also a feeling among many youngsters that these activities furnish a more practical preparation for making a living than the academic work.

talking with his classroom teacher, and so on. When she has grasped the relevant facts about the child and his background she makes a diagnosis and then tries to marshal all the forces possible to remove the causes of the troublesome behavior. At the college level mental hygiene service in the hands of competent psychiatrists is being introduced in many institutions to achieve the same result. The need to which this type of work corresponds is that for giving young people well-integrated lives in a time of much confusion and strain. Never before, perhaps, has there been such rapid change, and the result is that institutions are frequently so ill-adjusted to one another as to work at cross purposes. And the theatre of the conflict is the individual mind.

Formalism and Disorganization in Education. The general situation of our schools and colleges is an odd mixture of formalism and disorganization. Those who are enthusiastic for change find a great deal that seems to them out of date and formal, while those whose main concern is stability see an alarming disorganization. The truth is that in some places and in some aspects of the institution the shell of out-worn mechanism is persisting beyond its function, while in other places and in other aspects the old has been discarded and a period of trial and error has supervened in the attempt to find something better adapted. In few cases has there as yet developed a sound reorganization.

In the more backward parts of the country there are many schools that have the same curriculum and the same classroom procedure as fifty years ago. There has been no attempt to readjust to the needs and demands of modern life. On the other hand, some of our more enterprising school systems have pressed ahead enthusiastically, embracing new ideas in curriculum and procedure with a minimum of critical care. In striving to meet new requirements these schools have too commonly extended their system rather than their vital energies; they have perhaps grown more rapidly in the number of students, the variety of subjects taught, and in other numerable particulars, than in the inner and spiritual life, the ideals, the traditions, and the *personnel* of the teaching force. As in other expanding institutions life is spread out rather thin.

In our higher education there is a somewhat similar mixing of new materials, imperfectly integrated, with fragments of a decadent system. The old classical discipline has gone and it is perhaps best that it has, but surely nothing satisfactory has arisen to take its place.

Among the many things that might be said in this connection we will touch upon only one consideration, generally overlooked, namely, the value of *common* intellectual attainments, corresponding in this respect to what used to be known as "the education of a gentleman." Since the decay of the classical culture our higher education, notwithstanding so much that is excellent in it, has had practically no common content to serve as a medium of communication and spiritual unity among the educated class. In this connection as in so many others the question arises whether even an inadequate intellectual whole is not better than none at all.

If one has an assembly of university graduates before him, what, in the way of like-mindedness, can he count on their having? Certainly not Latin, much less Greek; he would be rash indeed to venture a quotation in these tongues, unless for mystification; nor would allusions to history or literature be much safer. The truth is that few of the graduates will have done serious work outside of their specialty; and the main thing they have in common is a collective spirit animated by the recollection of football victories and the like.

It may be that we are participating in the rise of a new type of intellectual heritage which shall revise rather than abandon the old traditions, and whose central current will perhaps be a study of the large principles of human life and of their expression in history, art, literature, and religion. And the belief that sociology is to have a part in this may not be entirely a matter of special predilection.

Adult Education. In the field of adult education we will content ourselves with mention of three of the most important movements—university extension, evening schools, and correspondence schools. These have all developed within the past fifty years and represent different adaptations to modern needs. University extension courses enroll about 200,000 annually in the United States. The instruction is given to qualified non-resident students either through extramural class work or through correspondence. The need here is for further knowledge on the part of those already out in the world, a need which the rapid changes of modern life make pressing.[8]

[8] For a survey of university extension work, see Alfred L. Hall-Quest, *The University Afield.*

Evening schools reach a less well-educated group than university extension. For the most part they are attended by adults from the industrial groups in our large cities. Usually the regular school buildings are used and teachers selected from the regular school personnel have charge of the classes. The work is mainly in the tool subjects and in vocational specialties.[9]

We have finally the correspondence school which has had a mushroom growth since 1873. All such schools in this country now enroll about two million yearly, which is more than twice as many as are registered in colleges and universities. A very small percentage of the work of these schools is broadly educational; rather their courses are for the most part narrowly vocational. The median age of the students is 26, and 83 per cent of them have had an eighth-grade education. They are thus fairly intelligent people who are seeking to better themselves vocationally by further training. However, this is not a very efficient means of accomplishing their purpose, for only about 6 per cent of the students in commercial correspondence schools complete the courses for which they have enrolled.[10]

The tremendous development of educational institutions which we have sketched in such brief compass here is obviously an illustration of the tentative method of social growth. Modern life has made many new needs felt and slowly and rather painfully human organization is trying to meet those needs. Old institutions change their traditional ways and take on new functions; new institutions gradually emerge, some of them to prove well adapted and to last, others to prove maladjusted and to pass from the scene. The whole picture is one of slow, uncertain, largely blind, but in the long run, adaptive, organization.

STUDY QUESTIONS

1. What differences do you find between educational institutions in primitive and modern life? What are the reasons for these differences?
2. Relate the trends in educational institutions discernible between the end of the middle ages and 1800 to underlying social forces.
3. Discuss the importance of the Industrial Revolution and modern

[9] For information on evening schools, see O. D. Evans, *Educational Opportunities for Young Workers.*

[10] For information on these schools, see John S. Noffsinger, *Correspondence Schools, Lyceums, Chautauquas.*

communication in producing the contemporary system of educational institutions.

4. Compare the amount of institutional education being received in the United States today with that received a century ago.
5. What are some of the newer tendencies in the curriculum of the elementary and secondary schools? Show that they are attempts to meet new needs.
6. What do you think of the recent tendency to emphasize extracurricular activities as educational agencies?
7. What are the social factors which have brought about the development of educational guidance, school health work, and mental hygiene programmes?
8. Do you agree that our educational institutions show a mixture of formalism and disorganization? Explain fully.
9. What are some of the developments in the field of adult education during the past 50 years? What has caused the rather sudden interest in this field?

CHAPTER XXVIII

THE CHURCH

The Problem of Religious Institutions. In religion our day is one of confusion and falling back upon human nature. The problem is to understand the reasons for this confusion and to appreciate the personal and institutional disorganization inevitable in the circumstances.

What is religion?

Religion is both an intellectual and an emotional experience, intensely personal and sharply to be distinguished from theology, on the one hand, and the church, on the other. As thought, religion is belief regarding the power underlying life and our relation to it. As feeling it is a various body of passion and sentiment associated with this belief—the sense of sin, perhaps, and dread, awe, reverence, love, and faith. Obviously, this is very different from theology, which is a system of theories about the nature of God, and from the church, which is the institutionalized totality of worshippers, forms, and symbols through which religion attains permanence and organization.

It is the cultural form, *i.e.,* the church, which determines the level, so to speak, on which the religious experience shall function. The symbols used and the meanings and values attached to them are supplied by the group culture. There is no such thing as a religion achieved *de novo* by the individual mind, any more than there is a mathematics which any individual invents. The religious life always rests upon a somewhat elaborate social structure—not necessarily a church, but something which does in fact what the church aims to do. The sentiments now possible to us are subtly evoked and nourished by language, music, ritual, and the other time-wrought symbols. And even more obviously are ideas—of God and of the larger being, of religious observances, government, and duty—matters of communal and secular growth.

In other words, religion as it appears with us is the outcome of a long cultural evolution. When did that evolution begin and why?

Origins of Religion. Traditional theories of the origins of particular religions seek them in *revelation.* Thus Judaism teaches that the Mosaic code was revealed by God to Moses; Mohammedanism presents itself as the revelations of the Angel Gabriel to Mohammed; and Christianity began with the teachings of Jesus who, according to the tradition, was himself divine.

In contrast to such theories philosophers and scientists trace the origins of religious phenomena in general to one or more of three kinds of sources: the *self-interest* of priests and rulers; *common psychological predispositions;* and *primitive attitudes.*

Self-interest.—That religion is a device of rulers and priests for their own benefit is a very old theory. Plato in the *Laws* mentions it as among the teachings of the sophists, and Cicero and other ancient writers touch on the same idea. In the sixth century B.C. heterodox Hindus were saying that all religions had been invented by priests for their own profit, and European heretics repeated the same idea centuries later.

Psychological Predispositions.—Many writers have derived religion from a universal "religious instinct." It is true that religious phenomena are very widespread, but no psychologist has ever isolated such an instinct. That there are always instinctive elements in religious behavior is quite a different proposition. Some anthropologists such as Wissler and Goldenweiser emphasize the biological and psychological factors in religion rather than the cultural. Thus Wissler includes religion in his universal culture pattern which he believes is based on biological predispositions. Goldenweiser has put forth a theory that the root of religion is the "religious thrill," *i.e.,* the thrill that results from the recognition of some "mysterious potency" in the environment.

Psychiatrists tend to see religion as "man's supreme method of sublimating the repressions of infancy and childhood and gratifying the unfulfilled desires of maturity and old age through the use of sacred rituals and fancies."[1] Religion may thus be regarded as a kind of weapon with which to combat the confusion of the inner thought-world; or, from another point of view, one method of overcoming man's sense of helplessness in the face of the universe.

Primitive Attitudes.—Certain French writers under the lead of Durkheim developed a theory that religion originated in the heightened emotional experiences of primitive group assemblies which first gave men the idea of the different, the peculiarly

[1] Edward J. Kempf, *Psychopathology,* St. Louis, 1920, p. 72.

potent, the sacred.[2] By association this feeling came to be attached to nearby plants and animals which were thus made into totems, or group symbols, and eventually the sense of group potency was expanded into the concept of *mana,* or non-personal force, which was probably one of the earliest of religious ideas. This theory is important in its emphasis on the group, but probably errs in assuming that the group was the only source of sanctity and that totemism was the earliest form of all religions.

Many other sources of religion have been suggested by students of primitive cultures. Sir Edward Tylor and Herbert Spencer thought *animism,* or the belief in spirits, was the root of all religion. Max Müller found the origin in *naturalism,* the tendency of savages to fear and revere natural objects of unusual impressiveness or power such as mountains, thunderstorms, etc. Sir J. G. Frazer, the author of *The Golden Bough,* saw religion as the child of *magic*. Other writers take *ancestor worship* as the starting point.[3]

All in all, four things seem to be fairly clear concerning religious origins:

1. Religion is very old, one of our oldest cultural forms, probably 25,000 and possibly many hundreds of thousands of years old.

2. As magic or as religion proper the religious impulse has expressed itself in every culture.

3. It has taken many forms.

4. No single theory of origins explains all the facts. Inspiration, the self-interest of priests and rulers, instinctive cravings, group influence, animism, naturalism, magic, ancestor worship, all may have had a share in its beginnings. Bye and large, religion seems to have originated in man's effort to adjust to what the Lynds call the "too-bigness" of life.

The Evolution of Religious Phenomena. If the theory of evolution is correct, there was probably a time when there was no religion at all just as there was no culture in general.

The first and most primitive level of religious phenomena seems to have been that of *animatism,* or the belief in some impersonal power without any theorizing about the nature of that power. This is the level of the Melanesian *mana,* the Algonquin *manitou,* the

[2] Emile Durkheim, *Elementary Forms of the Religious Life.*

[3] For a brief discussion of various theories, see E. Washburn Hopkins, *Origin and Evolution of Religion,* New Haven, 1923.

Iroquoian *orenda,* the Siouan *wakan,* all expressions symbolizing belief in some mysterious potency in nature.

A step beyond this is *animism.* Animism thinks of the mysterious potency as the property of spirits, usually believed to reside in a definite thing or place. Thus, the wood-sprite of the Trobriand Islanders lives in certain trees, and the terrible flying witches of the same people always come from the southern half of the island or from the east.

Eventually men begin to think of certain spirits as gods. "A god is a spirit endowed with a distinct personality and the object of a cult, as exercising certain supernatural functions in nature or human life."[4] Deified heroes and exalted nature spirits become gods. This, the level of *polytheism,* is the typical level of the early civilizations just as animitism and animism are the levels of savagery.

Gradually, however, the growing realization of the unity of life tends to narrow the field: one god is exalted as king over the rest, as with the Roman Zeus; or all the gods are identified with some one as in the Hindu Vedas; or one national god such as the vengeful, tribal Yahveh of the Jews is transformed by the labors of prophets into the one God, "creator and ruler of all things, the God of social justice, mercy, and love."

Thus out of *monolatry,* or the worship of one god among other possible gods, there emerges *monotheism,* or the belief that there is only one god to be worshipped. Under the leadership of the prophets, the ancient Hebrews were the first people in the world to reach this level of religious development. More than that, under the leadership of the later prophets, particularly Isaiah, they were the first people in the world to conceive of God as essentially an ethical being, righteous, just, and lovable.

Whether or not associated with monotheism, the ethical level of religious development is a relatively late achievement. There are five great ethical religions in the world today—in the order of their development, Judaism, Confucianism, Buddhism, Christianity, and Mohammedanism. All are products of the east or near-east; and all appeared (or reached a definitely socialized stage as in the case of Judaism) in the comparatively short span of 1372 years between the birth of Isaiah, 740 B.C., and the death of Mohammed, 632 A.D.

[4] L. T. Hobhouse, *Morals in Evolution,* New York, 1916, p. 402.

The World's Religions. About 37 per cent of the world's population can be classed as Christian, 48 per cent are distributed among seven great non-Christian religions—Judaism, Mohammedanism, Buddhism, Hinduism, Confucianism, Taoism, and Shintoism—and the remaining 15 per cent are animists or nature-worshippers.[5]

Of the Christians, about 331,000,000, or 48 per cent, are Roman Catholics; about 144,000,000, or 21 per cent, are Orthodox, or Greek, Catholics; and about 207,000,000, or 31 per cent, are Protestants.

The Growth of Christianity. It is unnecessary here to recount in detail the historical fortunes of Christianity: How a few followers were left after the departure of their Master; how a Pharisee named Paul took the heritage of this little Semitic sect and transformed it into a world-challenging religion; how that religion, the faith of slaves and outcasts at first, became in time the religion of the dying Roman Empire and lived on to conquer the conquering Teutons; how the Bishop of Rome became eventually the head of the Roman Catholic Church, on occasion the mightiest prince in Christendom; and how, in the end, abuse of power by the Popes led to the Reformation and the division of western Christendom into Catholic and Protestant camps. Neither is it necessary to do more than mention the diffusion of Catholicism to the New World following Columbus,[6] and the heroic work of the Catholic missionaries over a span of more than two centuries in Florida, New Mexico, California, and Canada. Until approximately the latter part of the nineteenth century the story of Christianity among the whites in what is now the United States is mainly the story of the various Protestant sects whose beginnings on this continent were protected by the English flag.[7]

[5] In a world population estimated at 1,849,500,000 in 1928, 682,400,000 were classed as Christians; 350,600,000 as Confucianists, and Taoists; 230,150,000 as Hindus; 209,020,000 as Mohammedans; 150,180,000 as Buddhists; 25,000,000 as Shintoists; 15,630,000 as Jews; and 186,520,000 as animists and miscellaneous.

[6] Catholicism reached the New World nearly four centuries before Columbus. There is a record in the Vatican of the appointment of a Roman Catholic bishop of Greenland, one Eric Gnupson or Upsi, in 1112, and the last entry relating to the ill-fated see of Greenland coincides almost exactly with the start of Columbus's expedition, 1492. See Thomas O'Gorman, *A History of the Roman Catholic Church in the United States,* American Church History Series, Vol. IX, New York, 1895, p. 6.

[7] At the time of the Revolution the Catholic population was less than 30,000 in a total population of nearly 4,000,000. The influx of immigrants from southeastern Europe after 1880 was largely responsible for the large increases in Catholic population added to the earlier increments from the Irish.

At the outbreak of the Revolution Protestantism in one form or another was the recognized state religion in nine of the thirteen colonies.

The Church in the United States.[8] The history of the Protestant churches in the United States has been marked by great fluctuations in popular interest and by marked cultural lag in readjusting to changed cultural conditions. The confusion and disorganization of the present can be traced largely to the tardiness with which the church is responding to the new social forces about it. Yet the church has passed through periods of less popularity than it enjoys today.

Fluctuations in Popular Interest. In early New England church membership was practically universal. While this was by no means true in Virginia and the other colonies, the seventeenth century was characterized by greater religious interest than marked the beginning of the eighteenth. Indifference became very widespread and lasted until the first Great Awakening which began in 1735 with the preaching of Jonathan Edwards. After a few years of revived interest, however, political events rather than the problem of the hereafter began to occupy men's minds and by the time of the Revolution it was estimated that not more than 4 per cent of the population of the colonies belonged to any church.[9] This condition continued for another twenty years and inspired many thoughtful observers with pessimism concerning the future of the church. Chief Justice Marshall was among those who said that "the church is too far gone ever to be revived." Yet in 1796 the second awakening began under the stimulus of the teaching of President Timothy Dwight of Yale and of a number of popular preachers in the West. The first awakening had led to the founding of Princeton college; the second led to the invention of the campmeeting and to an increased interest in the religious welfare of the settlers who were beginning to pour into the northwest territory.

At various times since 1800 waves of religious enthusiasm

[8] For the history of religion and religious institutions in America, see Thomas O'Gorman, *A History of the Roman Catholic Church in the United States*, American Church History Series, Vol. IX, New York, 1895; Leonard W. Bacon, *A History of American Christianity*, New York, 1897; Henry K. Rowe, *The History of Religion in the United States*, New York, 1924; William W. Sweet, *The Story of Religions in America*, New York, 1930; Woodbridge Riley, *American Thought from Puritanism to Pragmatism*, New York, 1915, etc.

[9] Henry Kalloch Rowe, *The History of Religion in the United States*, New York, 1924, p. 104.

have swept over local areas, particularly western New York where Mormonism, Spiritualism, and a number of other new faiths appeared.

As against a popular membership of 4 per cent in 1776, approximately 48 per cent of the population were listed as church members in the federal religious census of 1926, or, more accurately, 55 per cent of all persons 13 years of age and over. About 30 per cent of the church members 13 years old and over were Roman Catholics, 65 per cent were Protestants, and 5 per cent Jews.[10]

Readjustment to Cultural Changes. The current confusion and disorganization in the church can be traced to maladjustments due mainly to seven causes:[11] (1) science; (2) new theological ideas; (3) the growth of cities; (4) social reform; (5) the continental Sabbath; (6) changing morals; and (7) decline in supernaturalism.

In order to understand the present condition of the church it will be necessary to analyze each of these factors in some detail.

1. **The Impact of Science on the Church.** Probably the most revolutionary effect of science upon the church has been the tendency to substitute the idea of universal law for the old idea of an arbitrary God. In effect, science has outlawed miracle.[12]

As Robert A. Millikan, Nobel prize-winner and one of America's greatest physicists, has said,

"The idea of God, or Nature, or the Universe, whatever term you prefer, is not a being of caprice or whim as had been the case in all the main body of thinking of the ancient world, but is, instead, a God who rules through law, or a Nature capable of being depended upon, or a Universe of consistency, or orderliness and of the beauty that goes with order—that the idea has *made* modern science."[13]

It is against this conception of God and the Universe that Fundamentalism has unfurled its banners. The five fundamentals

[10] Estimates by C. Luther Fry for The President's Research Committee on Social Trends, 1932. *Recent Social Trends in the United States,* Vol. II, Chap. XX.

[11] In their study of Middletown in 1923–24 the Lynds found that the church had changed less since 1890 than any other institution in the city. Cf. *Middletown,* p. 497.

[12] The story of the church's resistance to this revolution in ideas has been ably told in A. D. White, *A History of the Warfare of Science with Theology in Christendom,* New York and London, 1896.

[13] *Science and the New Civilization,* New York, 1930, p. 177.

as laid down by the leaders of the movement in 1910 are: the Virgin Birth; the actual, physical Resurrection; the inerrancy of Scriptures; the substitutionary theory of the Atonement; and the imminent, physical Second Coming of Jesus Christ. Since each one of these doctrines posits an interruption, or break, in the sequences of cause and effect as science has observed them, scientists and many other religious people who take the scientific point of view have been unable to accept them.

Thus the church faces a problem of coming to terms with the scientific conception of the uniformity of nature.

2. **The Higher Criticism and the New Theology.** As one historian of the church has expressed it, the evolution of religion in America is a process by which it has been rationalizing its doctrine, socializing its practices, and spiritualizing its conception of the world.[14] We have already pointed out the need of rationalizing church doctrine to take account of modern science. In later sections we shall find church practices expanding to meet the demands of new social situations. For the moment we shall confine ourselves to the spiritualizing process in theology.

Under the lead of German scholars like Harnack the higher criticism revealed the fact that Christian tradition has not been a static thing, given once for all, but has passed through an interesting evolution during which, for example, the conception of Christ and His mission changed radically.

In accordance with such studies modern theologians have worked out new theories of the nature of God and of the meaning of Christ's message.

Schleiermacher, for example, stresses the fact that the great work of Christ in redemption is the transformation of character rather than any essentially supernatural benefit. Others have developed a theological position from which the modernist looks upon God as immanent and as ruling through law, not arbitrary will; a theology which humanizes Jesus and reinterprets His work. As a recent expression of this tendency has come the New Humanism which seeks God only in man's own will-to-goodness and addresses its prayers to the Spirit of On-Going Humanity. Fundamentalists see little difference between this and outright atheism, which, by the way, became an organized movement in 1925 and claimed 100,000 members by 1927.[15]

[14] Rowe, *op. cit.*, pp. 122 ff.

[15] Organized atheism—the Association for the Advancement of Atheism—demands the ultimate abolition of churches, and in the meantime advocates full

Such tendencies have created serious problems of disorganization within the Protestant churches themselves. Ministers and laymen reared in the old theology find it difficult to understand the newer movements while millions of people who have accepted the more liberal point of view recoil from the formalism which they think they see in the old tradition.

One result of all this has been a decrease in the emphasis on sectarianism. For at least a generation the tendency has been toward co-operation at least, if not unity, rather than further division and schism. Yet in 1926 the federal religious census enumerated no less than 213 different denominations maintaining more than 232,000 churches.

The decline in denominational emphasis is making it possible to apply business methods to church organization, but many small communities are still over-churched while whole sections of certain industrial cities are practically neglected.

3. **The Church in the Changing City.** Until about 1890 Protestant churches in cities seemed to be thriving. Then subtle changes set in. The old church members began moving away from neighborhoods invaded by newcomers. Business began encroaching on former "residential neighborhoods." In a few years many a city church found itself stranded in an area of deterioration or surrounded by immigrants who did not even speak the language of the minister. In this situation most churches sold out and followed their retreating congregations. Studies in St. Louis and other cities show two, three, and sometimes four migrations in a century—usually in the direction of the middle-class residential districts. The net result is that urban Protestantism now finds itself at a disadvantage in the competition for the industrial workers whose needs it has tended to neglect.[16]

Along with these readjustments to population movements have come readjustments in programme. Douglas in an intensive study of 26 representative urban churches in 1925–26 found that the average church was carrying on 30 activities, but that there were

taxation of church property. *Cf.* Homer Croy, "Organized Atheism in Our Midst," *World's Work,* May, 1927.

[16] The larger the community the smaller the percentage of church attendance, according to figures gathered by Mr. Roger W. Babson. In incorporated areas and villages under 2500 population the churches show an average attendance of 71 per cent; places 3500 to 5000, 66 per cent; 5000–10,000, 46 per cent; 10,000 to 50,000, 42 per cent; 50,000 and over, 30 per cent. *The Literary Digest,* August 6, 1932, p. 22.

60 different kinds of activities represented in all.[17] To meet a more complex situation in the cities the churches have been driven to develop a fuller programme, in many cases becoming "institutional churches" with activities available every day in the week.

4. **Social Reform.** During the Middle Ages men looked for happiness to the next world and accepted this life as a mere preparation for the hereafter. Crime, poverty, and suffering were interpreted either as probationary trials of the spirit or as punishments for sin. The church confined its ministrations to the individual soul.

As the Middle Ages passed away the first social condition to attract the attention of any religious body as a problem for the Christian conscience was slavery. In 1688 the English Quakers denounced this institution, and within a century were joined by the Methodists, the Baptists, and eventually by the Unitarians, and practically all the other denominations. By 1830 the churches in America were virtually unanimous in opposing slavery. Within a few years, however, conditions in the South had so changed as to swing the Southern ministers to the defense of their "peculiar institution"—a right-about-face that broke the Methodist and Baptist churches into Northern and Southern groups and estranged Presbyterians and Episcopalians North and South for two generations.

In 1811 the Presbyterians began the temperance movement which quickly became so powerful as to drive alcohol from the private home and thus open the way for the commercialization of liquor in the saloon. After the Civil War the liquor trade grew so rapidly as to alarm the churches. The result was a reorganization of the temperance movement, first in the Women's Christian Temperance Union and later in the Anti-Saloon League. It was the latter organization, with the backing of the Protestant churches, that was largely instrumental in securing the adoption of the 18th Amendment.

With the increase in industrialization that followed the Civil War the startling contrasts of wealth and poverty in the cities began to trouble the Christian conscience. Seeley's *Ecce Homo*, published in 1867, was probably the first clear expression of the modern emphasis on the social aspects of religion. In this awakening of the churches to the meaning of Christianity in an industrial

[17] Harlan Paul Douglass, *The Church in the Changing City*, New York, 1927, p. 445.

order some of the leaders were Washington Gladden, a Congregational minister of Columbus, Ohio, Walter Rauschenbusch, of the Rochester Theological Seminary, Shailer Matthews, of the University of Chicago, Graham Taylor, of the Chicago Theological Seminary, and Harry F. Ward, of the Union Theological Seminary. Between 1900 and 1930 practically all the leading churches adopted a "social creed," and in 1931 the Pope issued an Encyclical denouncing the selfish concentration of wealth. On the practical side the churches have been participating more and more widely in reform movements. It was, for example, the Interchurch World Movement investigation of the steel strike of 1919 that opened the way for a shorter work day in that industry.

This tendency of many ministers to meddle with the here and now instead of confining their interests to the hereafter has pained many good and prosperous parishioners. Hence the problem which the churches are facing today: Shall they merely preach the gospel of individual salvation—in which case the industrial masses show little interest? Or shall they go in for social reform even at the risk of alienating their chief contributors as the steel strike investigation alienated the financial backers of the Interchurch World Movement? The very demand of the Christian conscience that the social order shall square with the teachings of Jesus thus becomes itself a disorganizing influence for many devout Christians.

5. **The Church Loses Its Monopoly of the Sabbath.** Under the Puritan régime the church enjoyed a virtual monopoly of the Sabbath. Church attendance was obligatory in the early days of New England, and laws protecting the sanctity of the Sabbath remain scattered through our statute books. In Philadelphia at one time, for example, the churches had the legal right to stretch chains across the streets to stop all traffic during the time of worship.

While the early Puritanism had long been weakening, it was probably the Civil War that brought the first widespread loosening of the old restrictions. Not only was it impossible to enforce Blue Laws in the army, but back home the demand for news from the front on Sunday as well as on week days broke down the old taboo on secular reading on the Lord's Day and opened the way for the modern Sunday newspaper. After the war the influx of immigrants, untrained in the Puritan tradition and bringing with them the conception of Sunday as a day of relaxation and merrymaking, rapidly transformed the American Sabbath. The growth of co-operative services as cities increased in size also made it increasingly inconvenient to suspend all economic activities one day in seven. By 1880 even the leading advocates of the old-fashioned Sabbath realized that it was impossible to enforce their ideas in the large cities, although for more than another generation sporadic attempts continued to prohibit baseball and other Sunday amusements in the rural areas.

The net result is that today the church's monopoly of the Sabbath has been broken and it must compete with the Sunday newspaper, the automobile, the motion-picture show, the golf club, the radio, and various other forms of amusement and relaxation. Inevitably church attendance has suffered and many ministers have not yet adjusted themselves to a situation in which survival seems to depend on their ability to meet vivid and exciting competition on somewhat equal terms.

6. **Changing Morals.** The social and intellectual transformations which we have been tracing have had their repercussions on the moral life. Traditionally the Christian code has belittled sex and sanctioned large families and unbroken marriage. Discoveries in modern psychology have, however, shown the importance of sexual adjustment for individual mental health, and the economic liberation of women has brought in its train a fivefold increase in divorce since 1870. Birth control from being an unmentionable mystery for a century has emerged into the light of controversy and the falling birth rate testifies to its wide acceptance by millions among the middle and upper classes.

The sharp decline in the birth rate since the World War, while not all attributable to birth control, is one of the most revolutionary things that has ever happened in America. It has been impossible for the church to avoid the issue. The result has been a division of forces: The Catholic Church has officially condemned birth control; the Episcopal Church, on the other hand, has given it guarded approval. Other denominations find it a subject fruitful of controversy. Birth control like divorce remains among the new things toward which the church is being forced to clarify its position in the light of new conditions.

An interesting side-light has been thrown on the moral confusion in which the church must work by an experiment reported by Professor Pitkin. Having asked 500 men and women of superior intelligence, education, and educational background to rank the Ten Commandments in order of their importance, he found

> 102 individuals denying all moral significance to the first four, or religious commandments . . . 59 persons holding these same commandments high above all others as moral guides. And . . . 339 persons who accept all ten commandments as having some moral value but rank the religious well below the social.[18]

In other words, this test revealed three moral philosophies among that group of 500, running the whole gamut from the fundamentalist position to that of the extreme modernist who sees no value in the religious precepts.

Thus the church and its members have been driven to face far-reaching readjustments: Is God arbitrary or a God of law? What is the essence of Christ's message? What is the function of religion under urban conditions? How can the church meet Sunday competition? Can the church accept a revolution in morals? Questions of this kind are bringing confusion to many congregations and to many individuals. Nor does the matter end there: In every culture there is always a certain strain for consistency in the *mores,* a certain pressure to eliminate or shut out any beliefs or practices that do not fit into the prevailing pattern of the time. Thus the automobile culture presses for the elimination of unpaved roads and right-angle turns, vestiges of the horse culture; and efficiency experts from the business culture challenge college professors, whose creativeness depends on leisure, to account for their time in hours-per-day. In the same way the whole scientific-machine culture of our time bears hard on the supernaturalism of the old religious tradition.

7. **The Decline of Supernaturalism.** Undeniably the pressures of our practical lives—the constant presence of automobiles, radio sets, vacuum cleaners, airplanes, telephones, and all the rest—tend constantly toward naturalism rather than supernaturalism. More and more are modern inventions and the intricacies of modern culture forcing men and women to focus attention on this world and its workings. Day in and day out we cannot help observing that the engineer and the mechanic get results by a careful adaptation of means to ends; that the physician relieves suffering by

[18] Walter B. Pitkin, "Grading the Ten Commandments," as condensed in *The Reader's Digest,* Nov., 1926, p. 401, from *The Century,* October, 1926.

chemicals and the control of infection; that even moral behavior seems to be a matter of early habit-formation and social opportunities. Nowhere in the life of the average man or woman for six days a week is any break observable in the iron-bound sequences of cause and effect.

Inevitably this constant drumming on the here and now for six days a week must have its slow effect on the mind-set, or attitude, with which people face the seventh. Slowly the reality of the other world recedes in consciousness. It has by no means vanished. In most churches it still constitutes an essential element of the faith. But, unless it is fortified by a powerful tradition which sharply separates reason from faith, interest in things unseen must inevitably languish in the face of a triumphant material culture which claims so vastly much more of the average man's life than does the church.

It is precisely here that the church as an organized social body faces its basic problem: While the developing intricacies of modern life make its ethical and critical functions, *i.e.*, its socal functions, more important than ever, the whole tendency of that life is to subordinate supernaturalism—in other words, to reduce further and further the rewards that the church can promise to the individual for himself.

Now traditionally the church promised the individual eternal life and everlasting happiness if he would only obey its teachings. No more stupendous reward could be imagined. Beside it all earthly things shrank into insignificance. But only as he kept contact with the church could the individual attain that glittering prize. The Pope as God's vicar on earth held the keys to Heaven and only through the ministrations of the ordained priesthood could sinners reach salvation.

The Reformation changed all that. While still holding out the eternal reward as before, the weight of Protestant authority now said, "It is the Book and not the Church that is sacred. No man need wait on another to be saved." Thus the Reformation by substituting the Sacred Book for the Sacred Church made the church less essential than it had been before. And the process then begun has not yet ended. Modernism would replace the Sacred Book with something called Universal Law. And for the ultra-modernist there is even no question of life hereafter and no suggestion that the church is essential to the individual, however valuable it may claim to be to him and to the community. Hence the problem: Can a church which promises mainly a collective benefit instead of an individual one motivate individual participation? How far can the theoretical value of the church as a social institution and a centre of sociability and mental hygiene for the individual member overbalance a decline in its emphasis on supernatural values? Such a decline has already set in, and in accordance with the principle of consistency in the *mores* there is no reason to expect it to stop in the near future.

In fact the vanguard of the modernist position, the New Humanists, definitely turn their backs on the next world, refuse to stress questions of immortality, profess no interest in the problem of God, and pin their faith on personal insight and social reform. The same influences are at work in many denominations: "Peace with science," "Religion in the making," "Social service"—these are the slogans of a faith striving to be consistent with the world in which it finds itself.

The Dilemma of the Liberal Church. What it all means for the church may be made clearer by a glance at the figures of church membership at the begining and the end of a recent decade. Since 1890 adult church membership has been growing at about the population rate, and this despite the fact that the open-country church has been declining. Such gains are sometimes interpreted as meaning that despite the apparent confusion and personal disorganization characteristic of the time America is more religion-conscious than ever before and that therefore the church has no cause for alarm. Analysis of church growth from 1916 to 1926, however, in the light of the principle of cultural consistency reveals a somewhat different picture.

The accompanying table presents a comparison of population growth, growth of church membership in general, and the membership changes in three of the more "socialized" churches in particular for the decade in question. While theologically the Congregationalists may stand somewhat closer to other Protestant denominations than to the Unitarians and the Universalists, the well-known emphasis of the Congregational ministry on community service, *i.e.,* on the here and now, is the basis for the present classification. Socialized here means, therefore, churches which tend to appeal to members on the basis of social function with a corresponding lessening of emphasis on supernaturalism.

With no corrections for variations from denomination to denomination in the definition of a member, church membership grew on the books 30.2 per cent from 1916 to 1926. The so-called

TABLE 12

STATISTICAL EVIDENCE OF THE SOCIALIZED CHURCH'S DILEMMA[19]

	1916	1926	*Per cent Increase*
Population	100,757,735	117,135,817	16.2
Total membership of leading denominations	41,926,854	54,576,346	30.2
Membership of three socialized churches — Congregationalist, Unitarian, and Universalist	950,817	996,805	4.8
Congregationalists	809,236	881,696	8.9
Unitarians	82,515	60,152	—27.1
Universalists	58,566	54,957	— 6.2

"socialized" churches, however, taken together could show a growth of only 4.8 per cent, or about one sixth of the general rate. When the extremes of the movement alone are considered, the Unitarians and the Universalists, an actual loss in membership occurred. Certainly not all of this can be accounted for by the refusal of these churches to claim children as members. The figures support the inference that the more the church shifts its emphasis to its social functions as against supernatural rewards, the more tenuous its hold on its members.[20]

Where Is the Church Going? Responding to the various forces which we have enumerated—science, the city, the new Sabbath, the new morality, social reform, the naturalism of the time—the Protestant churches, because of the strain for consistency in the *mores,* tend slowly to shift their main emphasis from the supernatural to mental hygiene, social amelioration, ethics, and the like. Instantly the tie that binds the individual member to the church begins to weaken, or at least to grow more indirect and

[19] Figures compiled by the United States Census Bureau and supplied by *The World Almanac,* and the *Statistical Abstract of the United States,* 1925.

[20] This tenuousness is increased by the tendency of the more liberal churches to make religion a matter of individual choice. While the Catholic Church claims the child at birth certain Protestant churches will not accept a member under 18 years of age. Both the Unitarian and the Universalist churches have become more missionary in spirit since 1926.

subtle. Merely as a valuable social institution the church can no longer claim a unique personal loyalty but only the loyalty of a good citizen. We may grant that few of us would care to rear our children in a town without a church, but it does not follow that we personally must contribute either time or money in order to get the benefit. There is always the possibility that some one else will do it for us. The immediacy of the motivation has departed.

In the denominations in which this tendency has probably gone farthest, the Congregational, the Unitarian, and the Universalist, membership, as we have seen, is either growing more slowly than population or it is actually declining. True, the real strength of a church as a social force may be very inaccurately measured by church membership, as one sees in the churches of many college towns. Yet the trends of church membership suggest something at least of the success of the church in perpetuating itself as a social body. Lacking the insulation of a self-protecting tradition such as the Catholic, the great Protestant churches such as the Methodist, Baptist, and Presbyterian, which today still lean strongly on the supernatural, may be expected to find it increasingly difficult as the years go by to avoid shifting their emphasis to the civic and community values which they undoubtedly possess. As this shift occurs, and as the members increasingly become aware that it has occurred, it will become progressively harder to motivate individual participation except in time of crisis.

The Need of New Techniques. If the preceding analysis is sound, the need of further inventions in church salesmanship becomes apparent. Bereft of the old appeal to self-interest in the hereafter, the churches most affected by this trend are obviously trying other lines of attack. So far they have relied mainly on rationalism and on an increase in their social functions. But they could still utilize the self-interest appeal and they could knit up more skillfully their social values with the individual's self-feeling. For example, most of them could do much more than has yet been done in the direction of organizing themselves as cooperative societies to provide various practical services such as recreation, day nurseries, credit unions, collective purchasing, etc., for their own members. They could experiment usefully to make the church service itself an æsthetic experience worth seeking for itself. The tradition of Puritanism dies hard here, and the Puritan's fear of beauty. They could labor to increase the sociability satisfactions derivable from church membership in a hurly-burly, impersonal civilization. They could provide real opportunities for useful and significant community service.

Beyond these more or less obvious lines of appeal there is, of course, need for translating the modern religious experience into forms of art as the mediæval experience was translated into cathedrals, rich paintings, and sonorous masses. The modern religious experience needs to be felt as well as thought about, and art is the universal language of the emotions. Only as it arouses the creative imagination of artists, poets, and composers will the modern religious movement grip the hearts of men and women.

To date it seems plain that the decline of supernaturalism is leaving the Protestant churches without effective hold on the individual. They are no longer indispensable to him personally as the Catholic Church is indispensable to its members. That they can yet make themselves thus indispensable does not seem wholly impossible, but it will require an inventiveness and an artistic creativeness not yet marshalled in their service.

The Social Functions of the Church. In the early days of Christianity the church acted as the dispenser of supernatural gifts, as a salvager of social failures and as a critic of social values. Today supernaturalism, as we have said, is decreasing. Increasing specialization of social institutions has led to a transfer of many of the social salvaging functions of the early church to private philanthropy, public relief agencies, and psychiatry. And as a social critic the church has for generations been under heavy pressure to conform to the *mores* of nationalism and industrial capitalism. Under these circumstances many people are asking, what function has the church? Has the church outlived its usefulness and is it now only a vestigial appendage that society eventually will slough off?

The hostility of Communism to Christianity, the appearance of organized atheism in America, and the alleged indifference of youth to organized religion all give force to these questions.

What valuable social functions is the church still called upon to perform that no other institution is fitted to take over? Analysis reveals four such functions:

(1) *No other institution is specialized as is the church to provide a systematic way of adjusting the individual to the too-big-*

ness of life, the mystery of existence. Undoubtedly the advances of science and of modern invention have greatly dulled the average man's awareness of the too-bigness of life. Science has cushioned our lives against the Ultimate Mystery, but it has not removed that mystery, nor can it do so. Obviously all science can ever tell us about anything is how it *acts,* not what it *is.*[21] Energy, matter, cause, and effect, these are terms which science has to use, but back of which it cannot go. This means that when the last discovery has been made the Mystery will still remain. It is the function of the church uniquely among institutions to orient the individual emotionally as well as intellectually to this Mystery, and the net result of doing this for a group of individuals is to produce a community knit together by a sense of a common fate. That sectarianism has divided communities rather than unified them is a criticism not of religion or even of the church, but of sectarianism. The church remains the only institution equipped to orient the individual to the mysteries that lie beyond science.

(2) *No other institution is specialized as is the church to preserve, reinterpret, and enrich the ethical achievements of our culture.* In Chapter VI we saw that culture consists of three kinds of elements: Material traits; language; and non-material traits other than language, specifically folkways and *mores.* Included in the folkways and *mores* we found customs and institutions.[22]

The *mores* also include those esteems and disesteems or more accurately perhaps, systems of those esteems and disesteems which we call values. A system of values is a system of practical ideas or motives to behavior.

Now the process by which systems of values emerge and function in culture may be schematized somewhat as follows: First,

[21] When the chemist tells us that water is composed of a certain combination of hydrogen and oxygen he has told us what water is in terms of elements. These in turn, the physicist breaks up into atoms, electrons, protons, etc. But what are atoms, electrons, and protons? When they behave in certain ways we call them oxygen or hydrogen; but what *are* they? Ultimately the physicist gets back to hypothetical constructions based in turn on still broader hypothetical constructions such as energy and cause and effect. None of these terms is a final answer to the question of what the world is made of.

[22] The present usage of the term *mores* differs somewhat from the usage adopted by Professor Ellsworth Faris and most other sociologists. Professor Faris limits the term to those ideas and practices deemed essential to group welfare and enforced by public opinion. Institutions which are committed to the care of specialists armed with authority thus lie outside the *mores* in this sense. Such usage leaves us without an inclusive term for all conscious adjustment patterns of a group. *Mores* as here used is such an inclusive term.

there is a stage of insight and formulation on the part of some individual such as Socrates, Confucius, or Jesus. Then these values become traditional and various devices are set up for insuring their transfer to successive generations; *i.e.,* for "character-training" in the young. At the same time adults holding these esteems and disesteems tend to criticize existing conditions when such conditions fail to satisfy their value-systems. As conditions change, however, it becomes necessary to reinterpret old values to fit the new facts. Thus, the system grows and adapts itself to new conditions.

One of the great functions of all churches is to maintain a group of men who devote themselves to thinking about ethical values. Other institutions such as the school may utilize these values and even teach them more effectively than the church itself can do. But no other institution is specifically charged with the task of preserving the ethical tradition and reinterpreting it as conditions change.

To be more specific, what institution except the church has as its major objectives the furtherance of the ideals of brotherhood, service, and respect for personality? Any one who cares to compare the lot of the average man under modern conditions with that of the average man in earlier civilizations in which these values were only beginning to appear on the secondary group level will agree that such values are worth preserving. In primary groups they tend to realize themselves, but in secondary groups their extension must be specifically provided for. It is an elementary principle of social organization that to get a function well performed we must turn it over to specialists. On this principle we turn health protection over to physicians and education to the schools. On the same principle the function of preserving the tradition of the value of brotherhood, service, and respect for personality belongs primarily to an institution specializing in that field, namely, the church.

(3) *While perhaps seldom wholly free to provide moral initiative in community life, the church nevertheless enjoys a certain strategic advantage in that direction since it is uniquely charged with the custody of the moral tradition and is free from the taint of profit-seeking.*

Moral leadership in American communities centres in the churches. Hostile critics can easily point out that frequently leadership has been bigoted and intolerant, but at least it has been leadership. Every community stands on a moral order. In fact, community life is impossible without some kind of moral order. And until some other institution is prepared to take over the task of community criticism in terms of that moral order the church has an indispensable function to perform.

(4) *A final function of the church which it is coming to share in a measure with other agencies is that of providing mental hygiene service for individuals.* For the great majority of the people it is religion that supplies them with their world view, or theory of the universe and the meaning of life. Consequently it is to religion that they turn when life becomes baffling, uncertain, menacing. It is religion that holds up to them goals more enduring than mere individual success or self-indulgence; religion that tells them life is not useless nonsense but something beautiful and significant despite sorrow and suffering.

To bring this message home to the individual with sympathy and understanding, to help him make the emotional adjustments involved in adolescence, marital misunderstandings, disappointments, bereavements, and the like, is a tremendous service which thousands of ministers are today performing. Whether they talk in the terms of the old theology or of the new psychology the task is essentially the same, the task of mental hygiene. The minister cannot take the place of the trained psychiatrist, but he can furnish first aid for the more serious cases and lighten the emotional burdens of countless others who might well become serious cases if left to themselves. Mental hygiene service is, therefore, one of the functions of the church, as the Catholic confessional has recognized for ages.

Summary. Religion, then, as man's method of adjusting to the too-bigness of life, is passing through a period of stress due to the delayed readjustments of religious institutions to cultural changes.

Beginning in the very dawn of culture, religious phenomena have evolved from the level of primitive animatism to that of ethical monotheism and the accompanying refinements such as the New Humanism, and the like. In a cultural evolution covering at least 500,000 years, the five great ethical religions of the world all appeared within a span of less than fourteen centuries, *i.e.*, less than three tenths of 1 per cent of the total time.

Today Christianity claims 37 per cent of the world's population. Nearly half of the Christian world is Roman Catholic; 31 per cent is Protestant.

In the United States in 1926 Catholics constituted approximately 30 per cent of the adult church members, Protestants approximately 65 per cent and Jews about 5 per cent. Church members themselves made up 48 per cent of the population as compared with 4 per cent at the time of the Revolution.

Confusion and disorganization in the church can be traced to maladjustments resulting from the impact of modern science, new theological ideas, the growth of cities, social reforms, the continental Sabbath, changing morals, and the decline of supernaturalism. The decline of supernaturalism is a joint product of science and the machine and is evidence of the strain for consistency in the scientific-industrial *mores*. It may be interpreted as forecasting a decline in the membership of Protestant churches in days to come unless new techniques of religious salesmanship are applied and the modern religious experience is interpreted emotionally by artists, poets, and composers.

As we have seen, the church still has a fourfold social task to perform: To orient the individual to the too-bigness of life; to maintain, adapt, and enrich the ethical tradition; to furnish moral leadership to the community; and to provide a first-aid mental-hygiene service for the individual in the emotional crises of his life.

STUDY QUESTIONS

1. Define: religion, theology, church.
2. What similarity is there between religion and mathematics?
3. What theories have been offered to explain the origin of religion?
4. What are the five outstanding stages in the evolution of religious phenomena?
5. What percentage of the world's population is classed as Christian? What percentage of the population of the United States is classed as Protestant? Catholic? Jewish?
6. What marked flunctuations have occurred in popular interest in the church in this country?
7. Why have the churches of Middletown changed less since 1890 than any other institutions?
8. To what six conditions is the church readjusting?
9. In what way has modern science affected the church?

10. What changes have come from the higher criticism?
11. Compare the New Humanism with the old theology.
12. In what way does social reform embarrass the church?
13. If the church has lost its monopoly of the Sabbath what should the minister do about it?
14. In what way does the changing moral situation affect the church?
15. What is meant by the strain for consistency in the *mores?*
16. What evidence can you give that supernaturalism has declined?
17. What is happening to church membership in general? In the liberal churches in particular? What does it mean?
18. What is the rôle of art in holding or building church membership?
19. What four social functions has the church as an institution?

SUGGESTED ASSIGNMENT

Attend a church service and note what adjustments that particular church has made to each of the six factors mentioned in the text.

CHAPTER XXIX

SOCIAL SCIENCE AND VALUES

Is Man Morally Ready for the Power He Wields? At the 101st meeting of the British Association for the Advancement of Science at York, England, in September, 1932, the presiding officer, Sir Alfred Ewing, former principal of the University of Edinburgh, voiced in his presidential address a fear that has echoed more than once in the words of thoughtful men since the World War. Reviewing the recollections of his sixty-five years of contact with the Association—"surprises that are commonplace today: the dynamo, the electric motor, the phonograph, the telephone, the internal combustion engine, the airplane, the radio"—Sir Alfred asked:

Whither does this tremendous procession tend? Man was ethically unprepared for so great a bounty. In the slow evolution of morals he is still unfit for the tremendous responsibility which it entails. The command of Nature has been put into his hands before he knows how to command himself.

Are we children playing with fire? Is man morally ready for the enormous power over nature which science is placing in his hands? The question has troubled many another besides Sir Alfred since Herbert Spencer's easy identification of progress with evolution passed out of fashion. Long before the German invasion of Belgium, Samuel Butler, in *Erewhon,* had described a country in which the inhabitants had exterminated power-machines to prevent the machines, which had acquired powers of growth and replacement of their own, from enslaving or exterminating the human masters themselves. Mr. Edwin E. Slosson, late director of Science Service, Washington, put the same problem thus:

The question on which the future depends is whether men can muster up among them enough mentality and morality to manage the stupendous powers which applied science has recently placed in their hands. Once upon a time, before the oldest of us was born, before any man was born for that matter—I refer to the Jurassic Era—the ruling race was composed of creatures much larger and more powerful than we are. There were giants on the earth in those days, gigantic saurians which, when they stood up on their hind legs, would tower up four times as tall as a man. But their cranial cavity was smaller than ours. The Jurassic saurians had grown too big for their brains; so they perished. Now the addition of machine power to the natural strength of man is equivalent to adding more powerful arms and legs, more skilful hands, and sharper senses. It increases his physical capacity but does not directly enlarge his mental ability. . . . The physical sciences have evidently been developed so far beyond the political sciences as to constitute a menace to civilization. The modern man, like the Arabian fisherman, has liberated from the bottle genii that he does not know how to control.[1]

The Twofold Task of Commanding Ourselves. Man's problem of commanding himself, as Sir Alfred Ewing calls it, appears in reality to be two closely related problems: (1) There is first the problem of discovering what happens in society and how it is caused; then (2) there is the problem of determining the ends or purposes for which this knowledge, once it has been obtained, shall be used.

Now the unfortunate fact is that both in the understanding of social phenomena and in the morality of the purposes for which our understanding is used, man's self-control falls far below his control of nature. As Mr. Slosson remarked in the essay already quoted, the chemist during the World War did his job efficiently; the diplomat fell down on his. Yet somehow, if civilization is to survive, the efficiency of man's self-control must be raised. This means that his understanding of himself and of the associative life must be clarified and systematized and his purposes must be moralized to encompass the new world that he has created. The social sciences and socialized morality, in other words, are the answers to the double problem that confronts us.

Social Science. The social sciences have been slowly emerging during the last century from the centuries of speculation that preceded them. Of course, if one accepts the rigid criteria of the physical sciences and insists on quantitative measurement and the expression of relationships in mathematical formulas as the

[1] Edwin E. Slosson, "The Changing Mind of Man," an address delivered at Dartmouth College and reprinted in *Essays Toward Truth*, Robinson, Pressey, McCallum *et al.*, New York, 1924, pp. 100–1.

essence of science, then there are still no social sciences at all. But anthropologists, historians, political scientists, economists, geographers, and sociologists claim kinship with the natural scientists, not on the basis of measurement and mathematical formulas, but because, like the natural scientists, they are endeavoring to describe, analyze, and interpret objectively observed phenomena for the purpose of arriving at generalizations which may be expected to hold true under given conditions. Those who wish to use language with accuracy will, perhaps, prefer to speak of anthropology, economics, sociology, and similar studies as disciplines rather than sciences in the strict sense of the term.

Social Philosophy. Social philosophy, which may be defined as speculative thinking about society, has been the mother of all the social sciences. Just as physics and chemistry gradually differentiated themselves from natural philosophy, so sociology has gradually differentiated itself from social (or, as it was usually called, moral) philosophy.

The earliest social philosophies found expression in proverbs. Sayings such as "Birds of a feather flock together," "The child is father to the man," and "A soft answer turneth away wrath," show considerable insight into social processes.[2]

At a more sophisticated level we have attempts to bring together such generalizations into a definite and explicit social philosophy. From the earliest historical times there are such systems, though it is not for a long time that any clear separation is made between what actually occurs and what the writers think ought to be. Thus Plato's *Republic* is a description of his conception of an ideal state based upon his observation of the working of actual states. Aristotle, in his *Politics,* tried to get at the principles actually operating in life by studying intensively existing systems of government. Though he went on to sketch his own ideal state, he was nearer to the spirit of the modern social scientist than was Plato.

Utopias have been a favorite way of embodying social philosophy throughout the ages. St. Augustine's *City of God* in the early fifth century was based upon the ideals of Christianity. Sir Thomas More's *Utopia* in the late sixteenth century, Sir Francis Bacon's *New Atlantis* in the early seventeenth, the Ameri-

[2] Professor Bogardus has made an interesting collection of such proverbs from many cultures. See *A History of Social Thought,* Chap. II.

can Edward Bellamy's *Looking Backward* in the late nineteenth, and H. G. Wells's *The Time Machine,* are other interesting examples of this method. In order to sketch a plausible ideal society, all had to have considerable insight into the actual processes of social life.

A more realistic approach to the problems of politics is found in Machiavelli's *The Prince* (1513). He felt that the well-being of the state was all-important and therefore set forth those principles upon which he conceived the monarch must act if he is to preserve the state. His was a great contrast with the idealistic schemes of the framers of utopias, since he was disillusioned, not to say cynical, concerning the motives and capacities of men. However, his emphasis upon what actually takes place was salutary from a scientific point of view.

The Republic of Jean Bodin (1530–96) marked a further advance toward the scientific approach. One section of this work was devoted to the influence of geographical conditions, especially climate, upon political and social institutions. He recognized that no form of organization had absolute validity, but that the institutions of a people are an adaptation to their conditions of life. *Montesquieu* (1689–1758) in his famous *Spirit of the Laws* carried this same type of analysis further. He set out to consider the social causes of particular types of government and systems of law. Although he allowed his preconceptions to influence his results, his attitude was more thoroughly inductive than that of his predecessors. A contemporary of Montesquieu and another important precursor of modern social science was Giambattista Vico (1668–1744), an Italian. In his *New Science* he emphasized that what was needed was less abstract speculation and more attention to facts. He believed that history was governed by laws just as were the phenomena of the physical world.

Throughout the seventeenth and eighteenth centuries the general trend, however, was toward purely philosophical consideration of social relations and social processes. The far-reaching political readjustments then under way aroused speculation concerning natural law, the state of nature, and the social contract. Hugo Grotius, the philosopher of international law, Hobbes, the originator of the social-contract idea, Locke, who believed that the social contract depended upon the consent of the governed and who was therefore the philosopher most depended upon by the

American Revolutionists, Rousseau, whose somewhat similar doctrine was a theoretical buttress of the French Revolution, and Hume, who strongly opposed the contract theory and asserted that man was naturally social, were leaders in this discussion.

It will readily be seen that none of the work before the middle of the eighteenth century could be called social science in the strict sense. There had been some observation of the processes of human social life and some attempts to formulate laws which would cover the observations. But most of the writing dealt with broad areas of life and was necessarily rather speculative. It was only with the differentiation of thought into particular provinces that a more scientific method was possible. Perhaps the first discipline to be clearly separated from the general body of social philosophy was economics. Utilizing what was valuable in the work of the Physiocrats, Quesnay, Turgot, and Condorcet, Adam Smith in his *Wealth of Nations* (1776) laid the foundations of modern economics.

The Emergence of Sociology. Sociology did not emerge as a separate scientific discipline until Auguste Comte coined the word in his *Positive Philosophy* issued in six volumes between 1830 and 1842. He conceived of sociology as the general inclusive social science and made it the highest in his hierarchy of sciences. He was convinced of the superiority of the positive, or fact-finding approach to the theological or metaphysical and pointed out that the other sciences had evolved through these other stages into the positive stage. It was his ambition to bring this newest of all sciences, sociology, into this stage likewise. To this end he insisted upon observation and classification of phenomena with the hope of arriving at the natural laws which govern social life. For many of his ideas he was indebted to St. Simon, the socialist, under whose influence he came at an early age. Comte's importance lies not so much in what he accomplished as in what he pointed the way to. He indicated the broad outlines of a field of study, made many suggestive generalizations concerning the working of social phenomena, and outlined methods for future work in this unexplored field.

Perhaps the man who did more than any other to make sociology well-known and influential was Herbert Spencer (1820–1903). This English philosopher who took all the sciences of life for his province was particularly interested in working out a system of sociology. He was much influenced by Darwin's *Origin of Species,* the publication of which in 1859 led him to adopt the evolutionary point of view in his later works. Spencer had the impulses of a scientist in that he believed that his generalizations about social life must flow from a careful study of wide ranges of fact; and with the help of assistants he actually gathered an immense amount of data about primitive and civilized people. But his weakness was a tendency to formulate a theory on scant evidence and then to illustrate it by further collection of facts. Once he had made his hypothesis the facts had to be fitted in; there was no reshaping of the hypothesis. One theory of this kind which runs all through his work is that society is very similar to a biological organism. Although he admitted differences, in his treatment he largely ignored them. In general his sociology tended to be mechanical and analogical. However, despite the faults of his own work, Spencer made a tremendously valuable contribution in the way he attracted attention to the possibilities of sociology and stimulated younger men to pursue it in a scientific manner.

In sharp contrast to Spencer, who emphasized the passive aspect of social adaptation and inclined toward a *laissez-faire* viewpoint, was Lester Ward (1841–1913), an American, who was strongly impressed with man's ability to mould his own destiny through purposeful thinking. He erected a complete sociological system, which, because of the inadequate factual data at hand, had to be highly philosophical. Ward was the first American sociologist of any importance and his emphasis upon mental factors in social process was largely responsible for the psychological turn which American sociology took.

Later European Developments. It is impossible here to do more than mention a few of the outstanding sociologists of Germany, France, and England during the past fifty years by way of furnishing background for a glimpse of present-day movements in America.

Sociology in Germany has remained highly theoretical right down to our own time. However, hypotheses have been evolved which have proved stimulating and which have given orientation to more inductive work elsewhere. Ferdinand Tönnies (1855–) pointed out a fundamental dichotomy between "community" and "society," the former being a personal and habitual group, the latter, impersonal and volitional. It is somewhat the same distinction as that made between the primary and non-primary groups in this volume. More influential on the course of German sociology perhaps than any other individual was Georg Simmel (1858–1918). He developed the notion of a "formal" sociology, a science which would not concern itself with the content of social relations (that would be left to economics, political science, etc.) but with their forms. An admirer of Simmel who has developed a systematic sociology on somewhat the same lines but with more inductive emphasis is Leopold von Wiese (1876–). His work is now available in English.[3] The last of the Germans we shall mention is Max Weber (1864–1920). Coming into sociology late in life after having made his mark in history and economics, he nevertheless made important contributions to the methodology of historical sociology. Unlike the earlier sociologists, he tested the validity of his theories by rigid induction carried out in the most painstaking manner.

We will deal with only three Frenchmen. Frederic Le Play (1806–82) was quite unlike his contemporary Herbert Spencer. He was no systematizer, but introduced the method of monographic studies in different localities, or social surveys. Since he was an engineer by profession, he naturally inclined to the statistical method and his studies of working men's budgets were excellent pieces of research in their day. Gabriel Tarde (1834–1904), on the other hand, was a brilliant speculative thinker who is frequently credited with being the founder of social psychology. His *Laws of Imitation* was very stimulating but his theory of imitation as the all-important process of social life has not held up. The most important French sociologist is Emile Durkheim (1858–1917). His two great contributions were his demonstration that division of labor contributes to social unity through consciousness of supplementary difference and his hypothesis of a group mind. The latter conception has been widely challenged, but it has served a useful purpose by bringing about a more balanced emphasis than was given by such writers as Spencer, who saw in a group only an aggregation of separate individuals.

English sociology since Herbert Spencer need not detain us long, for there have been few contributors to it. L. T. Hobhouse (1858–1929) was a social philosopher who built his theories as far as possible upon inductive evidence. Graham Wallas (1858–),

[3] *Systematic Sociology* (with Howard Becker).

unlike Hobhouse, was no system builder. He dealt with specific questions in an illuminating way. His *The Great Society* is, perhaps, his best-known work. Edward Westermarck (1862–) is the author of a monumental *History of Human Marriage*. Bronislaw Malinowski (1884–) is more anthropologist than sociologist yet he does not hesitate to generalize certain principles from his data when he believes they warrant it. His various studies of the Trobriand Islanders make fascinating reading as well as being scientifically beyond reproach.

Contemporary American Sociology. Sociology has had a tremendous growth in America since Ward gave it its impetus. In no other country has it received such widespread recognition as a university discipline. Since the World War the number of graduate students in sociology has increased many-fold, while at the other end of the scale we find that the subject is slowly but steadily penetrating the high school curriculum.

There have, perhaps, been four strong currents contributing to the development of American sociological theory:

(1) *The Psychological Approach.*—This began with Ward as we have seen, and there has been no cessation of interest. Those who have contributed the most are James Mark Baldwin (1861–) with his theory of the dialectic of personal growth; Charles H. Cooley (1864–1929) with emphasis upon communication as the basic factor in personality development, social organization, and social process; Edward A. Ross (1866–) with his study of the psychology of social control; W. I. Thomas (1863–) with the theory of wishes which we have set forth in Chapter IX; and L. L. Bernard (1881–) who has done much to systematize the field as well as to make minor original contributions.

A related approach is that from the angle of man's biological organism and hereditary equipment. The "instinct determinism" of William McDougall was for some fifteen years very influential in American sociology. He attempted to show in his *Social Psychology* that the behavior of men is simply a working out of clear-cut instinctive drives. Since the publication of Bernard's *Instinct* in 1924 McDougall's point of view has been on the wane.

(2) *The Anthropological Approach.*—William G. Sumner (1840–1910), to whose work we referred in Chapter VI, was the first to tap primitive life as a source for sociological analysis. W. I. Thomas also followed this lead in his earlier work. It was

through this cross-fertilization with anthropological thought that the concept of culture came to bulk so large in modern sociology. The Lynds used this anthropological approach in their justly famous *Middletown* (1929).

(3) *The Statistical Approach.*—Since the World War there has been a growing emphasis on the use of statistics in sociological analysis. One of the first Americans to emphasize the dangers of subjective bias in the gathering of information was Franklin Giddings (1855–1931); William F. Ogburn (1886–) has perhaps done more with this technique than any other investigator,[4] although F. Stuart Chapin (1888–) and others are working in the same field.

(4) *The Ecological Approach.*—In the decade following the World War emphasis in American sociology turned strongly to objective research and especially to research in local areas. The leader in this movement was R. E. Park (1864–) of Chicago. The University of Chicago sociology department has been especially active in carrying out studies of Chicago from the ecological point of view.[5] R. D. McKenzie (1885–) has contributed notably to the development of ecological theory and methodology.

Sociology, Social Technology, and Social Engineering. We have distinguished sociology from social philosophy. It is now necessary to draw a distinction between the scientific study of human association, *i.e.*, sociology proper, and the formulation of principles for the control of certain practical problems or situations. When interest shifts from the mere description and understanding of phenomena to an effort to affect or to control those phenomena for some practical end, we have passed from the purely scientific level to the level of technology. Thus when the physicist ceases to be concerned with the laws of motion as such and begins to plan a machine he is no longer a physicist but a technologist. And when the sociologist ceases to ask, What is the law of change in this community? and asks instead, What can we do to change the rate of juvenile delinquency or the housing congestion or the distribution of wealth?—when that shift of interest occurs, the individual has ceased to function as a sociologist and is beginning to function as a social technologist. And when he actually begins to try to change conditions—to lower the juvenile delinquency rate,

[4] See, for instance, Groves and Ogburn, *American Marriage and Family Relationships*.
[5] See Shaw, *Delinquency Areas;* Burgess, *The City.*

to reduce congestion, to reduce poverty, and so on—he becomes, in so far as he actually uses the general principles of his technology, a social engineer, or, if emotional, a reformer.

A great deal of what now passes as sociology in our curricula is either social philosophy or social technology. This does not mean that it is any less valuable. The world is a highly complicated place in which wisdom and intelligent action are as badly needed as scientific information. But it should be noted that intelligent action in the social world requires vastly more scientific information than any one science can supply. Social technology, in other words, must draw on history, economics, psychology, psychiatry, political science, geography, and law as well as on sociology. Thus, while a considerable amount of social technology such as penology, social case work, and the like, is listed as sociology, the fact is that sociology constitutes only one of the many disciplines drawn upon in the formulation of the principles of each technique.

Nor is this all. Not only is the technology of community organization, for example, dependent on several disciplines, but it implies a philosophy of life. We must know what values we wish to have realized in community life before we can organize scientific knowledge to achieve them. The most science can do is to discover the most efficient way to reach a desired result; it can never judge as to the ultimate worth of the end. If it is felt that great opportunities for the few, even at the expense of the many, will in the long run prove more valuable, we can perhaps organize the community to obtain this result; if another point of view is accepted, we can probably change our technique to suit. But we must know whither it is desired to go. Thus we are brought back to the second phase of our problem of controlling ourselves: Not only do we need social sciences to provide the scientific information, and social technologies to weld this information into usable tools for social engineering, but *we need a socialized ethics to determine the purposes for which we shall use our tools.*

The Problem of Socializing Purpose. A distinguished American sociologist, Professor Hornell Hart, has written a very stimulating book, *The Technique of Social Progress,* dedicated to the demonstration of the proposition that "progress consists in those biological and cultural changes which, on the whole and in the long run, release, stimulate, facilitate, and integrate, the purposes of men"—but not once in 685 pages does he face the question of *what* purposes are to be released, stimulated, facilitated, and integrated. The German army marching into Belgium was probably the finest product of those biological and cultural changes which, on the whole, and in the long run, release, stimulate, facilitate, and integrate the purposes of men—but was the purpose which that army served, namely, war, a progressive purpose in the world of 1914? There are those who believe that war—any war—is an anachronism in a world market. It is as impossible to prove that they are wrong as to prove that the militarists are right.

The point is, the mere increase in the efficiency of our technology—even the technology of progress, as Doctor Hart defines it—does not automatically insure more human well-being in the world unless along with that increased technical efficiency there also goes an increase in man's determination to use his power for the common good. Now unfortunately it is not always easy to determine what constitutes the common good. As a matter of fact, Sir Alfred Ewing, Mr. Slosson, Dean Inge, Bertrand Russell, and many other thoughtful people are questioning whether this very increase in technical efficiency that Doctor Hart finds so progressive is really for the common good after all. There is certainly no questioning the fact that automobiles, airplanes, machine guns, and all the other products of technical evolution have enormously increased the individual's range of influence. Each one of us can affect for good or ill many times as many people as the average individual of George Washington's day. And there lies the rub, for the evil, the indifferent, and the vicious have been given this power to affect more and more people just as truly as the well-intentioned and the good have been given it.

What Values Are Worth While? A discussion of this problem would take us far into the field of ethics, and it would inevitably lead us into the whole range of the social philosophies that men have conceived. No one is properly equipped for modern life who has not faced such questions as, What is the good life? and, What kind of society seems most likely to produce it? But such questions are not properly the province of a discipline seeking to describe, classify, and analyze phenomena. We shall content ourselves, therefore, merely with suggesting one or two of the most challenging modern answers to the question, What values are worth while?

Since the time of the Greeks most thinkers have agreed that the highest human good consists in well-being, or happiness, but their definitions of happiness differ. According to the hedonists happiness consists in pleasure; according to the rigorists it is identical with virtue while unhappiness is vice; and according to the self-realizationists happiness consists in the normal exercise of man's faculties. Now whichever definition of well-being we adopt, one thing seems clear: It is through the developed personality that these values are achieved. In other words, the developed personality is the source in this world of the worth-while values of life. But this immediately involves a further question: Whose personality shall be developed?

In primitive life the answer to that question is not difficult: Practically all the men have an approximately equal chance for the meagre development that such culture affords. The women seldom count. But when complex social organization has superseded the face-to-face primary group and division of labor has created social classes the answer is not so simple.

Until the latter part of the eighteenth century every civilization that ever existed had found the answer by excluding all but a relatively small percentage of the population from the opportunities for full development. Then with the American Revolution came the groping attempt to realize the ideal that every white man at least should have an opportunity to make the most of himself. This was a new departure in human relations and set the new nation for generations in the forefront of social idealism. When, as a result of the Civil War, the theory was extended to black men as well as white and presently even women were increasingly recognized as possessing rights as human beings and not mere members of a sex, Americans could pride themselves for a time on a social order that theoretically at least was pointing the way for the cynics of the old world.

Unfortunately this attempt to provide equality of opportunity for the common man coincided with that tremendous overturn in the economic basis of society known as the Industrial Revolution. The coming of the machine enormously increased the power of the business class. The very Civil War which, in theory, extended equality of opportunity to the Negro actually set in motion economic forces which presently were to make the business class supreme. Gradually as wealth became more concentrated, it became more and more difficult to keep opportunity open, to say nothing of equal. At the end of nearly a century and a half of the American experiment the net result seems to be that real equality of opportunity for the great mass of the people is farther from realization than at the beginning. Wealth is more highly concentrated than in 1790, the frontier is gone, and the idealism that burned so brightly on the threshold of a new continent now flickers uncertainly in the fitful airs of an all-encompassing and cynical materialism. Millions are asking, Is it worth while even to try to equalize opportunity after all? Isn't the task beyond the reach of human skill and courage? Do not the judgments of history and the verdicts of science alike condemn it as an impossible ideal? The "best people" of all cultures have usually condemned it. Hamilton and the Federalists generally detested it. Calhoun and the Southern slave-owners ridiculed the idea. Successful business men and worshippers of efficiency today are lukewarm at best in their support of it. Unquestionably the task of giving the common man his chance is vastly more formidable today than in Jefferson's day. For one thing, modern biology and psychology have shown us that men are not born equal. For another thing, the forms of possible inequality have multiplied since the days of log cabins and pioneer poverty. And the power of vested interests is greater today than the early egalitarians ever dreamed possible. Facing these mounting difficulties and disillusioned by the failures of the past—the failure of the ballot to make even white men free, the failure of emancipation to emancipate the black man, the failure of the school to educate, the failure of the machine to banish poverty, the failure of this and the failure of that—is it any wonder that many a tired idealist gives up the struggle? Yet every generation must face the question anew: Is the American experiment a mistake? Was the vision of those revolutionary days just a dream and nothing more? Is it beyond human power to build a social system in which every normal human being shall have as real a chance as every other human being to lead the good life?

Recent Social Trends in the United States. This whole question received a significant turn in the minds of practical men and theorists alike as a result of the unparalleled depression which began in 1929. Under the impact of falling prices and mounting numbers of the unemployed, millions of people who had never before questioned the beneficence of *laissez-faire* began suddenly to realize that the world had changed since Adam Smith. One of the most significant expressions of the growing realization of the need of conscious social planning was the report of the President's Committee on Social Trends in January, 1933. Covering twenty-nine fields of national life from population and natural resources to social attitudes, religion, and government, this report—the work of 500 social scientists during the preceding three years—provides the most complete description of the American scene that has yet been available.

As we have implied throughout this book, problems of our physical and biological heritage seem far less serious to these social scientists than do the problems of our social heritage, or culture. Specifically the crucial problem, as the Committee sees it, almost in the terms used in the opening chapter of this book, is the surpassing efficiency of material invention as contrasted with the relative backwardness of social invention. In business, in the family, in the school, in the state, and in other fields, the result is a bewildering accumulation of maladjustment and strain. The only hope, as the Committee sees it, is for "cumulative thinking by many minds over years to come"; the focussing of collective attention, in other words, on the great task of stimulating social invention "to keep pace with mechanical invention."

The alternative to constructive social initiative may conceivably be a prolongation of a policy of drift and some readjustment as time goes on. More definite alternatives, however, are urged by dictatorial systems in which the factors of force and violence may loom large. In such cases the basic decisions are frankly imposed by power groups, and violence may subordinate technical intelligence in social guidance.

Unless there can be a more impressive integration of social skills and fusing of social purposes than is revealed by recent trends, there can be no assurance that these alternatives with their accompaniments of violent revolution, dark periods of serious repression of libertarian and democratic forms, the prescription and loss of many useful elements in the present productive system, can be averted.

Fully realizing its mission, the Committee does not wish to assume an attitude of alarmist irresponsibility, but on the other hand it would be highly negligent to gloss over the stark and bitter realities of the social situation, and to ignore the imminent perils in further advance of our heavy technical machinery over crumbling roads and shaking bridges. There are times when silence is not neutrality, but assent.[6]

[6] *Recent Social Trends in the United States,* Report of the President's Research Committee on Social Trends, New York and London, 1933, Vol. I, pp. lxxiv–lxxv.

All of which brings us to one final question: What makes a social system good or bad? As technologists seeking to effectuate certain values in the world, what criteria of judgment can we set up?

The Bases for Judging the Worth of a Social System.[7] Many people evaluate a social system merely on the basis of deep-rooted prejudices. Because things have always gone on thus and so, and because in going they have brought a certain amount of satisfaction, the social order must be good. Perhaps most defenders of the existing order in the United States really base their attitude not on the results of critical thinking but on socially inherited prejudice.

Another basis of judgment is the belief that the social system, actual or imagined, is such, or would be such, as to provide a desirable career for the kind of person that the individual thinks he is. As the Russells observe,

> One cannot imagine that Napoleon, even in youth, could have been very enthusiastic about dreams of universal peace, or that captains of industry would be attracted by Samuel Butler's *Erewhon*, where all machines were illegal.

A third means of evaluating is by determining whether or not the activities involved in creating the suggested system would be agreeable or not. People who are maladjusted to the present order not infrequently find pleasure in imagining their own rôle in constructing a very different order. Whether this rôle would be pleasing to them is the principal basis for their approval or disapproval of the proposed order.

Still a fourth basis of judgment is æsthetic: Does the proposed order constitute a pattern that is pleasant to contemplate? Philosophers, and others, sometimes find it difficult to think of a social order in terms of individuals. Yet the real test is not the harmony or symmetry of an ideal construction but the fullness of the lives of individual men and women.

A final and far more rational basis than any yet suggested is the present well-being of those who compose the social order and its capacity for developing into something better. Here again we are

[7] Adapted from Bertrand and Dora Russell, *Prospects of Industrial Civilization,* New York, 1923.

brought back to the problem discussed in the preceding section, the aristocratic fallacy, as the Russells call it, or the tendency to judge a society "by the kind of life it affords to a privileged minority." Perhaps, no social order has ever produced more cultural achievements than the classic Athenian. But essentially it consisted of a minority of free citizens supported by the labor of a multitude of underprivileged workers and slaves. Every other civilization has shown the same cleavage—a privileged minority and an underprivileged or actually enslaved majority. It is obviously fallacious to judge any society merely by considering the condition of the privileged and ignoring the condition of the underprivileged. What sort of life does the social order afford to the man in the ranks as well as to the headquarters staff? That is the question.

And since, with the advance of science, man's power to increase well-being obviously increases, it becomes important likewise that the realization of man's ideals keep step with his power to achieve them. In the end, *it is only a system that seems to be working toward a fuller measure of happiness for all that will command the faith of the average man in the days to come.*

All of which is not a matter of scientific demonstration but of belief and philosophical insight. Ultimately science can only provide the tools; it is our social philosophy, our scale of values, our world view, that must determine what the tools are used for. So the final question, beyond the power of sociology or of any social discipline to answer, confronts every serious-minded man and woman today: *What kind of society are we trying to build?*

Inexorably in a hundred million choices Americans are answering that question day by day. Whether we are morally ready for the power we wield the historian of 3000 A.D. will know. Even our own children may have some inkling of the answer.

STUDY QUESTIONS

1. It has been suggested that civilized nations should declare a 10-year holiday on inventions. What line of thought do you think lies behind this suggestion?
2. Discriminate carefully between the rôles to be played by social science and by ethics in man's control of his own destiny.
3. Give reasons for and against calling sociology a science.
4. Distinguish between social philosophy and social science.
5. Name several important Utopias and their authors. Of what value do you think such Utopias have been?

6. Discuss the importance in the evolution of sociology of Comte; of Spencer; of Ward.
7. What characteristics have Le Play, Weber, Malinowski, Westermarck, and von Wiese in common? Tönnies, Hobhouse, Tarde, and Simmel?
8. Discuss the four principal trends in American sociology, mentioning outstanding contributors to each.
9. What is the difference between sociology and social technology? Does social technology depend wholly on the scientific findings of sociology?
10. Show why the social sciences will never be able to dictate the path of social reform.
11. What is Professor Hart's notion of social progress? Why is it inadequate?
12. Explain how modern communication has rendered unsocialized purposes more injurious than formerly.
13. Discuss the values which have been thought most worth while by various schools of thought.
14. Explain the conflict between the American ideal of equal opportunity and industrial developments since the Civil War.
15. From what standpoints do people judge the value of a social system?

SELECTED BIBLIOGRAPHY

CHAPTER I. THE PROBLEM OF LIVING WITH OTHERS

Beard, Charles A., and others, *Whither Mankind.* New York, 1928.
Chase, Stuart, *Men and Machines.* New York, 1929.
Gras, N. S. B., *An Introduction to Economic History.* New York, 1922.
Kroeber, A. L., *Anthropology.* New York, 1923.
de Laguna, Theodore, *The Factors of Social Evolution.* New York, 1926.
Lull, Richard S., *Organic Evolution.* New York, 1920.
Lynd, Robert S. and Helen M., *Middletown.* New York, 1928.
Osborn, H. F., *Man Rises to Parnassus.* New York, 1927.
Ripley, W. Z., *The Races of Europe.* New York, 1899.
Robinson, James H., *The Mind in the Making.* New York, 1921.
Thompson, Warren S., *Population Problems.* New York, 1930.

CHAPTER II. THE BIOLOGICAL BASIS OF HUMAN ASSOCIATION

Bernard, L. L., *Instinct. A Study in Social Psychology.* New York, 1925.
Boas, Franz, *Anthropology and Modern Life.* New York, 1928.
Castle, W. E., *Genetics and Eugenics.* Cambridge, Mass., 1924.
Child, C. M., *Physiological Foundations of Behavior.* New York, 1924.
Conklin, E. G., *Heredity and Environment in the Development of Men.* Princeton, 5th ed., 1923.
Darwin, Charles, *The Origin of Species.* London, 1859.
Davenport, C. B., *Heredity in Relation to Eugenics.* New York, 1911.
Galton, Francis, *Hereditary Genius,* 2d ed. London, 1892.
Gates, R. R., *Heredity in Man.* London, 1929.
Gosnewy, E. S., and Popenoe, P., *Sterilization for Human Betterment.* New York, 1929.
Guyer, M. F., *Being Well-Born,* 2d ed. Indianapolis, 1927.
Herrick, C. J., *The Brains of Rats and Men.* Chicago, 1926.
Holmes, S. J., *Studies in Evolution and Eugenics.* New York, 1923.
Jennings, H. S., *The Biological Basis of Human Nature.* New York, 1930.
—— *Prometheus.* New York, 1925.
Morgan, T. H., *et al., The Mechanism of Mendelian Heredity.* New York, 1926.
Newman, H. H., *Evolution, Genetics and Eugenics,* 2d ed. Chicago, 1925.
Pearl, Raymond, *The Present Status of Eugenics.* Hanover, N. H., 1928.
Popenoe, P., and Johnson, R. H., *Applied Eugenics.* New York, 1918.

CHAPTER III. THE PSYCHO-SOCIAL BASIS OF ASSOCIATION—COMMUNICATION AND SYMPATHETIC INSIGHT

Allport, Floyd A., *Social Psychology,* Chaps. VIII, IX, X. Boston, 1924.

Darwin, Charles, *The Expression of the Emotions in Man and Animals.* London and New York, 1873.

Hunter, Walter S., "The Symbolic Process," *Psychological Review,* XXXI (1924), 478–502.

de Laguna, Grace A., *Speech: its Function and Development.* New Haven, 1927.

Markey, J. F., *The Symbolic Process and its Integration in Children.* New York, 1928.

Mead, George H., "A Behavioristic Account of the Significant Symbol," *Journal of Philosophy,* XIX (1922), 157–63.

Ogden, C. K., and Richards, I. A., *The Meaning of Meaning.* New York, 1923.

Park, R. E., and Burgess, E. W., *Introduction to the Science of Sociology,* 2d ed., Chap. IV. Chicago, 1924.

Piaget, Jean, *The Language and Thought of the Child.* New York, 1926.

Sapir, Edward, *Language: an Introduction to the Study of Speech.* New York, 1921.

CHAPTER IV. HUMAN NATURE AND PRIMARY GROUPS

Blanchard, Phyllis, *The Child and Society,* Chap. II. New York, 1928.

Dewey, John, *Human Nature and Conduct.* New York, 1922.

Edman, Irwin, *Human Traits and their Social Significance.* Boston, 1919.

Faris, Ellsworth, "The Nature of Human Nature," *Pub. Am. Sociological Society,* XX (1926), 15–29.

—— "The Primary Group—Essence or Accident," *Am. Journal of Sociology,* XXXVIII (1932), 41–50.

Puffer, J. A., *The Boy and his Gang.* Boston, 1912.

Thrasher, F. M., *The Gang.* Chicago, 1927.

Young, Kimball, *Social Psychology,* Chaps. XI, XII. New York, 1930.

CHAPTER V. THE INDIVIDUAL AND SOCIETY

Cooley, Charles H., *Social Organization,* Chaps. I and II. New York, 1909.

Follett, Mary P., *Creative Experience.* New York, 1924.

MacIver, Robert M., *Society: its Structure and Changes,* Chaps. I and II. New York, 1931.

Mackenzie, John S., *An Introduction to Social Philosophy.* New York, 1895.

CHAPTER VI. CULTURE—THE ACCUMULATED RESULTS OF ASSOCIATION

Chase, Stuart, *Men and Machines.* New York, 1929.
Goldenweiser, Alexander A., *Early Civilization.* New York, 1922.
Hobhouse, L. T., *Morals in Evolution.* London, 1906.
Kroeber, A. L., *Anthropology.* New York, 1923.
President's Research Committee, *Recent Social Trends in the United States,* Vol. I, Chap. III. New York and London, 1933.
Robinson, James Harvey, *Mind in the Making.* New York, 1921.
Stawell, F. M., and Marvin, F. S., *The Making of the Western Mind.* London, 1923.
Sumner, William Graham, *Folkways.* Boston, 1906.
Wallas, Graham, *Our Social Heritage.* New Haven, 1921.
Wissler, Clark, *Man and Culture.* New York, 1923.

CHAPTER VII. HOW EXTERNAL FACTORS CONDITION CULTURE

Chapin, F. Stuart, *An Introduction to the Study of Social Evolution,* Chap. V. New York, 1920.
Dexter, E. G., *Weather Influences.* New York, 1904.
Huntington, Ellsworth, *Principles of Human Geography.* New York, 1924.
—— *Civilization and Climate.* Yale University Press, 1925.
President's Research Committee, *Recent Social Trends in the United States,* Vol. I, Chap. II. New York and London, 1933.
Ridgely, D. C., *Geographic Principles.* New York, 1925.
Thomson, J. Arthur, *Outline of Science,* Vol. III, pp. 597 ff.
Turner, F. ., *The Frontier in American History.* New York, 1920.
Semple, Ellen Churchill, *Influences of Geographic Environment.* New York, 1911.
Smith, J. Russell, *North America.* New York, 1925.
Whitbeck, R. H., and Thomas, Olive J., *The Geographic Factor.* New York, 1932.

CHAPTER VIII. CULTURE AND PERSONALITY DEVELOPMENT

Boas, Franz, *The Mind of Primitive Man.* New York, 1913.
Bogardus, Emory S., "Personality and Occupational Attitudes," *Journal of Applied Sociology,* VIII (1924), 172–6.
—— "Social Distance and its Origins," *Journal of Applied Sociology,* IX (1925), 216–26.
Burgess, E. W. (Ed.), *Personality and the Social Group.* Chicago, 1929.
Case, C. M., "Instinctive and Cultural Factors in Group Conflicts," *Am. Journal of Sociology,* XXVIII (1922), 1–20.
Faris, Ellsworth, "The Subjective Aspect of Culture," *Pub. Am. Sociological Society,* XIX (1925), 37–46.

Hughes, Everett C., "Personality Types and the Division of Labor," *Am. Journal of Sociology,* XXIII (1928), 754–768.
Lévy-Bruhl, L., *Primitive Mentality.* New York, 1923.
Lumley, F. E., *The Means of Social Control.* New York, 1925.
Park, R. E., and Miller, H. A., *Old World Traits Transplanted,* Chap. V. New York and London, 1921.

CHAPTER IX. THE SELF

Cooley, Charles H., "A Study of the Early Use of Self-words by a Child," *Psychological Review,* XV (1908), 339–57. Reprinted in *Sociological Theory and Social Research.* New York, 1930.
Hall, G. Stanley, "Some Aspects of the Early Sense of Self," *Am. Journal of Psychology,* IX (1897–8), 351–93.
Mead, George H., "The Social Self," *Journal of Philosophy,* X (1913), 374–80.
—— "The Genesis of the Self and Social Control," *International Journal of Ethics,* XXXV (1925), 251–77.
Park, R. E., and Burgess, E. W., *Introduction to the Science of Sociology,* 2d ed., pp. 111–28. Chicago, 1924.
Thomas, W. I., *The Unadjusted Girl,* Chaps. I and II. Boston, 1923.
Todd, Arthur J., "Primitive Notions of the Self," *Am. Journal of Psychology,* XXVII (1916), 171–202.

CHAPTER X. EMULATION

Allport, Floyd, *Social Psychology,* Chap. XI. Boston, 1924.
Carlyle, Thomas, *On Heroes, Hero-Worship and the Heroic in History.*
Cooley, Charles H., "Personal Competition," *Economic Studies,* IV, No. 2. New York, 1899. Reprinted in *Sociological Theory and Social Research.* New York, 1930.
Parsons, E. W. C., *Fear and Conventionality.* New York, 1914.
Sorokin, Pitirim, *et al.,* "An Experimental Study of Efficiency of Work under Various Specified Conditions," *Am. Journal of Sociology,* XXXV (1929–30), 765–82.
Vincent, George E., "The Rivalry of Social Groups," *Am. Journal of Sociology,* XVI (1910–11), 469–84.

CHAPTER XI. CONSCIENCE AND DEGENERACY

Anderson, Nels, *The Hobo.* Chicago, 1923.
Blanchard, Phyllis, and Paynter, R. H., "The Problem Child," *Mental Hygiene,* VIII (1924), 26–54.
Burt, Cyril, *The Young Delinquent.* New York, 1925.
Glueck, Sheldon and Eleanor, *500 Criminal Careers.* New York, 1930.
Goddard, Henry, *Feeblemindedness: its Causes and Consequences.* New York, 1914.
Healy, William, and Bronner, Augusta, *Delinquents and Criminals, their Making and Unmaking.* New York, 1926.

President's Research Committee, *Recent Social Trends in the United States*, Vol. II, Chap. XXII. New York and London, 1933.

Reckless, Walter, and Smith, Mapheus, *Juvenile Delinquency*. New York, 1932.

Shaw, Clifford, *Delinquency Areas*. Chicago, 1929.

—— *The Jack-Roller*. Chicago, 1930.

—— *The Natural History of a Delinquent Career*. Chicago, 1931.

CHAPTER XII. THE CULTURAL ENLARGEMENT OF COMMUNICATION

Bent, Silas, *Ballyhoo*. New York, 1927.

Bücher, Carl, *Industrial Evolution*, Chap. VI. Translated from the German by S. M. Wickett. New York, 1901.

Duffus, R. L., *Books: Their Place in a Democracy*. Boston and New York, 1930.

Graves, W. Brooke, *Readings in Public Opinion*. New York, 1928.

—— "The Press and Public Opinion," Chap. IX.

—— "The Theater and Moving Pictures and Public Opinion," Chap. X.

—— "Literature and Public Opinion," Chap. XI.

—— "Music and Public Opinion," Chap. XII.

—— "Art and Public Opinion," Chap. XIII.

—— "The Power of the Spoken Word," Chap. XIV.

—— "The Radio and Public Opinion," Chap. XV.

Kingsbury, J. E., *The Telephone and Telephone Exchanges*. London and New York, 1915.

Mason, William A., *A History of the Art of Writing*. New York, 1920.

Park, Robert E., and Burgess, E. W., *Introduction to the Science of Sociology*, Chap. VI. Chicago, 1921.

Payne, George Henry, *A History of Journalism in the United States*. New York and London, 1920.

President's Research Committee, *Recent Social Trends in the United States*, Vol. I, Chap. IV. New York and London, 1933.

Ross, E. A., *Principles of Sociology*, Chap. X. New York, 1930.

Seabury, William M., *The Public and the Motion Picture Industry*. New York, 1926.

Tassin, Algernon, *The Magazine in America*. New York, 1916.

Whipple, Leon, "The Revolution on Quality Street," *Survey Graphic*, Nov. 1, 1926, p. 119 ff.

—— "Sat. Eve. Post, Mirror of These States," *Survey Graphic*, March 1, 1928, p. 699 ff.

Willey, Malcolm M. and Rice, Stuart A., "Communication," *American Journal of Sociology*, XXXVI (1931), 966–977.

Young, Kimball, *Source Book for Social Psychology*, Chap. XXVI, "The Organs of Public Opinion. New York, 1927.

CHAPTER XIII. PERSONALITY IN THE MODERN WORLD

Beard, C. A., "The Myth of Rugged American Individualism," *Harper's Magazine*, CLXIV (1931), 13–22.

Healy, William, *Mental Conflicts and Misconduct.* Boston, 1917.
Mumford, Lewis, *The Golden Day.* New York, 1927.
Myerson, Abraham, *The Foundations of Personality.* New York, 1923.
President's Research Committee, *Recent Social Trends in the United States,* Vol. II, Chap. XIX. New York and London, 1933.
Thomas, William I., "The Problem of Personality in the Urban Environment," *Am. Journal of Sociology,* XXXII (1926), No. 1, Part 2, pp. 30–39.
Tufts, J. H., "Individualism and American Life," in *Essays in Honor of John Dewey.* New York, 1929.
Turner, Ralph, *America in Civilization,* Chap. XIII. New York, 1925.
Van Waters, Miriam, *Youth in Conflict.* New York, 1925.

CHAPTER XIV. THE ENLARGEMENT OF MEN'S MINDS

Bagehot, Walter, *Physics and Politics.* New York, 1875.
Bryce, James, *Modern Democracies.* New York, 1921.
Lecky, W. E. H., *Democracy and Liberty.* London, 1896.
Pillsbury, W. B., *The Psychology of Nationalism and Internationalism.* New York and London, 1919.
Robinson, James H., *The Mind in the Making.* New York and London, 1921.
Rose, John H., *Nationality in Modern History.* New York, 1915.
Stawell, F. M., and Marvin, F. S., *The Making of the Western Mind.* New York, 1923.
de Tocqueville, Alexis, *Democracy in America.* London, 1838.
Turner, F. J., *The Frontier in American History.* New York, 1920.
Turner, Ralph, *America in Civilization,* Chap. XIV. New York, 1925.

CHAPTER XV. GROUPING AND THE RISE OF NON-PRIMARY ASSOCIATION

Allport, Floyd H., "Group and Institution as Concepts in a Natural Science of Social Phenomena," *Publications of the American Sociological Society,* Vol. XXII, 1928, 83–99.
Folsom, Joseph K., *Social Psychology,* Chap. VII. New York, 1931.
Giddings, Franklin H., *The Scientific Study of Human Society,* Chap. VII. Chapel Hill, N. C., 1924.
Graves, W. Brooke, *Readings in Public Opinion,* Chap. XXI. New York, 1928.
Hobhouse, L. T., *Morals in Evolution,* Chaps. IV, V. New York, 1916.
Lasker, Bruno, *Race Attitudes in Children.* New York, 1929.
LeBon, Gustave, *The Crowd.* New York, 1900.
Lowie, Robert H., *Primitive Society,* Chaps. X, XI. New York, 1920.
Lynd, Robert S. and Helen M., *Middletown.* New York, 1929.
McKenzie, R. D., *The Neighborhood: A Study of Local Life in the City of Columbus, Ohio.* Chicago, 1921.
Park, Robert E., and Burgess, E. W., *Introduction to the Science of Sociology,* Chaps. III, V, and XIII. Chicago, 1921.
Parsons, Alice B., *Woman's Dilemma.* New York, 1926.

President's Research Committee, *Recent Social Trends in the United States,* Vol. II, Chap. XIV. New York and London, 1933.
Ross, E. A., *Principles of Sociology,* Chaps. XVIII–XX. New York, 1930.
Russell, Dora, *Hypatia, or Woman and Knowledge.* New York, 1925.
Terpenning, Walter A., *Village and Open-Country Neighborhoods.* New York, 1931.
Woolbert, C. H., "The Audience," *University of Illinois Studies, Psychological Monograph No. 92,* XXI (1916), 36–54.
Young, Kimball, *Source Book for Social Psychology,* Chaps. IV, XXII, XXIII. New York, 1927.

CHAPTER XVI. THE COMMUNITY AND ITS STRUCTURE

Anderson, Nels, and Lindeman, E. C., *Urban Sociology.* New York, 1928.
Brunner, Edmund deS., *Village Communities.* New York, 1927.
Burgess, E. W., editor, *The Urban Community.* Chicago, 1926.
—— Editor, "The Relation of the Individual to the Community," *Publications of the American Sociological Society,* XXII (1928), 1–303.
—— Editor, "The Rural Community," *Publications of the American Sociological Society,* XXIII (1929), 1–359.
Burr, Walter, *Small Towns.* New York, 1929.
Duffus, R. L., *Mastering a Metropolis.* New York, 1930.
Galpin, Charles Josiah, *Rural Life.* New York, 1916.
Holmes, Roy H., *Rural Sociology.* New York and London, 1932.
Park, Robert E., Burgess, E. W., and McKenzie, R. D., *The City.* Chicago, 1925.
Shaw, Clifford R., *Delinquency Areas.* Chicago, 1929.

CHAPTER XVII. THE COMMUNITY AS A CENTER OF FUNCTION

Bowman, LeRoy E., and others, "Community Organization," "City Life," "Employment," "Medicine and Public Health," etc.—See May numbers of the *American Journal of Sociology,* 1929, 1930, etc., for articles reviewing conditions during previous year.
Inquiry, The, *Community Conflict.* New York, 1929.
Lorimer, Frank, *The Making of Adult Minds in a Metropolitan Community.* New York, 1931.
Lynd, Robert S., and Helen M., *Middletown.* New York, 1929.
Munro, W. B., *Municipal Government and Administration.* New York, 1923.
Pettit, Walter W., *Case Studies in Community Organization.* New York and London, 1928.
President's Research Committee, *Recent Social Trends in the United States,* Vol. I, Chap. V; Vol. II, Chaps. XVII, XVIII, XXI, XXIII–XXIX. New York and London, 1933.
Steiner, J. F., *The American Community in Action.* New York, 1928.

Thompson, J. G., *Urbanization, its Effects on Government and Society.* New York, 1927.
Wood, A. E., *Community Problems.* New York, 1928.

CHAPTER XVIII. REGIONS AND THE AMERICAN STATES

Angoff, Charles, and Mencken, H. L., "The Worst American State," *The American Mercury,* September, October, November, XXIV (1931), 1 ff.
Committee on the Regional Plan of New York and its Environs, *The Regional Survey of New York and its Environs.* New York, 1929–31.
Duffus, R. L., *Mastering a Metropolis.* New York, 1930.
Geddes, Patrick, *Cities in Evolution.* London, 1915.
Gras, N. S. B., *An Introduction to Economic History,* Chaps. V, VI. New York and London, 1922.
McKenzie, R. D., "Ecological Succession in the Puget Sound Region," *Publications American Sociological Society,* XXIII (1929), 60–80.
Mukerjee, R., *Regional Sociology.* New York and London, 1926.
President's Research Committee, *Recent Social Trends in the United States,* Vol. I, Chaps. IX, X. New York and London, 1933.
Rice, Stuart A., *Quantitative Methods in Politics,* Chaps. X, XI. New York, 1928.
Smith, J. Russell, *North America.* New York, 1925.

CHAPTER XIX. NATIONS, THE WORLD MARKET, AND THE PROBLEM OF WAR

Bakeless, J., *The Economic Causes of Modern War.* Williamstown, Mass., 1921.
Beard, Charles A., and Mary R., *The Rise of American Civilization.* New York, 1927.
Brown, P. M., *International Society, Its Nature and Interests.* New York, 1923.
Dublin, Louis I., and Lotka, A. J., "The Present Outlook for Population Increase," *Publications American Sociological Society,* XXIV (1930), 106 ff.
Dublin, Louis I., "Birth-Control: What It Is Doing to America's Population," *Forum,* LXXVI (1931), 270–75.
Follett, M. P., *The New State.* New York, 1918.
Gettell, R. G., *Problems in Political Evolution.* New York, 1914.
Laski, H. J., *Authority in the Modern State.* New Haven, 1919.
Moon, Parker Thomas, *Imperialism and World Politics.* New York, 1927.
Poole, DeWitt C., *The Conduct of Foreign Relations under Modern Democratic Conditions.* New Haven, 1924.
Potter, Pitman B., *Introduction to the Study of International Organization.* New York, 1922.
President's Research Committee, *Recent Social Trends in the United States,* Vol. I, Chaps. I, XII. New York and London, 1933.

Thompson, Warren S., *Population Problems.* New York, 1930.
Turner, Ralph E., *America in Civilization,* Chap. IX. New York, 1925.
Wallas, Graham, *The Great Society.* New York, 1920.

CHAPTER XX. SOCIAL CLASSES

Brawley, Benjamin, *A Social History of the American Negro.* New York, 1921.
Chicago Commission on Race Relations, *The Negro in Chicago.* Chicago, 1922.
Commons, John R., *The Legal Foundations of Capitalism.* New York, 1924.
Dewey, D. R., *Financial History of the United States.* New York, 1922.
Douglass, H. P., and others, *The Worker in Modern Economic Society.* New York, 1923.
Flynn, John T., *God's Gold.* New York, 1932.
Hobhouse, L. T., *Morals in Evolution,* Part I, Chap. VII. New York, 1915.
Holmes, Roy Hinman, *Rural Sociology.* New York, 1932.
Klein, Henry H., *Dynastic America.* New York, 1921.
Mallock, W. H., *Aristocracy and Evolution.* New York, 1898.
Myers, Gustave, *History of Great American Fortunes.* Chicago, 1910.
Phillips, Ulrich B., *American Negro Slavery.* New York, 1918.
President's Research Committee, *Recent Social Trends in the United States,* Vol. I, Chaps. VI, XI. New York and London, 1933.
Ripley, W. Z., *From Main Street to Wall Street.* New York, 1929.
Ross, E. A. *Principles of Sociology,* Chaps. XX, XXI. New York, 1930.
Sorokin, Pitirim, *Social Mobility.* New York, 1927.
Sorokin, Pitirim, and Zimmerman, Carl C., *Principles of Rural Urban Sociology,* Part I. New York, 1929.
Veblen, Thorstein, *The Theory of the Leisure Class.* New York, 1899.
Wesley, Charles R., *Negro Labor in the U. S.* New York, 1927.

CHAPTER XXI. CLASS TENSIONS IN THE MODERN WORLD

Adamic, Louis, *Dynamite, the Story of Class Violence in America.* New York, 1931.
Barnes, Harry E., Chase, Stuart, and others, *New Tactics in Social Conflict.* New York, 1926.
Beer, M., *History of British Socialism* (2 vols.). London, 1923.
Commons, John R., and Associates, *History of Labor in the United States,* two-volume edition. New York, 1921.
Ellwood, Charles E., *The Psychology of Human Society,* Chap. VIII. New York, 1925.
Hiller, E. T., *The Strike.* Chicago, 1928.
Hobson, John A., *The Evolution of Modern Capitalism.* New York and London, 1916.

Marx, Karl, *Capital.* Translated from the 3rd German edition by Samuel Moore and Edward Aveling and edited by Frederick Engels. London, 1887.

Parrington, Louis V., *Main Currents in American Thought* (3 vols.). New York, 1927–30.

President's Research Committee, *Recent Social Trends in the United States,* Vol. II. Chap. XVI. New York and London, 1933.

Trotsky, Leon, *The History of the Russian Revolution.* Translated from the Russian by Max Eastman (2 vols.). New York, 1932.

CHAPTER XXII. PUBLIC OPINION

Angell, Norman, *The Public Mind.* New York, 1927.

Bryce, James, *Modern Democracies,* Vol I. New York, 1921.

Elliott, Harrison S., *The Process of Group Thinking.* New York, 1928.

Ellwood, Charles E., *The Psychology of Human Society,* Chaps. VII, VIII. New York, 1925.

Graves, W. Brooke, *Readings in Public Opinion.* New York, 1928.

Lippmann, Walter, *Public Opinion.* New York, 1922.

Lowell, A. L., *Public Opinion in War and Peace.* Cambridge, 1923.

Mecklin, J. M., *Introduction to Social Ethics,* Chap. IX. New York, 1920.

Odegard, Peter, *The American Public Mind.* New York, 1930.

Park, Robert E., and Burgess, E. W., *Introduction to the Science of Sociology,* Chap. XII. Chicago, 1921.

President's Research Committee, *Recent Social Trends in the United States,* Vol. I, Chap. VIII. New York and London, 1933.

Ross, E. A., *Principles of Sociology,* Chaps. XXIX, XXXI. New York, 1930.

Young, Kimball, *Source Book for Social Psychology,* Chaps. XXV, XXVI. New York, 1927.

CHAPTER XXIII. PUBLIC OPINION AND LEADERSHIP

Burr, Walter, *Community Leadership.* New York, 1929.

Gowin, E. B., *The Executive and His Control of Men.* New York, 1915.

Kent, Frank R., *The Great Game of Politics.* Garden City, N. Y., 1923.

Macpherson, W., *The Psychology of Persuasion.* New York, 1920.

Miller, Arthur H., *Leadership.* New York, 1920.

Mumford, Eben, *The Origins of Leadership.* Chicago, 1909.

Munro, W. B., *Personality in Politics.* New York, 1924.

Young, Kimball, *Source Book for Social Psychology,* Chaps. XX, XXI. New York, 1927.

CHAPTER XXIV. PUBLIC OPINION AS GROUP INTELLIGENCE

Bernays, Edward L., *Crystallizing Public Opinion.* New York, 1923.

Bury, J. A., *A History of Freedom of Thought.* New York and London, 1913.

Chaffee, Zechariah, *Freedom of Speech.* New York, 1920.
Dewey, John, *The Public and its Problems.* New York, 1927.
Ellwood, Charles E., *The Psychology of Human Society,* Chap. X. New York, 1925.
Lasswell, Harold D., *Propaganda Technique in the World War.* New York, 1927.
Park, Robert E., and Burgess, E. W., *Introduction to the Science of Sociology, Chaps.* XIII, XIV. Chicago, 1921.
Pierce, Bessie L., *Public Opinion and the Teaching of History.* New York, 1926.
Ross, E. A., *Principles of Sociology,* Chaps. XXIX, XXXI. New York, 1930.
Ryan, Rev. John, *Our Vanishing Liberties.* New York, 1927.
Scott, J. F., *The Menace of Nationalism in Education.* London, 1926.
Strong, E. K., "The Control of Propaganda as a Psychological Problem," *Scientific Monthly,* XIV (1922), 234–52.
Whipple, Leon, *The Story of Civil Liberty in the United States.* New York, 1927.
Young, Kimball, *Source Book for Social Psychology,* Chap. XXVII. New York, 1927.

CHAPTER XXV. INSTITUTIONS

Allport, Floyd H., "The Nature of Institutions," *Social Forces,* VI (1927–8), 167–79.
Chapin, F. Stuart, "A New Definition of Social Institutions," *Social Forces,* VI (1927–8), 373–7.
Ginsberg, Morris, *The Psychology of Society,* Chap. VIII. New York, 1921.
Hertzler, Joyce O., *Social Institutions.* New York, 1929.
Judd, C. H., *The Psychology of Social Institutions.* New York, 1926.
MacIver, R. M., *Community,* Chap. IV. London, 1917.
Sumner, William G., *Folkways,* pp. 53–55. Boston, 1906.

CHAPTER XXVI. THE FAMILY

Burgess, E. W., "The Family as a Unit of Interacting Personalities," *The Family,* VII (1926), 3–9.
Colcord, Joanna, *Broken Homes.* New York, 1919.
Goodsell, Willystine, *A History of the Family as a Social and Educational Institution.* New York, 1915.
—— *Problems of the Family.* New York, 1928.
Groves, Ernest, and Ogburn, W. F., *American Marriage and Family Relationships.* New York, 1928.
Lichtenberger, J. P., *Divorce.* New York, 1931.
Mowrer, Ernest, *Family Disorganization.* Chicago, 1926.
President's Research Committee, *Recent Social Trends in the United States,* Vol. I, Chap. XIII. New York and London, 1933.

Reed, Ruth, *The Modern Family.* New York, 1929.
Reuter, Edward B., and Runner, J. R., *The Family.* New York, 1931.
Todd, A. J., *The Primitive Family as an Educational Agency.* New York, 1913.

CHAPTER XXVII. EDUCATIONAL INSTITUTIONS

Counts, George S., *The American Road to Culture.* New York, 1930.
Dewey, John, *The School and Society.* Chicago, 1915.
Finney, Ross M., *A Sociological Philosophy of Education.* New York, 1928.
Hambly, W. D., *Origins of Education Among Primitive Peoples.* London, 1926.
Hart, Joseph K., *A Social Interpretation of Education.* New York, 1929.
Payne, George (Ed.), *Readings in Educational Sociology.* New York, 1932.
Peters, C. C., *Foundations of Educational Sociology,* rev. ed. New York, 1930.
President's Research Committee, *Recent Social Trends in the United States,* Vol. I, Chap. VII. New York and London, 1933.
Smith, Walter, *Principles of Educational Sociology.* Boston, 1928.
Thomas, W. I. and Dorothy, *The Child in America.* New York, 1928.
Encyclopedia of the Social Sciences, Articles on Primitive Education, History of Education, Public Education, Sectarian Education, Part Time Education, and Educational Finance, Vol. V, pp. 399–432.

CHAPTER XXVIII. THE CHURCH

Bacon, Leonard W., *A History of American Christianity.* New York, 1897.
Bryan, W. J., *The Seven Questions in Dispute.* New York and Chicago, 1924.
Ellwood, Charles E., *The Reconstruction of Religion.* New York, 1922.
Hopkins, E. W., *Origin and Evolution of Religion.* New Haven, 1923.
James, William, *Varieties of Religious Experience.* New York, 1902.
Lake, Kirsopp, *The Religion of Yesterday and Tomorrow.* Boston and New York, 1926.
Moore, Edward C., *Christian Thought Since Kant.* New York, 1915.
Niebuhr, Reinhold, *Does Civilization Need Religion?* New York, 1928.
O'Gorman, Patrick, *A History of the Roman Catholic Church in the United States.* New York, 1895.
President's Research Committee, *Recent Social Trends in the United States,* Vol. II, Chap. XX. New York and London, 1933.
Riley, Woodbridge, *American Thought from Puritanism to Pragmatism.* New York, 1915.
Rowe, Henry K., *The History of Religion in the United States.* New York, 1924.
Sweet, William W., *The Story of Religions in America.* New York, 1930.

CHAPTER XXIX. SOCIAL SCIENCE AND VALUES

Barnes, H. E. (Ed.), *The History and Prospects of the Social Sciences.* New York, 1925.

Bogardus, Emory S., *A History of Social Thought,* 2d ed. Los Angeles, 1928.

Bouglé, C. C. A., *The Evolution of Values.* New York, 1926.

Bristol, Lucius M., *Social Adaptation.* Cambridge, Mass., 1915.

Bury, J. B., *The History of the Idea of Progress.* New York, 1920.

Case, C. M., *Social Process and Human Progress.* New York, 1931.

Hart, Hornell, *The Technique of Social Progress.* New York, 1931.

Hayes, E. C., *Sociology and Ethics.* New York, 1921.

Hertzler, Joyce O., *A History of Utopian Thought.* New York, 1923.

Hobhouse, L. T., *Social Development.* New York, 1924.

House, Floyd N., *The Range of Social Theory.* New York, 1929.

de Laguna, Theodore, *An Introduction to the Science of Ethics.* New York, 1914.

Lichtenberger, James, *The Development of Social Theory.* New York, 1923.

Lundberg, George, *Social Research.* Boston, 1929.

Mumford, Lewis, *The Story of Utopias.* New York, 1922.

Odum, H., and Jocher, K., *An Introduction to Social Research.* New York, 1929.

Sorokin, Pitirim, *Contemporary Sociological Theories.* New York, 1928.

Todd, A. J., *Theories of Social Progress.* New York, 1918.

INDEX

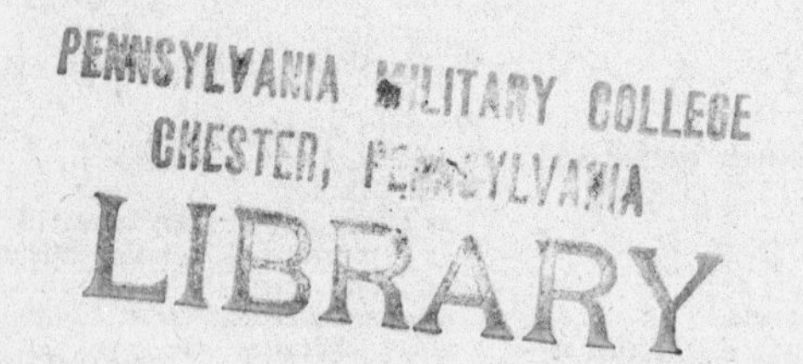